Special Edition Using

Linux

Fourth Edition

Jack Tackett, Jr.
Steve Burnett

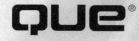

Special Edition Using Linux

International Standard Book Number: 0-7897-1746-8

Library of Congress Catalog Card Number: 98-85654

Printed in the United States of America

First Printing: September, 1998

01 00 99   4 3 2

Trademarks

Warning and Disclaimer

EXECUTIVE EDITOR
Jeff Koch

ACQUISITIONS EDITOR
Jane Brownlow

DEVELOPMENT EDITORS
Mark Cierzniak
Kate Shoup Welsh

MANAGING EDITOR
Sarah Kearns

PROJECT EDITOR
Christopher Morris

COPY EDITOR
Audra McFarland

INDEXER
Craig Small

TECHNICAL EDITOR
Eric C. Richardson

SOFTWARE DEVELOPMENT SPECIALIST
Jack Belbot

PRODUCTION
Steve Balle-Gifford
Maribeth Echard
Megan Wade

Contents at a Glance

VI | Using the Internet

VII | Setting Up a Linux Web Server

VIII | Appendixes

Table of Contents

IV Working with Linux

18 Understanding Linux Shells   337

19 Managing Multiple Processes   381

V Network Administration

About the Authors

Jack Tackett, Jr. is the Manager of System Operations for Nortel's Information Network, the leading outsource provider of Virtual Private Networks in the VPN industry. When not herding his system administrators (a practice very similar to herding cats), he sometimes breaks away to write (another practice very similar to herding cats and usually just as rewarding ;-). He fights for living space with his loving wife and their two dogs and three cats in Cary, NC. He invites your comments at tackett@netwharf.com.

Steve Burnett is an information technology consultant in Research Triangle Park, NC. His last degree was an M.S. in Technical Communication. For the last several years, his professional interests have centered on systems administration, integration, and interoperability. When he's not working, he likes to take his wife out for dinner, cooking not being a noted achievement of his.

Dedication

From Jack Tackett

To my wife Peggy and to my Mom, Mary Louise—love always.

From Steve Burnett

To my mother.

Acknowledgments

From Jack Tackett:

First, I want to thank all the readers of the first three editions for their patronage and for their helpful and insightful comments. Your comments are important and make a difference; you have made this a better project!

I want to say thank you for the tremendous efforts put forth by the Linux developers scattered across the globe. I also want to acknowledge the fine contributions begun by Linus Torvalds and continued by so many others around the world—thanks for creating Linux and breathing life into such a monumental effort! Also, thanks to Matt Welsh, et al., for the work on the Linux Documentation project. Also, a big thanks to the fine folks at Red Hat for their help in preparing this edition—and for a great lunch at Kanki's!

Next, I want to express my regards for the people at the Que Continuum. I especially want to thank Jane Brownlow and Mark Cierzniak for their help in getting this project off the ground and finished.

To Steve Burnett for stepping in at the last minute to provide aid and assistance to a haggard cat herder. Also thanks to Paul Barrett for his initial help with the research that eventually led to this book. And also thanks to David Gunter for his efforts with the first three editions.

To my friends Paul Barrett, Keith E. Bugg, Gregg and Beckie Field, Dave and Lola Gunter, Israel Janovich, Dianna Smith, Kell and Joy Wilson, Britney, Vicki, and Binh, and finally Joe Williams: Thanks for the memories! Thanks to my combined family—the Tacketts and the Martins—for their support in all my endeavors. Also, a big thank you to the best cousins in the world—Bill and Hope Tackett, Jr.

I'd like to thank my best instructor, Dr. Joe Daugherty of the University of North Carolina-Asheville. Also thanks to Myrtice Trent of the Blue Ridge Technical Community College. Thanks for the help and encouragement you both provided.

Next a great big thank-you to my coworkers at Nortel's Information Network for picking up the slack while I revised this book—thank you to everyone!

Finally, to my wife Peggy, who has yet again put up with me spending endless hours at the computer writing yet another computer book. Thanks, sweetheart, and I love you!

From Steve Burnett

First, without the mammoth amount of work put into Linux by Linus Torvalds and the rest of the Linux development community, there would be nothing to write about here. Since the first release, Linux has grown into a robust operating system that is used to meet a wide variety of needs, from home hobbyists up through business usage central to those companies. Secondly, without Jack and David's work on the previous editions, there wouldn't have been a book to invite me to help revise. Jack, thanks for inviting me in on this project. Although electronic mail works great, living within a local call range of each other helped keep my bills down while we tried to coordinate our actions.

Other people I'd like to thank include David Fugate for coordination, and Leland Wallace, Jay Cuthrell, and Cameron Wallace for fact-checking and offering occasional opinions when asked. Louis Popovsky also contributed by sending me frequent well-chosen technical updates throughout the writing period. Sanity checks were provided by the various staff and inhabitants of the Duke University Primate Center, reminding me there's more than computers out there. Finally and most importantly, I'd like to thank my wife Merrie.

Tell Us What You Think!

As the reader of this book, *you* are our most important critic and commentator. We value your opinion and want to know what we're doing right, what we could do better, what areas you'd like to see us publish in, and any other words of wisdom you're willing to pass our way.

As the Executive Editor for the Operating Systems team at Macmillan Computer Publishing, I welcome your comments. You can fax, email, or write me directly to let me know what you did or didn't like about this book—as well as what we can do to make our books stronger.

Please note that I cannot help you with technical problems related to the topic of this book, and that due to the high volume of mail I receive, I might not be able to reply to every message.

When you write, please be sure to include this book's title and author, as well as your name and phone or fax number. I will carefully review your comments and share them with the author and editors who worked on the book.

Fax: 317-581-4663

Email: **opsys@mcp.com**

Mail: Executive Editor
          Operating Systems
          Macmillan Computer Publishing
          201 West 103rd Street
          Indianapolis, IN 46290 USA

Introduction

Linux is no longer a "not ready for prime time" operating system! Many commercial uses of Linux abound, ranging from being used to create many of the fantastic special effects for James Cameron's mega hit *Titanic*, to being used as the OS for new network computers. As Linux evolves, one has to keep up with the changes; that's why you will find plenty of new material in this fourth edition of the popular *Special Edition Using Linux*.

Many chapters have been rewritten to highlight the Red Hat distribution—probably the most popular and easiest-to-install Linux distribution ever. In addition, the book contains updated coverage of such items as RPM (the Red Hat Package Manager), which offers the easiest way to install and upgrade your system; PAM, a leading security feature of most Linux distributions; and X Windows. You'll also find another CD-ROM containing a *lite* version of Caldera's OpenLinux Base product. Finally, on the third CD-ROM, you'll find a copy of Caldera's StarOffice, an integrated office application that includes several office automation programs. ■

However, if you're just tuning in, you might want to know just what the heck Linux is.

In 1991, Linus Torvalds, then a 23-year-old college student, began a personal project to expand the Minix operating system into a full-fledged clone of the UNIX operating system that was so popular on college campuses. The project is still evolving: Linux is continuously updated and expanded by literally hundreds of people around the world.

Therefore, Linux is a unique animal in the computer (r)evolution. It isn't a commercial product backed by a huge corporation; rather, it's an operating system born of frustration and built by a ragtag team of computer enthusiasts around the world. This team used Internet resources to communicate and build the operating system named Linux.

But don't think Linux is just a hobby for hackers around the world—it's not! Plenty of commercial products are being written specifically for Linux. In fact, several companies are porting their UNIX-based applications, such as Corel's WordPerfect, to Linux. As a matter of fact, Corel has adopted Linux for its new Network Computer and has released the resulting software to the development community.

N O T E While it is very hard to estimate the total number of Linux users or installations in the world, a working estimate shows between 5,000,000 and 10,500,000 active Linux users worldwide. For more information see the following URL:

http://www.redhat.com/redhat/linuxmarket.html ■

N O T E If you don't understand what a Uniform Resource Locator (URL) is or how to use it, don't despair! This book will help you learn how to make your way around the Internet using Linux. ■

▶ **See** "URLs," **p. 614**

Many Fortune 500 companies use Linux for internal projects and mission-critical applications. And recently, large companies such as Netscape Communications, are embracing the concept of open solutions by releasing their own software into the development community, just as Linus Torvald and others released their software to the world.

There are also plenty of free applications and utilities for Linux. Since the inception of Linux, almost the entire GNU library of utilities has been ported to Linux, and the X Windows GUI system—so popular on UNIX-type workstations—also has been ported. GNU (a recursive acronym for "GNU's Not UNIX") is a project started by one man to make software available to anyone who wants access. The GNU General Public License in Appendix D describes the philosophy under which Linux and many other fine software packages are distributed. The accompanying CD-ROMs contain many of these packages.

This book provides you with enough information to use and enjoy Linux. The accompanying CD-ROMs contain the Red Hat 5.1 distribution and Caldera's OpenLinux Lite, each of which use the 2.0.34 Linux kernel.

Probably the first order of business is to help you pronounce the word *Linux*. To most Americans, the pronunciation is LEN-nucks, with the short i sound. The official pronunciation is LIE-nucks, with the long i sound.

ON THE WEB

You can hear Linus pronounce Linux in English at the following URL:

ftp://ftp.linux.org/pub/kernel/SillySounds/english.au

Who Should Use This Book?

Anyone interested in the Linux phenomenon can use this book as a guide to installing, configuring, and using Linux. Linux is often called a UNIX clone, but it's actually a POSIX-compliant multiuser, multitasking operating system for Intel 386 and later processors. POSIX is an international standard for operating systems and software detailing interoperability standards. Linux doesn't require MS-DOS or Windows to operate; in fact, Linux can replace those programs on your computer.

Because Linux is still evolving, it's imperative that you understand the possibility of losing existing data on your system. *Do not install Linux without first backing up your system.* It might be necessary to repartition your hard drive to make room for this new operating system, although it's possible to install Linux on top of MS-DOS or to repartition your hard drive without losing data. If you take the proper precautions, anyone can install and enjoy Linux.

NOTE The most current version of Linux is always available on the Internet, from sources listed in Appendix A, "Sources of Information." The accompanying CD-ROMs contain the latest possible versions of Linux, but due to the rapid development of this popular operating system and the chaotic process in which it's developed, it's impossible to provide the latest and greatest on a CD-ROM. In fact, although all efforts are made to keep the book and CD-ROMs in synch, that also is nearly impossible. Unlike commercial software, which changes infrequently and under controlled conditions, Linux and related software are perpetually dynamic. ▪

Because Linux is very similar to UNIX, many of the operations and procedures necessary for using Linux also apply to many UNIX systems. By learning to use Linux, you also learn how to use most UNIX systems.

UNIX has evolved over the years to become the premier operating system used by hundreds of thousands of people throughout the world. This isn't an accident. Earlier versions of UNIX were harder to manipulate than other operating systems, but despite this, UNIX managed to amass a distinguished following in academic and scientific circles. These professionals realized not only what a powerful, flexible, and manageable operating system UNIX was, but also its potential to be the best operating system ever. Their efforts have culminated in the UNIX of today, with its marvelous utilities, bundled with the newest communications capabilities and graphical user interfaces (GUIs).

The UNIX of today promises again to revolutionize the personal computer industry, and perhaps redirect the industry's growth. UNIX has evolved from a minicomputer operating system to one that crosses all hardware platforms. There's no reason to think that this evolution will stop. UNIX may well become the standard for what most users dream of—complete standardization and compatibility of all computer systems eventually, regardless of size or power.

UNIX comes in several flavors from a variety of vendors, including versions for the Intel PC platforms, but most of these versions cost big bucks. Linux provides a relatively inexpensive—free if you have access to the Internet—solution to learning about UNIX-type procedures and commands, the X Windows GUI, and accessing the Internet via Linux.

Who Should *Not* Use This Book?

If you are a Linux kernel hacker or a UNIX guru, this book may not be your cup of tea. This book is a great resource for someone wanting to know more about Linux and UNIX who has never been involved with either operating system.

However, if you know how to install Linux and maneuver around in UNIX, you may still find this book of use, particularly if you are only a UNIX user and have never had the chance to perform system administration tasks. Several sections of the book explain the finer points of system administration and how to maintain a Linux/UNIX system. Typically, a normal UNIX user is never allowed to perform these system administration tasks, but with Linux you become king of the hill and ruler of the system, free to do whatever you want to do!

Now, if you don't have a clue what MS-DOS is or what a floppy disk looks like, you might want to brush up on some computer basics before tackling Linux. Linux isn't for the faint of heart—you must have some understanding of how a computer works. If the thought of repartitioning or reformatting your hard drive sends shivers down your spine, you probably should put off learning Linux for a while until you become more comfortable with your computer system.

Hardware Needed to Use This Book

Most of Linux has been written across the Internet by computer *hackers* (not *crackers*, but people who truly enjoy writing software that accomplishes something). Thus, the hardware supported by Linux is the hardware owned by the various hackers.

However, many hardware manufacturers are accepting Linux as a valid market and are beginning to write drivers for their hardware. They are also providing hardware specifications to the world so that Linux developers can write software to work with the hardware. Many companies are also farming out work to Linux developers to specifically write drivers for their hardware. These companies then release the code into the community under GNU guidelines. This is a dramatic change from a few years ago when many manufactures withheld information for proprietary and competitive reasons.

Table 1 is a brief list of the supported hardware. If you don't have the correct hardware, it's unlikely that you'll be able to boot Linux and productively use the system—forewarned is forearmed! Appendix C, "The Linux Hardware Compatibility HOWTO," provides a more in-depth listing of Linux-supported hardware.

I feel it's only fair to let you know what type of systems we used to create this book. The test machine was a Pentium II 233-based system with 64MB of RAM and a Buslogic SCSI controller, a 4 gigabyte Micropolis SCSI drive, an NE2000 PCI Ethernet card, a 24x ATAPI CD-ROM, and a Matrox Mystique video card. The name server used in our network is a no-name 486dx100 system with IDE drives and 32MB of memory running Red Hat Linux. This machine is also the main sendmail server for the site. The main Web server is a Digital Equipment Alpha also running Red Hat Linux. The entire site is connected to the Internet via an ISDN line using an Ascend Pipeline 75 router.

Table 1   A Brief List of Hardware Supported by Linux

Item	Description
CPU	Intel 386 and later (and compatibles), DEC Alpha, Sun Sparcs, and PowerMacs.
Bus	ISA, EISA, VESA local bus, and PCI; the MicroChannel bus isn't fully supported yet.
RAM	Minimum of 2MB of RAM; 4MB is recommended.
Hard drive controller	AT standard hard drive controller; Linux supports MFM, RLL, ESDI, and IDE controllers. Linux also supports several popular SCSI drive and CD-ROM drive controllers.
Disk space	Minimum of 20MB; 80MB is recommended.
Monitor	Linux supports Hercules, CGA, EGA, VGA, and SVGA video cards and systems; X Windows has other requirements detailed in Chapter 21, "Installing the X Windows System."
Mouse	Any standard serial mouse (for example, Logitech, Microsoft, or Mouse Systems) or bus mouse from Microsoft, Logitech, or ATIXL.
CD-ROM drive	Any CD-ROM drive that uses a true SCSI interface works; some proprietary CD-ROM drives such as the SoundBlaster series are also supported. CD-ROM drives known to work with Linux include NEC CDR-74, Sony CDU-45, Sony CDU-31a, Mitsumi CD-ROMs, and Texel DM-3042.
Tape drive	Any SCSI tape drive works; other drives hosted from a floppy controller may also be supported. Now, the Colorado Jumbo 120 and 250 using the QIC 80 format are supported.
Printer	If you can access your parallel printer from MS-DOS, you should be able to access it from Linux; some fancy features might not be accessible.
Ethernet card	If you have access to an Ethernet network, Linux supports several standard Ethernet cards for accessing your network. Cards supported include 3Com's 3C503, 3C509, and 3C503/16; Novell's NE1000 and NE2000; and Western Digital's WD8003 and WD8013.

ON THE WEB

The following Web site provides more information on MicroChannel bus support:

http://glycerine.itsmm.uni.edu/mca/

How to Use This Book

You may prefer to read this book from cover to cover. The information progresses from simple to complex as you read through the various sections and their chapters. Because the information is separated into seven parts and four appendixes, each with its own particular emphasis, you can choose to read only those parts that appeal to your immediate needs. Don't, however, let your immediate needs deter you from eventually giving attention to each chapter. Whenever you have the time, you can find a wealth of information in them all!

Part I: Installing Linux

Part I, "Installing Linux," provides a detailed overview of the Linux system as well as instructions to get Linux up and running. It consists of six chapters:

- Chapter 1, "Understanding Linux," introduces the Linux operating system and provides a general overview of the various components that make up the Linux system and various distributions.
- Chapter 2, "Linux Installation Overview," provides a general overview of installing various Linux distributions, with specific emphasis on supported hardware and potential problems and their resolutions.
- Chapter 3, "Installing Red Hat," gives detailed instructions for installing the version of Red Hat provided on the accompanying Red Hat CD-ROM.
- Chapter 4, "Installing Caldera OpenLinux Lite," gives detailed instructions for installing the version of OpenLinux provided on the accompanying CD-ROM.
- Chapter 5, "Running Linux Applications," provides a basic introduction to the process of running various applications on your Linux system after you get Linux up and running.
- Chapter 6, "Upgrading and Installing Software with RPM," provides you with the information needed to install new software using the Red Hat Package Management system (RPM). The chapter also covers installing software from the Internet and tells you how to patch existing programs.

Part II: System Administration

Part II, "System Administration," provides basic information on configuring and managing a typical Linux installation.

- Chapter 7, "Understanding System Administration," provides a brief background of the processes and procedures needed to configure and maintain a Linux system.
- Chapter 8, "Using the vi Editor," instructs you how to use UNIX's visual editor. Although vi isn't the most productive editor in the world, every Linux/UNIX system has it, and sometimes it's the only editor available for use.

- Chapter 9, "Booting and Shutting Down," details the various actions that happen when you boot up or shut down a Linux system, and explains why you can't simply switch off the power supply. This chapter contains a complete description of the files Linux uses to boot.
- Chapter 10, "Managing User Accounts," shows you how to add, delete, and manage user accounts on your machine.
- Chapter 11, "Backing Up Data," explains the necessity of backing up your data, as well as the procedures needed to back up your Linux system.
- Chapter 12, "Improving System Security," gives you a brief overview of system security on Linux systems and then explains the procedures needed to maintain a reasonably secure system.
- Chapter 13, "Configuring the Linux Kernel," illustrates how to configure a kernel, no matter what distribution you are using, for your hardware.

Part III: Managing the File System

Part III, "Managing the File System," provides detailed knowledge of how to be more productive with various Linux features. Everything you learn in these four chapters can be transferred easily to other UNIX-type systems:

- Chapter 14, "Managing File Systems," provides an overview of creating, mounting, and using a file system under Linux.
- Chapter 15, "Using Samba," provides a detailed explanation of Samba and how to configure Linux to use Samba with other Linux systems as well as with NT systems.
- Chapter 16, "Understanding the File and Directory System," provides an overview of file permissions, users, and file types.
- Chapter 17, "Managing Files and Directories," details the Linux file system structure and organization, file-naming conventions, and directory hierarchy. The chapter also teaches you how to successfully navigate the Linux file system.

Part IV: Working with Linux

Part IV, "Working with Linux," increases your skill at working with the Linux command-line tools and utilities.

- Chapter 18, "Understanding Linux Shells," introduces you to the magical world of Linux shells, the powerful capabilities that exist through the use of shell scripting, and the different shells you may encounter with different versions of Linux.
- Chapter 19, "Managing Multiple Processes," explores the capabilities of Linux when you run more than one process at a time. You learn how to initiate and manage multiple processes, as well as how to control and stop them.
- Chapter 20, "Printing," covers all the printing basics, from issuing print commands and checking printer status to canceling print jobs and dealing with common printing problems.
- Chapter 21, "Installing the X Windows System," provides you with the necessary information to get the X Windows system up and running under Linux. Under Linux, the X Windows system is called XFree86 and is similar to other GUI environments, such as Microsoft Windows or the OS/2 Workplace Shell.

- Chapter 22, "Using X Windows," provides you with information necessary to use the X Windows system under Linux.

Part V: Network Administration

Part V, "Network Administration," provides a greater understanding of the procedures and processes necessary to administer a robust Linux system.

- Chapter 23, "Understanding the TCP/IP Protocol Suite," provides an overview of the network transport protocol suite in use today on the Internet.
- Chapter 24, "Configuring a TCP/IP Network," shows you how to set up and configure TCP/IP on Linux.
- Chapter 25, "Configuring Domain Name Service," provides you with the necessary information to get your system up and running with Domain Name Service (DNS).
- Chapter 26, "Configuring Electronic Mail," provides you with the necessary information to get your e-mail system up and running with sendmail.
- Chapter 27, "Configuring a Usenet News Service," provides you with the necessary information to set up Usenet news on your system.
- Chapter 28, "Using the emacs Editor," teaches you how to use the ubiquitous UNIX editor written by GNU patriarch Richard Stallman.

Part VI: Using the Internet

The six chapters in Part VI, "Using the Internet," provide a basic overview of the Internet.

- Chapter 29, "Using SLIP and PPP," illustrates how to configure and use Serial Line Internet Protocol (SLIP) and Point-to-Point Protocol (PPP) lines to connect with the Internet.
- Chapter 30, "Accessing the Network with telnet, ftp, and the r- Commands," provides you with information on how to use various programs such as telnet and ftp to access information around the world.
- Chapter 31, "Surfing the Internet with the World Wide Web," gives you an overview of using various Linux utilities to search for and retrieve information from the Internet, with emphasis on the Web.
- Chapter 32, "Creating Web Documents with HTML," tells you how to create home pages for the World Wide Web by using HTML for your Linux system.
- Chapter 33, "Using Electronic Mail," gives you an overview of electronic mail (e-mail) and how to use it in Linux.
- Chapter 34, "Surviving Usenet News," provides you with an explanation of Usenet newsgroups, as well as instructions for accessing this global community of newsgroups.

Part VII: Setting Up a Linux Web Server

Part VII, "Setting Up a Linux Web Server," provides detailed information on setting up and running a Web server on Linux. Three chapters make up this part:

- Chapter 35, "Getting Started with Apache," gives you the basics so that you can get started with Apache. It covers compiling and installing Apache, and the basic configuration options.

- Chapter 36, "Configuring Apache," discusses the major configuration options within Apache, including MIME types, indexing, server-side includes, image maps, and virtual hosts.
- Chapter 37, "Managing an Internet Web Server," discusses the various administrative concepts involved with managing a Web server, including controlling the server child process, increasing server efficiency, managing log files, and dealing with security issues.

Appendixes

The appendixes provide supplementary information on installing and using Linux, as well as licensing information for using Linux. The book contains the following six appendixes:

- Appendix A, "Sources of Information," provides you with a detailed listing of books, magazines, Usenet newsgroups, and FTP sites dealing with Linux. Also, you get a brief glimpse of the myriad resources available to you as a Linux user.
- Appendix B, "The Linux HOWTO Index," provides a list of all the main and mini HOWTOs available. HOWTOs provide information on *how to* accomplish a specific task with Linux. This HOWTO comes directly from the Internet.
- Appendix C, "The Linux Hardware Compatibility HOWTO," provides important details on the hardware supported by the current Linux distribution. This HOWTO also comes directly off the Internet.
- Appendix D, "The GNU General Public License," is the verbatim license for using GNU applications. It describes your responsibilities when modifying, distributing, or using GNU programs.
- Appendix E, "Installing StarOffice," covers how to install and use StarOffice, Caldera's office suite of applications.
- Appendix F, "What's on the CD-ROM," discusses the contents of the three CD-ROMs included with this book.

Conventions Used in This Book

This book uses several special conventions that you need to become familiar with. These conventions are listed here for your reference.

Linux is a *case-sensitive* operating system; that means when this book instructs you to type something at a command or shell prompt, you must type exactly what appears in the book, exactly as it is capitalized. This book uses a `monospaced typeface` for Linux commands to set them off from standard text. If you're instructed to type something, what you are to type appears in **`bold monospace text`**. For example, if the book gives the following instruction:

Enter **`cat`**.

You must press the letters <c>, <a>, and <t> and then press the <Enter> key.

Keys are sometimes pressed in combination; when this is the case, the keys are presented like this: <Ctrl-h>. This example implies that you must press and hold the <Ctrl> key, press the <h> key, and then release both keys.

N O T E This book uses a convention for key names that may vary from what you are accustomed to. To avoid confusion in the case-sensitive UNIX environment, this book uses lowercase letters to refer to keys when uppercase letters may be the norm. For example, this book uses the form <Ctrl-c> instead of the form <Ctrl-C> (the latter form may make some readers wonder whether they should press <Ctrl> and <Shift> and <c>). ■

Some example listings show a portion of the screen after you type a specific command. These listings show the command prompt or shell prompt—usually a dollar sign ($)—followed by what you type in **bold**. Don't type the dollar sign when you follow the example on your own system. Consider this example:

```
$ lp report.txt &
3146
$
```

You should type only what appears in bold on the first line (that is, type lp report.txt & and then press <Enter>). The rest of the listing shows Linux's response to the command.

When discussing the syntax of a Linux command, this book uses some special formatting to distinguish between the required portions and the variable portions. Consider the following example:

```
lp filename
```

In this syntax, the *filename* portion of the command is a variable; that is, it changes depending on what file you actually want the lp command to work with. The lp is required because it's the actual command name. Variable information is presented in *italic*; information that must be typed exactly is not in italic.

In some cases, command information is optional—that is, it's not required for the command to work. Square brackets ([ ]) enclose optional parts of the command syntax. Consider the following example:

```
lp filename [device1] [abc]
```

Here, lp is the command name and is neither optional nor variable. The *device1* parameter is both variable and optional (it is in italic and enclosed in square brackets); this means that you can type any device name in place of *device1* (without the brackets), or you can type nothing at all for that parameter. The abc parameter is optional (you don't have to use it if you don't want to), but it's not variable; if you use it, you must type it exactly as it appears in the book—again, without the brackets.

Tips, notes, and cautions appear throughout the book in special formats to make the information they contain easy to locate. Longer discussions not integral to the flow of the chapter are set aside as *sidebars*, with their own heading.

The book also contains many cross-references to appropriate topics throughout the book. A typical cross-reference appears as follows:

▶ **See** "Using X Windows," **p. xxx**

Installing Linux

Understanding Linux

by Jack Tackett

In this chapter

To understand Linux, you must first understand the question, "What is UNIX?" The reason is that Linux is a project initiated to create a working version of UNIX on Intel-based machines, more commonly referred to as IBM PC-compatible computers that most people are familiar with.

UNIX is arguably the most versatile and popular operating system found today on scientific and high-end workstations. This chapter explains why you may want to select the UNIX-like Linux instead of one of the other operating systems available for Intel platforms, such as MS-DOS, Windows 95/98, Windows NT, or OS/2.

What Is Linux?

Linux is an operating system for several types of computer platforms, but primarily for Intel-based PCs. The system has been designed and built by hundreds of programmers scattered around the world. The goal has been to create a UNIX clone, free of any commercially copy-righted software, which the entire world can use.

Actually, Linux started out as a hobby of Linus Torvalds while he was a student at the University of Helsinki in Finland. He wanted to create a replacement for the Minix operating system, a UNIX-like operating system available for Intel-based PCs.

N O T E We'll explain many of the terms used within the chapter later, so don't worry if some of them are unfamiliar to you now. ▓

Linux is basically a UNIX clone, which means that with Linux you get many of the advantages of UNIX. Linux multitasking is fully *preemptive*, meaning that you can run multiple programs at the same time, and each program seems to process continuously. Other systems, such as Microsoft Windows 3.1, allow you to run multiple programs, but when you switch from one program to another, the first program typically stops running. Microsoft's Windows 95 and Windows NT are more like Linux because they allow preemptive multitasking. Linux allows you to start a file transfer, print a document, copy a floppy, use a CD-ROM, and play a game—all at the same time.

Linux is fully multiuser capable, which means that more than one person can log in to and use the system at the same time. Although the multiuser feature may not be very useful at home, it gives many people in a corporate or university setting access to the same resources at the same time, yet eliminates the need to duplicate expensive machines. Even at home, you'll find the capability to log in to separate accounts on what are called *virtual terminals* very useful. Also from home, you could provide your own personal online service by using Linux and several modems.

▶ **See** "Managing Users," **p. 107**

Linux is free—or nearly so. In fact, for only a portion of the price of this book, you've received two fully functioning distributions of Linux (RedHat Linux and Caldera OpenLinux) on the accompanying CD-ROMs. Everything you need to get Linux up and running is provided on the

CD-ROMs, including hundreds of applications. And on the third CD-ROM, you'll also find an integrated office productivity pack called StarOffice (also from Caldera).

Linux provides a learning opportunity unparalleled today. Here you have a complete working operating system, including source code, with which to play and learn what makes it tick. Learning what makes Linux tick is something you can't do in a typical UNIX environment, and it's definitely something you can't do with a commercial operating system because no vendor is willing to just give away the source code.

Finally, Linux gives you a chance to relive—or perhaps experience for the first time—the chaos of the early PC revolution. In the mid-1970s, computers were the provinces of large organizations, such as the government, big business, and universities. The ordinary person had no access to these marvels. But with the introduction of the microprocessor and the first personal computers, things changed. At first, PCs were the province of the *hackers*—dedicated computer enthusiasts—who hacked the early systems because those systems could do very little in the way of productive work. But as the hackers experimented and became entrepreneurs, and as the capabilities of PCs increased, PCs became commonplace.

N O T E   The term "hacker" has unfortunately taken on a negative connotation in today's society. See the section "Hackers" later in this chapter for more details on hackers and crackers. ▨

The same is true today of system software (that is, operating systems). Linux represents a breakaway from a system controlled by large organizations that stifle creativity and enhancements in the name of market share.

Why Use Linux?

You'll want to use Linux because it's the only operating system today that's freely available to provide multitasking and multiprocessing capabilities for multiple users on IBM PC-compatible hardware platforms. No other operating system gives you these same features with the power that Linux enjoys. Linux also separates you from the marketing whims of the various commercial providers. You aren't locked into upgrading every few years and paying outrageous sums to update all your applications. Many applications for Linux are freely available on the Internet, just as the source code to Linux itself is available on the Internet. Thus, you have access to the source code to modify and expand the operating system to your needs—something you can't do with commercial operating systems such as Windows NT, Windows 95, MS-DOS, and OS/2.

Freedom from commercial vendors is also a potential downside to using Linux. Because no single commercial vendor supports Linux, getting help isn't just a phone call away. Linux can be finicky and may or may not run properly on a wide range of hardware. The potential to damage or delete data files residing on your system also exists because Linux is constantly changing and doesn't go through a rigorous testing process before it's released.

Linux isn't a toy; it's a system designed to give users the feeling of tinkering with a new project, just like in the beginning of the PC revolution. However, Linux is relatively stable on many systems and presents you with an inexpensive opportunity to learn and use one of the most popular operating systems in the world today—UNIX. Many CD-ROM vendors and software companies, such as Red Hat and Caldera, now support the Linux operating system. Linux is an alternative to other UNIX systems and can be used in place of those sometimes-expensive systems. If you program on UNIX systems at work, for example, you might want a UNIX-like system at home. Are you a systems administrator of a UNIX system at work? If so, you can perform some of your duties from home by using Linux. Or do you not have a clue as to what UNIX is? Well, then, Linux provides a low-cost introduction to one of the most popular operating systems in the world—UNIX.

Linux also provides you with easy access to the Internet and the rest of the information superhighway.

Linux Distributions

Linux is distributed by many different organizations, each of which provides a unique collection of programs along with the core group of files that constitutes a Linux release. The current release of Linux on the accompanying CD-ROMs is kernel version 2.0.34. This distribution may also contain experimental kernels with drivers for unique hardware. Under Red Hat, the kernels are part of the Red Hat Package Management system (RPMs) and are installed as part of the system. Caldera's OpenLinux follows the same scheme because it is based on the Red Hat distribution.

Luckily for you, by having bought this book, you've made the decision of which distribution to use rather easy. The three CDs accompanying this book offer complete versions of both Red Hat's and Caldera's distributions (the companies' Internet versions, not the ones sold commercially). However, other distributions such as the following are available on the net:

- MCC Interim Linux
- TAMU Linux
- LST
- SLS
- Debian Linux
- Yggdrasil Plug-and-Play Linux CD-ROM and the Linux Bible
- Trans-Ameritech Linux plus BSD CD-ROM
- The Linux Quarterly CD-ROM
- Caldera (this vendor uses Red Hat's)
- Red Hat (Red Hat's commercial version includes a commercial X server called Metro X)

The Distribution HOWTO also provides an exhaustive list of Linux distributions. You'll learn later in this chapter how to access the various HOWTOs that accompany each Linux release.

Advantages of Using Linux

Using Linux has many advantages. Of the many operating systems available today, Linux is the most popular free system that's widely available. For the IBM PC, Linux provides a complete system with built-in multiuser and multitasking capabilities that take advantage of the entire processing power of your 386 and higher computer systems.

Linux comes with a complete implementation of the TCP/IP networking protocol. With Linux, you can connect to the Internet and the vast wealth of information it contains. Linux also provides a complete e-mail system to send messages back and forth through cyberspace.

Linux also has a complete graphical user interface (GUI), XFree86, that's based on the popular X Windows system. XFree86 is a complete implementation of the X Windows system that can be distributed free of charge with Linux. XFree86 provides the common GUI elements you find on other commercial GUI platforms, such as Windows and OS/2.

Today, all of this is available for Linux and is basically free. All you have to pay is the price for acquiring the programs from the Internet or via mail order (available from several different vendors). Of course, because you've purchased this book, you already have the entire Linux system on the accompanying CD-ROMs.

Open Systems Portability

In the never-ending quest for standardization, many organizations have taken a renewed interest in the direction in which operating systems are developing. UNIX hasn't gone unnoticed. The drive to standardize UNIX stems from the many UNIX variants now available. You'll learn more about how those variants were developed in the following section.

Efforts have been made to combine, collate, and otherwise absorb all versions of UNIX into a single all-encompassing version of the operating system. Initially, the effort met with guarded enthusiasm, and some effort was expended on coming to terms with blending the different versions. As with many noble efforts, this one was doomed to failure because developers weren't willing to sacrifice part of what they had already invested in their particular versions. (Sadly enough, many developers still feel that way.)

However, the continued existence of UNIX varieties isn't necessarily cause for alarm. Despite the different varieties, all are still inherently superior to all other operating systems available today because each contains the same elements described in the preceding pages.

Portability is merely the capability to transport an operating system from one platform to another so that it still performs the way it should. UNIX is indeed a portable operating system. Initially, UNIX could operate on only one specific platform—the DEC PDP-7 minicomputer. Today, the many UNIX variants can operate in any environment and on any platform, from laptops to mainframes.

Portability provides the means for different computer platforms running UNIX to communicate accurately and effectively with any of the other platforms. These systems can do this without the addition of special high-priced after-market communications interfaces. No other operating system in existence can make this claim.

Applications

Although using an operating system is sometimes fun in and of itself, it isn't the reason most people use a computer. Most people need to do productive work with their computers. Linux has literally thousands of applications available today, including programs for spreadsheets, databases, word processing, application development in a variety of computer languages, and telecommunications packages to get you online. Linux also comes with a wide range of games, both text- and graphics-based. When you need a break from the drudgery of the daily grind, Linux can provide a few minutes (or hours) of relaxation.

Advantages for Computer Professionals

If you're a computer professional, Linux provides a wealth of tools for program development. It includes compilers for many of the top computer programming languages today, such as C, C++, and Smalltalk. If you don't like those languages, Linux provides you with tools, such as Flex and Bison, that you can use to build your own computer languages. These tools come with the CD-ROMs accompanying this book, but their commercial counterparts can cost several hundred dollars each. If you want to learn one of the aforementioned languages but don't want to spend hundreds of dollars for another compiler, Linux and its development tools are for you.

Linux also allows you to communicate with your company's office systems. And if you're a UNIX systems administrator, Linux can help you perform your duties from home. Although working from home is just in its infancy, perhaps some day you can use Linux to do your job at home and then only occasionally visit the office for personal meetings.

Two of the industry's buzzwords are *open systems* and *interoperability*, both of which refer to the capability of many different systems to communicate with one another. Most open systems specifications require POSIX (Portable Operating System Interface) compliance, which means some form of UNIX. Linux meets those standards today. In fact, Linux was designed for source-code portability, so if you have a corporate program running on one version of UNIX, you should be able to port that system relatively quickly to a system running Linux.

Corporations are insisting on these types of open systems so that they aren't locked into using any one vendor. Remember the old adage "Don't put all your eggs in one basket?" Corporations today are becoming leery of systems controlled by single companies because those in control can dictate how the software behaves and what hardware systems the software supports. If that company chooses a direction that's not good for your corporation, tough luck. You're stuck with that company's decision whether you like it or not. With UNIX/Linux and open systems, however, you're in control of your own destiny. If the operating system doesn't have a feature you need, plenty of consultants are available who can make the necessary changes, which is possible because you have the source code to your operating system.

Education

Students, note that Linux provides you with editors to write your assignments and spell check-ers to proof those assignments. With Linux, you should be able to log in to your school's computer network. Of course, with access to the Internet, you also have an instant tap into the limitless wealth of information there. You also have access to thousands of experts in a wide variety of subjects who can answer your questions. Linux can be useful, even if your major isn't computer science.

Linux provides such advantages for so little because of the spirit and philosophy of the community that built and continues to build Linux. Linux is a great experiment that took on a life of its own. Literally hundreds of computer hackers from around the world contributed to its development. Linus Torvalds first developed what became Linux for himself and later released his brainchild to the world under the GNU copyleft.

▶ **See** "The GNU License," **p. 800**

Hackers

At the basic level, Linux is a system built by and for hackers. The popular definition of *hacker* has a negative connotation in today's society, but computer hackers aren't criminals by their definition of the word. Their definition deals with how one approaches any activity in life—not just when dealing with computers. Hackers feel a certain depth of commitment and an enhanced level of excitement at hacking a system. *Hacking* basically means learning all there is to know about a system, becoming immersed in the system to the point of distraction, and being able to fix the system if it breaks.

Hackers basically want to know how a system they find interesting works. Most are not interested in making money or seeking revenge, although certain hackers do cross that line to become what the hacker community calls *crackers*. Computer hackers become outraged when they're compared with these vandals and criminals the popular media now calls *hackers* (instead of *crackers*). Hopefully, Linux gives you a feeling of what it's like to be a hacker, and ideally, you will avoid becoming a cracker.

If you're simply the curious type and want to learn more about UNIX, Linux is for you. Here is a fully functional version of UNIX to which you have free, unrestricted access—something you seldom find in the real world. Most UNIX users are given accounts on UNIX machines that grant them only limited rights and privileges, and in such cases, a normal user can't use or experiment with certain UNIX/Linux commands. But this isn't conducive to learning all about UNIX. With Linux, however, you have complete run of the place and can do what you want whenever you want. Of course, with this great power comes great responsibility: You must learn how to manage a real UNIX system, which can be fun in and of itself.

Disadvantages of Using Linux

Perhaps the biggest disadvantage of using Linux is the fact that no single corporate entity is in charge of its development. If something goes wrong or you have a problem, no toll-free technical support numbers are available that you can call for help. But when you really think about it, do such numbers provide real support for current commercial systems? How often are you referred elsewhere—providing you get through to tech support—to have your question answered? How many times are you asked to post a question on an online service to get help? Well, with Linux, although there's no tech support number, there are literally thousands of users in the online communities to help answer your questions. (See Appendix A, "Sources of Information," for places to go for help.)

Lack of Technical Support

Having no source of technical support can be a problem with Linux, no doubt about it. The same is true of Linux applications. Although a few commercial programs are available for Linux, most programs are developed by small groups and then posted to the world. Many developers, however, do help out with questions.

> **N O T E** Many commercial companies are now building Linux applications that they sell. For people to use their applications, though, these companies typically provide a free copy of a Linux distribution along with their product and thus supply technical support for that version of Linux. ■

Hardware Problems

Another disadvantage is that Linux can be hard to install and doesn't work on all hardware platforms. Unlike a commercial program development operation, where a cohesive group spends months building and testing a program against a variety of conditions and hardware, Linux developers are scattered across the globe. There's no formal quality-assurance program. Developers release their programs when they feel like releasing them. Also, the hardware supported by Linux depends on the hardware each developer owns while writing that portion of the code. Thus, Linux doesn't work with all the hardware available for PCs today.

> **CAUTION**
>
> If your system doesn't have the hardware supported by Linux, you'll have problems installing and running the system. Chapter 3, "Installing Red Hat," Chapter 4, "Installing Caldera OpenLinux," and Appendix C, "Linux Hardware Compatibility HOWTO," provide details on the hardware you need in order to use Linux.

If you have the hardware that's supported, chances are you'll have no problem installing and using Linux. If you don't have the necessary hardware…well, Linux developers expect you to fix it. After all, this is a hacker's system.

Inability to Use Current Software

Another disadvantage is that your current applications for such operating systems as DOS and OS/2 more than likely won't work under Linux. Fortunately, those other systems can *coexist* with Linux; thus, although you can't use both operating systems at the same time, you can leave Linux and boot the other operating system to use your applications there.

Work is in progress on Linux emulators that run DOS and Windows programs, as well as the Executor project to run Macintosh programs under Linux. Although the DOS project is much further along than the Windows or Mac projects, all are in early phases and are not quite ready for prime time. But some day in the near future, Linux will be able to run your Mac, DOS, and Windows applications.

Also, Caldera, Inc. has ported Sun's WABI (Windows Applications Binary Interface) product to Linux. WABI allows Windows 3.1 applications to run under X on Linux. Unlike many Linux applications, Caldera sells this product along with several other Linux applications. However, Caldera provides the Red Hat distribution of Linux free of charge to run the applications the company sells. Caldera is also at work on porting a version of DOS, called DR DOS, to Linux.

To install Linux, you typically have to repartition your hard drive—although this is not always necessary. *Repartitioning* means erasing part of your drive, which wipes out your programs and data on that drive. Currently, there's no safe way to install Linux without repartitioning. If you plan to install Linux, you should back up your disk first (two or three backups is safest). Also, you might not have enough hard disk space to install Linux and keep your other software on the same disk, in which case you have to decide what goes and what stays. No matter what, you have to back up your system, repartition the drive, restore your old software, and then install Linux, which can be a time-consuming and error-prone process.

N O T E There are alternatives to repartitioning your hard drive. You can share space with Linux and DOS, or you can use a program that repartitions your drive without erasing files. These alternatives do work, but you still face the possibility of losing data while installing the system. Also, by repartitioning, you gain improved performance and better control over the amount of disk space used for Linux.

The amount of disk space you need to run Linux depends on the various applications you plan to install. You should have at least 120MB free on the drive that you want to install Linux on, in addition to the programs and data you want to keep from your other operating systems. If you have 200MB free, you should have more than enough space for a full installation of Linux. ■

Lack of Experience

Finally, unless you're already a UNIX guru, you must learn how to manage a Linux system. Unlike DOS, Windows, and OS/2, Linux and UNIX need to be managed. The manager, usually called the *systems administrator* or *sys admin*, is responsible for maintaining the system. The sys admin is responsible for performing such duties as adding and deleting user accounts, backing up the system on a regular basis, installing new software, configuring the system, and fixing things when they go wrong (which happens even on commercial versions of UNIX in use every day). Because UNIX doesn't run perfectly 100 percent of the time, the systems administrator must maintain the system. This presents a great opportunity for you to learn how to be a systems administrator on a UNIX system.

▶ **See** "Understanding Centralized-Processing Systems," **p. 166**

Overcoming the Disadvantages

At first, you might think that using Linux puts you all alone in the world, making you survive by yourself. This is partially true because Linux started life as a hacker's system, and hackers like to tinker and fix systems themselves. But today, because the popularity of Linux has grown, many sources of help are available.

Thousands of pages of documentation are provided with most distributions of Linux. You can find this information in the /DOCS directory on the accompanying Slackware 96 CD-ROM and in the /DOC directory on the Red Hat CD-ROM.

In addition, several magazines are devoted to Linux, and you'll find plenty of online sources of information and online users willing to help with your questions. If you're a commercial entity and need a professional contractor, these too are available. After you install Linux, you'll also find a wealth of online help providing information on almost every Linux command and program available. Check out Appendix A, "Sources of Information," to see that you're not alone.

Disappearing Disadvantages

Although all the disadvantages discussed in the preceding sections still exist, many are slowly disappearing as new companies come into existence to build on Linux and offer new solutions. Two such companies are Red Hat and Caldera. We chose Red Hat as the primary distribution for this book because of its ease of use and installation. Caldera also uses the Red Hat distribution for its line of Linux applications. Both Red Hat and Caldera provide online, fax, and e-mail–based technical support for their products and their versions of Linux.

The Commercial Side of Linux

Linux is just not a "toy" OS anymore. Many companies use Linux as an inexpensive Web server for their intranets. Linux is also used for various network applications (such as DNS), for routing, and as firewalls. Also, many Internet service providers (ISPs) use Linux as their main operating system.

Many commercial programs are also available for Linux, which you can check out in the Commercial HOWTO. Other organizations, such as NASA and Digital Domain, use Linux to render various images including high-resolution planetary images (NASA) or realistic special effects for movies such as Titanic (Digital Domain).

Commercial Programs from Red Hat

Although Red Hat released one of the most popular distributions of Linux, the company also has produced several commercial programs. Red Hat has also created a Linux package manager, called RPM, which it released under the GPL for other distributions to use.

Along with its GPL versions of Linux and RPM, Red Hat also provides an application framework called Applixware, which contains a word processor, a spreadsheet program, a presentation graphics program, a mail tool, and various development tools. Red Hat also provides a commercial version of Motif for developing and running X under Linux.

Commercial Programs from Caldera

Caldera originally provided a networking-based distribution based on Red Hat and technology from Novell, where many of Caldera's principals previously worked. Their second-generation product, Caldera OpenLinux Base, is a low-cost UNIX-like operating system based on the Linux 2.0 kernel and the OpenLinux distribution from Caldera. It includes a graphical user interface capable of managing system and networked resources, including client and server interaction with the Internet and all major networking systems. The menu-driven installation is provided in multiple languages. Caldera OpenLinux Base is a nondedicated gateway and includes all Internet client, server, and router protocols and services. OpenLinux Base also includes a commercial X server from MetroLink and a fully licensed Linux version of the Netscape Navigator.

Caldera also provides Corel's WordPerfect for Linux, as well as an Internet office suite containing a bundle of complete business applications. These commercial programs, as well as dozens more, are available from Caldera on the company's Solutions CD. You can use Netscape to browse the catalog and then follow the instructions on the Ordering page to place an order.

ON THE WEB

You can see Caldera's catalog online at **http://www.caldera.com/solutionscd**.

Caldera also licensed and ported Sunsoft's WABI technology to allow end users to run the most popular Windows 3.1 applications on Linux-based system software.

A Brief History of Linux

The history of Linux is tied to the history of UNIX and, to a lesser extent, a program called Minix. Minix was an operating system tutorial written by the well-known and respected computer scientist Andrew Tannebaum. This operating system became popular on several PC platforms, including MS-DOS-based PCs. But more on Minix later. First, a brief history of UNIX.

Although AT&T created the UNIX operating system, many other companies and individuals have tried to improve the basic idea over the years. The following sections examine a few of the leading variants in use today.

AT&T

Ken Thompson (a computer programmer for AT&T Bell Laboratories) and a group of people working under Ken's direction developed an operating system that was flexible and completely compatible with programmers' varied needs. Legend tells that Ken, who had been using the MULTICS operating system, dubbed this new product UNIX as he joked with others on his development team. He was lampooning the MULTICS multiuser operating system: UNIX was derived from *uni*, meaning *one* or *single*, followed by the homophone X. Perhaps the greater joke in this bit of folklore lies in the fact that MULTICS is remembered by few users today as a viable multiuser operating system, while UNIX has become the de facto industry standard for multiuser multitasking operating systems.

BSD

Berkeley Software Distribution (BSD), University of California at Berkeley, released its first version of UNIX, based on AT&T's Version 7, in 1978. BSD UNIX, as it's known throughout the industry, contained enhancements developed by the academic community at Berkeley that were designed to make UNIX more user-friendly. The user-friendly "improvements" in BSD UNIX were an attempt to make UNIX appeal to casual users in addition to the advanced programmers who liked its flexibility in conforming to their changing demands. Despite being less than 100 percent compatible with AT&T's original UNIX, BSD UNIX did accomplish its goals: The added features enticed casual users to use UNIX.

BSD has become the academic UNIX standard. The original creators of BSD have since released a version for the Intel platform called, appropriately enough, BSD. This version too has a limited distribution on the Internet and via CD-ROM vendors. The authors also wrote several articles a few years ago in the computer magazine *Dr. Dobb's Journal*, detailing the design and implementation of BSD386 or FreeBSD. Today, BSDI, the commercial version of FreeBSD, is another popular operating system similar to Linux.

USL

UNIX System Laboratories (USL) was an AT&T spinoff company that had been developing the UNIX operating system since the early 1980s. Before Novell purchased it in 1993, USL produced the source code for all UNIX System V derivatives in the industry. However, USL itself didn't sell a shrink-wrapped product at that time.

USL's last release of UNIX was UNIX System V Release 4.2 (SVR4.2). SVR4.2 marked USL's first entry into the off-the-shelf UNIX marketplace. In a joint venture with Novell, which temporarily created a company called Univel, USL produced a shrink-wrapped version of SVR4.2 called UnixWare. With Novell's purchase of USL, Novell shifted the focus of USL from source-code producer to UnixWare producer. Novell has now sold its version of UNIX to the Santa Cruz Operation (SCO).

Recently, SCO made a free single-user license available to the public for using SCO UNIX. The program costs $19 for the distribution media, not unlike Linux. However, whereas SCO provides a copy of its operating system, it doesn't provide the source code. Some in the Linux community suspect Linux is giving the UNIX community—or at least the SCO community—some stiff competition.

XENIX, SunOS, and AIX

Microsoft developed its UNIX version, XENIX, in the late 1970s and early 1980s, during the peak of the PC revolution. Processing power available in PCs began to rival that of existing minicomputers. With the advent of Intel's 80386 microprocessor, it soon became evident that XENIX, which had been developed specifically for PCs, was no longer necessary. Microsoft and AT&T merged XENIX and UNIX into a single operating system called System V/386 Release 3.2, which can operate on practically any common hardware configuration. XENIX is still available today from Santa Cruz Operation (SCO), a codeveloper with Microsoft, whose efforts to promote XENIX in the PC market have made this version of UNIX one of the most commercially successful.

Sun Microsystems has contributed greatly to UNIX marketability by promoting SunOS and its associated workstations. Sun's work with UNIX produced a version based on BSD. Interestingly enough, AT&T's SVR4 is compatible with BSD, too—no doubt an offshoot of AT&T and Sun Microsystems' collaboration in UNIX System V Release 4.0.

IBM's venture into the world of UNIX yielded a product called AIX (Advanced Interactive Executive). Although AIX isn't as well known as some other UNIX versions, AIX performs well and has no problem holding its share of the operating system market. It's perhaps the old belief that any UNIX version is an unfriendly, unforgiving operating system that has kept AIX from gaining a better market reception.

Linux

Linux is the brainchild of a computer science student named Linus Torvalds. Linux began life as a hobby project in 1991 for Linus, who was then 23. He hoped to create a more robust version of UNIX for Minix users. Minix, as mentioned earlier, is a program developed by computer science professor Andrew Tannebaum.

The Minix system was written to demonstrate several computer science concepts found in operating systems. Torvalds incorporated these concepts into a stand-alone system that mimics UNIX. The program was widely available to computer science students all over the world and soon generated a wide following, including its own Usenet newsgroups. Linus Torvalds set out to provide his fellow Minix users with a better platform that could run on the widely available IBM PC. Linus targeted the emerging 386-based computers because of the task-switching properties of the 80386 protected-mode interface.

What follows are some of the statements Linus made when announcing his Linux program.

> "After that it was plain sailing: hairy coding still, but I had some devices, and debugging was easier. I started using C at this stage, and it certainly speeds up development. This is also when I started to get serious about my megalomaniac ideas to make 'a better Minix than Minix.' I was hoping I'd be able to recompile gcc under Linux some day...."

> "Two months for basic setup, but then only slightly longer until I had a disk driver (seriously buggy, but it happened to work on my machine) and a small file system. That was about when I made 0.01 available [around late August of 1991]: it wasn't pretty, it had no floppy driver, and it couldn't do much [of] anything. I don't think anybody ever compiled that version. But by then I was hooked, and didn't want to stop until I could chuck out Minix."

N O T E   These announcements are from the "Linux Installation and Getting Started Guide," by Matt
Welsh (copyright 1992-94 by Matt Welsh, 205 Gray Street NE, Wilson, NC 27893,
mdw@sunsite.unc.edu). They're used subject to section 3 of Matt's copyright.

You can obtain the complete "Linux Installation and Getting Started Guide" from the Linux Documentation Project's various archives sites. You can find this book on **sunsite.unc.edu** in the directory
/pub/Linux/docs/LDP/install-guide. For information on how to access archives and download files,
refer to Chapter 31, "Surfing the Internet with the World Wide Web." ■

In a later announcement, made in **comp.os.minix** on Oct. 5, 1991, Linus introduced to the
world Linux version 0.02, the first official version of Linux.

> "Do you pine for the nice days of Minix 1.1, when men were men and wrote their own
> device drivers? Are you without a nice project and just dying to cut your teeth on an OS
> you can try to modify for your needs? Are you finding it frustrating when everything
> works on Minix? No more all-nighters to get a nifty program working? Then this post
> might be just for you."

> "As I mentioned a month ago, I'm working on a free version of a Minix lookalike for AT-
> 386 computers. It has finally reached the stage where it's even usable (though [it] may
> not be depending on what you want), and I am willing to put out the sources for wider
> distribution. It's just version 0.02, but I've successfully run bash, gcc, gnu-make, gnu-sed,
> compress, and so forth under it."

Who Owns Linux?

IBM owns the rights to OS/2, and Microsoft owns the rights to MS-DOS and MS Windows, but
who owns the rights to Linux? First and foremost, Linux isn't public domain software; various
components of Linux are copyrighted by many people. Linus Torvalds holds the copyright to
the basic Linux kernel. Red Hat, Inc. owns the rights to the Red Hat distribution version, and
Patrick Volkerding holds the copyright to the Slackware distribution. Many Linux utilities are
under the GNU General Public License (GPL). In fact, Linus and most Linux contributors have
also placed their work under the protection of the GNU GPL. You can find the license on each
of the accompanying CD-ROMs in the root directory in the file named "copying."

This license is sometimes referred to as the GNU Copyleft (a play on the word *copyright*). This
license covers all the software produced by GNU (itself a play on words—GNU's Not UNIX) and
the Free Software Foundation. The license allows programmers to create software for everyone.
The basic premise behind GNU is that software should be available to everyone, and that if someone wants to modify the program to his or her own ends, that should be possible. The only caveat
is that the modified code can't be restricted; others must also have the right to the new code.

▶ **See** "How to Apply These Terms to Your New Programs," **p. 805**

The GNU Copyleft, or GPL, allows a program's creators to keep their legal copyright, but allows others to take, modify, and sell the resulting new program. However, in doing so, the
original programmers can't restrict any of these same rights to modify the program from the
people buying the software. If you sell the program as is or in a modified form, you must provide the source code. That's why Linux comes with the complete source code.

From Here...

Linux is a viable alternative to UNIX on the desktop. The freely available source code and applications make Linux a reasonable alternative to other operating systems for PC-based platforms. For more information, check out the following:

- Chapter 3, "Installing Red Hat," provides information on putting the Red Hat distribution of Linux on your computer.

- Chapter 4, "Installing Caldera OpenLinux Lite," provides information on putting Caldera's distribution of Linux on your computer.

- Chapter 5, "Running Linux Applications," explains how to use some of the applications that come on the accompanying CD-ROMs.

- Appendix D, "The GNU General Public License," provides the verbatim license for using GNU applications.

Linux Installation Overview

by Jack Tackett

In this chapter

This chapter gives you the information you need to install almost any Linux distribution. Remember, Linux isn't a commercial product, and you might find some problems. Although this book leads the way, you may find the need to use the resources, such as the various HOWTOs, provided on the CD-ROM and available on the Internet.

N O T E This book assumes that you have a working knowledge of DOS and of such items as formatting your hard drive, partition tables, and sector sizes. If this information sounds like a foreign language, check out *Using MS-DOS 6.2, Special Edition*, or ask a computer guru buddy to help you through this. ■

 T I P You're about to make major changes to your system, so be careful. It's a good idea to have paper and pen nearby to take notes just in case something does go wrong; besides, you'll need to jot down some numbers along the way.

Understanding Linux's Hardware Requirements

To be able to install Linux successfully, you need supported hardware. Choosing the right level of hardware for your Linux system depends on such factors as the number of users to be supported and the types of applications to be run. All this translates into requirements for working memory, hard disk storage space, the types of terminals needed, and so forth.

 ON THE WEB

For current information on hardware that Red Hat 5.1 supports and doesn't support, see Red Hat's Web site

http://www.redhat.com/support/docs/rhl/intel/rh51-hardware-intel.html

Most Linux systems today consist of PCs. These Linux installations are often for only a single user, although they may also be tied into larger Linux or UNIX systems.

CAUTION

Linux is a constantly evolving system, and hardware support is sporadically updated. The Red Hat distribution on the accompanying CD-ROM is relatively stable, but new hardware support may have been provided by the time this book is printed and the CD-ROM is created. Although many hardware components have clones or compatible replacements, not all may work with Linux. If you do have the hardware discussed in this chapter, the odds are excellent that Linux installs, boots, and operates properly. If you don't have the equipment listed, Linux may or may not operate properly, but the odds are against you getting a system up and running.

If you're using a version of Linux in a single-user configuration (the most likely configuration), you're the system administrator. It's your responsibility to understand the system well enough to perform the administrative duties required to keep it operating at an optimum level. These duties include keeping enough space on the hard drive, backing up regularly, ensuring that all devices attached to the system have the proper software drivers, installing and configuring software, and so forth.

Choosing the level of hardware you need depends heavily on the hardware used by the myriad people who programmed the Linux system. Unlike commercial software developers who can afford to test their systems on many different hardware configurations, Linux developers typically have access only to their personal computers. Luckily, because so many Linux developers exist, most of the standard hardware found in the PC world is supported.

The System's CPU

A basic system requires an IBM-compatible PC with an Intel 80386 or later CPU in any of the various CPU types, such as the 80386SX, 80486DX/2, and Intel's various Pentium processors. Other CPU clones, such as the 80386 clone chips made by Cyrix and Advanced Micro Devices (AMD), are also compatible with Linux.

The 80386 and 80486SX processors don't have math coprocessors built in, but Linux doesn't require a floating-point math coprocessor. Linux can emulate the coprocessor by using software routines, but at a significant reduction in execution speed. For a fast system, you should consider getting a CPU with a math coprocessor built in, such as an 80486DX or Pentium.

The Linux kernel has also been ported to other processors. Among those now supported are the DEC Alpha, the PowerPC (Macs), Sun Sparcs, and even embedded systems processors such as those used in Caldera's Network PC.

The System's Bus

The type of bus used to communicate with the peripherals is also important. Linux works with only the ISA, EISA, and PCI buses. The MicroChannel Architecture (MCA) bus used on IBM's PS/2 isn't supported, although a port is in process. Some newer systems use a faster bus for such items as disk access and video displays, called the *local bus*. Linux does support the VESA Local Bus but may not support a non-VESA Local Bus architecture.

Memory Needs

Linux requires surprisingly little RAM to run, especially when compared to comparable operating systems such as OS/2 and Windows NT. Linux requires at least 2M of RAM, although 4M is highly recommended. If you have less than 4M of RAM, you need to use what's called a *swap file*. The basic rule of thumb is that the more memory your system contains, the faster your system runs.

The next memory consideration for Linux is the use of the X Windows clone called XFree86. XFree86 is a version of X Windows that's freely distributable and is included with Linux for that reason. XFree86 is a GUI similar to Microsoft Windows.

▶ **See** "Installing the XFree86 System," **p. 425**

To productively use X, your Linux system requires at least 16M of virtual memory. *Virtual memory* is the combination of physical memory and swap space on the hard drive. Again, the more physical memory the system contains, the more responsive the system will be, especially when using X.

Disk Drives and Space Requirements

Although it's possible to run Linux from a floppy-drive-only system, running Linux from your system's floppy drive isn't recommended.

N O T E You can boot Linux from a floppy drive. *Booting a system* refers to the process of starting a computer system and loading the operating system into memory to start the system. The term is derived from the phrase *bootstrapping*. ■

For a home-based system, you need a floppy drive—either 5 1/4 inch or 3 1/2 inch. You need a floppy drive even if you install and run Linux from your CD-ROM.

For better system performance, you want to install Linux on a hard drive. You must have an IBM AT standard drive controller. This shouldn't be a problem because most modern, non-SCSI controllers are AT compatible. Linux supports all MFM and IDE controllers, as well as most RLL and ESDI controllers. Linux may or may not support the newer high-capacity IDE drives from older 8-bit IDE controllers.

Linux supports a wide range of SCSI hard-drive controllers. If your controller is a true SCSI controller—that is, not a proprietary version of SCSI—Linux can use your controller. Linux now supports SCSI controllers from Adaptec, Future Domain, Seagate, UltraStor, the SCSI adapter on the ProAudio Spectrum 16 card, and Western Digital. The following card types are supported:

Adaptec 152x/1542/1740/274x/284x/294X	Always IN2000
Buslogic	Pro Audio Spectrum 16
EATA-DMA (DPT, NEC, AT&T)	Qlogic
Seagate ST-02	Trantor T128/T128F/T228
Future Domain TMC-8xx, 16xx	UltraStor
Generic NCR5380	7000FASST
NCR 53c7, 8xx	

▶ **See** "Controllers (SCSI)," **p. 676**

If you have the proper drive controller, you must worry about disk space requirements. Linux supports multiple hard drives and can be installed across drives. Unlike other operating systems, Linux doesn't need to be installed on the same hard drive; pieces can be installed on different drives.

Disk Space The one item to realize about disk space, however, is that Linux can't reside on the same partition as other operating systems, such as MS-DOS and OS/2. *Partitions* are areas of a disk drive specified during initialization of a drive and before formatting a drive. You typically use a program called fdisk to partition a drive. Some commercial products allow you to repartition a drive, and Linux provides a utility called FIPS to do the same. To use Linux efficiently, you should repartition your hard drive and allocate enough space for the Linux system files and your data files.

> **CAUTION**
>
> Unless you're installing Linux onto a brand-new hard drive, you'll need to repartition and reformat the drive. This destroys all information now stored on that portion of the drive. Thus, it's imperative to back up your files—twice—before installing Linux. If space permits, you can split a single hard drive into multiple partitions and copy your files back to one of the partitions.

The amount of disk space required depends on the software you install and the amount of data you expect that software will generate. Linux requires less disk space than most implementations of UNIX systems. You can run a completely functional Linux system, without X Windows support, in 20MB. For a complete installation of everything in the distribution, 150MB to 200MB is recommended.

Swap Space   Finally, as mentioned earlier in the section "Memory Needs," if you have limited RAM, you need swap space. Whereas systems such as Microsoft Windows create a swap file that resides on your hard drive as any other file, Linux allows the swap file to reside on a separate swap partition. Most Linux installations use partitions rather than files. Because you can place multiple partitions on the same physical hard drive, you can place the swap partition on the same drive as Linux, but for better performance you should place the swap partition on a separate drive.

Linux allows up to eight swap partitions that can be no larger than 16MB. A rule of thumb is to set the swap file size to twice the amount of physical RAM contained on your system. Thus, if you have 8MB of physical RAM, your swap partition should be 16MB in size.

Monitor Requirements

For text-based terminals, Linux supports all standard Hercules, CGA, EGA, VGA, and SuperVGA video cards and monitors. To take advantage of the color-coding directory listings available with Linux, you need a color monitor. So for text-based operation, any video/controller combination should work.

The big problems occur when you run the X Windows system distributed with Linux. To use XFree86, you need a video adapter that uses one of the chipsets listed in Table 2.1. *Chipsets* are a group of integrated circuits, or computer chips, used to take information from the computer and convert the data into a form displayable on a video monitor. To find out the chipset used by your video adapter, check the documentation included with your card to determine whether there are any problems using XFree86.

Table 2.1   Video Chipsets Supported by Linux

Manufacturer	Chipset(s)
Tseng	ET3000, ET40000AX, ET4000/W32
Western Digital	WD90C00, WD90C10, WD90C11, WD90C24, WD90C30, WD90C31
Trident	TVGA8800CS, TVGA8900B, TVGA8900C, TVGA8900CL, TVGA9000, TVGA9000i, TVGA9100B, TVGA9200CX, TVGA9320, TVGA9400CX, TVGA9420
ATI	28800-4, 28800-5, 28800-a
NCR	77C22, 77C22E, 77C22E+
Cirrus Logic	CLGD5420, CLGD5422, CLGD5424, CLGD5426, CLGD5428, CLGD6205, CLGD6215, CLGD6225, CLGD6235
OAK	OTI067, OTI077
S3	86C911, 86C924, 86C801, 86C805, 86C805i, 86C928
Compaq	AVGA
Western Digital/ Paradise	PVGA1

N O T E   The release notes for the current version of XFree86 distributed with Linux should contain a more recent list of supported and non-supported chipsets. ▓

Some problems encountered by the XFree86 developers are caused by adapter manufacturers who don't provide the necessary information on programming the cards to display information. Without this information, developers can't support X Windows on those adapters. Also, some manufacturers provide this information but require either royalty payments or non-disclosure agreements for others to use the information. These types of restrictions make it impossible to support these adapters on a freely distributed system like the XFree86 system for Linux.

N O T E   The Diamond video cards haven't been supported in the past, due to restrictions the company had on giving out proprietary information. The Diamond company has now begun work with the XFree team to support the company's video systems specifically under Linux and XFree86. ▓

▶ **See** "Video Cards," **p. 750**

CD-ROMs

To install the Linux system included on the accompanying CD-ROM, you must have a CD-ROM drive supported by Linux. Because most CD-ROMs use a SCSI interface controller, any SCSI controller listed earlier in the section "Disk Drives and Space Requirements" should also work with a CD-ROM attached to the controller. Linux also now supports many of the new EIDE and ATAPI CD-ROMs available on the market.

Many of the CD-ROMs included with multimedia packages may or may not work with Linux, depending on whether the controller is a true SCSI adapter or a proprietary adapter. Proprietary adapters for the most part won't work. However, Linux does specifically support the Creative Labs SoundBlaster line of CD-ROMs and provides a specific installation configuration for their CD-ROMs. Other CD-ROMs known to work with Linux include the following:

NEC CDR-74	Okano
Sony CDU-541	Wearnes CD with interface card
Sony CDU-31a or 33a	
Plextor DM-3024	Most IDE/ATAPI CD-ROMs
Aztech	Mitsumi CD-ROMs
Orchid	SoundBlaster, Panasonic Kotobuki, Matsushita, TEAC-55a, or Lasermate

▶ **See** "CD-ROM Drives Supported," **p. 773**

Network Access

You can connect a Linux system to the world in several ways, but the two most popular (and supported) methods are via network controller cards and modems. Network controller cards include Token Ring, FDDI, TAXI, and Ethernet cards. Most common business networks use an Ethernet controller card.

Network Access via Ethernet   Ethernet, a protocol invented by Xerox, has gained immense popularity in the networking world. Although it's unlikely you'll connect Linux to an Ethernet network at home, many business and educational institutions are connected via Ethernet. Table 2.2 lists several of the Ethernet adapters supported.

Table 2.2   Ethernet Controller Cards Supported by Linux

Manufacturer	Interface Card
3Com	3c503, 3c503/16, 3c509
Novell	NE1000, NE2000
Western Digital	WD8003, WD8013
Hewlett-Packard	HP27245, HP27247, HP27250

▶ **See** "Supported Ethernet," **p. 772**

Network Access via Modem   At home, you'll more than likely connect to the outside world via a modem and a communications protocol such as SLIP or PPP. Linux supports almost every type of modem on the market, internal and external. If you can access the modem from MS-DOS, you'll have no problem accessing the modem from Linux.

▶ **See** "Understanding the Requirements for SLIP and PPP," **p. 562**

Miscellaneous Hardware

The following sections list miscellaneous hardware supported by Linux, such as mice, tape drives, and printers. Although such hardware makes Linux easier to use and more robust, it isn't required.

Mice   Using text-based Linux doesn't require a mouse. Unlike many UNIX implementations, however, Linux does allow you to cut text from any area of the screen and paste it to the command line by using a mouse. If you intend to use the X Windows clone, XFree86, you must use a mouse.

Linux supports most serial mice, including the following mice:

- Logitech
- MM series
- Mouseman
- Microsoft
- Mouse Systems

Linux also supports the Microsoft, Logitech, ATIXL, and PS/2 bus mice. In fact, any pointing devices, such as trackballs and touch screens, that emulate the previously listed mice should work with Linux.

Tape Drives   Tape drives provide a great deal of storage space for backing up your computer system. Linux supports several SCSI-based tape systems, as shown in Table 2.3. Linux also supports the popular Colorado Memory Systems tape drives (120 and 250 versions), which are plugged into a system's floppy-disk controller. The versions that plug into the printer port aren't now supported. Most drives supporting QIC-02 should also work with Linux.

Table 2.3   Tape-Backup Drives Supported by Linux

Manufacturer	Model
Exabyte	All SCSI models
Sanko	CP150SE
Tandberg	3600
Wangtek	5525ES, 5150ES, 5099EN

▶ **See** "Tape Drives Supported," **p. 775**

Printers   Linux supports the complete range of parallel printers. Configuring Linux to support serial printers is tedious and error-prone. Serial printer support isn't well documented or supported by the basic Linux installation programs. If you have a serial printer, you may have problems using it under Linux. If you have a parallel printer, your biggest problem is most likely the *stair-step effect*:

```
This is line one.
                This is line two.
                            This is line three.
```

How UNIX, and hence Linux, treat carriage returns and line feeds produces the stair-step effect. Under most UNIX systems, the command to move the paper down one line (line feed) and then position the print head at the beginning of the line (carriage return) are represented by one control character. Under systems such as MS-DOS and Windows, however, each command is represented by a different control character. When you print a UNIX file under a printer configured for MS-DOS systems, you see the stair-step effect because the file contains only the line-feed control character and not the carriage-return control character.

▶ **See** "Knowing What You Need to Configure Printers," **p. 406**

Starting the Installation Process

To start the installation process, you need one or two (depending on the installation method) 3 1/2-inch 1.44MB formatted floppy disks. These disks will be used to create a boot disk for the Linux installation.

Next, you should make sure that you have enough hard disk space to install Linux. Everything on the CD-ROM, if installed, requires about 300MB of disk space, but you can get by with less, especially if you don't install the X Windows system. To decide on the amount of space, you should decide how much space you want for user accounts—that is, the space you want to provide to your users. On a single-user system, 30MB is more than enough.

Next, decide how much swap space your machine needs. If your machine has 8MB of RAM or less, you need a 16MB swap space. If you have 16MB or more, your swap space should equal the amount of RAM.

Finally, figure about 30MB for your root directory. This is the main directory from which all other directories under Linux are accessed.

▶ **See** "Linux Standard Directories," **p. 313**

Again, a minimal installation should fit in 200MB, whereas a full installation, with plenty of user space, should fit well on a 500MB drive.

N O T E   You can also run part of the Linux file system from the CD-ROM without installing all the software. You can choose to do so during installation. ▪

Part

I

Ch

2

If you decide to install and configure X (highly recommended), you should also write down what type of chipset your video card uses. If you have a serial mouse and modem, write down the serial port that each is using. You need this information later during the configuration process.

Understanding the Various Installation Methods

We, the authors, envision most of you installing Red Hat from the accompanying CD-ROM. However, you can use one of the following four methods to install Red Hat: from CD-ROM, via NFS, via FTP, or from a hard drive.

To install directly from CD-ROM, you need access to DOS. From the DOS prompt, execute the command

```
[cdrom-drive]:\dosutils\autoboot
```

where [*cdrom-drive*] is the drive letter for your system's CD-ROM.

> **CAUTION**
>
> This method will erase your hard drive. Back up any files you fear losing.

If you have another partition available, you can install Linux to coexist with your system without erasing what's already there. To do this, you need the CD-ROM, an empty partition, and a boot disk. You learn later in this chapter how to create the boot disk, as well as how to repartition your hard drive.

NFS (Network File System) provides a way to install Red Hat across a network. First, you must mount the CD-ROM drive on a machine supporting the ISO-9660 file system with RockRidge extensions and then export the file system via NFS. You need to know the path to the exported file system and the IP number, or, if DNS is configured, the name of the system.

FTP (File Transfer Protocol) is a method for transferring files across the Internet. (Chapter 30, "Accessing the Network with telnet, ftp, and the r- Commands," explains FTP in more detail.) To install via FTP requires a boot disk and the supplemental disk described later in this chapter.

Installing Red Hat from a hard drive requires the same boot and supplemental disks used for an FTP installation. First, create a directory named RedHat. Then copy the corresponding directory from the CD-ROM, and all the subdirectories there, to the RedHat directory. You can use the following DOS commands to do so:

```
cd \RedHat
xcopy /s e:\RedHat
```

The cd command assumes that you're already on the installation hard drive; the xcopy command assumes that your CD-ROM drive is drive E.

No matter which method you use, you'll need at least the boot disk to proceed with installation. But first, you should gather some information.

Compiling Needed Information

Before starting the installation, you need the following information about your system:

- The type of video card, chipset, and monitor used
- The serial port used by your mouse
- The serial port used by your modem
- The network information for your computer, if it's connected to a network (items such as its IP address, gateway, and domain name)
- The type of hard drive and CD-ROM drive in your system and their controller types
- The name you intend to call your system

If you're connecting to the Internet, you can get most of this information from either your network administrator or your Internet service provider.

If you intend to use other operating systems on the same computer (such as Windows 95, Windows NT, or OS/2), you'll need to create the necessary partitions for these operating systems. Typically, you need to use the operating system's partitioning software, because Linux can't handle these other partition types.

ON THE WEB

A product named System Commander, from V Communications, lets you install and switch between 32 different operating systems. You can find more information about this product at

http://www.v-com.com/

Next, you should check for any last-minute changes to the Red Hat distribution. The reasons are many, but the two major reasons are that Linux is constantly updated, and this chapter is being written at least a month before the CD-ROM is cut. In the interim, new material or bug fixes may have been released.

ON THE WEB

You can also check for updated material on the Web at

http://www.redhat.com/errata

Table 2.4 lists the currently available update packages that fix known problems in the Red Hat 5.1 distribution.

▶ **See** "Installing Packages with RPM," **p. 150**

Table 2.4   Red Hat Errata Listing

Date Released	Package
01-Jun-1998	linuxconf
01-Jun-1998	xosview
01-Jun-1998	bootp
01-Jun-1998	metamail
02-Jun-1998	initscripts
02-Jun-1998	dhcpcd
05-Jun-1998	netkit-base
05-Jun-1998	glint
05-Jun-1998	fstool, usercfg, cabaret
10-Jun-1998	xscreensaver
10-Jun-1998	findutils
10-Jun-1998	emacs
10-Jun-1998	inn
10-Jun-1998	libjpeg, et al
10-Jun-1998	Netscape
10-Jun-1998	kernelcfg
10-Jun-1998	tmpwatch
10-Jun-1998	patch
11-Jun-1998	XFree86
11-Jun-1998	dhcp
12-Jun-1998	mailx

For information on Caldera, see the file /pub/OpenLinux/updates/README at **ftp://ftp.caldera.com/pub/OpenLinux/updates/**.

These directories contain various updated boot disk images and update packages in RPM format for the releases of Caldera OpenLinux. Table 2.5 lists the update packages available.

Table 2.5   Caldera Errata Listing

File/Directory	Description
update.col-1.2.007.12.tgz	Upgrade script for OpenLinux 1.2
update.col.README	Instructions for using upgrade script
README	Instructions on how to get update materials
1.0/	Updated packages for OpenLinux Base release 1.0
1.1/	Updated packages for OpenLinux release 1.1
1.2/	Updated packages for OpenLinux release 1.2

If you're not installing directly off the CD-ROM, you next need to repartition your current hard drive to make room for Linux. This may cause problems, because repartitioning a hard drive destroys any data contained on the affected partitions. After making room for Linux, you need to boot the Linux system and create its new partitions and file systems. Typically, Linux systems need a primary partition to store the files on and a swap file partition, especially if you have a machine with 8MB or less of memory.

N O T E   A *file system* is basically a section of your hard drive specially formatted to hold certain types of files. UNIX and Linux use file systems to represent entire sections of the directory tree. This is in contrast to MS-DOS, which places subdirectories in the directory tree on the same logical drive. UNIX systems use the directory tree format because placing subdirectories on different drives is safer. If one drive malfunctions, only the information on that drive needs to be replaced or fixed.

▶ **See** "Understanding File Systems," **p. 266** ▓

After creating the file systems, you then install the Linux operating system, its support files, and various application packages distributed with the system. To install Linux, you must first boot a stripped-down version of the operating system. You do this by creating a boot disk and a supplemental disk set containing the stripped-down OS.

Creating the Boot and Supplemental Disks

You need to create the boot and supplemental disks by using the rawrite program. You can find this program on the accompanying CD-ROM in the /dosutils subdirectory. For this step, you need two formatted floppies: one labeled *boot* and the other labeled *supp*. Place the boot disk in the A drive and enter the following:

```
E:\dosutils>rawrite

Enter disk image source file name: e:\images\boot.img
Enter target diskette drive: A:
Please insert a formatted diskette into drive A: and press -ENTER-
```

If you want to abort the process, simply press <Ctrl-c> to stop. If rawrite fails, try a new formatted disk. If the problem persists, you should have your hardware checked for possible problems.

After writing the boot disk, you need to create the supplemental disk. Simply use the supp image file name (supp.img) as the source filename in the preceding command sequence.

Partitioning Your Hard Drive

After you back up your system and make the necessary boot and supplemental disks, you must prepare your system's hard drive for Linux.

> **CAUTION**
>
> This process is the most dangerous because maximum data loss is assured. If you haven't backed up your system, do so now. Although you can use an experimental program called FIPS and commercial programs such as Partition Magic to do non-destructive repartitioning, a full backup is recommended, just in case problems occur.

Understanding Partitions

In the early days of PCs, hard drives were few and far between. Most computers used floppies to hold the operating system, programs, and their data. With the introduction of the IBM PC XT, IBM introduced a 10MB hard drive. Early operating systems such as DOS could access only a limited amount of space on hard drives. Then hard drive manufacturers kept expanding the space on their hard drives more quickly than the operating system's capability to access the additional space. The operating system got around this problem by letting the user split the hard drive into sections, called *partitions*. These partitions can hold program files, other operating systems, or data.

Typical MS-DOS systems have one partition, which is referred to as drive C. If you split the drive into partitions, these partitions are typically referred to in alphabetical order as D, E, and so on. MS-DOS also allows you to install multiple hard drives, so that the next drive in this chain might be referred to as F.

UNIX and Linux don't use drive letters to refer to partitions; instead, they use directory names to refer to partitions. Also, as indicated earlier, Linux users can place different directories on different partitions and even on different drives. You can also place different operating systems on different partitions.

Partitions are specified in a section of the hard drive referred to as the *boot record* in what's called a *partition table*. This table is used by the various operating systems to determine what operating system to boot and where their files can physically be found on the hard drive. The boot record is used to *boot*, or start up, the machine's operating system. Linux's boot program, LILO (LInux LOader), and other boot managers use this section of the hard drive, typically found on the first sectors of the drive, to control which operating system to start.

The partition table holds information about the locations and sizes of the various partitions on the hard drive. There are three kinds of partitions: primary, extended, and logical. DOS and some other operating systems must boot from primary partitions. Hard drives can contain only four primary partitions. An extended partition doesn't contain data itself; instead, it allows the user to define other, logical partitions on the drive. Thus, to get around the limit of four primary partitions, you can define an extended partition and then define other logical partitions within the extended partition.

Some operating systems, such as MS-DOS and versions of OS/2 before version 2.0, require that they be installed in a primary partition, but they can access logical drives in extended partitions. This is important to remember if you're going to have a DOS system and a Linux system reside on the same drive. DOS must go in a primary partition.

Using *FDISK*

Partitions are created, destroyed, and managed by a program usually called FDISK. Each operating system has its own version of FDISK, so be sure to use the correct one. If you're now using DOS or are planning to use DOS, you must first repartition the DOS drive by using DOS's FDISK. You later use the Linux version of fdisk to create the Linux partitions. If you're using OS/2, you also need to use the OS/2 version of FDISK to prepare the OS/2 partitions.

Partition Requirements   First, you should plan what partitions you need. DOS requires a primary partition; Linux and OS/2 can reside in other partitions. If you're using the OS/2 boot manager, which also works well with Linux, you must prepare for its use. You must also be aware that if you're shrinking a current DOS partition to make room for Linux, not all of your files can be restored to the new, smaller DOS partition.

> **N O T E**   You can access DOS partitions from Linux, thus moving, saving, and editing DOS files under Linux. But you can't execute DOS programs under Linux.

Two experimental components of Linux allow you to emulate DOS under Linux and also install Linux under DOS. Both systems are still in the implementation stage and are, thus, more suited for Linux hackers. Also, one of the methods, UMSDOS, is incompatible with Red Hat, so you can't use that method at all. You can find plenty of information on these topics in the Linux world.

▶ **See** "Running DOS Programs Under Linux," **p. 127** ▨

Next, you should jot down the number of partitions you need and how much disk space to provide each with.

DOS Requirements   If you want to boot DOS, it must go in a primary partition. A bootable version of DOS doesn't require much space—just enough for the system files, COMMAND.COM, CONFIG.SYS, and any driver files needed to start your system. For example, I provide a 5MB DOS partition on my first drive to boot DOS.

When DOS is loaded and running, you can access any of the other extended and logical drives on the system. Unfortunately, whereas Linux can access DOS files in a DOS partition, DOS can't access Linux files in a Linux partition.

OS/2 Requirements   OS/2 versions 2.0 and later don't need a primary partition. The OS/2 system can install and boot from an extended partition. Thus, you can install DOS on a primary partition and create an extended partition area for OS/2 and Linux. The space required for OS/2 is version- and feature-dependent; you should consult your OS/2 documentation for space requirements. You should also subtract 1MB from available space if you intend to use the OS/2 boot manager.

Linux Requirements   As explained earlier, Linux stores files on file systems, and these file systems can reside on different partitions, basically as safety precautions. Linux requires one partition for each file system. The next consideration is for a swap partition. Linux, like most operating systems that use disk space for memory (called a *virtual memory configuration*), needs a swap file or a swap partition to simulate physical memory using disk space. Linux typically uses a swap partition.

The size of the swap partition depends on the amount of physical RAM your system contains. A rule of thumb is to make your swap partition twice the size of your amount of RAM. Thus, if you have 8MB of RAM in your system, you should create a swap partition 16MB in size. If you have 4MB of RAM or less, you must activate a swap partition.

Linux swap partitions can be no more than 128MB in size, so if you need more space, you have to create multiple swap partitions. Thus, if you have a Linux system that needs two partitions for Linux (one for the system files and one for user files), plus a swap partition, you need to define two Linux partitions and one 32MB swap partition.

Repartitioning Your DOS Drive

This section assumes that you need to repartition a DOS drive. First, you execute FDISK by typing fdisk at the DOS prompt. The FDISK Options screen appears (see Figure 2.1).

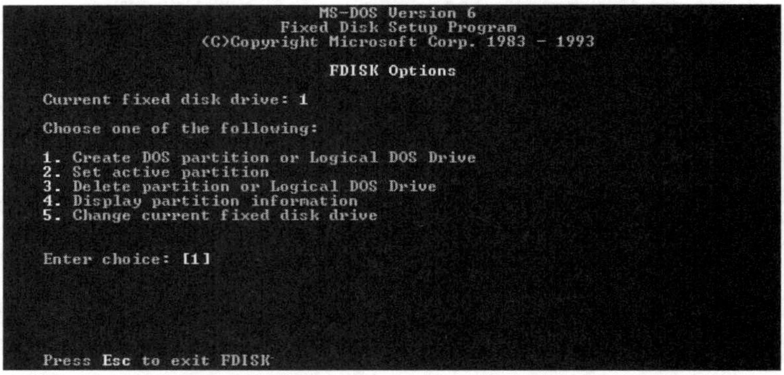

FIG. 2.1
From the FDISK Options screen, you can look at current partitions, create new partitions, and delete old partitions.

```
                        MS-DOS Version 6
                     Fixed Disk Setup Program
             (C)Copyright Microsoft Corp. 1983 - 1993

                           FDISK Options

Current fixed disk drive: 1

Choose one of the following:

  1. Create DOS partition or Logical DOS Drive
  2. Set active partition
  3. Delete partition or Logical DOS Drive
  4. Display partition information
  5. Change current fixed disk drive

Enter choice: [1]




Press Esc to exit FDISK
```

The screen shown in Figure 2.1 might look different depending on which version of MS-DOS you're using. Pick menu option 4, Display Partition Information. The Display Partition Information screen appears (see Figure 2.2). Write down the information in this screen. You need the current partition table information if you decide to abort the Linux installation and put your system back the way it was before you started.

FIG. 2.2

You can look at current partition information by using the Display Partition Information screen in MS-DOS 6.x.

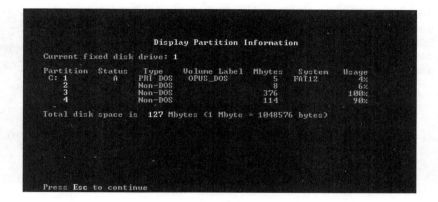

```
                        Display Partition Information
Current fixed disk drive: 1

Partition  Status    Type    Volume Label  Mbytes   System    Usage
  C: 1       A     PRI DOS    OPUS_DOS        5      FAT12       4%
     2             Non-DOS                    8                  6%
     3             Non-DOS                  376                100%
     4             Non-DOS                  114                 90%

Total disk space is  127 Mbytes (1 Mbyte = 1048576 bytes)



Press Esc to continue
```

An Alternative to Repartitioning Your Hard Drive

You may not need to repartition your hard drive, although it's thought that repartitioning offers the best introduction to Linux. You can use FIPS to non-destructively repartition your hard drive.

FIPS stands for *First non-destructive Interactive Partition Splitting*. A program developed by Arno Schaefer as a result of the Linux project, FIPS is used to move around DOS partitions to make room for Linux partitions.

You can find the complete instructions for using FIPS in the document fips.doc located on the accompanying Red Hat CD-ROM in the /utils/fips directory. This program can help only if you have enough free space left on your drive to install Linux; otherwise, you need to delete unneeded files or use the process described earlier to repartition your hard drive.

Under Slackware Linux, you can install Linux on the same partition as DOS with UMSDOS. UMSDOS is a project to allow Linux to exist on DOS partitions. UMSDOS lets you create the Linux root file system under an existing DOS directory. Unfortunately, you can't use UMSDOS under Red Hat.

Deleting Partitions   Unfortunately, FDISK doesn't allow you to simply resize a partition; you must first delete the partition and then add it back with the desired size. From the FDISK Options screen, choose menu option 3, Delete Partition or Logical DOS Drive, which deletes the necessary partitions. The Delete DOS Partition or Logical DOS Drive screen appears (see Figure 2.3).

Pick the appropriate menu option for the type of partition you're deleting, such as a primary DOS partition. For example, option 1, Delete Primary DOS Partition, allows you to delete primary DOS partitions.

Choose option 1 to display the Delete Primary DOS Partition screen (see Figure 2.4). The screen asks for a volume name of the partition and then a confirmation to see whether you really want to delete the partition. Because all information on the partition will be destroyed, FDISK wants to make absolutely sure that you want to delete the primary DOS partition.

FIG. 2.3

Use the Delete DOS
Partition screen to
delete a specific
partition or logical drive.

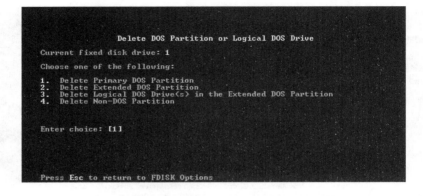

FIG. 2.4

MS-DOS warns you
when you try to delete a
primary DOS partition.

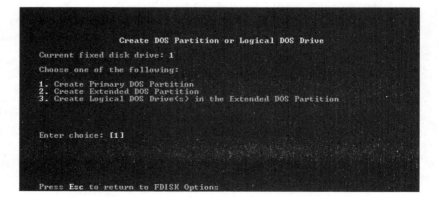

Adding Partitions   After you delete all the necessary partitions, you must add the appropriate partitions for your DOS system by selecting the Create a DOS Partition menu item on the FDISK Options screen. Figure 2.5 shows the Create a DOS Partition or Logical DOS Drive screen.

FIG. 2.5

Most operating systems
require a primary active
partition to boot
properly.

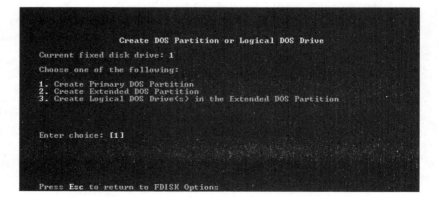

N O T E You can't add the Linux or OS/2 partitions with the DOS FDISK program. Partitioning the hard drive for Linux is covered later in the section "Using the Linux *fdisk* Command." ◼

Providing all the space available for the partition and making the partition the active partition are the FDISK defaults, as shown in Figure 2.6.

FIG. 2.6
You can use all the disk space for one partition or spread out the free space across several partitions.

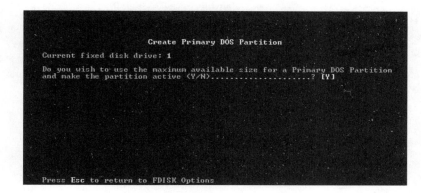

Active indicates that the partition is bootable. To boot DOS, you must specify the primary partition as active. Choose N (no) for this first selection so that you can specify the exact amount of disk space to provide to your DOS partition. Answering no to the question in Figure 2.6 displays the Specify Disk Space for the Partition screen. Specify the desired space for your DOS partition either in megabytes or in percentage of space available and press <Return>.

Next, you must set this partition as active. From the FDISK Options screen, choose menu option 2, Set Active Partition, and simply follow the instructions on the set active menu screen.

Formatting the Partition   After you repartition your hard drive, you need to prepare the new partition for DOS and restore the appropriate files back to the DOS partition. Reboot your computer with the boot disk you made earlier. Then format the appropriate drive and transfer the system files by using the following DOS command:

```
format c: /s
```

When the partition is formatted, you can restore your backup to the new drive. Remember, if you reduced the size of the partition, not all the files will fit on the new drive. It might be necessary to place the files that don't fit on the new drive onto other DOS drives or partitions.

Using the Linux *fdisk* Program

At the fdisk prompt, type m for a list of commands. Table 2.6 lists the available commands.

Table 2.6 The Linux *fdisk* Commands

Command	Description
a	Toggles a bootable flag
c	Toggles the DOS compatibility flag
d	Deletes a partition
l	Lists known partition types
m	Displays this menu
n	Adds a new partition
p	Displays the partition table
q	Quits without saving changes
t	Changes a partition's system ID
u	Changes display/entry units
v	Verifies the partition table
w	Writes the table to disk and exits
x	Provides extra functionality for experts only

To begin the partitioning, select the p command (press <p><Return>) to display the current partition table, which should reflect the drive you partitioned earlier with the DOS FDISK program. Listing 2.1 shows a possible listing from the p command.

Listing 2.1 Example of a Current Partition Table

```
Disk /dev/hda: 15 heads, 17 sectors, 1024 cylinders
Units = cylinders of 255 * 512 bytes

Device        Boot    Begin   Start   End    Blocks   Id   System
/dev/hda1     *       1       1       41     5219     1    DOS 12-bit FAT
dev/hda2              1024    1024    4040   384667+  51   Novell?
Partition 2 has different physical/logical endings:
phys=(967, 14, 17) Logical=(4096, 14.17)
```

N O T E Your screen may appear different than what's shown in Listing 2.1, because the values are different for each drive type and the partitions already defined on that drive. ▨

Listing 2.1 indicates the various partitions already defined that it can detect, the start and ending locations of the partition, and how big it is in blocks. The listing also indicates the partition type. Table 2.7 shows all the different types of partitions you can define with the Linux fdisk program. The primary partition types you used are 83-Linux Native and 82-Linux Swap. You can get a similar listing with the l command.

Table 2.7   The Known Linux Partition Types

Reference Number	Type
0	Empty
1	DOS 12-bit FAT
2	XENIX root
3	XENIX usr
4	DOS 16-bit < 32M
5	Extended
6	DOS 16-bit >= 32M
7	OS/2 HPFS
8	AIX
9	AIX bootable
a	OS/2 Boot Manager
40	Venix 80286
51	Novell?
52	Microport
63	GNU HURD
64	Novell
75	PC/IX
80	Old MINIX
81	MINIX/Linux
82	Linux Swap
83	Linux Native
93	Amoeba
94	Amoeba BBT
a5	BSD/386
b7	BSDI fs
b8	BSDI swap
c7	Syrinx
db	CP/M
e1	DOS access

Part

I

Ch

2

continues

Table 2.7 Continued

Reference Number	Type
e3	DOS R/O
f2	DOS secondary
ff	BBT

In Listing 2.1, Linux prints a note about the different physical and logical endings at the bottom of the screen. The difference exists because on the system used to write this chapter, a prior partition containing the DOS D drive was left intact, whereas the C drive was repartitioned to a smaller C drive to make room for Linux. Thus, there's space between the C drive and the D drive. This is where the necessary partitions required by Linux will be created.

The begin, start, and end numbers from Listing 2.1 are very important and you should write them down. You'll need them in a later step to specify the necessary sizes of the partitions you'll add.

Adding the Necessary Partition

Because you've repartitioned the drive for DOS, you shouldn't have to delete any partitions for Linux. You should only have to add partitions. To add a partition, issue the n command, which displays this:

```
Command Action
e extended
p primary(1-4)
```

Press <p><Return>. fdisk then asks for the partition number; enter your selection and press <Return>. If you indicate a partition number already in use, fdisk reports this fact and asks you to delete the partition before trying to add it to the partition table. For this example, enter **3** to add a third primary partition that's referred to as /dev/hda3.

Next, fdisk asks for the location of the first cylinder. This is usually the first available cylinder; in fact, fdisk displays a default range for your selection—for example:

```
First cylinder (42-1024) :
```

Notice that the first partition ends at cylinder 41 and that the next partition begins at cylinder 1024. Thus, the range supplied by fdisk here allows you to start the next partition anywhere in the range of 42-1024. It's a very good idea not to place partitions just anywhere throughout the disk; instead, choose the next available location, which in this case is cylinder 42. Enter **42** and press <Return>.

N O T E Linux can have trouble booting from partitions defined to start at cylinders above 1024. If you can create a Linux partition only in this range, you may have to boot Linux from a floppy. You learn how to create a boot floppy (different from the boot floppy used for installation) later in this chapter. The only downside is that it takes a little longer to boot Linux from a floppy than it does from the hard drive. ■

Now `fdisk` wants you to specify how much space to allocate for this partition. You can express this size in number of cylinders or by the number of bytes (+*size*), kilobytes (+*size*K), or megabytes (+*size*M). Because you should already know the approximate size you need for the swap file, define this partition first, and then leave the rest of the disk space for the Linux program partitions. Thus, for this example, your machine has 8MB of RAM, so you need to specify a 16MB partition size by replying

```
Last cylinder or +size or +sizeM or +sizeK (42-1023): +16M
```

You should then use the p command to look at the new partition table you've defined. In this example, the new partition table looks like

```
Disk /dev/hda: 15 heads, 17 sectors, 1024 cylinders
Units = cylinders of 255 * 512 bytes

Device      Boot Begin Start End   Blocks  Id   System
/dev/hda1    *    1     1     41    5219 1  DOS  12-bit FAT
/dev/hda2         1024  1024  4040  384667+ 51  Novell?

Partition 2 has different physical/logical endings:
phys=(967, 14, 17) Logical=(4039, 14.17)
/dev/hda3         42    42    170   16447+  83       Linux native
```

By default, `fdisk` made the new partition a Linux Native type. To change this to a swap partition, you need to use the t command. Enter **t**, and then enter the partition number you want to change; in this example, enter **3**. `fdisk` then requests that you enter the hexadecimal value of the desired partition type from Table 2.7 (if you don't have the table handy, you can type **1** to get the list of codes). Because you want a swap partition, enter **82** at the prompt.

As you can see, `fdisk` reports the new partition type, but you can also use the p command to double-check that partition 3 is now a Linux swap partition.

Now you can add your Linux partitions. For this example, add only one partition, but if you want to have multiple partitions for various reasons, you can also do so at this time. To add a partition, press <n>, specify p for another primary partition, and then specify the number for this partition (4). To keep from fragmenting different partitions across the drive, start the last partition where the other left off, at cylinder 171. For the last cylinder, because you want to use the rest of the space for the Linux system, you can specify the last cylinder instead of an exact byte count. Thus, enter **1023**, as shown here:

```
Command (m for help):n
Command action
e     extended
p     primary partition (1-4)
p
Partition number (1-4): 4
First cylinder (171-1024):171
Last cylinder or +size or +sizeM or +sizeK (171-1023):1023
```

Now use the p command to verify the new partitions. If you need to make any changes, do so now.

When you're satisfied with the layout of your partitions, you can use the w command to write the partition table information to the hard disk. None of your changes are permanent until you use the w command; thus, if you feel you've made some changes in error, you can use the q command to exit without altering the partition table. If you use the w command, Linux tells you the partition table has been altered and then resynchronizes the disks to match the new partition table. If your Linux system hangs at this point, reboot with the installation boot and root disks until you're back at the # prompt.

> **CAUTION**
>
> Don't use the Linux fdisk program to create or modify partitions for other operating systems. This could leave the hard drive in a useless state for both operating systems.

Troubleshooting Problems

After your machine reboots, the LILO prompt should appear. Make sure that you can boot to your old operating system if you left it on the hard drive. If that system was DOS, press <Shift> and then type the short word you used to identify the DOS partition when you installed LILO. If you enter an invalid word, press <Tab> to get a list of valid operating system types. If you're having problems at that point, place your DOS boot disk in the boot drive and reboot.

You should be able to boot from your boot disk. When your system is up and running under DOS, try the Linux boot disk you created during installation—not the ones you created to originally install the entire system. If that boot disk doesn't work, you may have to reinstall Linux. Potential problems to check initially are the kernels and your hardware. Before starting over, make sure that you have the appropriate hardware. If you made notes during the installation process, check which kernel you installed against what hardware you have. Make sure your hardware is supported by Linux.

Below are some answers to common problems listed on Red Hat's Web site. These troubleshooting tips are used under the provisions of GNU's GPL.

Q: Can I use a hard drive that has more than 1023 cylinders?

A: The infamous 1023 cylinder question. Yes, but not to boot Linux. You can install Linux on partitions above the 1023 cylinder, but to boot Linux, the root directory and specifically the /boot directory must be installed on the first hard drive below 1024.

Q: How do I add arguments for LILO at the prompt?

A: Some hardware requires that extra parameters be fed to the kernel before the kernel will recognize the hardware. You can accommodate this by editing the /etc/lilo.conf file to provide the necessary parameters, or you can provide them manually during boot up. See the LILO HOWTO for more examples of LILO parameters.

Q: Why does LILO hang on LI?

A: This is a symptom of the 1023 cylinder problem addressed previously. If you have installed the boot system above 1023, LILO will not be able to boot the system. You can try to boot from a floppy using the rescue disk you made during installation, or you can repartition your hard drive and reinstall Linux.

Q: The installation will not find the SCSI card.

A: To remedy this, you need to add a boot-time argument such as the following:

```
LILO: linux qlogicfas=0x230,11,5
```

This option can be made permanent so you don't have to re-enter it. See the LILO configuration option append in the lilo.conf man page.

Q: How do I uninstall LILO?

A: If you want to uninstall LILO and reinstall the original boot record, try using this command

```
lilo -u /dev/hda
```

which represents the boot record of the first IDE drive. Parameters may vary for your machine, for example, if your first hard drive is a SCSI drive, you would use /dev/sda.

Q: Can I use LILO and Win95 on one installation?

A: Yes, install Windows 95 first and then install Linux. During the installation, tell Linux to place LILO in the MBR. You can also use a commercial program such as System Commander.

Q: How do I mount a CD-ROM?

A: Installing Red Hat 5.1 should place the proper entries in your /etc/fstab file, as shown below:

```
#
# /etc/fstab
#
# You should be using fstool (control-panel) to edit this!
#
# <device>      <mountpoint>    <filesystemtype> <options> <dump> <fsckorder>
/dev/sda1       /                               ext2    defaults 1 1
/dev/sda5       /home                           ext2    defaults 1 2
/dev/cdrom      /mnt/cdrom                      iso9660 noauto,ro 0 0
/dev/fd0        /mnt/floppy                     ext2    noauto 0 0
/dev/sda6       /var                            ext2    defaults 1 2
/dev/sda2       none                            ignore 0 0 0
none            /proc                           proc    defaults
/dev/sda7       none                            swap    sw
```

Note the use of noauto for the cdrom entry. Without this setting, Linux will try to automount the CD-ROM when it boots, which isn't really a problem unless there's no CD in the drive.

If there is not an entry in your fstab file, you can either edit /etc/fstab or use the X Window Control Panel tool to add the appropriate mount information. Also, make sure the mount point /mnt/cdrom does indeed exist. If the entry is correct, you can cd to the mount point and issue the following commands:

```
cd /mnt
mount cdrom
```

Q: I have Red Hat 5.0 and have upgraded to the ld.so RPM package listed in the errata, but my libc5 applications still create a seg fault. What is wrong?

A: The problem with crashing libc5 applications can be caused by several things.

Before or after the upgrade, another version of libc might have been installed that was not obsoleted by the upgrade process, or the libc5 libraries might have been placed in a location that causes conflict.

To find out if this is the case, run this command:

```
rpm -qa ¦ grep libc
```

It should produce the following output:

```
glibc-devel-2.0.5c-12
libc-5.3.12-24
glibc-debug-2.0.5c-12
rpm-2.4.10-1glibc
rpm-devel-2.4.10-1glibc
glibc-profile-2.0.5c-12
glibc-2.0.5c-12
```

If you see items like libc-debug-5.3.12-18 or libc-5.4.44-2, you will need to remove these packages (with the command rpm -e libc-debug) and run ldconfig -v.

Your /etc/ld.so.conf file has been changed from an optimal setting. For optimal loading, set your /etc/ld.so.conf file in the following order:

```
/usr/i486-linuxaout/lib
/usr/i486-linux-libc5/lib
/usr/openwin/lib
/usr/X11R6/lib
```

Q: Some of my older applications get the incorrect time.

A: Some libc5 apps want /usr/lib/zoneinfo. You can either recompile them for libc6, or you can provide a symlink with the following command so things will work.

```
ln -s ../share/zoneinfo /usr/lib/zoneinfo
```

Q: I have all the latest updates installed, but my programs still get the incorrect time.

A: If you have installed all the latest updates and your programs still get the incorrect time, try checking the settings in /etc/sysconfig/clock. They probably look something like this:

UTC=true

ARC=false

This means that Linux will assume your BIOS clock is set to the UTC or GMT time zone. More than likely, the clock is set to your local time zone, and you need to change the UTC line to the following:

UTC=false

Q: When the system boots up, I see a message that says I have unknown PCI hardware. What does this mean?

A: The error "unknown PCI device" can occur for several reasons. The first and most harmless one is that PCI isn't responding to Linux's queries in a way it understands, but Linux is able to keep going. The more common occurrence is that the system hangs on, querying PCI bus cards, and cannot get any further.

Because this is a hardware problem in the kernel, there is not much that Red Hat can do except point you to the maintainer of that section of the kernel. That person might be able to let you know what is going on and might want to look at what hardware you do have in your system so she can better handle it in the future. The maintainer can be reached at:

linux-pcisupport@cck.uni-kl.de

Include the following information

/proc/pci

which is your exact hardware description. Try to find out which device is unknown. It may be your main board chipset, your PCI-CPU bridge, or your PCI-ISA bridge. If you can't find the actual information in your hardware booklet, try to read the references of the chip on the board.

Q: Linux isn't detecting my NE2000 compatible network card.

A: It has been found that some NE2000s that worked with earlier kernels do not work with the later 2.0.x kernels. For some, the following workaround will enable them to work.

You can try to get the card to work by entering the following settings:

```
insmod 8390
insmod ne io=0XXXX irq=Y
```

(Note: Replace *XXXX* and *Y* with your IO address and IRQ. Most common values for the IO address are 0x300 and 0x310. The IRQ can be anything.)

After this, use `ifconfig` or `netcfg` to configure the card. Sometimes, even though the card is recognized, it fails to transfer TCP/IP packets. This is being looked into.

If the above settings work, add them to /etc/conf.modules. It should look something like this:

```
alias eth0 8390
alias eth0 ne
options eth0 io=0xXXX irq=Y
```

Part

I

Ch

2

Q: I have installed Linux, and it seems to initially start booting. However, when it gets down to something called sendmail, the machine seems to hang. What is happening, and what should I do?

A: If after the install the machine seems to hang when it reaches certain processes like sendmail, apache, or SMB, there is probably a network problem. The most common cause is that Linux cannot look up the name of the machine you have called the box (if you set up networking to have a machine name). The machine is currently paused waiting for the network timeout of DNS lookups and will eventually bring up the login prompt. When you get the prompt, log in as root and check the usual culprits for a problem.

If you are directly on a network with a DNS server, make sure that the /etc/resolv.conf file has the correct values for your machine's DNS server. Check with your systems administrator for the correct values.

If you are using Linux on a network without a DNS server (or if this box is going to be the DNS server), you will need to edit the /etc/hosts file to have the hostname and IP address so that the lookups will occur correctly. The format of the /etc/hosts file is like the following example

```
127.0.0.1               localhost localhost.localdomain
192.168.200.1           mymachine mymachine.mynetwork.net
```

where the example machine is called mymachine.

From Here...

When you have your system up and running, you can read the following chapters for further information about Linux:

- ▓ Chapter 5, "Running Linux Applications," gets you up to speed on the various programs you just installed.
- ▓ Chapter 6, "Upgrading and Installing Software with RPM," provides instructions on how to reinstall packages you may have left out during the initial setup of your Linux system.
- ▓ Chapter 21, "Installing the X Windows System," provides you with information on installing X if something went amiss during your Red Hat installation. Although designed for the Slackware distribution, the XFree86 software is the same for any Linux distribution version.
- ▓ Chapter 22, "Using X Windows," is interesting if you've installed the X system.
- ▓ Chapter 31, "Surfing the Internet with the World Wide Web," briefs you on the basics about how to get to the Internet.

## CHAPTER 3

Installing Red Hat

by Jack Tackett

In this chapter

This chapter gives you the information you need to install the Red Hat distribution of Linux. Remember, the Red Hat Linux included with this book isn't a commercial product, and you might find some problems. Although this book leads the way, you may find the need to use the resources, such as the various HOWTOs, provided on the Red Hat CD-ROM. However, Red Hat is one of the easiest distributions to install, so take heart!

N O T E For basic information on the hardware required and disk partitioning, see Chapter 2. ■

Starting the Installation Process

To start the installation process, you need one or two (depending on the installation method) 3 1/2-inch 1.44MB formatted floppy disks. These disks will be used to create a boot disk for the Linux installation. You should also have an extra disk available to create a rescue disk.

Next, you should make sure that you have enough hard disk space to install Linux. Everything on the CD-ROM, if installed, requires about 300MB of disk space, but you can get by with less, especially if you don't install the X Windows system. To decide on the amount of space, you should decide how much space you want for user accounts—that is, the space you want to provide to your users. On a single-user system, 50MB is adequate.

Next, decide how much swap space your machine needs. If your machine has 8MB of RAM or less, you need a 24MB swap space. If you have 16MB or more, your swap space should equal the amount of RAM.

Finally, figure about 50MB for your root directory. This is the main directory from which all other directories under Linux are accessed.

▶ **See** "Linux Standard Directories," **p. 313**

Again, a minimal installation should fit in 200MB, whereas a full installation, with plenty of user space, should fit well on a 500MB drive. Table 3.1 outlines the pros and cons of the various installation methods.

Table 3.1 Installation Pros and Cons

Method	Pro	Con
CD-ROM	Fast; reliable	Distribution quickly outdated
FTP	Convenient; up-to-date software; accessible worldwide	Unreliable; slow
NFS	Convenient; great if no CD-ROM drive is available	Requires network; slow
SMB	Convenient in an MS Windows network	Requires network and some understanding of Samba
Hard drive	Works when all other methods fail	Requires lots of extra space

N O T E You can also run part of the Linux file system from the CD-ROM without installing all the software. You can choose to do so during installation. ▨

If you decide to install and configure X (highly recommended), you should also write down what type of chipset your video card uses. If you have a serial mouse and modem, write down the serial port that each is using. You need this information later during the configuration process.

Understanding the Various Installation Methods

We envision most of you installing Red Hat from the accompanying CD-ROM. However, you can use one of the following five methods to install Red Hat: from CD-ROM, via NFS, via FTP, via an SMB image on a shared drive, or from a hard drive.

To install directly from CD-ROM, you need access to DOS. From the DOS prompt, execute this command

```
[CD-ROM-drive]:\dosutils\autoboot
```

where [*CD-ROM-drive*] is the drive letter for your system's CD-ROM.

Part

I

Ch

3

CAUTION

This method will erase your hard drive. Back up any files you fear losing.

If you have another partition available, you can install Linux to coexist with your system without erasing what's already there. To do this, you need the CD-ROM, an empty partition, and a boot disk. You learn later in this chapter how to create the boot disk, as well as how to repartition your hard drive.

For those of you who have systems that can boot from a CD-ROM (check your BIOS settings), you can boot and install from the Red Hat CD-ROM.

NFS (Network File System) provides a way to install Red Hat across a network. First, you must mount the CD-ROM drive on a machine supporting the ISO-9660 file system with RockRidge extensions and then export the file system via NFS. You need to know the path to the exported file system and the IP number, or, if DNS is configured, the name of the system.

FTP (File Transfer Protocol) is a method for transferring files across the Internet. (Chapter 30, "Accessing the Network with `telnet`, `ftp`, and the `r-` Commands," explains FTP in more detail.) To install via FTP requires a boot disk and the supplemental disk described later in this chapter.

Installing Red Hat from a hard drive requires the same boot and supplemental disks used for an FTP installation. First, create a directory named RedHat. Then copy the corresponding directory from the CD-ROM, and all the subdirectories there, to the RedHat directory. You can use the following DOS commands to do this:

```
cd \RedHat
xcopy /s e:\RedHat
```

The `cd` command assumes that you're already on the installation hard drive; the `xcopy` command assumes that your CD-ROM drive is drive E.

No matter which method you use, you'll need to gather some information.

Compiling Needed Information

Before starting the installation, you need the following information about your system:

- The type of video card, chipset, and monitor used
- The serial port used by your mouse
- The serial port used by your modem
- The network information for your computer, if it's connected to a network (items such as its IP address, gateway, and domain name)
- The type of hard drive and CD-ROM drive in your system and their controller types
- The directory structure you want to use on your system, such as placing /home on a separate hard drive and /var on a separate partition from your swap file
- The name you intend to call your system (the hostname)

If you're connecting to the Internet, you can get most of this information from either your network administrator or your Internet service provider.

If you intend to use other operating systems on the same computer (such as Windows 95, Windows NT, or OS/2), you'll need to create the necessary partitions for these operating systems. Typically, you need to use the operating system's partitioning software, because Linux can't handle these other partition types.

ON THE WEB

A product named System Commander, from V Communications, lets you install and switch between 32 different operating systems. You can find more information about this product at

http://www.v-com.com/

Next, you should check for any last-minute changes to the Red Hat distribution. The reasons are many, but the two major reasons are that Linux is constantly updated, and this chapter is being written at least a month before the CD-ROM is cut. In the interim, new material or bug fixes may have been released. You can contact InfoMagic, the manufacturers of the accompanying CD-ROM, for more information.

ON THE WEB

You can also check for updated material on the Web at

http://www.redhat.com/errata

If you're not installing directly off the CD-ROM, you next need to repartition your current hard drive to make room for Linux. This may cause problems, because repartitioning a hard drive destroys any data contained on the affected partitions. After making room for Linux, you need to boot the Linux system and create its new partitions and file systems. Typically, Linux systems need a primary partition to store the files on and a swap file partition, especially if you have a machine with 8MB or less of memory.

> **N O T E** A *file system* is basically a section of your hard drive specially formatted to hold certain types of files. UNIX and Linux use file systems to represent entire sections of the directory tree. This is in contrast to MS-DOS, which places subdirectories in the directory tree on the same logical drive. UNIX systems use the directory tree format because placing subdirectories on different drives is safer. If one drive malfunctions, only the information on that drive needs to be replaced or fixed.

▶ **See** "Understanding File Systems," **p. 266** ▓

After creating the file systems, you then install the Linux operating system, its support files, and various application packages distributed with the system. To install Linux, you must first boot a stripped-down version of the operating system. You do this by creating a boot disk and a supplemental disk set containing the stripped-down OS.

Creating the Boot, Supplemental, and Rescue Disks

You need to create the boot and supplemental disks by using the `rawrite` program. You can find this program on the accompanying CD-ROM in the /dosutils subdirectory. For this step, you need two formatted floppies: one labeled *boot* and the other labeled *supp*. Place the boot disk in the A drive and enter the following:

```
E:\dosutils>rawrite

Enter disk image source file name: e:\images\boot.img
Enter target diskette drive: A:
Please insert a formatted diskette into drive A: and press -ENTER-
```

If you want to abort the process, simply press <Ctrl-c> to stop. If `rawrite` fails, try a new formatted disk. If the problem persists, you should have your hardware checked for possible problems.

After writing the boot disk, you need to create the supplemental disk. Simply use the supp image file name (supp.img) as the source file name in the preceding command sequence.

Next you should create a rescue disk. Unlike previous releases of Red Hat, with 5.1, you cannot use the installation disk to boot the system in case of problems. To provide for better problem resolution, Red Hat has introduced a rescue disk image (rescue.img). To create the rescue disk, use rescue.img as the source file in the preceding `rawrite` commands.

▶ **See** "Partitioning Your Hard Drive," **p. 42**

Part

I

Ch

3

Installing the Linux System

To start the Linux installation, place the boot disk you created into your disk drive and reset your computer. After your system does its hardware/BIOS checks, you should see the following boot messages on your system:

```
                        Welcome to Red Hat Linux
■ To install or upgrade a system running Red Hat 2.0 or later, press the <ENTER>
key.
■ To enable expert mode, type expert <ENTER>. Press <F3> for more information
about expert mode.
■ This disk can no longer be used as a rescue disk. Press <F4> for more
information on the new rescue disk.
■ Use the Function Keys listed below for more information
[F1-Main] [F2-General] [F3-Expert] [F4-Rescue] [F5-Kickstart] [F6-Kernel]
boot:
```

Table 3.2 provides information on the various function keys and their uses. Typically, you only need to press the Enter key to continue installation.

Table 3.2 Installation Function Keys

Function Key	Description
F1	Displays the main screen shown above. Pressing <F1> always returns you to this screen.
F2	Provides general information on the installation process.
F3	Explains expert mode. Basically, the Linux installation process autoprobes the hardware trying to determine what is installed. This probing can hang a system. If this happens, you must enter expert mode and specify your system's hardware during installation.
F4	Provides instructions on creating and using the rescue disk.
F5	Red Hat 5.1 allows you to perform an unattended installation using a configuration file. This screen provides information on performing such an installation.
F6	If Linux can't boot properly, you may have to pass some extra parameters to the kernel during bootup. This screen tells you how to perform this operation.

NOTE   For more information on passing boot parameters, see the Linux BootPrompt HOWTO on the CD-ROM at **/doc/HOWTO/BootPrompt-HOWTO**. ■

The system displays the following prompt and then begins initializing the system:

```
Loading initrd.img….
loading vmlinuz....
```

After booting, your system will display the Welcome screen (see Figure 3.1).

FIG. 3.1
The Red Hat Linux
Welcome screen.

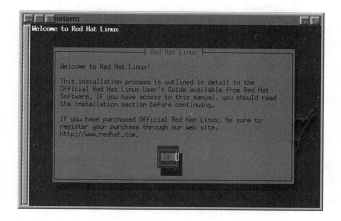

Part
I
Ch
3

Press <Enter> to continue. The next screen (see Figure 3.2) asks you which language to use during installation.

FIG. 3.2
For a laugh, try installing Red Hat Linux using the Redneck language!

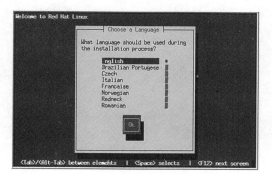

N O T E Moving around in the dialog boxes is easy, and the installation program provides reminders at the bottom of most screens. To move from element to element (field), press <Tab> or <Alt-Tab>. Use the Spacebar if you need to select an item from a list or check a check box. To choose a button (typically OK or Cancel), press <Enter>. To scroll through a list of selections, use the arrow keys. ▦

The next dialog box (see Figure 3.3) asks you to select the type of keyboard used by your system.

T I P Use /usr/sbin/kbdconfig to change your keyboard selection in the future.

FIG. 3.3

Linux uses the selections you make about your keyboard during installation and when you boot your system in the future.

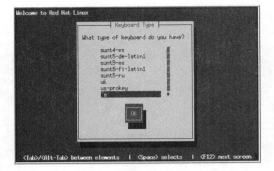

The next screen asks whether you need PCMCIA (PC Card) support for your system (see Figure 3.4). Select the appropriate answer with the <Tab> key and press <Enter>.

FIG. 3.4

Red Hat Linux provides optional support for PCMCIA (PC) cards.

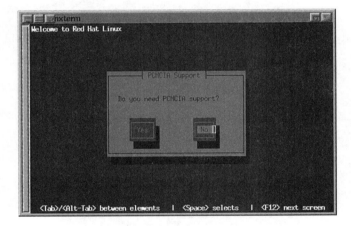

Next you need to select the installation method. Select your installation method and press <Enter>. The installation program asks you to insert the Red Hat CD-ROM into the CD-ROM drive. When you're done, simply press <Enter> to continue.

FIG. 3.5

Red Hat lets you install the system by using a variety of methods, including NFS and ftp.

N O T E The rest of this chapter assumes that you're installing from the local CD-ROM drive. If you select another method of installation, see the appropriate help topics or Red Hat's Web site at **http://www.redhat.com.** ▨

Next, the installation program attempts to autoprobe the system's CD-ROM type. If the program determines the CD-ROM correctly, installation continues; if not, you must select the type from the following selections:

SCSI	Use this selection for true SCSI devices
Other CD-ROM	Use this selection for NON-IDE or soundcard compatible CD-ROMs

If you select Other, the installation program displays the selection dialog box shown in Figure 3.6. Select the appropriate drive type and press <Enter> to continue installation.

FIG. 3.6
The Red Hat Linux installation program needs to know what type of CD-ROM is used in your system.

The Other CDROM category includes such drives as those sold by Creative Labs (SoundBlaster) and other multimedia kit-based CD-ROMs, as well as the following:

Aztech CD	Sanyo
Goldstar R420	Sony CDU-31A
Mitsumi	Sony CDU-5xx
Optics Storage 8000	SoundBlaster/Panasonic
Phillips CM206/CM260	

Depending on your selection, the installation program may ask for some parameters, such as IRQs or DMA addresses. Or the program may try to determine these values automatically by probing your hardware. It's best to let the program autoprobe first before providing parameters.

N O T E Anytime the installation program probes the system's hardware, the system may hang. If that happens, you must reboot and redo the installation. Be sure to try to collect the needed information, such as IRQs and DMA addresses, before attempting to reinstall. ▨

After detecting your CD-ROM type, the system starts its installation from the CD-ROM drive. First, it asks you whether you're installing a new system or upgrading an existing Red Hat system. Red Hat 5.1 easily upgrades over versions 2.0 or greater, but no Linux distribution easily upgrades over a different distribution version. So if you have a prior distribution version, such as Slackware, just performing a new install and blowing away your prior system is best—after backing up important data files, of course. If you're upgrading from a previous version of Red Hat, the installation program will save any current configuration files with a .rpmsave extension.

▶ **See** "Updating Packages with RPM," **p. 152**

All actions performed by the installation program are also saved in the file /tmp/upgrade.log.

 T I P To see what the installation program is doing, press <ALT-F3> to change to the virtual terminal that displays every action taken.

Next, the installation program probes for any SCSI devices. The program may ask you to select a SCSI controller and will display the Configuration dialog box, where you tell the system whether you have any SCSI adapters in your system. Choose the appropriate button and continue.

If you have a SCSI adapter, the program displays the load module dialog box from which you can select from the following SCSI drivers:

Adaptec 152x	Iomega PPA3 (Parallel port Zip)
Adaptec 1542	NCR 5380
Adaptec 1740	NCR 53c406a
Adaptec 2740, 2840, 2940	NCR 53C810/53C820 PCI
AdvanSys Adapters	Pro Audio Spectrum/Studio 16
Always IN200	Qlogic FAS
Buslogic Adapters	Qlogic ISP
DTC 3180/3280	Seagate ST01/02
EATA DMA Adapters	Trantor T128/T128F/T228
EATA PIO Adapters	UltraStor 14F/34F
Future Domain TMC-885, TMC-950	UltraStor 14F/24F/34F
Future Domain TMC-16x0	Western Digital wd7000

ON THE WEB

For current information on hardware that Red Hat 5.1 supports and doesn't support, see Red Hat's Web site at

http://www.redhat.com/support/docs/rhl/intel/rh51-hardware-intel.html

Next, you must partition your disks—or at least select the partitions you've already created. The installation program displays the Disk Setup dialog box shown in Figure 3.7. You can use the command line fdisk program or the GUI-based Disk Druid program. If you want to use fdisk, move to the fdisk button and press <Enter>. This drops you into the fdisk program to partition the selected hard drive. If you want to use the Disk Druid program, skip forward to the section "Using Disk Druid."

FIG. 3.7
You have to prepare your hard drives for installation. You can use the GUI program Disk Druid or the command line fdisk program.

Using the Linux *fdisk* Program

At the fdisk prompt, type m for a list of commands. Table 3.3 lists the available commands.

> **CAUTION**
> You will use the fdisk program native to Linux for these actions. Please be careful because this program is different than the fdisk programs included with other operating systems such as MS-DOS, Windows 98/95, and OS/2. You cannot use these programs interchangeably! For example, you cannot use Linux's fdisk to rearrange a partition for a DOS partition. Although you can use any fdisk to create partitions, you must use the appropriate operating system's version of fdisk to perform such actions as setting file types.

Table 3.3   The Linux *fdisk* Commands

Command	Description
a	Toggles a bootable flag
c	Toggles the DOS compatibility flag

continues

Part

I

Ch

3

Table 3.3 Continued

Command	Description
d	Deletes a partition
l	Lists known partition types
m	Displays this menu
n	Adds a new partition
p	Displays the partition table
q	Quits without saving changes
t	Changes a partition's system ID
u	Changes display/entry units
v	Verifies the partition table
w	Writes the table to disk and exits
x	Provides extra functionality for experts only

To begin the partitioning, select the p command (press <p><Enter>) to display the current partition table, which should reflect the drive you partitioned earlier with the DOS FDISK program. Listing 3.1 shows a possible listing from the p command.

Listing 3.1 Example of a Current Partition Table

```
Disk /dev/hda: 15 heads, 17 sectors, 1024 cylinders
Units = cylinders of 255 * 512 bytes

Device      Boot   Begin   Start   End    Blocks   Id   System
/dev/hda1    *      1       1       41     5219     1    DOS 12-bit FAT
dev/hda2            1024    1024    4040   384667+  51   Novell?
Partition 2 has different physical/logical endings:
phys=(967, 14, 17) Logical=(4096, 14.17)
```

> **N O T E** Your screen may appear different than what's shown in Listing 3.1, because the values are different for each drive type and the partitions already defined on that drive. ∎

Listing 3.1 indicates the various partitions already defined that it can detect, the start and ending locations of the partition, and how big it is in blocks. The listing also indicates the partition type. Table 3.4 shows all the different types of partitions you can define with the Linux fdisk program. The primary partition types you used are 83-Linux Native and 82-Linux Swap. You can get a similar listing with the l command.

Table 3.4   The Known Linux Partition Types

Reference Number	Type
0	Empty
1	DOS 12-bit FAT
2	XENIX root
3	XENIX usr
4	DOS 16-bit < 32M
5	Extended
6	DOS 16-bit >= 32M
7	OS/2 HPFS
8	AIX
9	AIX bootable
a	OS/2 Boot Manager
40	Venix 80286
51	Novell?
52	Microport
63	GNU HURD
64	Novell
75	PC/IX
80	Old MINIX
81	MINIX/Linux
82	Linux Swap
83	Linux Native
93	Amoeba
94	Amoeba BBT
a5	BSD/386
b7	BSDI fs
b8	BSDI swap
c7	Syrinx
db	CP/M

Part
I

Ch
3

continues

Table 3.4 Continued	
Reference Number	**Type**
e1	DOS access
e3	DOS R/O
f2	DOS secondary
ff	BBT

In Listing 3.1, Linux prints a note about the different physical and logical endings at the bottom of the screen. The difference exists because on the system used to write this chapter, a prior partition containing the DOS D drive was left intact, whereas the C drive was repartitioned to a smaller C drive to make room for Linux. Thus, there's space between the C drive and the D drive. This is where the necessary partitions required by Linux will be created.

The begin, start, and end numbers from Listing 3.1 are very important and you should write them down. You'll need them in a later step to specify the necessary sizes of the partitions you'll add.

Adding the Necessary Partition

Because you've repartitioned the drive for DOS, you shouldn't have to delete any partitions for Linux. You should only have to add partitions. To add a partition, issue the n command, which displays this:

```
Command Action
e extended
p primary(1-4)
```

Press <p><Enter>. fdisk then asks for the partition number; enter your selection and press <Enter>. If you indicate a partition number already in use, fdisk reports this fact and asks you to delete the partition before trying to add it to the partition table. For this example, enter 3 to add a third primary partition that's referred to as /dev/hda3.

Next, fdisk asks for the location of the first cylinder. This is usually the first available cylinder; in fact, fdisk displays a default range for your selection—for example:

```
First cylinder (42-1024) :
```

Notice that the first partition ends at cylinder 41 and that the next partition begins at cylinder 1024. Thus, the range supplied by fdisk here allows you to start the next partition anywhere in the range of 42-1024. It's a very good idea not to place partitions just anywhere throughout the disk; instead, choose the next available location, which in this case is cylinder 42. Enter 42 and press <Enter>.

N O T E Linux can have trouble booting from partitions defined to start at cylinders above 1024. If you can create a Linux partition only in this range, you may have to boot Linux from a floppy. You learn how to create a boot floppy (different from the boot floppy used for installation) later in this chapter. The only downside is that it takes a little longer to boot Linux from a floppy than it does from the hard drive. ▧

Now `fdisk` wants you to specify how much space to allocate for this partition. You can express this size in number of cylinders or by the number of bytes (+*size*), kilobytes (+*size*K), or megabytes (+*size*M). Because you should already know the approximate size you need for the swap file, define this partition first, and then leave the rest of the disk space for the Linux program partitions. Thus, for this example, your machine has 8MB of RAM, so you need to specify a 16MB partition size by replying as follows:

```
Last cylinder or +size or +sizeM or +sizeK (42-1023): +16M
```

You should then use the p command to look at the new partition table you've defined. In this example, the new partition table looks like this:

```
Disk /dev/hda: 15 heads, 17 sectors, 1024 cylinders
Units = cylinders of 255 * 512 bytes

Device      Boot Begin Start  End   Blocks  Id   System
/dev/hda1    *    1     1     41    5219 1  DOS  12-bit FAT
/dev/hda2         1024  1024  4040  384667+ 51   Novell?

Partition 2 has different physical/logical endings:
phys=(967, 14, 17) Logical=(4039, 14.17)
/dev/hda3         42    42    170   16447+  83   Linux native
```

By default, `fdisk` made the new partition a Linux Native type. To change this to a swap partition, you need to use the t command. Enter t, and then enter the partition number you want to change; in this example, enter 3. `fdisk` then requests that you enter the hexadecimal value of the desired partition type from Table 3.5 (if you don't have the table handy, you can type 1 to get the list of codes). Because you want a swap partition, enter 82 at the prompt.

As you can see, `fdisk` reports the new partition type, but you can also use the p command to double-check that partition 3 is now a Linux swap partition.

Now you can add your Linux partitions. For this example, add only one partition, but if you want to have multiple partitions for various reasons, you can also do so at this time. To add a partition, press <n>, specify p for another primary partition, and then specify the number for this partition (4). To keep from fragmenting different partitions across the drive, start the last partition where the other left off, at cylinder 171. For the last cylinder, because you want to use the rest of the space for the Linux system, you can specify the last cylinder instead of an exact byte count. Thus, enter 1023, as shown here:

```
Command (m for help):n
Command action
e    extended
p    primary partition (1-4)
p
```

Part

I

Ch

3

```
Partition number (1-4): 4
First cylinder (171-1024):171
Last cylinder or +size or +sizeM or +sizeK (171-1023):1023
```

Now use the p command to verify the new partitions. If you need to make any changes, do so now.

When you're satisfied with the layout of your partitions, you can use the w command to write the partition table information to the hard disk. None of your changes are permanent until you use the w command; thus, if you feel you've made some changes in error, you can use the q command to exit without altering the partition table. If you use the w command, Linux tells you the partition table has been altered and then resynchronizes the disks to match the new partition table. If your Linux system hangs at this point, reboot with the installation boot and root disks until you're back at the # prompt.

> **CAUTION**
>
> Don't use the Linux `fdisk` program to create or modify partitions for other operating systems. This could leave the hard drive in a useless state for both operating systems.

Creating the Swap Partition

Some distributions of Linux provide automatic creation and activation of the swap file during installation, so you don't have to worry about creating the swap file. However, if you're using a different distribution, you may need to create and activate the swap file before continuing with the installation.

> **NOTE** If you get an "out-of-memory" type error during the installation procedures that follow, you should increase the size of your swap file. If you already have the maximum of 16MB, you need to create and activate another swap partition by following these instructions. Remember, the Red Hat installation program allows only one swap partition. ▓

To create the swap space, use the `mkswap` command and tell it which partition to use and how much size to use for virtual RAM. For example, to create a swap space on the /dev/hda3 partition that you previously defined, enter the following command at the # prompt:

`# mkswap -c /dev/hda3 16447`

The 16447 represents 16MB and can be found in the blocks column of the `fdisk` p command output screen. The optional `-c` flag tells `mkswap` to check for bad sections on the partition.

Next, you need to activate the swap system with the `swapon` command:

`# swapon /dev/hda3`

Again, if you're using the accompanying Red Hat CD-ROM, you shouldn't have to worry about activating the swap system as long as you create the partition for one. During installation, the install program detects the swap partition and automatically starts the system for installation.

After creating your partitions on the various hard drives and returning to the Partitioning Disks dialog box, choose the Done button to continue with the installation.

Next, the system asks you to select the active swap space, which should be the partition you created and marked as type Linux Swap (82) in the preceding section. Select this partition and choose OK. The program then initializes the swap space.

After creating the swap space, the program displays the Select Root Partition dialog box. The root partition is your main file system for Linux where all the boot files are located. Select the device (hard drive) for your root partition from the list box and press <Enter>. Now you can mount the other partitions, if any, from the Partition Disk dialog box. From here, you also can mount any DOS or OS/2 file systems so that you can access them from Linux. Select the partition to edit from the list box and press <Enter>. From the Edit Mount Point dialog box, you can specify a mount point—that is, a directory—to which you want this partition mounted.

▶ **See** "Mounting and Unmounting File Systems," **p. 269**

After you select the root and mount points for your various partitions, the program formats those you selected. You select the partitions to format from the Format Partition dialog box.

Using Disk Druid

Selecting the Disk Druid button on the Disk Setup dialog box (refer to Figure 3.7) displays the Disk Druid main screen shown in Figure 3.8.

FIG. 3.8

Disk Druid makes partitioning disks and creating mount points a snap.

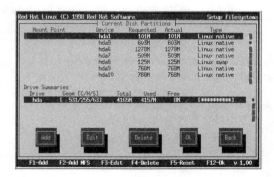

Disk Druid allows you to create partitions, set mount points on specified devices, set sizes of partitions, and specify file system types, and it provides information on these attributes. Table 3.5 lists the various fields on the Disk Druid main screen. Table 3.5 also describes what task each button performs.

▶ **See** "Understanding File Systems," **p. 266**

Table 3.5   Disk Druid Fields

Field/Button	Description
Mount Point	Another term for a directory; the location in which the specified directory and all subdirectories will be placed.
Device	The physical hard drive and partition to which this mount point belongs.
Requested Size	You can specify either a default size for a partition or an initial size that can be allowed to grow.
Actual Size	The actual size allocated for the partition.
Type	File system type of the partition.
Drive Summaries	This portion of Disk Druid's main screen provides information on the specified device (hard drive/patron) including such information as amount of space available. Remember, a hard drive device can have several partitions.
Add	Adds a new partition.
Edit	Edits the selected mount point.
Delete	Deletes the selected mount point.
Ok	Commits the specified changes to your system and continues with the installation program.
Back	Returns to the previous dialog box in the installation program and aborts all changes you have specified.

To add a new partition, click the Add button or the press the <F2> function key. This displays the Edit New Partition dialog box shown in Figure 3.9.

FIG. 3.9

No need to remember all those different file systems types. The Edit New Partition dialog presents them all in a list box.

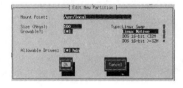

Enter the mount point for this new partition in the Mount Point field. Examples are the root partition (/) or the var partition (/var). Next, specify the size of the partition in megabytes and indicate if you want the partition to grow in size as necessary when you add and delete other partitions. Next you must select from the Type: list box what type of file system will exist on the partition. Finally, you can select which physical hard drive to place the partition on by selecting the appropriate hard drives from the list of Allowable Drives.

N O T E   If you specify a size that's too big for the space available on the indicated device, Disk
Druid will tell you and ask you to reduce the amount of requested space. Disk Druid will
also warn you of other potential problems and provide you with possible solutions. ▨

Installing the Software Components

Congratulations! Your system is now prepped for Linux, but you're only halfway finished. Now
you must select the various software components to install and then configure them.

The installation program displays the Components to Install dialog box, which allows you to
select the various packages. Table 3.6 describes each package.

Table 3.6   The Installation Components

Component	Description
Printer Support	Allows you to print from your Linux system.
X Windows System	Provides the GUI for all UNIX—hence, Linux—workstations; X is a powerful GUI like Windows 95 and OS/2.
Mail/WWW/News tools	Provides programs to use e-mail, surf the World Wide Web, and read and post Usenet news.
DOS/Windows Connectivity	Allows you to access DOS files, run DOS programs, and run some Windows programs (with limited success).
File Managers	Provides tools to manipulate your file systems such as Midnight Commander.
BRU Backup Util	Provides a single-user version of the popular tape backup program.
BRU X11 Front End	Provides a GUI interface under X to BRU.
Real Media Client	Allows you to access Real Media programs on the Internet.
Real Media Server	Allows your Linux server to provide Real Media content to the Internet.
Graphics Manipulation	Provides programs to work with graphic images such as xv and the popular The GIMP.
X Games	Provides popular strategic and arcade type games that run under X.
Console Games	Provides games that run on a text console.
X Multimedia Support	Provides multimedia support for X.

continues

Part

I

Ch

3

Table 3.6 Continued

Component	Description
Console Multimedia Support	Provides multimedia support for text consoles.
Print Server	Allows your Linux box to act as a print server on your network.
Networked Workstation	Provides networking applications and SNMP support.
Dialup Workstation	Allows you access to the Internet via dial-up lines—that is, via a modem.
News Server	Allows your system to act as a news server (if you can get a news feed), thus providing news to your users.
NFS Server	Allows your system to export and attach to other file systems on your network.
SMB (Samba) Connectivity	Provides SMB services, both client and server.
IPX/NetWare Connectivity	Provides access to Novell NetWare networks.
Anonymous FTP/Gopher Server	Allows you to set up your system so that others may access it via anonymous FTP.
Web Server	Includes the most used Web server software today, Apache.
DNS Name Server	Provides the software needed to run your own Domain Name Server on your Linux system.
PostGress (SQL) Server	Allows you to run the PostGress SQL database system.
Network Management Workstation	Provides utilities and tools to help troubleshoot and monitor your network, including SNMP services.
TeX Document Formatting	Provides a series of programs used to add formatting codes to documents.
Emacs	Installs the ubiquitous editor for Linux (you can do anything with emacs, or so the emacs gurus say).
Emacs with X Windows	Provides an X front end to the powerful emacs editor.
C Development	Provides the GNU gcc compiler and tools.
Development Libraries	Provides various libraries needed by the various development tools, such as gcc and g++.
C++ Development	Installs the GNU C++ compiler, gcc.

Component	Description
X Development	Provides the tools, libraries, and miscellaneous items (such as fonts) needed to develop X applications.
Extra Documentation	Provides the Linux documentation project containing the important HOWTOs, along with other helpful information.
Everything	Installs everything on the CD-ROM; you need about 350MB available, not counting free space for your data files.

N O T E   You can select individual packages by checking the appropriate check box in the dialog box, or you can install everything by selecting that list option. To select a package to install, simply move to the desired component and press the Spacebar. After you select all your components, tab to the OK button and press <Enter>. ■

T I P   You can use the RPM program described in Chapter 6 to install any package in the future.

The next dialog box after installation informs you that you can see the files installed by viewing the file /tmp/install.log. Press <Enter> to continue with the installation.

Now comes the hard part—waiting. Transferring and decompressing upward of 350MB of programs can take a while. Setup firsts installs a file system on your indicated partitions and then starts installing software. The system informs you of its progress as it installs the various files you selected in the Install Status dialog box. Installation time varies depending on what you're installing and how fast your machine can process the information. Relax and order a pizza!

Configuring Your System

After installing the software, the installation program begins to configure your system. It first configures your mouse by displaying the Configure Mouse dialog box. Simply select the mouse type from the list box that best describes your mouse. Remember, many mice can emulate the Microsoft serial mouse if they have to. The Emulate 3 Buttons check box is there because many PC mice have only two buttons, and X Windows usually uses three buttons to maneuver and make program selections. By checking this box, the system will make clicking both mouse buttons at the same time the same as pressing the middle button on a three-button mouse. Make your selection and choose OK.

T I P   You can use the following command
`/usr/sbin/mouseconfig`

to reconfigure your mouse at any time in the future.

Next, you must specify the serial port that your mouse connects to. After making the selection from the list box, tab to the OK button and press <Enter>. The program then asks you to select the type of video card in your system.

> **CAUTION**
>
> Try to select the correct video card, because of all things software-based, the only subsystem that software can easily destroy is your video card and monitor. If you make the wrong decision, you might fry your monitor! Although this is highly unlikely, there's still the slight possibility, so choose wisely, young Linux walker.

The system now tries to install the proper XFree86 server for your hardware.

▶ **See** "Installing the XFree86 System," **p. 425**

Next, you must select your monitor. Again, be as specific as possible. After selecting your monitor, the program asks for the amount of video memory your card contains. Make the appropriate selection and choose OK to continue.

Remember all those warnings about frying your monitor? Well, now you really have a chance to toast it, so be careful. The next screen asks you to select the clockchips located on your video card. These chips are used to drive the video signals through your card and into your monitor. If they're way out of synchronization, the signals can—you guessed it—fry your monitor (few actually explode, most just fizzle and smoke). Please be careful! If you have no clue as to what clockchips your card is using, take the default selection, No Clockchip Setting, and choose OK.

After selecting your clockchips (or lack thereof), the system can autoprobe and try to configure X. The autoprobe may hang your system, but as long as nothing is seriously wrong (for example, you selected outrageous clock speeds for your card), you can simply reboot and continue with the installation. You do have the option to skip the autoprobe and continue with the installation.

> **N O T E** I have installed Red Hat many times and have yet to have the installation software properly configure my X system. You may have better luck than me, so don't worry if your X installation fails. I've always been able to configure X after installation with the various configuration programs available.

▶ **See** "Configuring XFree86," **p. 430** ▦

If the autoprobe succeeds, the system displays an information screen on selecting the resolutions you want to use with your system. You can select more than one, as long as your video card and monitor can handle the resolutions. Finally, the program tells you how to start and stop your X Windows system.

Configuring Your Network

After configuring X Windows, the installation program continues with your network. If your machine is or will be connected to the Internet and you installed the networking components, choose Yes and continue.

First, the system asks which Ethernet driver to use with the Load Module dialog box. Select the appropriate driver for your Ethernet card and choose OK.

Again, the installation program might try to autoprobe your hardware to determine certain values for the card. This probing can hang the system and force you to reboot. If this happens, hang in there. First make sure that you selected the correct driver. Then see whether you need to pass any special parameters to the device, such as IRQ or DMA address settings. You can do this by selecting the Specify Parameter option instead of the autoprobe option.

> **N O T E** Ethernet is the most popular network interface for Linux today. Other technologies, such as Token Ring, ISDN, and ATM, have some support, but they're not ready for prime time yet under Linux. Many are still in alpha or beta stage and are dependent on vendor-specific hardware. ■

If the system can detect your network card, it leads you through setting up your TCP/IP network.

Part

I

Ch

3

Configuring the TCP/IP Network

The installation software uses the Configure TCP/IP dialog box to gather your system's TCP/IP information. Your network administrator or Internet service provider can provide the following information: your machine's IP number, netmask, network address, and broadcast address.

Next, the system must configure your network. It gathers information from the Configure Network dialog box. You must specify your network's domain name and your system's host name. The domain name is typically the last two parts of an Internet address. For example, if the name is www.netwharf.com, then netwharf.com is the domain name and www is the host name.

Next, your network administrator must give you the values for your system's default gateway and the primary name server. Your network may also have a secondary name server, too, so enter the value in the appropriate place.

> **N O T E** Be careful what you name your host, because this name will appear on your default prompt line, in mail messages, and in log reports. Do you really want your boss to receive mail from uradork.netwharf.com? ■

Configuring the Clock

Next, you have to specify how your system will keep time and in what time zone it exists. This is done with the Configure Timezones dialog box. Check whether you want to use local time or

GMT time, and then pick your time zone from the list box. After making your selections, choose OK.

Selecting the Services to Start on Reboot

Next you need to specify the services (programs and daemons) that your system will start automatically when it boots. You select from the list of services displayed in the Services dialog box, shown in Figure 3.10. Table 3.7 provides a list of the available services and a description of their uses. Those services marked with an * have been selected by Red Hat to start on reboot by default.

▶ **See** "Understanding the Boot Process," **p. 206**

FIG. 3.10
Linux gives you control of which programs to start at boot time, which is similar to the startup folder under Microsoft Windows.

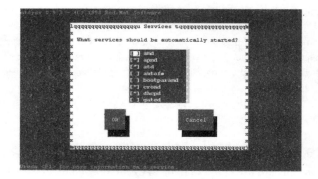

Table 3.7 Startup Services

Service	Description
amd	Runs the automount daemon
apmd *	Monitors battery status and can shut down the system on low battery conditions
atd *	Runs at commands at their scheduled times
autofs	Automatically mounts file systems when you use them
bootparamd	Allows Sun servers to boot from a Linux box using bootp
crond *	Runs the cron daemon
dhcpd *	Provides DHCP services
gated	Runs the gate daemon to provide routing services for BGP and other protocols
gpm *	Runs the program that provides mouse support to Linux
httpd *	Runs the Apache Web server
Inet *	Starts the internet super daemon (inetd) that provides all the sevices specified in /etc/inet.conf

Service	Description
inmd	Starts the Usenet news server innd
kerneld *	Starts the kerneld daemon, which loads and unloads kernel modules as they are needed
keytable *	Loads the appropriate keyboard map
lpd *	Provides printing services to Linux
mars-new	Loads the MArs NetWare file and print server daemon
mcserv	Provides midcommander remote file services
named *	Provides DNS services
network *	Provides control of all the network interfaces
nfs *	Provides Network File System server services
nfsfs *	Mounts and unmounts all NFS mount points specified in /etc/exports
pcmcia	Provides access to PCMCIA (PC Cards) services
pnserver	Starts the Real Media services
portmap *	Provides Remote Procedure Call (RPC) support for other protocols like NFS
postgresql	Runs the postgres database and provides SQL services
random *	Saves and restores a random value to help generate better random numbers (which are used for various security systems)
routed	Provides for automatic router table updates using the RIP protocol
rusersd	Provides services that allow users to find one another over the network
rwalld	Provides users the ability to use the rwall command to write messages on remote terminals
rwhod	The rwho protocol lets remote users get a list of all of the users logged into a machine by running the rwho daemon
sendmail *	Runs the sendmail daemon to provide e-mail
smb *	Provides SMB (Samba) client/server services
snmpd *	Provides Simple Network Management Protocol support to Linux
sound *	Provides access to sound cards
squid *	Runs the squid proxy Web server
syslog *	Provides logging capability to your Linux system
xntpd	Starts the NTPv3 daemon
ypbind	Binds YP/NIS clients to a yellow pages server
yppasswd	Allows users to change their passwords on systems running YP/NIS
ypserv	This daemon provides the YP/NIS server functions

Part

I

Ch

3

TIP While you can manually change the services that run on startup by editing the appropriate rc.d files (see Chapter 9), the /usr/sbin/ntsysv command brings you back to the Services dialog box and allows you to reconfigure the services with the GUI.

Selecting Your Root Password

Now you must select your root password. This is the ultimate key into your system, so some care should be given. The superuser, or root, on a Linux/UNIX system can do great things— and can also wreak awesome damage. Pick a secure password and be careful who you give it to. The Root Password dialog box shown in Figure 3.11 lets you enter the password twice to confirm what you've typed.

FIG. 3.11
You must choose a root password wisely "young Linux Walker."

Although you can fix users' accounts when they forget their password, if you forget the root password, you may be forced to reinstall the system. However, booting from a floppy and editing the password file may allow a recovery.

▶ **See** "Dealing with Password Security," **p. 237**

Installing LILO

Next you will be asked to create a boot disk, as shown in the Bootdisk dialog box in Figure 3.12. We highly recommend you create a disk, just in case you cannot boot your computer in the future. A boot disk is your first tool for repair, followed by the rescue disk you created.

After creating the boot disk, you will be asked to install LILO. LILO stands for LInux LOader. LILO is a program executed at system startup that lets you choose which operating system is used to boot the computer. You can use LILO to boot several different operating systems, such as Linux and MS-DOS. Press <Tab> to get a list of operating systems LILO can boot.

With LILO, you can specify a default operating system to boot and a default time limit before it boots that system. For example, if you have MS-DOS and Linux on your computer, you can configure LILO to boot either one. You could then tell LILO to boot MS-DOS if no one intervenes after 30 seconds. Before that 30 seconds is up, however, a user can specify another operating system to boot instead of the default. You can press the <Ctrl>, <Alt>, or <Shift> key to stop the timed process.

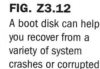

FIG. Z3.12
A boot disk can help you recover from a variety of system crashes or corrupted configuration files.

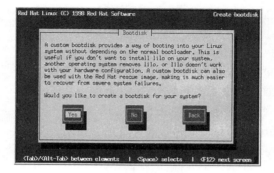

You specify all this information while configuring LILO. You can later directly edit the lilo.conf file located in the /etc directory. If you don't want to boot Linux automatically, you can select the Skip button to continue. Otherwise, select a hard drive to install LILO and press <Enter> to edit the entry.

Congratulations! After you load LILO, your system is up and running—and, let's hope, problem-free.

Part

I

Ch

3

Installing Red Hat Linux on DEC Alphas

Unlike other distributions, Red Hat also provides Linux for DEC Alphas. This distribution isn't included on the accompanying Red Hat CD-ROM, but it's available from Red Hat. For more information on getting this distribution, see Red Hat's Web site at **http://www.redhat.com/products/rhl-alpha.html**. When you have the correct distribution, you can use the following instructions to install Red Hat Linux on an Alpha.

N O T E Red Hat also has a distribution for Sun's line of Sun Sparc processors. See Red Hat's Web site for more information. ■

Before installing the distribution on an Alpha, you should read the installation instructions in the first part of this chapter, because many of the steps are the same. You'll also need access to a computer capable of reading and writing MS-DOS disks, because you must create an installation floppy.

Using Supported Alpha Hardware

Red Hat supports various Alpha hardware from both Digital Equipment Corporation (DEC) and other vendors. The following hardware is supported:

- AlphaPC64 (Cabriolet, Aspen Telluride)
- AxpPCI133 (Noname)
- EB64+ (Aspen Alpine)

- EB66 (NekoTek Mach 1)
- EB66+
- Jensen (DEC PC 150, 2000 model 300, Cullean)
- Universal Desktop Box (UDB, aka Multia)
- AlphaStation 200, 250, 255, 400 (Avanti machines)
- EB164 (Aspen Avalanche, Timerline, Summit)
- Kinetic's Platform 2000 machines
- PC164 (Durango)
- Alcor AlphaStations 500, 600 (Maverick, Brett)
- Alpha-XL
- Alpha-XLT (XL 300, XL 366)
- Mikasa AlphaServer 1000 —the 1000A is NOT supported

All of these systems have SCSI systems supported by Red Hat Linux. The video systems should work too, although S3 support for the Jensen systems isn't included by default. To run X with a Jensen system, you need to download the X server from **ftp://ftp.azstarnet.com/pub/linux/axp/jensen**. Finally, all Ethernet solutions for these systems are supported, and the kernels for these machines also support Token-Ring adapters.

The hardware list changes frequently, so you should check the up-to-date list on Red Hat's Web site at **http://www.redhat.com**.

Creating the Boot and Root Disks

You need to create a boot and root floppy for an Alpha installation. The boot disk contains a program image allowing you to boot the system. The root floppy provides an image of the Linux kernel for the system to use during installation. Just as for Intel machines, you use the rawrite program to create these disk images.

The boot disk image depends on the type of Alpha used. These images are located in the /images directory with a README file that provides more information on each image described in Table 3.8.

Table 3.8   Boot Images Available for DEC Alphas

Image	Description
cab.img	AlphaPC64, Cabriolet
noname.img	AxpPCI33, Noname, Universal Desktop Box (Multias)
eb64p.img	EB64+, Aspen Timberlines
eb66.img	EB66
eb66p.img	EB66+
jensen.img	Jensens

Image	Description
avanti.img	AlphaStation 200, 250, and 400
xl.img	Alpha XL
xlt.img	Alpha XLT
eb164.img	EB164-based machines
p2000.img	Platform 2000
alcor.img	Alcor-based machines
mikasa.img	Mikasa-based machines

To create a boot image for a Universal Desktop Box, you use the command

```
E:\dosutils\rawrite -f E:\images\noname.img -d a: -n
```

where E: represents the drive letter of your CD-ROM. After creating the boot disk, you must create the root disk, which contains the RAM disk image of the Linux kernel. You create the root disk with the following command:

```
E:\dosutils\rawrite -f E:\images\ramdisk.img -d a: -n
```

Installing the Main Red Hat Distribution

After you have your boot media ready, you can install Linux. The installation procedure is very much like the one outlined earlier in the section "Installing the Linux System." The installation program guides you through the process, asking you to make selections from a list of possible choices.

To begin, place your boot disk into the floppy drive and restart your system. At the prompt, enter the following command:

```
boot fd0:vmlinux.gz root=/dev/fd0 load_ramdisk=1
```

You may see several SCSI messages flash by on-screen. Don't worry about them unless you see a message such as scsi0 : 1, which indicates that you have a SCSI termination problem that needs to be fixed before continuing with the installation. If all goes well, you should see the message VFS: Insert Root floppy to be loaded into ramdisk. Insert the root disk you created and press <Enter> to continue the installation process.

Going Back to the Beginning

After you complete the setup and configuration of your system, you should reboot the system so that all of your setup and configurations can take effect.

Rebooting Linux is more involved than rebooting DOS—you can't just turn off the power and turn the system back on. If you do so in Linux, you can damage the file structures and systems. Linux tries to repair itself on boot-up. Don't turn off the power while running Linux.

▶ **See** "Performing Backups and Restoring Files," **p. 229**

Part

I

Ch

3

To exit Linux, use the following command:

```
shutdown [-r] time
```

The optional -r indicates that the system should reboot after shutting down, and *time* indicates the time that the system should shut down. You can use now in place of *time* to indicate imme- diate shutdown. Linux also recognizes the warm boot keys used by DOS to reboot the ma- chine, <Ctrl-Alt-Delete>, which Linux interprets as the command

```
shutdown -r now
```

Make sure that you've removed the root disk from the drive and reboot your new Linux machine.

Troubleshooting Problems

After your machine reboots, the LILO prompt should appear. Make sure that you can boot to your old operating system if you left it on the hard drive. If that system was DOS, press <Shift> and then type the short word you used to identify the DOS partition when you installed LILO. If you enter an invalid word, press <Tab> to get a list of valid operating system types. If you're having problems at this point, place your DOS boot disk in the boot drive and reboot.

▶ **See** "Troubleshooting Problems," **p. 52**

You should be able to boot from your rescue disk. When your system is up and running under DOS, try the Linux rescue disk you created during installation. If that rescue disk doesn't work, you may have to reinstall Linux. Potential problems to check initially are the kernels and your hardware. Before starting over, make sure that you have the appropriate hardware. If you made notes during the installation process, check which kernel you installed against what hardware you have.

From Here...

When you have your system up and running, you can read the following chapters for further information about Linux:

- ■ Chapter 2, "Linux Installation Overview," provides detailed information on installing Linux. The chapter also provides information on potential problems and their resolu- tions.
- ■ Chapter 5, "Running Linux Applications," gets you up to speed on the various programs you just installed.
- ■ Chapter 6, "Upgrading and Installing Software with RPM," provides instructions on how to reinstall packages you may have left out during the initial setup of your Linux system.
- ■ Chapter 21, "Installing the X Windows System," provides you with information on installing X if something went amiss during your Red Hat installation. Although designed for the Slackware distribution, the XFree86 software is the same for any Linux distribu- tion version.
- ■ Chapter 22, "Using X Windows," is interesting if you've installed the X system.

Installing Caldera OpenLinux Lite

by Jack Tackett

In this chapter

This chapter gives you the information you need to install the Caldera OpenLinux distribution. Like Red Hat and Slackware, OpenLinux is a complete distribution of a multiuser, multitasking operating system based on the Linux 2.0 kernel. The CD-ROM accompanying this book contains a *lite* edition—that is, a non-commercial version—of Caldera's OpenLinux distribution. The version on the CD-ROM is a subset of Caldera's commercial OpenLinux Base product. Table 4.1 summarizes the differences between Caldera's commercial product and the product on the accompanying CD-ROM.

Table 4.1   OpenLinux Base Versus OpenLinux Lite

Component	OpenLinux Base (Official)	OpenLinux Lite (on CD-ROM)
Linux OS and utilities	Yes	Yes
System Admin and installation tools	Yes	Yes
250-page manual	Yes	No
Technical support	Yes	No
Netscape Navigator	Yes	No
Looking Glass Desktop	Yes	Yes (30-day trial)
CrispLite Graphical Editor	Yes	Yes (30-day trial)

ON THE WEB

For more information on Caldera's product line, visit the company's Web site at

http://www.caldera.com

What You Need to Install Linux

Caldera made arrangements with Red Hat to use its distribution, so many installation procedures are the same for Caldera and Red Hat. You should be able to use Chapter 3, "Installing Red Hat," to help you install OpenLinux Lite.

Your system must have the following components to successfully install OpenLinux Lite:

- An 80386 or above Intel-based PC (Caldera doesn't support other processors at this time)
- A 3 1/2-inch floppy drive
- At least 8MB of RAM
- About 250MB of disk space, but a minimal system without X Windows requires only about 50MB. A full installation with everything installed requires almost 690MB.
- A mouse and video card supported by XFree86

▶ **See** "Video Cards," **p. 750**

To briefly recap, you need to partition your hard drive, create the boot floppy, and then install and configure the system.

▶ **See** "Partitioning Your Hard Drive," **p. 42**

> **CAUTION**
>
> You're about to make major changes to your system, so be careful.

Installation

First, you need a distribution of Caldera OpenLinux, which is supplied on the accompanying CD-ROM. To start the installation process you need two formatted high-density floppy disks.

You should also decide how you intend to boot Linux. You have two choices:

- You can boot Linux from a floppy disk, in which case you need an extra formatted disk—for a total of three disks.
- You can use a program called LILO (the LInux Loader). LILO allows you to specify which operating system to boot. Such programs as OS/2, Windows 98, and Windows NT provide similar functionality.

Next, you should make sure that you have enough disk space to install Linux. Most people can get by with 200MB devoted to Linux—less if you plan not to use such applications as TeX and X Windows.

Having paper and pen nearby is a good idea, so you can take notes just in case something goes wrong. Besides, you'll need to jot down some numbers along the way. For configuring XFree86, the X Windows program distributed with Linux, you should write down what type of chipset your video card uses. If you have a serial mouse and modem, write down the serial port that each is using. You'll need this information later during the configuration process.

Part

I

Ch

4

Making the Preparations

If you have a brand new system, or if you have an existing system but don't care what happens to the data already stored on the computer, you can skip most of the following sections and go directly to "Creating the Boot and Root Disks." If, however, you're already using a system and you simply want to add Linux, you must do some planning because Linux is another operating system, not just a collection of programs.

In general, when you install Linux—a new operating system—you must do the following:

- *Create the Linux boot disks.* You must create two floppies because you need to bootstrap Linux onto the new system. (The term *bootstrap* comes from the old saying, "Pull yourself up by your boot straps.")

- *Repartition the hard drive to make room for Linux.* Repartitioning a hard drive may cause problems because it destroys any data stored on the affected partitions.

- *Boot Linux.* After making room for Linux, you need to boot the Linux system to gain access to the tools required to create its new partitions and file systems.

- *Create the Linux partitions.* Typically, Linux systems need a primary partition to store the files on and a swap file partition, especially if you have a machine with 8MB or less of memory.

- *Create the file systems.* A *file system* is basically a section of your hard drive specially formatted to hold files. UNIX and Linux use file systems to represent entire sections of the directory tree. This is in contrast to MS-DOS, which places subdirectories in the directory tree on the same logical drive. UNIX systems use the file system structure because placing subdirectories on different drives is safer. If one drive malfunctions, only the information on that drive must be replaced or fixed.

- *Install the Linux system and software applications.* After creating the file systems, you install the Linux operating system, its support files, and various application packages distributed with the system, such as the games and networking support packages.

Preparing the Installation Floppies

You must make a system disk for your PC. To install Linux, you need to repartition your hard drive to make room for the new operating system. Unfortunately, you just can't simply copy the files over to an MS-DOS, OS/2, or Windows NT file system.

If your system can boot a CD-ROM, or if you have free partitions on your current hard drive, or if you don't mind destroying your current file system, you can install directly from the CD-ROM and not bother with making the installation disk. It is recommended that you make the modules disk, however, because you might need one of the drivers found on that disk.

NOTE To launch an OpenLinux installation from the CD-ROM, change directory to d:/col/launch (using the series of commands d:, cd col, and then cd launch) and proceed according to the instructions in that directory's README.us file. Remember to create the modules disk discussed in the next section. ▪

Creating the Install and Modules Disks

You need to create the installation disks for Linux. Two floppies are needed with Caldera: the installation and the modules floppies. You create these floppies with an MS-DOS program called rawrite that's provided with most Linux distributions.

rawrite writes the contents of a file directly to a floppy without regard to the format. You use rawrite to transfer the images to the appropriate floppies.

NOTE The examples in this chapter assume that your CD-ROM is drive D:. If it is not, you need to substitute the appropriate drive letter for your CD-ROM. ▪

To create the installation disk, issue the following command:

`D:/col/launch/floppies/rawrite3.com`

This starts the `rawrite` program, and you can follow the prompts. When you're asked for the file, indicate the appropriate installation file. For 1.44MB floppies, use the install.144 file (as in d:/col/launch/floppies/install.144). For 2.88MB installation floppies, use the install.288 file.

Next, following the same instructions, create the modules disk. This disk can be placed on either a 1.44MB floppy or a 2.88MB floppy. Specify the filename D:/col/launch/floppy/modules.144.

Installing Linux

To use the disks you made, simply place the installation disk into the drive and reboot your system. If you are installing from a DOS system, read the instructions found in the file d:/col/launch/dos/README.us. No matter which way you boot the system, the installation program displays a splash screen and welcomes you to Caldera's OpenLinux product. You are then asked to boot the system.

If you have any parameters to pass to the kernel before it boots, enter them at the `boot:` prompt. (For information on these parameters, see the BootPrompt HOWTO in /doc/HOWTO.) If you don't need to pass on any parameters, press <Return> to continue the installation.

The system now goes through a series of probes trying to determined what type of equipment your system uses. Then the Linux Installation and System Administration (LISA) program begins. During the installation, you can maneuver around the various dialog boxes with the cursor keys to select choices from list boxes. The Tab key moves you from one item to another in a dialog box, such as from list boxes to buttons. At any time, you can press the <Escape> key to cancel a selection. To enter your selections, press the <Return> key.

 T I P During installation, you can use the key sequence <ALT-F6> to see the progress of the installation.

The first screen allows you to select the language that will be used during installation. You can choose from English, German, French, Italian, Spanish, or Portuguese. After you make a selection, LISA asks you to select a keyboard to use. The Linux system will use configuration information based on your selection to bind certain keys to certain language characters.

Using a Previous Configuration

Next LISA asks you if you want to use a previously saved configuration. The Caldera distribution allows you to create several installation configurations and save them. Then if you want to reinstall at a later date, you can reuse this predefined configuration so you don't have to go through the entire configuration process again. Because this is your first time installing the OpenLinux system, simply answer no.

Part
I

Ch
4

Configuring LISA

Next you must configure LISA. Typically the defaults shown on the Change LISA Setup dialog box are acceptable. If you need to make changes, select the following options and make the appropriate change.

- *Disable Plug and Play Cards* turns off the BIOS setting that interacts with Plug and Play cards. During autoprobing and configuration, these cards can cause problems with Linux.

- *Automatic Network Configuration with bootp* allows another computer to issue network configuration to the current machine via the bootp protocol. At least initially, you should configure your own network options instead of trying to use bootp. However, this option is not fully supported yet in Caldera OpenLinux Lite.

- *Automatic Network Configuration with Netprobe* provides for network setup using Netprobe. Netprobe is a Caldera product similar in function to a computer running bootp, which allows remote network configuration.

- *Use Selection and Continue* tells the program to accept your selections and continue with the installation.

Probing for Hardware

Next the system will autodetect all the hardware it can. If LISA does not locate all your hardware, you will have to use the modules disk created earlier to load the appropriate hardware drivers. First the system probes for IDE and ATAPI equipment. Review the hardware list displayed by the Hardware Found (IDE/ATAPI) dialog box to see if all your hardware has been detected. Click the Continue button, and LISA asks if all hardware has been detected. If not, select no and continue with the hardware probes.

If the probe still does not find all your hardware, LISA will display the Kernel Module Manager dialog box. This dialog box gives you the following options:

- Continue with installation
- Analyze kernel modules
- Load kernel modules
- Remove modules

During installation, your typical selections will be to load and analyze kernel modules. How much hardware you have to add support for will determine how many times you cycle through the various dialog boxes associated with the Kernel Module Manager.

Analyzing Kernel Modules   Select the Analyze Kernel Modules function if you want to see what hardware was detected. You can also use this function to see what modules you or LISA have added through the course of installation. You can also review any messages the system has generated during the boot process. Table 4.2 describes each function in the Analyze Kernel dialog box.

Table 4.2 The Analyze Kernel Functions

Function	Description
Return to Previous Screen	Returns you to the Kernel Modules dialog box.
Show Hardware That Has Already Been Found	Displays all the hardware found so far in your system.
Show Loaded Kernel Modules	Displays all kernel modules currently installed on your system.
Verbose System Analysis	Provides more detailed information messages during installation.
Display Boot Process Messages	Similar to the information displayed by the <ALT-F6> key sequence. All information generated during the boot process is listed. This information includes the results of probing your system and installing various kernel modules.
Store Information on a DOS Floppy	Allows you to create a copy of all the information available from the Analyze Kernel Module functions.

Loading and Removing Kernel Modules The Load Kernel Modules function allows you to load various device drivers into Linux to support your hardware. These drivers are on the modules disk you created earlier. Table 4.3 lists the various subfunctions available in the Load Kernel Modules dialog box.

Table 4.3 The Load Kernel Module Functions

Function	Description
Return to Previous Menu	Returns you to the Kernel Modules dialog box
Load Driver for CD-ROM	Allows you to select a driver for your CD-ROM from the modules disk
Load Driver for SCSI Adapter	Allows you to load a driver for your systemís SCSI adapter
Load Driver for Network Card	Allows you to select a driver for your Ethernet card

To load a driver not currently available in the installation program, you must remove the installation disk from the floppy drive and then insert the modules disk. For example, several SCSI controllers are available from the installation disk, including Adaptec 2940s. However, the default installation disk does not contain drivers for Buslogic adapters. Therefore, to support a buslogic controller, you will need the modules disk. You will be led through a series of dialog boxes to select the desired driver and also to provide any additional configuration information for the device. LISA offers context-sensitive help throughout the process; simply press <F1> at any time to get help.

You should work your way down the function list, first installing support for your CD-ROM, then for any SCSI devices, and then for your network card. If you find you have installed the wrong driver, or if LISA's autoprobe installed the wrong driver, select the Remove Kernel Module function and indicate which module is to be removed.

Preparing the Hard Disks

Notice the first information line printed by `fdisk`: `Using /dev/hda as default device!` Remember that MS-DOS refers to most partitions and hard drives with a letter such as C or D. Linux refers to them in a very different manner. Linux refers to everything—devices, files, and so on—in the same manner.

Linux and MS-DOS communicate with hardware via a series of programs called *device drivers*. Whereas MS-DOS device drivers usually have a .SYS extension and can reside anywhere on the system, Linux stores all such device drivers in the /dev directory. The drivers Linux uses in installation were specified above using the Kernel Modules dialog box. The important point to remember, though, is that because the hard drive, floppy drives, and CD-ROM drives are hardware, Linux uses device drivers in the /dev directory to access the drives. Linux also references these drives by their subdirectory names instead of by letters. Table 4.4 displays a typical Linux device directory.

Table 4.4   Linux Devices

Device	Name
Floppy drive A	/dev/fd0
Floppy drive B	/dev/fd1
First hard drive	/dev/hda
First primary partition on hard drive A	/dev/hda1
Second primary partition on hard drive A	/dev/hda2
First logical partition on hard drive A	/dev/hda4
Second hard drive	/dev/hdb
First primary partition on hard drive B	/dev/hdb1
First SCSI hard drive	/dev/sda

Notice that the entire hard drive is referred to as /hd*letter*. The primary partitions are given the next set of four numbers, followed by the logical partitions. Thus, logical partitions always start at /dev/hda4. SCSI hard drives and CD-ROMs follow the same convention, except the hd is replaced by sd.

Using the Linux *fdisk* Program

At the `fdisk` prompt, enter `m` for a list of commands. Table 4.5 shows a list of available commands.

Table 4.5 The Linux *fdisk* Commands

Command	Description
a	Toggles a bootable flag
c	Toggles the DOS compatibility flag
d	Deletes a partition
l	Lists known partition types
m	Displays this table
n	Adds a new partition
p	Prints the partition table
q	Quits without saving changes
t	Changes a partition's system ID
u	Changes display/entry units
v	Verifies the partition table
w	Writes the table to disk and exits
x	Extra functionality (experts only)

To begin the process of partitioning, select the p command to display the current partition table, which should reflect the drive you partitioned earlier with the DOS FDISK program. Listing 4.1 shows a possible display from the p command.

Listing 4.1 An Example of a Current Partition Table

```
Disk /dev/hda: 15 heads, 17 sectors, 1024 cylinders
Units = cylinders of 255 * 512 bytes

Device          Boot    Begin   Start    End     Blocks    Id     System
dev/hda2                1024    1024     4040    384667+   51     Novell?
Partition 2 has different physical/logical endings:
phys=(967, 14, 17) Logical=(4096, 14.17)
```

N O T E You may see different information than what's shown here because the values are different for each type of drive and the partitions already defined on that drive. ∎

The display in Listing 4.1 indicates the various partitions already defined, the start and ending locations of the partition, and how big each partition is in blocks. The display also indicates the partition type. Table 4.6 lists all the different partition types you can define with the Linux fdisk command. The primary partitions you used are 83-Linux Native and 82-Linux Swap. You can get a similar listing with the l command.

Table 4.6   The Known Linux Partition Types

Reference Number	Type
0	Empty
1	DOS 12-bit FAT
2	XENIX root
3	XENIX usr
4	DOS 16-bit <32M
5	Extended
6	DOS 16-bit >=32M
7	OS/2 HPFS
8	AIX
9	AIX bootable
a	OS/2 Boot Manager
40	Venix 80286
51	Novell?
52	Microport
63	GNU HURD
64	Novell
75	PC/IX
80	Old MINIX
81	MINIX/Linux
82	Linux Swap
83	Linux Native
93	Amoeba
94	Amoeba BBT
a5	BSD/386
b7	BSDI fs

Reference Number	Type
b8	BSDI swap
c7	Syrinx
db	CP/M
e1	DOS access
e3	DOS R/O
f2	DOS secondary
ff	BBT

Notice the note about the different physical and logical endings at the end of Listing 4.1. The difference exists because, on the system used to write this chapter, a prior partition containing the DOS D drive was left intact, whereas the C drive was repartitioned to a smaller C drive to make room for Linux. As a result, there is space between the C drive and D drives. This is where the necessary partitions required by Linux will be created.

The begin, start, and end numbers from the display are very important. You should write them down because you'll need them in a later step to specify the necessary sizes of the partitions you'll add.

Adding the Necessary Partition

Because you've repartitioned the drive for MS-DOS, you shouldn't have to delete any partitions for Linux. You only should have to add partitions. A standard set of partitions should include the following:

- A / (root) partition for the whole system
- A swap partition for the swap file
- A /usr partition for software
- A /home partition for user directories
- A /var partition for log files

To add a partition, issue the n command, which displays the following:

```
Command Action
e extended
p primary(1-4)
```

Press <p> and then <Return>. fdisk asks for the partition number; enter your selection and press <Return>. If you indicate a partition number that's already in use, fdisk reports this fact and asks you to delete the partition before trying to add it to the partition table. For this example, enter **3** to add a third primary partition that's referred to as /dev/hda3.

Next, fdisk asks for the location of the first cylinder. This is usually the first available cylinder. In fact, fdisk displays a default range for your selection, such as this:

```
First cylinder (42-1024) :
```

From the preceding example, you can infer that the first partition ends at cylinder 41, and the next partition begins at cylinder 1024. Thus, the range supplied by fdisk allows you to start the next partition anywhere in the range of 42 to 1024. It's a very good idea not to place partitions just anywhere throughout the disk, so choose the next available location—in this case, cylinder 42.

> **N O T E**   Linux can have trouble booting from partitions defined to start at cylinders above 1024. If you create a Linux partition starting above 1024, you may have to boot Linux from a floppy. You learn how to create a boot floppy (which is different than the boot floppy used for installation) later in this chapter. The only downside is that booting Linux from a floppy takes a little longer than booting from the hard drive. If you have an IDE drive with more than 1024 cylinders, read the troubleshooting section in Chapter 2. ∎

▶ **See** "Troubleshooting Problems," **p. 52**

Now fdisk wants you to specify how much space to allocate for this partition. You can express this size in number of cylinders or by the number of bytes (+*size*), kilobytes (+*size*K), or megabytes (+*size*M). Because you should already know the approximate size you need for the swap file, define this partition first, and then leave the rest of the disk space for the Linux program partitions. For this example, because your machine has 8MB of RAM, you need to specify a 16MB partition size by replying like this:

```
Last cylinder or +size or +sizeM or +sizeK (42-1023): +16M
```

You should then use the p command to look at the new partition table you've defined. In this example, the new partition table looks like this:

```
Disk /dev/hda: 15 heads, 17 sectors, 1024 cylinders
Units = cylinders of 255 * 512 bytes

Device     Boot Begin Start  End   Blocks    Id     System
/dev/hda1    *    1     1     41    5219 1    DOS    12-bit FAT
/dev/hda2         1024  1024  4040  384667+   51     Novell?

Partition 2 has different physical/logical endings:
phys=(967, 14, 17) Logical=(4039, 14.17)
/dev/hda3          42    42    170   16447+    83     Linux native
```

Note that by default, fdisk made the new partition a Linux native type. To change this to a swap partition, you need to use the t command. Enter **t** and then enter the partition number you want to change (in this example, enter **3**). fdisk then requests that you enter the hexadecimal value of the desired partition type (refer to Table 4.8). If you don't have Table 4.8 handy, you can enter **1** to get the list of partition type codes. Because you want a swap partition, enter **82** at the prompt.

As you can see, fdisk reports the new partition type, but you can also use the p command to verify that partition 3 is now a Linux swap partition.

Now you can add your Linux partitions. For this example, you will add only one partition. But if you wanted multiple partitions for various reasons, you could add them at this time. To add a partition, press <n>, specify p for another primary partition, and then specify the number for this partition, which is **4**. To keep from fragmenting different partitions across the drive, start the last partition where the first left off, at cylinder 171. For the last cylinder, because you want to use the rest of the space for the Linux system, you can specify the last cylinder instead of an exact byte count. Thus, enter **1023**, as in the following example:

```
Command (m for help):n
Command action
e    extended
p    primary partition (1-4)
p
Partition number (1-4): 4
First cylinder (171-1024):171
Last cylinder or +size or +sizeM or +sizeK (171-1023):1023
```

Now use the p command to verify the new partitions. If you need to make any changes, do so now. When you're satisfied with the layout of your partitions, you can use the w command to write the partition table information to the hard disk.

None of your changes are permanent until you use the w command; thus, if you feel you've made some changes in error, you can use the q command to exit without altering the partition table. When you issue the w command, Linux tells you that the partition table has been altered and then resynchronizes the disks to match the new partition table. If your Linux system hangs at this point, reboot with the installation disk.

Creating the Swap Partition

After you partition your system as you see fit, LISA asks you to set up a swap partition. From the Configure Swap Space dialog box, select the partition you created for swap and select the Continue button. LISA will then configure, format, and activate the swap area.

Installing the Linux Software System

Now that the system is partitioned for Linux, you can install the various software packages that form the OpenLinux system. LISA displays the Installation Source Selection dialog box. From here, select the installation media: CD-ROM, hard disk, or NFS (Network File System).

Installing from the CD-ROM is a breeze with the enclosed CD package. However, you could copy the contents of the CD-ROM to a hard drive partition and access it from there. Also if you have a working network connection, you could connect to another computer and install from that machine. You may want to perform such an installation if OpenLinux could not recognize your CD-ROM.

After you make your selection, follow the instructions to begin software installation. (Remember that help is available by pressing F1.) For example, if you choose to install from the CD-ROM, you will be asked to select the appropriate hardware device. LISA typically already has this device selected.

You then need to select the root partition (/) to which all the software will be copied. After you select from the list of partitions, LISA formats and prepares the root partition for installation.

During this time, you will see a screen of numbers and hear lots of disk activity, but don't worry, this is normal.

After preparing the root partition, LISA asks if you want to place other directories under the root onto their own partition. Be careful here: The default answer is no, but you do want to place the /usr, /home, and /var directories onto the partitions you created earlier. So answer yes and repeat the process for each directory.

After creating the mount points for your file systems, LISA asks you what packages you want to install. A basic system will require about 50MB; a full install requires around 700MB. You can select from the following list:

> Minimal System without X (49MB)
>
> Minimal System with X (68MB)
>
> Small Standard System (121MB)
>
> Standard System (349MB)
>
> All Packages (688MB)

LISA generates a package listing after you select the installation size. LISA then begins the automated package installation. You can relax, sit back, and watch the installation.

Configuring Your System

After package installation you will need to configure your system. If you are connected to a network you will need the appropriate information from your service provider or network coordinator. You also need to select a root password. This is an important password, so choose wisely and don't forget it.

To begin, LISA asks for a host name. This is the name others on the network will call your machine. You'll also need to provide your domain name, which is typically something like company.com. The hostname and domain name create the fully qualified domain name for your computer (such as opus.netwharf.com).

▶ **See** "IP Addresses," **p. 469**

You need to provide the IP address of your computer, along with its netmask and the default gateway. After supplying this information, you need to specify your network's domain name server, or DNS machine.

After setting up your network, you need to configure your clock and time zone information. It is recommended that you use local time, even though most Internet servers use GMT. This is because most PCs have their BIOS clocks set to local time, not GMT. Setting a PC to GMT may cause problems, especially if you use other operating systems on the machine. Select local or GMT time, and then specify your time zone, such as EST.

Next you must specify what type of mouse you are using. Most ATX system use a PS/2 style mouse. If you are using a serial mouse, make sure you remember which serial port your mouse uses. Next, select the printer you intend to use with your system, if necessary.

▶ **See** "Understanding Key Terms Used in This Chapter," **p. 146**

Now you must select a root password. This is the super user's account and allows anyone to do anything they want to your system. Do not give this password to just anyone! And do not forget the root password. If you do forget, more than likely you will have to reinstall the system.

N O T E See Chapter 12, "Improving System Security," for password tips and rescue options. ■

After setting your root password, you need to create your first user account. LISA uses a default value of col (for Caldera OpenLinux), but you can specify any name you want—even your own. This first user account allows you to use the system as a regular user instead of as the super user (root). Typically you should not use the root account for day-to-day user tasks because of the potential for creating problems. After you specify the new account name, simply accept the default values for the other items requested. These fields, such as group, are explained in Chapter 10, "Managing User Accounts."

▶ **See** "Adding a User" **p. 220**

Next you indicate how you want your system to boot.

Installing LILO

LILO stands for the LInux LOader. LILO is a program executed at system startup that lets you choose which operating system will be used to boot the computer. You can use LILO to boot several different operating systems, such as Linux and MS-DOS. With LILO, you also can specify a default operating system to boot and a default time limit the system should wait before it boots that system. For example, if you have MS-DOS and Linux on your computer, you can configure LILO to boot either one. You can tell LILO to boot MS-DOS if no one intervenes within 30 seconds. Before that 30 seconds is up, however, a user can specify another operating system to boot instead of the default. You can press the <Ctrl>, <Alt>, or <Shift> key to stop the timed process. Press <Tab> to get a list of operating systems LILO can boot.

You specify all this information while configuring LILO. Although you can directly edit the lilo.conf file located in the /etc directory, the LILO INSTALLATION screen provides a better interface for editing the file.

After you configure your system, Setup lets you install LILO with the option to configure LILO.

Uninstalling LILO

If you're running LILO version 0.14 or newer, you can uninstall LILO with the following command:

```
opus:~# lilo -u
```

If you have a previous version, you must remove or disable LILO from its primary partition first. You can use the Linux fdisk or MS-DOS FDISK program to make another partition active.

Part
I

Ch
4

If you placed LILO within the MBR (master boot record), you must replace it with another MBR from another operating system. With MS-DOS 5.0 or above, the command `c:\>fdisk /mbr` restores the MS-DOS MBR.

When LILO is removed from the active partition or the MBR, you're free to remove the files from /etc/lilo.

▶ **See** "Removing Files or Directories," **p. 323**

Going Back to the Beginning

After you complete the setup and configuration of your system, the Setup program returns you to the main menu. From there, you can choose the EXIT option to leave Setup. If you want to change options, you can do so here. (In case you don't change the options during installation, Chapter 6, "Upgrading and Installing Software with RPM," provides information on updating and installing software after your initial installation.) Choose EXIT to leave the Setup program.

Choosing EXIT returns you to the system prompt, indicated by the # sign. You're now in Linux and can issue simple commands, such as ls for a directory listing of files. At this time, though, you should reboot the system so that all your setup and configurations settings can take effect.

Rebooting Linux is more involved than rebooting DOS. You can't turn off the power and turn the system back on. If you do so in Linux, you can damage the file structures and systems. Linux tries to repair itself on bootup. Don't turn off the power while running Linux. To exit Linux, use the following command:

```
shutdown [-r] time
```

The optional -r flag indicates that the system should reboot after shutting down. *time* indicates the time that the system should shut down; you can use now in place of *time* to indicate immediate shutdown. Linux also recognizes the warm-boot keys used by DOS (<Ctrl-Alt-Delete>) to reboot the machine, which Linux interprets as the command

```
shutdown -r now
```

▶ **See** "Shutting Down Linux," **p. 215**

Make sure you've removed all the floppy disks from the drive and reboot your new Linux machine.

Resolving Problems

After you reboot your machine, the LILO prompt should appear. Make sure that you can boot to your old operating system if you left it on the hard drive. If that system was DOS, press the <Shift> key and then type the short word you used to identify the DOS partition when you installed LILO. If you enter an invalid word, press <Tab> to get a list of valid operating system types. If you're having problems at this point, place your DOS boot disk in the boot drive and reboot.

From Here...

After you have your system up and running, you can read the following chapters for further information about Linux:

- Chapter 3, "Installing Red Hat," because much of the installation process for Caldera is based on an older version of RedHat's Linux distribution, including the use of RPM.
- Chapter 5, "Running Linux Applications," gets you up to speed on the various programs you just installed.
- Chapter 6, "Upgrading and Installing Software with RPM," provides instructions of how to reinstall packages you may have left out during the initial setup of your Linux system.
- Chapter 12, "Improving System Security," provides tips and tricks for providing passwords and recovering from errors.

Part

I

Ch

4

Running Linux Applications

by Jack Tackett

Now that you've installed your Linux system, this chapter presents a brief introduction to setting up a user account for you to use and some basic commands to get you moving around your new system. This is your very own multitasking, multiuser system; experimenting is encouraged, so go ahead and play with your system. You may never get this type of opportunity on a typical UNIX system.

However, just playing with an operating system is no fun; it doesn't get your daily job done. After all, you don't use DOS all day, right? You use applications. Linux provides access to literally thousands of applications from around the world. You've installed several from the Slackware or Red Hat distribution from the accompanying CD-ROMs. There are plenty more where they came from, too. Programs that rival those costing hundreds of dollars for the PC platform are readily available for Linux.

Maneuvering Through Linux

After installing Linux and rebooting, you're faced with a system prompt based on the name you gave your system during installation. The prompt looks similar to this:

```
Red Hat Linux release 5.0 (Hurricane)
Kernel 2.0.31 on an I486
web login:
```

The prompt may indicate a different version of Linux, however, because Linux is an evolving system.

You must now supply a user name and a password. A user name identifies you to the operating system because Linux can support many different users, both at different times and concurrently. An account also provides each user with a default directory, called the *home directory*. Many accounts are also set up to restrict users to certain directories on the system and to prevent them from using certain commands, primarily to protect the files of one user from the prying eyes of another.

Entering Commands

You enter commands in Linux much as you do in DOS and other command-line-oriented operating systems. Linux, like UNIX, is case-sensitive; if Linux doesn't know a command, make sure that you've spelled it correctly and that you've entered it in the proper case. Most commands are executed after you press <Return>.

Recalling Command History

Linux also provides a history function to recall previous commands. This history is kept across sessions, too. You can press the <↑> key to recall previous commands and then press <Return> to activate that command. To get a complete listing of all the prior commands you've entered, you use the history command:

```
[tackett@web~]$ history
1 clear
```

```
2 adduser
3 history
```

When you have the preceding history list, you can repeat the command by using the <↑> key and cycling through the commands until the proper one appears on the command line, or you can press <!> (the *bang* character) and enter the number of the command you want to re-execute. For example, if you wanted to repeat the adduser command in the previous list, you would enter the following:

```
[tackett@web~]$ !2
```

The number of entries in the history list is user-defined in the user account's .profile configuration file. See Chapter 18, "Understanding Linux Shells," for more information on the .profile configuration file.

NOTE Linux provides many different command shells, some of which don't provide the history functions. ▪

Making Selections

If you have a mouse with your system and installed the selection program, you can also use your mouse to copy text from other areas of your screen to the command line. To select the text, simply move the mouse cursor (which appears as soon as you click the left mouse button) by holding down the left mouse button as you drag the cursor across the desired text, and then press the right mouse button to copy the text to the command line. This is useful if you need to enter a long filename on the command line.

Completing Commands

Linux also offers another nice feature when entering commands. You can start to type a filename and then press <Tab>. Linux searches the directory for a file beginning with the same letters you've typed and completes the filename it finds. If Linux can't find a unique filename, it beeps and completes the filename to the last common character. For example, if you wanted to copy a file called todo_monday to the file todo_today, you type **cp to** at the prompt and then press <Tab>, Linux beeps and fills out the command line like so:

```
[tackett@web~]$ cp todo_
```

If you then type an **m** and press <Tab>, Linux will place the entire todo_monday filename on the command line.

Managing Users

On many systems, the person responsible for maintaining the user accounts is referred to as the *systems administrator.* The systems administrator sets up user accounts and performs other duties. For more information on the various aspects of systems administration, check out the chapters in Part II, "System Administration." On your Linux system, you're the systems administrator, so it's your responsibility to set up accounts for yourself, family, and friends.

Part

I

Ch

5

To add an account for yourself, you must create that account as the systems administrator. Systems administrators are also sometimes referred to as *superusers* because they have so much control over the system. To begin your trek through Linux, you must first log in as the superuser via the root account.

Logging In and Out

To log in as root, enter **root** at the login prompt. Linux asks for a password.

By using a password, you prevent unauthorized users from logging in to any account. Linux wants to make sure that the user name is in fact the correct user. You shouldn't share your passwords with just anyone. Linux protects the password you type by not *echoing*—that is, not displaying—the letters on-screen, so make sure that you enter the correct password.

If you enter an invalid user name or password, Linux gives the following error message and starts the process over:

```
web login: jack
Password: password
Login incorrect

web login:
```

Because this is your first time logging in to the system since installation, the root account has no password set, so after entering **root**, you're presented with a command prompt. Then you can enter Linux commands. You enter most commands the same way you do in DOS: Type the command with any necessary parameters and press <Return>.

To log out, enter **logout**. This command returns you to the login prompt. If this command doesn't work, try the exit command.

Adding Users Under Slackware

After you log in as root, you should add an account for yourself. To add an account, enter the following command and follow the prompts:

```
[root@web~]# adduser

Adding a new user. The user name should be not exceed 8 characters
in length, or you many run into problems later.

Enter login name for new account (^C to quit):
```

Look at this screen for a second. Notice the command prompt after which you entered the command. The prompt begins with the host name of the computer. This is the name you entered while installing the *n* package of disks. The next item is the tilde character (~). Linux uses this character to refer to the account's home directory (described later). Here, it represents the directory the user is now located in. If you issued the adduser command from the /usr/bin directory, the prompt reads:

```
[root@web~]#/usr/bin#
```

The next character is the pound sign (#). This prompt, by convention, belongs to any superuser account. A normal user account usually has a dollar sign ($) as a prompt.

Next, you may have noticed the misspellings and improper grammar in the prompts—that is, should be not and you many run. These errors don't affect the performance of the system, but they help highlight the fact that Linux, while fully functional and a great system, isn't a commercial venture.

Now enter a user name of up to eight characters and press <Return>. An example session to create an account for Jack Tackett follows:

```
Enter login name for new account (^C to quit): jack

Editing information for new user [jack]

Full Name: Jack Tackett, Jr.
GID[100]:<Return>

Checking for an available UID after 500
501...
First unused uid is 502

UID [502]:<Return>

Home Directory [/home/jack]:<Return>

Shell [/bin/bash]:<Return>

Password: opus

Information for new user [jack]:
Home directory: [/home/jack] Shell: [/bin/bash]
Password: [opus] uid: [502] gid: [100]

Is this correct? [y/N] :y

Adding login [jack] and making directory [/home/jack]

Adding the files from the /etc/skel directory:
./ .kermc -> /home/jack/ ./ .kermc
./ .less -> /home/jack/ ./ .less
./ .lessrc -> /home/jack/ ./ .lessrc
./ .term -> /home/jack/ ./ .term
./ .term/termrc -> /home/jack/ ./ .termrc
./ .emacs -> /home/jack/ ./ .emacs

[root@web ~]#
```

As you move through the process, you must enter a full name for the user to help identify the user account further. Next, you're asked to enter a group ID and a user ID. Don't worry about these items at this time. Linux uses them to determine the directories and files that you have access to by default. You can safely accept the default values (within the brackets) by simply pressing <Return> after each request.

Part

I

Ch

5

Next, you're asked to enter a home directory for the user. This is where the user is automatically placed when he or she first logs in. This is the user's account area for storing files and for working storage. Linux provides a default directory based on the user's name. If this default directory is acceptable, press <Return>; otherwise, enter a directory and press <Return>. Accept, for now, the defaults offered by the adduser command.

You're now asked to specify a shell for the user. The shell is a command interpreter much like COMMAND.COM is for DOS. The shell accepts the input and runs specified commands. You've been using a shell called bash since installing Linux. For the time being, simply accept the default bash option.

▶ **See** "Understanding Shells," **p. 339**

The final parameter is the password for the account. It's highly recommended that you provide every account with a password. Linux then displays all the information entered and asks whether it's correct. If the information isn't correct, enter **n** (or simply press <Return>, because No is the default choice); you must go back and correct the errors. If everything is correct, enter **y**.

Linux displays a series of files it copies from a skeletal user account located in the ./etc/skel directory to the new user's home directory. These files are configuration files for such items as the user's terminal and how such programs as emacs and less run from their accounts. The users can modify these files at any time to change the default behavior of the programs.

After adding the account, you can verify its existence in one of two ways; the quickest is to use a utility called finger to see whether the user has an account. The general form of the command is finger *name*. For example, you can test for the account you just created by entering this:

```
[root@web ~]#finger jack

Login: jack    Name Jack Tackett, Jr.
Directory: /home/jack    Shell: /bin/bash
Never logged in.
No Mail.
No Plan.
[root@web ~]#
```

If the user has an account, the appropriate information is displayed; otherwise, a message indicating no such user has an account is displayed.

The next way to verify the account is to actually log in to the account to see whether Linux will let you. You can do this in one of several ways:

- You can log out and then log in as the new user.
- You can use the su command, which stands for *switch user*.
- You can use the login command.
- You can use one of the six virtual terminals provided by Linux to log in to a new account. Remember, Linux is multiuser.

Table 5.1 presents an overview of each method.

Table 5.1   Logging In to a Newly Created User Account

Command	Description
`logout`	Logs you out of the root account and brings you back to the login prompt. You no longer have access to the root account until you log in as root.
`su` *username*	Logs you out of the account, doesn't ask for the user name to log in as, and then prompts you for the password. If you don't specify *username*, su assumes that you're trying to log in as root and expects you to enter the root password.
`login` *username*	Almost the same as su, except that leaving off *username* merely places you at the normal login prompt.
`<Alt-Fx>`	Lets you use the virtual terminals. You can access a virtual terminal by pressing the <Alt> key and one of the function keys (F1 through F6). This takes you to another login screen, where you can log in as the new user. The best feature of using the virtual terminals is that you're still left in the other account and can swap back and forth by using the <Alt-Fx> keys; you aren't logged out of the other account.

N O T E   If you try to add a user later from an account you know you've created, you may not be able to use the command adduser because certain commands can be entered only by the superuser, and adduser is one of them. If you have trouble adding a user to the system, make sure that you're logged in as root. ■

Adding Users with Red Hat

Red Hat Linux automates many of the adduser functions. To add a new user from the command line, enter the following command:

`[root@web /root]#`**adduser jack**

This command is a shell script located in /usr/sbin. You must be the superuser—that is, root—to issue this command.

▶ **See** "Working with Shell Scripts," **p. 325**

The script, which is just an ASCII file, creates the necessary directories and files needed by the new user. The only thing left is to set the user's password when he or she first logs in. Changing passwords is discussed later in the section "Changing Passwords."

▶ **See** "Viewing the Contents of a File," **p. 365**

Using Red Hat's Control Panel to Manage Users

If you installed XFree86 with your Red Hat installation, you can use the Control Panel's User/Group Manager configuration window (see Figure 5.1) to add users, modify user

Part

I

Ch

5

settings, and delete or deactivate users. To manipulate a user's account, select the user in the dialog box and click the appropriate button. Table 5.2 describes each button's function.

FIG. 5.1

The RHS Linux User/Group Manager dialog box lets you see and manipulate the information stored in /etc/passwd.

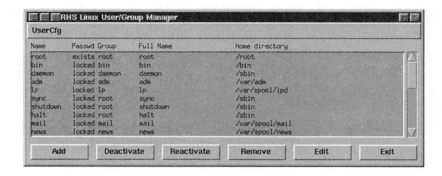

Table 5.2   The RHS Linux User/Group Manager Buttons

Button	Description
Add	Displays the Add User dialog box, which lets you set the various required attributes for a user, such as home directory and password.
Deactivate	Allows you to deactivate the account of a user who you know will need the account again in the future. You may want to deactivate an account for a user who's on sabbatical or is being disciplined for some infraction. You can choose to compress the user's files to save space on your system until you reactivate that user later.
Reactivate	Allows you to reactivate a user's account.
Remove	Deletes a user from your system. The user's various files and directories will be removed. You may want to back up these files before deleting them.
Edit	Allows you to edit user accounts for such items as passwords (if they forget their password), their groups, or the shell they want to use.
Exit	Exits the RHS Linux User/Group Manager.

Clicking the Add button displays the Add User dialog box shown in Figure 5.2. You can set up the user's account from this dialog box by filling in the information for the various fields. Table 5.3 describes the fields and their functions.

Table 5.3   The Options of the Add User Dialog Box

Field	Description
Username	The name the user uses to log in to your system.
Password	The user's password. To give the user a password, you must use the combo box arrow and choose Edit from the menu. This displays a new

Field	Description
	dialog box that lets you enter a new password for the user. The password combo box also lets you either blank out the password field by selecting the "none" value or lock the password.
UID	A field generated by the system. For more information on UIDs and groups, see Chapter 10, "Managing User Accounts."
Primary Group	The primary group to which the user belongs. Groups allow you to put users into similar groupings, all having the same permissions.
Full Name	The user's full name.
Home	The user's home directory. Typically, it's located in a directory under /home or /usr/home.
Shell	The default shell the user's account starts with. This combo box allows you to select any shell offered by the Red Hat system for the user.

FIG. 5.2
Red Hat's graphical
admin tools make
adding new users a
breeze.

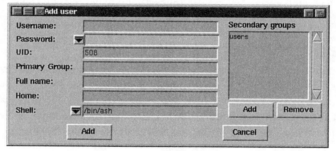

Changing Passwords

In the future, you may want to change your password or add a password to an account that doesn't have one, such as the current root account. You should always password-protect the root account.

To change a password under any version of Linux or UNIX, you use the passwd command, specify the old and new password, and then verify the new password. If you don't have (or—worse—don't remember) the old password, you can't use the passwd command to change your password. The typical sequence for passwd follows:

```
[tackett@web ~]$ passwd
Changing password for jack
Enter old password: password
Enter new password: new-password
Re-type new password: new-password
```

If you make an error, Linux informs you that the password hasn't been changed. Linux also requires at least six characters for a valid password, and this minimum is enforced.

Part

I

Ch

5

> **CAUTION**
>
> *Don't forget your passwords!* If you forget a user password, you must change the account information. If you forget the root account password, you must use the boot floppy created during installation to boot the system and change the password. Typically, you can set the password to empty by selecting none in the RHS Add/Edit User dialog box, and then let the user set a new password with the `passwd` command. You can also edit the /etc/passwd file and remove the encrypted password from the user's record.

▶ **See** "Setting User Passwords," **p. 221**

Using Basic Commands

You need to know some basic commands to get around the system. The following sections provide some of the commands you need to use your Linux system. Finally, many of the "commands" presented in the following sections are actually utility programs that Linux uses to extend its command set. These programs are found in the /bin, /sbin, and /usr/bin directories.

Getting Help for Commands with *man*

To get online help for each of the various Linux commands, you can type `man`. Linux then displays, a screen at a time, any information it has on the command. If you aren't sure of what command to use, you can try the `-k` parameter and enter a simple keyword that represents the topic of interest. `man` then searches through its help files (called man, or manual, pages) for a topic that contains the keyword. Linux also provides an alias for this command, called `apropos`.

If you enter the command `man ls`, Linux provides help on the `ls` command, including all its parameters. The command `man -k cls` provides a listing of commands that have the word `cls` in the help file; the command `apropos cls` is the same as `man -k cls`.

Using Directory-Manipulation Commands

Linux provides many commands to work with directories. Like other operating systems you may have used, Linux allows you to create, delete, and move directories, as well as display information about the directory.

Changing the Current Working Directory with *cd* Linux, like DOS and other operating systems, stores files in a tree structure called a directory. You can specify a file via a path from the root directory, specified with the / character, to the file itself. Thus, the configuration file for emacs for the user jack can be exactly specified like so:

```
/home/jack/.emacs
```

If you're familiar with the DOS limits of eight characters for a filename and three characters for an extension, you'll be pleasantly surprised to learn that Linux has no such limit on filenames.

▶ **See** "Understanding File and Path Names," **p. 304**

Linux also uses the concept of a home directory, which is specified when an account is added to the system. A user's home directory is usually specified with the tilde character (~). You can use the tilde in place of the directory name when the user wants to copy a file from the current directory \usr\home\jack to his or her home directory:

```
cp .emacs ~
```

To move around the Linux directory structure, you use the change directory command, cd. If you enter **cd** without any parameters, Linux immediately returns you to your home directory. To move from one directory to another directory, you use the cd command much as you do in DOS—that is, cd *new-directory*. Linux also uses the single dot (.) to represent the current directory and the double dot (..) to represent the parent directory. In fact, it's DOS that emulates UNIX, not UNIX/Linux emulating DOS.

N O T E Be careful how you specify the directory separator. DOS uses as its directory separator the backslash (\) character, which Linux uses as the character for continuing a command on another line. To separate directory names in Linux, you must use the forward slash (/) character.

Also, although DOS doesn't mind if you fail to use spaces when specifying the . and .. parameters, Linux does. Linux doesn't understand cd.., but it understands cd .. Linux needs the space separating the command and the parameter. ■

Displaying Information About Files and Directories with *ls*

ls stands for *list* and is used by Linux to display a list of files. This command is the counterpart to the DOS DIR command. (Linux also accepts the dir command to list files in a directory.) Under Linux, the ls command displays all the main files in a directory in color. By default, blue indicates directories and green indicates executable programs. You can change the default colors by modifying the file /etc/DIR_COLORS.

▶ **See** "Listing Files," **p. 318**

ls takes many parameters to specify not only how to display a file but what files to display. The most common parameter is -la, which tells ls to display information in a long format for every file in a directory.

The command ls -la lists all information about every file in the current directory. The command ls .emacs lists the file .emacs, whereas ls -l .emacs lists all information about the file .emacs.

The command options –ltar (used as ls –ltar) list the same information as the above ls command, except the file listings are displayed in order from oldest to most recent.

Creating New Directories with *mkdir*

Because Linux's file system is based on directories, Linux provides the mkdir command so users can create new ones. Unlike DOS, which has an alias for the mkdir command called MD, Linux requires that the full mkdir command be spelled out. You must specify a name for each new directory, as shown in the following example:

```
mkdir backup
```

Part
I

Ch
5

N O T E Linux does provide a way, via the command shell, to make aliases for command names; thus, if you simply can't live without the DOS MD command and hate typing `mkdir`, you can alias md to the `mkdir` command. ■

▶ **See** "Command Aliasing," **p. 364**

Deleting Directories with *rmdir* The `rmdir` command deletes Linux directories. The command takes the name of the directory to delete. This directory must be empty—otherwise, Linux can't remove it.

For example, if the /backup directory had two directories within it, the command `rmdir /backup` fails. The command `rmdir /backup/jack/*` removes all files in the /backup/jack directory, and then `rmdir /backup/jack` removes the now-empty /backup/jack directory.

> **CAUTION**
>
> You can't delete a directory that contains files with the `rmdir` command. Instead, you can use the `-r` flag to the `rm` command. For example,
>
> `rm -r *`
>
> deletes everything from the current directory and every directory below the current directory. Be very careful using this command, because the moment you delete a directory, you can't recover the directory or the files that were located in the directory. Make backups.

Using File-Manipulation Commands

Because Linux treats directories and files similarly, it provides similar commands for manipulation.

Copying Files with *cp* The `cp` command is similar to the DOS COPY command. You use this command to copy one or more files from one directory to another directory. The syntax of `cp` is as follows:

`cp from-filename to-filename`

You must supply a *from-filename* and a *to-filename* for the files to be copied. If you want to preserve the filename, use the dot (.) as a placeholder for the *to-filename* parameter. This is in contrast to DOS, where you could leave off the *to-filename*.

The command `cp fred1 fred1.old` copies the file fred1 to a backup file named fred1.old, whereas the command `cp ~fred1.old /backup/jack` copies the file fred1.old from the home directory to the /backup/jack directory. (The ~ character represents the user's home directory.)

Moving Files with *mv* The `mv` command, which is similar to the DOS MOVE command, allows you to move files from one directory to another directory. When you move a file, it has the same effect as if you had copied the files to a new directory and then deleted the files in the old directory. `mv` doesn't make a copy of the files.

The syntax of the `mv` command is identical to the `cp` command:

```
mv from-filename to-filename
```

The command `mv fred1 fred1.old` copies the file fred1 to a backup file named fred1.old and deletes the old fred1 file, whereas the command `mv ~fred1.old /backup/jack` moves the fred1.old file from the home directory to the /backup/jack directory.

Deleting Files with *rm*   To delete files under Linux, you use the `rm` command. The `rm` command is dangerous because as soon as a file is deleted, you can never recover it. For safety reasons, you should use the following form of the `rm` command:

```
rm -i filename
```

The `-i` parameter tells the command to query, or inquire, the user to see if that's the file they really want to remove. For example, the command `rm fred1` removes the file named fred1, whereas the command `rm -i fred1` deletes the fred1 file after asking whether the user really wants to remove this file.

> **CAUTION**
>
> As soon as you delete a file under Linux, that file is gone. You can't undelete a file or directory under Linux like you can with DOS. If you delete a file, your only hope is a backup copy.

Displaying File Contents with *more*   The `more` command displays a screen of a text file. You can look through a text file without invoking an editor, printing the file, or trying to pause the terminal as it displays the file. To display the contents of your `emacs` configuration file, for example, you can type the following:

```
more .emacs
```

> **N O T E**   If you try to pass a binary data file to `more`, you could have some unpleasant effects—for example, your terminal can lock up. If your terminal does lock up, try pressing <Ctrl-q> or <Ctrl-s>. ■

A disadvantage with `more` is that you can't back up to see a screen of information once it passes. But the command discussed in the following section overcomes that problem.

Using *less*—a Better *more*   `less` displays information a screen at a time on your terminal. The program's name is a play on words for the program it's meant to replace—more. Like `more`, `less` can display a screen of information in a text file, but unlike `more`, `less` allows you to page back and forth within the file. You can use the following command to browse through the readme file located in the info directory:

```
less /info/readme
```

Clearing the Screen with *clear*   Sometimes after filling your terminal screen with information, you want a blank screen while you sit and contemplate your next action. Under DOS, you can use the `cls` command, but under Linux, you must use the `clear` command.

Part
I

Ch
5

Dealing with DOS Files Under Linux

During installation, you were given the chance to make any DOS partitions you had available visible to Linux. These partitions were then placed in a directory you specified during configuration—for example, /dosc.

▶ **See** "Repartitioning Your DOS Drive," **p. 70**

If you want to copy these files to a floppy, using the cp command may cause problems because UNIX and Linux treat text files a little differently than DOS, especially when dealing with carriage returns and line-feeds. To overcome this problem, a group of programs was developed to help deal with MS-DOS files under a UNIX environment. These are the m- commands, which include such commands as mcopy and mdir. mcopy works just like the DOS COPY command, and mdir provides a directory listing. As you may notice, they resemble their DOS counterparts, except that they begin with the letter m, hence the name "m- commands." The m- commands are part of the mtools package, which is a collection of public-domain programs that allows UNIX to interact with DOS files much more easily.

These commands also make copying files to floppy disks much easier because you can use the DOS designation, like A, instead of the Linux designation /dev/fd0. For more information on the m- commands, enter the following:

```
man mtools
```

Table 5.4 provides a brief listing of the various m- commands.

Table 5.4 The _m-_ Commands

Command	Description
mattrib	Displays the file attributes for the specified file(s)
mcd	Changes directory to the specified path
mcopy	Copies the files specified to the new path
mdel	Deletes the specified files
mdir	Provides a directory listing
mformat	Formats a floppy
mlabel	Labels the DOS file system
mmd	Makes a directory
mrd	Removes a directory (must be empty, just as in DOS)
mren	Renames an existing DOS file
mtype	Displays the text contents of a DOS file

NOTE Although you can see a DOS file with Linux and even do some editing on text files in DOS partitions that Linux can see, you can't execute DOS or Windows programs under Linux. However, projects are under way across the Internet to supply such emulation for Linux. Although the prospects look very good for such emulators in the future, at this time DOS and Windows emulation isn't fully available. You'll have a brief introduction to both items later in this chapter. ■

Shutting Down Linux

When you're finished using a DOS machine, you can typically just turn off the power and walk away. You could also do the same under Windows, although there's a great possibility for file damage. Under Linux, there are even more chances for damaging your system, both to hardware and file systems, by simply turning off the power. You must shut down Linux in an orderly fashion, or you might corrupt the operating system to the point where it can't boot the next time you try.

Linux keeps a lot of information about itself and files in memory, in areas called *buffers*, before writing the information to disk. This process helps improve system performance and control access to the hardware—something a multitasking operating systems needs to maintain so that one user doesn't try to use a hardware device that another user is using. If you turn off the power, this information is lost and you can corrupt your file system.

▶ **See** "Shutting Down Linux," **p. 215**

Because Linux is a multiuser and multitasking operating system, it must make sure that every user stops processing gracefully and saves any work in progress before shutting the system down, to prevent data loss and file damage. This also gives each user logged in to the system time to log out. To shut down Linux in an orderly fashion, you must use the shutdown command. The shutdown command syntax is this:

shutdown [-r] *time-to-shutdown* [*message*]

The optional -r flag indicates that Linux should immediately reboot after it shuts down. This is useful if you want to quit Linux and boot to another operating system.

time-to-shutdown indicates when the system should shut down. The time is specified on a 24-hour clock, so you can tell the machine to shut down at 11 p.m., for example by entering the following:

shutdown 23:00

The *message* parameter is a message sent to each user logged in to the system. This message is then displayed on their terminals. You can use this message to tell users why you're shutting down the system. For example, if you needed to do weekly backups, you could use the following message to make sure that everyone logged out of the system:

[root@web /root]# **shutdown -r 23:00 Shutting down at 11:00pm for system maintenance**

Remember, don't simply turn off the computer or press the Reset button to exit Linux.

Part
I

Ch
5

> **CAUTION**
>
> On some systems, Linux traps the <Ctrl-Alt-Del> reboot keystroke and executes an orderly shutdown as though the user had typed the shutdown command. However, on some systems Linux can't detect this keystroke combination and reboots immediately.
>
> If you do accidentally turn off your system and damage the file structure, you can use the fsck command to try and repair the file system.
>
> ▶ **See** "Using the fsck Command," **p. 279**

Running Linux Programs

When you're familiar with moving around Linux and executing basic commands, you can try several applications installed when you set up the system. These applications cover a broad range of utilities, from a calculator to full-featured C and C++ compilers. Some of these programs cost hundreds of dollars; thanks to the GNU philosophy, however, many are readily available, and the only monetary outlay is the cost of getting the program from the Internet.

Luckily, many programs for Linux are also available on local bulletin boards, which you can reach via the telecommunications program included with the Slackware and Red Hat distributions of Linux. Also, many CD-ROM vendors supply CD-ROMs with hundreds of UNIX programs in source code. You can retrieve these programs from the CD-ROM and, by using the gcc and g++ compilers distributed with Linux, get those programs up and running on your PC—even if you've never compiled a program before.

Finally, these programs are text-based and don't require the X Windows system to operate; thus, they may not have flashy graphics, but they work with most Linux installations.

Using the *workbone* CD Player

workbone is installed with the Slackware distribution. workbone is a text-based CD player written by Thomas McWilliams. If you have a CD-ROM capable of playing audio CDs, you should give it a try.

McWilliams wrote the program for his own enjoyment by hacking an X Windows-based program. Because he did this for his own enjoyment, workbone may not work correctly with every CD-ROM drive.

With this program, you use the numeric keypad to control the CD, so make sure that you have the <Num Lock> key engaged. Table 5.5 lists the controls and their uses.

Table 5.5   *workbone* Commands

Key	Description
0	Exits workbone and leaves music playing
DEL	Displays the help screen

Key	Description
1	Goes backward 15 seconds
2	Aborts workbone and stops music
3	Goes forward 15 seconds
4	Goes to the previous selection
5	Restarts the current selection
6	Goes to the next selection
7	Stops
8	Pauses/resumes
9	Plays

As workbone plays, the display updates the time and current selection. If you want to continue working while your CD plays, you have two choices:

- You can exit workbone and leave the music playing (key 0).
- If you want to keep the display up and running, you can simply switch to another virtual terminal via the <Alt> key and log in to another account. When you want to check on the display, you can switch back to the proper virtual terminal and check on the status of the CD.

You can also stop the CD with the 0 key and then later simply re-execute the program to see what tracks are playing. For more information, check out the man page by typing **man workbone**.

Using the *sc* Spreadsheet Calculator

Do spiffy computers sell software, or does software sell computers? This is an age-old question whose answer tends to side with the concept that the proper application can sell thousands of computers. When the program called VisiCalc entered the market, PC use in business exploded. Why? Because for years, business people had played what-if games with their businesses on pieces of paper called ledgers, or spreadsheets. VisiCalc was an electronic version of the paper spreadsheet; it revolutionized how business did its forecasting and planning. Today, the successors of VisiCalc, such as Microsoft Excel and Lotus 1-2-3, still carry on the legacy started by VisiCalc. In the world of Linux, sc carries on that same legacy.

sc is a spreadsheet calculator containing rows and columns of cells. Each cell can contain a numeric value, a label string, or an expression or formula that evaluates to a numeric value or label string. These label strings can also be based on other cells to form complex relationships across a multiple collection of information.

If you've worked with other spreadsheet programs, you should have no problem getting up to speed on using sc. If you do need help, you can run a tutorial program to help you learn by entering the following command:

```
sc /usr/lib/sc/tutorial.sc
```

This tutorial provides an excellent introduction to using sc. If you need a quick reference card, you can print one by entering this command:

```
scqref ¦ lpr
```

The solid bar is referred to as a *pipe* because you're piping, or passing on, the results of one command, scqref, to another command, lpr.

N O T E   Check out Chapter 20, "Printing," if you have any problems printing with Linux. The biggest problem you may face, besides the possibility of not being able to print at all, is a bad case of the *jaggies*, which are the stair-step effects caused by the difference between how UNIX/Linux treats carriage returns and line feeds versus how MS-DOS treats them when printing text files containing these characters. ■

For online help about sc, simply type **man sc**.

Using the *bc* Calculator

bc is a command-line calculator for those quick-and-dirty calculations. bc is actually a sophisticated programming language that allows you to evaluate arithmetic expressions interactively.

When executed, bc responds with a short copyright notice and then leaves you at the command prompt, a blank line. You can then enter simple addition and subtraction functions. You can also perform division and multiplication—however, the version of bc distributed with Linux truncates the result of division and multiplication operations. (This is one of the hazards to be aware of when dealing with GNU software.) bc is great for simple calculations, as long as you're aware of the possible problems with its division and multiplication operations.

Another great feature is bc's capability of storing values from one operation to the next with a simple syntax, *variable-name = expression*. The following example calculates the value of 125 * 5 and stores the result in the var1 variable. To see what the results of the calculation are, you can type the name of the variable, and bc prints the value on the next line, as shown in the example. Next, the example sets the variable var2 to the contents of var1 divided by 5.

```
var1 = 125 * 5
var1
625
var2 = var1 / 5
var2
```

Using the *minicom* Telecommunications Package

Let's hope that after you read the chapters in Part VI, "Using the Internet," you can get your Linux system up and running on the Internet (the global Information Superhighway that's in the news so much today). Until then, however, you can still connect with the rest of the world if you have a modem and a telecommunications package. Linux supplies the package, called minicom, so all you have to do is supply the modem connected to one of your serial ports.

minicom, like a lot of Linux software, was written by a single person with help from many people on the Internet. The main author of minicom is Miquel van Smoorenburg. minicom is a very robust application that rivals many other commercial applications. With it you can connect to various bulletin-board services, maintain a list of numbers to dial, and download and upload files as soon as you connect. Help for most of minicom's functionality is available on the man page.

The first thing to remember is that minicom uses the key sequence <Ctrl-Shift-a> to access the various functions, such as auto-dial and file downloading. To get help at any time while in minicom, simply press <Ctrl-a><z> to display a brief command summary screen. Table 5.6 lists a few of those commands.

Table 5.6   *minicom* Command Summary

Key	Description
D	Accesses dialing directory
S	Sends files
P	Lists communication parameters
L	Toggles on or off capturing the session to a file
F	Sends a BREAK to the other terminal
T	Sets terminal emulation between vt100, Minix, or ANSI
W	Toggles line wraps on or off
G	Runs a minicom script file
R	Receives a file
A	Adds a line-feed character to the end of lines
H	Hangs up the phone line
M	Initializes the modem
K	Runs the kermit protocol
E	Toggles on or off local echo
C	Clears the local screen
O	Allows you to configure minicom
J	Jumps to a new command shell
X	Quits and resets the modem
I	Cursor key mode
Z	Displays the help screen
B	Scrolls back through the terminal window

Part
I

Ch
5

While in the help window, you can simply press the appropriate letter to execute the command. From the minicom program, however, you must preface the appropriate letters with <Ctrl-a>.

minicom has four file-transfer protocols: zmodem, ymodem, xmodem, and kermit. If possible, you should try to use zmodem because of its superior error-recovery capabilities. If zmodem isn't available on the other system you're dialing, you should try each of the protocols in the order given. This isn't to say kermit is a bad protocol (it's not)—it's just slower than most of the others. The upside to using kermit is that more than likely almost any system you log in to supports kermit.

The second thing you should be aware of is that minicom takes advantage of some commands that give it access to the same type of power controlled by the superuser; thus, anyone running minicom has access to certain features of Linux that you may not want him or her to have.

▶ **See** "File Security," **p. 240**

Playing Games

If you installed the y package, you have access to myriad games. Most are text-based, so you don't need the X Windows system up and running to enjoy a few minutes of fun. To get an idea of the variety of games, check out the /usr/games directory. By listing the files, you can see the available games. If you don't know what a game is or does, you can try to get help on the game with the man command. Of course, if you're adventurous, you can simply start the game and explore. Have fun!

Tetris

Tetris originated in the former Soviet Union. In the game, various shapes drop from the sky and pile up at the bottom of the screen. The object of the game is to eradicate those shapes building up and keep the game area from filling. You accomplish the elimination by completely filling a row across the playing field. When you connect one wall of the playing field with the other so that there are no gaps, that row disappears and all the shapes above it fall down to take up the vacated row. The catch to this strategy is that the shapes fall in a variety of patterns. To fill a row, you must decide how to orient a shape and then where to place it before it touches another block. When a shape touches another block, it remains at that position.

This game has been ported to most platforms, so if you've played the game on other systems, you should have no problem playing Tetris under Linux.

This version of the game is meant to be played only from the terminal, so don't expect fancy graphics. Also, the biggest pain is that on other systems you can position and orient the falling shapes with the keyboard arrow keys—not so with this version of Tetris. You must use the keys listed in Table 5.7 for positioning and orienting the various blocks.

Table 5.7   Tetris Command Keys

Command	Key
Move left	<,>
Move right	</>
Rotate	<.>
Drop	Spacebar
Pause	<s>
Quit	<q>
Refresh the screen	<Ctrl-l>

Dungeon

Dungeon is a text adventure based on the ancient Adventure text games, but instead of caves, you deal with dungeons. You interact with this text-based world in search of treasures and adventure; if you've played other text adventures, this one is very similar. If you've used only glittery graphics, sit back and use the brain. You interact with the game by issuing commands and requests in the form of verbs and nouns. For instance, at the beginning of the game it tells you that you're in an open field west of a big, white house with a boarded front door. There's a small mailbox here. At the prompt, you can issue the following command to read whatever is in the box:

```
There is a small mailbox here.
> open box
Opening the mailbox reveals:
a leaflet.
> read leaflet
```

The game then provides a brief overview of the game and the talented programmers who built it. The last line of the information in the leaflet tells you to get assistance by entering the command help or info.

Trek

Trek is a text-based game based on the popular TV series *Star Trek*. Your goal is to survive the bloody battles with the Klingons and rid your star sector from their scourge. When you start the game by typing **trek**, you're asked a series of questions to set up the game:

- You're asked for the length of the game you want to play.
- You can restart a saved game from a logfile. To do so, you specify a logfile on the command line. This filename then becomes the name of the game saved.
- You're asked what skill level you want to play.
- You can enter a password so that others can't claim your glory. No, really—you need a password so that no one but you can blow up your ship.

Part

I

Ch

5

At any point—during setup or while playing—you can type a question mark to get help on the possible answers and actions available to you. Table 5.8 lists some of the possible actions.

Table 5.8   Trek Commands

Command	Description
abandon	Quits Trek
damages	Lists the damages your starship has sustained
impulse	Goes to impulse power
ram	Goes to ramming speed
srscan	Engages short-range scan
undock	Leaves starbase
capture	Captures the Klingons
destruct	Self-destructs
lrscan	Engages long-range scan
dump	Who knows?
visual	Looks at the Klingons' position
cloak	Cloaks the ship
dock	Enters starbase
move	Plots and follows course
rest	Rests for a while
terminate	Quits
Warp	Engages warp engines
computer	Finds out some information
help	Calls a starbase for help
phasers	Fires phasers
shields	Shields up
torpedo	Fires torpedoes

The game begins by telling you how many Klingons are in your sector and how many starbases are here and their location. Docking at a starbase can replenish and repair your ship. Unfortunately, the game doesn't tell you where the nasty Klingon warships are located. Make sure that you pay attention to energy use; otherwise, you're in for some bad surprises.

Although this text-based game has no glitzy graphics, you can get a short-range scan with the srscan command, which displays your sector and all known objects at their respective coordinates. srscan also provides you with valuable information on the condition of your ship. All coordinates refer to a Cartesian matrix that you can maintain on paper—better yet, graph paper—so you don't have to remember from one srscan command to the other.

Running DOS Programs Under Linux

After you have enough of running various Linux applications, you occasionally might want to run some of your DOS or Windows programs. Although not yet a complete reality, work is progressing to allow you to do just that, by emulating the various operating systems under Linux. DOSEMU is a program that lets programs based on MS-DOS (and variants such as PC-DOS) run under Linux. DOSEMU stands for DOS EMUlator.

N O T E   Some distributions of Linux include a command called simply dos, which starts a DOS editor. Commercial distributions of RedHat Linux 5.1 and above include this command. ■

Also, a project is under way to allow users access to Windows programs under Linux. This project, called Wine, is discussed later in the section "Running MS Windows Programs Under Linux."

Installing DOSEMU

You can find the current version of DOSEMU on the accompanying Slackware CD-ROM under the name /contrib/dosemu_0.000 and contrib/dosemu_0.060. This file archive and its files need to be placed in the /usr/src directory and then unzipped and untarred by using the following commands:

```
[root@web src]# gzip -d dosemu_5.tgz
[root@web src]# tar -xvf dosemu_5.tar
```

Next, you must build the various files by using the following commands:

```
[root@web src]#make config
[root@web src]#make depend
[root@web src]#make most
```

These commands should install the DOSEMU files in the /var/lib/dosemu directory. You must be logged in as root and have at least 10M of virtual memory available for the build.

N O T E   You must have installed package d, the program development package. You need the various compilers and tools within this package to build the DOS emulator. ■

Configuring DOSEMU

After the emulator is built, you must configure the system. To start, make a bootable DOS disk and copy the following DOS files on the disk: command.com, fdisk.exe, and sys.com.

Next, copy the following DOSEMU files from the dosemu subdirectory onto the floppy: emufs.sys, ems.sys, cdrom.sys, and exitemu.com. You can use the m- commands mentioned earlier in "Dealing with DOS Files Under Linux" to copy the files from the Linux partitions to the floppy drive.

T I P   If you have trouble finding the Linux files, you can use the `find` command to locate the necessary files. For example, this command

```
find -name emufs.sys -print
```

will display the location of the file on your system, providing that it exists.

DOSEMU requires a configuration file, dosemu.conf, to operate correctly. You must customize this file for your system. You can find an example file in the examples directory on your system with the name config.dist. Listing 5.1 shows config.dist. Remarks are indicated with a pound symbol (#), and most options take the form of *parameter value*. If a parameter has more than one value, the values are placed within braces ({}).

Listing 5.1   A Sample dosemu.conf File

```
# Linux dosemu 0.51 configuration file.
# Updated to include QuickStart documentation 5/10/94 by Mark Rejhon
# James MacLean, jmaclean@fox.nstn.ns.ca, 12/31/93
# Robert Sanders, gt8134b@prism.gatech.edu, 5/16/93
#
# NOTICE:
#   - Although QuickStart information is included in this file, you
#     should refer to the documentation in the "doc" subdirectory of the
#     DOSEMU distribution, wherever possible.
#   - This configuration file is designed to be used as a base to make
#     it easier for you to set up DOSEMU for your specific system.
#   - Configuration options between lace brackets { } can be split onto
#     multiple lines.
#   - Comments start with # or ; in column 1. (beginning of a line)
#   - Send Email to the jmaclean address above if you find any errors.

#************************DEBUG*********************************************
#
# QuickStart:
#   This section is of interest mainly to programmers. This is useful if
#   you are having problems with DOSEMU and you want to enclose debug info
#   when you make bug reports to a member of the DOSEMU development team.
#   Simply set desired flags to "on" or "off", then redirect stderr of
#   DOSEMU to a file using "dos 2>debug" to record the debug information
#   if desired. Skip this section if you're only starting to set up.
#
debug { config off    disk  off    warning off    hardware off
port  off    read  off    general off    IPC    off
video off    write off    xms   off    ems    off
serial off    keyb  off    dpmi  off
printer off    mouse off
}

#************************MISCELLANEOUS************************************
#
```

```
#   Want startup DOSEMU banner messages? Of course :-)
dosbanner on
#
#   timint is necessary for many programs to work.
timint on


#*************************KEYBOARD*************************************
#
# QuickStart:
#  With the "layout" keyword, you can specify your country's keyboard
#  layout. The following layouts are implemented:
#    finnish        us      dvorak    sf
#    finnish_latin1 uk      sg        sf_latin1
#    gr          dk        sg_latin1  es
#    gr_latin1    dk_latin1 fr        es_latin1
#    be          no        fr_latin1
#  The us-layout is selected by default if the "layout" keyword is omitted.
#
#  The keyword "keybint" allows more accurate keyboard interrupts,
#  It is a bit unstable, but makes keyboard work better when set to "on".
#
#  The keyword "rawkeyboard" allows for accurate keyboard emulation for
#  DOS programs, and is only activated when DOSEMU starts up at the
#  console. It only becomes a problem when DOSEMU prematurely exits
#  with a "Segmentation Fault" fatal error, because the keyboard would
#  have not been reset properly. In that case, you would have to reboot
#  your Linux system remotely, or using the RESET button. In reality,
#  this should never happen. But if it does, please do report to the
#  dosemu development team, of the problem and detailed circumstances,
#  we're trying our best! If you don't need near complete keyboard
#  emulation (needed by major software package), set it to "off".
#
keyboard { layout us keybint on rawkeyboard on }
# keyboard { layout gr-latin1 keybint on rawkeyboard on }
#
#  If DOSEMU speed is unimportant, and CPU time is very valuable to you,
#  you may want to set HogThreshold to a non-zero value. This means
#  the number of keypress requests in a row before CPU time is given
#  away from DOSEMU. A good value to use could be 10000.
#  A zero disables CPU hogging detection via keyboard requests.
#
HogThreshold 0


#*************************SERIAL*************************************
#
# QuickStart:
#  You can specify up to 4 simultaneous serial ports here.
#  If more than one ports have the same IRQ, only one of those ports
#  can be used at the same time. Also, you can specify the com port,
#  base address, irq, and device path! The defaults are:
#    COM1 default is base 0x03F8, irq 4, and device /dev/cua0
#    COM2 default is base 0x02F8, irq 3, and device /dev/cua1
#    COM3 default is base 0x03E8, irq 4, and device /dev/cua2
#    COM4 default is base 0x02E8, irq 3, and device /dev/cua3
#  If the "com" keyword is omitted, the next unused COM port is assigned.
```

Part

I

Ch

5

continues

Listing 5.1 Continued

```
#  Also, remember, these are only how you want the ports to be emulated
#  in DOSEMU. That means what is COM3 on IRQ 5 in real DOS, can become
#  COM1 on IRQ 4 in DOSEMU!
#
#  Also, as an example of defaults, these two lines are functionally equal:
#  serial { com 1 mouse }
#  serial { com 1 mouse base 0x03F8 irq 4 device /dev/cua0 }
#
#  If you want to use a serial mouse with DOSEMU, the "mouse" keyword
#  should be specified in only one of the serial lines. (For PS/2
#  mice, it is not necessary, and device path is in mouse line instead.)
#
#  Uncomment/modify any of the following if you want to support a modem
#   (or any other serial device).
#serial { com 1 device /dev/modem }
#serial { com 2 device /dev/modem }
#serial { com 3 device /dev/modem }
#serial { com 4 device /dev/modem }
#serial { com 3 base 0x03E8 irq 5 device /dev/cua2 }
#
#  If you have a non-PS/2 mouse, uncomment/modify one of the following.
#serial { mouse com 1 device /dev/mouse }
#serial { mouse com 2 device /dev/mouse }
#
#  What type is your mouse? Uncomment one of the following.
#  Use the 'internaldriver' option with ps2 and busmouse options.
#mouse { microsoft }
#mouse { logitech }
#mouse { mmseries }
#mouse { mouseman }
#mouse { hitachi }
#mouse { mousesystems }
#mouse { busmouse }
#mouse { ps2 device /dev/mouse internaldriver }
#  The following line won't run for now, but I hope it will sometime
#mouse { mousesystems device /dev/mouse internaldriver cleardtr }

#************************NETWORKING SUPPORT****************************
#
#  Turn the following option 'on' if you require IPX/SPX emulation.
#  Therefore, there is no need to load IPX.COM within the DOS session.
#  The following option does not emulate LSL.COM, IPXODI.COM, etc.
#  NOTE: MUST HAVE IPX PROTOCOL ENABLED IN KERNEL !!
ipxsupport off
#
#  Enable Novell 8137->raw 802.3 translation hack in new packet driver.
#pktdriver novell_hack

#*************************VIDEO***************************************
#
# !!WARNING!!: A LOT OF THIS VIDEO CODE IS ALPHA! IF YOU ENABLE GRAPHICS
# ON AN INCOMPATIBLE ADAPTOR, YOU COULD GET A BLANK SCREEN OR MESSY SCREEN
# EVEN AFTER EXITING DOSEMU. JUST REBOOT (BLINDLY) AND THEN MODIFY CONFIG.
#
```

```
# QuickStart:
#  Start with only text video using the following line, to get started.
#  then when DOSEMU is running, you can set up a better video configura-
#  tion.
#
# video { vga console }      # Use this line, if you are using VGA
# video { cga console }      # Use this line, if you are using CGA
# video { ega console }      # Use this line, if you are using EGA
# video { mda console }      # Use this line, if you are using MDA
#
# Even more basic, like on an xterm or over serial, use one of the
# following :
#
#  For Xterm
# video { vga chunks 25 }
#  For serial at 2400 baud
# video { vga chunks 200 }
#
# QuickStart Notes for Graphics:
#   - If your VGA-Bios resides at E000-EFFF, turn off video BIOS shadow
#     for this address range and add the statement vbios_seg 0xe000
#     to the correct vios-statement, see the example below.
#   - Set "allowvideoportaccess on" earlier in this configuration file
#     if DOSEMU won't boot properly, such as hanging with a blank screen,
#     beeping, or the video card bootup message.
#   - Video BIOS shadowing (in your CMOS setup) at C000-CFFF must be dis-
#     abled.
#
#   *> CAUTION <*: TURN OFF VIDEO BIOS SHADOWING BEFORE ENABLING GRAPHICS!
#
#   It may be necessary to set this to "on" if DOSEMU can't boot up properly
#   on your system when it's set "off" and when graphics are enabled.
#   Note: May interfere with serial ports when using certain video boards.
allowvideoportaccess on
#
#  Any 100% compatible standard VGA card _MAY_ work with this:
#video { vga console graphics }
#
#  If your VGA-BIOS is at segment E000, this may work for you:
#video { vga console graphics vbios_seg 0xe000 }
#
#  Trident SVGA with 1 megabyte on board
#video { vga console graphics chipset trident memsize 1024 }
#
#  Diamond SVGA
#video { vga console graphics chipset diamond }
#
#  ET4000 SVGA card with 1 megabyte on board:
#video { vga console graphics chipset et4000 memsize 1024 }
#
#  S3-based SVGA video card with 1 megabyte on board:
#video { vga console graphics chipset s3 memsize 1024 }
```

Part

I

Ch

5

continues

Listing 5.1 Continued

```
#************************MISCELLANEOUS********************************
#
# QuickStart:
#  For "mathco", set this to "on" to enable the coprocessor during DOSEMU.
#  This really only has an effect on kernels prior to 1.0.3.
#  For "cpu", set this to the CPU you want recognized during DOSEMU.
#  For "bootA"/"bootC", set this to the bootup drive you want to use.
#  It is strongly recommended you start with "bootA" to get DOSEMU
#  going, and during configuration of DOSEMU to recognize hard disks.
#
mathco on      # Math coprocessor valid values: on off
cpu 80386      # CPU emulation valid values: 80286 80386 80486
bootA          # Startup drive valid values: bootA bootC


#***********************MEMORY***************************************
#
# QuickStart:
#  These are memory parameters, stated in number of kilobytes.
#  If you get lots of disk swapping while DOSEMU runs, you should
#  reduce these values. Also, DPMI is still somewhat unstable,
#  (as of early April 1994) so be careful with DPMI parameters.
#
xms 1024       # XMS size in K, or "off"
ems 1024       # EMS size in K, or "off"
dpmi off       # DPMI size in K, or "off". Be careful with DPMI!


#*********************PORT ACCESS************************************
#
# !!WARNING!!: GIVING ACCESS TO PORTS IS BOTH A SECURITY CONCERN AND
# SOME PORTS ARE DANGEROUS TO USE. PLEASE SKIP THIS SECTION, AND
# DON'T FIDDLE WITH THIS SECTION UNLESS YOU KNOW WHAT YOU'RE DOING.
#
# ports { 0x388 0x389 } # for SimEarth
# ports { 0x21e 0x22e 0x23e 0x24e 0x25e 0x26e 0x27e 0x28e 0x29e } # for
# jill


#******************SPEAKER*****************************************
#
# These keywoards are allowable on the "speaker" line:
#  native   Enable DOSEMU direct access to the speaker ports.
#  emulated Enable simple beeps at the terminal.
#  off      Disable speaker emulation.
#
speaker native    # or "off" or "emulated"


#*****************HARD DISKS***************************************
#
# !!WARNING!!: DAMAGE MIGHT RESULT TO YOUR HARD DISK (LINUX AND/OR DOS)
# IF YOU FIDDLE WITH THIS SECTION WITHOUT KNOWING WHAT YOU'RE DOING!
#
# QuickStart:
#  The best way to get started is to start with a boot floppy, and set
#  "bootA" above in the configuration. Keep using the boot floppy
#  while you are setting this hard disk configuration up for DOSEMU,
#  and testing by using DIR C: or something like that.
```

```
#   If you want DOSEMU to be able to access a DOS partition, the
#   safer type of access is "partition" access, because "wholedisk"
#   access gives DOSEMU write access to a whole physical disk,
#   including any vulnerable Linux partitions on that drive!
#
#   !!! IMPORTANT !!!
#   You must not have LILO installed on the partition for dosemu to boot
#   off.
#   As of 04/26/94, doublespace and stacker 3.1 will work with wholedisk
#   or partition only access. Stacker 4.0 has been reported to work with
#   wholedisk access. If you want to use disk compression using partition
#   access, you will need to use the "mkpartition" command included with
#   dosemu to create a partition table datafile for dosemu.
#
#   Please read the documentation in the "doc" subdirectory for info
#   on how to set up access to real hard disk.
#
#   "image" specifies a hard disk image file.
#   "partition" specifies partition access, with device and partition
#    number.
#   "wholedisk" specifies full access to entire hard drive.
#   "readonly" for read only access. A good idea to set up with.
#
#disk { image "/var/lib/dosemu/hdimage" }   # use diskimage file.
#disk { partition "/dev/hda1" 1 readonly }  # 1st partition on 1st IDE.
#disk { partition "/dev/sda2" 1 readonly }  # 1st partition on 2nd SCSI.
#disk { wholedisk "/dev/hda" }              # Entire disk drive unit

#*****************DOSEMU BOOT**********************************************
#
#   Use the following option to boot from the specified file, and then
#   once booted, have bootoff execute in autoexec.bat. Thanks Ted :-).
#   Notice it follows a typical floppy spec. To create this file use
#   dd if=/dev/fd0 of=/var/lib/dosemu/bdisk bs=16k
#
#bootdisk { heads 2 sectors 18 tracks 80 threeinch file /var/lib/dosemu/#bdisk }
#
#   Specify extensions for the CONFIG and AUTOEXEC files. If the below
#   are uncommented, the extensions become CONFIG.EMU and AUTOEXEC.EMU.
#   NOTE: this feature may affect file naming even after boot time.
#   If you use MSDOS 6+, you may want to use a CONFIG.SYS menu instead.
#
#EmuSys EMU
#EmuBat EMU


#*****************FLOPPY DISKS*********************************************
#
# QuickStart:
#   This part is fairly easy. Make sure that the first (/dev/fd0) and
#   second (/dev/fd1) floppy drives are of the correct size, "threeinch"
#   and/or "fiveinch". A floppy disk image can be used instead, however.
#
#   FOR SAFETY, UNMOUNT ALL FLOPPY DRIVES FROM YOUR FILESYSTEM BEFORE
#   STARTING UP DOSEMU! DAMAGE TO THE FLOPPY MAY RESULT OTHERWISE!
#
```

continues

Listing 5.1   Continued

```
floppy { device /dev/fd0 threeinch }
floppy { device /dev/fd1 fiveinch }
#floppy { heads 2 sectors 18 tracks 80
#       threeinch file /var/lib/dosemu/diskimage }
#
#  If floppy disk speed is very important, uncomment the following
#  line. However, this makes the floppy drive a bit unstable. This
#  is best used if the floppies are write-protected.
#
#FastFloppy on

#*******************PRINTERS*********************************************
#
# QuickStart:
#  Printer is emulated by piping printer data to a file or via a unix
#  command such as "lpr". Don't bother fiddling with this configuration
#  until you've got DOSEMU up and running already.
#
#printer { options "%s" command "lpr" timeout 20 }
#printer { options "-p %s" command "lpr" timeout 10 }  # pr format it
#printer { file "lpt3" }
```

You must then use a text editor to change the settings from the example configuration file to match your system. Such items as processor type and video cards must match.

N O T E   You can also boot DOSEMU from a hard drive partition, instead of from a floppy. To access a hard drive, simply configure a drive/partition in the dosemu.conf file. ■

Running DOSEMU

To run DOSEMU, simply type **dos** at any Linux prompt. To exit, use the exitemu command from the prompt. Table 5.9 provides a listing of command-line options you can pass to DOSEMU. You also can use -? to get a complete, up-to-date listing of command-line parameters.

Table 5.9   DOSEMU Command-Line Parameters

Parameter	Description
-A	Boots from the A drive
-C	Boots from the hard drive
-c	Optimizes video performance from virtual terminals
-D	Sets debug options
-e	Specifies the amount of EMS memory
-F#	Indicates number (#) of floppies to use from dosemu.conf

Parameter	Description
-f	Flips the definition of the A and B floppy drives
-H#	Indicates number (#) of hard disks to use from dosemu.conf
-k	Uses the raw keyboard console defined in the rawkeyboard parameter of dosemu.conf
-P	Copies the debug information to a file
-t	Delivers the time interrupt 9
-V	Activates VGA emulation
-x	Specifies the amount of XMS memory
-?	Displays summary help for each command
-2	Emulates a 286
-3	Emulates a 386
-4	Emulates a 486

From the DOS prompt supplied by DOSEMU, you can run most DOS programs except those that require DPMI (DOS Protected Mode Interface) support. Simply type the name of the program and—providing that DOSEMU can find the program in your path—DOSEMU will load and run the program.

Table 5.10 shows some of the programs known to operate under Linux, but more are added every day (check the file EMUsuccess.txt, in the directory where DOSEMU was installed, for an up-to-date listing). Table 5.11 lists some of the programs that don't work with Linux.

Table 5.10   Programs Known to Run with DOSEMU

Name	Function	Success Story Posted By
1st Wordplus	GEM word processor	jan@janhh.hanse.de
4desc	4dos desc editor	piola@di.unito.it
4DOS 4.2	Command interp.	rideau@clipper.ens.fr
4dos 5.0c	Command interp.	J1MCPHER@VAXC.STEVENS-TECH.EDU
ack3d	3-D engine	martin5@trgcorp.solucorp.qc.ca
ACU-COBOL	Compiler	fjh@munta.cs.mu.OZ.AU
Alite 1.10		ph99jh42@uwrf.edu
AmTax 93 & 94	Tax software	root@bobspc.canisius.edu

continues

Part

I

Ch

5

Table 5.10   Continued

Name	Function	Success Story Posted By
ansi.sys	Screen/keyboard driver (display functions)	ag173@cleveland. Freenet.Edu
arj v2.41a	[Un]archiver	tanner@winternet.mpls.mn.us
As Easy As 5.01	Spreadsheet	ph99jh42@uwrf.edu
Autoroute Plus	Route planner	hsw1@papa.attmail.com
Axum	Sci. graphics	miguel@pinon.ccu.uniovi.es
battle chess	Chess game	jvdbergh@wins.uia.ac.be
Binkley 2.50eebd	Fidomailer	stub@linux.rz.tu-clausthal.de
Blake Stone_	Game	owaddell@cs.indiana.edu
bnu 1.70	Fossil (Fido)	stub@linux.rz.tu-clausthal.de
Borland C++ 2.0	86/286 C/C++ IDE	rideau@clipper.ens.fr
Boston Business EDT+		keegstra@csdr2.fsfc. nasa.gov
Cardbox Plus	Database	hsw1@papa.attmail.com
Castle Wolfenstein	3-D game	gt8134b@prism.gatech.EDU
Checkit diagnostics		
clipper 5.1	dBASE compiler	jvdbergh@wins.uia.ac.be
COMPRESS	Compressed fs	rideau@clipper.ens.fr
CCM (Crosstalk)	Modem program	
cshow 8.61	Picture viewer	jvdbergh@wins.uia.ac.be
cview	Picture viewer	lotov@avarice.ugcs.caltech.edu
d86/a86		
DataPerfect 2.1	Database	fbennett@uk.ac.ulcc.clus1
Dbase 4		corey@amiganet.xnet.com
Derive 1.2	Math package	miguel@pinon.ccu.uniovi.es
Disk Freedom 4.6	Disk utility	
diet 1.45f	File compression	stub@linux.rz.tu-clausthal.de
dosnix 2.0	UNIX utilities	miguel@pinon.ccu.uniovi.es
Dosshell task	Swapper	jmaclean@fox.nstn.ns.ca
dtmm	Molecular models	miguel@pinon.ccu.uniovi.es

Name	Function	Success Story Posted By
Dune 2	Game	COLIN@fs1.in.umist.ac.uk
dviscr	EMTEX dvi preview	ub9x@rz.uni-karlsruhe.de
Easytrax	Layout editor	maehler@wrcd1.urz.uni-wuppertal.de
Elvis	vi clone	miguel@pinon.ccu.uniovi.es
Epic Pinball	Game	krismon@quack.kfu.com
ETen 3.1	Chinese terminal	tyuan!root@mp.cs.niu.edu
Eureka 1.0	Math package	miguel@pinon.ccu.uniovi.es
Falcon 3.0	Fighter simulator	rapatel@rockypc.rutgers.edu
FastLST 1.03	FidoNdlstcompiler	stub@linux.rz.tu-clausthal.de
FormGen II		root@bobspc.canisius.edu
freemacs 1.6d	Editor	ph99jh42@uwrf.edu
Frontier (Elite II)	Game	COLIN@fs1.in.umist.ac.uk
FW3		Sebastian.Bunka@vu-wien.ac.at
MS Flight Simulator 5	Game (runs *slow!*)	newcombe@aa.csc.peachnet.edu
Foxpro 2.0	Database	
Framework 4		corey@amiganet.xnet.com
Freelance Graphics 2.1	Graph/drawing application	jwest@jwest.ecen.okstate.edu
GEM/3	GUI	jan@janhh.hanse.de
GEM Draw	GEM drawing app	jan@janhh.hanse.de
GEM Paint	GEM painting app	jan@janhh.hanse.de
gmouse	Mouse driver	tk@pssparc2.oc.com
God of Thunder	Game	ensor@cs.utk.edu
Gravity	Simulation package	miguel@pinon.ccu.uniovi.es
GWS for DOS	Graphic file conv	bchow@bchow.slip
Gzip 1.1.2	File compression	miguel@pinon.ccu.uniovi.es
Harpoon	Game	wielinga@physics.uq.oz.au
Harvard Graphics 3.0	Graph/drawing package	miguel@pinon.ccu.uniovi.es

Part
I

Ch
5

continues

Table 5.10   Continued

Name	Function	Success Story Posted By
Hero's Quest I	Game	lam836@cs.cuhk.hk
Hijaak 2.0	Graphic file conv	bchow@bchow.slip
hocus pocus	Apogee game	kooper@dutiws.TWI.TUDelft.NL
Image Alchemy Pro	Graphic file conv (-v doesn't work)	J1MCPHER@VAXC. STEVENS-TECH.EDU
Incredible Machine	Game (slow)	sdh@po.cwru.edu
Key Spreadsheet Plus	Spreadsheet (on non-doublespaced disks)	jwest@jwest.ecen.okstate.edu
Lemmings		sdh@po.cwru.edu
less 1.7.7	More than more	miguel@pinon.ccu.uniovi.es
LHA	File compression	
Lotus Manuscript	Word processor	miguel@pinon.ccu.uniovi.es
Managing Your Money	Financial	newcombe@aa.csc.peachnet.edu
Manifest	(dies during memory timings)	hsw1@papa.attmail.com
Mathcad 2.01	Math package	root@bobspc.canisius.edu
MathCad 2.06	Math package	miguel@pinon.ccu.uniovi.es
mcafee 9.23 v112	Virus scanner	jvdbergh@wins.uia.ac.be
Microemacs	Editor	hjstein@MATH.HUJI.AC.IL
MicroLink Yaht 2.1		root@bobspc.canisius.edu
Microsoft C 6.0	Compiler	ronnie@epact.se
Microsoft Assembler 5.0	Assembler	ronnie@epact.se
Microsoft Library 2.0		root@bobspc.canisius.edu
Microsoft Make	make	ronnie@epact.se
MicrosoftMouse Drv 8.2	Mouse driver	hsw1@papa.attmail.com
MoneyCounts 7.0	Accounting package	raeburn@cygnus.com
mscmouse	Mouse driver	tk@pssparc2.oc.com
nnansi.com	ANSI driver	mdrejhon@undergrad. math.uwaterloo.ca

Name	Function	Success Story Posted By
Netzplan	GEM project mgr	**jan@janhh.hanse.de**
NHL Hockey	Game	**krismon@quack.kfu.com**
NJStar 2.1	Chinese word proc	**aab2@cornell.edu**
Norton Utils 4.5	Disk utils	**rideau@clipper.ens.fr**
Norton Utils 7.0	Disk utils	**rideau@clipper.ens.fr**
PAF	Geneology package	**geek+@CMU.EDU**
Paradox	Database	**hp@vmars.tuwien.ac.at**
PC Paintbrush IV	Paint program	**bchow@bchow.slip**
PCtools 4.20	Disk utils	**rideau@clipper.ens.fr**
pcwdemo		**vinod@cse.iitb.ernet.in**
PC-Write 3.0	Word processor	
pcxlab 1.03	PCX viewer	**miguel@pinon.ccu.uniovi.es**
peachtree complete 6.0	Accounting	**stjeanp@math.enmu.edu**
Pinball Dreams	Game	**ronnie@lysator.liu.se**
PKzip/unzip	File compression	
pklite 1.15	File compression	**stub@linux.rz.tu-clausthal.de**
Pong Kombat	Game	**ensor@cs.utk.edu**
PrintShop	Greeting card pkg	**geek+@CMU.EDU**
Procomm Plus 2.0	Communication	**newcombe@aa.csc.peachnet.edu**
Procomm 2.4.3	Communication	**hsw1@papa.attmail.com**
Pspice 5.0	Circuit sim.	**root@bobspc.canisius.edu**
Q&A	Word proc/database	**newcombe@aa.csc.peachnet.edu**
Qbasic/edit	Interpreter (from DOS 5.0)	
Qedit	Editor	
QuickC	Compiler	**martin@trcsun3.eas.asu.edu**
Quicken 4.0 for DOS	Accounting pkg	**juphoff@nrao.edu**
Quicken 6.0 for DOS	Accounting pkg	
Quicken 7.0 for DOS	Accounting pkg	**juphoff@astro.phys.vt.edu**
Railroad Tycoon		**juphoff@astro.phys.vt.edu**

Part
I

Ch
5

continues

Table 5.10 Continued

Name	Function	Success Story Posted By
Red Baron	Game	wielinga@physics.uq.oz.au
RM/COBOL	compiler	fjh@munta.cs.mu.OZ.AU
Rpro 1.6		root@bobspc.canisius.edu
scan109	Antivirus	miguel@pinon.ccu.uniovi.es
scan112	Antivirus	piola@di.unito.it
Scorch	Tank game	geek+@CMU.EDU
Shez94	Arcer-Shell	stub@linux.rz.tu-clausthal.de
sled	Editor	piola@di.unito.it
Space Quest IV	Game	lam836@cs.cuhk.hk
Spell Casting 301		mancini@phantom.com
SPSS/PC+4.0	Statistical pkg	jr@petz.han.de
Squish 1.01	Fido Scan/Tosser	stub@linux.rz.tu-clausthal.de
Stacker 3.1	Compressed fs	mdrejhon@undergrad math.uwaterloo.ca
Stacker 4.00	Compressed fs	J1MCPHER@VAXC. STEVENS-TECH.EDU
StatPhys	Simulation pkg	miguel@pinon.ccu.uniovi.es
STSORBIT	Orbit simulation	troch@gandalf.rutgers.edu
Stunts	Game?	gt8134b@prism.gatech.EDU
Superstor	Compressed fs	rideau@clipper.ens.fr
TAG 2.02	Polish word proc	rzm@oso.chalmers.se
TASM 2.51	MACRO assembler	rideau@clipper.ens.fr
Telix	Modem program	jou@nematic.ep.nctu.edu.tw
THelp from BC++2.0	Popup help	rideau@clipper.ens.fr
TimED/beta	Fido MSGeditor	stub@linux.rz.tu-clausthal.de
TLINK 4.0	LINKER	rideau@clipper.ens.fr
Topspeed Modula-2	Compiler	mayersn@hermes. informatik.uni-stuttgart.de
Turbo Debugger 2.51	Realmode debugger	rideau@clipper.ens.fr
Turbo Pascal 5.5	Compiler	

Name	Function	Success Story Posted By
Turbo Pascal 6.0	Compiler	**t2262dj@cd1.lrz-muenchen.de**
Turbo Pascal 7.0	Compiler	**mdrejhon@undergrad.** **math.uwaterloo.ca**
Turb-opoly 1.43		**root@bobspc.canisius.edu**
Ultima 6	Game	**msphil@birds.wm.edu**
Vpic 6.1		**root@bobspc.canisius.edu**
warlords II	Game	**buckel@cip.** **informatik.uni-wuerzburg.de**
Warrior of Destiny	Game	**msphil@birds.wm.edu**
WITWI Carmen Sandiego	Game	**tillemaj@cae.wisc.edu**
Windows 3.0	Windows (real mode)	**cjw1@ukc.ac.uk**
Wolf3d	Game	**owaddell@cs.indiana.edu**
WordPerfect 5.1	Word processor	**sdh@po.cwru.edu**
WordPerfect 6.0	Word processor (needs >1M RAM)	**lujian@texmd.minmet.mcgill.ca**
Xtpro 1.1	Disk util	**root@bobspc.canisius.edu**
XWing	Game (very slow)	**ronnie@lysator.liu.se**
Zarkov 2.6	Chess	**a-acero@uchicago.edu**
zoo	File compression	

Part

I

Ch

5

Table 5.11 Programs Known *Not* to Run with DOSEMU

Name	Function	Posted By
4D-box	Boxing game	**jvdbergh@wins.uia.ac.be**
Apple][emulator	Emulator	**ph99jh42@uwrf.edu**
Borland C++ 3.1 IDE	Compiler	**juphoff@uppieland.async.vt.edu**
brief	Editor	**bchow@bchow.slip**
Chuck Yeager Aircombat	Flight simulator	**jvdbergh@wins.uia.ac.be**
CIVILIZATION	Game	**miguel@pinon.ccu.uniovi.es**

continues

Table 5.11   Continued

Name	Function	Posted By
DesqView 2.51	(Alt key doesn't work)	hsw1@papa.attmail.com
doom	Game	rideau@clipper.ens.fr
dpms from Stacker 4.0		J1MCPHER@VAXC. STEVENS-TECH.EDU
dxma0mod.sys	Token-ring driver	adjihc4@cti.ecp.fr
dxmc0mod.sys	Token-ring driver	adjihc4@cti.ecp.fr
ELDB	Economics database	hjstein@math.huji.ac.il
FIPS 0.2.2	Disk util (hdimage FAT problem)	
Howitzer	Tank game	geek+@CMU.EDU
Lahey Fortran	Fortran compiler	hjstein@math.huji.ac.il
Maple V2	Math package	ralf@ark.btbg.sub.de
MSDOS 5/6 QBASIC/EDIT	Editor	bchow@bchow.slip
NORTON UTILITIES 7.0	Disk utils	bchow@bchow.slip
Quattro Pro 4.0	Spreadsheet	jwest@jwest.ecen.okstate.edu
Raptor	Game	ensor@cs.utk.edu
Silent Service II	Submarine game	jvdbergh@wins.uia.ac.be
thunderByte scan	Virus scanner	jvdbergh@wins.uia.ac.be
Ventura Publisher 3.0	Desktop pub	niemann@swt. ruhr-uni-bochum.de
wildunix	Wild cards	miguel@pinon.ccu.uniovi.es
Windows 3.1		
		juphoff@uppieland.async.vt.edu

Running programs under DOSEMU has several problems, mostly because the computer is emulating DOS and the underlying machine instead of actually running DOS. Emulation slows down the system. The slowdown can become annoying, especially when you're also running other Linux programs in other virtual terminals. Video updates are also rather slow under DOSEMU.

Many DOS programs hog the CPU, because they believe they're the only program running. This prevents other Linux programs from receiving access to the CPU. To alleviate this problem, Thomas G. McWilliams wrote a program called `garrot` to release access of the processor back to Linux from DOS-hogging programs. You can find `garrot` on the **sunsite.unc.edu** FTP site in the /pub/linux/alpha/dosemu directory.

Running Windows Programs Under Linux

DOSEMU can't run Microsoft Windows programs, so the Linux community has embarked on creating a program that will allow Linux users to run such programs. This Windows emulator is called Wine. Wine isn't a standard acronym; it can stand as *WIN*dows *E*mulator or, because Wine can be built as a static library instead of an emulator, *Wine Is Not* a *Windows Emulator*. Both acronyms are from the Windows FAQ.

The Windows FAQ is required reading if you want to experiment with Wine, because Wine isn't as far along in development as DOSEMU. Thus, it's very experimental and error-prone. Also, not many Windows programs are supported. In fact, to use Wine, you must have Windows installed on a partition accessible to Linux, because Wine still relies on many parts of Windows to work. Wine also requires the X system to be installed and operational.

To experiment with Wine, you'll need the following:

- A Linux kernel, version 99.13 or above
- Source code for Wine, because it's available only in source code format
- The d package installed for the compiler tools to build the source code
- At least 8MB of RAM and at least a 12M swap drive
- At least 10MB of disk space
- X Windows installed and configured
- A pointing device such as a mouse
- Microsoft Windows installed on a partition accessible to Linux

Because Wine is under heavy development, new versions are released almost weekly. The newest source code is located at **sunsite.unc.edu** (and other major FTP sites) in the /pub/Linux/ALPHA/wine/development directory. The file is named after the date of its release—for example, wine-961201.tar.tgz.

▶ **See** "Using FTP for Remote File Transfer," **p. 580**

Because Wine is changing so fast and is so unstable, it's not included on the accompanying CD-ROMs. If you want to experiment with Wine, feel free to download the newest files and read over the FAQs and HOWTOs. These documents are located on the CD-ROM in the /docs directory and provide the information needed to compile, install, configure, and use Wine.

Part

I

Ch

5

Installing Wine is very similar to installing DOSEMU, with the exception that you can place the source tar file anywhere. Use the `tar` command to unarchive the file in the directory, as shown here:

```
[root@web wine]# gzip -d 950606.tar.gz
[root@web wine]# tar -xvf 950606.tar
```

Building Wine is a little more involved than building DOSEMU—in fact, it's more like building a new kernel. You must answer several questions to configure the build process. The Wine HOWTO explains the full process in detail.

Next, you must answer several questions to configure Wine with runtime parameters. These configuration parameters are stored in a file named /usr/local/etc/wine.conf. Although you can edit this file by hand, it's best to use the supplied configure program to do so.

After you configure the compilation files and the runtime parameter file, you can build Wine with the simple command `make`. This process takes several minutes. To use Wine, you invoke the emulator and provide the path name to a Windows executable file:

```
[tackett@web ~]$wine /dosc/windows/winmine.exe
```

The programs now supported by Wine are calc.exe, clock.exe, notepad.exe, and winmine.exe. This list is continuously expanding, so check the FAQ and HOWTO for current programs supported by the Windows emulator.

N O T E MS-DOS and Microsoft Windows aren't the only operating systems emulated under Linux. There are also emulators for the old Apple II, CPM, and the newer Macintosh operating systems. You can generally find these emulators on FTP sites in the \pub\Linux\system\emulators directory. ▪

From Here...

This chapter has just lightly touched on getting started with Linux and the various application programs available. For more information, see the following chapters:

- Chapter 6, "Upgrading and Installing Software with RPM," explains how to install new software from CD-ROM or the Internet.

- Chapter 8, "Using the `vi` Editor," discusses the popular `vi` text editor for Linux.

- Chapter 22, "Using X Windows," deals with the graphical user interface provided with Linux, XFree86.

Upgrading and Installing Software with RPM

by Jack Tackett

In this chapter

The base Linux system initially contains only a core set of utilities and data files. The system administrator installs additional commands, user application programs, and various data files as required. Applications get updated frequently. System software changes as new features are added and bugs are fixed. The system administrator is responsible for adding, configuring, maintaining, and deleting software from the Linux system.

The word *installing* means copying the associated program files onto the system's hard disk and *configuring* the application (assigning resources) for proper operation on a specific system. The configuration of a program instructs it as to where parts of the application are to be installed and how it is to function within the system environment in general.

Both the Red Hat and Caldera distributions of Linux ease the pain of installing and upgrading software by including the rpm command. However, you'll also find yourself installing software that isn't in rpm format. Many of the software packages available on the Internet are in compressed tar format.

On large systems, an administrator usually installs applications because most users don't have access to the tape or floppy drives. Administrative permission is also often needed to install components of the applications into system directories. Components may include shared libraries, utilities, and devices that need to go into directories that a normal user can't access.

Understanding Key Terms Used in This Chapter

As you may have surmised if you read the introduction to this chapter, the installation of applications involves an expanded vocabulary. Table 6.1 lists some terms and definitions that you should become familiar with.

Table 6.1   Terms Related to Application Installation

Term	Definition
superuser	The highest privileged user on the system. Also called the *root user*.
systems administrator	The person in charge of keeping the Linux system optimized and properly running. The system administrator has superuser privileges and can install new software onto the system.
installing applications	The initial installation or update of a program for a UNIX system. The process usually requires superuser privileges and access to the computer's tape or floppy disk drive.
configuring	The act of setting up an application to work with your particular system. Configuring can include setting up the application for many users to use, putting it in accessible directories, or sharing it with the network.

Understanding the Politics of Upgrading

What software should you upgrade? How often should you upgrade? The answers to these questions are largely determined by the purpose of your system—personal or business—and the demands of your users. Software versions are changing all the time. Various parts of the Linux system are constantly being updated. You wouldn't have time to use your system if you tried to keep up with each and every upgrade that comes out.

Typically, you shouldn't have to reinstall the entire Linux system when you upgrade your system software. Usually, only a tiny portion of the system software changes with a new release. You may have to upgrade your kernel or upgrade your system libraries, but you probably won't have to do a full reinstall. However, when you upgrade software packages, you quite often have to completely install a new version, especially if you're several versions behind when you upgrade.

> **N O T E** Making a current backup of your system before upgrading software is a good idea. That way, if something goes wrong, you can always get back to your original system.
>
> ▶ **See** "Considering Backup Tips," **p. 227** ▓

In general, you should upgrade your system if a new version of either system or application software becomes available that either fixes a serious problem or adds functionality that you need. It's up to you to determine what constitutes a serious problem. If a new release of a software package fixes something that has caused problems on your system or fixes a bug that could damage your system, it's probably worth the time it takes to install it.

> **N O T E** Don't try to keep up with every release of every piece of software; upgrading for the sake of upgrading takes too much time and effort. With a little research, you can keep your system working in good condition and update only the parts that need upgrading as you go along. ▓

Installing Software

Installing a major program onto a Linux system is more complicated than installing a similar program on a single-task operating system, such as MS-DOS or Apple Macintosh System 7.6. The multiuser nature of Linux means that every application on the system sometimes receives simultaneous calls for access.

To further complicate installation, most application programs—with the exception of very simple ones—require configuration to your specific system before they can be used. It's up to the system administrator installing the software to identify items specific to the system's configuration when prompted during an application's configuration process.

For example, one user may have only an older character-based terminal, whereas another has a fancy new X Windows terminal. The superuser must make sure that the application responds correctly to the older terminal, sending only ASCII characters—that is, letters and numbers—and that the X Windows terminal receives full advantage of the application's colors and

Part
I

Ch
6

graphics. The system administrator manages the system and has the responsibility of keeping it optimized (all programs up to current versions, proper user accounts assigned, and so forth).

As already stated, loading a program onto a Linux system is more complicated than doing so on single-user operating systems. The system administrator who's installing an application may have to create new directories to house the files associated with a particular program. Some software packages call for the configuring or reconfiguring of system devices. Although the end user worries only about learning the new program's features and operating commands, the superuser must make sure that system resources are properly allocated, configured, and maintained for the program (while, of course, not messing up any already installed applications).

Installing software by using menus or commands is outwardly a relatively simple task; to the system itself, however, the task is complex. Applications for single-user operating systems, such as DOS programs, usually run only one copy of themselves at a time and have no competing programs. In even a simple Linux installation with only one user logged in, many processes can be running at the same time. Multiply this activity by several users all running programs—including some users who utilize the same application—and the complexity increases dramatically.

The Linux operating system excels at juggling a multitude of processes, programs, users, and peripherals simultaneously. To live in a Linux environment, an application must be properly loaded. An ill-behaving application, or one improperly installed, can cause a system *crash* (when a process or program goes wild and locks the CPU, causing it to lose control of all the currently running programs). The system shuts down, all users are kicked off, and their programs are interrupted. There's often much wailing and gnashing of teeth from frustrated persons in the midst of some complicated task.

As the one loading a new application, the system administrator or superuser is responsible for making sure that the application is compatible with the system and testing the application after it's installed. Understanding the loading of software onto a Linux system first requires a basic knowledge of the responsibilities and privileges of the system administrator.

Understanding the System Administrator's Job

If you use Linux on a small system, you're probably your own system administrator. You install and run your applications. It's your responsibility to keep a current backup of files, maintain a proper amount of free space on the hard disk, make sure that the system runs optimally through memory management and other means, and do everything else required in the administration of an efficient and productive system. If you're a user in a larger system environment, a specific person probably handles system administration. The following list briefly summarizes what the system administrator does:

- Starts and stops the system, as needed.
- Makes sure that there's enough free disk space and that file systems are free of error.
- Tunes the system so that the maximum number of users have access to the system's hardware and software resources and so that the system operates as fast and as efficiently as possible.

- Protects the system from unauthorized entry and destructive actions.
- Sets up connections to other computer systems.
- Sets up or closes user accounts on the system.
- Works with software and hardware vendors and with those with training or other support contracts for the system.
- Installs, mounts, and troubleshoots terminals, printers, disk drives, and other pieces of system and peripheral hardware.
- Installs and maintains programs, including new application programs, operating system updates, and software-maintenance corrections.
- And nothing else. Too often users log in as root and do everything from there, but this can cause a myriad of problems on your system. Use root for system administration tasks, and use your user account for day-to-day tasks!

Using the Red Hat Package Manager

Both the Red Hat and the Caldera OpenLinux distributions make use of packages for managing software installation. A package contains a complete, fully tested and configured program. The package is typically built from a source code package so that developers and users know what they are getting. To manage these packages, Red Hat Software developed the Red Hat Package Manager (RPM) and released it to the world.

ON THE WEB

See **http://www.rpm.org** for more information on RPM.

RPM has six modes of operation, five of which can be used from either the command line or the X Windows-based tool called Glint. The various modes are installing, uninstalling, updating, querying, verifying, and building. You can only build an RPM package from the command line.

N O T E For more information on building packages with RPM, see the book *Maximum RPM* (SAMS Publishing) or Red Hat software's *Maximum RPM*. ■

You use RPM from the command line in this format:

```
rpm [options] package-name
```

where *options* is one of many different flags used by RPM to manipulate packages and *package-name* indicates the software package to be used. The package name usually looks like this: quota-1.55-4.i386.rpm. The package-name follows this format:

name	quota
version	1.55
release	4

Part

I

Ch

6

| **computer architecture** | i386 |
| **extension** | .rpm (typically) |

However, the package file can be any name because the information about the package itself is contained inside the file.

Locating Packages

Most packages provided with your distribution will be found on the CD-ROM under the directory /RedHat/RPMS. To mount the CD-ROM and list the various packages available, use the following commands:

```
cd /mnt
mount CD-ROM
cd CD-ROM/RedHat/RPMS
ls ¦ more
```

Most of these packages were installed during your installation of Linux. However, if you decided not to install certain packages, you could install them now from this collection of packages.

▶ **See** "Installing the Software Components," **p. 75**

RPM also allows you to install packages located on other computers using FTP, as you will see in the next section.

Installing Packages with RPM

To install a package from the command line you use the -i option like this:

```
rpm -i quota-1.55-4.i386.rpm
```

This command installs the quota package on your system. The -i option instructs the RPM command to install the package quota-1.55-4.i386.rpm onto the local system. To run the installation, RPM goes through a series of steps:

Dependency checks. Each package may depend on other software already being installed.

Conflict checks. RPM checks to see if a component is already installed or that the component is not older than the one currently installed.

Processing configuration files. RPM attempts to provide a proper configuration file, and if it finds a previous config file, it saves it for future reference.

Installing files. RPM unpacks the various components from the package and places them in the proper directories.

Post installation processing. After installing the various components, RPM performs any necessary tasks to properly configure the system.

Updating the database. RPM keeps track of all its action via a database.

The command provides no feedback during this installation, but you can use the –v (verbose) option to get more information. Table 6.2 provides a list of other options you can use during installation.

Table 6.2   Installation Options

Option	Description
-vv	Provides very verbose information.
-h	Prints hash marks(#) periodically during installation. This allows you to see that RPM is actually doing something and is not just hung.
--percent	Instead of #, this option prints the percent completed during installation.
--test	Does not install the package, but performs a dry run to test installation and reports any errors.
--replacefiles	Replaces files from other packages.
--force	Tells RPM to ignore certain conflict errors and install the package anyway.

To install a package located on another machine, you can use an FTP-type URL to designate the package:

```
rpm -i ftp://ftp.netwharf.com/pub/RPMS/quota-1.55-4.i386.rpm
```

This command assumes that the remote machine accepts anonymous FTP.

▶ **See** "Using FTP with a Web Browser," **p. 601**

If you need to specify a username and password to install the file, you can use the following command:

```
rpm -i ftp://mark@ftp.netwharf.com/pub/RPMS/quota-1.55-4.i386.rpm
Password for mark@ftp.netwharf.com:  <enter your password here>
```

N O T E   You can enter your username and password in the command at the same time like this:

```
rpm -i ftp://mark:password@ftp.netwharf.com/pub/RPMS/
quota-1.55-4.i386.rpm
```

However, this is not a secure method for entering commands because someone could look over your shoulder or (more likely) recall the command from your history file. ■

Part

I

Ch

6

Uninstalling Packages with RPM

One of the benefits of using RPM is the ease of installing new programs. If you've heard about a new program on the Internet, you can install the package and test out the new program. What happens, then, if you decide the software is not for you and you want to get rid of it? Fortunately, RPM makes uninstalling a package just as easy as installing one. To uninstall a package, use the -e option:

```
rpm -e quota-1.55-4.i386.rpm
```

When erasing a package from your system, RPM goes through the following sequence of actions:

Checks dependencies. RPM checks its database to see if any other packages depend on this database. If so, RPM will not delete the package unless explicitly told to do so.

Executes scripts. RPM will execute a pre-uninstall script.

Checks config files. RPM will save a copy of any modified config files.

Deletes files. RPM deletes every file associated with the specified package.

Executes scripts. RPM executes a post uninstall script.

Updates database. RPM removes all references to the package from its database.

As with the `-i` option, you can use the `-v` and `-vv` options to get verbose information from the `erase` command. You can also use the `--test` option to see what problems might occur if you were to really remove the package. Finally, you can use the `--nodeps` option to tell RPM to ignore dependencies and go ahead and remove the package.

> **CAUTION**
>
> Be careful using the `--nodeps` option. If you remove a package on which another program depends, that program may not work correctly in the future.

Updating Packages with RPM

After you install a package, there will eventually be upgrades either for bug fixes or for new features. RPM makes the typically horrendous task of upgrading a program effortless with the `-U` (note it's uppercase!) option. Let's say someone has added several new features to the quota program and released a new package called quota-1.55-4.i386.rpm. To upgrade to the new version you would use the following command:

```
rpm -U quota-1.55-4.i386.rpm
```

While upgrading, RPM installs the specified package and then erases all the older versions of the packages (if any exist). RPM also spends a great deal of time processing any configuration files associated with the package. Thus, while RPM is upgrading a package, you might see a message like the following, indicating that a configuration file is being saved to a new file:

```
Saving syslog.conf to syslog.conf.rpmsave
```

This indicates RPM has created a new configuration file that may be compatible with your system. After upgrading you should compare the two configuration files and make any necessary modifications to the new file.

Querying Packages with RPM

To see what packages are installed on your system, you can use the following command:

```
rpm -qa
```

This will list every package currently installed on your system. To get information on a specific package, just use the `-q` option. Table 6.3 provides the various options you can use with rpm `-q` command to query RPM packages.

Table 6.3 RPM Query Options

Option	Description
-q *name*	Provides package name, version, and release number.
-qa	Lists all packages currently installed.
-qf *file*	Queries the package associated with *file*.
-qp *package*	Queries *package*.
-qi *package*	Provides the name, description, release, size, build date, installation date, and other miscellaneous information about *package*.
-ql *package*	Lists the files associated with *package*.

CAUTION

The various -q options do not work well when specifying symbolically linked files. For best results, cd to the appropriate directory where the real file is located before using the -q options.

▶ **See** "Links," **p. 308**

As an example, if you found a new package and wanted to know more information about it, you could use the following query command:

```
rpm -qip quota-1.55-4.i386.rpm
```

The command would display output similar to the following:

```
Name        : quota                    Distribution: Manhattan
Version     : 1.55                         Vendor: Red Hat Software
Release     : 9                         Build Date: Thu May  7 22:45:48 1998
Install date: (not installed)          Build Host: porky.redhat.com
Group       : Utilities/System         Source RPM: quota-1.55-9.src.rpm
Size        : 82232
Packager    : Red Hat Software <bugs@redhat.com>
Summary     : Quota administration package
Description :
Quotas allow the system administrator to limit disk usage by a user and/or
group per filesystem. This package contains the tools which are needed to
enable, modify, and update quotas.
```

Verifying Packages with RPM

The final RPM mode verifies a package. You may need to check the consistency of a file on your system at some point. Let's say you suspect that a file has been corrupted accidentally by an errant program or a user. You will need to compare the current files against the originals you installed. RPM allows you to do this with the -V option (note the uppercase V). Verifying a package compares the size, MD5 checksum, file permissions, file type, and file owner and group settings. To verify that a particular package's files have not been modified since they were installed, use `rpm -V packagename`. For example, to verify the quota package, you would enter this:

```
rpm -V quota
```

If nothing has changed, RPM will not display any output. If something had changed, RPM will display a string of eight characters indicating what has changed and the name of the file that has changed. You would then need to inspect the various files in the package and determine if you need to reinstall the damaged package. Table 6.4 lists the possible output codes.

Table 6.4   Verification Failure Codes

Code	Meaning
c	The file is a configuration file.
5	The file failed the MD5 checksum test.
S	File size has changed since installation.
L	Problem with symbolic links.
T	File modification time does not match original.
D	Device attribute.
U	User setting is different.
G	Group setting is different.
M	Mode differs, either in permission or file type.

Installing Non-Linux Software

Unfortunately, most of the software programs you'll find aren't in RPM package format. Typically, these pieces are downloaded via anonymous FTP from some archive site.

The process of installing software can range from extremely simple to almost impossible. It all depends on how well the software authors wrote their installation scripts and how good their installation documentation is.

Deciphering Software Package Formats   The software packages that you get via anonymous FTP will virtually all be in the form of a compressed tar file. These files can be created in a couple of different ways. Typically, a directory tree contains source files, libraries, documentation, executables, and other necessary files that are bundled into a tar file by using the `tar` program. This tar file is then usually compressed to save space.

The software package will probably have an extension at the end of the file name that tells you what format it's in. If the file ends in .gz, it was compressed with the GNU gzip program. This is the most common file-compression format for Linux software packages. If the archive name ends with a .Z, it was compressed with the compress program. For example, the software package foo.tar.gz is a tar archive that has been compressed with gzip.

N O T E Sometimes, a tar file that has been compressed with gzip is written with the .tgz extension instead of .tar.gz.

▶ **See** "Using tar," **p. 229** ■

Installing the Software The next thing that you have to do after you figure out the package format is figure out where you want to place the source files so that you can build the software package. Some software packages are fairly large, so it's a good idea to place them on a file system that has a good bit of free space. Some people create a separate file system for sources and mount it under a directory, such as /usr/local/src or /src. Wherever you decide to build your software packages, make sure that you have enough disk space so that the software can be compiled successfully.

Now, you can go ahead and move the software package to the source tree that you've set up and decompress it and expand the archive. If a file is compressed with gzip, you can decompress it with the gzip -d command. For example, this command

```
gzip -d foo.tar.gz
```

expands the compressed file foo.tar.gz and replaces it with the tar archive named foo.tar. See Table 6.5 for gzip command line flags.

Table 6.5 Flags for the *gzip* Command

Flag	Flag Name	Description
-a	ascii	ASCII text; converts end-of-line characters by using local conventions.
-c	stdout	Writes on standard output; keeps original files unchanged.
-d	decompress	Decompresses.
-f	force	Forces overwrite of output file and compresses links.
-h	help	Gives a help listing.
-l	list	Lists compressed file contents.
-L	license	Displays software license.
-n	no-name	Doesn't save or restore the original name and time stamp.
-N	name	Saves or restores the original name and time stamp.
-q	quiet	Suppresses all warnings.

Part

I

Ch

6

continues

Table 6.5   Continued

Flag	Flag Name	Description
-S *suffix*	suffix .*suf*	Uses suffix .*suf* on compressed files.
-t	test	Tests compressed file integrity.
-v	verbose	Changes to verbose mode.
-V	version	Displays the version number.
-1	fast	Compresses faster.
-9	best	Compresses better (that is, the file is smaller).
file		Specifies file(s) to (de)compress; if none given, uses standard input.

For files that have been compressed with the compress command, use the uncompress command to expand them. For example, the command

```
uncompress foo.tar.Z
```

expands the compressed file foo.tar.Z and replaces it with the tar archive named foo.tar.

After you expand the compressed file, you need to expand the tar file into a directory tree. You want to put the sources for each separate package in its own directory in your source tree. Before untarring the file, you should look at its tar listing to see whether it was created with a directory as the first entry. Use the command

```
tar -tvf tarfile-name ¦ more
```

to see whether the first entry in the tar file is a directory. If so, the tar file creates the directory when it's expanded. If there's no directory entry at the top level of the tar file, all the files at the top level are extracted into the current directory. In this case, you need to make a directory and move the tar file into it before you expand it.

N O T E   Always check for a top-level directory before expanding a tar file. It can be quite a mess if the tar file expands and places a few hundred files in the current directory instead of in a subdirectory. ▨

When you have the tar file where you want to expand it, you can use this command to expand the source tree in the tar file.

```
tar -xvf tarfile-name
```

The next step depends on how the software package that you're installing was written. Typically, you change directory to the top-level directory of the software sources and look for a file named something like README.1ST. There should be a few documentation files in the top-level source directory that explain the installation process.

N O T E On most versions of Linux, you can decompress a tar file "on-the-fly" as you extract it.
Simply add the z flag to the `tar` command, as in `tar -zxvf foo.tar.gz`. ■

The typical installation process involves editing the file named Makefile to edit the destination directories where the software places its compiled binaries. You then usually run `make` followed by `make install`.

The `make` process probably varies with each package that you install. For some packages, some sort of configuration shell script may ask you questions and then compile the software for you. Make sure that you read the documentation files that come with the package.

Reviewing File Permissions

Setting permissions for a software package usually occurs automatically during installation. The installation script that comes with your application usually installs each file with the proper ownership and permissions. Only when something goes wrong and a user who should be able to access the program can't do so are you required to find the directory the application was copied to and check the permissions.

Typically, the executable file that you run to start the application is installed with permissions that let any user run the file; however, only the superuser can delete or overwrite it. The application usually is installed in a directory with read and execute permissions, but no write permissions.

▶ **See** "File Permissions," **p. 310**

Solving Problems

A well-written and well-supported application installs onto your system with minimal requests for information from you. It sets permissions properly so that all you have to do is test the program and inform your users—often through e-mail—that the application is now available. But things can and do go wrong in the installation of programs and their subsequent operation (or non operation). If, for whatever reason, the program doesn't complete the loading process or fails to operate correctly after installation, it's your responsibility to determine why and to fix the problem.

If a program doesn't install completely, your troubleshooting efforts often require no more than reading the documentation and README files supplied with the application and looking for a list of exceptions or problems and their solutions. However, no one expects you to possess expertise and familiarity with the scores of software packages available for Linux. Occasionally, you'll require outside help.

If you can't solve the problem by using the information that came with the package, you should try looking on Usenet news to see whether there's any discussion of the package in question. A question posted in the appropriate Linux group on Usenet can solve a lot of problems. If you can't find help on the Net, you can try to contact the application developer, usually via e-mail. Remember, Linux is free, and so are most of the software packages that exist for Linux. Don't expect shrink-wrapped manuals and 24-hour technical support lines. But if you weren't the adventurous type, you wouldn't be using Linux—right?

Part
I

Ch
6

Removing Applications

If an application is superseded by a better package or is no longer used by any user on the system, removing it is a good idea. Disk space is always precious; you certainly don't want old, unused programs to hog space required by new applications.

Like installation, removal of a program on a Linux system is more complicated than for single-user operating systems. It's sometimes not enough just to erase the application's files and remove its directory. Drivers and other software connections must be disconnected to avoid future problems. By taking notes and capturing the installation messages to a logfile, you can usually figure out what was changed when the software was installed. You can then deduce what files to remove and which files to change in order to successfully delete a package.

Upgrading Your Kernel

Along with upgrades for other software, new versions of the kernel sources are released regularly. These versions may fix bugs or add new functionality. Alternatively, you may decide to upgrade your kernel because you need to reconfigure it or add new device drivers. In any case, the process is fairly straightforward. You should make sure that you have a backup of your system software and a Linux boot floppy before you start so that you can recover if you should damage your system. For a complete description of how to rebuild the Linux kernel, see Chapter 13, "Configuring the Linux Kernel."

▶ **See** "Building a New Kernel," **p. 254**

The process for upgrading your kernel is detailed in the Kernel HOWTO document, which is regularly posted to the Linux newsgroups on the Internet and is available on the various Linux FTP sites, including **sunsite.unc.edu**. Be sure to get a copy of this HOWTO and read it thoroughly before you start your kernel upgrade.

The first step in the basic process of upgrading your kernel is getting the new kernel sources, which are available via anonymous FTP from the various Linux archive sites. When you have the sources, you need to preserve your current kernel sources. To do so, move your /usr/src/linux directory to another name, such as /usr/src/linux.old. Unpack the kernel sources in the /usr/src directory, which creates the linux subdirectory in the process. At that point, change to the linux directory and look at the documentation and the README files. Things may change as new kernels are released, so be sure to read the documentation.

From here, the process may vary a bit. Typically, you enter make config, which runs a configuration script and asks you questions about your system. If the configuration phase completes successfully, you then enter something similar to make dep. This checks for all the file dependencies to make sure that the new kernel finds all the files it needs to compile.

After the dependency check is complete, you typically enter make clean to delete any old object files that are left lying around in the kernel source directory. If everything has gone okay up to this point, you can enter make to compile the new kernel. After it compiles, you can install it with the LILO boot manager, and off you go.

Again, be sure to read the Kernel HOWTO before trying to do this. It goes into deep detail on setting up your kernel and will probably save you hours of frustration. Also, it may keep you from trashing your current Linux system in the process.

From Here...

You can find more information about installing and upgrading software in the following chapters:

- Chapter 3, "Installing Red Hat," provides a detailed discussion about how to install and set up the Red Hat distribution of the Linux operating system.
- Chapter 4, "Installing Caldera OpenLinux Lite," provides a detailed discussion about how to install and set up the Caldera OpenLinux distribution of Linux.
- Chapter 5, "Running Linux Applications," provides a basic introduction to setting up your Linux system.
- Chapter 11, "Backing Up Data," looks at the process for making system backups.
- Chapter 13, "Configuring the Linux Kernel," provides all the details you need to install a new Linux kernel.

Part

I

Ch

6

System Administration

Understanding System Administration

by Jack Tackett

In this chapter

A Linux system should have at least one person designated as the systems administrator to manage the system and oversee its performance. The systems administrator is responsible for seeing that the system is functioning properly, and he or she knows who to call if things can't be fixed locally, as well as how to provide software and hardware facilities to current and new users.

A Linux system requires initial configuration and continuous attention to ensure that the system remains effective, trustworthy, and efficient for all users. The systems administrator is the person responsible for attending to the Linux system's needs. As such, this person is responsible for many different tasks.

This chapter discusses some of the major tasks and issues confronting a systems administrator in a networked multiuser environment. Assuming that you bought this book to learn about and install Linux, you'll probably find yourself in the role of a systems administrator almost immediately. Some of the topics in this chapter are geared to systems administration in a larger organization. However, even if you're a single user who wants to play with Linux at home, you should be familiar with the topics discussed in this chapter so that you can be aware of the larger issues involved in system administration.

In many cases, your Linux system is networked with other computers that aren't running Linux. These other computers might be running other types of UNIX, or they might be running a different operating system entirely. Because Linux is a specific flavor of UNIX, much of the information in this chapter is applicable to Linux *and* UNIX. In some places in this chapter, UNIX and Linux are referred to interchangeably.

Understanding the Importance of Proper Administration

All UNIX systems are different in one way or another, and each is unique in the way it must be administered. Linux is no exception. Your administrative duties vary, based on such variables as the number of users you manage, the kinds of peripherals (printers, tape drives, and so on) attached to the computer, networking connections, and the level of security you require.

A systems administrator, alone or with a support staff, must provide a secure, efficient, and reliable environment for system users. The administrator has the power and responsibility to establish and maintain a system that provides effective and dependable service. In a multiuser environment, a number of competing purposes and priorities exist. The administrator exercises the power and responsibility necessary to provide a well-functioning system.

Delegation of administrative responsibilities varies from system to system. On large systems, administrative tasks can be divided among several people. Conversely, some small systems don't even require a full-time administrator; such systems simply designate a certain user to act as systems administrator. If you work in a networked environment, your system may be administered over the network by a network administrator.

Each Linux system has a single user who can perform virtually any operation on the computer. This user is called the *superuser* and has a special login name called *root*. The home directory for the root user, when logged in to the system, is typically / (the root directory of the file system) or a specific home directory, such as /home/root.

The systems administrator logs in as the superuser to perform tasks that require special access privileges. For normal system work, the systems administrator logs in as an ordinary user. The superuser's login name—root—is used only for limited special purposes. The number of users who can log in as root should be kept to a minimum (two or three at most). When any person logs in to the system as root, that person is a superuser and has absolute power on the system. With this privilege, the superuser can change the attributes of any file, stop the system, start the system, back up the system's data, and perform many other tasks.

The administrator must be aware of many of the technical aspects of the computer system. Also, the administrator must be aware of the users' needs, as well as the system's primary purpose. Any computer system is a finite resource, and therefore, policies regarding its use must be established and enforced. Thus, the administrator must play a policy-enforcing role as well as a technical role. That policy-enforcing role, combined with the power to perform virtually any possible action, requires a responsible, skillful, and diplomatic person in the role of administrator.

The precise job description of the systems administrator often depends on the local organization. As systems administrator, you might find yourself involved in a wide variety of activities, from setting policy to installing software to moving furniture. However, all systems administrators have to perform or manage a number of tasks, such as the following:

- *Manage users*. Add users, delete users, and modify users' capabilities and privileges.
- *Configure devices*. Make available and share such devices as printers, terminals, modems, and tape drives.
- *Make backups*. Schedule, make, and store backups for possible restoration in case the system's files are lost or damaged.
- *Shut down the system*. Shut down the system in an orderly manner to avoid inconsistencies in the file system.
- *Train users*. Provide or obtain training for users so that they can use the system effectively and efficiently.
- *Secure the system*. Keep users from interfering with one another through accidental or deliberate actions.
- *Log system changes*. Keep a log book to record any significant activity concerning the system.
- *Advise users*. Act as the "local expert" to aid the system's ordinary users.

Understanding Multiuser Concepts

A multiuser system employs two main concepts: multitasking and multiuser services. Linux has the apparent capability to execute multiple tasks concurrently—though transparently to the user. For example, you can read your e-mail while compiling a program.

Each task—whether it's a simple command entered on the command line or a complex application—starts one or more processes. Everything running on a Linux system is associated with a process. And because Linux can run many processes simultaneously, Linux is a multitasking operating system.

You can connect to a computer running UNIX (referred to as a *server*) in many ways. You can use a terminal or a computer; you can be located physically near the server and connected with a cable, or you can be on the other side of the planet connected with high-speed data lines or ordinary phone lines. Whether you're using a terminal or computer and how you're connected to the server determine whether the computer's resources are considered to be distributed or centralized.

A single-user computer operating system, such as DOS, is designed to be used by one person at a time. All the processing is done on one computer that has sole access to resources, such as printers, storage area, and processing.

Multiuser systems use the centralized-processing and distributed-processing models described here to accommodate many users simultaneously.

- In a *centralized-processing environment*, many users (large systems can have hundreds of users) access the resources of one computer; storage, printer, memory, and processing tasks are all performed by that one computer.

- In the *distributed-processing environment*, processing can occur on the user's own workstation, and the central processor is used to distribute applications and data. Printers and storage can be connected to the user's workstation or to the main server.

Understanding Centralized-Processing Systems

As technology during the 1950s and '60s advanced, operating systems began to allow multiple users to share resources from separate terminals. By using a batch-processing sequence, two users could execute two sets of instructions while sharing a processor, storage, and output.

With the advent of a switched telephone network, computers began to use telephone resources to extend computer resources geographically. In this model, each processor used communications-processing resources to connect with remote terminals. This created a need for computers and terminals to communicate in a better way. The result was the development of *front-end processing* for communications tasks and the centralized-processing model.

Until personal computers became inexpensive, powerful, and ubiquitous, most UNIX systems used the centralized-processing model. With centralized processing, mainframe computers handled all the processing. Users connected to the mainframe and shared its resources. This model is used less and less today, although it's still appropriate for computing sites where users are separated geographically.

For example, your bank may have one main processing center, yet all the bank's branches can access the data center regardless of their locations. On each user's desk is a terminal, including a keyboard, a monitor, and a direct connection to the mainframe so that the terminal can access the centralized resources: processing, printing, and storage (see Figure 7.1). The centralized-processing model is usually made up of many elements, such as the server, front-end processors, terminals, modems, and multiport adapters.

FIG. 7.1
This figure shows the centralized-processing model of a computing environment.

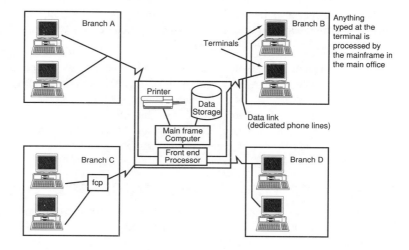

When a user requests data, the request is processed by the computer in the bank's main office. Results of the processing are then sent back to the terminal in the branch office. All data is processed and stored by the mainframe computer.

Elements of the Centralized-Processing Model

To make the centralized-processing model work, you need many elements, including the server, front-end processors, terminals, modems, and multiport adapters.

A *server* can be defined as any computer set up to share its resources (processing power, storage, printers, and so on). For example, you can use an IBM-compatible PC as a server as long as it has enough hard disk space and RAM.

A *front-end processor* connects the communication channels and the server. It handles the details of communication so that the server is free to process its data.

Two popular types of terminals are used today: *dumb terminals* and *smart terminals*. Traditionally, UNIX is used with dumb terminals, which have keyboards and monitors but nothing else. The most important thing to realize about dumb terminals is that they have no local processing power. The communications port on the terminal is connected—directly or through a modem—to the server. When you type at a dumb terminal, each keystroke is transmitted to the server, where it's processed. Smart terminals can complete minimal processing at the local site. Cash registers and other point-of-sale devices are examples of smart terminals, as are the familiar automated teller machines (ATMs). The local device stores the transaction request and then transmits the entire request instead of transmitting each keystroke as a dumb terminal does.

Part
II

Ch
7

To connect your terminal to a telephone line, you use a *modem*. Modems translate the digital signals of terminals and computers into analog signals required by telephone lines. Modems are always used in pairs. The first one connects your terminal to the telephone line; the second connects the server to the telephone line. To make the connection, you dial out on the terminal. When the modem on the other end (the one connected to the server) answers, your terminal can communicate with the server.

To expand the number of available ports that users can connect to, you can install a *multiport adapter*. Typically, a PC has only two serial ports: COM1 and COM2. If you want to use a PC as a server for more than two users, however, you need more ports. The multiport adapter, in this case, consists of a card that you install inside the computer, a small box with eight or more connectors, and a cable that connects the box and the card. Software is supplied with the adapter to permit the added connectors to function as additional serial ports.

Understanding Distributed-Processing Systems

In distributed processing, the terminal is replaced by a workstation, which is itself a computer usually running DOS or UNIX. Programs can be located and run from the server or from your workstation. Similarly, files can be located on either system. If you process a file on your workstation, you store it on the server so that others can access it. You can print on local printers connected to your workstation or on printers connected to the server.

Because workstations are in common use, your bank probably uses a distributed-processing system instead of the centralized system described in the preceding section. Figure 7.2 shows the same bank with a distributed-processing system.

FIG. 7.2

This figure shows the distributed-processing model of a computing environment.

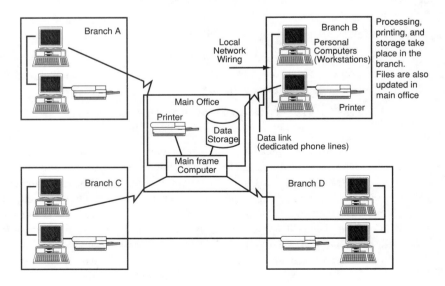

Elements of the Distributed-Processing Model

Distributed processing uses file servers, workstations, network interface cards, hubs, repeaters, bridges, routers, and gateways. The purpose of the *file server* is to distribute files and segments of programs to workstations, print from a central location, and control flow on the connection between workstations. More than 90 percent of processing occurs at the workstation level, leaving 5 to 10 percent of the load at the file server for administrative tasks.

In addition to using it as a file server, you can use a personal computer as a Linux *workstation*. Linux was designed to run in a very minimal hardware configuration. In fact, you can run Linux with a 386SX microprocessor and 4MB of RAM! Because most current systems are more powerful than Linux's minimum requirements, you should have no problem with computing power. The amount of hard drive space required depends on how much software you want to install. If you want to run entirely off CD-ROM, you need only about 5MB of hard disk space. A minimal hard-disk installation takes 10MB to 20MB of space; a full installation takes more than 100MB.

Generally, resources should be applied to the workstation level, where most of the processing occurs. The amount of additional resources depends on the types of tasks you plan to do. For example, word processors take minimal resources (hard drive, RAM, quality of monitor) compared with graphics-intensive tasks such as those you might perform in multimedia and computer-aided design (CAD) programs. For applications involving CAD, you need very large hard disks (1 gigabyte or more), a lot of RAM (16MB, 32MB, or even 64MB), and high-resolution monitors and video cards (1,280×1,024 or higher). You might even want a tape drive for backing up your system and a CD-ROM drive for loading large applications.

A *network interface card* (NIC) attaches to a slot on the motherboard and is the physical link between the computer and the cabling for the network. Network interface cards are generally available for coaxial or twisted-pair cabling.

The *hub* serves as a connecting point for network cables, such as 10BaseT Ethernet, and can be passive or active. A passive hub usually has four connectors. An active hub usually has at least eight ports and amplifies or relays the signal.

Repeaters amplify or regenerate the signal over the network so that you can extend the normal distance limitations of network cabling.

Use a *bridge* when you need to connect two similar network types.

Routers are used in large, complex networks that provide many paths for network signals to travel to the same destination. The router determines which is the most effective route and sends the signal along that route.

Use a *gateway* when you need to connect dissimilar network types, which use different protocols. The gateway performs the necessary protocol conversions so that the two networks can communicate. For example, an SNA network connected to a TCP/IP network would require a gateway.

Topologies

The term *topology* refers to how workstations and file servers are connected in a network. The names of various topologies are derived from the pattern the cables make after you connect the various terminals, workstations, and file servers. The most common topologies are *star*, *bus*, and *ring*. When more than one topology is used in a network, it's referred to as a *hybrid network*.

Star Topology   With the star topology, all workstations are connected to a central file server or hub (see Figure 7.3). You can have passive or active hubs in this scheme.

FIG. 7.3

All workstations connect to a central file server in a star topology.

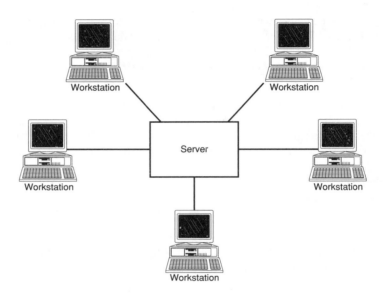

A passive hub is simply a connecting point for the workstations. An active hub also offers amplification of the signal. AT&T's StarLan is an example of a network using star topology.

Bus Topology   In a bus topology (see Figure 7.4), all workstations and file servers share a common pathway. They are, in fact, connected directly. The bus topology is the foundation for Ethernet and token bus.

Ring Topology   A ring topology looks like a wagon wheel without the hub (see Figure 7.5). The server is connected to the workstations in bus fashion, except that the last items along the network are connected to make a closed loop. Ring topologies use a repeater, which IBM refers to as a Multistation Access Unit (MAU). The IBM Token-Ring Network is an example of a ring topology.

Hybrid Topology   In the 1970s and '80s, firms with decentralized purchasing departments experienced the growth of different topologies on their networks. For example, the accounting department in a given company used a bus network; the purchasing department installed Token-Ring machines; manufacturing used an Ethernet bus; and administration relied on mainframe technology. This combination of networks planted the seeds for enterprise computing and hybrid wide area networks. The integration of these networks linked dissimilar topologies, such as rings, stars, and buses.

FIG. 7.4
All workstations and file servers share a common pathway in a bus topology.

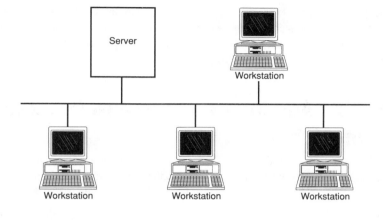

FIG. 7.5
In a ring topology, the server is connected to the workstations in bus fashion.

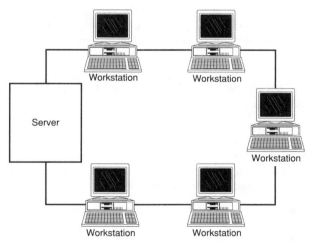

Understanding the Client/Server Model

The result of the development of distributed processing is the *client/server model*. Today, Linux can be used in this model as the client, the server, or both.

To understand a client/server setup, assume that several Linux workstations (the clients) are connected in a bus topology to a server (a high-end PC with lots of disk space, also running Linux). The server has directories for each client where important files can be stored and backed up with the server's nightly backup. The server also has directories from which clients

Part
II

Ch
7

can share files. Connected to the server is a fast laser printer that everyone can access and a tape drive suitable for backing up the large hard disks. Also, several of the clients have their own slower, less-expensive laser printers connected locally.

N O T E The server in this example is a PC running Linux—just like the clients' PCs, although the server is more powerful. There's no reason why the server can't act like a client at times and share resources from the clients. In other words, any Linux system can function as both a client and a server. ■

Performing Administration in a Networked Environment

A UNIX network usually takes the form of many computers, large and small, tied together over directly connected wires or common telephone lines. Administering the network is usually the task of a person or persons located at one of the sites in the network.

Most people can learn Linux and administer a network. In a production environment, it would be nice to find a qualified person right away; however, such people are somewhat rare—and usually well paid. With practice and patience, even people with limited backgrounds in computers can learn to administer a corporate UNIX/Linux computer.

Defining the Role of the Network Administrator

Anytime you have more than a few UNIX/Linux systems connected in a network, you should probably have a dedicated network administrator. Some expertise is needed to decide how systems are connected (LANs or modems), the level of security needed, and how shared peripherals (printers, tape backups, and so on) are distributed. On a day-to-day basis, the administrator maintains lists of system names, network addresses, and user access and generally makes sure that the network is running properly.

Corporations with networks of hundreds of computers can afford to have several administrators with extensive training in selected topics. This can be a necessity if you have complex printing needs, for example. Administering printers and printing can require extensive knowledge of specific printers and how to interface that equipment to Linux.

Understanding Hardware and Software Issues

If, as systems administrator, you're required to choose the networking software and hardware for the computers under your control, you should consider several things. As with most things in life, you balance what you need with what you can afford.

If your systems are close together in the same building, a local area network is a low-cost, high-speed means of networking your computers. Put an Ethernet board in each Linux system and use TCP/IP as the networking protocol software. TCP/IP is a standard component of Linux distributions.

To connect over greater distances, you can use modems for lower-speed transmissions and Point-to-Point Protocol (PPP) or Serial Line Internet Protocol (SLIP) to provide asynchronous TCP/IP connections. You also can use UUCP software for e-mail, news, and file transfers (although UUCP has limitations). For higher speeds over long distances, you can use ISDN or get leased lines from the telephone company.

Don't buy just any old networking hardware. Although many off-the-shelf networking hardware products come with the drivers needed to make them work with DOS, the same isn't true with Linux. As a result, Linux systems have many standard networking drivers built in. Table 7.1 shows some of the Ethernet cards now supported by Linux. Check the Ethernet HOWTO for updates to this list (see Appendix A for information about HOWTOs).

Table 7.1   Some Ethernet Cards Now Supported Under Linux

Manufacturer	Cards
3Com	3c503, 3c503/16, 3c509, 3c579
SMC (Western Digital)	WD8003, WD8013, SMC Elite, SMC Elite Plus, SMC Elite 16 ULTRA
Novell Ethernet	NE1000, NE2000, NE1500, NE2100
D-Link	DE-600, DE-650, DE-100, DE-200, DE-220-T
Hewlett-Packard	27245A, 27247B, 27252A, 27247A, J2405A
Digital	DE200, DE210, DE202, DE100, DEPCA (rev. E)
Allied Telesis	AT1500, AT1700
PureData	PDUC8028, PDI8023

Applications that aren't integrated with networking products can be used in a network environment. For example, you can install an application on a Linux system and have many users from other computers use the application by running the remote execution commands built into UNIX. Or you can share an application by remotely mounting the file system that contains the application and then running it from the local system.

Performing Common Networking Administrative Tasks

Administration of a network takes on several dimensions. Most networks don't just occur; typically, they evolve. In the ideal situation, the administrators are involved with the purchase of the computers and software so that they know what's expected of them as administrators and what the users are getting.

Setting Up the System   Network software should be installed and ready to connect onsite. If you're using Ethernet for your Linux network segment, it's a good idea to have the continuity tests completed. If you're using telephone lines, have them tested as well. Wiring and terminals for users also should be tested and ready. Installation should be Plug and Play, but it never is. There are always connection problems.

Part

II

Ch

7

The advantage of buying a computer for a situation in which the operating system isn't yet installed is that you can set up file systems to accommodate your specific needs. You must know what software is going on the computer, the number of users who will be using the system, and the intensity of their usage.

TIP You've invested time and money in setting up the network to this point. Immediately back up the configuration files you've set up.

When the system is fully functional, the application software should be installed. Software on a Linux computer is often more complex than on a single-user system, so be prepared to spend some time installing, tuning, and making the software fully operational. This task can take from a couple of hours to several days—or longer.

You're now ready to start adding users to the system, although you're still not onsite. Add login IDs for a few key users and put in a common startup password, such as *temp01*. This provides some initial security and gives you a chance to get key people onto the system and operational right away when you install the system.

After installation, the computer should be attached to the network. Make sure that you can communicate from any point in the network to any other point. Test communications by moving large and small files from one computer to another. Electronic mail should be directed to and from other nodes in the network. All computers must "know" this new computer in the network. This means that you need to add it to your host name database that's used by any other computers on your network. If you use the Domain Name System (DNS) locally, you must add the host name to the DNS name database. If you aren't using DNS, add the name to the /etc/hosts files on your other systems.

Handling Peripherals   Printing can present a major issue to an administrator. Monitoring and maintaining printers is a significant task and can take a lot of an administrator's time. Understanding the spooling of print jobs, interface tools, and equipment peculiarities requires time and patience.

Modems are the cheapest way to link a network that spans long distances. Modems and PPP or UUCP are tools that can make it practical for a small staff to administer many computers. As with printers, however, modems have some problems that require time to get them running right. Choose one or two brand names and really learn their idiosyncrasies.

Monitoring the System   When the installation is complete, you can set up UNIX tools to monitor this new system. The administrators should start getting a feel for how the system is performing.

Monitoring running systems in a network is an ongoing process, but the administrative load should stabilize after a while if you aren't constantly adding peripherals or software. Occasionally, something fails, or tweaking may be necessary. A good administrator learns to determine whether the problem is related to hardware or software.

Coping with Software Upgrades   Some software packages are constantly being updated. Although this is a concern with commercial UNIX, it's a special issue under Linux because much of the software is publicly available over the Internet and is continually modified. The good news might be that a bug is fixed. The bad news might be that each system in the network has to be updated. Expect a new challenge with each update.

The best advice isn't to immediately put all new versions on your systems, but to test the upgrade or patch on one noncritical system. When you're sure that the new version is okay, upgrade the other systems. A good administrator learns how to install these patches or new versions without going to the other sites in the network. This sounds impossible at first, but you'll find that many UNIX tools facilitate the installation of patches and upgrades.

Training the Administrator

Training in most organizations is very hit-or-miss. Perhaps the person has some computer background in some computer topic, but little is done to formally train that person to administer the system. Administration requires attention and a solid knowledge of the following topics:

- *Linux/UNIX design and usage.* The administrator has to have a thorough understanding of such issues as redirection, pipes, background processing, and so on.

- *The vi editor.* The vi editor is on virtually every credible UNIX computer put out during the last 10 years, including Linux. Many people criticize it, and many people substitute other editors for their own use, but it's advisable to have an administrator learn and become proficient in the use of vi because it's the "common denominator" among UNIX editors.

- *Shell script programming.* Many of the key programs used to administer UNIX are written in shell script language and might require modification for your specific needs. Many of the tools outlined in this chapter require knowledge of how to put together and use a shell program. Almost every user has a favorite shell.

  bash, the Bourne Again shell, is a Bourne shell clone that's the default shell under Linux. Also, the Z and T shells are available in the distribution. You should, however, stay with the common Bourne shell until you master this shell language. Also, virtually all the shell programs written by the Linux creators are written in the Bourne shell. You should also investigate the Perl system administration language. It provides a very robust set of tools for system administration in one programming environment.

- *Communications.* Communications training is generally not very good as of this writing. To set up computer networking effectively, knowledge of TCP/IP and the related protocols is essential. Similarly, you'll want to understand PPP if you're going to set up an asynchronous Internet connection. Ideally, these protocols should be taught in a laboratory environment with the many options available. Attend classes or at least buy manuals on the subject, but accept that you'll be spending much time experimenting.

- *UNIX conventions.* UNIX conventions aren't taught or even mentioned in many UNIX classes, and you'll probably have to pick them up by observing as you go through training. For example, you'll learn that binary executable programs are generally stored in the bin directories, such as /usr/bin, /bin, and /usr/local/bin. You can put your own executable programs in /usr/local/bin. Likewise, the lib directories, such as /usr/lib, are used for library files, and you can put your own libraries in a directory such as /usr/local/lib. Understanding and following standard Linux/UNIX conventions such as these can save time when it comes to finding and fixing problems.

Several reputable companies, perhaps including the company that you bought your computer from, offer training on all these topics. However, this training is probably not specific to Linux. A few vendors sell various distributions of the Linux operating system and offer classes on selected topics. You should also look for user groups in your area and check the **comp.os.linux** newsgroup hierarchy on Usenet news on the Internet.

Training is best done in small pieces. You should take a course and then come back and use what you learned right away on your network. Linux has an elaborate set of tools that will probably never be completely mastered, but you have to know where to find information in manuals.

From Here...

You can find more information about system administration topics in the following chapters:

- Chapter 9, "Booting and Shutting Down," discusses proper procedures for starting and stopping the Linux system.
- Chapter 10, "Managing User Accounts," describes how to create and manage user accounts under Linux.
- Chapter 14, "Managing File Systems," shows how to create, update, and manage your file systems.

## CHAPTER 8

Using the *vi* Editor

by Jack Tackett

Introducing *vi*

Earlier chapters have shown you how convenient and advantageous it is to have sequences of commands or shell programs stored in a file. You probably have to create data, e-mail, lists, memos, notes, reports, and so on; you use some type of text editor to do these tasks. You may have several editors or word processors available on your Linux system to help you with those tasks. To put commands or shell programs in a file, however, you need an editor that can save your work in a text file—a file in ASCII format. Linux comes with a standard text editor called vi, which you can use for all but the most complex writing and editing projects.

vi is very useful to system administrators because it is available on every UNIX platform. Thus, once you learn how to use vi, you can use it on any system running UNIX. vi is also useful because it takes up very few resources when executing, which means you can use vi when other programs might not run because of hardware or other system problems.

The vi and ex editors that ship with the Red Hat distribution are actually other names for an editor called vim (for VI iMproved). The names vi and ex are symbolically linked to vim, so when you type **vi**, you're actually running vim. Read /usr/share/vim/vim_diff.txt for a summary of the differences between vim and vi.

Your Linux system also has other text editors: a graphical editor for use under the XFree86 system and two standard nongraphical text editors called ed and ex. They're both line-oriented editors—that is, you work with only one line at a time. Another editor, called emacs, is also supplied with most Linux distributions. vi and emacs are full-screen editors; when you use them, you see a screen's worth of information, so you can make changes or additions in context. This chapter doesn't discuss ed or ex very much because you'll find vi easier to use and available on every UNIX machine, including Linux.

To understand vi (pronounced *vee eye*), you need to understand some of vi's history within the UNIX world. Moreover, although today's systems (including Linux) have much more user-friendly and robust editors, you should learn how to use vi because every UNIX (and, thus, Linux) system has a copy of vi available. Sometimes vi is the only editor available at a crucial moment; therefore, you need to know some of its basic operations.

UNIX was developed in an environment in which the user's terminal was a teletype or some other slow, hard copy terminal; video display monitors generally weren't used. A natural editor for that environment was a line-oriented editor—one that the user sees and works on one line of text at a time. Two line-oriented editors are on UNIX systems today: ed and ex.

In its early days, UNIX was made available to universities essentially free of charge. Students and faculty at several universities made many contributions to the UNIX working environment. Several notable improvements came out of the University of California at Berkeley, including a full-screen editor—one that lets you work with a screen of information at once rather than a single line of text. That full-screen editor is called vi, which stands for *visual*. The time was right for the transition to screen-oriented work. Users were working with video terminals rather than hard copy devices.

T I P You don't have to become an expert to use `vi`. Simply type **man vi** at the command prompt for help. You also can ask for help by pressing <Esc> and then entering **:help**.

N O T E This chapter doesn't cover all of `vi`'s features; that requires more space than is available. (In fact, entire books are written just on `vi`.) Instead, you learn the commands to do the most necessary editing tasks. If you want to know about the more advanced features of `vi`, consult the man pages supplied with Linux. ■

What Is *vi*?

Because it's part of the standard UNIX environment, `vi` has been learned and used (to one degree or another) by millions of UNIX users. You will find that `vi` starts quickly and can be used for simple and complex tasks. As you would expect, you use it to enter, modify, or delete text; search or replace text; and copy, cut, and paste blocks of text. You also see that it can be customized to match your needs. You can move the cursor to any position on-screen and move through the file you're editing. You use the same methods with any text file, regardless of its contents.

The `vi` editor isn't a word processor or desktop publishing system. There are no menus and virtually no help facilities.

N O T E The original version of `vi` doesn't have a help facility. However, newer versions of `vi`, such as `vim` for the Red Rat distribution, provide some online help. ■

Word processing systems usually offer screen and hard copy formatting and printing, such as representing text as **bold**, *italic*, or underlined, but `vi` doesn't. Other Linux commands can perform some of these functions—for example, `lp` can print and `nroff` can format text. Some text processing programs, such as TeX (pronounced tek) and LaTeX, can process embedded commands into text, such as bold and underlined attributes.

The `vi` editor operates in two modes:

- ■ In command mode, your keystrokes are interpreted as commands to `vi`. Some of the commands allow you to save a file, exit `vi`, move the cursor to different positions in a file, and modify, rearrange, delete, substitute, and search for text.

- ■ In input or text-entry mode, your keystrokes are accepted as the text of the file you're editing. When `vi` is in input or text-entry mode, the editor acts as a typewriter.

In an editing session, you can freely switch between modes. You have to remember the mode you're using and know to change modes. Some people may find this uncomfortable at first. Later in this chapter, you learn about the `showmode` option, which tells you `vi`'s current mode. With a little practice, however, you'll find `vi` extremely convenient for editing Linux ASCII files, especially configuration files and shell scripts.

Understanding the Editing Process

You edit text by creating new text or by modifying existing text. When you create new text, you place the text in a file with an ordinary Linux file name. When you modify existing text, you use the existing file name to call a copy of the file into the editing session. In either case, as you use the editor, the text is held in the system's memory in a storage area called a *buffer*. Using a buffer prevents you from directly changing the contents of a file until you decide to save the buffer. This is to your benefit if you decide you want to forget the changes you've made and start over.

As you make changes and additions to the text, these edits affect the text in the buffer not in the file stored on disk. When you're satisfied with your edits, you issue a command to save the text. This command writes the changes to the file on the disk. Only then are the changes made permanent. You can save changes to disk as often as you like (it's usually a good idea to save any file you're editing frequently in case of lockups or power loss). You don't have to exit the editor when you save changes. This chapter shows you several ways to exit the editor; some of those ways write the buffer to the text file on the disk.

The vi editor is said to be *interactive* because it interacts with you during the editing session. The editor communicates with you by displaying status messages, error messages, or sometimes nothing on-screen (in typical Linux fashion). The last line on-screen, called the *status line*, holds the messages from Linux. You see the changes you make in the text on-screen.

You use the editor to modify, rearrange, delete, substitute, and search for text. You conduct these editing operations while using the editor in command mode. In several instances, a command is a single letter that corresponds to the first letter of an action's name. For example, i corresponds to the insert action, and r is used when replacing a character.

Most commands operate on a single line or range of lines of text. The lines are numbered from 1 (the top line) to the last line in the buffer. When you add or delete lines, the line numbers adjust automatically. A line's number is its address in the buffer. An address range is simply two addresses or line numbers separated by a comma. If you want to specify the range consisting of the third through the eighth line of the buffer, you use 3,8.

The position of the cursor always indicates your current location in the editing buffer. Some of the commands you issue in command mode affect the character at the cursor position. Unless you move the cursor, changes take place at that position. Naturally, vi has several commands for moving the cursor through the edit buffer.

You know now that vi is a full-screen editor. You give vi commands to move the cursor to different positions in a file, and you see the changes you make as you make them. So vi has to be able to move to and modify the text on your terminal as well as on a host of other terminal types. It knows what terminal you're using and what its video capabilities are by checking the shell variable TERM. Linux uses the TERM variable to determine your terminal's capabilities, such as underlining, reverse video, the screen-clearing method, function-key assignment, and color capability.

TROUBLESHOOTING

My *vi* editor doesn't appear to be working correctly with my terminal or screen; I see "strange" characters. The TERM variable may not be set correctly. Another symptom of an improper terminal setup is that blocks of characters overwrite legible text. The $TERM expression gives the value of your current terminal setting. To check the value of TERM, enter **echo $TERM**. If you work at a terminal that is—or emulates—a vt100, this command displays the following result (type the command on the terminal, not while in the *vi* editor):

```
vt100
```

If the proper terminal type isn't echoed back, set the value of TERM by entering the following command, if you're using the bash shell:

```
TERM=vt100
export TERM
```

If you're using the C shell, enter the following (the spaces around the = sign are important):

```
setenv TERM = vt100
export TERM
```

Your specific terminal type may be different from vt100; set TERM accordingly.

▶ **See** "Setting the Shell Environment," **p. 344**

I start *vi* but don't get the expected responses. Check to see whether your terminal is properly set up. Your terminal type isn't the same as the name of your terminal; your terminal type must match one of the terminal types contained in the directory /usr/lib/terminfo.

Using *vi*

To start *vi*, simply type its name at the shell prompt (command line). If you know the name of the file you want to create or edit, you can issue the *vi* command with the file name as an argument. For example, to create the file myfile with *vi*, enter **vi myfile**.

When *vi* becomes active, the terminal screen clears, and a tilde character (~) appears on the left side of every screen line, except for the first. The ~ is the empty-buffer line flag. The following is a shortened version of what you should see on your screen (only five lines are listed to save space):

```
_
~
~
~
~
```

The cursor is at the leftmost position of the first line (represented here as an underscore character). You'll probably see 20 to 22 of the tilde characters at the left of the screen. If that's not the case, check the value of TERM (as described in the preceding troubleshooting section) and perhaps talk with your system administrator.

When you see this display, you've successfully started vi; vi is in command mode, waiting for your first command.

N O T E   Unlike most word processors, vi starts in command mode. Before you start entering text, you must switch to input mode with the <a> or <i> keys, both of which are described in the next section.

Looking at *vi*'s Two Modes

As mentioned earlier, the vi editor operates in two modes: command mode and input mode. In command mode, vi interprets your keystrokes as commands; there are many vi commands. You can use commands to save a file, exit vi, move the cursor to various positions in a file, or modify, rearrange, delete, substitute, or search for text. You can even pass a command to the shell. If you enter a character as a command but the character isn't a command, vi beeps. Don't worry; the beep is an audible indication for you to check what you're doing and correct any errors.

You can enter text in input mode (also called *text-entry mode*) by appending characters after the cursor or inserting before the cursor. At the beginning of the line, this doesn't make much difference. To go from command mode to input mode, press one of the following keys:

    <a>   To append text after the cursor

    <i>   To insert text in front of the cursor

Use input mode only for entering text. Most word processors start in input mode, but vi doesn't. When you use a word processing program, you can type away, entering text; to issue a command, you have to use function keys or keys different than those you use when typing normal text. vi doesn't work that way: You must go into input mode by pressing <a> or <i> before you start entering text, and then explicitly press <Esc> to return to command mode.

Creating Your First *vi* File

The best way to learn about vi is to use it. This section gives a step-by-step example of how to create a file by using vi. In each step, you see an action to perform and then the necessary keystrokes. Don't be concerned with complete accuracy here. The example takes you through the motions and concepts of using vi to create a file, moving between command and input modes, and saving your results. If you run into difficulties, you can quit and start over by pressing <Esc>; then enter :q!.

1. Start vi by entering **vi**. You see the screen full of flush-left tildes.

2. Go into input mode to place characters on the first line. Press the <a> key; don't press <Return>. Now you can append characters to the first line. You shouldn't see the character *a* on-screen.

3. Add lines of text to the buffer by typing the following:

```
Things to do today.
a. Practice vi.
b. Sort sales data and print the results.
```

You can use the <Backspace> key to correct mistakes on the line you're typing. Don't worry about being precise here; this example is for practice. You learn other ways to make changes in some of the later sections of this chapter.

4. Go from input mode to command mode by pressing <Esc>. You hear a beep from your system if you press <Esc> when you're already in command mode.

5. Save your buffer in a file called vipract.1 by entering **:w vipract.1**. The characters :w vipract.1 appear on the bottom line of the screen (the status line). The characters shouldn't appear in the text. The :w command writes the buffer to the specified file. This command saves or writes the buffer to the file vipract.1.

6. Look at your action confirmed on the status line. You should see the following on the status line:

```
"vipract.1" [New File] 3 lines, 78 characters
```

This statement confirms that the file vipract.1 has been created, is a new file, and contains 3 lines and 78 characters. Your display may be different if you didn't type the information exactly as specified.

7. Exit *vi* by entering **:q**.

When you type **:q**, you're still in command mode and see these characters on the status line. When you press <Return>, however, *vi* terminates, and you are returned to the login shell prompt.

You use these steps, or variations of them, for all your editing tasks. Make sure that you can work through them before continuing.

Things to Remember About *vi*

- *vi* starts in command mode.

- To move from command mode to input mode, press <a> (to append text) or <i> (to insert text).

- You add text when you're in input mode.

- You give commands to *vi* only when you're in command mode.

- You give commands to *vi* to save a file and can quit only when you're in command mode.

- To move from input mode to command mode, press <Esc>.

Starting *vi* by Using an Existing File

To edit or look at a file that already exists in your current directory, type **vi** followed by the file name. Try this with the file you created in the preceding section by entering the following:

vi vipract.1

You see the following display (the number of lines shown here are fewer than you will actually see on-screen):

```
Things to do today.
a. Practice vi.
b. Sort sales data and print the results.
~
~
~
"vipract.1" 3 lines, 78 characters
```

As before, tilde characters appear on the far left of empty lines in the buffer. Look at the status line: It contains the name of the file you're editing and the number of lines and characters.

TROUBLESHOOTING

I type a file name that I know exists, but vi acts as though I'm creating a new file. No one is a perfect typist; you may have typed the name of a file that doesn't exist in your current directory. Suppose that you type **vi vipract.1**, but there's no file named vipract.1 in your current directory. You still start vi, but vi acts as though you were creating a new file.

I try to edit a file, but vi displays a message about read permission denied and I see the shell prompt again. You've tried to edit a file you aren't permitted to read. Also, you can't edit a directory— that is, if you type **vi *directory_name***, where *directory_name* is the name of a directory, vi informs you that you opened a directory and doesn't let you edit it. If you try to use vi with a file that's an executable program in binary, as opposed to ASCII, you'll see a screen full of strange (control) characters. It won't be something you can read and edit. vi expects files to be stored as lines.

I open a file in vi, but I see a message that the line is too long. You're trying to use vi on a data file that's just one long string of bytes. You can modify this file, but doing so will probably corrupt the data file.

I open a file in vi, but I'm seeing some very strange characters on-screen. You may be using vi with a file produced by a word processor.

In all these cases, exit vi to return to your login shell prompt by pressing <Esc> to go to command mode and then typing **:q!**. Using :q! ensures that you quit vi and make no changes to the existing file.

Exiting *vi*

You can exit or quit vi in several ways. Table 8.1 lists the commands you can use to exit vi.

N O T E   Remember that you must be in command mode to quit vi. To change to command mode, press <Esc>. (If you're already in command mode when you press <Esc>, you hear a harmless beep from the terminal.) ■

Table 8.1 Ways to Quit or Exit *vi*

Command	Action
:q	Exits after making no changes to the buffer, or exits after the buffer is modified and saved to a file
:q!	Exits and abandons all changes to the buffer since it was last saved to a file
:wq, :x, or ZZ	Writes the buffer to the working file and then exits

As you can see in Table 8.1, several keystrokes accomplish the same end. To practice, use *vi* to edit the file vipract.1 created earlier in this chapter. To edit the file, enter **vi vipract.1**. You see a display similar to this:

```
Things to do today.
a. Practice vi.
b. Sort sales data and print the results.
~
~
~
"vipract.1" 3 lines, 78 characters
```

The cursor is indicated by an underscore character. When you first open the file, it's under the first character of the file (the *T* in "Things"). Because you haven't made any changes to the file since you opened it, you can exit by entering **:q**. You see the shell prompt. You can also type **:wq** to exit the file; if you do so, you see the following message before the shell prompt appears:

```
"vipract.1" 3 lines, 78 characters
```

This message appears because *vi* first writes the buffer to the file vipract.1 and then exits.

Start *vi* again with the same file (type **vi vipract.1**). You see a display similar to this:

```
Things to do today.
a. Practice vi.
b. Sort sales data and print the results.
~
~
~
"vipract.1" 3 lines, 78 characters
```

Although *vi* starts in command mode, just to be sure, press <Esc>. Now press the Spacebar enough times so that the cursor moves under the period following today in the first line. To replace that character with an exclamation mark, press <r> (for replace) and type **!**. The first line now looks like this:

```
Things to do today!
```

Because you've changed the buffer, *vi* won't let you exit unless you save the changes or explicitly give a command to quit without saving the changes. If you try to exit *vi* by typing :q, *vi* displays the following message to remind you that you haven't written the file to disk since you changed it:

```
No write since last change (:quit! overrides)
```

To abandon the changes you've made to the file, quit by typing `:q!`. To save the changes, quit by typing `:wq` or any other equivalent form (**ZZ** or `:x`).

> **N O T E**   vi doesn't keep backup copies of files. After you enter `:wq`, the original file is modified and can't be restored to its original state. You must make your own backup copies of vi files.

▶ **See** "Performing Backups and Restoring Files," **p. 229** ■

CAUTION

Use the `:q!` command sparingly. When you enter `:q!`, all the changes you've made to the file are lost.

Rather than issue a `:q!` command, it's often safer to save the file to a different filename. That subject is covered later in the section "Saving as a New File."

Undoing a Command

In vi, you can "undo" your recent actions or changes to the buffer as long as you haven't saved that change to the disk file. You do this in command mode. Suppose that you've inadvertently deleted a line of text, changed something you shouldn't have, or added some text incorrectly. Press <Esc> to change to command mode and then press <u>. This returns things to the way they were before the buffer was changed with the undo command sequence.

The following is an example of using the undo command. Start vi again with the file vipract.1 (enter **vi vipract.1**). You see a display similar to the following:

```
Things to do today!
a. Practice vi.
b. Sort sales data and print the results.
~
~
~
"vipract.1" 3 lines, 78 characters
```

To add the phrase "for 60 minutes" between vi and the period on the second line, move to the second line by pressing <Return>. The cursor now appears under the first character of the second line. Now move the cursor to the period after vi by pressing the Spacebar until the cursor moves to that location. Insert the phrase "for 60 minutes" by pressing <i> to give the input command and then typing the characters of the phrase. Press <Esc> to return to command mode. Your screen now looks like this:

```
Things to do today!
a. Practice vi for 60 minutes.
b. Sort sales data and print the results.
~
~
~
```

Is 60 minutes a good idea? Maybe not. To undo the change to the second line, make sure that you're in command mode (press <Esc>) and then press <u>. The second line of the file now looks like this:

```
a. Practice vi.
```

Then again, maybe it was a good idea to practice for 60 minutes. Press <u> again (you're already in command mode), and you see the phrase "for 60 minutes" reappear. Will you or won't you practice for that long? You decide. Use the undo command to undo the change (and undo the undo) as many times as you want. Even if you decide to leave the buffer in its original form, *vi* assumes that the buffer has changed and you must exit with :q! (abandon changes) or :wq (save the changes).

If you decide to save the file with the changes, save it to another file by entering :w **vipract.2**.

 T I P You can use the <Backspace> key to correct mistakes you make while typing a single line. Unfortunately, as you backspace, you erase all the characters you go back over. The left-arrow key (< ← >) doesn't erase characters. The arrow keys are covered later in this chapter.

Writing Files and Saving the Buffer

You've seen how to write the buffer to a file and quit *vi*. Sometimes, however, you want to save the buffer to a file without quitting *vi*. You should save your file regularly during an editing session. If the system goes down because of a crash or a power failure, you may lose your work if you haven't saved it recently. To save the buffer, issue the :w (write) command from command mode.

N O T E Before you issue the write command, first press <Esc> to change to command mode if you aren't already there. If you're already in command mode, you hear a harmless beep. ■

There are some variations to the steps you follow to save a file. The form of the write command you use depends on the case, of which there are four distinct ones. The following sections describe these cases; Table 8.2 lists the variations of the write command.

Table 8.2   Commands to Save or Write a File

Command	Action
:w	Writes buffer to the file *vi* is editing
:w *filename*	Writes buffer to the named file
:w! *filename*	Forces *vi* to overwrite an existing file

Saving a New File   If you started *vi* without specifying a filename, you must provide a filename if you want to save the file to disk. The write command you issue in this case has the following format:

```
:w filename
```

This command writes the buffer to the file *filename*. If the command is successful, you see the name of the file and the number of lines and characters in the file. If you specify the name of an existing file, an appropriate message appears on the status line:

```
File exits - use "w! filename" to overwrite.
```

This condition is described in later in the section "Overwriting an Existing File."

Saving to the Current File   You may want to save the buffer to the file you're now editing. For example, if you started vi with an existing file, made some changes to the file, and want to save the changes to the original file, you can simply enter **:w**, a form of the write command.

 Save the changes you're making to a file regularly. Use the :w command frequently—at least every 15 minutes—during an edit session. You never know when the system might go down.

The :w command saves the buffer to the file you're now working with (your working file). The status line tells you the name of the file and the number of lines and characters written to the file.

Saving As a New File   You may want to save the buffer to a new file, giving it a different filename from the one you originally started with. For example, if you started vi with the file vipract.1, made some changes to the file, and want to save the changes to a new file without losing the original vipract.1 file, you can save the file as a new file. Type this form of the write command to save the file with a new filename:

```
:w filename2
```

This form of the write command is essentially the same as the original form described earlier in the section "Saving a New File." The buffer is written to the file named *filename2*. If the command is successful, you see the name of the file and the number of lines and characters in the file. If you specify the name of an existing file, an appropriate message appears on the status line:

```
File exists - use ! to overwrite.
```

The following section explains this scenario.

Overwriting an Existing File   If you try to save the buffer to an existing file different from the one you started with, you must explicitly tell vi that you want to overwrite or replace the existing file. If you specify an existing filename when you try to save the buffer, vi displays the following message:

```
File exists - use ! to overwrite.
```

If you really want to save the buffer over the existing file, use this form of the write command:

```
:w! existing_file
```

In this syntax, *existing_file* is the name of the file you want to replace. Be careful; after you overwrite a file, you can't restore it to its original form.

Positioning the Cursor

When you edit text, you need to position the cursor where you want to insert additional text, delete text, correct mistakes, change words, or append text to the end of existing text. The commands you enter in command mode to select the spot you want are called *cursor-positioning commands*.

The Arrow Keys   You can use the arrow keys on many, but not all, systems to position the cursor. It's easy to see whether the arrow keys work: Start vi with an existing file and see what effects the arrow keys have. You should also be able to use the <Page Up> and <Page Down> keys on the Linux keyboard, providing you have the correct terminal type indicated in your TERMCAP environment variable.

To create a new file called vipract.3 that contains a list of the files and directories in the directory usr, enter the following command:

```
ls /usr > vipract.3
```

You can use this file to experiment with cursor-positioning commands.

After the file is created, start vi with the vipract.3 file (enter **vi vipract.3**). Now try using the arrow keys and the <Page Up> and <Page Down> keys to move around the editing buffer.

It may be the case that, although it appears as though the cursor-positioning keys work, they're introducing strange characters into the file. To check whether the keys are entering characters instead of just moving the cursor, press <Esc> to make sure that you're in command mode and then enter **:q**. If vi allows you to quit and doesn't complain that the file was modified, everything is fine.

T I P   In vi, you can clear the screen of spurious or unusual characters by pressing <Ctrl-l>.

Other Cursor-Movement Keys   You can position the cursor in vi without using the arrow keys in other ways. You should become familiar with these methods in case you can't or don't want to use the arrow keys. This section also shows you some ways to position the cursor more efficiently than using the arrow keys.

When vi was developed, many terminals didn't have arrow keys. Other keys were and still are used to position the cursor. vi uses the <h>, <j>, <k>, and <l> keys to position the cursor, because they're in a convenient position for touch-typists. It takes a little practice to get comfortable with these keys, but some experienced vi users prefer these keys over the arrow keys.

The following are some other keys that move the cursor:

- Press the Spacebar or <l> to move the cursor one position to the right.
- Press <Return> or <+> to move to the beginning of the next line. (Note that using the <j> key to go down one line preserves your position in the line.)
- Press the minus sign (<->) to move to the beginning of the previous line. (Note that using the <k> key to go up one line preserves your position in the line.)

- Press <h> to move one character to the left.
- Press <0> (zero) to move to the beginning of a line.
- Press <$> (the dollar sign) to move to the end of a line.

Some *vi* commands allow you to position the cursor relative to words on a line. A *word* is defined as a sequence of characters separated from other characters by spaces or usual punctuation symbols such as these:

. ? , -

Those commands include the following:

Keystroke	Action
<w>	Moves forward one word
<b>	Moves to the beginning of the current word
<e>	Moves to the end of the current word

The following example demonstrates some of these actions. Start *vi* and open the vipract.1 file by entering **vi vipract.1**. Now use any of the cursor-positioning commands just described to move the cursor (indicated by an underscore) to the *t* in the word "data" on the third line of the file. The third line looks like this:

```
b. Sort sales data and print the results.
```

To move to the beginning of the next word, press <w>; the cursor is positioned under the *a* of the word "and." To move to the end of that word, press <e>; the cursor is positioned under the *d* in "and." To move to the beginning of that word, press <b>; the cursor is positioned under the *a* in "and" again.

You can move forward several words to the beginning of another word by pressing a number key before pressing <w>. For example, to move the cursor from its current position (under the *a* of the word "and") to the beginning of the word three words forward (under the *r* of the word "results"), press <3><w>. Likewise, you can move backward four words by pressing <4><b>; you can move forward to the end of the second word by pressing <2><e>.

You can also use this whole-number technique with the keys <h>, <j>, <k>, <l>, <+>, and <->. For example, press <1><5><j> to position the cursor down 15 lines. If 15 lines aren't left in the buffer, you hear a beep, and the cursor stays where it is.

Big-Movement Keys   You can quickly position the cursor to the top, middle, or bottom of the screen. In each case, the cursor appears at the beginning of the line. The following commands allow you to position the cursor on-screen:

- Press <Shift-h> to move to the first line of the screen. This is sometimes called the *home position*.
- Press <Shift-m> to move to the line in the middle of the lines now displayed.
- Press <Shift-l> to move to the last line on-screen.

If you want to move through a file one screen at a time (which is more efficient than pressing <Return> or <j> 23 times), use commands that scroll through a file. Pressing <Ctrl-f> moves you forward one screen. Pressing <Ctrl-b> moves you backward one screen.

To move quickly to the last line of the file or buffer, press <Shift-g>. To move to the first line of the file, press <1><Shift-g>. In fact, to move to a specific line in the buffer, type the line number before you press <Shift-g>. For example, to move to line 35 of the file (if there is a line 35), press <3><5><Shift-g>.

N O T E Take a little time to practice positioning the cursor by using the commands described in these last few sections. Remember that you must be in command mode for the cursor-positioning commands to work. Press <Esc> before you issue a cursor-positioning command. ■

Adding Text

To add text to the editing buffer, you must go from command mode to input mode. Any usual text characters you type are then added to the buffer. If you press <Return> while you're in input mode, *vi* "opens," or adds, a line to the buffer. Before you start adding text, first position the cursor at the location you want to add text. Press <a> to go to input mode and append text after the cursor position. Press <i> to go to input mode and insert text in front of the cursor position. When you're done adding text, press <Esc> to return to command mode.

The following are two examples of typing in input mode. The position of the cursor is represented by an underscore character. For each case, a before-and-after view is shown.

- Example showing the use of <i> (the insert command) to add text.

  Before:

  ```
  This report is important.
  ```

  Press <i> to insert text in front of the word "important," type **very**, press the <Spacebar>, and press <Esc>.

  After:

  ```
  This report is very_important.
  ```

  Note that the cursor is positioned under the last character you added (in this case, the space).

- Example showing the use of <a> (the append command) to add text.

  Before:

  ```
  This report is important.
  ```

  Press <a> to append text after the word "is," press the <Spacebar>, type **very**, and press <Esc>.

  After:

  ```
  This report is very important.
  ```

  Note again that the cursor is positioned under the last character you added (in this case, the *y* in "very").

When you want to append text at the end of a line, you can position the cursor at the end of a line and press <a>. You can also position the cursor anywhere in the line and press <Shift-a> to position the cursor at the end of the line, put you in input mode, and allow you to append text—all with one command. Likewise, you can move to the beginning of the current line and insert text at the beginning of a line by pressing <Shift-i>.

To add a line of text below or above the current line, you press <o> or <Shift-o>, respectively. Each keystroke "opens" a line in the buffer and allows you to add text. In the following two examples, you add a line to some existing text.

■ Example showing the use of <o> to insert lines below the current line.

Before:

```
All jobs complete
please call
if you have any questions.
```

The cursor is on the second line. Press <o> to add a line or lines below that line. Now type the following lines:

```
Jack Tackett, Jr.
555-1837
```

Press <Esc>.

After:

```
All jobs complete
please call
Jack Tackett, Jr.
555-1837
if you have any questions.
```

■ Example showing the use of <Shift-o> to insert lines above the current line

Before:

```
All jobs complete
please call
if you have any questions.
```

The cursor is on the third line. Press <Shift-o> to add a line or lines above that line. Now type the following lines:

```
Jack Tackett, Jr.
555-1837
```

Press <Esc>.

After:

```
All jobs complete
please call
Jack Tackett, Jr.
555-1837
if you have any questions.
```

In both cases, when you press <Esc>, the cursor is positioned under the last character you typed (the *7* in the phone number). Although you added only two lines, you could have added more lines by pressing <Return> at the end of each line. Naturally, you could have added only one line by not pressing <Return> at all.

Table 8.3 summarizes the commands for adding text. Press <Esc> to make sure that you're in command mode before using these commands.

Table 8.3   Commands for Adding Text

Keystroke	Action
<a>	Appends text after the cursor position
<Shift-a>	Puts you in input mode and appends text to the end of the current line
<i>	Inserts text in front of the cursor position
<Shift-i>	Puts you in input mode and inserts text at the beginning of the current line
<o>	Opens a line below the current line to add text
<Shift-o>	Opens a line above the current line to add text

Deleting Text

Making corrections or changes to a file may involve deleting text. You must be in command mode to delete characters. If you're in input mode when you type the delete-character commands, the letters of the commands appear as characters in the buffer file. If that should happen, press <Esc> to go to command mode and press <u> to undo the mistake.

With vi, you can delete a character, a word, a number of consecutive words, all the text to the end of a line, or an entire line. Because vi is a visual editor, the characters, words, or lines are removed from the screen as you delete them. Table 8.4 describes the delete commands.

Table 8.4   Commands for Deleting Text

Keystroke	Action
<x>	Deletes character at the cursor position
<d><w>	Deletes from the cursor position in the current word to the beginning of the next word
<d><$>	Deletes from the cursor position to the end of the line
<Shift-d>	Same as <d><$>: deletes the remainder of the current line
<d><d>	Deletes the entire current line, regardless of cursor position in the line

All these commands take effect from the current cursor position. Move the cursor to the character, word, or line you want to change, and then issue the desired delete command. Practice using them to see their effect. You'll find they're helpful in making corrections to files.

These commands can be applied to several objects—characters, words, or lines—by typing a whole number before the command. (This whole-number technique was introduced earlier in this chapter in the section on positioning the cursor.) Some examples are as follows:

- Press <4><x> to delete four characters.
- Press <3><d><w> to delete three words.
- Press <8><d><d> to delete eight lines.

 To have vi display line numbers, press <Esc> to make sure that you're in command mode, and then enter **:se number**. To turn off the line numbers, enter **:se nonumber**.

You can also specify a range of lines to delete. To do that, press the colon (<Shift-;>), type the two line numbers you want to delete (inclusive) separated by a comma, press <d>, and press <Return>. For example, to delete lines 12 through 36 (inclusive), type **:12,36d** and press <Return>.

When you delete two or more lines, the status line states how many lines were deleted. Remember that you can press <u> to undo the deletion.

Searching

Finding a word, phrase, or number in a file can be difficult if you have to read through each line yourself. Like most editors and word processors, vi has a command that allows you to search for a string of characters. You can search forward or backward from your current position in the buffer. You also can continue searching. vi starts searching from the beginning of the buffer file when it reaches the end, and vice versa. Table 8.5 summarizes the commands for searching. In each case, vi searches for the string you specify in the direction you specify and then positions the cursor at the beginning of the string.

Table 8.5   The Search Commands

Command	Action
/*string*	Searches forward through the buffer for *string*
?*string*	Searches backward through the buffer for *string*
<n>	Searches again in the current direction
<Shift-n>	Searches again in the opposite direction

When you type the search command, it appears on the status line. To search forward for the string sales > 100K in a file, for example, first you would make sure you're in command mode, and then you would enter the following:

/sales > 100K

The typed command appears on the status line. If the string is in the buffer, vi positions the cursor under the first *s* in the word "sales." If the string isn't in the buffer, vi displays the message `Pattern not found` on the status line. To search for another occurrence of the string, press <n>; `vi` positions the cursor under the next occurrence of the string or, if there's no "next occurrence," the cursor doesn't move.

TROUBLESHOOTING

I typed a string I know exists in the file, but `vi` can't find it. The most common cause for this error is that you typed the string incorrectly. `vi` (and computers in general) doesn't do a good job of thinking; `vi` has a terrible time figuring out what you really mean when you type something. If you're looking for the string "vegi-burger" but you type "vigi-burger," `vi` can't find what you want (unless you happened to misspell "vegi-burger" in the buffer, and it matches the search string). Check the search string carefully before you press <Return>.

I searched for a phrase that incorporates a punctuation mark, and `vi` returned some odd results. Searching in `vi` may not give you the results you want if you're looking for characters that are "special" to `vi`. For example, if you want to find a word you know is located at the end of a sentence (for example, the string "*end.*"), you must "escape" the period; to `vi`, the period means "any character," not "end of sentence." If you enter /**end.** and press <Return>, `vi` would locate such things as the word "ending," the word "end" followed by a space, and the word "end" followed by a period. To find only "end" followed by a period, you would enter /**end\.**.

Searching in `vi` is also case-sensitive. If you're looking for the word "Tiger" in your buffer, you must enter /**Tiger**, not /`tiger`.

Changing and Replacing Text

Another often-faced editing task is changing text or replacing one text string with another (there isn't too much difference between the two operations). The change commands in `vi` allow you to change a word or the remainder of a line. In effect, you're replacing one word or the remainder of a line with another. You use the replace commands to replace or change a single character or sequence of characters. Table 8.6 summarizes the change and replace commands. After you enter the command, simply type the new material as appropriate.

Table 8.6   The Change and Replace Commands

Keystroke	Action
<r>	Replaces a single character
<Shift-r>	Replaces a sequence of characters
<c><w>	Changes the current word, from the cursor position to the end of the word
<c><e>	Changes the current word, from the cursor position to the end of the word (same as <c><w>)
<c><b>	Changes the current word, from the beginning of the word to the character before the cursor position

continues

Table 8.6 Continued

Keystroke	Action
<c><$>	Changes a line, from the cursor position to the end of the line
<Shift-c>	Changes a line, from the cursor position to the end of the line (same as <c><$>)
<c><c>	Changes the entire line

The changes take place relative to the position of the cursor. You must be in command mode before you can use these commands. Position the cursor at the location in the buffer file you want to correct and press <Esc> before using these commands. Because vi is visual, the changes are made to the buffer as you execute the commands.

Each of these commands puts you into input mode. Except for when you use <r> to replace a single character, you must press <Esc> to finish making changes and return to command mode.

TIP To change several words, use a whole number (representing the number of words to change) before pressing <c><w>.

Here are three examples of how to use the change and replace commands, with a before-and-after scenario for each.

■ Example showing the use of <c><e> to change to the end of the word.

Before:

```
The report demonstraits thw,strengths of are apporach.
```

The cursor is located at the point in the incorrectly spelled word where corrections are to begin. To change the spelling, press <c><e>, type **tes**, and press Esc.

After:

```
The report demonstrates thw,strengths of are apporach.
```

■ Example showing the use of <Shift-r> to replace a sequence of characters.

Before:

```
The report demonstrates thw,strengths of are apporach.
```

The cursor is located at the point in the incorrectly spelled word where you want to start replacing characters. To change "thw," to "the" and a space, press <Shift-r>, type **e**, press the <Spacebar>, and press <Esc>.

After:

```
The report demonstrates the_strengths of are apporach.
```

- Example showing the use of <c><w> to change text, beginning with the current word and continuing for two words.

  Before:

  ```
  The report demonstrates the strengths of are apporach.
  ```

  The cursor is positioned under the letter of the word where you want to begin making changes. To fix the last two words on the line, press <2><c><w>, type **our approach**, and press <Esc>.

  After:

  ```
  The report demonstrates the strengths of our approach.
  ```

Remember to press <Esc> after you make changes to the lines and return to command mode.

Copying, Cutting, and Pasting

When you delete or cut characters, words, lines, or a portion of a line, the deleted object is saved in what's called the *general-purpose buffer*. The name isn't too important; what's important is that you can put or paste the contents of that buffer anywhere in the text you're editing. You do that with the <p> or <Shift-p> command. The <p> command pastes the object to the right of or after the cursor position; the <Shift-p> command pastes the object to the left of or before the cursor.

Here are some examples of cutting and pasting text, with a before-and-after scenario for each.

- Example showing the use of <p> to paste the contents of the general-purpose buffer after the cursor.

  Before:

  ```
  Carefully carry these out instructions.
  ```

  Delete the characters "out" and a space by pressing <d><w>. Now move the cursor to the space after the *y* in "carry" and press <p>.

  After:

  ```
  Carefully carry out these instructions.
  ```

- Example showing the use of <Shift-p> to paste the contents of the general-purpose buffer in front of the cursor.

  Before:

  ```
  Carefully carry these out instructions.
  ```

  Delete the characters "these" and a space by pressing <d><w>. Now move the cursor to the first *i* in "instructions" and press <Shift-p>.

  After:

  ```
  Carefully carry out these instructions.
  ```

 TIP To change the order of two characters, position the cursor under the first character and press <x><p>.
Try it to change the word "tow" to the word "two," for example.

The preceding examples showed you how to paste after deleting text. But you don't have to delete before you can paste. You can use an operation called *yank*, which is the same as the copy operation in some word processors. The forms of the yank command are similar to the forms of the delete command. The idea is that you yank, or copy, a portion of text and then paste it somewhere else by pressing <p> or <Shift-p>. The list names some of the yank commands (notice that most of the yank commands use the lowercase letter *y*):

Keystroke	Action
<y><w>	Yanks from the cursor position in the current word to the beginning of the next word
<y><$>	Yanks from the cursor position to the end of the line
<Shift-y>	Same as <y><$>: yanks the remainder of current line
<y><y>	Yanks the entire current line

All these commands can be applied to several objects—characters, words, or lines—by typing a whole number before the command.

To copy a sequence of four lines to another portion of the text, follow these steps:

1. Position the cursor at the beginning of the first of the four lines.
2. Press <4><y><y> to yank from the cursor to the end of the line four times. The buffer (what you see on-screen) is unchanged.
3. Position the cursor elsewhere in the text.
4. Press <p> to paste the yanked lines below the line holding the cursor.

You can also search and replace words throughout the file or within a specified range of lines. The format of the command is as follows:

`:[range]s/oldstring/newstring/g`

where

range	Indicates the range on which to operate; for example, you can use the percent symbol (%) to operate on the entire file, or you can use specific line numbers (such as 1,4) to operate on specific lines (in this case, lines 1 through 4)
s	Indicates this is a search and replace operation
oldstring	The string to search for in the file and replace with *newstring*
newstring	The string to insert; *newstring* replaces *oldstring*

For example, to replace the incorrectly spelled word "recieved" with the correct spelling throughout an entire file, you can use the following command:

`:%s/recieved/received/g`

Repeating Commands

Not only does vi keep the text just deleted or yanked for future use, it also stores the last command you used for future use. You can repeat the last command that changed the buffer by pressing <.>.

Suppose that you've completed a report but think it would be a good idea to put two lines containing this text at key points in the report:

```
*************** Please comment ******
*************** On this section ******
```

To do so, follow these steps:

1. Position the cursor in the buffer file where you want to place these lines the first time.
2. Insert the lines by pressing <o> to open a line and typing the two lines of asterisks and text.
3. Press <Esc> to make sure that you're in command mode.
4. As often as necessary, position the cursor to another section of the report and press <.> to insert these same two lines again and again.

vi Command Summary

You now have a basic understanding of using vi for text processing. Table 8.7 provides a summary of the keystrokes and commands you can use in vi.

Table 8.7   *vi* Command Summary

Keystroke/Command	Description
<i>	Inserts text before cursor
<I>	Enters text at start of line
<a>	Inserts text after cursor
<A>	Enters text at end of line
<o>	Opens a new line below cursor
<O>	Opens a new line above cursor
<d><w>	Deletes word
<d><d>	Deletes entire line
<D>	Deletes to end of line
<x>	Deletes character under cursor
<c><w>	Changes word
<c><c>	Changes line

continues

Table 8.7   Continued

Keystroke/Command	Description
\<C\>	Changes to end of line
\<R\>	Replaces character under cursor
\<J\>	Joins lines together
\<e\>	Moves to end of word
\<w\>	Moves to next word
\<$\>	Moves to end of line
\<l\>	Moves one space right
\<k\>	Moves one line up
\<j\>	Moves one line down
\<h\>	Moves one space left
\<f\>\<x\>	Moves cursor to first occurrence of x
\<F\>\<x\>	Moves cursor to last occurrence of x
\<;\>	Repeats the last f/F command
number\<|\>	Moves cursor to specified column *number*
\<H\>	Moves cursor to top line on-screen (not top line of file)
\<L\>	Moves cursor to bottom line on-screen
\<M\>	Moves cursor to middle line on-screen
\<G\>	Moves cursor to bottom line of file
number\<G\>	Moves cursor to specified line *number* (same as \<ESC\>:*number*)
\<^\>	Moves to beginning of line
\<m\>*x*	Marks current position with letter *x*
\<Ctrl-d\>	Scrolls forward one half of the screen
\<Ctrl-u\>	Scrolls backward one half of the screen
\<Ctrl-f\>	Scrolls forward one screen
\<Ctrl-b\>	Scrolls backward one screen
\<Ctrl-l\>	Redraws the screen
\<Ctrl-G\>	Shows the filename, current line, and column number
\<z\>\<z\>	Redraws the screen with current line in middle of screen
\<y\>\<y\>	Yanks entire line into buffer

Keystroke/Command	Description
<p>	Puts contents of buffer below cursor
<P>	Puts contents of buffer above cursor
x"[*number*]"<y><y>	Yanks the indicated number of lines into the buffer named *x* (*x* can be any single character a–z)
x<p>	Places the contents of buffer *x* after the cursor
:w [*file*]	Writes contents to disk as *file*
:q	Quits vi
:q!	Quits file without saving changes
:wq	Saves changes and quits vi
:r *file*	Reads specified *file* into editor
:e *file*	Edits *file*
:!*command*	Executes specified shell *command*
:*number*	Moves to specified line number
:f	Prints out current line and filename (same as <Ctrl-G>)
/*string*	Searches forward for *string*
?*string*	Searches backward for *string*
:*x*,*y*s/*oldstring*/*newstring*	Replaces *oldstring* with *newstring* from line *x* to line *y* (entering y = $ will replace to end of file)
<ESC><u>	Undoes last command
<n>	Finds next occurrence of string
.	Repeats last command
~	Changes character to opposite case
<ESC>	Switches to command mode

Setting the *vi* Environment

The vi editor has several options you may or may not choose to use. Some of these options can be set on a system-wide basis by the system administrator. You can customize your environment with a number of options that are in effect whenever you start vi. Table 8.8 summarizes all the environment options you can set for vi. When setting environment options (as described in the next section), you can use the abbreviation shown in the first column of the table or the full name used in the second column.

Table 8.8   Environment Options for *vi*

Abbreviated Option	Full Name and Function of Option
ai	autoindent indents each line to the same level as the line above (useful for writing programs). The default is autoindent off.
ap	autoprint prints the current line to the screen when the line is changed. The default is autoprint on.
eb	errorbells causes the computer to beep when you introduce a command error. The default is errorbells off.
nu	number displays line numbers when editing a file. The default is number off.
redraw	redraw keeps the screen up-to-date as changes occur. The default is redraw on.
report	report sets the size of an editing change that results in a message on the status line. For example, report=3 triggers a message when you delete three lines but not when fewer than three lines are deleted. The default is report=5.
sm	showmatch shows a matching open parenthesis when the closing parenthesis is entered. This option is useful mainly for programmers writing program code. The default is showmatch off.
smd	showmode displays INPUT, REPLACE, or CHANGE on the right side of the status line when the associated command is given. The default is showmode off.
warn	warn displays a warning message when an attempt is made to exit vi if the buffer has been changed and not saved to the disk file. The default is warn on.
wm=*n*	wrapmargin defines the right margin. In the syntax of this command, *n* is a whole number. If *n* is greater than 0, the command forces a carriage return so that no word is *n* or less characters from the right margin. For example, wm=5 tells vi to wrap the line when a character occurs within five characters of the end of the line. Turn this option off by specifying wm=0, which is the default.
ws	word search (called wrapscan on some systems) wraps from the <eof> (end-of-file) character to the <bof> (beginning-of-file) character during a search. Default is word search on.

Using *set* to See and Set Options

To see the options now set for your system, enter `:set` while in command mode in `vi`. The options now set for this session of `vi` are displayed on the status line. The options displayed with the `set` command vary depending on the default options and on your particular implementation of `vi`. Here is an example of what you might see when you issue the `set` command:

```
autoprint errorbells redraw report=1 showmatch showmode term=vt100 wrap margin=5
```

> **N O T E** Issuing the `set` command with no arguments results in a display of only the user-set options. You can abbreviate the `set` command as `se`. To set a number of options on the same line, use the `se` command and separate the options with a space, as in the following example:
>
> `:se ap eb redraw report=1 sm smd warn wm=5 ws`
>
> Notice that the first character is the colon character, which indicates to `vi` that a command is to be entered. ■

To see the list of all possible options and their settings, enter `:set all`. The options and their settings listed in Table 8.7 are displayed.

Setting the *showmode* Option

One of the most used options is `showmode`. To learn about the `showmode` option, start `vi` again with the vipract.1 file (enter `vi vipract.1`).

When `vi` executes, you see the text from your first `vi` session on-screen. In your first session, you may have noticed that there was no way to determine whether you were in input mode when you entered the text for this file. You can tell `vi` to inform you when you're in input mode by using the `showmode` option. The `showmode` option identifies the mode you're in on the status line.

When you set the `showmode` option, `vi` displays whatever type of input mode it's in: regular INPUT MODE, APPEND MODE, REPLACE 1 CHAR mode, and so on. To set `showmode` in `vi`, press <Esc> to make sure that you're in command mode and then enter `:set showmode`. Now go to input mode (press <i>). You should see the message INPUT MODE on the status line. Press <Esc> to return to command mode. You may want to see what happens when you give the commands to replace or change text.

Setting Toggle Options

Any option that doesn't take a number argument is like a toggle switch: You can turn it on or off. For example, as you learned in the preceding section, you set the `showmode` option by entering this command:

`:se showmode`

To turn the `showmode` option off, you simply add `no` in front of the option like this:

`:se noshowmode`

Changing Options for Every *vi* Session

Setting an option during a `vi` session sets that option for the current session only. You can customize your `vi` sessions by putting the `set` commands in a file named .exrc in your home directory. To see whether such a file exists, type the following commands:

```
cd
vi .exrc
```

The first command takes you to your home directory. The second starts `vi` by using the .exrc file. If the file exists, it appears on the `vi` screen. If the file doesn't exist, `vi` lets you know it's a new file.

The `set` commands in the .exrc file start with the word `set` but no colon. For example, the following line sets the options `number` and `showmode`:

```
set number showmode
```

> **N O T E** The .exrc file is read when you start `vi`. If you create it while you're in `vi`, you must restart `vi` to put the settings into effect. ■

The options you set and the values you give to some options depend on your preferences and the type of editing you'll be doing. Experiment with some options or talk with more experienced users.

From Here...

Although this chapter can't discuss all the options or features of `vi`, you know where to start and how to use the basic features of `vi`. `vi` is a very important editor for you to learn because it's available on every Linux/UNIX box. The editor is also quick to load and doesn't require many system resources, so you can use it when other editors may not be able to load. System administrators use `vi` for many quick-and-dirty editing tasks. For more information, see the following chapters:

- Chapter 11, "Backing Up Data," discusses how to protect your text files from accidental erasure. This chapter shows you how to back up those important files you create with `vi`.

- Chapter 16, "Understanding the File and Directory System," shows you how to deal with files and how those files are treated under Linux. You should have a basic understanding of the file system when using `vi` or any other editor.

- Chapter 20, "Printing," shows you how to print your text files after you create them with `vi`.

- Chapter 28, "Using the `emacs` Editor," discusses one of the other editors available with Linux. `emacs` provides many enhancements over `vi`. `emacs` also provides you with an environment from which you can do many tasks you would normally do with other programs, such as read mail and read news.

## CHAPTER 9

Booting and Shutting Down

by Jack Tackett

In this chapter

Two of the most common tasks that you encounter when administering a Linux system are booting the system and shutting it down. As you might have guessed, booting and shutting down Linux are operations that require special consideration.

To use Linux, you must boot the operating system. Although this sounds pretty straightforward, you need to consider that most people run at least one additional operating system on their PCs other than Linux. This means that you must have some way to specify which operating system you want to boot when you start the system. You can do this in two basic ways: You can boot Linux from a floppy, or you can boot from your hard drive by using a boot manager.

Understanding the Boot Process

Red Hat and most modern distributions of Linux use the SysV `init` boot process instead of the older BSD style `init`. `init` is the first program the kernel executes at startup and, hence, is given the process id (or PID) of 1. This becomes the parent process for all other processes running in the Linux system.

NOTE   The PID of a process is a number the operating system uses to identify that process. Many Linux commands use this PID number as a qualifying parameter. ▪

Linux follows these steps to boot:

1. The kernel runs the `init` program, which is located in the /sbin directory.
2. `init` runs the shell script /etc/rc.d/rc.sysinit.
3. rc.sysinit sets various system variables and performs other startup initializations.
4. `init` runs all the scripts specified for the default run level.
5. `init` runs the script /etc/rc.d/rc.local.

▶ **See** "Understanding Processes," **p. 349**

This program starts various processes and writes information to the console and to the system log file /var/log/messages about the status of each process that's started. Listing 9.1 shows a typical startup sequence.

TIP   The /var/log/message log file is an excellent aid for debugging startup problems. The kernel stores all error messages here, so you don't have to worry about writing down the messages as they scroll by during startup.

Listing 9.1   Typical Log Entries for Bootup

```
May 22 23:23:42 ns syslogd 1.3-3: restart.
May 22 23:23:43 ns kernel: klogd 1.3-3, log source = /proc/kmsg started.
May 22 23:23:45 ns kernel: Loaded 4189 symbols from /boot/System.map.
May 22 23:23:45 ns kernel: Symbols match kernel version 2.0.31.
May 22 23:23:45 ns kernel: Loaded 2 symbols from 3 modules.
May 22 23:23:45 ns kernel: Console: 16 point font, 400 scans
```

May 22 23:23:45 ns kernel: Console: colour VGA+ 80x25, 1 virtual console
➥(max 63)
May 22 23:23:45 ns kernel: pci_init: no BIOS32 detected
May 22 23:23:45 ns kernel: Calibrating delay loop.. ok - 49.97 BogoMIPS
May 22 23:23:45 ns kernel: Memory: 30816k/32768k available (736k kernel code,
➥384k reserved, 832k data)
May 22 23:23:45 ns kernel: This processor honours the WP bit even when in
supervisor mode. Good.
May 22 23:23:45 ns kernel: Swansea University Computer Society NET3.035 for
➥Linux 2.0
May 22 23:23:45 ns kernel: NET3: Unix domain sockets 0.13 for Linux NET3.035.
May 22 23:23:45 ns kernel: Swansea University Computer Society TCP/IP for
➥NET3.034
May 22 23:23:45 ns kernel: IP Protocols: IGMP, ICMP, UDP, TCP
May 22 23:23:45 ns kernel: VFS: Diskquotas version dquot_5.6.0 initialized
May 22 23:23:45 ns kernel:
May 22 23:23:45 ns kernel: Checking 386/387 coupling... Ok, fpu using
➥exception 16 error reporting.
May 22 23:23:45 ns kernel: Checking 'hlt' instruction... Ok.
May 22 23:23:45 ns kernel: Linux version 2.0.31 (root@porky.redhat.com)
➥(gcc version 2.7.2.3) #1 Sun Nov 9 21:45:23 EST 1997
May 22 23:23:45 ns kernel: Starting kswapd v 1.4.2.2
May 22 23:23:45 ns kernel: Serial driver version 4.13 with no serial options
➥enabled
May 22 23:23:45 ns kernel: tty00 at 0x03f8 (irq = 4) is a 16550A
May 22 23:23:45 ns kernel: tty01 at 0x02f8 (irq = 3) is a 16550A
May 22 23:23:45 ns kernel: Real Time Clock Driver v1.07
May 22 23:23:45 ns kernel: Ramdisk driver initialized : 16 ramdisks of
➥4096K size
May 22 23:23:45 ns kernel: hda: Micropolis 2217A, 1551MB w/508kB Cache,
➥CHS=3152/16/63
May 22 23:23:45 ns kernel: hdb: Maxtor 72700 AP, 2583MB w/128kB Cache,
➥CHS=20746/15/17
May 22 23:23:45 ns kernel: ide0 at 0x1f0-0x1f7,0x3f6 on irq 14
May 22 23:23:45 ns kernel: Floppy drive(s): fd0 is 1.44M
May 22 23:23:45 ns kernel: FDC 0 is an 8272A
May 22 23:23:45 ns kernel: md driver 0.35 MAX_MD_DEV=4, MAX_REAL=8
May 22 23:23:45 ns kernel: scsi : 0 hosts.
May 22 23:23:45 ns kernel: scsi : detected total.
May 22 23:23:45 ns kernel: Partition check:
May 22 23:23:45 ns kernel: hda: hda1
May 22 23:23:45 ns kernel: hdb: hdb1 hdb2
May 22 23:23:45 ns kernel: VFS: Mounted root (ext2 filesystem) readonly.
May 22 23:23:45 ns kernel: Adding Swap: 3300k swap-space (priority -1)
May 22 23:23:45 ns kernel: sysctl: ip forwarding off
May 22 23:23:45 ns kernel: Swansea University Computer Society IPX 0.34
➥for NET3.035
May 22 23:23:45 ns kernel: IPX Portions Copyright 1995 Caldera, Inc.
May 22 23:23:45 ns kernel: Appletalk 0.17 for Linux NET3.035
May 22 23:23:45 ns kernel: eth0: 3c509 at 0x300 tag 1, 10baseT port,
➥address 00 60 97 13 30 e1, IRQ 10.
May 22 23:23:45 ns kernel: 3c509.c:1.12 6/4/97 becker@cesdis.gsfc.nasa.gov
May 22 23:23:45 ns kernel: eth0: Setting Rx mode to 1 addresses.
May 22 23:23:50 ns named[243]: starting. named 4.9.6-REL Thu Nov 6 23:29:57
➥EST 1997
^Iroot@porky.redhat.com:/usr/src/bs/BUILD/bind-4.9.6/named

init starts all the processes required by the OS to perform its duties, such as allowing network operations, use of the mouse, and basic functions like I/O to the terminal. The SysV init program knows which processes to start by reading config files located in /etc/rd.d. These files are further segregated according to run levels, specified by directories.

A run level specifies what types of services are available, from single-user mode (run level 1) to full multiuser, multitasking, all-processes-running mode (run level 3). Table 9.1 outlines the various run levels available in Linux.

Table 9.1   Linux Run Levels

Run Level	Description
0	halt
1	single-user mode
2	multiuser, no NFS
3	full multiuser mode
4	unused
5	X11
6	reboot

The init program uses the following directory structure:

    init.d
    rc0.d
    rc1.d
    rc2.d
    rc3.d
    rc4.d
    rc5.d
    rc6.d

The various numbers in the directory names correspond to the run levels in Table 9.1. Each directory contains various shell scripts that start or stop the necessary services required in each run level. These scripts also initialize the file system and lock files to a known state.

▶ **See** "Working with Shell Scripts," **p. 365**

Each directory contains various shell scripts. Each script's filename begins with either an S or a K (for Start or Kill) and a two-digit number. The numbers are used to order the sequence and have no other meaning.

Each script usually accepts either a start or stop command line argument, although it can accept other parameters. init supplies only either a start or stop to the script, depending on whether rc has been called to change run levels. You can also execute the scripts by hand if you need to reconfigure a service; for example, you can use sendmail with the following command (you must be logged in as root in order to execute the init scripts):

```
/etc/rc.d/init.d/sendmail stop
/etc/rc.d/init.d/sendmail stop
/etc/rc.d/init.d/sendmail start
```

You should notice two things about this command. First, the command was repeated twice with the stop parameter. This ensures that the system has time to stop the process. Then the start command is called. Next you notice we executed the script from the init.d directory, and not from the directory for the run level. Also, the script does not have a letter (S or K) or a number. If you list the files in any run level directory, you will note that they are actually linked to files in the init.d directory, as you can see in Listing 9.2. Following the listing, Table 9.2 outlines a few crucial startup scripts in this directory.

Listing 9.2   Directory Listing of a Typical rc3.d Directory

```
lrwxrwxrwx  1 root    root    16 Jan 25 21:56 K08autofs -> ../init.d/autofs
lrwxrwxrwx  1 root    root    18 Dec 14 12:17 K10pnserver -> ../init.d/pnserver
lrwxrwxrwx  1 root    root    17 Dec 14 12:17 K20rusersd -> ../init.d/rusersd
lrwxrwxrwx  1 root    root    15 Dec 14 12:17 K20rwhod -> ../init.d/rwhod
lrwxrwxrwx  1 root    root    15 Dec 14 12:17 S15nfsfs -> ../init.d/nfsfs
lrwxrwxrwx  1 root    root    16 Dec 14 12:17 S20random -> ../init.d/random
lrwxrwxrwx  1 root    root    16 Dec 14 12:17 S30syslog -> ../init.d/syslog
lrwxrwxrwx  1 root    root    13 Dec 14 12:17 S40atd -> ../init.d/atd
lrwxrwxrwx  1 root    root    15 Dec 14 12:17 S40crond -> ../init.d/crond
lrwxrwxrwx  1 root    root    14 Dec 14 12:17 S50inet -> ../init.d/inet
lrwxrwxrwx  1 root    root    15 Dec 14 12:17 S55named -> ../init.d/named
lrwxrwxrwx  1 root    root    13 Dec 14 12:17 S60lpd -> ../init.d/lpd
lrwxrwxrwx  1 root    root    13 Jan 31 20:17 S72amd -> ../init.d/amd
lrwxrwxrwx  1 root    root    18 Dec 14 12:17 S75keytable -> ../init.d/keytable
lrwxrwxrwx  1 root    root    18 Dec 14 12:17 S80sendmail -> ../init.d/sendmail
```

Table 9.2   rc.3 init Scripts

Script Name	Daemon	Description
S15nfsfs	nfs	Handles Network File Services (NFS)
S30syslog	syslog	Allows logging of system messages in /var/log/messages
S40atd	atd	Allows user to perform a task at an indicated time
S40crond	cron	Batch scheduler for Linux
S50inet	inetd	The super server (PID 1)
S55named	Name server	Provides DNS name services
S60lpd	lpd	Line printer daemon to allow printing

`init` loops through the files in the specified run level directory and passes either the `start` or `stop` parameter as indicated by the first character of the filename.

▶ **See** "Links," **p. 308**

The rc.d directory also contains three files called rc, rc.local, and rc.sysinit. The `rc` shell script is responsible for restarting the system in a different run level. That script takes one parameter, which is a number corresponding to the new run level. The rc.local file is executed after all the other scripts are executed during startup. You can place any local initialization instructions in this file. The rc.local file (the contents of which are shown in Listing 9.3) provides an example of starting a local process, called *secure shell*, which allows secure remote access to the system.

Listing 9.3   A Sample rc.local Shell Script

```
#!/bin/sh
# This script will be executed *after* all the other init scripts.
# You can put your own initialization stuff in here if you don't
# want to do the full Sys V style init stuff.

if [ -f /etc/redhat-release ]; then
        R=$(cat /etc/redhat-release)
else
        R="release 3.0.3"
if
arch=$(uname -m)
a="a"
case "_$arch" in
        _a*) a="an";;
        _i*) a="an";;
esac
# This will overwrite /etc/issue at every boot.  So, make any changes you
# want to make to /etc/issue here or you will lose them when you reboot.
echo "" > /etc/issue
echo "Red Hat Linux $R" >> /etc/issue
echo "Kernel $(uname -r) on $a $(uname -m)" >> /etc/issue
cp -f /etc/issue /etc/issue.net
echo >> /etc/issue
## Start sshd
##  Added By Lance Brown 1/29/1998
/usr/local/sbin/sshd
```

The rc.sysinit file is the first file `init` runs at startup. This script performs various functions, such as setting system wide variables (like the hostname), checking the file system and starting repairs, turning on user quotas, and mounting the /proc file system. The script in Listing 9.3 also starts a local process called sshd, which is the secure shell deamon that provides secure Telnet and remote commands to Linux.

N O T E ssh is not part of the standard Red Hat distribution because of export restrictions on munitions (the United States government has classified encryption utilities in the same category as nuclear weapons). You can install the utility yourself, though. Just check out the following Web site for more information: **http://www.cs.hut.fi/ssh/**. ▪

The default run level is decided in /etc/inittab with the following command:

```
id:3:initdefault:
```

This command tells the system to start in run level 3 (full multiuser and multitasking). Listing 9.4 shows a sample /etc/inittab file.

Listing 9.4   A Sample /etc/inittab File

```
# inittab       This file describes how the INIT process should set up
#               the system in a certain run-level.
#
# Author:       Miquel van Smoorenburg, <miquels@drinkel.nl.mugnet.org>
#               Modified for RHS Linux by Marc Ewing and Donnie Barnes
#

# Default run level. The run levels used by RHS are:
#   0 - halt (Do NOT set initdefault to this)
#   1 - Single user mode
#   2 - Multiuser, without NFS (The same as 3, if you do not have networking)
#   3 - Full multiuser mode
#   4 - unused
#   5 - X11
#   6 - reboot (Do NOT set initdefault to this)
#
id:3:initdefault:

# System initialization.
si::sysinit:/etc/rc.d/rc.sysinit

l0:0:wait:/etc/rc.d/rc 0
l1:1:wait:/etc/rc.d/rc 1
l2:2:wait:/etc/rc.d/rc 2
l3:3:wait:/etc/rc.d/rc 3
l4:4:wait:/etc/rc.d/rc 4
l5:5:wait:/etc/rc.d/rc 5
l6:6:wait:/etc/rc.d/rc 6

# Things to run in every run level.
ud::once:/sbin/update

# Trap CTRL-ALT-DELETE
ca::ctrlaltdel:/sbin/shutdown -t3 -r now

# When our UPS tells us power has failed, assume we have a few minutes
# of power left.  Schedule a shutdown for 2 minutes from now.
# This does, of course, assume you have powerd installed and your
# UPS connected and working correctly.
pf::powerfail:/sbin/shutdown -f -h +2 "Power Failure; System Shutting Down"
```

continues

Listing 9.4 Continued

```
# If power was restored before the shutdown kicked in, cancel it.
pr:12345:powerokwait:/sbin/shutdown -c "Power Restored; Shutdown Cancelled"


# Run gettys in standard run levels
1:12345:respawn:/sbin/mingetty tty1
2:2345:respawn:/sbin/mingetty tty2
3:2345:respawn:/sbin/mingetty tty3
4:2345:respawn:/sbin/mingetty tty4
5:2345:respawn:/sbin/mingetty tty5
6:2345:respawn:/sbin/mingetty tty6

# Run xdm in run level 5
x:5:respawn:/usr/bin/X11/xdm -nodaemon
```

Do not specify either run level 0 or run level 6 as the default run level because either one will render your system unusable. If, for some reason, your inittab file does become corrupted, you can boot to single-user mode and fix the problem. To do this, at the LILO boot prompt, enter the parameter "Linux single," like this:

```
LILO boot:    Linux single
```

LILO is the Linux loader and is discussed later in this chapter.

▶ **See** "Understanding LILO, the Linux Loader," **p. 214**

Booting Linux from a Floppy

Many people use a boot floppy to start Linux. This boot floppy contains a copy of the Linux kernel that points to the root Linux file system on the appropriate hard drive partition. The Red Hat and Caldera Linux installation programs give you the opportunity to create a bootable floppy during the installation process.

> **CAUTION**
>
> You should make a bootable Linux floppy disk during the installation, even if you intend to install a boot manager on your hard drive. If your hard disk should crash, the bootable floppy might be the only way to boot your system! Also if you try to use a "generic" boot disk made up after a crash from another Linux computer, it probably won't work!

You can also use the installation diskettes in an emergency. At the boot prompt, pass the option rescue to the kernel. After asking a few questions, the system will ask you to insert the supplementary disk to finish the boot process.

▶ **See** "Creating the Boot, Supplemental, and Rescue Disks," **p. 61**

After booting, the system will provide you a minimal command shell called ash, as well as several other utilities. Table 9.3 lists the utilities provided, which should be enough to repair your system.

Table 9.3   Rescue Utilities

Utility	Description
cat	Displays the contents of a file
chmod	Changes the access permissions of files
cpio	Copies files from archives
e2fsck	Checks a Linux second extended file system
fdisk	Partitions table manipulator for Linux
gzip/gunzip	Compresses or expands files
insmod	Installs loadable kernel module
ls	Lists files
mkdir	Creates a directory
mke2fs	Creates a Linux second extended file system
mount	Mounts a file system
rm	Removes a file
rmmod	Unloads loadable module

▶ **See** "Using Basic Commands," **p. 114**

T I P For Intel systems with the root partition on an IDE hard drive, you can also use the boot disk to boot Linux. At the boot prompt, enter the following command:

```
Linux single root=/dev/hda1 initrd=
```

Be sure to specify the appropriate device for your root filesystem if it is on an IDE device other than /dev/hda1. This command mounts the root partition, dumps you into single-user mode immediately, and then skips the rest of the boot process on the boot disk. Unfortunately, this procedure does not work if your root partition is on a SCSI device.

Booting from a Boot Manager

Linux comes with a boot manager known as LILO, which stands for LInux LOader. This program modifies the master boot sector of your boot hard disk and allows you to choose which operating system you want to boot when you turn on your computer.

Boot Managers

Using a boot manager has its advantages and disadvantages. With a boot manager, you don't need a floppy disk to boot your system. Also, you can choose to boot different operating systems from a menu at boot time, or have the system default to a given operating system.

As for the disadvantages, a boot manager adds another level of complexity to the boot process. It must be modified or possibly reinstalled if you add, delete, or upgrade a version of any of the operating systems on your disk. It modifies the master boot record of your hard disk, so if something goes wrong, you might not be able to boot with anything other than a floppy disk until you reformat your hard drive. Also, the boot manager that you choose might not be compatible with some operating systems.

You should consider your own computing needs carefully before deciding whether to use a floppy or boot manager for booting Linux.

It's also possible to set up LILO so that it can be started from the OS/2 boot manager.

Understanding LILO, the Linux Loader

LILO is a boot manager that comes bundled as part of the Red Hat and Caldera Linux distributions. It can be installed in the master boot record, on a formatted floppy disk, or on the boot partition's super block for booting OS/2.

▶ **See** "Installing LILO," **p. 82** and **101**

When LILO is installed, you can use the master boot record to select from a set of different operating systems at boot time. Depending on its configuration, LILO counts to a timeout value and then boots a default operating system.

The easiest way to install LILO is to do it via the Red Hat or Caldera Linux installation program, which takes you through a menu-driven system that automates much of the installation process.

> **CAUTION**
>
> It's highly recommended that you install LILO from the Red Hat or Caldera installation program. Installing a boot manager is an inherently dangerous process; you can easily corrupt data on your hard disk if the installation isn't done correctly.

Configuring LILO

LILO reads a configuration file, /etc/lilo.conf, and uses it to figure out what operating systems are installed on your system and where their boot information is located. The /etc/lilo.conf file starts with some information that tells LILO how to operate in general. It then contains several sections that list the boot information specific to each operating system that LILO can boot. LILO is configured to boot one section for each operating system on your Linux system.

Two sections from a LILO configuration file follow:

```
# Section for the Linux partition
image=/vmlinuz
label=Linux
root=/dev/hda1

# Section for MS-DOS
other=/dev/hda3
table=/dev/hda
label=msdos
```

The first section gives the boot information for Linux. The `image` line tells LILO where the Linux kernel is located. The `label` line that appears in both sections gives the name of the operating system that appears in the LILO boot menu. The `root` line specifies the location of the Linux root file system.

In the MS-DOS section, the `other` line indicates that the partition for an additional operating system is located on the disk partition hda3. The `table` line tells LILO where to find the partition table for /dev/hda3.

Using LILO

When you install LILO, you typically want to set a default timeout value and a default operating system to boot. This allows you to have a certain amount of time to select another operating system at boot time. In the event that you don't select an operating system, LILO boots the one that you've set as the default at the end of the timeout count.

When you boot your computer with LILO installed, you get a prompt that reads `LILO:`. At this point, you have several options. You can wait and have Linux boot your default operating system, or you can press <Ctrl>, <Alt>, or <Shift> to have LILO boot the default operating system immediately. You can also type the name of one of the operating systems to have LILO boot the one you specify. Finally, you can press <Tab> to have LILO display a list of the different available operating systems.

Shutting Down Linux

With a Linux system, you have to be careful when you shut the system down. You can't simply turn the power off. Linux maintains file system I/O information in memory buffers. If you just power down a Linux system, file system corruption can result.

> **CAUTION**
>
> You should never turn off a Linux system without shutting down properly. The file systems need to synchronize properly when the system is shutting down. You can cause severe damage to the Linux file system if you just power the system off.

Part

II

Ch

9

The best way to shut down a Linux system is with the shutdown command. The syntax of the command is as follows:

```
/sbin/shutdown [flags] time [warning-message]
```

[warning-message] is a message sent to all users who are currently logged on, and *time* is the time that the shutdown is to occur. The *time* argument can take a couple of formats:

- It can be specified as an absolute time in the format *hh:mm*, where *hh* is the hour (in one or two digits) and *mm* is the minute of the hour. The *mm* value must be specified with two digits.

- The *time* value can also be given in the format +*m*, where *m* is the number of minutes to wait before the shutdown. You can substitute the word now for +0.

Table 9.4 lists the flags that can be used with the shutdown command.

Table 9.4   Command-Line Flags for the *shutdown* Command

Flag	Message to Linux
-t *sec*	Wait the specified number of seconds between sending the warning and the kill signal to all processes. This delay gives processes time to finish any shutdown processing that they have to do.
-k	Don't really shut down the system, just send the warning message to all users.
-r	Reboot after shutdown.
-h	Halt after shutdown.
-n	Don't sync disks before rebooting or halting. *Use this flag with caution; it can cause your data to become corrupted.*
-f	Do a "fast" reboot. This creates the /etc/fastboot file. The rc boot script should check for this file and should not do an fsck if it's found.
-c	Cancel an already running shutdown. With this option, it's not possible to specify the *time* argument.

The shutdown command prevents any users from logging on, notifies all users on the system that the system will be shut down, waits until the time that you specify, and then sends a SIGTERM signal to all processes so that they can exit cleanly. shutdown then calls halt or reboot, depending on your command-line choice in the shutdown command.

CAUTION

It's possible to halt or reboot the system by entering **halt** or **reboot** directly. However, if you use either of these commands, no warning is given to the users, and the system goes down immediately. These commands should be used only if you're the only user on the system. To see who is logged on to the system, either press <w> or use the command who.

From Here…

Obviously, there's more to systems administration than just booting and shutting down the system. You can find more information about systems administration in the following chapters:

- Chapter 7, "Understanding System Administration," provides an overview of the various tasks that the average system administrator faces.
- Chapter 10, "Managing User Accounts," shows how to create and maintain user login accounts on your Linux system.
- Chapter 14, "Managing File Systems," discusses how to manage and maintain file systems properly.
- Chapter 18, "Understanding Linux Shells," shows how to write various shell scripts under several of the command shells included with Linux.

Part
II

Ch
9

Managing User Accounts

by Steve Burnett

In this chapter

Working with Users

As the systems administrator, you're in charge of managing users. Managing involves adding users so that they can log in to the system, setting user privileges, creating and assigning home directories for users, assigning users to groups, and deleting users when necessary. In this chapter, you will learn about the various tools and techniques that enable you to perform user account management.

Every user should have a unique login name. Login names make it possible to identify each user and avoid the problem of one user deleting another's files.

Each user also must have a password. About the only exception to having a password is when only one user is on a system, and the system has absolutely no connection by modem or network to any other computer.

▶ **See** "Dealing with Password Security," **p. 237**

When there's no real reason for a person to have access to your system, you must make sure that individual can't log in. That person's login name should be removed, along with any files that your remaining users no longer need.

Adding a User

When you add a user, the result is an entry for the user in the password file, /etc/passwd. That entry has the following form:

```
login_name:encrypted_password:user_ID:group_ID:user_information:
↪login_directory:login_shell
```

In this syntax, fields are separated by colons. Table 10.1 lists the fields.

Table 10.1   Fields in an /etc/passwd File Entry

Field	Description
login_name	The name used to log in.
encrypted_password	The password required to authenticate the user; this is the primary line of defense against security violations.
user_ID	A unique number the operating system uses to identify the user.
group_ID	A unique number or name used to identify the primary group for this user. If a user is a member of multiple groups, he or she can switch group membership to another group if permitted by the administrator.
user_information	A description of the user, such as the user's name or title.
login_directory	The user's home directory (where the user ends up after logging in).
login_shell	The shell used by a user when logging in (for example, /bin/bash if using the bash shell).

The `adduser` command enables you to add a user to your Linux system. You invoke the command with the name of the user that you want to add. The following section provides greater detail on this subject.

▶ **See** "Shadow Passwords: What Good Are They?," **p. 248**

Using the *adduser* Command

When you add a user, you simply use the `adduser` command and provide the name of the user you want to add (see Listing 10.1).

Listing 10.1   An Example of an *adduser* Session

```
# ./adduser jschmoe

#
```

The `adduser` command copies the files whose names begin with . (dot) from the /etc/skel directory into the user's home directory. The /etc/skel directory should contain template files you want every user to have. These typically include "personal" configuration files, such as .profile, .cshrc, and .login for shell configuration; .mailrc for e-mail setup; .emacs for your users using `emacs` as an editor; and so on.

The `adduser` command is a Bourne shell script located in the /usr/sbin directory. As such, you can customize this script if you need to perform some additional actions when you create a user account. A common modification is to have `adduser` prompt for the user's full name, rather than hard-code a default user name into the password file. If you don't change the script so that it asks for the user's name, you'll have to change it by hand with the `chfn` command as shown here:

```
# chfn jschmoe
Changing finger information for jschmoe.
Name [RHS Linux User]: Joseph A. Schmoe
Office []:
Office Phone []:
Home Phone []:

Finger information changed.
#
```

The `adduser` command doesn't set the password for the account. You'll have to do that by using the `passwd` command.

Setting User Passwords

You set a user's password by using the `passwd` command. You should set a password for each user added to the system; users can then change their passwords when they log in. The following steps outline the basic procedure for using `passwd`:

1. Type the command and login name (for example, **passwd jschmoe**) and press <Return>.

2. At the `New password:` prompt, enter the password (you won't see the password on-screen).

3. You're prompted to type the password again. Enter the password again:

   `New password (again): `**`newpassword`**

   The password is encrypted and put into the /etc/passwd file.

It's important that you take the time to make sure your password follows these rules:

- Passwords should be at least six (preferably eight) characters long.

- Passwords should contain both upper- and lowercase letters as well as punctuation symbols and numerals.

▶ **See** "Dealing with Password Security," **p. 237**

When you're adding a number of users, you'll be tempted to enter short, easy passwords. Don't fall for it. Good passwords are your first line of defense against intruders. Be sure to tell your users why you've assigned that type of password. Further, it's a good idea to change passwords regularly, but remember to educate system users about the choice of good passwords.

After a user is assigned a password, the file entry looks something like this:

`jschmoe:Zoie.89&^0gW*:123:21:Joseph A. Schmoe:/users/jschmoe:/bin/bash`

The second field is the password—not as it was typed, but in encrypted form.

N O T E Users occasionally forget their passwords. It isn't possible for you to tell users their own passwords. You can delete a forgotten password, however, by editing the /etc/passwd file and deleting the second field in the user's file entry. You can then set the user's new password with the `passwd` command. You should establish a procedure for dealing with such a situation, and let your users know about it. ▪

Removing a User

There are several different degrees of user removal. Removing a user from the system doesn't have to be a final, irrevocable act. Here are some possibilities:

- *Remove only the capability to log in.* This is useful if the user is away for a while and needs to be reinstated some time in the future. The user's directory, files, and group information are kept intact. Edit the password file (/etc/passwd) and put an * in the second field of the user's entry like this:

  `jschmoe:*:123:21:Joseph A. Schmoe:/users/jschmoe:/bin/bash`

- *Remove the user from the password file but keep the user's files on the system.* This is useful if the files are used by others or if a new person will be taking over the duties of the old user. Delete the user's entry from the password file or files. You can do this by using an editor or with the `userdel` *login_name* command. You can then change the ownership and location of the deleted user's files by using the `chown` and `mv` commands.

- *Remove the user from the password file and remove all files the user owns.* This is the ultimate and complete form of deleting a user. You must delete the user's entry from the password file and delete the user's files from the system. You can do this by using the `find` command:

```
find user's-home-directory -exec rm {} \;
```

Then remove the directory with `rmdir user's-home-directory` and remove the appropriate entry from the password file or files.

N O T E If you use other configuration files at your site, such as e-mail alias files, you'll also have to remove the user from those files. ■

Working with Groups

Each user is a member of a group. You can give different types of groups different capabilities or privileges. For example, it's reasonable to give a group of users who use the system to analyze the company's sales data access to a different set of files than a user group whose main function is researching new products.

The password file contains information for a single user. Information about groups is kept in the /etc/group file. The following is a sample entry:

```
sales::21:tuser, jschmoe, staplr
```

In this example, the group name is sales, the group ID number is 21, and the members are tuser, jschmoe, and staplr. Files and directories have permissions associated with them for the owner, group, and others. A user can be a member of more than one group, and you can change group memberships.

Adding a Group

You create a new group by editing the /etc/group file directly and entering the new group information.

Each group in the /etc/group file has a unique group ID number associated with it. Linux pays attention to the number that you assign, not to the name. Hence, if you assign two groups with the same number, they will be treated as though they're the same group.

Deleting a Group

You delete a group by editing the /etc/group file and removing the entry for the specific group that you want to delete. Also, you should reassign all files that have that associated GID to a different group. An easy way to do this is with the `find` command, as in this example:

```
find / -gid group-id find users-home-directory -exec chgrp newgroup {} \;
```

Managing Home Directories

You should give some thought to grouping your home directories logically if you plan to have a lot of users on your system. In general, you should try to place all the home directories on a given machine under one single top-level directory. That way, they can be grouped according to whatever arrangement makes sense for your needs.

▶ **See** "Mounting and Unmounting File Systems," **p. 269**

For example, you can specify that /home be the top-level directory for user directories. Under /home, you can group users by department. The sales users would have accounts under /home/sales, development under /home/develop, and so on. Your user home directories would then fall under these directories or under another set if additional grouping is needed. Because user directories can use a lot of disk space, you could consider placing logical groups of users on different physical file systems. As you need additional space, you can simply create an additional category for home directories and mount it on a file system as a mount point under /home.

Web-Based Administration

The Red Hat 5.1 distribution of Linux includes Jacques Gelinas' system administration tool called Linuxconf. Linuxconf enables you to manage many system administration tasks, including working with users and groups. In addition to the familiar character-line and X Windows access, Linuxconf supports administration of the Linux system over the World Wide Web. If the option "Linuxconf HTML Access Control" is selected in Linuxconf, you can enter the URL **http://<hostname>:98/** to display the top Web page of the Linuxconf tool.

N O T E   To do anything to the system, you'll need to go to one of the sub-pages. You will be prompted for the root password at that time, so have it ready. ■

From Here...

As the systems administrator, you're responsible for managing and supporting the users that log in to your system. Proper user management procedures can help simplify creating and deleting accounts. Linux provides a complete set of tools for managing user account and group information. It's important to understand how user accounts can be grouped logically. By considering how to set up their directory structures so that they reflect this grouping, you can make the most out of limited disk space and make file system maintenance a less-taxing job.

You can find more information about systems administration in the following chapters:

- Chapter 7, "Understanding System Administration," gives an introduction to common systems administration tasks.
- Chapter 11, "Backing Up Data," discusses how to plan and implement plans for data backups.
- Chapter 14, "Managing File Systems," describes how to set up and manage file systems on your Linux system.

Backing Up Data

by Jack Tackett

Various kinds of problems can result in loss of data: files get accidentally removed, hardware fails, important information stored in files is no longer available. Users should feel confident that, in such cases, they can access a timely backup of the "lost" files.

Your company's future—and your future with your company—may depend on making those backup files available. At such times, you and others will be thankful that you've taken the time and effort to copy files to some sort of storage media according to a regular, rigorous, and well-documented schedule. Backing up files isn't very glamorous, but no administrator can ignore the process.

Considering Backup Issues

The following are several issues to consider when backing up a system:

- *Full or incremental backups.* A *full backup* copies every file. Is it necessary to do that every day? A full backup usually requires a good deal of time and enough media to hold all the files on the system. An *incremental backup* copies the files that have changed since the last full backup.

- *File systems to back up.* Naturally, active file systems must be backed up regularly. Others can be backed up less frequently. Make sure that you have current copies of all the file systems.

- *Types of backup media.* Depending on the devices on your system, you may be able to use nine-track tape, 1/4-inch cartridge tape, 4mm or 8mm DAT tapes, or floppy disks. Each has advantages over the other in terms of sheer bulk, storage capacity, and cost for devices and media. Choose the backup medium to fit your budget, remembering that the least-expensive medium may be the most time-consuming.

- *Effect of backups on users.* Performing a backup operation increases the load on a system. Will that be an unreasonable burden on users? Also, files that are changed during the backup process may not be backed up, which can merely be an inconvenience or a very important consideration if you're backing up an active database. Should you perform backups when the system is quiet?

- *Commands to use for backups.* Some relatively simple, time-honored commands are available for creating backups, such as `tar` and `cpio`. Are they sufficient?

- *Documentation of the backed-up files.* You must label all backed-up material so that you can use it to recover files when necessary. Some procedures and commands allow you to prepare a table of contents or list of the material that has been backed up.

From an administrator's point of view, the file system should be backed up according to some automated process with as little operator intervention as possible. It should also be done when the system is relatively quiet so that the backup is as complete as possible. This consideration must be balanced with convenience and costs. Should an operator or administrator have to stay until midnight on Friday to perform a full backup? Is it worth $2,000 for a DAT tape drive so that the entire system can be backed up automatically at 3 a.m. with no operator intervention?

Consider the alternatives, determine the true costs, and make a decision or recommend a course of action. It's generally a lot cheaper and always easier to restore well-managed backup information than to re-create it or do without it.

Considering Backup Tips

The purpose of performing backups is being able to restore individual files or complete file systems as rapidly and easily as possible. Whatever you do about backups should be focused on that central purpose.

Set up a backup plan. Include the files to be backed up, how often they'll be backed up, and how the files are to be restored. Let all users know the backup schedule and how they can request restoration of files. Be sure to stick with the plan.

Be sure to verify your backups. This could include reading a table of contents from the backup medium after it's stored or restoring an arbitrarily chosen file from the medium. Remember that it's possible for the backup medium—disk or tape—to have flaws.

Make backups so that files can be restored anywhere on the file system or on another computer system. Use backup or archive utilities that create archives that can be used on other Linux or UNIX computer systems.

Be sure to label all media—tapes, disks, whatever—used in a backup. If you have to use multiple tapes or disks, make sure that they're numbered sequentially and dated. You must be able to find the file or files you need.

Plan for a disaster. Make copies of the files on your system so that the entire system can be restored in a reasonable amount of time. Store copies of backup tapes or disks off-site. The last sentence is very important! You should store at least one copy of your backup material off-site, away from your computers. If a disaster (such as a fire) wipes out your system, it will more than likely also destroy your nearby backups. Many businesses rent a safe deposit box to store their tapes and disks in. You should store a complete hardware list in the same off-site location so that you would be able to reorder identical parts should a disaster occur.

Plan to re-evaluate your backup procedures periodically to make sure that they're meeting your needs.

Several tools are available that can help automate your backup procedure. Check out the Linux archives on **sunsite.unc.edu** for more information. Also, Linux supports the FTAPE extensions. FTAPE lets you perform backups to QIC-80 magnetic tape units that run off a floppy controller on your system. For detailed information, refer to the FTAPE HOWTO guide.

Part

II

Ch

11

Planning a Backup Schedule

It's important to come up with a backup schedule that meets your needs and makes it possible to restore recent copies of files. After you decide on a schedule, stick to it.

The ideal situation is to be able to restore any file at any time. Taken to an extreme, that's not possible, but you should be able to restore files on a daily basis. To do this, you use a combination of complete and incremental backups. A *complete backup* is one that contains every file on the system. An *incremental backup* is one that contains files that have changed since the last backup. Incremental backups can be at different levels—incremental to the last complete backup or incremental to the last incremental backup. It's convenient to think of backups as occurring at different levels:

Level 0: full backup

Level 1: incremental to the last complete backup

Level 2: incremental to the last level 1 backup

The following are some sample backup schedules:

- *Full backup one day, incremental other days.*

Day 1	Level 0, complete backup
Day 2	Level 1, incremental backup
Day 3	Level 1, incremental backup
Day 4	Level 1, incremental backup
Day 5	Level 1, incremental backup

  If you create and save an index of each backup, you should need only one day's backup to restore an individual file and only two days' backups (that of day 1 and another day) to completely restore the system.

- *Full backup once a month, weekly incremental, and daily incremental.* (This example is built around Tuesday, but it could be any day of the week.)

First Tuesday	Level 0, complete backup
Any other Tuesday	Level 1, incremental backup
Any other day	Level 2, incremental backup

  To restore an individual file under this schedule, you may need the complete backup if the file wasn't changed during the month, the level 1 backup if the file was changed the previous week but not this week, or the level 2 backup if the file was changed this week. This schedule is more complex than the previous example, but backups take less time per day.

You also might want to consider keeping backup files for an extended period, in case you need to restore an older version. A common schedule is to keep one weekly copy of a full backup for four weeks. For periods of longer than four weeks, you might consider keeping a biweekly backup for about three months.

Performing Backups and Restoring Files

Several different utilities are available for backing up and restoring files in a Linux system. Some are simple and straightforward; others are more complex. The simple methods have their limitations, however. Choose the one that meets your needs.

Because backing up and restoring files is very important, a number of available software systems are dedicated to that task. The following sections present two of them:

- `tar` is a tape archive utility available on every Linux or UNIX system. This easy-to-use Linux version can use several tapes or disks.

- `cpio` is a general-purpose utility for copying files available on every UNIX system. `cpio` is easy to use and more robust than `tar`, and it can use several tapes or disks.

Using *tar*

The UNIX `tar` utility was originally designed to create a tape archive (to copy files or directories to tape and then to extract or restore files from the archive). You can use it to copy to any device. It has the following advantages:

- It's simple to use.
- It's reliable and stable.
- Archives can be read on virtually any Linux or UNIX system.

It also has a few disadvantages:

- For some versions of `tar`, the archive must reside on one disk or tape, which means that if a portion of the medium fails—from a bad sector on a disk or bad block on a tape, for example—the entire backup may be lost.

- `tar` can't back up special files, such as device files.

- On its own, `tar` can perform only complete backups. If you want to do incremental backups, you have to do a little shell programming.

▶ **See** "Working with Shell Scripts," **p. 365**

Table 11.1 lists some options that are commonly used with `tar`. You can use many other command parameters with `tar`; refer to the man page for a complete list.

Table 11.1   Common Options for the *tar* Command

Option	Description
c	Creates an archive.
x	Extracts or restores files from the archive that's on the default device or on the device specified by the f option.
f *name*	Creates the archive or reads the archive from *name*, where *name* is a filename or a device specified in /dev, such as /dev/rmt0.

continues

Table 11.1	**Continued**
Option	**Description**
Z	Compresses or decompresses the tar archive.
z	Compresses or decompresses the tar archive with gzip.
M	Creates a multivolume tar backup.
t	Creates an index of all files stored in an archive and lists on stdout.
v	Uses verbose mode.

Consider some examples of the use of tar in backing up and restoring files. The following command copies the directory /home to the floppy drive /dev/fd0:

```
tar -cf /dev/fd0 /home
```

In this case, the f option specifies that the archive is created on the floppy drive device /dev/fd0.

The following command also archives the directory /home:

```
tar -cvfzM /dev/fd0 /home ¦ tee homeindex
```

The v option indicates verbose mode, the z option indicates that the archive should be compressed to save space, and the M option tells tar to create a multivolume backup. When one floppy disk is full, tar prompts you for another. A list of the copied files is directed to homeindex. It's a good idea to look at that file to see what was copied.

The find command is useful for locating files that have been modified within a certain time period so that they can be scheduled for incremental backups. The following example uses the command find to create a list of all files that have been modified in the last day:

```
find /home -mtime -1 -type f -print > bkuplst tar cvfzM /dev/fd0
↪'cat bkuplst' ¦ tee homeindex
```

To use the list as input to the tar command, place the command cat bkuplst in back quotes (backward single quotation marks, also known as *grave accents*—'cat bkuplst'). This tells the shell to execute the command as a subshell and place the output from the command on the command line in the location of the original back-quoted command.

The following command restores the /home/dave/notes.txt file from the device /dev/fd0 (note that you have to give the complete filename to restore it):

```
tar xv /usr2/dave/notes.txt
```

TIP You can automate any of these commands by putting them in root's crontab file. For example, you could put the following entry in the root's crontab file to perform a backup of /home every day at 1:30 a.m.:

```
30 01 * * * tar cvfz /def/fd0 /home > homeindex
```

If you need to do more complicated backups, you can create shell scripts to control your backups. These shell scripts can also be run via `cron`.

▶ **See** "Scheduling Commands with `cron` and `crontab`," **p. 388**

You also can use the `tar` command to create archive files in the Linux file system rather than write to a backup device. This way, you can archive a group of files along with their directory structure in one file. To do this, simply give a file name as the argument to the `f` option instead of a device name. The following is an example of archiving a directory and its subdirectories with the `tar` command:

```
tar cvf /home/backup.tar /home/dave
```

This creates the file /home/backup.tar, which contains a backup of the /home/dave directory and all files and subdirectories below /home/dave.

N O T E The tar command by itself doesn't perform any file compression. To compress the resulting tar file, either specify the z option with the tar command or use a compression program, such as gzip, on the final tar file. ■

When you use `tar` to make archive files, it's usually a good idea to try to make the top-level entry in the tar file a directory. This way, when you extract the tar file, all the files in it are placed under a central directory in your current working directory. Otherwise, you could end up with hundreds of files in your directory if you extract a tar file in the wrong place.

Suppose that you have below your current directory a directory named data, which contains several hundred files. There are two basic ways to create a tar file of this directory. You can change directories to the data directory and create the tar file from there, as in this example:

```
$ pwd
/home/dave
$ cd data
$ pwd
/home/dave/data
$ tar cvf ../data.tar *
```

This creates a tar file in /home/dave that contains just the contents of data without containing an entry for the directory. When you extract this tar file, you don't create a directory to put the files in—you just get several hundred files in your current directory.

Another way to create the tar file is to start from data's parent directory and specify the directory name as the thing to archive. Here's the command sequence:

```
$ pwd
/home/dave
$ tar cvf data.tar data
```

Part
II

Ch
11

This also creates an archive of the data directory, but it puts the directory entry as the first thing in the archive. This way, when the tar file is extracted, the first thing that's created is the directory data, and all the files in data are placed in the data subdirectory.

N O T E If you want to create a tar file of all the files in the directory, it's a good idea to specify a different location for the tar file (other than the current directory). That way, if you try to archive all the files in the current directory, tar won't get confused and try to add its tar file recursively to the tar that it's creating. ▪

Using *cpio*

cpio is a general-purpose command for copying file archives. You can use it to create backups by using the -o option, or to restore files by using the -i option. It takes its input from standard input and sends its output to standard output.

The advantages of cpio include the following:

- It can back up any set of files.
- It can back up special files.
- It stores information more efficiently than tar.
- It skips bad sectors or bad blocks when restoring data.
- Its backups can be restored on almost any Linux or UNIX system.

Some people find cpio's syntax to be a bit more confusing than tar's syntax. Also, to perform incremental backups, you have to do some shell programming.

Table 11.2 lists the commonly used options for cpio. See cpio's man page for a complete description of the options you can use with this command.

Table 11.2 Commonly Used Options for *cpio*

Option	Description
-o	Copy out. Creates an archive on standard out.
-B	Blocks input or output at 5,120 bytes per record; useful for efficient storage on magnetic tape.
-i	Copy in. Extracts files from standard input. This is typically used when the standard input is the result of a copy out action of another cpio command.
-t	Creates a table of contents of the input.

The following list provides some examples of using cpio to back up and restore files:

- The following command copies the files in the directory /home to the device /dev/fd0:

  ```
  ls /home ¦ cpio -o > /dev/fd0
  ```

- The following command extracts the files on the device /dev/fd0 and creates an index in the bkup.indx file:

  ```
  cpio -it < /dev/fd0 > bkup.indx
  ```

- The following example uses the find command to create a list of all files in /home that have been modified in the last day:

  ```
  find /home -mtime 1 -type f -print ¦ cpio -oB > /dev/fd0
  ```

  The output of that command is piped to cpio, which creates an archive on /dev/fd0, where the data is stored at 5,120 bytes per record.

- The following command restores the file /home/dave/notes.txt from the device /dev/fd0:

  ```
  echo "/home/dave/notes.txt" ¦ cpio -i < /dev/fd0
  ```

N O T E You must give the complete filename to restore a file with cpio. ▥

T I P You can automate any of these commands by putting them in root's crontab file. For example, you could put the following entry in the root's cron file to perform a daily backup of /home at 1:30 a.m.:

```
30 01 * * * ls /home ¦ cpio -o > /dev/fd0
```

If you need to do more complicated backups, you can create shell scripts to control your backups. You also can run these shell scripts via cron.

Part
II

Ch

11

From Here...

You can find more information about system administration in the following chapters:

- Chapter 7, "Understanding System Administration," gives an overview of the duties of a systems administrator.
- Chapter 10, "Managing User Accounts," shows how to create and manage user access to your Linux system.
- Chapter 14, "Managing File Systems," discusses the ins and outs of file systems and the various issues that you need to consider.

## CHAPTER 12

Improving System Security

by Steve Burnett

In this chapter

Unless your system is locked in a closet, you're the only one with a key, and you keep the key on a chain around your neck at all times, you should be concerned about system security. This really isn't a joke. If there are multiple users, if the system is connected to the outside world by modems or a network, or if there are times when the system isn't attended, there's the real risk that someone may gain unauthorized access to it.

Sometimes, unauthorized access is benign—but it can still be unnerving. If someone takes the time to gain access to your system, that person probably has the skill to copy information you want to keep confidential, make unauthorized use of your system's resources, and modify or delete information.

In most organizations, the systems administrator has the responsibility for system security. You don't have to be paranoid about it, but you should be aware of the risks and be able to take steps to keep your system secure. Be assertive and professional when addressing security issues.

This chapter discusses ideas and policies for increasing computer security, as well as actual techniques that you can use to make your system more secure. Some of these ideas are of little use to the home computer user and tend to apply to larger installations. Other points in this chapter are very applicable to home users.

N O T E Over the past several years, the mass media has changed the meaning of the word *hacker* from "a computer enthusiast" to "someone who breaks into computers." In the computer community, the commonly accepted term for someone who breaks into computers is *cracker*. This is the term used throughout this chapter. ▪

Handling Physical Security

With all the mass media hype about viruses, computer break-ins, and diabolical computer crackers with their modems and network connections, too little attention is paid to the physical security of computer systems. Computer equipment is fairly sensitive to various environmental conditions.

Fire and smoke can obviously mean a quick end for your computing equipment. If you have any sort of business computer installation, you should consider installing smoke detectors, automatic fire extinguishers, and a fire alarm system.

In addition to fire and smoke, dust can wreak havoc with computer equipment. Dust is abrasive and can shorten the life of magnetic media and tape and optical drives. Dust can collect in ventilation systems and block the airflow, letting computers overheat. Also, dust can be electrically conductive and can cause circuit boards to short out and fail.

Electricity poses a special threat to computer equipment. Computers are very sensitive to surges in electrical current. All computer equipment should be connected to surge suppression equipment to reduce the chances of damage. This includes modems connected to telephone lines. Many areas suffer from "dirty power" that fluctuates in current and voltage.

N O T E Although surge suppressors can help protect against spikes in the electrical current, they're virtually worthless against any kind of lightning strike. If lightning hits an incoming line to your house or business, simple surge suppressors are unlikely to save your equipment. In the case of a severe thunderstorm, it's best to unplug your surge suppressor and wait it out. ■

Computers are also common targets for theft. Many computer components are small and expensive. As a result, they're easily stolen and sold. You should evaluate how secure your computers are and try to protect them against theft as you would any valuable possession.

Another aspect of physical computer security is preventing access by unauthorized persons. If someone can walk into your computer room, sit down at a console, and start working unchallenged, you have a problem. By controlling access to your computers, you make it more difficult for someone to steal or damage data or equipment. Establish access policies for your computing facilities and educate your users as to these policies.

The following are some steps you can take to improve the physical security at your installation:

- Don't leave a system, tape drives, disk drives, terminals, or workstations unattended for a prolonged period of time. It's a good idea to have some restrictions regarding access to the rooms that house your primary system and associated tape and disk drives. A lock on the door goes a long way in providing security. An unauthorized person can remove backup media—disks or tapes—from an unlocked area.

- Don't leave the system console or other terminal device logged in as root and unattended. If users know the system, they can easily give themselves root privileges, modify important software, or remove information from the system.

- Educate system users about physical security risks. Encourage them to report any unauthorized activity they may witness. Feel free to courteously challenge someone you don't recognize who is using the system.

- If possible, don't keep sensitive information on systems that have modem or network connections.

- Keep backups in a secure area and limit access to that area.

Part

II

Ch

12

Dealing with Password Security

The first line of defense against unauthorized access to a system is password protection. This is also often the weakest link in the chain. This section describes some steps you can take to keep passwords secure.

The reality is that users want simple, easy-to-remember passwords. They don't want to change their passwords. They like to write them down so that they can reference them. Unfortunately for you, the systems administrator, these are all bad approaches from a computer security standpoint. Password security requires almost constant attention.

The root password is special. Anyone who knows it can access anything on your system and perhaps other systems that your computer is connected to through a network. Change the root password often, choose it wisely, and keep it secure. It's best committed to memory. In most organizations, it's a good idea for two people to know it—but no more than that!

Passwords should be at least six characters long; however, only the first eight characters in any password are recognized. This means that your password is truncated to eight characters if you enter one that's longer than eight characters.

It's not too difficult to write a program that can attempt to guess a password. If the password-guessing program is trying to guess a random password, it will take longer to be successful if the password itself is longer.

Computers are very good at doing the same thing over and over, such as encrypting every word in a dictionary and comparing it to your password to try to break into your system. You should never choose a password that's a dictionary word. Also, try not to choose a password that's easily associated with you. Your name, address, spouse's name, child's name, pet names, phone number, driver's license number, and so on are all obvious targets for a cracker.

So how do you pick a good password if all the easy ones are also easy to guess? One technique is to pick two random short words and connect them with a punctuation character. This makes an almost random sequence of characters as far as a password guesser is concerned, but is fairly easy for a user to remember. The following are a few examples of passwords that use this technique:

joe&day

car!pan

modem!at

Another method for picking passwords is to take a phrase that you'll remember and use the first letter from each word for the password. This results in a random sequence of characters, but one that you can easily recall. For example, the phrase "Ladies and Gentlemen, Elvis has left the building" translates into the password L&GEhltb.

The crucial point is that the password should be remembered. It shouldn't be written down anywhere. If your users feel they must write down their password at all, give them a tip to disguise it in some type of list or sentence. For instance, if your password is modem!at, a note on a small piece of paper saying "Don't forget to pick up modem! At computer shop for repairs" looks like an ordinary reminder in case another person sees the paper, but the password is well disguised.

Developing Login Security

Each account on your Linux system is a door into your computer. All someone needs is the right key—the password. If you've instituted good password-management practices, you already have a head start toward developing a more secure system. One aspect of computer security that goes hand in hand with password security is login or account security.

Login or account security involves looking for accounts on your system that may be potential security problems and dealing with them. Login security can pose several different kinds of problems.

Accounts Without Passwords

Many computer crackers succeed in breaking into a computer by simply finding an account that doesn't have a password. You should check your password file regularly for such accounts and disable them. The password is stored in the second field of the password file under Linux. You can check for a blank password field with several tools, such as grep, awk, or perl. You can disable logins to an account by editing the password file and changing the password field to a * character. This prevents anyone from logging in with that login ID.

▶ **See** "Setting User Passwords," **p. 221**

Unused Accounts

If a login name won't be used anymore, you should delete the account so that it can't be compromised. At the very least, you should edit the password file and set the password to the * character, which will prevent anyone from logging in to the account. If you choose to delete the account, you should use the find command to locate all files owned by the account and then change their ownership or delete them.

▶ **See** "Removing a User," **p. 222**

> **N O T E** If you use other configuration files, such as system mail alias lists, you'll have to remove the account from those files as well. ■

Default Accounts

Linux comes with several standard login IDs that are required for the operating system to work correctly. For example, the root account has no password when Linux is first installed. You should check the password file when you've finished your installations to make sure that all your default accounts have good passwords or have been disabled by setting the password field to a * character.

Some software packages automatically create accounts on your system during their installation processes. Remember to disable them or set their passwords accordingly.

Guest Accounts

It's not uncommon for computer centers to provide some type of guest access accounts for visitors so they can use the local computers temporarily. These accounts usually don't have passwords or have passwords that are the same as the login ID. For example, the login *guest* might not have a password or has a password of guest. As you might guess, these are security disasters waiting to happen.

Because these accounts and passwords are probably widely known, an intruder could use one to gain initial access to your system. When a cracker has broken into your system, the intruder can then try to get root access from the inside or use your system as a waypoint from which to attack other computers over a network. Tracing an attack back to an open public account makes it much harder to find the true source of the attack.

Guest or open accounts really aren't a good idea on any system. If you really must use one, keep it disabled until it's needed. Randomly generate a password for the account when it needs to be used and, when you can, disable it immediately. Remember not to send the password via e-mail.

Command Accounts

It's common for computers to have several *command accounts*—login IDs that run a given command and then exit. For example, finger is an account that has no password. When a user logs in as finger, the `finger` program is run, showing who is on the system, and then the session terminates. Other such accounts may be sync and date, which typically don't have passwords. Even though they don't run a shell and run only one command, they can still pose a security risk.

If you allow command accounts on your system, you should ensure that none of these commands accepts command-line input. Also, these commands shouldn't have any type of shell escape that can allow a user to get to an interactive shell.

A second reason for not using these types of accounts is that they can give away information about your system that can be useful to an intruder. Using programs such as `finger` or `who` as command accounts can allow intruders to get the login IDs of users on your system. Remember that the login ID/password combination protects your accounts. If an intruder gets the login ID of a user, that person now has half the information that's needed to log in to that account.

Group Accounts

A group account is an account for which more than one person knows the password and logs in under the same ID. You guessed it—a bad idea. If you have an account shared by several people that is broken into and is being used as a base to attack other computers, finding the person who gave out the password is difficult. If you have an account that's shared by five people, it may in fact be shared by 25. There's no way to know.

▶ **See** "Working with Groups," **p. 223**

Linux allows you to provide file access based on group membership. This way, a group of people who need access to a set of files can share them without needing to share an account. Rather than create group accounts, make wise use of groups under Linux. Stay with the "One Login ID, One Person" philosophy.

Handling File Security

The file system under Linux is a tree structure that's built from files and directories. Linux stores several types of information about each file in its file system, including the following:

- The filename
- The file type
- The file size
- The file's physical location on disk
- Various access and modification times
- The owner and group ID of the file
- The access permissions associated with the file

If a user can modify some of the file information on certain files, security breaches can occur. As a result, the file system plays a very important role in system security.

Permissions

Linux file permissions control which users can access which files and commands. These permission bits control access rights for the owner, the associated group members, and other users. By using the ls -l command, you can generate a file list that shows the permissions field. The leftmost field shown by ls -l specifies the file permissions. For example, this field may look like -rw-r--r--. The first - in the field shows the file type. For regular files, this field is always -.

The next nine characters represent the file access permissions for the owner, group, and world, respectively. Each category takes up three characters in the permissions field, consisting of the characters r (for read permission), w (for write permission), and x (for execute permission). Any or all of these characters may be present.

If one of the permissions has been granted, the corresponding character is present. If permission isn't granted, there's a - instead. For example, if a file has a permission field that looks like -rw-r--r--, this indicates that the file is a regular file (the first character is -), the owner has permissions rw- (which means read and write, but no execute), and the other group members and the world at large both have permissions r-- (which means read permission but no write or execute access). File permissions are changed via the chmod command.

▶ See "File Permissions," **p. 310**

> **N O T E** You can specify the permissions to the chmod command as octal values instead of the rwx symbolic values. Simply treat the three characters in a permission field as bits in an octal number—if the character is present, count it as a 1. So, the permissions -rw-r--r-- are represented numerically as 644. ▪

SUID and SGID Programs

Two additional permission bits are associated with a file: the SUID and SGID bits. SUID stands for *Set User ID*, and SGID is *Set Group ID*. Programs with these permissions behave as though they were owned by different UIDs when they're run. When an SUID program is run, its effective UID is set the same as the user that owns the program on the file system, regardless of who is actually running the program. SGID is similar except that it changes the group ID instead.

Although the SUID/SGID feature can be useful, it can present a big security hole. SUID programs are generally used when a program needs special permissions, such as root permission, to run.

Programmers usually go to great lengths to ensure that their SUID programs are secure. Most security holes in SUID programs occur when the program executes a command line, activates a shell, or runs a file that users can change to contain their own commands. Although some SUID programs are necessary, you should try to keep them to a minimum. You should also regularly scan your file systems to check for new SUID programs by using the `find` command (refer to the man page for the exact syntax).

Avoiding Social Engineering Threats

With all the different security features available on a Linux system, the biggest security hole is typically your users. After all, your users already have valid accounts.

But what does this have to do with social engineering? What is social engineering, anyway? *Social engineering* is about convincing people to do what you want, either by playing on their assumptions or behavior, or by outright misrepresentation and lying. People, in general, want to be helpful. And, if given the opportunity, they usually try to help out as much as possible. Crackers with good social engineering skills play on this characteristic.

Assume that you have a computer user named Mr. Jones. He's just your average user—not a guru at all. One day, Mr. Jones gets a call at the office that goes something like this:

Mr. Jones:	Hello?
Caller:	Hello, Mr. Jones. This is Fred Smith in tech support. Due to some disk space constraints, we're going to be moving some user home directories to another disk at 5:30 this evening. Your account will be part of this move and will be temporarily unavailable.
Mr. Jones:	Uh, okay. I'll be home by then, anyway.
Caller:	Good. Be sure to log out before you go. I just need to check a couple of things. What was your login ID again—jones?
Mr. Jones:	Yes, it's jones. None of my files will get lost during the move, will they?
Caller:	No sir. But I'll check your account just to make sure. What was the password on that account so I can get in to check your files?
Mr. Jones:	My password is tuesday.
Caller:	Okay, Mr. Jones. Thanks for your help. I'll be sure to check your account and verify that all the files are there.
Mr. Jones:	Thank you. Bye.

So what just happened here? Someone called one of your users on the phone and managed to get both a valid user name and password in the course of the conversation. And you guessed it—if Mr. Jones calls tech support tomorrow, he'll probably find that no Fred Smith is working there!

How do you prevent things like this from happening? Educate your users. Your users should never give out a password over the phone to a caller. They should never leave one on e-mail or voice mail. Crackers use social engineering by convincing users to give them what they want; they don't even have to try to break into your system.

Recording Use of the *su* Command

Linux verifies your identity by your login ID/password combination. As you log in, your process is tagged with an ID that identifies you to the system. It's this UID that's checked for file and directory access.

Linux offers the capability to switch to another UID while you're working. When users use the su command, they can become root or another user. They must know the password of the user that they're changing to. For example, for a user to change user ID to that of user ernie, the command is

```
su ernie
```

The user is then prompted for the password associated with the login ID ernie.

To change to root, the command is

```
su root
```

The user is then prompted for the root password.

Typically, all attempts at using su are automatically logged in a system logfile, such as /var/adm/syslog. Examine this file periodically to check on this sort of activity.

Developing a Secure System

Along with power comes responsibility. If not handled carefully, Linux's power to share information, processing resources, and peripherals can leave your system open to abuse. Your job is to set up system security so that only the right users and systems can connect to yours, and that they can use only the parts of your computer you want to share.

Security Threats

You can monitor your system for security threats. To determine who is using your system and the type of work they're doing, use the ps command.

Be wary of jobs that seem to be running a very long time or users who seem to be using more resources than normal. These can be an indication that a login has been compromised and an unauthorized user is running a program to guess passwords.

Controlling the Root

The root login is reserved for your administrators. The person who logs in as the root has the power to erase any file, restrict use by any person on the network, and quite literally to cause havoc among users. That's the downside of the picture. Linux was designed to give the people having root access the tools to do their jobs better than in other environments.

Many proprietary operating systems have blockages established by the creators to avoid accidental damage to files and other operating factors on the system. The creators of UNIX and Linux took a different attitude toward the administrator. You'll find tools that permit you to connect almost any computer device. You'll find software that monitors the performance of the computer. You can create an endless array of software and adapt it to just about any business environment.

Also, you can force your users to do only specified things on the computer, or you can give them limited rights until they grow in their knowledge. The root user, the administrator, has the power to do these things.

N O T E   Because access to the root is so important, some companies restrict use to a select few. ■

Controlling Modems and Crackers

Allowing access from a common modem, similar to those that people have at home, can permit someone to "crack" the system and destroy important data. As a result, many companies insist that the computer have elaborate security mechanisms, which can make these computers almost impossible to work with. Some companies put a dial-back option on the computer so that you must dial the computer and then wait for a return call before you can interact with the system.

Most of the time, a traditional UNIX/Linux approach is recommended. Make sure that all your user logins have passwords. Restrict the systems that can connect to your system. Keep permissions closed on sensitive files. Be careful of set UID bit programs (those that give the user who runs the program the permissions to run as another user). Most break-ins occur because someone left the door open.

N O T E   Ultimately, security is a problem with people rather than systems. You can't allow passwords to be etched in the wall near a terminal or have DOS computers with root passwords embedded in communication programs. ■

Preventing Idle Terminals

Users should log out or use some kind of terminal lock program when they leave at the end of the day. Most UNIX systems have such a program that shuts down terminals left on beyond a prescribed length of time.

Enforcing Security

Security in defense firms is clearly understood. Companies that have highly sensitive products in the design cycle understand the need for security. But employees in a small distributor of plumbing parts may have a hard time understanding what everybody is so concerned about. Security in this example isn't an issue until you can't figure out who removed a file that included a key proposal.

Employees should have a quick lesson about the sensitivity of data on your computer. A business has a significant investment in the data on the computer. Loss of data can be a distraction or it can mean chaos. Employees who are unwilling to participate in securing a computer should understand that this can be cause for dismissal.

For an administrator, the task becomes apparent. If you're the chief security officer for the network, how can you be sure that files and directories are adequately secured? Fortunately, there are many tools to help you, such as umask, cron, and Linux itself.

Permissions seem to be a significant source of worry for most administrators. New administrators typically tighten up permissions and then field calls from people saying they can't gain access to a file they need or can't execute a program on the system. After a while, these administrators loosen up the permissions so that anybody can do anything. The balancing act of securing the computer while permitting the proper people the tools to do their jobs is sometimes frustrating.

Handling Security Breaches

Security on a computer can require a little detective work. For example, look at the following:

```
# who -u
root    tty02   Jan 7 08:35   old    Ofc #2
martha ttym1d Jan 7 13:20   . Payroll #1
ted     ttyp0   Jan 7 08:36   8:25   Warehouse
margo   ttyp2   Jan 7 07:05   9:45   CEO Ofc
root    ttyp4   Jan 7 08:36   . Modem #1
# date
Tue Jan 7 19:18:21 CST 1997
```

Suppose that you know that Martha left the office at 5 p.m. Has someone found her password, or did she leave the terminal on when she left? You can see that she logged in at 13:20 today. It's now 19:18, and somebody is active on the system using her login. Do you dispatch security?

But what do you do if someone does break into your system? First, try to determine whether you really do have an intruder. Many times, what you notice may just be the result of human error. If you do have an intruder, you have several options. You need to decide whether any damage was done, and the extent of the damage. Do you prosecute those responsible if you can catch them? If so, you should start trying to gather and protect evidence.

You must decide how to go about securing your system and restoring any damage from your backups. Probably the most important thing of all is to document what you do. Start a log immediately. Sign and date any printouts showing evidence of intrusion; these may be useful as evidence. Your log may be invaluable in helping you figure out what you've done when you have to change or restore files.

Two other preventive measures that you should take are to make printouts of your basic system configuration files, such as /etc/fstab, and establish a site security policy. You must make sure that your users are aware of your site policy and that they're reminded frequently.

Another area of concern is when an employee leaves the company. When an employee leaves, for whatever reason, personnel should contact the computer staff to retire the login.

With all the different security considerations, how much security is enough? Can you have too much? You may be surprised to learn that yes, you can have too much security. In general, if the cost of recovering from a security breach is less than the cost of security, you should reduce the security level for your systems. Note that these cost factors include much more than monetary costs. Among other things, you should take into consideration the content of your files, the amount of time and money that it will take to replace them, any lost productivity time that an attack would produce, and the effect that publicity of a computer security problem will have on your organization.

Performing Backups

Few issues that the typical Linux administrator deals with are as important as the backup or archiving of a system. An administrator can be fired or a company can literally fail because of the loss of valuable data. The disk or disks on a computer are electromechanical devices, and they will fail at some time.

Most new hard disks are rated at around 150,000 hours mean time between failures—more than five years. But the mean-time statistic can be deceptive. Your disk could fail at the 50,000 hour mark or it might last for more than 10 years (highly unlikely). You're gambling if you back up your systems only occasionally, and you take an even greater chance if you aren't checking your backup tapes regularly.

▶ **See** "Planning a Backup Schedule," **p. 227**

PAM: The Pluggable Authentication Modules Architecture

Users need to be able to perform the tasks they want, even if their desired goal is winning that game of Solitaire. In order to do this, users will affect the system and its contents in varying degrees. In general, users should be able to run applications and create, change and delete files that do not affect the system's continued performance or change items belonging to another user that that user has not decided to share. One way of assigning authority over a system is based on your login name and password combination: When you log in, the system asks you for a name and password. Based on the proof that you are who you say you are, the system allows you to do essentially anything you want to your own area of the system and restricts you if you try to affect a part of the system you're not supposed to.

Other methods exist for verifying a user's identity besides the name-password combination. The Pluggable Authentication Modules (PAM) architecture allows you to change authentication policy without having to change the applications themselves. This section presents the structure and relationship of the PAM module architecture.

These are the four types of PAM modules:

- *Auth* performs the authentication activity.
- *Account* defines if the authentication is allowed. For example, consider a user who's only supposed to be on the system during the daytime and not work evenings or weekends. An account module would detect the user if she attempted to perform an action in the middle of the night.
- *Password* sets passwords.
- *Session* provides services to the user after the account module allows the authentication module to verify the user's identity.

Modules may be *stacked* in sequence to allow multiple methods of access or to restrict access by requiring success of multiple methods.

Understanding PAM Configuration Files

The configuration files for PAM are located in the directory /etc/pam.d/.

N O T E In older Linux systems, the file /etc/pam.conf provided configuration definitions. /etc/pam.conf is still supported for backwards compatibility, but its use is discouraged. ■

The best way to understand the syntax is to examine a configuration file. Here's the PAM file for passwd. If you installed PAM as part of your Linux installation, this is the default file /etc/pam.d/passwd:

```
#%PAM-1.0
auth        required    /lib/security/pam_pwdb.so shadow nullok
account     required    /lib/security/pam_pwdb.so
password    required    /lib/security/pam_cracklib.so retry=3
password    required    /lib/security/pam_pwdb.so use_authtok nullok
```

Line 1 is a comment, indicated by the octothorp (# sign) at the beginning of the line. Line two causes the user to be prompted to enter a password and for that password to be checked. The third line does the same if shadow passwords aren't being use (more on shadowing later). Line four calls a password-cracking application to see if the new password is a good one, and line five specifies which module should be used to change the password.

Required, Requisite, and Optional: Module Order and Necessity

You can see that all four of the called modules are marked as "required." Labeling a module as required means that that module is called regardless of the success or failure of earlier modules. As a security guideline, all of them are called, so the reply from a failure at any point looks the same. By hiding the location of the failure, a malicious attacker's task is made harder.

If every module is required, the order of the modules is unimportant. However, PAM allows for these other control flags to be used instead of required:

- Optional
- Sufficient
- Requisite

"Optional" is entirely secondary to all other modules; the success or failure of an optional module does not affect the success of the authentication, IF there is another module in the PAM configuration file. If an optional module is the only one defined for authentication, its success or failure determines the success or failure of the authentication itself. A "sufficient" module acts like an optional module, except it overrides any or all optional modules. A required or requisite module's response supersedes a sufficient module, however. If a "requisite" module fails, control is directly returned to the application. If you want a PAM stack to stop at a particular module, you can edit the configuration file and change the control flag from required to requisite.

For more information, Red Hat Software provides documentation for PAM on its Web site at **http://www.redhat.com/linux-info/pam/**.

Shadow Passwords: What Good Are They?

On a Linux system without the Shadow Suite installed, user information (including passwords) is stored in the /etc/passwd file. The password is stored in an encoded format: Although the password looks like gibberish to a human, it is simply encoded with the UNIX crypt command, with the text set to [null] and the password used as the key.

It is difficult but possible to take a given encoded password and re-create the original password. However, because people may get lazy sometimes, on any system with more than a few users, some of the passwords are likely to be common words or simple variations. It's quite possible, and within the means of many, to encrypt a dictionary list and compare it to the password list in /etc/passwd. Other attacks are possible and used often, but this brute force approach is simple and easy to do. In addition to passwords, the /etc/passwd file also contains information such as user IDs and group IDs that are read by many system programs, so the /etc/passwd file must remain world readable.

Shadow passwording moves the passwords to another file, usually /etc/shadow, which is set to be readable only by root. Moving the passwords to the /etc/shadow file prevents an attacker from having access to the encoded passwords with which to perform a dictionary attack.

The Shadow Suite is included with most of the standard distributions of Linux.

However, in some cases such as the following, installing the Shadow Suite would NOT be a good idea:

- The system does not contain user accounts.
- The system is running on a LAN and uses NIS (Network Information Services) to get or supply usernames and passwords to other machines on the network.

- The system is used by terminal servers to verify users via NFS (Network File System), NIS, or some other method.
- The system runs other software that validates users, AND there is no shadow version available, AND you don't have the source code.

The /etc/password and /etc/shadow Files

A non-shadowed /etc/passwd file has the following format:

```
username:passwd:UID:GID:full_name:directory:shell
```

For example:

```
username:Npje044eh3mx8e:507:200:Full Name:/home/username:/bin/csh
```

A shadowed /etc/passwd file would instead contain:

```
username:x:507:100:Full Name:/home/username:/bin/csh
```

The *x* in the second field in this case is now a placeholder for the real passwords stored in the shadow file /etc/shadow. The /etc/shadow file has the following format:

```
username:passwd:last:may:must:warn:expire:disable:reserved
```

Table 12.1 outlines the fields in the /etc/shadow file.

Table 12.1   Fields in an /etc/shadow File Entry

Field	Description
username	The name used to log in.
password	The encoded password.
last	Days since Jan 1, 1970 that password was last changed.
may	Days before password may be changed.
must	Days after which password must be changed.
warn	Days before password is to expire that user is warned.
expire	Days after password expires that account is disabled.
disable	Days since Jan 1, 1970 that account is disabled.
reserved	A reserved field.

Part
II

Ch
12

Adding, Changing, and Deleting Users with Shadowed Passwords

The Shadow Suite adds the following command line oriented commands for adding, modifying, and deleting users: useradd, usermod, and userdel.

useradd   The *useradd* command is used to add users to the system. You also invoke this command to change the default settings.

The first thing that you should do is examine the default settings and make changes specific to your system with the following command:

```
useradd -D
```

usermod The usermod utility is used to modify the information on a user and is very similar to the useradd program.

userdel userdel enables you to delete the user's account with this command:

```
userdel -r username
```

The -r deletes all files in the user's home directory to be removed, along with the home directory itself. A less drastic way to eliminate a user from the system is to use the passwd command to lock the user's account.

passwd In addition to setting and changing passwords, the root user can use the *passwd* command to perform the following tasks:

- Lock and unlock accounts (with the -l and -u options)
- Set the maximum number of days that a password remains valid (-x)
- Set the minimum days between password changes (-n)
- Set the number of days of warning that a password is about to expire (-w)
- Set the number of days after the password expires before the account is locked (-i)

pwck The program pwck enables you to check on the consistency of the /etc/passwd and /etc/shadow files. It checks each username and verifies that each entry has the following:

- correct number of fields
- unique user name
- valid user and group identifier
- valid primary group
- valid home directory
- valid login shell

Finally, pwck also warns of any account that has no password.

> **N O T E** It's a good idea to run pwck after installing the Shadow Suite. It's also a good idea to run it periodically—perhaps weekly or monthly. If you use the -r option, you can use cron to run it on a regular basis and have the report mailed to you. ▓

grpck grpck is the consistency checking program for the /etc/group and /etc/gshadow files. It checks for the correct number of fields, unique group names, and a valid list of members and administrators.

Again, the -r option generates an automated report, so you can use cron to trigger this check automatically.

Enabling Dial-Up Passwords   If you want to limit who can dial in and connect, dial-up passwords allow you to control who accesses the systems remotely. To enable the use of dial-up passwords, you must examine the file /etc/login.defs and see that DIALUPS_CHECK_ENAB is set to Yes.

Two files contain the dial-up information:

- */etc/dialups* contains the ttys (one per line, with the leading "/dev/" removed). If a tty is listed, dial-up checks are performed.
- */etc/d_passwd* contains the fully qualified path name of a shell, followed by an optional password.

If a user logs into a line that is listed in /etc/dialups and his shell is listed in the file /etc/d_passwd, he will be allowed access only by entering the correct dial-up password.

The command dpasswd assigns passwords to the shells in the /etc/d_passwd file.

From Here...

You can find more information about security issues in the following chapters:

- Chapter 10, "Managing User Accounts," discusses the issues relating to creating and maintaining user accounts on Linux.
- Chapter 11, "Backing Up Data," describes how to set up and maintain backups of your system.

Part

II

Ch

12

Configuring the Linux Kernel

by Jack Tackett

In this chapter

This chapter gives you the information you need to configure and install a new Linux kernel. The kernel is the core of the Linux operating system and provides the basic system services to the rest of Linux. Remember, Linux isn't a commercial product, so you might find some problems after a new distribution is released. Or someone may discover a serious security hole in the kernel. This happens all the time with both commercial and "free" operating systems. The difference is that with Linux, because the source code is available, you can patch any problems immediately after they are discovered. You do not have to wait for your commercial vendor to release a new service pack to fix a hole in your system.

In addition, a new feature in the current releases of the Linux kernel enables you to load specific device and program support into the kernel without precompiling the support into a large kernel. This allows Linux to load into memory only those parts of the kernel it needs. Modules also provide a way to modify the kernel to solve a problem or to add a new feature without recompiling the entire system.

Preparing to Build a New Kernel

Sometimes a problem has only one solution—a new kernel. The kernel is the core operating system for Linux. Although not for the faint of heart, downloading a new kernel from the Net and building the kernel is sometimes necessary. If you have some programming experience and know your way around the C programming language, you should be able to build and install a new kernel. If not, you might want to skip this section.

You may have to install a new kernel for a few reasons:

- A patch is released to run new hardware.
- You want to remove features you don't use from the kernel in order to lower the memory requirements for your system.

The starting point is to determine what kernel version you're now running. You can find out the kernel version with the following command:

```
uname -a
```

The response indicates which version of the kernel is running and when it was created. The version numbers are in the form of

MajorVersionNumber.MinorVersionNumber.PatchLevel

Linus Torvalds is the official release point for new kernels, although anyone can modify Linux (due to the GPL). Because Linus is the official release point, the Linux development and user community has a common baseline from which to work and communicate.

N O T E   Be sure to read the Kernel HOWTO for up-to-date information before actually trying to build and configure a new kernel. If you mess up, you could render your system useless. You should also make sure to keep an older, working copy of a kernel around just in case of problems. You can then boot that kernel instead of the worthless kernel. ■

Configuring a New Kernel

To build a new kernel, you first need to configure the source code files. The source files should be located in the /usr/src/Linux directory. You also must have the C compiler package loaded. If you didn't install that package during installation, use RPM to do so now with the following commands:

```
rpm -i kernel-source-2.0.34-0.6.i386.rpm
rpm -i gcc-2.7.2.3-11.i386.rpm
```

You may also have to install the kernel headers and various compiler libraries.

▶ **See** "Installing Packages with RPM," **p. 150**

First, you must get the new kernel sources or patches. The new sources are usually found on the Internet; check **sunsite.unc.edu** for the latest and greatest kernels. (If you're modifying your current kernel, this step is, of course, unnecessary.) The source files are usually in a tar file and will need to be unarchived.

Making a backup copy of your current kernel with the following commands is a very good idea:

```
cd /usr/src
cp Linux linux.sav
```

These commands copy the entire Linux source directory to another directory called linux.sav.

Next, you should use the patch command to apply any patch files. After preparing the source files, you can configure and build your new system. Depending on your personal preferences and hardware available, three methods are available for configuring the kernel: a text-based program, a text-based menu program, and if you have installed X Windows, an X-based program.

In order to use kernel modules, you must answer Yes to kerneld support and module version (CONFIG_MODVERSIONS) support during your kernel configuration.

The Interactive Text-Based Program

If you are using the text-based interactive program, you start by entering the following command from the /usr/src directory:

```
# make config
```

The make command asks you various questions about the drivers you want to install or configure. Pressing <Return> accepts the default value for each question; otherwise, you must supply the answer. Some of the questions are listed in Table 13.1. You may have to answer other questions depending on the version of the kernel you're installing or the patches you've applied. This list of options is supported by all the configuration utilities described in this chapter.

Part
II

Ch

13

Table 13.1   Some Configuration Options

Configuration Option	Description
Code Maturity Level	For use with experimental components in this kernel.
Loadable Module Support	Needed if you intend to use modules instead of a monolithic kernel.
General Setup	Asks a series of questions about general components, such as math coprocessor support and PCI BIOS support.
Floppy, IDE, and Other Block Devices	Asks questions about the type of IDE hard drives and other block I/O devices.
Networking Options	Asks several questions about how to support various network support features, such as firewalls and IP Masquerading.
SCSI Support	Enables support for SCSI controllers.
SCSI Low-Level Support	Enables low-level support for SCSI controllers and for reporting on various SCSI statistics.
Network device support	Enables support for various network controllers and processes.
ISDN subsystem	Enables kernel support for Integrated Services Digital Network (ISDN).
CD-ROM drivers (not for SCSI or IDE/ATAPI drivers)	Support for proprietary CD-ROM drives.
Filesystems	Lets you configure support for various filesystems, including foreign language DOS codepages.
Character Devices	Provides support for various character and similar devices, such as system watchdogs.
Sound	Provides configuration support for various sound cards.
Kernel Hacking	Provides for profiling support in the kernel.

Using the Menu-Based Program

If you are using the text-based interactive program, start by entering the following command from the /usr/src/linux directory:

```
# make menuconfig
```

Linux then displays the main screen, as shown in Figure 13.1.

FIG. 13.1

The Linux kernel configuration screen. Using a graphical menu system can help speed configuration of a new kernel.

The advantage to using the graphical system is that you need to configure only those parts of the kernel that need to be modified. The interactive text-based system leads you through the entire configuration process.

Using the X Windows-Based Program

If you are using the text based interactive program, start by entering the following command from the /usr/src/linux directory:

```
# make xconfig
```

Linux then displays the main screen, as shown in Figure 13.2.

FIG. 13.2

The X-based Linux kernel configuration screen. X Windows provides a less cluttered system of configuring a new kernel.

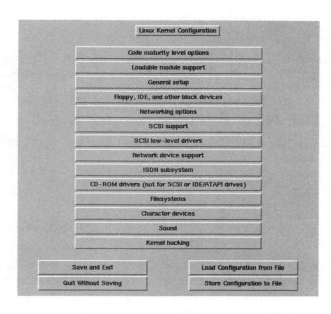

The X-based configuration tool allows you to configure only those kernel components you wish to change, just as the graphical text-based tool does. When you click on a button, you are presented with another dialog box you use to configure various components. For example, Figure 13.3 displays the Loadable Module Support dialog box. From this dialog box, you can configure the entire kernel for module support.

FIG. 13.3

The Loadable Module Support dialog box. You must specify module support during configuration in order to enable such support in your new kernel.

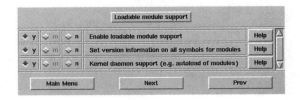

To select an item, simply click the appropriate radio button (the diamonds). If you need help on a specific topic, such as "Enable Loaded Module Support," you can click the Help button along the right-hand side of the dialog box. The resulting dialog box provides helpful information (see Figure 13.4).

FIG. 13.4

The CONFIG_MODULES help screen. Helpful information about the component is just a mouse click away.

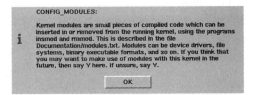

You must save your configuration after answering the appropriate questions. Simply click the Save and Exit button to save your new kernel configuration and exit the configuration system.

Compiling the New Kernel

After you answer the various questions to configure your new kernel, you must compile it. The following commands will build the new kernel:

```
make dep
make clean
make
```

The build process can take anywhere from a few minutes to many hours, depending on your hardware. So relax and order another pizza!

When the compilation is complete, you need to set up your system to use the new kernel on boot. The new kernel is /usr/src/linux/arch/i386/boot/zImage, and you need to copy this image into the boot directory. But before that you should create a copy of your current kernel image, just in case something goes wrong. To save the old kernel use the following command:

```
mv /boot/vmlinuz.old /boot/vmlinuz.old
```

Then you can copy over the new kernel with this command:

```
cp /usr/src/linux/arch/i386/boot/zImage /boot/vmlinuz
```

▶ **See** "Configuring LILO," **p. 214**

To change the default kernel that Linux boots into, you edit the /etc/lilo.conf file and add another entry for a new kernel. The example in Listing 13.1 shows the addition of the older kernel to the list of operating systems the machine can boot. To do this, you must rename /boot/vmlinuz to /boot/vmlinuz.old with the above commands and then change its label to "old" in lilo.conf as shown in Listing 13.1.

Listing 13.1   A Sample /etc/lilo.conf File

```
boot=/dev/hda
     map=/boot/map
     install=/boot/boot.b
     prompt
     timeout=50
     image=/boot/vmlinuz
            label=linux
            initrd=/boot/initrd
            root=/dev/hda1
            read-only
     image=/boot/vmlinuz.old
            label=old
            root=/dev/hda1
            read-only
```

After making the changes to /etc/lilo.conf, run the following command

```
/sbin/lilo -v
```

and the updated lilo will be written to the boot device. From then on when you reboot, the machine will boot into the new kernel (linux) as default instead of the older kernel, with a 50-second delay to give you time to choose the old kernel at the boot prompt if you want to boot that kernel.

Building a Modularized Kernel

With the introduction of modularization in the Linux 2.0.x kernel, there have been some significant changes in building customized kernels. In the past, you were required to compile support into your kernel if you wanted to access a particular hardware or filesystem component. For some hardware configurations, the size of the kernel could quickly reach a critical level, so to require ready support for items that were used only occasionally was an inefficient use of system resources. With the capabilities of the 2.0.x kernel, if certain hardware components or filesystems are used infrequently, driver modules for them can be loaded on demand. To see the current modules in use, use the following command:

```
lsmod
```

Part
II

Ch
13

The output, shown below, lets you know what modules are loaded and how they loaded, as well as how many pages of memory they are using:

```
Module          Pages   Used by
isofs             5               1 (autoclean)
ne2k-pci          1               1 (autoclean)
8390              2     [ne2k-pci]     0 (autoclean)
BusLogic         20               4
```

Only Red Hat Linux/Intel and Red Hat Linux/SPARC support modular kernels; Red Hat Linux/Alpha users must build a monolithic kernel as described in the earlier section "Building a New Kernel." These instructions provide you with the knowledge required to take advantage of the power and flexibility available through kernel modularization.

N O T E   You need to have already installed the kernel-headers and kernel-source packages. Also, you must issue all commands from the /usr/src/linux directory. ▓

To make the modules, go to /usr/src/linux and run the following command:

```
make modules
```

Then use this command to install the modules run:

```
make modules-install
```

Working with Kernel Modules

Now that you have compiled and installed the modules, you are ready to extend your kernel with loadable modules. Table 13.2 shows the basic commands that are available.

Table 13.2   Module Commands Available in Linux

Command	Description
lsmod	Lists the modules currently loaded in the kernel
insmod	Inserts a specified module into the kernel
rmmod	Removes the specified module from the kernel
depmod	Creates a dependency file for use by modprobe
modprobe	Loads modules from a list generated by depmod

If you are running X Windows, you can take advantage of the kerneld daemon from the Control Panel (shown in Figure 13.5) to work with modules from a GUI instead of from a command line. Clicking this button brings up the Kernel Configurator dialog box shown in Figure 13.6.

To list the currently loaded modules, use the lsmod command. To add a module you have compiled to the kernel, either you can use the following command

```
insmod module-name
```

or you can click the Add button on the kerneld dialog box and specify the module (see Figure 13.7).

FIG. 13.5

The kerneld menu button. The Control Panel provides access to many administrative functions, including working with kerneld.

The kerneld button ——

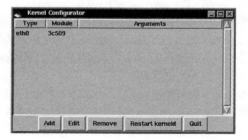

FIG. 13.6

The Kernel Configurator dialog box. Working with kernel modules is easy with the X interface to kerneld.

FIG. 13.7

The Choose Module Type dialog box. Adding modules is a breeze using X Windows.

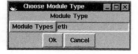

Part
II

Ch
13

To delete a module from the kernel, either use this command

```
rmmod module-name
```

or select the module from the list displayed in Figure 13.6 and click the Remove button.

Restarting *kerneld*

The changes you make with the Kernel Daemon Configuration tool will be made in the /etc/conf.modules file, which `kerneld` reads whenever it is started. Listing 13.2 provides a sample listing.

Listing 13.2   A Sample /etc/conf.modules File

```
alias scsi_hostadapter BusLogic
alias eth0 ne2k-pci
```

To restart `kerneld`, you can use the tool shown in Figure 13.6 and click the Restart Kerneld button. You can also restart the daemon via the command line, as shown here:

```
/etc/rc.d/init.d/kerneld stop
/etc/rc.d/init.d/kerneld start
```

Restarting `kerneld` does not cause any modules that are currently in use to be reloaded, but `kerneld` will use the configuration when it loads modules in the future.

From Here...

In this chapter, you learned about configuring and building a new kernel for your system. You also learned how to add functionality to your system using modules. The following chapters provide more information:

- Chapter 3, "Installing Red Hat," explains how to install the Red Hat Linux distribution.

- Chapter 5, "Running Linux Applications," shows you how to run various Linux applications, such as the compiler and X Windows.

- Chapter 6, "Upgrading and Installing Software with RPM," provides you with the necessary information to install and upgrade new packages, such as those needed for new kernel source code and compilers to build the source.

- Chapter 22, "Using X Windows," provides you with the information about using X under Linux.

Managing the File System

Managing File Systems

by Jack Tackett

File systems form the basis for all data on a Linux system. Linux programs, libraries, system files, and user files all reside on file systems. Proper management of file systems is critical because all your data and programs exist on top of file systems.

Many of the steps outlined in this chapter are performed automatically when you install Linux. However, you should learn to manage your file systems so that you can create, manage, and maintain your Linux system. Understanding file-system management is critical to successful systems administration. Your file system must work properly for your Linux system to work at all.

Understanding File Systems

Under Linux, the file space that's visible to users is based on a tree structure, with the root at the top. The various directories and files in this space branch downward from the root. The top directory, /, is known as the *root directory*. Figure 14.1 gives a graphical example of a tree structure.

FIG. 14.1

Picture the Linux file system as an upside-down tree, with the root at the top and the branches and leaves spreading downward.

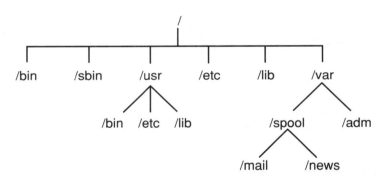

To users, this directory tree looks like a seamless entity—they just see directories and files. In reality, many of the directories in the file tree are physically located on different partitions on a disk, on different disks, or even on different computers. When one of these disk partitions is attached to the file tree at a directory known as a *mount point*, the mount point and all directories below it are referred to as a *file system*.

The Linux operating system is made up of several directories and many different files. Depending on how you selected your installation, these directories may be different file systems. Typically, most of the operating system resides on two file systems: the root file system, known as /, and a file system mounted under /usr (pronounced *user*).

If you change directories to the root directory with the cd / command and ask for a directory listing, you see several directories. These make up the contents of the root file system and provide the mount points for other file systems as well.

The /bin directory contains executable programs, known as *binaries*. (In fact, the directory named /bin is short for *binary*.) These programs are essential system files. Many Linux commands, such as ls, are actually programs found in this directory.

The /sbin directory is also used to store system binary files. Most files in this directory are used for system administration purposes.

The /etc directory is very important, containing many of the Linux system configuration files. Essentially, these files give your Linux system its "personality." The password file, passwd, is found here, as is the list of file systems to mount at startup, fstab. Also, this directory contains the startup scripts for Linux, the list of hosts with IP addresses that you want permanently recorded, and many other types of configuration information.

The shared libraries that programs use when they run are stored in the /lib directory. By using shared libraries, many programs can reuse the same code, and these libraries can be stored in a common place, thus reducing the size of your programs at run time.

The /dev directory contains special files known as *device files*, which are used to access all the different types of hardware on your system. For example, the /dev/mouse file is for reading input from the mouse. By organizing access to hardware devices in this way, Linux effectively makes the interface to a hardware device look like any other piece of software. This means that you, in many cases, can use the same syntax that you use with software to perform operations on computer hardware devices. For example, to create a tape archive of your home directory on a floppy drive, you can use the following command:

```
tar -cdf /dev/fd0 ~tackett
```

/dev/fd0 indicates that the `tar` command should use the floppy drive identified by fd0.

▶ **See** "Using `tar`," **p. 229**

Many of the devices in the /dev directory are in logical groups. Table 14.1 lists some of the most commonly used devices in the /dev directory.

Table 14.1   Commonly Used Devices in the /dev Directory

Device File	Description
/dev/console	The *system console*, which is the computer monitor physically connected to your Linux system.
/dev/hd	The device driver interface to IDE hard drives. The /dev/hda1 device refers to the first partition on hard drive hda. The device /dev/hda refers to the entire hard disk hda.
/dev/sd	The device driver interface for SCSI disks. The same conventions for SCSI disks and partitions apply as they do to the IDE /dev/hd devices.
/dev/fd	Device drivers that provide support for floppy drives. /dev/fd0 is the first floppy drive and /dev/fd1 is the second floppy drive.
/dev/st	The device driver for SCSI tape drives.
/dev/tty	Device drivers that provide different consoles for user input. The name comes from when terminals known as *teletypes* were physically hooked

Part

III

Ch

14

continues

Table 14.1 Continued	
Device File	**Description**
	to a UNIX system. Under Linux, these files provide support for the virtual consoles that can be accessed by pressing <Alt-F1> through <Alt-F6>. These virtual consoles provide separate simultaneous local login sessions.
/dev/pty	Device drivers that provide support for pseudo-terminals, which are used for remote login sessions such as login sessions using Telnet.
/dev/ttyS	The serial interface ports on your computer. /dev/ttyS0 corresponds to COM1 under MS-DOS. If you have a serial mouse, /dev/mouse is a symbolic link to the appropriate ttyS device that your mouse is connected to.
/dev/cua	Special call-out devices used with modems.
/dev/null	A very special device—essentially a black hole. All data written to /dev/null is lost forever. This can be very useful if you want to run a command and throw away the standard output or the standard error. Also, if /dev/null is used as an input file, a file of zero length is created.

The /proc directory is actually a virtual file system. It's used to read process information from memory.

The /tmp directory is used to store temporary files that programs create when running. If you have a program that creates a lot of large temporary files, you may want to mount the /tmp directory as a separate file system rather than just have it as a directory on the root file system. If /tmp is left as a directory on the root file system and has lots of large files written to it, the root file system can fill up.

The /home directory is the base directory for user home directories. It's common to mount this as a separate file system so that users can have plenty of room for their files. In fact, if you have many users on your system, you may need to separate /home into several file systems. To do so, you could create subdirectories such as /home/staff and /home/admin for staff members and administrators, respectively. Mount each of these as different file systems and then create the users' home directories under them.

The /var directory holds files that tend to change in size over time. Typically, various system log files are located below this directory. The /var/spool directory and its subdirectories are used to hold data that's of a transitory nature, such as mail and news that's recently received from or queued for transmission to another site.

 TIP You can create other mount points under the / directory if you want. You might want to create a mount point named /cdrom if you routinely mount CD-ROMs on your system.

The /usr directory and its subdirectories are very important to the operation of your Linux system. It contains several directories with some of the most important programs on your system. Typically, subdirectories of /usr contain the large software packages that you install. Table 14.2 discusses some of the /usr subdirectories. The /usr directory is almost always mounted as a separate file system.

Table 14.2   Important Subdirectories in the /usr File System

Subdirectory	Description
/usr/bin	This directory holds many of the executable programs found on your Linux system.
/usr/etc	This directory contains many miscellaneous system configuration files.
/usr/include	Here and in the subdirectories of /usr/include is where you find all the include files for the C compiler. These header files define constants and functions and are critical for C programming.
/usr/g++-include	This directory contains the include files for the C++ compiler.
/usr/lib	This directory contains various libraries for programs to use during linking.
/usr/man	This directory contains the various manual pages for programs on your Linux system. Below /usr/man are several directories that correspond to the different sections of the man pages.
/usr/src	This directory contains directories that hold the source code for different programs on your system. If you get a package that you want to install, /usr/src/*packagename* is a good place to put the source before you install it.
/usr/local	This directory is designed for local customizations to your system. In general, much of your local software is installed in this directory's subdirectories. The format of this directory varies on almost every UNIX system you look at. One way to set it up is to have a /usr/local/bin for binaries, a /usr/local/etc for configuration files, a /usr/local/lib for libraries, and a /usr/local/src for source code. The entire /usr/local directory tree can be mounted as a separate file system if you need a lot of room for it.

Mounting and Unmounting File Systems

By now, you should have a good feel for what a file system is. So how do you set up a directory as a separate file system?

To mount a file system in the Linux directory tree, you must have a physical disk partition, CD-ROM, or floppy disk that you want to mount. You also must make sure that the directory to which you want to attach the file system, known as the *mount point*, actually exists.

Mounting a file system doesn't create the mount point directory. The mount point must exist before you try to mount the file system. Suppose that you want to mount the CD-ROM in drive /dev/sr0 under the mount point /mnt. A directory named /mnt must exist, or the mount fails. After you mount the file system under that directory, all the files and subdirectories on the file system appear under the /mnt directory. Otherwise, the /mnt directory is empty.

T I P Use the command df . if you need to know which file system the current directory is located on. The command's output shows the file system as well as the free space available.

Mounting File Systems Interactively

As you may have guessed by now, Linux uses the mount command to mount a file system. The syntax of the mount command is as follows:

mount *device mountpoint*

device is the physical device that you want to mount; *mountpoint* is the point in the file system tree where you want it to appear.

N O T E The mount command can be used only by superusers. This is to help ensure system security. Several software packages are available that allow users to mount specific file systems, especially floppy disks. ▧

mount accepts several command-line arguments in addition to the two mentioned above (see Table 14.3). If a needed command isn't given, mount attempts to figure it out from the /etc/fstab file.

Table 14.3   Command-Line Arguments for the *mount* Command

Argument	Description
-f	Causes everything to be done except for the actual mount system call. This "fakes" mounting the file system.
-v	Verbose mode; provides additional information about what mount is trying to do.
-w	Mounts the file system with read and write permissions.
-r	Mounts the file system with read-only permission.
-n	Mounts without writing an entry in the /etc/mtab file.
-t *type*	Specifies the type of the file system being mounted. Valid types are minux, ext, ext2, xiafs, msdos, hpfs, proc, nfs, umsdos, sysv, and iso9660 (the default).
-a	Causes mount to try to mount all file systems in /etc/fstab.

Argument	Description
-o *list_of_options*	When followed by a comma-separated list of options, causes mount to apply the options specified to the file system being mounted. Many options are available here; for a complete list, refer to the mount man page.

N O T E Several forms of the mount command are very common. For example, the command mount /dev/hdb3 /mnt will mount the hard disk partition /dev/hdb3 under the directory /mnt. Similarly, mount -r -t iso9660 /dev/sr0 /mnt mounts the SCSI CD-ROM drive /dev/sr0, which is read-only and of the ISO 9660 file format, under the directory /mnt. And the command mount -vat nfs mounts all the NFS file systems listed in the /etc/fstab file. ■

T I P If a file system doesn't mount correctly, use the command mount -vf *device mountpoint* to see what mount is doing. This gives a verbose listing and tells mount to do everything except mount the file system. This way, you can fake out the mount command and get a lot of information about what it's trying to do.

Mounting File Systems at Boot Time

Under most circumstances, the file systems that your Linux system uses won't change frequently. For this reason, you can easily specify a list of file systems that Linux mounts when it boots and that it unmounts when it shuts down. These file systems are listed in a special configuration file named /etc/fstab, for *file system table*.

The /etc/fstab file lists the file systems to be mounted, one file system per line. The fields in each line are separated by spaces or tabs. Table 14.4 lists the different fields in the /etc/fstab file.

Table 14.4   Fields in the /etc/fstab File

Field	Description
File system specifier	Specifies the block special device or the remote file system to be mounted.
Mount point	Specifies the mount point for the file system. For special file systems such as swap files, use the word none, which makes swap files active but not visible within the file tree.
Type	Gives the file system type of the specified file system. The following types of file systems are supported: minix: a local file system supporting filenames of 14 or 30 characters

Part

III

Ch

14

continues

Table 14.4 Continued	
Field	Description
	ext: a local file system with longer filenames and larger inodes (this file system has been replaced by the ext2 file system and should no longer be used)
	ext2: a local file system with longer filenames, larger inodes, and other features
	xiafs: a local file system
	msdos: a local file system for MS-DOS partitions
	hpfs: a local file system for OS/2 High Performance File System partitions
	iso9660: a local file system used for CD-ROM drives
	nfs: a file system for mounting partitions from remote systems
	swap: a disk partition or special file used for swapping
	umsdos: a UMSDOS file system
	sysv: a System V file system
Mount Options	A comma-separated list of mount options for the file system. At a minimum, it must contain the type of mount for the file system. See the mount man page for more information on mount options.
Dump Frequency	Specifies how often the file system should be backed up by the dump command. If this field isn't present, dump assumes that the file system doesn't need to be backed up.
Pass Number	Specifies in what order the file systems should be checked by the fsck command when the system is booted. The root file system should have a value of 1. All other file systems should have a value of 2. If a value isn't specified, the file system won't be checked for consistency at boot time.

TIP It's recommended that you mount your file systems at boot time via the /etc/fstab file instead of by using the mount command. Remember, only superusers can use mount.

The following is a sample fstab file:

```
# device        directory     type      options
/dev/hda1       /             ext2      defaults
```

```
/dev/hda2      /usr       ext2     defaults
/dev/hda3      none       swap     sw
/dev/sda1      /dosc      msdos    defaults
/proc          /proc      proc     none
```

In this sample file, you can see several different file systems. First, notice that comments in the file are prefixed by a # character. In this fstab file, two normal Linux file systems are mounted—the disk partitions /dev/hda1 and /dev/hda2. These are listed as being of type ext2 and are mounted under the root directory, /, and /usr respectively.

The entry defaults listed under the options field indicates that this file system should be mounted by using a common set of default options. Specifically, the file system is mounted read/write enabled, it's to be interpreted as a block special device, all file I/O should be done asynchronously, the execution of binaries is permitted, the file system can be mounted with the mount -a command, the set UID (user ID) and set GID (group ID) bits on files are interpreted on this file system, and ordinary users aren't allowed to mount this file system. As you can see, it's a lot easier just to type **defaults** for the option instead.

▶ **See** "Creating the Swap Partition," **p. 72** and **p. 99**

The partition /dev/hda3 is a swap partition that's used for kernel virtual-memory swap space. Its mount point is specified as none because you don't want it to appear in the file system tree. It still has to be in the /etc/fstab file, so the system knows where it's physically located. Swap partitions are also mounted with the option sw.

The /proc file system is a virtual file system that points to the process information space in memory. As you can see, it doesn't have a corresponding physical partition to mount.

 T I P For full information on all options available in the /etc/fstab file, refer to the man page for fstab.

MS-DOS file systems can also be mounted automatically. The partition /dev/sda1 is the first partition on the SCSI hard drive sda. It's mounted as an MS-DOS partition by specifying msdos as the type and by giving /dosc as its mount point. You can place the mount point for the MS-DOS file system anywhere—there's no requirement that it be under the root directory.

Unmounting File Systems

Now that you know all sorts of stuff about mounting file systems, it's time to look at how to unmount. You use the umount command to unmount file systems. You would want to unmount a file system for several reasons: so that you can check/repair a file system with fsck, unmount NFS-mounted file systems in case of network problems, or unmount a file system on a floppy drive.

N O T E This command is umount, not "unmount." Make sure that you type it correctly. ■

There are three basic forms of the umount command:

```
umount device ¦ mountpoint
```

```
umount -a

umount -t fstype
```

device is the name of the physical device to unmount; *mountpoint* is the mount point directory name (specify only one or the other). The umount command has only two command-line parameters: -a, which unmounts all file systems, and -t *fstype*, which acts only on file systems of the type specified.

> **CAUTION**
>
> The umount command doesn't unmount a file system that's in use. For example, if you have some file system mounted under /mnt and you try
>
> **cd /mnt**
>
> **umount /mnt**
>
> you get an error telling you that the file system is busy. You have to change to a different directory in another file system to unmount the file system mounted under /mnt.

Understanding the Network File System

The Network File System (NFS) is a system that allows you to mount file systems from a different computer over a TCP/IP network. NFS allows you to share data among PC, Mac, UNIX, and Linux systems. Under NFS, a file system on a remote computer is mounted locally and looks just like a local file system to users. The illusion of being mounted locally has numerous uses. For example, you can have one machine on your network with a lot of disk space acting as a file server. This computer has all the home directories of all your users on its local disks. By mounting these disks via NFS on all your other computers, your users can access their home directories from any computer.

NFS has three essential components:

- The computers with the file systems that you want to NFS mount must be able to communicate with each other via a TCP/IP network.
- The computer with the file system that you're interested in as a local file system must make that file system available to be mounted. This computer is known as the *server*, and the process of making the file system available is known as *exporting the file system*.
- The computer that wants to mount the exported file system, known as the *client*, must mount the file system as an NFS file system via the /etc/fstab file at boot time or interactively via the mount command.

The following sections discuss exporting the file system and mounting it locally.

Exporting an NFS File System

For clients to mount an NFS file system, this file system must be made available by the server. Before the file system can be made available, you must ensure that it's mounted on the server.

If the file system is always going to an NFS exported file system, you should make sure that you have it listed in the /etc/fstab file on the server so that it automatically mounts when the server boots.

When you have the file system mounted locally, you can make it available via NFS. This is a two-step process. First, you must make sure that the NFS daemons `rpc.mountd` and `rpc.nfsd` are running on your server. These daemons are usually started from the startup /etc/rc.d/init.d/nfs script. Usually, all that's needed is to make sure that the following lines are in your script:

```
daemon rpc.mountd
daemon rpc.nfsd
```

> **N O T E** As RPC-based programs, the `rpc.mountd` and `rpc.nfsd` daemons aren't managed by the `inetd` daemon but are started up at boot time, registering themselves with the portmap daemon. You must be sure to start them only after `rpc.portmap` is running. ■

Second, you must enter the NFS file system in a configuration file named /etc/exports. This file contains information about what file systems can be exported, what computers are allowed to access them, and what type and level of access is permitted.

Understanding the /etc/exports File

The /etc/exports file is used by the `mountd` and `nfsd` daemons to determine what file systems are to be exported and what restrictions are placed on them. File systems are listed in /etc/exports, one per line. The format of each line is the name of the mount point for a local file system, followed by a list of computers that are allowed to mount this file system. A comma-separated list of mount options in parentheses may follow each name in the list. Table 14.5 lists the mount options available in the /etc/exports file.

Table 14.5 Mount Options Available in the */etc/exports* File

Option	Description
`insecure`	Permits non-authenticated access from this machine.
`secure`	Requires secure RPC authentication from this machine.
`root_squash`	Maps any requests from root, UID 0 on the client, to the UID NOBODY_UID on the server.
`no_root_squash`	Doesn't map any requests from UID 0 (default behavior).
`ro`	Mounts the file system as read-only (default behavior).
`rw`	Mounts the file system as read-write.
`link_relative`	Converts absolute symbolic links (where the link contents start with a slash) into relative links by prefixing the link with the necessary

Part

III

Ch

14

continues

Table 14.5 Continued

Option	Description
	number of ../ characters to get from the directory containing the link to the root on the server.
link_absolute	Leaves all symbolic links as they are (normal behavior for Sun NFS servers). This is the default behavior for Linux.
map_daemon	Maps local and remote names and numeric IDs by using an lname/uid map daemon on the client where the NFS request originated. Used to map between the client and server UID spaces.
all-squash	Maps all UIDs and GIDs to the anonymous user. This option is useful for NFS-exported public directories, such as those housing FTP and news.
no-all-squash	The opposite of the all-squash option. This is the default option for Linux.
squash-uids	Specifies a list of UIDs subject to anonymous mappings. A valid list of IDs looks like this: squash uids=0-15,20,25-50
squash-gids	Specifies a list of GIDs subject to anonymous mappings. A valid list of IDs looks like this: squash gids=0-15,20,25-50
anonuid	Sets the UID for the anonymous account. This option is useful for PC/NFS clients.
anongid	Sets the GID for the anonymous account. This option is useful for PC/NFS clients.
noaccess	Used to exclude certain subdirectories from a client. Makes everything below the directory inaccessible to the client.

Here is a sample /etc/exports file:

```
/home                   bill.tristar.com(rw) fred.tristar.com(rw)
➥george.tristar.com(rw)
/usr/local/bin/bin          *.tristar.com(ro)
/projects               develop.tristar.com(rw) bill.tristar.com(ro)
/pub                    (ro,insecure,root_squash)
```

In this example, the server exports four different file systems. /home is mounted with read/write access on three different computers: bill, fred, and george. This indicates the directory probably holds user home directories because of the directories' names. The /usr/local/bin file system is exported as read-only with access allowed for every computer in the tristar.com domain.

The /projects file system is exported with read/write access for the computer develop.tristar.com but with read-only access for bill.tristar.com.

For the /pub file system, there's no list of hosts that are allowed access. This means that any host is allowed to mount this file system. It has been exported as read-only with non-authenticated access allowed, and the server remaps any request from root on a remote machine that accesses this file system.

Mounting NFS File Systems

Mounting an NFS file system is similar to mounting any other type of file system. You can mount NFS file systems from the /etc/fstab file at boot time or interactively via the mount command.

> **CAUTION**
>
> You must be sure to separate the host name and *file/system/path* portions of the remote file system name with a colon, such as
>
> `mailserver:/var/spool/mail`
>
> when using the mount command or when making an entry in /etc/fstab. If you don't separate the host name from the directory, your system won't mount the remote directory correctly.

Mounting NFS File Systems via /etc/fstab   When you specify an NFS file system in the /etc/fstab file, you identify the file system with the format

`hostname:/file/system/path`

where *hostname* is the name of the server where the file system is located, and */file/system/path* is the file system on the server.

The file-system type is specified as nfs in the mount options field of the file system entry. Table 14.6 lists the most commonly used mount options.

Table 14.6   Commonly Used Options for NFS Mounts

Option	Description
rsize=*n*	Specifies the datagram size in bytes used by the NFS clients on read requests. The default value is 1,024 bytes.
wsize=*n*	Specifies the datagram size in bytes used by the NFS clients on write requests. The default value is 1,024 bytes.
timeo=*n*	Sets the time, in tenths of a second, that the NFS client waits for a request to complete. The default value is 0.7 seconds.
hard	Mounts this file system by using a hard mount. This is the default behavior.
soft	Mounts this file system by using a soft mount.
intr	Allows signals to interrupt an NFS call. This is useful for aborting an operation when an NFS server doesn't respond.

Part

III

Ch

14

Hard Mounts Versus Soft Mounts

Hard mounts and *soft mounts* determine how an NFS client behaves when an NFS server stops responding. NFS file systems are hard-mounted by default. With either type of mount, if a server stops responding, the client waits until the timeout value specified by the `timeo` option expires and then resends the request (this is known as a *minor timeout*). If the requests to the server continue to time out and the total timeout reaches 60 seconds, a *major timeout* occurs.

If a file system is hard mounted, the client prints a message to the console and starts the mount requests all over again by using a timeout value that's twice that of the previous cycle. This has the potential to go on forever. The client keeps trying to remount the NFS file system from the server until it gets it.

Soft mounts, on the other hand, just generate an I/O error to the calling process when a major timeout occurs. Linux then continues on its merry way.

Typically, important software packages and utilities that are mounted via NFS should be mounted with hard mounts. This is why hard mounts are the default. You don't want your system to start acting strange if the Ethernet gets unplugged for a moment; you want Linux to wait and continue when the network is back up. On the other hand, you might want to mount non-critical data, such as remote news spool partitions, as soft mounts so that if the remote host goes down, it won't hang your current login session.

A typical NFS file system entry in the /etc/fstab file might look like this:

```
mailserver:/var/spool/mail   /var/spool/mail   nfs timeo=20,intr
```

This entry mounts the /var/spool/mail file system located on the host mailserver at the local mount point /var/spool/mail. It specifies that the file system type is `nfs`. Also, it sets the timeout value to 2 seconds (20 tenths of a second) and makes operations on this file system interruptible.

Mounting NFS File Systems Interactively NFS file systems can be mounted interactively, just like any other type of file system. However, you should be aware that the NFS `mount` command isn't very pretty due to all the options that you can specify on the command line.

By using the previous example, the interactive `mount` command that you use to mount the /var/spool/mail file system becomes

```
# mount -t nfs -o timeo=20,intr mailserver:/var/spool/mail   /var/spool/mail
```

If you need to specify datagram sizes and timeouts, interactive `mount` commands can become very complex. It's highly recommended that you place these `mount` commands in your /etc/fstab file so that they can be mounted automatically at boot time.

Maintaining File Systems

As the systems administrator, you're responsible for maintaining the integrity of the file systems themselves. Typically, this means checking the file systems periodically for damaged or corrupted files. Linux automatically checks file systems at boot time if they have a value greater than 0 specified in the pass number field of the /etc/fstab file.

N O T E The ext2 file system commonly used under Linux has a special flag known as a *clean bit*. If the file system has been synchronized and unmounted cleanly, the clean bit is set on the file system. If the clean bit is set on a file system when Linux boots, it's not checked for integrity. ■

Using the *fsck* Command

It's a good idea to check your file systems occasionally for damaged or corrupt files. Under the Slackware distribution of Linux, you use the fsck (file system check) command to check your file systems. The fsck command is really a "front end" for a series of commands that are designed to check specific file systems. The syntax for the fsck command is as follows:

```
fsck [-A] [-V] [-t fs-type] [-a] [-l] [-r] [-s] filesys
```

However, the most basic form of the command is this:

```
fsck filesys
```

Table 14.7 describes the command-line options for the fsck command.

Table 14.7   Command-Line Arguments for *fsck*

Argument	Description
-A	Goes through the /etc/fstab file and tries to check all file systems in one pass. This option is typically used during the Linux boot sequence to check all normally mounted file systems. If you use -A, you can't use the *filesys* argument as well.
-V	Verbose mode. Prints additional information about what fsck is doing.
-t *fs-type*	Specifies the type of file system to be checked.
filesys	Specifies which file system is to be checked. This argument can be a block special device name, such as /dev/hda1, or a mount point, such as /usr.
-a	Automatically repairs any problems found in the file system without asking any questions. Use this option with caution.
-l	Lists all the filenames in the file system.
-r	Asks for confirmations before repairing the file system.
-s	Lists the superblock before checking the file system.

The fsck command is actually a front-end program that calls the command to check the file system that matches the type you specify. To do so, Linux needs to know the file system type that it's checking. The easiest way to make sure that fsck calls the right command is to specify a file system type with the -t option to fsck. If you don't use the -t option, Linux tries to figure out the file system type by looking up the file system in /etc/fstab and by using the file type specified there. If fsck can't find the file type information in /etc/fstab, it assumes that you're using a Minix file system.

Part
III

Ch
14

> **CAUTION**
>
> The `fsck` command assumes that the file system you're checking is a Minix file system if you don't tell it differently—either with the `-t` argument or by listing the type in /etc/fstab. Because your Linux file systems are probably of type `ext2` and not Minix, you should be careful and make sure that `fsck` knows the correct type. This is especially important if you're checking a file system that isn't listed in the /etc/fstab file.

It's a good idea to unmount a file system before checking it. This ensures that none of the files on the file system are in use when they're being checked.

> **NOTE** Remember, you can't unmount a file system if any of the files on it are busy. For example, if a user is now in a directory on a file system that you try to unmount, you get a message saying that the file system is busy. ▪

Trying to check the root file system presents an additional problem. You can't directly unmount the root file system, because Linux must be able to access it in order to run. To check the root file system, you should boot from a maintenance floppy disk that has a root file system on it, and then run `fsck` on your real root file system from the floppy by specifying the special device name of your root file system. If `fsck` makes any changes to your file system, it's important that you reboot your system immediately. This allows Linux to reread important information about your file system and prevents your file system from further corruption.

> **CAUTION**
>
> Be sure to reboot your computer immediately after you run `fsck` if any changes were made to your file system to prevent further corruption to your file system. Use the `shutdown -r` command or the `reboot` command to reboot.

Creating and Formatting File Systems

When you add a new hard disk to your computer or want to change the partition information on an old hard disk, you go through the steps of creating a file system from a raw disk. Assuming that you've added a new hard disk to your system, you must set the disk partition information and then create the actual file systems on the disk before Linux can use the disk. To change disk partition information, you use the `fdisk` command. After you partition the hard drive, you need to create the file systems by using the `mkfs` command.

Using *fdisk* to Create Disk Partitions

The `fdisk` command is used to create disk partitions and set the attributes that tell Linux what type of file system is on a particular partition. If you installed Linux from scratch on an MS-DOS system, you had to run `fdisk` to change the disk partition information before you could install Linux.

> **CAUTION**
>
> Using `fdisk` on a disk can destroy all data on the disk. Because `fdisk` completely rewrites the file table on the disk, all your former files may be lost. Make sure that you have a complete, current backup of your disks before using `fdisk`.

You should always run the `fdisk` command on an unmounted file system. `fdisk` is an interactive, menu-driven program, not just a single command. To start `fdisk`, type this command

fdisk [*drive*]

where *drive* is the physical disk drive that you want to work on. If you don't specify a disk, the disk /dev/hda is assumed. For example, to run `fdisk` on the second IDE hard drive in your system, enter

fdisk /dev/hdb

at the superuser command prompt. Because `fdisk` is a menu-driven program, several different commands are available when you're using `fdisk`, as summarized in Table 14.8.

Table 14.8   Commands Available from the *fdisk* Menu

Command	Description
a	Toggles the bootable flag on a partition
c	Toggles the DOS compatibility flag on a partition
d	Deletes a partition
l	Lists partition types known to `fdisk`
m	Displays a menu listing all available commands
n	Adds a new partition
p	Prints the partition table for the current disk
q	Quits without saving any changes
t	Changes the file system type for a partition
u	Changes display/entry units
v	Verifies the partition table
w	Writes the table to disk and exits
x	Lists additional functions for experts:
	b Moves the beginning location of data in a partition
	c Changes the number of cylinders

Part

III

Ch

14

continues

Table 14.8	Continued
Command	**Description**
d	Prints the raw data in the partition table
e	Lists extended partitions on disk
h	Changes number of heads on disk
r	Returns to main menu
s	Changes number of sectors on disk

fdisk can set the file system type of a disk partition to any of several different types. Only use Linux fdisk to create partitions used under Linux. For MS-DOS or OS/2 partitions, you should use the fdisk tool that's native to that operating environment, and then use Linux's fdisk to tag the partitions as Linux native or Linux swap.

Table 14.9 lists the partitions supported by Linux fdisk. Each partition type has an associated hexadecimal code that identifies it. You must enter the appropriate code in fdisk when you want to set a partition type.

Table 14.9	Partition Codes and Types in Linux *fdisk*
Hex Code	**Partition Type**
0	Empty
1	DOS 12-bit FAT
2	XENIX root
3	XENIX usr
4	DOS 16-bit file system, less than 32MB
5	Extended
6	DOS 16-bit file system supporting more than 32MB
7	OS/2 High Performance File System (HPFS)
8	AIX
9	AIX bootable
a	OS/2 Boot Manager
40	Venix 80286
51	Novell?
52	Microport

Hex Code	Partition Type
63	GNU HURD
64	Novell NetWare
65	Novell NetWare
75	PC/IX
80	Old MINIX
81	Linux/MINIX
82	Linux swap, used for swap files under Linux
83	Linux native, common Linux file system type
93	Amoeba
94	Amoeba BBT
a5	BSD/386
b7	BSDI file system
b8	BSDI swap file system
c7	Syrinx
db	CP/M
e1	DOS access
e3	DOS R/O
f2	DOS secondary
ff	BBT

The following sections show how to use `fdisk`. Here is an example of how to use `fdisk` to set up the partitions on a hard disk for use by Linux. Assume that you want to configure the first IDE drive in your system for Linux. Make sure that you have a backup of your data. All data on your hard disk is destroyed in the process. The name of the first IDE hard disk is /dev/hda, which is the default device for Linux.

Running *fdisk*   You run `fdisk` with this command

```
# fdisk
```

and `fdisk` responds with the following:

```
Using /dev/hda as default device!
Command (m for help):
```

This tells you that `fdisk` is using disk /dev/hda as the device that you're working with. Because this is what you wanted, you're fine. You should always check to make sure that you're really on the disk that you think you're on. Linux then displays the `fdisk` command prompt.

Part
III

Ch
14

Displaying the Current Partition Table   The first thing you want to do is display the current partition table. This is done with the p command:

```
Command (m for help): p
Disk /dev/hda: 14 heads, 17 sectors, 1024 cylinders
Units = cylinders of 238 * 512 bytes

Device      Boot    Begin    Start    End    Blocks    Id    System

Command (m for help):
```

This listing shows that the current disk, /dev/hda, has a geometry of 14 heads, 17 sectors, and 1,024 cylinders. The display units are in cylinders of 238 * 512 (121,856) bytes each. Because there are 1,024 cylinders and each cylinder is 121,856 bytes, you can deduce that the disk can hold 1,024×121,856 = 124,780,544 bytes, or about 120MB. You can also see that /dev/hda has no partitions.

Creating a New Partition   Assume that you want to create a 100MB Linux file partition for user home directories and a 20MB swap partition. Your next step is to use the n command to create a new partition:

```
Command (m for help): n
Command action
e   extended
p   primary partition (1-4)
p
Partition number (1-4): 1
First cylinder (1-1023):   1
Last cylinder or +size or +sizeM or +sizeK (1-1023):   +100M
```

Using the n command to create a new partition displays another menu. You must choose whether you want to create an extended partition or a primary partition. You typically want to create a primary partition unless you have more than four partitions on a disk. fdisk then asks you for the partition number that you want to create. Because this is the first partition on the disk, you answer 1. You're then prompted for the first cylinder for the partition. This determines where on the disk the data area starts. Again, because this will be the first partition on the disk, you can start the partition at cylinder 1.

The next line asks you how large you want the partition to be. You have several options as to how to answer this question. fdisk accepts either a number, which it interprets as the size in cylinders, or the size in bytes, kilobytes, or megabytes. The size in bytes is specified as +*bytes*, where *bytes* is the size of the partition. Similarly, +*size*K and +*size*M set the partition size to size kilobytes or size megabytes, respectively. You know that you want a 100MB partition, so the easiest answer to the prompt is +100M.

Rechecking the Partition Table   Now you should check the partition table again to see what fdisk has done:

```
Command (m for help): p
Disk /dev/hda: 14 heads, 17 sectors, 1024 cylinders
Units = cylinders of 238 * 512 bytes
```

```
Device      Boot    Begin   Start    End    Blocks     Id     System
/dev/hda1                1      1      861    102400    81     Linux/MINIX
Command (m for help):
```

The partition table shows that you have 1 partition, /dev/hda1, that goes from cylinder 1 to cylinder 861 and uses 102,400 blocks. It's listed as being type 81, Linux/MINIX.

Creating the Swap Partition   Now you need to create the 20MB swap partition by using the remaining disk space. This is just like creating the first partition:

```
Command (m for help): n
Command action
e    extended
p    primary partition (1-4)
p
Partition number (1-4): 2
First cylinder (862-1023):  862
Last cylinder or +size or +sizeM or +sizeK (862-1023): 1023
```

TIP   It's usually better to go ahead and enter the size of the last partition in cylinders to make sure that you use all the disk space.

Here you specified partition number 2 for the second partition. When fdisk prompts for the first cylinder, notice that it gives a range of 862 to 1023. This is because the first partition takes up everything before cylinder 862. So enter **862** as the starting cylinder for the second partition. You want to use all the remaining space on the disk for the swap partition. You should have about 20MB left, but if you specify the size in megabytes, the internal fdisk calculations could leave you with a couple of unused cylinders. So you enter **1023** for the last cylinder on the size prompt.

N O T E   You might see an error similar to this

```
Warning: Linux cannot currently use the last xxx sectors of this
partition.
```

where *xxx* is some number. Such an error can be ignored. It's left over from the days when Linux couldn't access file systems larger than 64MB. ■

Making Sure the Sizes Are Correct   At this point, you've created both partitions that you wanted to create. You should take a look at the partition table one more time to check that the sizes are correct:

```
Command (m for help): p
Disk /dev/hda: 14 heads, 17 sectors, 1024 cylinders
Units = cylinders of 238 * 512 bytes

Device      Boot    Begin   Start    End    Blocks     Id     System
/dev/hda1                1      1      861    102400    81     Linux/MINIX
/dev/hda2              862    862     1023     19159    81     Linux/MINIX
Command (m for help):
```

As you can see, /dev/hda1 uses cylinder 1 through cylinder 861 with a size of 102,400 blocks, which is approximately 100MB. Partition /dev/hda2 goes from cylinder 862 to cylinder 1023 with a size of 19,156 blocks, or almost 20MB.

Changing the Partition Type   The next thing that you need to do is change the partition type for each partition. To change the partition type, use the t command at the fdisk command prompt. The most common choice for a standard Linux file system partition is to set it to partition type 83, Linux native. Swap partitions should be set to partition type 82, Linux swap.

```
Command (m for help): t
Partition number (1-4): 1
Hex code (type L to list codes): 83
Command (m for help): t
Partition number (1-4): 2
Hex code (type L to list codes): 82
```

When you use the t command, you're prompted for the partition number that you want to change. You're then prompted for the hex code for the file system ID that you want to set the partition to. Typically, Linux file systems are set to type 83 for normal file systems, and type 82 for swap partitions. You can type 1 at this point to see a list of file systems, if you want.

Finishing Up   Now that you've created the partitions and labeled them, you should take one last look at the partition table before you exit just to make sure that everything is okay.

```
Command (m for help): p
Disk /dev/hda: 14 heads, 17 sectors, 1024 cylinders
Units = cylinders of 238 * 512 bytes

Device     Boot    Begin   Start    End    Blocks    Id    System
/dev/hda1             1      1      861    102400    83    Linux native
/dev/hda2           862    862    1023     19159    82    Linux swap
Command (m for help):
```

As you can see, the partitions are in the right place, they're the right size, and the file system types are set correctly. The last thing that you need to do is use the w command to write the partition table to disk and exit:

```
Command (m for help):  w

#
```

None of the changes that you make during an fdisk session take effect until you write them to disk with the w command. You can always quit with the q command and not save any changes. This said, you should still always have a backup of any disk that you want to modify with fdisk.

After you make changes to a disk with fdisk, you should reboot the system just to make sure that Linux has the updated partition information in the kernel.

Using *mkfs* to Build a File System

After you create a file system partition with fdisk, you must build a file system on it before you can use it for storing data. This is done with the mkfs command. Think of building a parking lot. If you think of fdisk as physically building the parking lot, mkfs is the part of the process that paints the lines so that the drivers know where to park.

Just like fsck is a "front-end" program for checking different types of file systems, mkfs actually calls different programs to create the file system, depending on what file system type you want to create. The syntax of the mkfs command is this

```
mkfs  [-V] [-t fs-type] [fs-options] filesys [blocks]
```

where *filesys* is the device of the file system that you want to build, such as /dev/hda1.

> **CAUTION**
>
> The mkfs command also accepts the name of a mount point, such as /home, as the file system name. You should be extremely careful about using a mount point. If you run mkfs on a mounted "live" file system, you might very well corrupt all the data on that file system.

Table 14.10 lists the various command-line parameters that you can specify with mkfs.

Table 14.10   Command-Line Parameters for the *mkfs* Command

Option	Description
-V	Causes mkfs to produce verbose output, including all file system-specific commands that are executed. Specifying this option more than once inhibits execution of any file system-specific commands.
-t fs-type	Specifies the type of file system to be built. If the file system type isn't specified, mkfs tries to figure it out by searching for *filesys* in /etc/fstab and using the corresponding entry. If the type can't be deduced, a MINIX file system is created.
fs-options	Specifies file system–specific options that are to be passed to the actual file system–builder program. Although not guaranteed, the following options are supported by most file system builders: -c Checks the device for bad blocks before building the file system -l *file-name* Reads a list of the bad blocks on the disk from *file-name* -v Tells the actual file system builder program to produce verbose output
filesys	Specifies the device on which the file system resides. This parameter is required.
blocks	Specifies the number of blocks to be used for the file system.

Part

III

Ch

14

Although -t fs-type is an optional argument, you should get in the habit of specifying the file system type. Just like fsck, mkfs tries to figure out the type of the file system from the

/etc/fstab file. If it can't figure it out, it creates a MINIX file system by default. For a normal Linux file system, you probably want an ext2 partition instead.

Using Swap Files and Partitions

Swap space on your Linux system is used for virtual memory. A complete discussion of all the issues involved with virtual memory is beyond the scope of this book. Any good general computer operating system text book discusses the issue in detail.

Linux supports two types of swap space: swap partition and swap files. A *swap partition* is a physical disk partition with its file system ID set to type 82, Linux swap, and is dedicated for use as a swap area. A *swap file* is a large file on a normal file system that's used for swap space.

You're better off using a swap partition instead of a swap file. All access to a swap file is performed through the normal Linux file system. The disk blocks that make up the swap file are probably not contiguous and, therefore, performance isn't as good as it is with a swap partition. I/O to swap partitions is performed directly to the device, and disk blocks on a swap partition are always contiguous. Also, by keeping the swap space off a normal file system, you reduce the risk of corrupting your regular file system if something bizarre happens to your swap file.

Creating a Swap Partition

To create a swap partition, you must have created a disk partition by using `fdisk` and tagged it as type 82, Linux swap. After you create the swap partition, you have two additional steps to follow to make the swap partition active.

First, you must prepare the partition in a manner similar to creating a file system. Instead of `mkfs`, the command for preparing the partition is `mkswap`. The syntax of the `mkswap` command is as follows:

```
mkswap [-c] device size-in-blocks
```

where *device* is the name of the swap partition, such as /dev/hda2, and *size-in-blocks* is the size of the target file system in blocks. You can get the size in blocks by running `fdisk` and looking at the partition table. In the example in the section "Making Sure the Sizes Are Correct," the size of /dev/hda2 was 19,159 blocks. Linux requires that swap partitions be between 9 and 65,537 blocks in size. The `-c` argument tells `mkswap` to check the file system for bad blocks when creating the swap space, which is a good idea.

Following the example in "Making Sure the Sizes Are Correct," the command for setting up a swap partition on /dev/hda2 is this:

```
mkswap -c /dev/hda2 19159
```

After you run `mkswap` to prepare the partition, you must make it active so that the Linux kernel can use it. The command to make the swap partition active is `swapon`. The syntax for the swapon command is as follows:

```
swapon filesys
```

where *filesys* is the file system that you want to make available as swap space. Linux makes a call to swapon -a during boot, which mounts all available swap partitions listed in the /etc/fstab file.

N O T E   Remember to put an entry for any swap partitions or swap files that you create into the /etc/fstab file so that Linux can automatically access them at boot time. ▓

Creating a Swap File

Swap files can be useful if you need to expand your swap space and can't allocate disk space to create a dedicated swap partition. Setting up a swap file is almost identical to creating a swap partition. The main difference is that you have to create the file before you can run mkswap and swapon.

To create a swap file, you use the dd command, which is used for copying large chunks of data. For a full description of this command, see the man page for dd. The main things that you have to know before creating the file are the name of the swap file you want to create and its size in blocks. A block under Linux is 1,024 bytes. For example, to create a 10MB swap file named /swap, enter

```
# dd if=/dev/zero of=/swap bs=1024 count=10240
```

of=/swap specifies that the file to be created is named /swap, and count=10240 sets the size of the output file to be 10,240 blocks, or 10MB. You then use mkswap to prepare the file as a swap space:

```
# mkswap /swap 10240
```

Remember that you have to tell mkswap how big the file is. Before you run swapon, you need to make sure that the file is completely written to disk by using the /etc/sync command.

Now you're ready to make the swap file active. Like with the swap partition, you use the swapon command to make the file active; for example,

```
# swapon /swap
```

If you need to get rid of a swap file, you must make sure that it's not active. Use the swapoff command to deactivate the swap file, as in

```
# swapoff /swap
```

You can then safely delete the swap file.

From Here...

In this chapter, you've looked at many different aspects of the Linux file system, from a tour of the basic directory structure to mounting and unmounting file systems. You've explored accessing remote file systems with NFS and looked in detail at how to create file systems and prepare them for use. Finally, this chapter discussed the creation of swap partitions and swap files.

Part
III

Ch
14

You can find more information about systems administration in the following chapters:

- Chapter 7, "Understanding System Administration," introduces you to common systems administration tasks.
- Chapter 10, "Managing User Accounts," describes how to set up and manage user accounts on your Linux system.
- Chapter 11, "Backing Up Data," discusses how to plan and implement plans for data backups.

Using Samba

by Jack Tackett

In this chapter

This chapter gives you the information you need to install, configure, and use the Session Message Block (SMB or Samba) protocol services under Linux. With Samba you can

- Share a Linux filesystem with Windows 95, 98, or NT.
- Share a Windows 95, 98, or NT filesystem with Linux.
- Share a printer connected to a Linux system with Windows 95, 98, or NT systems.
- Share a Windows 95, 98, or NT printer with Linux.

Samba is the protocol used by Microsoft's operating systems to share files and printer services. Microsoft and Intel developed the SMB protocol system in 1987, and later Andrew Tridgell ported the system to various UNIX systems and then Linux.

N O T E   Microsoft is currently proposing another file sharing standard, called Common Internet File System (CIFS). The standard has been submitted to the Internet Engineering Task Force but CIFS has yet to be widely adopted, including in the Linux development community. ■

The Samba suite is made up of several components. The smbd daemon provides the file and print services to SMB clients, such as Windows for Workgroups, Windows NT, or LanManager. The configuration file for this daemon is described in smb.conf. The nmbd daemon provides NetBIOS nameserving and browsing support. It can also be run interactively to query other name service daemons.

The smbclient program implements a simple FTP-like client. This is useful for accessing SMB shares on other compatible servers, such as Windows machines, and it can also be used to allow a UNIX box to print to a printer attached to any SMB server, such as a PC running Windows 98.

The testparm utility allows you to test your smb.conf configuration file. The smbstatus utility allows you to tell who is currently using the smbd server.

Installing Samba

Samba can be installed during installation or later using RPM. If you need to install the package, first download the current version from Red Hat's Web site (**http://www.redhat.com**). You can then install the package (the current version is samba-1.9.18p5-1.i386.rpm) with the following command:

```
rpm -ivh samba-1.9.18p5-1.i386.rpm
```

▶ **See** "Installing Packages with RPM," **p. 150**

The package should contain all the files needed to run Samba, including the two primary programs smbd and nmbd. However, you might have to recompile the various programs if you are using a different distribution.

Configuring Samba on Linux

The main configuration file is called smb.conf and is located in the /etc directory. Listing 15.1 provides the default listing shipped with Red Hat 5.1

N O T E   A semicolon character (;) at the beginning of a line indicates that the line is a comment and is to be ignored when processed by the Samba server. ▦

Listing 15.1   The Sample smb.conf Samba Configuration File

```
; The global setting for a RedHat default install
; smbd re-reads this file regularly, but if in doubt stop and restart it:
; /etc/rc.d/init.d/smb stop
; /etc/rc.d/init.d/smb start
;======================= Global Settings =======================================
[global]

; workgroup = NT-Domain-Name or Workgroup-Name, eg: REDHAT4
   workgroup = WORKGROUP

; comment is the equivalent of the NT Description field
   comment = RedHat Samba Server

; volume = used to emulate a CDRom label (can be set on a per share basis)
   volume = RedHat4


; printing = BSD or SYSV or AIX, etc.
   printing = bsd
   printcap name = /etc/printcap
   load printers = yes

; Uncomment this if you want a guest account
;  guest account = pcguest
   log file = /var/log/samba-log.%m
; Put a capping on the size of the log files (in Kb)
   max log size = 50

; Options for handling file name case sensitivity and / or preservation
; Case Sensitivity breaks many WfW and Win95 apps
;   case sensitive = yes
   short preserve case = yes
   preserve case = yes

; Security and file integrity related options
   lock directory = /var/lock/samba
   locking = yes
   strict locking = yes
;   fake oplocks = yes
   share modes = yes
; Security modes: USER uses Unix username/passwd, SHARE uses WfW type passwords
;         SERVER uses a Windows NT Server to provide authentication services
```

continues

Listing 15.1   Continued

```
    security = user
; Use password server option only with security = server
;    password server = <NT-Server-Name>

; Configuration Options*****Watch location in smb.conf for side-effects*****
; Where %m is any SMBName (machine name, or computer name) for which a custom
; configuration is desired
;    include = /etc/smb.conf.%m

; Performance Related Options
; Before setting socket options read the smb.conf man page!!
    socket options = TCP_NODELAY
; Socket Address is used to specify which socket Samba
; will listen on (good for aliased systems)
;    socket address = aaa.bbb.ccc.ddd
; Use keep alive only if really needed!!!!
;    keep alive = 60

; Domain Control Options
; OS Level gives Samba the power to rule the roost. Windows NT = 32
;        Any value < 32 means NT wins as Master Browser, > 32 Samba gets it
;    os level = 33
; specifies Samba to be the Domain Master Browser
;    domain master = yes
; Use with care only if you have an NT server on your network that has been
; configured at install time to be a primary domain controller.
;    domain controller = <NT-Domain-Controller-SMBName>
; Domain logon control can be a good thing! See [netlogon] share section below!
;    domain logons = yes
; run a specific logon batch file per workstation (machine)
;    logon script = %m.bat
; run a specific logon batch file per username
;    logon script = %u.bat
; Windows Internet Name Serving Support Section
; WINS Support - Tells the NMBD component of Samba to enable its WINS Server
;        the default is NO.
;    wins support = yes
; WINS Server - Tells the NMBD components of Samba to be a WINS Client
;        Note: Samba can be either a WINS Server, or a WINS Client, but NOT both
;    wins server = w.x.y.z
; WINS Proxy - Tells Samba to answer name resolution queries on behalf of a non
;        WINS Client capable client, for this to work there must be at least one
;        WINS Server on the network. The default is NO.
;    wins proxy = yes

;=========================== Share Declarations ===============================
[homes]
    comment = Home Directories
    browseable = no
    read only = no
    preserve case = yes
    short preserve case = yes
    create mode = 0750
```

```
;  Un-comment the following and create the netlogon directory for Domain Logons
;  [netlogon]
;     comment = Samba Network Logon Service
;     path = /home/netlogon
;  Case sensitivity breaks logon script processing!!!
;     case sensitive = no
;     guest ok = yes
;     locking = no
;     read only = yes
;     browseable = yes  ; say NO if you want to hide the NETLOGON share
;     admin users = @wheel

;  NOTE: There is NO need to specifically define each individual printer
[printers]
   comment = All Printers
   path = /var/spool/samba
   browseable = no
   printable = yes
;  Set public = yes to allow user 'guest account' to print
   public = no
   writable = no
   create mode = 0700

;[tmp]
;     comment = Temporary file space
;     path = /tmp
;     read only = no
;     public = yes

;  A publicly accessible directory, but read only, except for people in
;  the staff group
;[public]
;     comment = Public Stuff
;     path = /home/samba
;     public = yes
;     writable = yes
;     printable = no
;     write list = @users

;  Other examples.
;
;  A private printer, usable only by fred. Spool data will be placed in fred's
;  home directory. Note that fred must have write access to the spool directory,
;  wherever it is.
;[fredsprn]
;     comment = Fred's Printer
;     valid users = fred
;     path = /homes/fred
;     printer = freds_printer
;     public = no
;     writable = no
;     printable = yes
;
;  A private directory, usable only by fred. Note that fred requires write
;  access to the directory.
```

continues

Listing 15.1 Continued

```
;[fredsdir]
;    comment = Fred's Service
;    path = /usr/somewhere/private
;    valid users = fred
;    public = no
;    writable = yes
;    printable = no
;
; a service which has a different directory for each machine that connects
; this allows you to tailor configurations to incoming machines. You could
; also use the %u option to tailor it by user name.
; The %m gets replaced with the machine name that is connecting.
;[pchome]
;   comment = PC Directories
;   path = /usr/pc/%m
;   public = no
;   writeable = yes
;
;
; A publicly accessible directory, read/write to all users. Note that all files
; created in the directory by users will be owned by the default user, so
; any user with access can delete any other user's files. Obviously this
; directory must be writable by the default user. Another user could of course
; be specified, in which case all files would be owned by that user instead.
;[public]
;    path = /usr/somewhere/else/public
;    public = yes
;    only guest = yes
;    writable = yes
;    printable = no
;
;
; The following two entries demonstrate how to share a directory so that two
; users can place files there that will be owned by the specific users. In this
; setup, the directory should be writable by both users and should have the
; sticky bit set on it to prevent abuse. Obviously this could be extended to
; as many users as required.
;[myshare]
;    comment = Mary's and Fred's stuff
;    path = /usr/somewhere/shared
;    valid users = mary fred
;    public = no
;    writable = yes
;    printable = no
;    create mask = 0765
```

The smb.conf file layout consists of a series of named sections. Each section starts with its name in brackets, as in [global]. Within each section, the parameters are specified by *key* = value pairs, such as comment = RedHat Samba Server.

smb.conf contains three special sections and one or more custom sections. The special sections are [global], [homes], and [printers].

The [global] Section

The [global] section controls parameters for the entire smb server. The section also provides default values for the other sections.

```
[global]

; workgroup = NT-Domain-Name or Workgroup-Name, eg: REDHAT4
   workgroup = WORKGROUP

; comment is the equivalent of the NT Description field
   comment = RedHat Samba Server

; volume = used to emulate a CDRom label (can be set on a per share basis)
   volume = RedHat4
```

The first line from the global section in Listing 15.1 defines the workgroup that this machine will belong to on your network. Next the file specifies a comment for the system and identifies a volume label.

```
; printing = BSD or SYSV or AIX, etc.
   printing = bsd
   printcap name = /etc/printcap
   load printers = yes
```

The next entry tells the Samba server what type of printing system is available on your server, and the line after that indicates where the printer configuration file is located.

▶ **See** "Understanding the /etc/printcap File," **p. 411**

The next line instructs Samba to make available on the network all the printers defined in the printcap file.

```
; Uncomment this if you want a guest account
;   guest account = pcguest
   log file = /var/log/samba-log.%m
; Put a capping on the size of the log files (in Kb)
   max log size = 50
```

The next entry indicates a username for a guest account on your sever. This account is used to authenticate users for Samba services available to guest connections.

The log file entry specifies the location of the log file for each client who accesses Samba services. The %m parameter tells the Samba server to create a separate log file for each client. The max log size entry sets a maximum file size for the logs created.

The [homes] Section

The [homes] section allows network clients to connect to a user's home directory on your server without having an explicit entry in the smb.conf file. When a service request is made, the Samba server searches the smb.conf file for the specific section corresponding to the service request. If it does not find the service, Samba checks to see if there is a [homes] section. If the [homes] section exists, Samba searches the password file to find the home directory for the user making the request. When it's found, this directory is shared with the network.

```
[homes]
    comment = Home Directories
    browseable = no
    read only = no
    preserve case = yes
    short preserve case = yes
    create mode = 0750
```

The comment entry is displayed to the clients to let them know which shares are available. The browseable entry instructs Samba how to display this share in a network browse list. The read-only parameter controls whether a user can create and change files in his home directory when it is shared across the network. The preserve case and short preserve case parameters instruct the server to preserve the case of any information written to the server. This is important because Windows filenames are not typically case-sensitive, but Linux filenames are case-sensitive. The final entry sets the file permissions for any files created on the shared directory.

▶ **See** "File Permissions," **p. 310**

The [printers] Section

The [printers] section defines how printing services are controlled if no specific entries are found in the smb.conf file. Thus like the [homes] section, if no specific entry is found for a printing service, Samba uses the [printers] section (if it's present) to allow a user to connect to any printer defined in /etc/printcap.

```
[printers]
    comment = All Printers
    path = /var/spool/samba
    browseable = no
    printable = yes
; Set public = yes to allow user 'guest account' to print
    public = no
    writable = no
    create mode = 0700
```

The comment, browseable, and create mode entries mean the same as discussed above in the [homes] sections. The path entry indicates the location of the spool file to be used when servicing a print request via SMB.

▶ **See** "Selecting a Printer to Work with Linux," **p. 406**

The printable value, if set to yes, indicates that this printer resource can be used to print. The public entry controls whether the guest account can print.

Sharing Directories

After configuring your defaults for the Samba server, you can create specific shared directories limited to just certain groups of people or to everyone. For example, suppose you want to make a directory available to only one user. To do so you would create a new section and fill in the needed information. Typically you'll need to specify the user, the directory path, and configuration information to the SMB server as shown here:

```
[jacksdir]
comment = Jack's remote source code directory
path = /usr/local/src
valid users = tackett
browsable = yes
public = no
writable = yes
create mode = 0700
```

This sample section creates a shared directory called jacksdir. The path to the directory on the local server is /usr/local/src. Because the browsable entry is set to yes, jacksdir will show up in the network browse list. However, because the public entry is set to no, only the user named tackett can access this directory using Samba. You can grant access to other users by listing them in the valid users entry.

Testing the smb.conf File

After creating the configuration file you should test it for correctness with the testparm program. testparm is a very simple test program to check the /etc/smb.conf configuration file for internal correctness. If this program reports no problems, you can use the configuration file with confidence that smbd will successfully load the configuration file.

> **CAUTION**
>
> Using testparm is NOT a guarantee that the services specified in the configuration file will be available or will operate as expected.

testparm has the following command line:

```
testparm [configfile [hostname hostip]]
```

where *configfile* indicates the location of the smb.conf file if it is not in the default location (/etc/smb.conf). The *hostname hostIP* optional parameter instructs testparm to see if the host has access to the services provided in the smb.conf file.

The following example shows a sample output from running testparm. If the smb.conf file contains any errors, the program will report them along with a specific error message.

```
# testparm
Load smb config files from /etc/smb.conf
Processing section "[homes]"
Processing section "[printers]"
Loaded services file OK.
Press enter to see a dump of your service definitions
```

When you press the <Enter> key, testparm will begin evaluating each section defined in the configuration file.

Running the Samba Server

The Samba server consists of two daemons, smbd and nmbd. The smbd daemon provides the file and print sharing services. The nmbd daemon provides NetBIOS name server support.

You can run the Samba server either from the init scripts as detailed in Chapter 9 or from inetd as a system service.

▶ **See** "Understanding the Boot Process," **p. 206**

Because Red Hat and Caldera both start SMB services from the init scripts instead of as a service from inetd, you can use the following command to start or stop the SMB server:

```
/etc/rc.d/init.d/samba start¦stop
```

Using *smbclient*

The smbclient program allows Linux users to access SMB shares on other, typically Windows, machines. This is because if you want to access files on other Linux boxes, you can use a variety of methods including FTP, NFS, and the r- commands (like rcp).

▶ **See** "Using the r- Commands," **p. 589**

smbclient provides an FTP-like interface that allows you to transfer files with a network share on another computer running an SMB server. Unfortunately, unlike NFS, smbclient does not allow you to mount another share as a local directory.

smbclient provides command line options to query a server for the shared directories available or to exchange files. For more information on the available command line options, consult the man page for smbclient. Use the following command to list all available shares on the machine win.netwharf.com:

```
smbclient -L -I win.netwharf.com
```

The -L parameter requests the list. The -I parameter instructs smbclient to treat the following machine name as a DNS specified entry instead of a NetBIOS entry.

To transfer a file, you must first connect to the Samba server by using the following command:

```
smbclient '\\WORKGROUP\PUBLIC' -I win.netwharf.com -U tackett
```

The parameter '\\WORKGROUP\PUBLIC' specifies the remote service on the other machine. This is typically either a file system directory or a printer. The -U option allows you to specify the username with which you want to connect. Samba will prompt you for a password (if this account requires one) and then place you at this prompt

```
smb: \
```

where \ indicates the current working directory.

From this command line, you can issue any of the various commands shown in Table 15.1 to transfer and work with files.

Table 15.1 *smbclient* Commands

Command	Parameters	Description
? or help	[*command*]	Provides a help message on *command*, or in general if no command is specified.
!	[*shell command*]	Executes the specified shell command or drops the user to a shell prompt.
cd	[*directory*]	Changes to the specified directory on the server machine (not the local machine). If no directory is specified, smbclient will report the current working directory.
lcd	[*directory*]	Changes to the specified directory on the local machine. If no directory is specified, smbclient will report the current working directory on the local machine.
Del	[*files*]	The specified files on the server will be deleted if the user has permission to do so. Files can include wildcard characters.
dir or ls	[*files*]	Lists the indicated files. You can also use the command ls to get a list of files.
exit or quit	none	Exits from the smbclient program.
get	[*remote file*] [*local name*]	Retrieves the specified remote file and saves the file on the local server. If local name is specified, the copied file will be saved with this filename instead of with the filename on the remote server.
mget	[*files*]	Copies all the indicated files—including those matching any wildcards—to the local machine.
md or mkdir	[*directory*]	Creates the specified directory on the remote machine.
rd or rmdir	[*directory*]	Removes the specified directory from the remote machine.
put	[*file*]	Copies the specified file from the local machine to the server.
mput	[*files*]	Copies all the specified files from the local machine to the server.
print	[*file*]	Prints the specified file on the remote machine.
queue	none	Displays all the print jobs queued on the remote server.

From Here...

You can read the following chapters for further information about Linux as related to using Samba:

■ Chapter 9, "Booting and Shutting Down," covers the process and files used when starting and stopping the various services for Linux.

■ Chapter 16, "Understanding the File and Directory System," discusses the basics of files and directories. You should have a basic understanding of the file system when using emacs or any other editor. Whereas the editor creates and modifies files, it's up to you to name them and place them in the appropriate directories.

■ Chapter 20, "Printing," provides information on printing your text files under Linux. Printing files under Linux can be tricky; this chapter helps you prepare your system for printing.

■ The SMB-HOWTO provides sample configuration files and scripts for printing from Samba. See Appendix A for information on how to access the various HOWTOs.

## CHAPTER 16

Understanding the File and Directory System

by Jack Tackett

In this chapter

The term *Linux file system* has two different and often conflicting meanings: the file system of disks and mechanisms of the disks, and the logical file system that the user sees and manipulates. This chapter is about the logical Linux file system that you see and manipulate. If you're familiar with PC operating systems such as MS-DOS and OS/2, you'll find many of the following topics familiar because the file structures of MS-DOS from version 2.0 onward were modeled on those of UNIX, which is the file structure used by Linux.

Every physical and logical entity in Linux is represented as a file in the Linux file system. The physical entities include disks, printers, and terminals; logical entities include directories and, of course, ordinary files—the kind that store documents and programs.

Understanding File and Path Names

In Linux, just as in other operating systems such as MS-DOS, you must distinguish between a filename and a path name. A *filename* consists of a simple series of contiguous letters, numbers, and certain punctuation marks. Filenames can't contain spaces or any characters that represent a field separator. For example, the filename "johns.letter" is valid, but "johns letter" isn't.

A filename shouldn't contain any characters that have special meaning to the shell. These are the "forbidden" special characters:

> ! @ # $ % ^ & * ( ) [ ] { } ' " \ / | ; < > `

Also, a filename can't contain the front slash character (/) because this character is used to indicate path names. (Path names are discussed later in this section.)

> **N O T E** Actually, you can use any of the "forbidden" characters if you place double quotation marks around the filename like this:
>
> "! johns.letter"
>
> However, you'll have a hard time accessing such a file with most programs, and the file isn't very portable to other UNIX systems. ▪

Most early versions of UNIX, on which Linux is based, limited filenames to 14 characters; however, Linux allows 256 characters in a filename. Some recent UNIX versions, such as the Berkeley version (BSD), allow 64-character filenames, but only the first 14 are significant. Because one of the goals of Linux is portability, in the interest of writing portable programs and shell scripts, you might want to limit yourself to 14-character filenames.

A path name can contain any number of characters. In Linux, files don't exist in a vacuum; they exist in a directory. The highest directory in Linux is called the *root* and is symbolized by the slash character (/). If a file named fred exists in the root directory, its absolute path name is /fred. When you add a user to the system with the adduser command, he or she is assigned a home directory. By convention, this home directory is usually found under root in a directory named, appropriately enough, home. Therefore, if a user named Fred is assigned a directory named /home/fred, all files that Fred creates are attached to the /home/fred directory. An absolute path name for one of Fred's files might be /home/fred/freds.file. An absolute path name specifies exactly where a file is stored in the file system.

Another kind of path name is a *relative path name*, which unambiguously points to a file's location as relative to the current directory. If Fred is in his home directory, for example, the filename freds.file is also a relative path name, relative to his current directory. To find out which directory is your current directory, use the command pwd (print working directory). You can also check the contents of the $PWD environment variable with the command echo $PWD to see which directory is the current working directory.

Part
III
Ch
16

You can define a file anywhere in the Linux file system with relative path names by using two pseudonyms found in all directories. The single dot (.) refers to the current directory, and the double dot (..) refers to the parent directory. MS-DOS and OS/2 use this same convention.

If Fred is in /home/fred, he can point to /fred by using ../../fred. In this relative path name, the second double dot points to /home (the parent directory of /home/fred), and the first double dot points to the parent directory of /home—namely, the root.

The pseudonym for the current directory, the single dot, comes in handy if you want to move files. If Fred wants to move /fred to his current directory, he can do so with absolute path names by using this command:

```
mv /fred fred
```

Alternatively, Fred can use the pseudonym for the current directory by using this command:

```
mv /fred .
```

Most Linux commands operate on path names. In most cases, the path name you use is the name of a file in the current directory. The default path name points to your current directory. If Fred is in his home directory (/home/fred), all three of the following are equivalent commands:

```
command freds.letter
```

```
command /home/fred/freds.letter
```

```
command ./freds.letter
```

N O T E Although a difference exists between filenames and path names, directories are files, too. When naming directories, remember that you must follow the same naming guidelines as for ordinary files.

Also note that unlike many PC-based operating systems, Linux doesn't have the concept of disk-drive letters, only directory paths. Linux deals with disk drive letters only when working with MS-DOS file systems on floppies with the m- commands (such as mcopy).

▶ **See** "Understanding File Systems," **p. 266** ▧

File Types

Linux lumps everything into four basic types of files: ordinary files, directories, links, and special files. There are several kinds of ordinary files, links, and special files and a large number of standard directories. The basic file types are described in the following sections.

You can use the command `file` to determine the type of a file. `file` can recognize a file type as executable, text, data, and so on. Many UNIX commands are only shell scripts or are interpreted programs similar to MS-DOS batch files, and `file` can report whether a UNIX command is a binary executable program or simply a shell script. It's also useful for determining whether the file is text-based and, therefore, whether it can be viewed or edited. The syntax for the `file` command is as follows:

```
file [-vczL] [-f namefile] [-m magicfile] filelist
```

Table 16.1 explains the arguments for the `file` command.

Table 16.1 *file* **Command Arguments**

Argument	Description
`-c`	Prints out the parsed form of the *magic file* (/usr/lib/magic), which is a number in the first part of a binary file that identifies the file type. This is usually used with `-m` to debug a new magic file before installing it.
`-z`	Looks inside a compressed file and tries to figure out the file type.
`-L`	Causes symbolic links to be followed.
`-f namefile`	Tells `file` that the list of files to identify is found in *namefile*, which is a text file. This is useful when many files must be identified.
`-m magicfile`	Specifies an alternative file of magic numbers to use for determining file types. The default file is /usr/lib/magic.
`filelist`	Lists space-delimited files whose type you want to know.

Ordinary Files

Ordinary files are what you spend most of your time manipulating. Ordinary files can contain text, C language source code, shell scripts (programs interpreted by one of the Linux shells), binary executable programs, and data of various types. As far as Linux is concerned, a file is a file. The only difference that Linux knows is files marked as executable. Executable files can be executed directly—provided, of course, that the file contains something to execute and that it's in your search path. Basically, the search path is a list of path names you've specified that Linux searches to find an executable file.

▶ **See** "Understanding Shells," **p. 339**

Executable files are binary files—that is, files that execute machine code and shell scripts. The Linux `file` command discussed in the preceding section looks at the data in a file and makes a reasonable guess as to what's inside. If you type `file *`, for example, you might see something similar to this:

```
INSTALL:       symbolic link to /var/adm
ghostvw.txt: ascii text
linux:         symbolic link to /usr/src/linux
mbox:          mail text
mterm.txt:     English text
seyon.txt:     English text
xcalc.txt:     English text
xclock.txt:    English text
xeyes.txt:     English text
xgrap.txt:     English text
xlock.txt:     English text
xspread.txt: English text
xtris.txt:     empty
```

All the files named in the first column are ordinary files that contain different kinds of data. All the files are located within the directory where the `file` command was executed.

Directory Files

Directories are files that contain the names of files and subdirectories, as well as pointers to those files and subdirectories. Directory files are the only place that Linux stores names of files. When you list the contents of a directory with the `ls` command, all you're doing is listing the contents of the directory file. You never touch the files themselves.

When you rename a file with the `mv` command and that file is in the current directory, all you're doing is changing the entry in the directory file. If you move a file from one directory to another, all you're doing is moving the description of the file from one directory file to another—provided, of course, that the new directory is on the same physical disk or partition. If not, Linux physically copies each byte of the program to the other disk.

Directories and Physical Disks

Every file in a Linux system is assigned a unique number called an *inode*. The inode is stored in a table called the *inode table*, which is allocated when the disk is formatted. Every physical disk or partition has its own inode table. An inode contains all the information about a file, including the address of the data on the disk and the file type. File types include such things as ordinary files, directories, and special files.

The Linux file system assigns inode number 1 to the root directory. This gives Linux the address on disk of the root directory file. The root directory file contains a list of file and directory names and their respective inode numbers. Linux can find any file in the system by looking up a chain of directories, beginning with the root directory. The contents of the root directory file might look like this:

```
1      .
1      ..
45     etc
230    dev
```

```
420   home
123   .profile
```

Notice that the files . (dot) and .. (double dot) are shown in the directory. Because this is the root directory, . and its parent directory, .., are identical. The contents of the /home directory file would be different and might look something like this:

```
420   .
1     ..
643   fred
```

Notice that the inode of the current directory (.) matches the inode for /home found in the root directory file, and the inode for the parent directory (..) is the same as that of the root directory.

Linux navigates its file system by chaining up and down the directory file system. If you want to move a file to a directory on another physical disk, Linux detects this by reading the inode table. In such a case, the file is physically moved to the new disk and assigned a new inode on that disk before being deleted from its original location.

As with the mv command, when you delete a file with the rm command, you never touch the file itself. Instead, Linux marks that inode as free and returns it to the pool of available inodes. The file's entry in the directory is erased.

▶ **See** "Moving and Renaming Files," **p. 323**

Links

Ordinary links aren't really files at all; they're actually directory entries that point to the same inode. The inode table keeps track of how many links there are to a file, and only when the last directory reference is deleted is the inode finally released back to the free pool. Obviously, ordinary links can't cross device boundaries because all the directory references point to the same inode.

To create a link you use the ln command, which has the following form:

```
ln [options] source destination
```

For example to create a link between a file named mainfile.txt and a file named tempfile.txt, you would enter the following command:

```
ln mainfile.txt tempfile.txt
```

Linux, as well as most modern versions of UNIX, has another kind of link called a *symbolic link*. For such a link, the directory entry contains the inode of a file that is itself a reference to another file somewhere else in the logical Linux file system. A symbolic link can point to another file or directory on the same disk, another disk, or to a file or directory on another computer.

One major difference between an ordinary link and a symbolic link is that with ordinary links, every link has equal standing (that is, the system treats every link as though it were the original file), and the actual data isn't deleted until the last link to that file is deleted. With symbolic links, when the original file is deleted, all symbolic links to that file are also deleted. Symbolically linked files don't have the same standing as the original file.

To create a symbolic link you use the -s option to the ln command. For example, to create a symbolic link from a file called named in the /etc/rc.d/initd directory to the file S55named, you would use the following command:

```
ln -s /etc/rc.d/initd/named /etc/rc.d/rc3.d/S55named
```

Other than these subtle differences between links and files, links are treated and accessed exactly as files are.

You can tell a file is a link by using the ls -l command. If it is a link, the response shows the local filename and then an indication of the linked file like this:

```
lrwxrwxrwx  1 root    root    4 Oct 17 15:27 Info -> info/
```

The file permission flags begin with l to indicate that the file is a linked file.

Part
III

Ch
16

Special Files

Every physical device associated with a Linux system, including disks, terminals, and printers, are represented in the file system. Most, if not all, devices are located in the /dev directory. For example, if you're working on the system console, your associated device is named /dev/console. If you're working on a standard terminal, your device name might be /dev/tty01. Terminals, or serial lines, are called *tty devices* (which stands for *teletype*, the original UNIX terminal). To determine what the name of your tty device is, type the command **tty**. The system responds with the name of the device to which you're connected.

Printers and terminals are called *character-special devices*. They can accept and produce a stream of characters. Disks, on the other hand, store data in blocks addressed by cylinder and sector. You can't access just one character on a disk; you must read and write entire blocks. The same is usually true of magnetic tapes. This kind of device is called a *block-special device*. To make life even more complex, disks and other block-special devices must be able to act like character-oriented devices, so every block-special device has a matching character-special device. Linux makes the translation by reading data being sent to a character device and translating it for the block device. This happens without you doing anything.

You might run into at least one other type of special device: a FIFO (first-in-first-out buffer), also known as a *named pipe*. FIFOs look like ordinary files: If you write to them, they grow. But if you read a FIFO, it shrinks in size. FIFOs are used mainly in system processes to allow many programs to send information to a single controlling process. For example, when you print a file with the lp command, lp sets up the printing process and signals the lpsched daemon by sending a message to a FIFO. A *daemon*, sometimes called a *demon*, is a system process that acts without a user requesting an action.

One device-special file—the bit bucket, or /dev/null—is very useful. Anything you send to /dev/null is ignored, which is useful when you don't want to see the output of a command. For example, if you don't want any diagnostic reports printed on the standard error device, you can pour them into the bit bucket with the following command:

```
ls -la> /dev/null
```

File Permissions

File permissions mean more in Linux than just what permissions you have on a file or directory. Although permissions determine who can read, write, or execute a file, they also determine the file type and how the file is executed.

You can display the permissions of a file with the long form of the listing command, ls -l. The -l flag tells the ls command to use the long listing. If you type **ls -l**, you might see a directory listing that looks like this:

```
Drwx------ 2 sglines  doc     512 Jan 1 13:44  Mail
Drwx------ 5 sglines  doc    1024 Jan 17 08:22 News
-rw------- 1 sglines  doc    1268 Dec 7 15:01  biblio
drwx------ 2 sglines  doc     512 Dec 15 21:28 bin
-rw------- 1 sglines  doc   44787 Oct 20 06:59 books
-rw------- 1 sglines  doc   23801 Dec 14 22:50 bots.msg
-rw-r---- 1 sglines  doc  105990 Dec 27 21:24 duckie.gif
```

This listing shows virtually everything that can be known about a file from the directory entry and the inode of the file. The first column shows the file permissions, the second column shows the number of links to a file (or extra blocks in a directory), and the third column shows who owns the file. (In Linux, ownership has three possibilities: the owner, the owner's group, and everyone else. Ownership is detailed later in this chapter.) The fourth column shows the group to which the file belongs. The fifth column shows the number of bytes in the file, the sixth column shows the date and time of creation, and the seventh column shows the name of the file itself.

The permissions field (the first column) can be broken into four distinct subfields:

```
- rwx rwx rwx
```

The first subfield defines the file type. A normal file has a hyphen (-) as a placeholder; directories are marked with a d. Table 16.2 shows the permissible values for the file-type subfield.

Table 16.2	Valid Entries for the File-Type Subfield
Character	**Meaning**
-	Ordinary file
b	Block-special file
c	Character-special file
d	Directory
l	Symbolic link

The next three subfields show the read, write, and execute permissions of the file. For example, an rwx in the first of these subfields means that the file has read, write, and execute permission for the owner. The next three characters show the same information for the group ownership of the file. Finally, the third set of characters shows the permissions allowed for everyone else.

These permission subfields can show more information; in fact, several attributes are packed into these three fields. Unfortunately, what these attributes mean is determined by the version of Linux you use and whether the file is executable.

N O T E Normally, a running program is owned by whoever ran it. If the user ID bit is on, the running program is owned by the owner of the file. This means that the running program has all the permissions of the owner of the file. If you're an ordinary user and the running program is owned by the root user, that running program has automatic permission to read and write any file in the system regardless of your permissions. The same is true of the set group ID bit. ■

Part
III

Ch
16

The *sticky bit* can also be set in these subfields. The sticky bit tells the system to save a copy of a running program in memory after the program completes. If the program is used often, the sticky bit can save the system a little time the next time it runs the program because the program doesn't have to be reloaded into memory from disk each time someone runs it.

You can change permissions on any file you have write permission for by using the chmod command. This command has two different syntaxes: absolute and relative. With absolute permissions, you define exactly what the permissions on a file will be in octal, or base 8. An octal number can have a value from 0 to 7. UNIX was originally created on a series of DEC minicomputers that used the octal numbering system, hence the current use of octal numbers. The octal numbers are added together to arrive at a number that defines the permissions. Table 16.3 lists the valid octal permissions.

Table 16.3 Absolute Octal Permissions Used with the *chmod* Command

Octal Value	Permissions Granted
0001	Execute permission for the owner
0002	Write permission for the owner
0004	Read permission for the owner
0010	Execute permission for the group
0020	Write permission for the group
0040	Read permission for the group
0100	Execute permission for all others
0200	Write permission for all others
0400	Read permission for all others
1000	Sticky bit on
2000	Group ID bit on if the file is executable; otherwise, mandatory file locking is on
4000	User ID bit on if the file is executable

Group and user IDs refer to who has permission to use, read, or execute a file. These initial file permissions are granted by the systems administrator when the user's account is first created. Only users of an indicated group can access files in a group, and only if the user has given group members permission to those files.

To give a file read and write permissions for everyone, you must add the required permissions together, as in the following example:

0002	Write permission for the owner
0004	Read permission for the owner
0020	Write permission for the group
0040	Read permission for the group
0200	Write permission for all others
0400	Read permission for all others

0666	Read and write permission for everyone

To give a file these permissions, you would use the following command:

```
chmod 666 file
```

Relative permissions use a slightly different format. With relative permissions, you must state the following:

- Whom you're giving permissions to
- What operation you intend (add, subtract, or set permissions)
- What the permissions are

For example, if you type **chmod a=rwx file**, you give read, write, and execute permission to all users. Table 16.4 summarizes the commands for relative permissions.

Table 16.4 Relative Permissions Used with the *chmod* Command

Value	Description
Whom	
a	All users (the user, their group, and all others)
g	Owner's group
o	All others not in the file's group
u	Just the user
Operator	
+	Adds the mode
-	Removes the mode
=	Sets the mode absolutely

Value	Description
Permission	
x	Sets execute
r	Sets read
w	Sets write
s	Sets user ID bit
t	Sets sticky bit

If a file has been marked as having the user ID bit on, the permissions displayed by the `ls -l` command look like this:

```
-rws------ 1 sglines    3136 Jan 17 15:42 x
```

If the group ID bit is added, the permissions look like this:

```
-rws--S--- 1 sglines    3136 Jan 17 15:42 x
```

If you then turn on the sticky bit for the file, the permissions look like this:

```
-rws--S--rws--S--T 1 sglines    3136 Jan 17 15:42 x
```

Note the use of uppercase S and T to indicate the status of the user ID bit and the sticky bit, respectively.

Linux Standard Directories

You're already familiar with the concept of directories. When you log in, the system places you in your home directory. The PATH environment variable is set to point to other directories that contain executable programs. These other directories are part of the standard Linux directory structure.

There is the classic set of directories for UNIX and what can be called the "emerging standard set of directories," which Linux basically follows. These are described in the following sections.

Classic UNIX Directories

Before UNIX System V Release 4 (for example, UNIX System V Release 3.2 and earlier), most versions of UNIX settled on a regular system of organizing the UNIX directories that looked like this:

```
/
      /etc
      /lib
      /tmp
      /bin
      /usr
            /spool
            /bin
```

```
/include
/tmp
/adm
/lib
```

The /etc directory contains most of the system-specific data required to boot, or bring the system to life. It contains such files as passwd and inittab, which are necessary for the proper operation of the system.

The /lib directory contains a library of functions needed by the C compiler. Even if you don't have a C compiler on your system, this directory is important because it contains all the shared libraries that application programs can call. A shared library is loaded into memory only when the command calling it is run. This arrangement keeps executable programs small. Otherwise, every running program contains duplicate code, requiring a lot more disk space to store and a lot more memory to run.

The /tmp directory is used for temporary storage. Programs that use /tmp generally clean up after themselves and delete any temporary files. If you use /tmp, be sure to delete any files before logging out. Because the system automatically deletes the contents of this directory periodically, don't keep anything you might need later in it.

The /bin directory keeps all the executable programs needed to boot the system and is usually home for the most commonly used Linux commands. Note, however, that an executable program doesn't have to be binary (which the name *bin* implies). Several smaller programs in /bin are, in fact, shell scripts.

The /usr directory contains everything else. Your PATH variable contains the string /bin:/usr/bin because the /usr/bin directory contains all the Linux commands that aren't in the /bin directory. This arrangement has a historical precedence. In the early days of Linux, hard disks weren't very big. Linux needs at least the /etc/tmp/ and /bin directories to *bootstrap* (that is, start executing) itself. Because the disks of the early Linux era held only those three directories, everything else was on a disk that could be mounted after Linux was up and running. When Linux was still a relatively small operating system, placing additional subdirectories in the /usr directory wasn't much of a burden. It allowed a moderately sized Linux system to exist with just two disks: a root disk and a /usr disk.

The /usr/adm directory contains all the accounting and diagnostic information needed by the system administrator. If both system accounting and diagnostic programs are turned off, this directory is effectively empty.

The /include directory contains all the source code used by #include statements in C programs. You'll have at least read permission for this directory because it contains all the code fragments and structures that define your system. You shouldn't modify any of the files in this directory because they were crafted (carefully, you can assume) by your system vendor.

The /usr/spool directory contains all the transient data used by the lp print system, the cron daemon, and the UUCP communications system. Files "spooled" to the printer are kept in the /spool directory until they're printed. Any programs waiting to be run by cron, including all the crontab files and pending at and batch jobs, are also stored here.

The /usr/lib directory contains everything else that's part of the standard Linux system. In general, the /usr/lib directory represents the organized chaos hidden beneath the relatively well-disciplined Linux system. This directory contains programs called by other programs found in /bin and /usr/bin as well as configuration files for terminals and printers, the mail system, cron, and the UUCP communications system.

The /usr directory contains all the subdirectories assigned to users. The general convention is this: If your login ID is "mary," your home directory is /usr/mary.

This directory arrangement made a lot of sense when disks were small and expensive, but with the advent of very large disks at (relatively) inexpensive prices, there are better ways of organizing Linux, as evidenced by the new directory structure discussed in the next section.

Linux Directories

One problem with the classical structure of UNIX is that backing up your data files is difficult with a fragmented /usr directory. Three different levels of backup generally are required in a system: the basic system itself, any changes to the tables that define the basic system for a specific site, and user data.

The basic system should be backed up only once with changes to the controlling tables backed up when there are changes. User data changes all the time and should be backed up frequently. The typical Linux directory structure is shown here, but your structure might be a little different depending on what packages you installed:

```
/
      /etc
            /passwd      (user database)
            /rc.d     (system initialization scripts)
/sbin
/bin
/tmp
/var
/lib
/home
      / <your user name here>      (user accounts)
/install
/usr
      /bin
/proc
```

The /bin, /etc, and /tmp directories have the same function as they do in the classic structure. System definition tables are moved into the /var directory so that whenever the operation of the system changes, you can back up only that directory.

What's new is that all system programs are moved into the /sbin directory. All the standard Linux programs are in /usr/bin, which is linked to /bin. For compatibility, all the classic directories are maintained with symbolic links. The /usr directory, which no longer contains user data, has been reorganized to make sense from the chaos that once was the /usr/lib directory.

From Here...

In this chapter, you examined how Linux uses files and directories and how the file permission system protects your data. You learned how to change the permissions on files and directories and what the meaning of a special file is. Finally, you studied the names and functions of the most common directories found in Linux. For more information, see the following chapters:

- Chapter 7, "Understanding System Administration," explains how to set up new users with file permissions.
- Chapter 14, "Managing File Systems," discusses the concept of file systems and how they're organized.
- Chapter 17, "Managing Files and Directories," discusses how to organize and use your files and directories.

Managing Files and Directories

by Jack Tackett

In this chapter

The vast majority of Linux commands manipulate files and directories. Indeed, Linux shell scripts are particularly adept at manipulating files and directories. File manipulations that are difficult in a conventional language (even in C) are made easy from within a shell, largely because of the rich selection of file-manipulation commands available in Linux.

File-manipulation commands can be grouped roughly into two categories:

- Commands that manipulate files as objects
- Commands that manipulate the contents of files

This chapter concentrates on commands that manipulate files as objects—commands that move, rename, copy, delete, locate, and change the attributes of files and directories. This chapter also takes a quick look at commands that manipulate the contents of files.

Listing Files

The basic command to list files is `ls`. The way `ls` displays files depends on how you use the command. If you use the `ls` command in a pipe, every file is displayed on a line by itself. This is also the default for some versions of UNIX, such as SCO UNIX. Other versions of UNIX list files in several columns. For most uses, the columnar format is more convenient; systems that list files one per row often have an alternative command, usually `lc`, for lists in column format.

The `ls` command's behavior is modified with the use of flags that take the form -abcd. In general, versions of the `ls` command fall into two categories: versions of `ls` derived from Linux System V and those derived from Berkeley. Because the Berkeley Linux systems are slowly giving way to Linux System V, this chapter concentrates on the flags used by System V. If you're in doubt about which version of `ls` you have, consult the manuals for your system or try the command `man ls`.

N O T E Most man pages for commands in this chapter are no longer being maintained and may be inaccurate or incomplete under Red Hat Linux because the system is moved to more graphical-based systems such as HTML and Texinfo. However, for the time being, this information is accurate for this release of Red Hat Linux 4.0. ■

Flags used with the `ls` command can be concatenated or listed separately. This means that the following commands are effectively identical:

```
ls -l -F
```

and

```
ls -lF
```

Table 17.1 lists in alphabetical order several of the flags used with `ls` and their uses.

Table 17.1   Flags for the *ls* **Command**

Flag	Description
-a	Lists all entries. In the absence of this or the -A option, entries whose names begin with a period (.) aren't listed. Linux has a way of "hiding" files; all files that begin with a period by default aren't listed because they're generally files used to customize applications. For example, .profile is used to customize the Bourne and Korn shells, and .mailrc is used to customize your system-wide e-mail configuration file. Because almost every major command you use has a startup file, your home directory looks cluttered if the ls command lists all those startup files by default. If you want to see them, use the -a flag.
-A	Same as -a, except that . and .. aren't listed. (Recall from Chapter 16, "Understanding the File and Directory System," that . is a pseudonym for the current directory, and .. is a pseudonym for the parent directory.) Because these filenames begin with a period, the -a flag lists them. If you don't want to see these pseudonyms, use the -A flag instead.
-b	Forces printing of nongraphic characters to be in octal \ddd notation. -b is more useful than the -q flag because it allows you to figure out what the characters are.
-c	Uses time of last edit (or last mode change) for sorting or printing. Linux maintains three time and date stamps on every file: the file creation date, the date of last access, and the date of last modification. Normally, files are listed in *ASCII order* (which is the same as alphabetical order except that capitals are sorted before lowercase letters).
-C	Forces multicolumn output with entries sorted down the columns. This is the default format of ls when output is to a terminal.
-d *filename*	If the argument is a directory, this flag lists only its name (not its contents); often used with the -l flag to get the status of a directory. Normally, the contents of a directory are listed if a directory name is explicitly listed or implied with the use of a wildcard. Thus, the simple command ls lists just the directory names themselves, but ls * lists files, directories, and the contents of any directories encountered in the current directory.
-F	Marks directories with a trailing slash (/), marks executable files with a trailing asterisk (*), marks symbolic links with a trailing at sign (@), marks FIFOs with a trailing bar (|), and marks sockets with a trailing equal sign (=).
-i	Prints each file's inode number (*inodes* are described in Chapter 16, "Understanding the File and Directory System") in the first column of the report. If you list linked files, notice that both files have the same inode number.

continues

Table 17.1 Continued

Flag	Description
-l	Lists directory entries in long format, giving mode, number of links, owner, size in bytes, and time of last modification for each file. If the file is a special file, the size field instead contains the major and minor device numbers. If the time of last modification is greater than six months ago, the month, date, and year are shown; otherwise, only the date and time are shown. If the file is a symbolic link, the path name of the linked-to file is printed, preceded by the characters ->. You can combine -l with other options, such as -n, to show user and group ID numbers instead of names.
-n	Lists the user and group ID numbers, instead of names, associated with each file and directory. Usually, only the names are listed. If you're setting up networking products, such as TCP/IP, it's useful to know ID numbers when you're setting up permissions across several systems.
-q	Displays nongraphic characters in filenames as the character ?. For ls, this is the default action when output is to a terminal. If a file has accidentally been created with nonprintable characters, the -q flag displays the file.
-r	Reverses the sort order to show files in reverse alphabetical or oldest-file-first order, as appropriate.
-s	Gives the size of each file, including any indirect blocks used to map the file, in kilobytes. If the environment variable POSIX_CORRECT is defined, the block size is 512 bytes.
-t	Sorts by time modified (latest first) instead of by name. If you want to see the oldest file first, use the -rt combination.
-u	Uses time of last access, instead of last modification, for sorting (with the -t option) or printing (with the -l option).
-x	Forces multicolumn output with entries sorted across instead of down the page.

If you installed the Slackware distribution of Linux, you'll find ls also provides color output for each file type. The color definitions are defined in the configuration file DIR_COLORS in the /etc directory. The default configuration highlights executable files in green, directories in blue, and symbolic links in cyan. To customize the colors, you must copy the DIR_COLORS file to your home directory and change its name to .dir colors. Table 17.2 provides the color definitions available; see the man pages and the DIR_COLORS file for more information.

N O T E For the Red Hat distribution, you must type **ls --color** to get the color effect. ▪

Table 17.2   DIR_COLORS Values for Creating Color Highlighting

Value	Description
0	Restores default color
1	For brighter colors
4	For underlined text
5	For flashing text
30	For black foreground
31	For red foreground
32	For green foreground
33	For yellow (or brown) foreground
34	For blue foreground
35	For purple foreground
36	For cyan foreground
37	For white (or gray) foreground
40	For black background
41	For red background
42	For green background
43	For yellow (or brown) background
44	For blue background
45	For purple background
46	For cyan background
47	For white (or gray) background

Part
III

Ch
17

More options are available than those shown here. To find them, consult the man pages for ls.

Organizing Files

There are no fixed rules for organizing files in Linux. Files don't have extensions (such as .EXE for executables) as they do in MS-DOS. You can (and perhaps should) make up your own system of naming files, but the classic system of organizing files in Linux is with subdirectories.

More and more, however, Linux applications that have come from the DOS world are bringing their conventions to Linux. Although they may not require it, vendors encourage you to name files that you use with their applications with certain extensions.

If you're going to write your own commands, a useful way to organize your directories is to mimic Linux's use of the /bin, /lib, and /etc directories. Create your own structure of subdirectories with these names, perhaps under your /home directory, and follow the Linux tradition of placing executable commands in your /bin directory, subsidiary commands in your /lib directory, and initialization files in your /etc directory. Of course, you aren't required to do this, but it's one way of organizing your files.

You create directories with the `mkdir` command. Its syntax is simple:

```
mkdir directory-name
```

In this syntax, *directory-name* represents the name you want to assign to the new directory. Of course, you must have write permission in the directory in order to create a subdirectory with `mkdir`, but if you're making a subdirectory within your home directory, you should have no problem.

Suppose you've written three programs called prog1, prog2, and prog3, all of which are found in $HOME/bin. Remember that $HOME is your home directory. If you want your private programs to run as though they were a standard part of the Linux command set, you must add `$HOME/bin` to your `PATH` environment variable. To do so, you would use the following command in the Bourne or Korn shell:

```
PATH=$PATH:$HOME/bin;export PATH
```

In the C shell, you would use this command:

```
setenv PATH "$PATH $HOME/bin"
```

N O T E   Remember that $HOME is the placeholder for the complete path that refers to your home directory. If your home directory is /home/ams, $HOME/bin is interpreted as /home/ams/bin. ■

If your programs call subsidiary programs, you may want to create subdirectories within your $HOME/lib directory. You can create a subdirectory for each program. The private command `pgm1` can then explicitly call, for example, $HOME/lib/pgm1/pgm1a.

Similarly, if your command `prog1` requires a startup table, you can name that table $HOME/etc/pgm1.rc; your data can be in your $HOME/data/pgm1 directory.

Copying Files

The command for copying files is `cp from to`. You must have read permission for the file you're copying from and write permission for the directory you're copying to (and the file if you're overwriting an existing file). Other than that, you are not restricted when it comes to copying files.

You need to watch for a few things as you copy files:

■ If you copy a file and give it the name of a file that already exists and that you have write permission for, you'll overwrite the original file.

- If you give the name of a directory as the destination of the cp command, the file is copied into that directory with its original name. For example, if you type the command **cp *file directory***, the file is copied into *directory* as *directory/file*.

- You can copy a list of files into a directory with the command cp *file1 file2 file3 ... directory*. If the last item in the list isn't a directory, an error message appears. Likewise, if any element in the list other than the last item is only a directory, an error message appears.

- Be careful when you use wildcards with the cp command because you can accidentally copy more than you intend to.

N O T E Because many Linux users also have MS-DOS files on their systems and usually make the DOS file system accessible from Linux, most of the Linux commands recognize when a file is being copied to or from a DOS partition. Thus, Linux can handle the necessary file translation when copying files. This translation is required because most DOS files embed the carriage return/line-feed characters into an ASCII file to indicate a line break. Most Linux and UNIX systems embed only a line-feed character, called *newline*, in the file to indicate a line break. ■

Part
III

Ch
17

Moving and Renaming Files

In Linux, moving and renaming files are accomplished with the same command: mv. The syntax and rules are the same for mv as they are for the copy command, cp. That is, you can move as many files as you want to a directory, but the directory name must be last in the list and you must have write permission to that directory.

One thing you can do with mv that you can't do with cp is move or rename directories. When you move or rename a file, the only thing that happens is the entry in the directory file is changed. Unless the new location is on another physical disk or partition, the file and the contents of the directory are physically moved.

If you try to use rm (for *remove*) or cp without options on a directory, the command fails and displays a message telling you that the item you're dealing with is a directory. To remove or copy directories, you must use the -r flag (for *recursive*) with rm and cp. The mv command, however, moves directories quite happily.

Removing Files or Directories

The command to remove a file is rm. To delete a file you don't own, you need read and write permission. If you own the file, you're allowed to delete it, provided that you haven't closed off your own permission to the file. For example, if you turn off write permission to a file by typing **chmod 000 *file***, you must open permission again with the chmod command (by typing **chmod 644 *file***) before you can delete it.

If you accidentally type rm *, you delete all the files you have permission to delete in the current directory; you don't delete the subdirectories. To delete subdirectories, you must use the recursive option (-r).

Some versions of rm stop and ask whether you really want to delete files that you own but don't have at least write permission for. Other versions of rm prompt you for any files marked for removal with wildcards. Indeed, you can write a macro or shell script that gives you a second chance before actually deleting a file.

If your version of rm balks at removing files you own but don't have write permission for, you can partially protect yourself from accidentally deleting everything in your directory by following these steps:

1. Create a file named 0. In the ASCII string sequence, the number 0 is listed before any files that begin with letters.

2. Remove all permissions from the file named 0 by typing the command **chmod 000 0**. This command removes read, write, and execute permissions for everyone, including yourself.

3. If you type the command **rm ***, the file named 0 is the first file that rm attempts to remove.

If your version of rm balks at removing the 0 file when you type **rm ***, you have the chance to think about what you just did. If you didn't intend to delete everything in your directory, press <Del> or <Ctrl-c> to kill the rm process. To test this out, try removing just the file named 0. Don't use rm * because if your version of rm doesn't stop at the file 0, you'll erase all the files in your directory.

A better way to protect yourself from accidentally deleting files is to use the -i flag with rm. The -i flag stands for *interactive*. If you give the command rm -i *filename*, you're asked whether you really want to delete the file. You must answer yes before the file is actually deleted. If you type the command **rm -i ***, you must answer yes for every file in your directory. This should give you enough time to think about what you really want to do.

> **CAUTION**
>
> Think before you delete files. Unlike in Windows, DOS, or MAC, when you delete a file (in most versions of Linux), it's gone and the only way to recover a lost file is from a backup. You did make a backup, didn't you?

▶ **See** "Performing Backups and Restoring Files," **p. 229**

If you use the rm -i command frequently, you can implement it in two ways: by writing a shell script or by creating a shell function. If you write a shell script, remember that the shell searches for commands in the directories listed in your PATH variable in the order in which they're listed. If your $HOME/bin directory is listed last, a shell script named rm will never be found. You can place your $HOME/bin directory first in the PATH variable's list or create a new command, such as del. If you create a shell script called del, you must mark it as executable with the chmod command for the shell to recognize it. When you create your del command, you need to give it only one command: rm -i $*. If you then type the command **del ***, the shell translates it into rm -i *.

▶ **See** "Editing and Aliasing Shell Commands," **p. 364**

Another way to accomplish the same task is with an *alias*, which takes precedence over commands that must be looked up. You can think of an alias as an internal shell command (similar to the `doskey` commands introduced in MS-DOS version 5.0).

To add an alias if you're using the C shell, you must edit the file named .cshrc. You can use any text editor, such as `vi` (see Chapter 8, "Using the `vi` Editor"), to edit this file. For the C shell, add the following lines to the top of your .cshrc file:

```
rm ()
{
/bin/rm -i $*
}
```

To add an alias to the Korn shell, add the following line to your $HOME/.kshrc file:

```
alias rm 'rm -i $*'
```

If you try to delete a directory with the `rm` command, you're told that it's a directory and can't be deleted. If you want to delete empty directories, use the `rmdir` command, as with MS-DOS.

Linux offers another way to delete directories and their contents, but it's far more dangerous. The `rm -r` command recursively deletes any directories and files it encounters. If you have a directory named ./foo that contains files and subdirectories, the command `rm -r foo` deletes the ./foo directory and its contents, including all subdirectories.

If you give the command `rm -i -r`, each directory that the `rm` command encounters triggers a confirmation prompt. You must answer yes before the directory and its contents are deleted. If you left any files in the directory you were attempting to delete, `rm` balks, just as it does if you attempt to remove the nonempty directory with the `rm` command with no options.

> **N O T E** You don't have to issue each flag individually for a Linux command. If the flag doesn't take an argument, you can combine the flags. Thus, `rm -i -r` can be issued as `rm -ir`. ■

Viewing the Contents of a File

Almost every Linux command prints to the standard output device, typically your screen. If the command takes its input from a file after manipulating the file in some way, the command prints the file to your screen. The trick in choosing a Linux command depends on how you want the file displayed. You can use three standard commands: `cat`, `more`, and `less`.

> **N O T E** Linux, as all UNIX systems do, opens four system files at startup: standard input, standard output, standard error, and AUX. These files are actually physical devices:

Name	Alias	Device
Standard input	standard in (stdin)	The keyboard
Standard output	standard out (stdout)	The screen
Standard error	standard err (stderr)	The screen
AUX	auxiliary	An auxiliary device

Using *cat* to View a File

For displaying short ASCII files, the simplest command is cat, which stands for *concatenate*. The cat command takes a list of files (or a single file) and prints the contents unaltered on standard output, one file after another. Its primary purpose is to concatenate files (as in cat *file1 file2>file3*), but it works just as well to send the contents of a short file to your screen.

If you try to display large files by using cat, the file scrolls past your screen as fast as the screen can handle the character stream. One way to stop the flow of data is to alternatively press <Ctrl-s> and <Ctrl-q> to send start and stop messages to your screen, or you can use one of the page-at-a-time commands, more or less.

Using *more* to View a File

Both more and less display a screen of data at a time. Although they both do roughly the same thing, they do it differently. more and less determine how many lines your terminal can display from the terminal database and from your TERM environment variable.

The more command is older than less, and it's derived from the Berkeley version of UNIX. It proved so useful that, like the vi editor, it has become a standard. This section covers just the basics of the command.

The simplest form of the more command is more *filename*. You see a screen of data from the file. If you want to go on to the next screen, press the space bar. If you press <Return>, only the next line is displayed. If you're looking through a series of files (with the command more *file1 file2 ...*) and want to stop to edit one, you can do so with the e or v command. Pressing <e> within more invokes whatever editor you've defined in your EDIT shell environment variable on the current file. Pressing <v> uses whatever editor has been defined in the VISUAL variable. If you haven't defined these variables in your environment, more defaults to the ed editor for the e command and to the vi editor for the v command.

▶ **See** "Setting the Shell Environment," **p. 344**

The more command has only one real drawback—you can't go backward in a file and redisplay a previous screen. However, you can go backward in a file with less.

Using *less* to View a File

One disadvantage to the less command is that you can't use an editor on a file being displayed. However, less makes up for this deficiency by allowing you to move forward and backward through a file.

The less command works almost the same way that more does. To page through a file, type the command **less *filename***. One screen of data is displayed. To advance to the next screen, press the Spacebar as you did with the more command.

To move backward in a file, press the <b> key. To go to a certain position expressed as a percentage of the file, press <p> and specify the percentage at the : prompt.

Searching Through a File and Escaping to the Shell

The less and more commands allow you to search for strings in the file being displayed. The less command, however, allows you to search backward through the file as well. Use the search syntax less /string to search backward through the file. With the less and more commands, if a string is found, a new page is displayed with the line containing the matching string at the top of the screen. With less, pressing the <n> key repeats the previous search.

The more and less commands also allow you to escape to the shell with the ! command. When you escape to the shell with the ! command, you're actually in a subshell; you must exit the subshell just as you do when you log out from a session. Depending on which shell you're using, you can press <Ctrl-d> or type exit to return to the same screen in more or less that you escaped from. If you press <Ctrl-d> and get a message to use logout instead of <Ctrl-d>, use the logout command.

Viewing Files in Other Forms

Other commands display the contents of files in different forms. For example, if you want to look at the contents of a binary file, display it with the od command, which stands for *octal dump*. The od command displays a file in octal notation, or base 8. By using various flags, od can display a file in decimal, ASCII, or hexadecimal (base 16).

Octal, Decimal, and Hexadecimal Notation

Representing binary data is an intriguing problem. If the binary data represents ASCII, you have no problem displaying it (ASCII is, after all, what you expect when you look at most files). If the file is a program, however, the data most likely can't be represented as ASCII characters. In that case, you have to display it in some numerical form.

The early minicomputers used 12-bit words. Today, of course, the computer world has settled on the 8-bit byte as the standard unit of memory. Although you can represent data in the familiar decimal (base 10) system, the question becomes what to display—a byte, a word, or 32 bits? Displaying a given number of bits compactly requires that base 2 be raised to the required number of bits. With the old 12-bit systems, you could represent all 12 bits with four numbers (represented by 2^3, which was the octal or base 8 format). Because early UNIX systems ran on these kinds of minicomputers, much of the UNIX—and, thus, Linux—notation is in octal. Any byte can be represented by a three-digit octal code that looks like this (this example represents the decimal value of 8):

\010

Because the world has settled on an 8-bit byte, octal is no longer an efficient way to represent data. Hexadecimal (base 16 or 2^4) is a better way. An 8-bit byte can be represented by two hexadecimal digits; a byte whose decimal value is 10 is represented as 0A in hexadecimal.

The od command lets you choose how to display binary data. The general form of the command is one of the following:

od [option]... [file]...

or

```
od —traditional [file] [[+]offset [[+]label]]
```

Table 17.3 summarizes the flags you can use with od.

Table 17.3 The *od* Command Flags

Short Flag	Full Flag	Description
-A	--address-radix=*radix*	Determines how file offsets are printed
-N	--read-bytes=*bytes*	Limits dump to *bytes* input bytes per file
-j	--skip-bytes=*bytes*	Skips *bytes* input bytes first on each file
-s	--strings[=*bytes*]	Outputs strings of at least *bytes* graphic characters
-t	--format=*type*	Selects output format or formats
-v	--output-duplicates	Prevents use of * to mark line suppression
-w	--width[=*bytes*]	Outputs *bytes* bytes per output line
	--traditional	Accepts arguments in pre-POSIX form
	--help	Displays this help and exits
	--version	Outputs version information and exits

The pre-POSIX format specifications in Table 17.4 may be intermixed with the commands in Table 17.3, in which case their effects accumulate.

Table 17.4 Pre-POSIX Format Specifications for *od*

Short Flag	POSIX Equivalent	Description
-a	-t a	Selects named characters
-b	-t oC	Selects octal bytes
-c	-t c	Selects ASCII characters or backslash escapes
-d	-t u2	Selects unsigned decimal shorts
-f	-t fF	Selects floats
-h	-t x2	Selects hexadecimal shorts
-I	-t d2	Selects decimal shorts
-l	-t d4	Selects decimal longs
-o	-t o2	Selects octal shorts
-x	-t x2	Selects hexadecimal shorts

For older syntax (second-call format), *offset* means -j *offset*. *label* is the pseudoaddress at first byte printed, incremented when the dump is progressing. For *offset* and *label*, a 0x or 0X prefix indicates hexadecimal. Suffixes may be . (dot) for octal and may be multiplied by 512. The *type* parameter is made up of one or more of the specifications listed in Table 17.5.

Table 17.5   Type Parameters

Parameter	Description
a	Named character
c	ASCII character or backslash escape
d[*size*]	Signed decimal, *size* bytes per integer
f[*size*]	Floating point, *size* bytes per integer
o[*size*]	Octal, *size* bytes per integer
u[*size*]	Unsigned decimal, *size* bytes per integer
x[*size*]	Hexadecimal, *size* bytes per integer

In Table 17.5, *size* is a number and also may be C for sizeof(char), S for sizeof(short), I for sizeof(int), or L for sizeof(long). If *type* is f, *size* may also be F for sizeof(float), D for sizeof(double), or L for sizeof(long double).

N O T E   sizeof is a C language function that returns the number of bytes in the data structure passed as the parameter. For example, you would use the following function call to determine the number of bytes in an integer on your system, because the number of bytes in an integer is system-dependent:

```
sizeof( int );
```

radix in Table 17.3 stands for number system and is d for decimal, o for octal, x for hexadecimal, or n for none. *bytes* is hexadecimal with a prefix of 0x or 0X; it's multiplied by 512 with a b suffix, by 1,024 with k, and by 1,048,576 with an m suffix. -s without a number implies 3; -w without a number implies 32. By default, od uses -A o -t d2 -w 16.

Searching for Files

If you can't find a file by looking with the ls command, you can use the find command. The find command is an extremely powerful tool, which makes it one of the more difficult commands to use. The find command has three parts, each of which can consist of multiple subparts:

- Where to look
- What to look for
- What to do when you find it

If you know the name of a file but don't know where in the Linux file structure it's located, the simplest case of the `find` command works like this:

```
find / -name filename -print
```

> **CAUTION**
>
> Be careful when searching from the root directory; on large systems, it can take a long time to search every directory beginning with the root directory and continuing through every subdirectory and disk (and remotely mounted disk) to find what you're looking for.

It may be more prudent to limit the search to one or two directories, at most. For example, if you know that a file is probably in the /usr or /usr2 directory, use the following command instead:

```
find /usr /usr2 -name filename -print
```

You can use many different options with `find`; Table 17.6 lists just a few. To see all the available options, use the `man find` command.

Table 17.6   A Sample of the *find* Command Flags

Command	Description
`-name file`	The *file* variable can be the name of a file or a wildcarded filename. If it's a wildcarded filename, every file that matches the wildcards is selected for processing.
`-links n`	Any file that has *n* or more links to it is selected for processing. Replace *n* with the number you want to check.
`-size n[c]`	Any file that occupies *n* or more 512-byte blocks is selected for processing. A c appended to *n* means to select any file that occupies *n* or more characters.
`-atime n`	Select any file that has been accessed in the past *n* days. Note that the act of looking for a file with `find` modifies the access date stamp.
`-exec cmd`	After you select a list of files, you can run a Linux command that uses the selected files as an argument. You use two simple rules with `-exec`: the name of a selected file is represented by {}, and the command must be terminated by an escaped semicolon, which is represented by \;. Suppose you create a user directory while logged in as root. As a result, all the files are owned by root, but the files should be owned by the user. You would issue the following command to change the owner of all the files in /home/jack and all subdirectories from root to jack: `find /home/jack -exec chown jack {} \;`
`-print`	This instruction, the most often used, simply prints the name and location of any selected files.

The `find` command allows you to perform many logical tests on files as well. For example, if you want to find a selection of filenames that can't be collectively represented with wildcards, you can use the *or* option (`-o`) to obtain a list:

```
find /home ( -name file1 -o -name file2 ) -print
```

You can combine as much selection criteria as you want with the `find` command. Unless you specify the `-o` option, `find` assumes you mean *and*. For example, the command `find -size 100 -atime 2` means find a file that's at least 100 blocks in size and that was last accessed at least two days ago. You can use parentheses, as in the above example, to prevent ambiguous processing of your criteria, especially if you combine an and/or selection criteria.

Changing File Time and Date Stamps

Each Linux file maintains three time and date stamps: the date of the file's creation, the date of the file's last modification, and the date of the last access. The file creation date can't be changed artificially except by deliberately copying and renaming a file. Whenever a file is read or opened by a program, the file's access date stamp is modified. As mentioned in the preceding section, using the `find` command also causes the access date to be modified.

If a file is modified in any way—that is, if it's written to, even if the file is actually not modified—the file modification and file access date stamps are updated. The date stamps on a file are useful if you need to back up selectively only files that have been modified since a given date. You can use the `find` command for this purpose.

If you want to modify the date stamps on a file without actually modifying the file, you can do so with the `touch` command. By default, `touch` updates the access and modification date stamps on a file with the current system date. By default, if you attempt to touch a file that doesn't exist, `touch` creates the file.

You can use `touch` to fool a command that checks for dates. For example, if your system runs a backup command that backs up only files modified after a particular date, you can touch a file that hasn't been changed recently to make sure that it's picked up.

The `touch` command has the following three flags that you can use to modify its default behavior:

`-a`	Updates only the file's access date and time stamp
`-m`	Updates only the file's modification date and time stamp
`-c`	Prevents `touch` from creating a file if it doesn't already exist

The default syntax for `touch` is `touch -am filelist`.

Compressing Files

If space is tight on a system or you have large ASCII files that aren't used often, you can reduce the size of the files by compressing them. The standard Linux utility for compressing files is gzip. The gzip command can compress an ASCII file by as much as 80 percent. Most UNIX systems also provide the command compress, which typically is used with tar to compress groups of files for an archive. A file compressed with the compress command ends with a .z extension—for example, archive1.tar.Z. Red Hat's distribution also provides the zip and unzip programs for compressing and archiving lists of files.

 T I P It's a good idea to compress a file before you mail it or back it up.

If a file is successfully compressed with the command gzip *filename*, the compressed file is named *filename*.gz, and the original file is deleted. To restore the compressed file to its original components, use the gunzip *filename* command.

N O T E You don't have to append the .gz to the filename when you uncompress a file. The .gz extension is assumed by the gunzip command. ▪

If you want to keep the file in its compressed form but want to pipe the data to another command, use the zcat command. The zcat command works just like the cat command but requires a compressed file as input. zcat decompresses the file and then prints it to the standard output device.

▶ **See** "Connecting Processes with Pipes," **p. 355**

For example, if you've compressed a list of names and addresses stored in a file named namelist, the compressed file is named namelist.gz. If you want to use the contents of the compressed file as input to a program, use the zcat command to begin a pipeline, as follows:

```
zcat namelist ¦ program1 ¦ program2 ...
```

zcat suffers from the same limitation cat does: It can't go backward within a file. Linux offers a program called zless that works just like the less command, except zless operates on compressed files. The same commands that work with less also work with zless.

The compress command's legal status is in limbo; someone has claimed patent infringement. The compression program of choice for Linux is the freely distributed compression utility gzip. The gzip command has none of the potential legal problems of compress, and almost all the files installed by Linux that are compressed were compressed with gzip. gzip should work with most compressed files, even those compressed with the older compress program.

For those of you familiar with PKWARE's PKZIP line of products, you can use the zip and unzip programs provided with the Red Hat distribution. The zip command compresses several files and stores them in an archive, just like PKZIP. The unzip command extracts files from an archive. See the man pages for zip and unzip for more information.

From Here...

Managing files and utilities in Linux is a relatively simple chore. Organizing files into directories is easy. Finding, moving, copying, renaming, and deleting files and directories are simple with the commands `find`, `mv`, `cp`, and `rm`. For more information, see the following:

- Chapter 14, "Managing File Systems," which discusses practices for keeping your file system under control.

- The man pages for the various commands discussed in this chapter: `ls`, `mkdir`, `mv`, `cp`, `rm`, `rmdir`, `cat`, `less`, `more`, `find`, `touch`, `gzip`, `compress`, `tar`, `zip`, and `unzip`.

Part

III

Ch

17

Working with Linux

Understanding Linux Shells

by Steve Burnett

In this chapter

Although graphical interfaces have been added to the UNIX system in recent years, most of the utilities for using and administering Linux (and other UNIX-like systems) are run by typing commands. In Linux, the command-line interpreter is called the *shell*. This chapter describes how to use the features of the various shells to work with Linux utilities and file systems.

Logging In

As a new user and novice system administrator on your Linux system, you've chosen a login ID and password. Because Linux is a multiuser operating system, it must be able to distinguish between users and classes of users. Linux uses your login ID to establish a session in your name and determine the privileges you have. Linux uses your password to verify who you are.

Because any user can log in to any terminal in theory (there is an exception), the UNIX operating system begins by displaying a login prompt on every terminal. Because it's unlikely you'll have multiple terminals connected to your initial Linux system (although connecting multiple terminals is certainly possible), you'll have the alternate, or virtual, terminals available to you.

To switch to the various virtual terminals, press the <Alt> key and any of the first six function keys to switch between the various virtual terminals. For example, to log in to virtual terminal one as root, press <Alt-F1>, which displays the following prompt:

```
Red Hat Linux release 5.1 (Manhattan)
Kernel 2.0.34 on an i686

login:
```

N O T E   The prompt line in the code line declares this example session to be running under the 2.0.34 version of the Linux kernel. As newer kernels are released, this number is incremented, so you may see a different version on the accompanying CD-ROMs. The stable released kernels are given even numbers for the middle number and the odd numbers indicate the latest (and beta) releases. ∎

Enter your user ID (root) and password.

When you log in to any terminal, you own the session on that terminal until you log out. When you log out, Linux displays the login prompt for the next user. Between logging in and logging out, Linux makes sure that all the programs you run and any files you might create are owned by you. Conversely, Linux doesn't allow you to read or alter a file owned by another user unless that user or the system administrator has given you permission to do so. Your login ID and password allow Linux to maintain the security of your files and those of others.

As the system administrator for your Linux system, you assign every user a user ID, temporary password, group ID, home directory, and shell. This information is kept in a file named /etc/passwd, which is owned and controlled by the system administrator, also known as root or the superuser. After you successfully log in, you can change your password, which is then encrypted in a form that no one else can read. If you forget your password, you (the system administrator) have to log in as the root user to create a new password. You can change your own password with the passwd command (although you have to type in the old password).

N O T E For more information on basic system administration duties, such as adding users and fixing forgotten passwords, see the chapters in Part II, "System Administration," particularly Chapter 10, "Managing User Accounts." ▨

Understanding Shells

After you log in, Linux places you in your home directory and runs a program called a *shell*. A shell is really nothing more than a program designed to accept commands from you and execute them. Many kinds of programs can be used as shells, but several standard shells are available with almost all versions of Linux.

N O T E Linux shells are equivalent to COMMAND.COM used by MS-DOS. Both accept and execute commands, run batch files, and execute programs. ▨

Looking at Different Shells

Red Hat Linux provides the following shells: sh, bash (Bourne Again SHell), tcsh, csh, pdksh (Public Domain Korn SHell), zsh, ash, and mc. Try each shell and pick one you like. This chapter concentrates on the sh and bash shells, because most Linux distributions install bash as the default shell. Also, sh is available on most UNIX systems, and you'll find many shell scripts written with sh commands.

Because the shell serves as the primary interface between the operating system and the user, many users identify the shell with Linux. They expect the shell to be programmable, but the shell isn't part of the kernel of the operating system. With enough background in systems programming and knowledge of the Linux operating system, you can write a program that can become a shell.

Although many different shells have been created, there are several prevalent shells: the Bourne, C, T, and Korn shells. The Bourne shell is the oldest, and the others have some features not in the Bourne shell. In fact, Linux uses a variation of the Bourne shell, the bash shell, as its default shell. (To the novice user, the Bourne and Korn shells look identical; indeed, the Korn shell was developed from the Bourne shell.)

N O T E The Slackware 96 distribution doesn't provide a copy of the Korn shell. The Red Hat distribution provides a version of the Korn shell called pdksh, which stands for Public Domain Korn Shell. ▨

The C shell was developed at the University of California at Berkeley as a shell more suitable for programmers than the Bourne shell. The T shell is a derivative of the C shell. The Korn shell has all the features of the C shell but uses the syntax of the Bourne shell. If all of this sounds confusing at the moment, don't worry. You can do a lot without knowing or worrying about the shell you're using.

In their simplest forms, the Bourne and Korn shells use the dollar sign ($) as the standard prompt; the C shell uses the percent sign (%) as the prompt. Fortunately (or not, depending on your disposition), these prompts can be changed so that you may or may not see either the dollar or the percent sign when you first log in.

The Bourne shell, known as sh, is the original UNIX shell. It was written by Steve Bourne with some help and ideas from John Mashey, both of AT&T Bell Laboratories, and is available on all Linux systems. The executable program for this shell is in the file /bin/sh. Because the Bourne shell is available on all Linux systems and it has all the properties described in the preceding sections as well as powerful programming capabilities, it has become a widely used shell.

N O T E   Many of the shell script examples in this chapter are written so that they can be used with the Bourne shell. *Shell scripts* are sequences of shell commands, normally written with an ASCII editor such as vi. You can think of shell scripts as similar to DOS batch files. ■

▶ **See** "Introducing vi," **p. 178**

The C shell, known as csh, was developed by Bill Joy at the University of California at Berkeley. The students and faculty at Berkeley have had a great deal of influence on UNIX and hence Linux. Two results of that influence are the C shell and the vi text editor. The Bourne shell has superior shell programming capabilities, but the C shell was developed to reflect the fact that computing was becoming more interactive. The executable program for the C shell is in the file /bin/csh.

The syntax of the C shell closely resembles the C programming language. This is one reason that shell scripts written for the C shell often can't run under the Bourne or Korn shell (executables compiled under the C shell will often behave properly, though). But the C shell has some desirable features not available in the Bourne shell: command editing, history, and aliasing.

The default Linux shell is the bash shell. bash is located in /bin/bash and provides several enhanced features detailed in the next few paragraphs, such as command editing, command history, and command completion.

All Linux systems have the bash shell. You also might have installed several other shells during installation—for example, the C shell or the T shell. To determine which shell you're using, enter

`echo $SHELL`

The echo command prints whatever follows the word echo to the terminal screen. SHELL is a variable, maintained by the shell, that holds the name of your current shell; $SHELL is the value of that variable.

To see whether the C shell is available, enter this command:

`csh`

If you see the percent sign (%) as the prompt, the C shell is available and running (enter `exit` to return to your previous shell). If you're logged in as root, the prompt for the C shell is #. If you get an error message, the C shell isn't available to you.

The shell you use as a login shell is specified in the password file. Each login ID is represented by a record or line in the password file; the last field in the record specifies your login shell. To change your login shell, you must change that field. The act of changing to another shell is relatively easy. Before you change shells, however, decide whether learning a new syntax and operating method are worth the change. See the man pages for detailed information on your shell's syntax.

> **CAUTION**
>
> Never directly edit the password file (/etc/passwd) in Linux. Because of the security features added to these releases, the password file should be manipulated only with the appropriate commands. For example, with Slackware Linux, to change to the C shell by using `usermod`, enter `usermod -s /bin/csh user`, where *user* is the user ID of the user for whom you're changing the shell. This caution is especially important if you are using the shadow suite of utilities.

Several other shells are available; some are proprietary and others are available on the Internet or through other sources. To determine which shell you want to use, simply read the man pages for the various shells and give each a try. Because shells are programs, you can run them just like any other application.

Configuring Your Login Environment

Before you see the shell prompt, Linux sets up your default environment. The Linux environment contains settings and data that control your session while you're logged in. Of course, as with all things in Linux, you're completely free to change any of these settings to suit your needs.

Your session environment is divided into two components:

- The first component, called the *terminal environment*, controls your terminal (more properly, the behavior of the computer's port to which you connect the cable from your terminal).

> **N O T E** Because Linux runs on a PC, the "terminal" is actually your monitor and keyboard. You may or may not have other terminals connected to your Linux system. Of course, you do have six virtual terminals that you can log in from. ■

- The second component, called the *shell environment*, controls various aspects of the shell and any programs you run.

You should first know about your terminal environment.

Setting the Terminal Environment Your login session actually consists of two separate programs that run side by side to give you the appearance of having the machine to yourself.

Although the shell is the program that receives your instructions and executes them, before the shell ever sees your commands, everything you type must first pass through the relatively transparent program called the *device driver*.

The device driver controls your terminal. It receives the characters you type and determines what to do with them—if anything—before passing them on to the shell for interpretation. Likewise, every character generated by the shell must pass through the device driver before being delivered to the terminal. This section is first concerned with how to control the behavior of your device driver.

Linux is unique in that every device connected to the system looks, to a program, just like every other device, and all devices look like files. It's the task of the different device drivers in your system to accomplish this transformation. A hard disk in the system behaves very differently from your terminal, yet it's the job of their respective device drivers to make them look identical to a program.

For example, a disk has blocks, sectors, and cylinders, all of which must be properly addressed when reading and writing data. Your terminal, on the other hand, accepts a continuous stream of characters, but those characters must be delivered to the terminal in an ordered and relatively slow manner. The device driver orders this data and sends it to you at 1200, 2400, 9600, or higher bits per second (bps) and inserts stop, start, and parity bits in the data stream.

Because your terminal is always connected to the system, the device driver allows you to define special characters, called *control characters*, that serve as end-of-file and end-of-line markers for your shell. The device driver also allows you to define control characters that send signals to a running process (such as the interrupt signal, which can, in most cases, stop a running process and return you to the shell). Figure 18.1 shows one way that the Linux kernel, shell, and device driver behave.

FIG. 18.1
You can understand how Linux interacts with the user through the command shell.

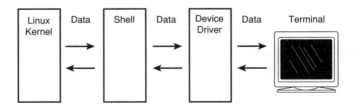

You can set dozens of parameters for your terminal, but most of them are handled automatically. However, you should know about a few parameters and modes.

The device driver has two modes of operation, called *cooked* and *raw*. In raw mode, all the characters you type pass directly to the shell or to a program run by the shell. Programs such as editors and spreadsheets require raw mode and set it up automatically. When such programs end, they normally reset your terminal to cooked mode—but not always. When your terminal is in raw mode, it doesn't respond to control keys such as the interrupt key.

When your terminal is in cooked mode, every key you type is interpreted by the device driver. Normal keys are stored in a buffer until the end-of-line key is pressed. In most cases, the end-of-line key is the <Enter> or <Return> key (however, this key can be changed). When the device driver receives the end-of-line character, it interprets the entire line before passing the interpreted or parsed line on to the shell or application program. Table 18.1 lists the most important control keys.

Table 18.1   Control Keys

Key Name	Description
Interrupt	Interrupts the execution of a running program. When you give Linux a command and press the end-of-line key, a program normally runs until normal completion. If you press the interrupt key, you send a signal to the running program, telling it to stop. Some programs ignore this signal; if your terminal is in raw mode, the interrupt key passes directly to the program and may not have the desired effect. The UNIX convention is to use the <Del> key as the interrupt key, but Linux changes this key to <Ctrl-c> for the convenience of people familiar with MS-DOS and other systems that use this key combination.
Erase	Deletes the last character in the buffer. This key is defined as the <Backspace> key. The erase key works just like the Backspace key on a typewriter. On some terminals and systems, there's confusion between the <Delete> and <Backspace> keys.
Kill	Deletes everything in the buffer before it passes to the shell or application program. This key is normally defined as the @ character. Unlike pressing the interrupt key, you don't see a new shell prompt when you press the kill key—the device driver simply waits for you to type more text.
End-of-line	Tells the device driver that you've finished entering text and want the text interpreted and passed on to the shell or application program. Linux uses the <Enter> or <Return> key.
End-of-file	Tells the shell to exit and display the login prompt. The end-of-file character is the <Ctrl-d> character. Linux treats all devices as though they were files; because your terminal is a source of virtually unlimited characters, Linux uses the end-of-file key as a way for you to signal that you're done with your login session.

Part

IV

Ch

18

The command used to set and display these control-key parameters is stty, which stands for *set teletype*. In the "old days," a teletype terminal was the only terminal available; a lot of UNIX terminology is left over from this era. For example, your terminal is defined as a tty device with a name such as tty14. To display all your present settings, enter **stty -a** from the command line. If you use this command, you see something like this:

```
speed 38400 baud; rows 25; columns 80; line = 0;
intr = ^C; quit = ^\; erase = ^?; kill = ^U; eof = ^D; eol = <undef>;
eol2 = <undef>; start = ^Q; stop = ^S; susp = ^Z; rprnt = ^R; werase = ^W;
lnext = ^V; flush = ^O; min = 1; time = 0;
-parenb -parodd cs8 hupcl -cstopb cread -clocal -crtscts
```

```
-ignbrk -brkint -ignpar -parmrk -inpck -istrip -inlcr -igncr icrnl ixon ixoff
-iuclc -ixany -imaxbel
opost -olcuc -ocrnl onlcr -onocr -onlret -ofill -ofdel nl0 cr0 tab0 bs0 vt0 ff0
isig icanon iexten echo echoe echok -echonl -noflsh -xcase -tostop -echoprt
echoctl echoke
```

Notice that on this system, the interrupt key (`intr`) is defined as <Ctrl-c> (shown as ^C), and the kill key is <Ctrl-u>. Although you can set all the settings listed here, as a matter of practicality, users usually only reset the interrupt and kill keys. For example, if you want to change the kill key from ^U to ^C, enter the following:

`stty kill '^C'`

> **N O T E** If your terminal is behaving strangely, reset it to a "most reasonable" setting by giving the command `stty sane`. ▓

> **T I P** If you want a certain setting to take effect every time you log in, place the command in your .profile file (located in your home directory) if you're running the `bash`, Bourne, or Korn shell. For the C shell, place the command in your .login file.

Setting the Shell Environment   Part of the process of logging in—that is, of creating a Linux session—is the creation of your environment. All Linux *processes* (as running programs are called) have their own environment separate and distinct from the program itself. It could be said that a program runs from within an environment. The Linux environment, called the *shell environment*, consists of a number of variables and their values. These variables and values allow a running program, such as a shell, to determine what the environment looks like.

Environment refers to things such as the shell that you use, your home directory, and what type of terminal you're using. Many of these variables are defined during the login process and either can't or shouldn't be changed. You can add or change as many variables as you like as long as a variable hasn't been marked "read-only."

Variables are set in the environment in the form *VARIABLE=value*. The meaning of *VARIABLE* can be set to anything you like. However, many variables have predefined meanings to many standard Linux programs. For example, the `TERM` variable is defined as being the name of your terminal type, as specified in one of the standard Linux terminal databases. Digital Equipment Corporation for years made a popular terminal named the VT-100. The characteristics of this terminal have been copied by many other manufacturers and often emulated in software for personal computers. The name of such a terminal type is vt100; it's represented in the environment as `TERM=vt100`.

Many other predefined variables exist in your environment. If you use the C shell, you can list these variables with the `printenv` command; with the Bourne or Korn shell, use the `set` command. Table 18.2 lists the most common environment variables and their uses. The Variable column shows what you type at the command line.

> **N O T E** Some environment and system variables can be changed, and some can't be changed. ▓

Table 18.2   Common Bourne Shell Environment Variables

Variable	Description
HOME=/home/*login*	HOME sets your home directory, which is the location that you start out from. Replace *login* with your login ID. For example, if your login ID is jack, HOME is defined as /home/jack.
LOGNAME=*login*	LOGNAME is automatically set the same as your login ID.
PATH=*path*	The *path* option represents the list of directories that the shell looks through for commands. For example, you can set the path like this: PATH=/usr:/bin:/usr/local/bin.
PS1=*prompt*	PS1 is the primary shell prompt that defines what your prompt looks like. If you don't set it to anything specific, your prompt is the dollar sign ($). If you prefer, you can set it to something more creative. For example, PS1="Enter Command >" displays Enter Command > as your command-line prompt.
PWD=*directory*	PWD is automatically set for you. It defines where you are in the file system. For example, if you checked PWD (by entering **echo $PWD** at the command line) and Linux displays /usr/bin, you're in the /usr/bin directory. The pwd command also displays the current directory.
SHELL=*shell*	SHELL identifies the location of the program that serves as your shell. For example, you can set SHELL in your .profile or .login file as SHELL=/bin/ksh to make the Korn shell your login shell.
TERM=*termtype*	Sets the name of your terminal type, as specified by the terminal database. For example, you can set TERM in your .profile or .login file as TERM=vt100.

Part
IV

Ch
18

N O T E   If you want an environment variable defined every time you log in, place the definition in your .profile file (located in your home directory) if you're running the bash or Bourne shell. For the C shell, place the definition in your .login file. ■

Perhaps the single most important variable in your environment is the PATH variable.

N O T E   DOS users should be familiar with the PATH variable. It performs the same function under both DOS and Linux. ■

The PATH variable contains a colon-delimited string that points to all the directories containing the programs you use. The order in which these directories are listed determines which directories are searched first. The list order is important on systems that support several different forms of the same command. Your system may also have locally created commands you may want to access. For example, your PATH variable may contain the following values:

```
/usr/ucb:/bin:/usr/bin:/usr/local/bin
```

This statement tells your shell to explore the /usr/ucb directory first. If the shell finds the command in the first directory it searches, it stops searching and executes that command. The /bin and /usr/bin directories contain all the standard Linux commands. The /usr/local/bin directory often contains the local commands added by you and other users of your system. This task of adding local commands is usually the responsibility of the system administrator.

If you are acting as the system administrator, or if you want access to the more system-oriented commands, you will probably want to add /usr/sbin or /usr/local/sbin or both to shorten the effort of typing /usr/sbin/traceroute.

If you intend to create your own commands, you can modify the PATH variable to include directories that contain your own commands. How you do this depends on which shell you use. For example, if you use the Bourne or Korn shell, you can add a directory to your PATH variable by typing the following at the command prompt:

```
$ PATH=$PATH:newpath
```

When you place a $ in front of the name of a variable, its current value is substituted. In this command, the $PATH variable represents whatever the current path is; the colon and the *newpath* parameters add to the current path.

The following section describes several other ways of manipulating variables in your environment. For now, it's sufficient to say that the shell environment contains variables and functions and that these objects can be manipulated by both shells and application programs. Application programs can access and modify the environment, but they generally manipulate variables within the program. Shells, on the other hand, can only manipulate variables in the environment.

Using Special Shell Variables   The shell keeps track of a number of special variables. You can see what they are with the env command, which lists the variables available to you within your working environment. Following is an abbreviated list of what you might see when you enter **env**:

```
HOME=/usr/wrev
SHELL=/bin/sh
MAIL=/usr/mail/wrev
LOGNAME=wrev
PATH=/bin:/usr/bin:.
TZ=PST8PDT
PS1=$
TERM=vt100
```

Any of these special variables can be used in the same way you use any other shell variable. Table 18.3 defines the special variables.

Table 18.3   Special Environment Variables

Variable Name	Meaning
HOME	Full path name of your home directory
SHELL	Name of your current shell

Variable Name	Meaning
MAIL	Full path name of your mailbox
LOGNAME	Your login name
PATH	Directories the shell searches for commands
TZ	Time zone for the date command
SECONDS	Number of seconds since invoking shell
PS1	System prompt
TERM	The type of terminal you're using

The HOME *Variable* The HOME variable always specifies your home directory. When you log in, you're in your home directory. Occasionally, you use the cd command to move to other directories. To change to the directory /usr/local/games, for example, enter **cd /usr/local/ games**. To get back to your home directory, all you have to do is enter cd. You can use the HOME variable when you're writing shell scripts that specify files in your home directory. Rather than write a command such as grep $number /usr/wrev/sales/data.01, it's better to enter the command as **grep $number $HOME/sales/data.01** for these reasons:

- The command line is easier to read.
- If your home directory is moved, the command still works.
- $HOME always represents the home directory of whoever is using the command. If you enter the command by using $HOME, others can use the command as well.

The PATH *Variable* The PATH variable lists the directories in which the shell searches for commands. The shell searches those directories in the order they're listed. If PATH=/bin:/usr/ bin:., whenever the shell interprets a command, it first looks in the directory /bin. If it can't find the command there, the shell looks in the directory /usr/bin. Finally, the shell searches the . directory (remember that the dot represents your current directory). When you enter cal to print this month's calendar, the shell first looks in /bin. Because the command isn't there, the shell then looks in /usr/bin and finds it.

TIP If you have a personalized command named cal, the shell never finds it; the shell executes the cal command in /usr/bin first whenever you give the command. Give your commands names that aren't the same as system commands.

You may want to put all your shell scripts in one directory and change the PATH variable to include that directory. This arrangement allows you to execute your shell scripts from whatever directory you happen to be in. To do this, follow these steps:

1. Create a directory to hold the scripts. Use the mkdir $HOME/bin command to create the bin subdirectory in your home directory.
2. Move each shell script to that subdirectory. For example, to move a shell script named stamp to your bin subdirectory, use the mv stamp $HOME/bin command.

Part

IV

Ch

18

3. Add the script subdirectory to your PATH variable with the PATH=$PATH:$HOME/bin command. Do this in your .profile file so that the change takes effect every time you log in to your system.

You need to create that new bin directory and modify the PATH variable only once. Under Linux, the directory called /usr/local/bin is created to hold "local" commands and scripts that aren't part of the standard Linux package but that you've added locally and have made available to all users. In this case, you should expect that /usr/local/bin is also part of PATH.

The MAIL Variable The MAIL variable contains the name of the file that holds your e-mail. Whenever mail comes into the system for you, it's put into the file specified by the MAIL variable. If you have a program that notifies you when new mail has arrived, it checks the file associated with the MAIL variable.

The PS1 Variable The PS1 variable holds the string of characters you see as your primary prompt. The prompt is the string of characters the shell displays whenever it's ready to receive a command. You see how you can change this variable—and any of the others—in the section "Customizing Linux Shells" near the end of this chapter.

The TERM Variable The TERM variable is used to identify your terminal type. Programs that operate in full-screen mode, such as the vi text editor, need this information.

The TZ Variable The TZ variable holds a string that identifies your time zone. The date program and some other programs require this information.

Your computer system keeps track of time according to Greenwich Mean Time (GMT). If the TZ variable is set to PST8PDT, the time and date are determined as Pacific Standard Time (PST), eight hours west of GMT, with support for Pacific Daylight Savings Time (PDT). Your computer system automatically changes between daylight savings time and standard time.

The LOGNAME Variable The LOGNAME variable holds your login name, the name or string of characters that the system associates you with. Among the things the LOGNAME variable is used for is to identify you as the owner of your files, as the originator of any processes or programs you may be running, and as the author of mail or messages sent by the write command.

The following example is an extension of safrm, a shell script created for the safe removal of files. The LOGNAME variable is used to remove all the files you own from the directory /tmp. To do that, the shell script uses the find command. The find command has a number of options; the shell script uses this find command line:

```
find /tmp -user $LOGNAME -exec rm {} \;
```

The first parameter, /tmp, is the directory to search. The option -user indicates that you want to search for all files that belong to a specified user. Before the command is executed, the shell replaces $LOGNAME with the current user's login name. The option -exec indicates that the following command is to be applied to every file found by the find program. In this case, the rm program is used to remove the found files. The braces ({}) represent the position of each filename passed to the rm command. The last two characters, \;, are required by the find command (an example of using the backslash to pass a character on to a program without being interpreted by the shell). Add this command line to the shell script in Listing 18.1 to obtain a program that removes files safely and also cleans up anything a user has in the /tmp directory that's more than 10 days old.

Listing 18.1   The *safrm* Shell Script

```
# Name:     safrm
# Purpose:  copy files to directory /tmp, remove them
#           from the current directory, clean up /tmp,
#           and finally send mail to user
# first copy all parameters to /tmp
cp $* /tmp
# remove the files
rm $*
# create a file to hold the mail message
#   The file's name is set to msg
#   followed by process ID number of this process
#   For example, msg1208
msgfile=/tmp/msg$$
# construct mail message
date > $msgfile
echo "These files were deleted from /tmp" >>$msgfile
# get list of files to be deleted from tmp
# -mtime +10 gets all files that haven't been
# modified in 10 or more days, -print displays the names.
find /tmp -user $LOGNAME -mtime +10 -print >> $msgfile
# remove the appropriate files from /tmp
find /tmp -user $LOGNAME -mtime +10 -exec rm {} \;
# mail off the message
mail $LOGNAME < $msgfile
# clean up
rm $msgfile
```

Understanding Processes

A running program in Linux is called a *process*. Because Linux is a multitasking system, many processes can run at the same time. To distinguish between processes, Linux assigns each new process a unique ID called a *process ID*.

The process ID is simply a number that uniquely identifies each running process. To see what process IDs are now associated with your process, use the ps command. To look at most of the process IDs now running on your system, issue the command with the flags -guax, and you see something like the following:

```
USER   PID  %CPU %MEM SIZE  RSS TTY STAT START    TIME COMMAND
jack   53   3.2  7.0  352   468 p 1 S   02:01   0:01 -bash
jack   65   0.0  3.5  80    240 p 1 R   02:01   0:00 ps -guax
root   1    0.8  3.1  44    208 con S   02:00   0:00 init
root   6    0.0  1.8  24    124 con S   02:00   0:00 bdflush (daemon)
root   7    0.0  1.9  24    128 con S   02:01   0:00 update (bdflush)
root   40   1.0  3.5  65    240 con S   02:01   0:00 /usr/sbin/syslogd
root   42   0.2  2.9  36    200 con S   02:01   0:00 /usr/sbin/klogd
root   44   0.5  3.2  68    216 con S   02:01   0:00 /usr/sbin/inetd
root   46   0.2  3.0  64    204 con S   02:01   0:00 /usr/sbin/lpd
```

```
root   52  0.1  2.0   32  140 con S    02:01   0:00 selection -t ms
root   58  0.2  2.4   37  164 p 6 S    02:01   0:00 /sbin/agetty 38400 tt
```

The process ID is identified by the column titled PID. Also note the boldfaced line, which indicates the first process started by the system—init. The init process is also described later in this chapter.

When Linux is told to run a program (that is, to create a process), it does so by making an exact copy of the program making the request. In the simplest case, you request that a program be run by telling your shell; the shell makes a fork request to the Linux kernel.

Fork, *init*, and the *exec* Process   A *fork* is the process of cloning an existing process. Linux creates all new processes through the mechanism of forking. When a process is forked, an almost exact duplicate of an existing process (including its environment and any open files) is created; what keeps the duplicate from being exactly the same as its parent application is a flag that tells the forked process which is the parent and which is the child.

Because all processes are created in this fashion, all processes have a parent process and a parent-process ID. Every process running on a Linux system can trace its lineage back to init, the mother of all processes. init itself, process ID 1, is the only process run directly by the Linux kernel that you as a user have any contact with. Every process you create during a session has your login shell as an ancestor, and your login shell has init as its parent.

After a process successfully forks, the child process calls the exec routine to transform itself into the process you requested. The only thing that changes after an exec function is the identity of the running process; the environment of the new process is an exact copy of the environment of its parent.

Standard Input and Output   Every new process is created with three open "files." Because Linux treats files and devices exactly the same, an open "file" can be a real file on a disk or a device such as your terminal. The three open files are defined as standard input (stdin), standard output (stdout), and standard error output (stderr). All Linux commands, as well as application programs, accept input from the standard input and place any output on the standard output. Any diagnostic messages are automatically placed on the standard error output.

When you first log in, the standard input, output, and error files are attached to your terminal; any programs you run (processes you create) inherit your terminal as the three open files.

Understanding Shell Command Parsing

Parsing is the act of splitting the command line, or what you type, into its component parts for processing. In Linux, parsing constitutes a lot more than simply splitting the command line. The command string is first split into its component parts: the filenames expanded if you used any wild cards, shell variables expanded, I/O redirection set up, any command groupings or subshells set up, and command substitution performed. Only then can the command line, as you typed it, be executed.

If terms such as *wild cards* and *I/O redirection* are new to you, you can find explanations of them, in the order they're performed, later in this chapter. You must first start, however, with the basic command syntax.

Using Commands, Flags, and Parameters

To execute a Linux command, you merely type the name of the file. The command to list files is ls; you can find a file by that name in the /bin directory. If /bin is listed in your PATH variable (and it should be), your shell finds and executes /bin/ls.

Some Linux commands aren't independent files. These commands are built into the shells themselves. For example, the cd (change directory) command is built into most shells and executed directly by the shell without looking up a file. Read the man pages for the shell you're using to determine what commands are executed internally or externally. Some shells have a command file that contains commands executed directly by the shell.

Flags   If a command is to execute properly, you must present it to your shell in the proper fashion. The command name itself must be the first item on the line; it's followed by any flags and parameters. Flags (sometimes called *options*) are single letters preceded by a hyphen (-) that modify the behavior of a command. For example, the list command, ls, simply lists the names of the files in the current directory in alphabetical order. By adding various flags, you can list the contents of a directory in many different ways. You can list files and all their attributes with the "long" flag, -l. This command takes the following form:

```
ls -l
```

▶ **See** "Listing Files," **p. 318**

-l is the flag. When you want to use more than one flag, simply string the flags together, as in ls -lF. The -F flag displays an asterisk (*) if the file is executable, an at sign (@) if the file is a symbolic link, and a slash (/) if the file is a subdirectory. The man page for every command usually lists all the modifying flags and their meanings before describing any parameters. Flags can also be listed separately; the shell parses them before passing them on to the program. For example, you can write the ls -lF command as ls -l -F.

> **N O T E**   Linux provides a popular feature—color highlighting. When you issue the ls command, Slackware Linux displays files in different colors depending on the file's type. This allows you to quickly identify files that are executable, directories, or linked to other files located in other directories. Also, if you redirect the output from ls to a file, this file contains the control codes used to indicate color. The control codes' information may cause problems with other programs, such as less, when used with this file. For Red Hat Linux, you must provide the --color flag to ls to get the same effect:

```
ls --color ▮
```

One type of flag signals that the next parameter has some special meaning. For example, the -t flag in the sort command is used to indicate that the next character is a field separator. If you want to sort the /etc/passwd file, whose fields are separated by a colon (:), you can enter

```
sort -t: /etc/passwd
```

In the case of the sort command, the -t flag is needed only if the file uses a field separator other than the default. The default field separator is defined in the IFS (Inter Field Separator) environment variable. The shell uses the IFS variable to parse the command line so that the shell knows to use the standard field separator unless the -t flag indicates otherwise.

Parameters   Flags must be presented to the command before any other parameters. *Parameters* are strings separated by any of the characters defined in the IFS environment variable. The default string in IFS is a space, a tab, and a newline character. You can place any number of field-separator characters between parameters; when the shell parses the command line, it reduces these characters to one character before proceeding. For example, if a command is followed by three spaces, a tab character, and then the first parameter, the shell automatically reduces the three spaces and a tab to one tab character. Thus, the following line

command<space bar><space bar><space bar><Tab>*parameter*

becomes

command<Tab>*parameter*

Parameters are usually filenames or strings that tell the command to perform some function. If a parameter contains an embedded space, the string must be placed in quotation marks to prevent the shell from expanding it. The following command line contains two parameters; the shell attempts to find the word New in a file named York:

```
grep New York
```

If the intent is to find the string "New York" in the standard input, the command must be entered as

```
grep "New York"
```

In this case, the string "New York" is passed to the grep command as one parameter.

Performing Filename Matching

Most modern operating systems (including all versions of Linux and DOS) support the use of wild cards for file and string searches. Table 18.4 summarizes the filename completion characters, otherwise known as *wild cards*.

Table 18.4   Filename Completion Characters

Character	Meaning
*	Represents any collection of characters except a period when it's the first character in a filename. For example, the command cat sales* > allsales combines all files whose names begin with sales into a file named allsales.
?	Represents a single character. For example, the command lp sales.9? prints a collection of files with names in the form of sales.*yy*, where *yy* represents a year in the nineties (such as sales.90, sales.91, and so on).

Character	Meaning
[]	Represents a single character in a range. For example, the command rm sales.9[0-3] removes the collection of files with the names sales.90, sales.91, sales.92, and sales.93.

N O T E If you place a filename wild card or expression inside quotation marks, the filename expansion is suppressed during command-line parsing. For example, if you type ls *, you will get all files in the current directory. On the other hand, if you type **ls "*"**, you probably will get the file not found error message because you're instructing ls to search for a file named *. ▪

The * Wild Card The asterisk (*) is the most universal wild card used. It simply means any and all characters. For example, the string a* means all files beginning with a. You can use as many asterisks in a single expression as you need to define a set of files. For example, the expression *xx*.gif means any filename with the .gif extension that has xx anywhere in the rest of the name. Matches include the filenames abxx.gif, xxyyzz.gif, and xx.gif.

Use the asterisk character (*) to represent any sequence of characters. For example, to print all files in your current directory with names that end with .txt, enter

```
lp *.txt
```

Pay attention when using the asterisk wild card. If you enter the following command, you print all files whose names end with txt:

```
lp *txt
```

The file named reportxt is included with the files printed with the second command but not with the first. If you enter the following command, the shell passes the name of every file in your directory, as well as the single file named txt, to the command lp (the file named txt in your directory is passed twice to lp):

```
lp * txt
```

In the last example, the lp command first prints the files represented by the *; that is, it prints all files. The lp command then moves to the second item in the list of files it is to print (Linux interprets the space character between the * and txt as a delimiter—in effect, as a comma in an English command). The lp command processes txt as the name of the next file it is to print.

The * symbol can be used anywhere in a string of characters. For example, if you want to use the ls command to list the names of all files in your current directory whose names contain the characters *rep*, enter this command:

```
ls *rep*
```

Linux lists files with names such as frep.data, report, and janrep. There's one exception: Files with names starting with a period aren't listed. To list files with names starting with a period (often called *hidden files*), you must specify the leading period. For example, if you have a file named .reportrc and want to see it listed, enter the following variation of the preceding command:

```
ls .*rep*
```

Part
IV

Ch

18

CAUTION

Be careful of using the asterisk wild card when you're deleting or removing files. The command `rm *` removes *all* files in your directory. An all-too-common mistake is to accidentally delete all files when you mean to delete a collection of files with a common suffix or prefix. If, instead of `rm *txt` (which would remove all files with names ending in txt), you enter `rm * txt`, Linux first deletes all files and then attempts to delete a file named txt. But at that point, no files are left.

To be safe, use the `-i` option with `rm` if you use the asterisk for filename completion. The `rm -i *txt` command prompts you for confirmation before each file is deleted.

The ? Wild Card   Use the question mark (?) wild card to represent a single character. Suppose that you have the files report1, reportb, report10, reportb3, report.dft, and report.fin in your current directory. You know that the `lp rep*` command prints all the files, but to print just the first two (report1 and reportb), enter this:

```
lp report?
```

To list the names of all files whose names are three characters long and end with the character *x*, enter the following:

```
ls ??x
```

This command lists a file with the name tax but not trax.

Because the question mark represents a single occurrence of any character, the string ??? represents all files consisting of just three letters. You can generate a list of files with three-letter extensions with the string *.???. For example, if you're searching a directory containing graphic images as well as other data, the following command lists all files with extensions such as .tif, .jpg, and .gif, as well as any other files with three-letter extensions:

```
ls *.???
```

N O T E   Remember that Linux isn't MS-DOS; filenames aren't limited to eight characters with a three-character extension. Also remember that filenames are case-sensitive under Linux. ■

The [] Expression   Sometimes you must be more selective than either of the more general-purpose wild cards allow. Suppose that you want to select the files job1, job2, and job3, but not jobx. You can't select the right files with the ? wild card because it represents one occurrence of any character. You can, however, use job[123] as the file descriptor.

You can also represent a single character by enclosing a range of characters within a pair of square brackets. To list the names of all files that begin with an uppercase letter, enter the following:

```
ls [A-Z]*
```

Suppose that you have files named sales.90, sales.91, sales.92, and sales.93 and want to copy the first three to a subdirectory named oldstuff. Assuming that the subdirectory oldstuff exists, you could enter this:

```
cp sales.9[0-2] oldstuff
```

Like the question mark, items inside square brackets ([]) represent exactly one character. You can describe a discrete series of permissible values, such as [123], which permits only the characters 1, 2, or 3; you can also describe a range of characters, as in [A–Z], which represent any character between uppercase A and uppercase Z, inclusive.

You can also specify a set of ranges, which incorporates more than one range. For example, if you want to specify only alphabetic characters, you can use [A–Z,a–z]. In the ASCII character set, there are special characters between ASCII Z and ASCII a; if you specified [A–z], you include those special characters in your request.

Connecting Processes with Pipes

Frequently, you need to use the output of one program or command as the input of another. Rather than enter each command separately and save results in intermediate files, you can connect a sequence of commands by using a pipe (|).

For example, to sort a file named allsales and then print it, enter this:

```
sort allsales ¦ lp
```

The name *pipe* is appropriate. The output of the program on the left of the pipe (the vertical bar) is sent through the pipe and used as the input of the program on the right. You can connect several processes with pipes. For example, to print a sorted list of the data in all files with names that begin with sales, enter the following command:

```
cat sales* ¦ sort ¦ lp
```

Redirecting Input and Output

Many programs expect input from the terminal or keyboard; many programs send their output to the terminal screen. Linux associates keyboard input with a file named stdin; it associates terminal output with a file named stdout. You can redirect input and output so that rather than come from or go to the terminal, it comes from a file or is sent to a file.

Use the < (less than) symbol to redirect input into a command or program so that it comes from a file instead of the terminal. Suppose that you want to send a file named info by e-mail to someone whose address is sarah. Rather than retype the contents of the file to the mail command, give this command to use the info file as the input (stdin) to the mail command:

```
mail sarah < info
```

Use the > (greater than) symbol to redirect the output of a program to a file. Instead of going to the terminal screen, the output is put into a file. The command date displays the current time and date on the terminal screen. If you want to store the current time and date in a file named now, enter this command:

```
date > now
```

> **CAUTION**
>
> If the filename on the right side of the > already exists, it will be overwritten. Be careful not to destroy useful information this way.

If you want to append, or concatenate, information to an existing file, use the two-character >> symbol. To append the current date to a file named report, enter the following command:

```
date >> report
```

For a slightly more lengthy example, suppose that the file named sales consists of sales data; the first field of each line contains a customer ID code. The first command line puts the output of the date command into a file named sales_report. The second command line uses the sales file as input to the sort command and appends the output to the sales_report file. The last line sends the sales_report file to users sarah and brad by e-mail:

```
date > sales_report
sort < sales >> sales_report
mail sarah brad < sales_report
```

> **CAUTION**
>
> Be careful not to redirect the same file as both input and output to a command. Most likely, you'll destroy the contents of the file.

Table 18.5 summarizes the redirection symbols used in Linux.

Table 18.5 Linux's Redirection Symbols

Symbol	Meaning	Example
<	Take input from a file	`mail sarah < report`
>	Send output to a file	`date > now`
>>	Append to a file	`date >> report`

Substituting Shell Variables

You learned about shell variable expansion earlier in this chapter when you set your PATH variable to PATH=$PATH:*newpath*. The shell replaced $PATH with the current values of the PATH variable. Shells are really interpreted languages, almost like BASIC; the shell variable is the primary object manipulated. Because shell variables are frequently manipulated, each shell provides methods of testing and defining the shell variables.

Shell variables are stored as strings. When two variables are placed together, their respective strings are concatenated. For example, if you have two variables, X=hello and Y=world, the expression XY results in the string helloworld. If you give the following command, the shell parses the two parameters and the values of X and Y (the two strings hello and world) are substituted before being passed to the echo command:

```
echo $X $Y
```

The echo command then prints hello world.

> **NOTE** If you place a dozen tab characters between $X and $Y, the output results are still the same. ■

If the substitution can be ambiguous, the shell picks the most obvious substitution—often with unpredictable results. For example, if you type **echo $XY**, the shell substitutes helloY. If you also had a variable XY, its value is substituted instead. To get around these ambiguities, the shell has a simple mechanism to allow you to define exactly what you mean. If you type **${X}Y**, the shell substitutes the value of X before appending the character Y to the string.

The Bourne and Korn shells have a rich collection of shell-variable expansion techniques that perform various tests on the variable before making the substitution. See the man pages for sh and ksh for more details.

Substituting Command Results

After the shell performs its substitution of variables, it scans the line again for commands to be run before the command line is finally ready. *Command substitution* means that Linux substitutes the results of a command for a positional parameter. This is specified in the following way:

```
command-1 parameter 'command-2'
```

Be careful in the use of apostrophes, or single quotes ('), and backquotes (`, also known as grave accents). Table 18.6 lists what each mark does.

Table 18.6 Quotation Marks and Apostrophes

Symbol	Meaning
"	Quotation marks disable filename generation and suppress parameter expansion; however, shell-variable and command substitution still take place.
'	The apostrophe disables all parsing. Whatever is enclosed within the apostrophes is passed on as a single parameter.
`	The backquote, or grave accent, implies command substitution. Whatever is enclosed within backquotes is executed as though the command was performed on a line by itself. Any output placed on the standard output then replaces the command. The command line is then parsed again for parameters.

Consider the following command line:

```
echo Today\'s date and time are 'date'
```

It produces this output:

```
Today's date and time are Mon May 18 14:35:09 EST 1994
```

To make the echo command behave properly, the 's in *Today's* in the preceding command was preceded by a backslash (\), also called the *escape character* (Today\'s). Virtually every non-alphanumeric character on your keyboard has some special meaning to the shell. To use any of the special characters in a string and to prevent the shell from interpreting the character, you must "escape" the character—that is, you must precede it with the backslash. If you want to pass the backslash character itself, use \\. To pass a dollar sign to a command, use \$.

Regular Expressions

A regular expression is a series of standard characters and special operators. Regular expressions are useful for searching for a string of characters in a file. Regular expressions are often used with the grep family of tools: grep, egrep, and fgrep, but are also used with other UNIX commands.

The simplest kind of regular expression is a string. A string is a set of characters, such as *and*. The syntax for a grep command is as follows:

```
grep string filename
```

For example, to search for the word hand in a specific file named michael, you would enter this command:

```
grep hand michael.txt
```

which might return the result

```
on the other hand, michael has been working hard this past
```

if that was the only line of the text file that contained the word hand. Grep will return every line of a text file that has a match to the string.

Regular expressions use special characters. The special characters used with regular expressions are the period (.), asterisk (*), square brackets ([]), backslash (/), caret (^), and dollar sign ($). Table 18.7 summarizes these special characters and their behavior in regular expressions.

Table 18.7   Special Characters in Regular Expressions

Character	Description
.	Matches a single character, unless the single character is a line-return. For example, b.d will match bad and bod.
*	Matches zero or more of the preceding regular expression. So the pattern 4* matches no 4s, 1 4, 2 4s, and so on.
[]	Used to group a set of multiples for matches. Remember that unlike DOS, UNIX is case-sensitive. So to search for all instances of the name Michael, you

Character	Description
	could use [Mm]ichael to search for both michael and Michael, but not MICHAEL. If you want to search for an actual] character, either you can use []], or you can use the backslash as an escape character to treat the right bracket as a text character, like so: /]. A dash inside brackets acts as a range, so [a–j] is the same as [abcdefghij].
/	Used to escape the special behavior of these special characters and treat them as text to be searched for in a string. So * matches everything, but /* matches only a line with the * character in it. // is used to search for a backslash character, of course.
^	If ^ is at the beginning of the string, it matches a line only if the string is at the beginning of the line. So if you have a text file of telephone numbers sorted by area code, the regular expression ^704 will match all telephone numbers with the area code 704, but not a telephone number 407-555-7043.
$	If a $ is the last character in a regular expression, it matches the expression to a line in the file if the expression is at the end of the file.

You can define how many of a given character to match by using the curly bracket pair {}. For example, the command

```
g\{3,4}
```

matches any line in the text file that contains either *ggg* or *gggg*.

If you maintain a large file of older mail, the command

```
grep 'whatever' ~/mail/*
```

will search for the string whatever in the mail directory. This is useful if you recall that your recent acquaintance Dave Quigman included his telephone number in his sigfile, but you can't remember what folder you saved his message into. This command

```
grep 'Quigman" ~/mail/*
```

will match all instances of the name.

However, a more efficient way may be to match the telephone number itself. Let's say his telephone number is in the area code 408. So the command

```
grep '408.[0-9]\{3\}.[0-9]\{4\}' ~/mail/*
```

finds all telephone numbers that start with 408. Notice the periods separating the 408, the [0–9]\{3\} and [0–9]\{4\}. The period matches any single character, which allows you to match the telephone number 408-555-1212 or 408.555.1212, because some people use periods to separate the telephone numbers.

Understanding Command Groups, Subshells, and Other Commands

You terminate a simple command with a carriage return. If you want to place more than one command on the command line before pressing <Return>, you can delimit individual commands with a semicolon (;), thus forming a group of commands. When the shell parses the command line, it treats the semicolon as an end-of-line character. If you type the following string, the shell executes each command sequentially as though you had typed each on a line by itself:

```
command-1;command-2;command-3
```

For example, you can enter `clear;ls` to clear your screen and display a directory listing.

Command Groups   If you want to redirect input or output to all the commands as a group, you can do so by making the command line a command group. A *command group* is defined as any number of commands enclosed in braces ({}). For example, the following command string directs the output of both commands to the file named output-file:

```
{command-1;command-2} > output-file
```

Any form of redirection can also be used. The output of a command group can be piped, as in the following example:

```
{command-1;command-2} ¦ command-3
```

In this case, the output of *command-1* is fed into the pipe, the output of *command-2* is then fed into the same pipe, and *command-3* sees just one stream of data.

N O T E   Commands executed in a command group run in the current shell. That means that they may modify the environment or change directories. ■

Subshells   When you run a series of commands as a command group, those commands run in the current shell. If one of the commands modifies the environment or changes directory, the changes are in effect when the command group finishes running. To avoid this problem, run a command group in a *subshell*.

A subshell is a clone of the present shell, but because child processes can't modify the environment of their parent process, all commands run in a subshell have no effect on the environment when the command group finishes. To run a command group in a subshell, replace the braces with parentheses. The command-group example in the preceding section then becomes the following:

```
(command-1;command-2) ¦ command-3
```

Only *command-3* runs in the current shell, but the output of the subshell is piped into the standard input of *command-3*.

Doing Background Processing

Because Linux is a multitasking operating system, you can run commands in the background in several ways. The simplest form of background processing allows you to run a command concurrently with a command in the foreground. Other methods place commands deeper and deeper in the background.

Arranging for Processes to Run in the Background

The shell allows you to start one process and, before the first one completes, start another. When you do this, you put the first process in the background. You put a process in the background by using the ampersand (&) character as the last character on the line containing the command you want to run in the background. Consider the following command:

```
sort sales > sales.sorted &
```

If you enter this command, you see a number on-screen. This number is the process ID (PID) number for the process you put in the background. The PID is the operating system's way of identifying that process.

Normally when you run a command, the shell suspends operation until the command is complete. If you append the ampersand to the end of a command string, the command string runs concurrently with the shell. By placing the ampersand *after* a command string, the shell resumes operation as soon as the background command is launched. Unless you use I/O redirection with the background command, the background command and the present shell expect input from and produce output to your terminal. Unless your background command takes care of I/O itself, the proper syntax for background processing is as follows:

```
command-string [input-file] output-file &
```

For example, to copy a collection of files whose names end with the characters .txt to a subdirectory named oldstuff and, without waiting for that process to finish, print a sorted list of the data in all files with names that begin with sales, use the following two commands:

```
cp *.txt oldstuff &
cat sales* ¦ sort ¦ lp
```

TIP Put jobs in the background when you don't want to wait for one program to finish before starting another. You can also put jobs in the background when you have a collection of tasks in which at least one can run on its own. Start that one and put it in the background.

You can also use the virtual terminals offered by Linux to execute a command and then log in to another terminal.

Because the background process is a child of your shell, it's automatically killed when you log out. All child processes are killed when their parent dies.

Part
IV

Ch

18

Using the *nohup* Command

To place a command deeper in the background than the & operator allows, use the nohup command (which stands for *no hang up*). The nohup command takes as its arguments a command string. However, nohup must be used with the & operator if you want the command to actually be placed in the background. If a command is run with nohup in the foreground, the command is immune to being killed when you disconnect your terminal or hang up a modem (its original purpose). The syntax for the nohup command is as follows:

```
nohup command-string [input-file] output-file &
```

Using the *cron* Daemon

If you run a command with the nohup command, the command executes immediately. If you want to run the command at a later time or on a "time-available" basis, you must invoke the services of the cron daemon.

The cron daemon is a command run in the background by Linux—or, more specifically, by init, the master program. cron provides scheduling services to all Linux processes. You can ask cron to run a program at a specific time, periodically, at a particular time every day, or whenever the load on cron permits.

▶ **See** "Scheduling Commands with cron and crontab," **p. 388**

The *at* Command   The at command expects a time or date as a parameter and takes any number of command strings from its standard input. When the at command detects an end-of-file marker, it creates a Bourne shell script for execution at the time you specified.

The at command is flexible about the types of dates and times it accepts. For example, if you enter the command **at now + 1 day**, the next commands, taken from the standard input, are executed tomorrow at this time. One way to use the at command is from within a shell script.

A *shell script* is nothing more than a file containing all the commands necessary to perform a series of commands. The name of the file then becomes your own addition to the Linux command language. One way of using the at command is shown here:

```
at now + 1 day
command-1
command-2
```

When placed in a shell script, these lines let you conveniently run one or more commands the next day. To run any number of different commands, simply enter new commands after the at command line. You can run any number of commands from this script.

The *batch* Command   The batch command is the logical equivalent of at now. If you attempt to use the at now command, you see an error message that says something along the lines of now has passed. The batch command works exactly as at now works if it were logically possible, with one minor exception: The cron daemon maintains a separate queue for commands generated by at, batch, and cron. Suppose that you entered the following commands into the file named backup:

```
tar -cvf tackettbkup /usr/home/tackett
```

Then you can tell the system to back up the directory /usr/home/tackett by using this command

```
batch backup
```

▶ **See** "Creating Your First vi File," **p. 182**

The *crontab* Command   One of the best uses of the cron daemon is in automating the maintenance of a system. With cron, you as the system administrator can set up automatic backups of your system every morning at 4 a.m., Monday through Saturday. You install, delete, and list commands you want run in this fashion with the crontab command.

To run commands periodically, you must create a file in the crontab format. The crontab file consists of six fields separated by spaces or tabs. The first five fields are integers specifying minute (00–59), hour (00–23), day of the month (01–31), month of the year (01–12), and day of the week (0–6, with 0 referring to Sunday). The sixth field is a command string. Each numeric field can contain an inclusive range of numbers (such as 1–5 to indicate Monday through Friday) or discrete sets of numbers (such as 0,20,40 to indicate that an instruction should be run every 20 minutes). A field can also contain an asterisk to indicate all legal values.

The following example runs the calendar command every 20 minutes, starting at midnight Monday and ending at 11:40 p.m. Friday:

```
0,20,40 * * * 1-5 calendar -
```

If you name this file cronfile, you can install it in the cron system by issuing the command crontab cronfile.

The cron daemon has a time granularity of one minute—meaning, the shortest time duration you can work with is one minute. You, as system administrator, can place limits on the number of commands allowed to be run at any one time. Just because you ask cron to run an at, batch, or crontab file doesn't mean that it runs at precisely the time you've indicated.

Understanding Command Feedback

Linux provides instant feedback for commands that abort for one reason or another. In most cases, errors are limited to misspellings of the command name or badly formed filenames. If you attempt to run a nonexistent command, Linux replies with

```
command: command not found
```

If you try to use a nonexistent filename, Linux responds with

```
command: file: No such file or directory
```

If the error is caused by something other than a command-line error, the command itself usually reports what happened—although not always in an easily decipherable form.

If you try to run a command with nohup and haven't redirected the standard error, Linux automatically places any error messages in a file named nohup.out in the directory from which the command was run.

Part
IV

Ch
18

Because commands run by cron have less urgency, any errors—indeed, any output placed on the standard output and not redirected—is sent to you through e-mail.

Editing and Aliasing Shell Commands

Different shells include features that provide shortcuts for running commands. *Command editing* lets you modify commands that have already been typed in. By using Linux's *command history* feature, you can recall commands you've previously entered. *Aliasing* lets you create commands that represent other commands. *Command completion* lets you fill in the rest of a filename after you type part of it.

Editing Commands

Command editing means that after you type a command—and before you press <Return>—you can edit or change parts of the command without having to retype most of it. To edit a command, press <Esc> to get into editing mode and then use any of the line-movement commands from the vi editor to modify the command. You can use <Backspace> to return to the portion of the command you want to change, and use other vi commands, such as x to delete a character, r to replace a character, and so on.

Viewing Command History

The command history feature allows you to look back at previously entered commands and recall them. This feature saves you the time and trouble of retyping commands. When you combine this feature with command editing, you can easily correct mistakes in complicated commands and deal effectively with some repetitive tasks.

In both shells, the history command displays the list of past commands the shell has saved. The commands are numbered. To execute command 10, for example, enter ! 10. The bash shell also takes advantage of your PC's arrow keys; you can recall previous commands by pressing the <↑> key.

Aliasing Commands

Command aliasing allows you to define a name for a command. Consider this example: The man command displays Linux documentation, or *man pages*. To make the word help an alias, or alternative, for man, enter the following:

```
alias help=man
```

Now you can enter **help cp** or **man cp** to display Linux man pages about the cp command.

You also can use aliases with commands that have options or arguments. For example, if you want to list the names of all the files in the current directory sorted in descending order by the time they were last modified (so that the most recent files are at the bottom of the list), you can use this command:

```
ls -art
```

The ls command is the command to list files; the -a option specifies all files, the -r option arranges the files in reverse, descending order, and the -t option sorts by time last modified. That's a lot to remember. You can assign the alias timedir to this complex command with the following command:

```
alias timedir="ls -art"
```

The quotation marks ("") are necessary because the shell expects the alias for timedir to be terminated by a space or <Return>. Now, if you enter timedir, you get the directory listing you want.

N O T E Setting an alias from the command line keeps that alias in effect only for the current session. To have the alias active whenever you log in, include the alias definition in the .profile file if you use the Bourne shell; keep it in the .login file if you use the C shell. ■

Completing Commands

Command completion allows you to type the beginning of a filename and then press the <Tab> key to expand the filename. This can save time and spelling mistakes when entering a command. If two files share a common prefix, Linux expands the command to the last common character, stops expanding the filename, and then beeps. You need to provide the unique filename.

Adding Text with Cut and Paste

Red Hat Linux and Slackware Linux both offer a program that can be started at boot time that allows you to use the mouse to select text from anywhere on-screen and then paste the text onto the command line for the shell to interpret. To get a mouse cursor, you simply press one of the mouse buttons. You then select the desired text from anywhere on-screen by first clicking with the left mouse button on the beginning of the text and, while holding down the button, dragging the cursor to the desired end point of the text. After you select the text, click with the right mouse button to copy the text to the command line.

Part
IV

Ch
18

Working with Shell Scripts

The shell accepts commands, interprets them, and arranges for the operating system to execute the commands in the manner you specify. In the previous sections, you saw how the shell interprets special characters to complete filenames, redirects input and output, connects processes through pipes, and puts jobs or processes in the background.

You can type commands at the terminal, or they can come from a file. A *shell script* is a collection of one or more shell commands in a file. To execute the commands, you type the name of the file. The advantages to this approach include the following:

■ You don't have to retype a sequence of commands.

■ You determine the steps to accomplish a goal once.

■ You simplify operations for yourself and others.

By using variables and keywords, you can write programs that the shell can interpret. This is useful because it allows you to create general shell scripts you or others can use in various situations.

Suppose that after you log in, you regularly like to see who's logged in to your system, run a program named `calendar` that displays your appointments for today and tomorrow, and print the current date and time to the screen. To do all that, you enter the following commands:

```
who
calendar
date
```

If you put these three commands into a file named whatsup and make that file executable, you have a shell script that you can execute just like any other command. The file whatsup must be a text file. You can use the `vi` or `emacs` text editor to put the commands in the whatsup file. To make the file executable, enter this command:

chmod +x whatsup

The `chmod` command modifies or sets the permissions for a file. The +x option makes the file executable—that is, it makes the file work just like a standard Linux command. Putting commands into the file and making the file executable are both one-time operations. From that point on, you can enter whatsup to execute your shell script. You can use the shell script just like any other command. For example, to print the results of the whatsup command, enter the following:

whatsup ¦ lp

To put the results of the whatsup command into a file named info for future reference, enter this:

whatsup > info

As a review, follow these steps to create a shell script that you can use whenever you want:

1. Use a text editor, such as `vi` or `emacs`, to put the shell commands into a text or ASCII file. In the preceding example, the commands were put in the file named whatsup.

2. Make it so that you have execute permission on the file. Use `chmod +x` *filename* (for example, `chmod +x whatsup`).

3. Test the command by typing the name of the command and pressing <Return>.

After using this process a few times, you'll see how easy it is to create useful scripts. Of course, the hardest part is figuring out which shell commands to use and how to use the shell's programming capabilities to express the steps you need to carry out.

You can test a shell script and see all the steps it goes through by entering this command:

sh -x *script-name*

In this syntax, *script-name* is the name of the file that holds the script you're considering. The `sh -x` command displays all the steps the script goes through and is useful when you're trying to debug a script.

Writing Programs with the Shell

To write programs that use the shells, you must know about *variables* and *control structures*. Don't let either term scare you. A variable is an object that, at any one time, has one of possibly many different values assigned to it. Control structures specify the way you can control the flow of execution of a script. There are two basic types of control structures: decision structures (such as `if...then...else` structures or `case` structures), and iterative structures or loops (such as a `for` or `while` loop). With a decision structure, you choose a course of action from one or more alternatives, usually depending on the value of a variable or the outcome of a command. With an iterative structure, you repeat a sequence of commands. The earlier section "Setting the Shell Environment" discusses shell variables; the later section "Programming with Control Structures" provides more information on control structures.

Using *echo*   You can use the `echo` command to display informative messages about what's happening in a shell script. The `echo` command displays its arguments—that is, whatever follows the word `echo`—on-screen. Putting a string of characters in quotation marks ensures that all the characters are displayed. You also can redirect the results of `echo` to a file.

This command:

```
echo "Please stand by ..."
```

displays the following line on the terminal screen:

```
Please stand by ...
```

The following command puts `Please stand by ...` in the file named messg:

```
echo "Please stand by ..." > messg
```

T I P   Using the echo command can make users feel as though something is happening when they enter a command–a particularly good idea if the command doesn't give any output for several seconds or longer.

The `echo` command is also useful when you want to trace a shell script. Using the `echo` command at key points tells you what's happening in a script. Here is the file whatsup with an `echo` command or two added:

```
echo " Let's see who is on the system."
who
echo " Any appointments? "
calendar
date
echo " All done"
```

When you run the whatsup file, you see the following:

```
$ whatsup
 Let's see who is on the system.
sarah      tty01     Dec 20 08:51
brad       tty03     Dec 20 08:12
ernie      tty07     Dec 20 08:45
 Any appointments?
```

Part
IV
Ch
18

```
12/20      Sales meeting at 1:45
12/21      party after work!
Mon Dec 20 09:02 EST 1993
 All done
$
```

Using Comments It's always possible that after you write a shell script and don't use it for a while, you'll forget what the shell script does or how it accomplishes its task. Put comments in your shell scripts to explain the purpose of the task and how the task is achieved. A *comment* is a note to yourself or whoever is reading the script. The shell ignores comments; they're important to and for human beings.

The pound sign (#) signals the beginning of a comment to the shell. Every character from the pound sign to the end of the line is part of that comment. Here's how you might comment the shell script whatsup:

```
# Name:      whatsup
# Written:   1/19/97, Patty Stygian
# Purpose:   Display who's logged in, appointments, date
    echo "Let's see who is on the system."
    who            # See who is logged in
    echo " Any appointments? "
    calendar       # Check appointments
    date           # Display date
    echo " All done"
```

Run the shell script again, and you see the same results as before. The comments don't change the behavior of the shell script in any way.

Using Variables in Shell Programs To use variables, you must know how to give a variable a value and how to access the value stored in a variable. Using the value of a variable is straightforward, but there are four ways of giving a variable a value:

- Using direct assignment
- Using the read command
- Using command-line parameters
- Substituting the output of a command

Using Direct Assignments The most direct way to give a variable a value is to write an expression such as this:

```
myemail=edsgar@crty.com
```

This expression gives the variable myemail the value edsgar@crty.com. Don't include spaces on either side of the equal sign (=). The direct-assignment method of assigning a value to a variable takes the following form:

```
variable-name=variable-value
```

If *variable-value* contains blanks, enclose the value in quotation marks. To assign an office address of Room 21, Suite C to the variable myoffice, for example, use the following command:

```
myoffice="Room 21, Suite C"
```

The shell retrieves the value of the variable whenever it sees a dollar sign ($) followed by the name of a variable. You can see that when the following two statements are executed:

```
echo " My e-mail address is $myemail"
echo " My office is $myoffice"
```

Suppose that you frequently copy files to a directory named /corporate/info/public/sales. To copy a file named current to that directory, enter this command:

```
cp current /corporate/info/public/sales
```

To make this easier, you can assign the long directory name to the variable corpsales with the following expression:

```
corpsales=/corporate/info/public/sales
```

Now, to copy the current file to that directory, you enter the following:

```
cp current $corpsales
```

The shell replaces $corpsales with the value of the variable corpsales and then issues the copy command.

Using the read Command   The read command takes the next line of input and assigns it to a variable. The following shell script extends the preceding corpsales example to ask the user to specify the name of the file to be copied:

```
# Name: copycorp
# Purpose: copy specified file to
#          /corporate/info/public/sales
     corpsales=/corporate/infor/public/sales
     echo "Enter name of file to copy"       # prompt user
     read filename                           # get file name
     cp $filename $corpsales                  # do the copy
```

The read command pauses the script and waits for input from the keyboard. When <Return> is pressed, the script continues. If <Ctrl-d> (sometimes represented as ^D) is pressed while the read command is waiting for input, the script is terminated.

Using Command-Line Parameters   When the shell interprets a command, it attaches variable names to each item on the command line. The items on the command line are the sequences of characters separated by blanks or tab characters. (Use quotation marks to signal that a collection of characters separated by spaces represents one item.) The variables attached to the items in the command line are $0, $1, $2, and so on through $9. These 10 variables correspond to the positions of the items on the line. The command name is $0, the first argument or parameter for the command is $1, and so on. To demonstrate this concept, consider the following sample shell script named shovars:

```
# Name:      shovars
# Purpose:   demonstrate command-line variables
     echo $0
     echo $2 $4!
     echo $3
```

Part

IV

Ch

18

Now suppose that you enter this command:

shovars -s hello "look at me" bart

The output of the shell script is this:

```
shovars
hello bart!
look at me
```

In this output, the first line is the command's name (variable $0), the second line is the second and fourth arguments (variables $2 and $4), and the last line is the third argument (variable $3).

Following is a more serious example. This shell script deletes a file but first copies it to the directory /tmp so that you can retrieve it if necessary:

```
# Name:    safrm
# Purpose: copy file to directory /tmp and then remove it
#          from the current directory
# first copy $1 to /tmp
    cp $1 /tmp
# now remove the file
    rm $1
```

If you enter safrm abc def, only the file abc is removed from the current directory because the safrm shell script deletes only variable $1. You can, however, represent all the parameters on the command line with $*. Make safrm more general by replacing each occurrence of $1 with $*. If you then enter safrm abc def xx guio, all four files (abc, def, xx, and guio) are removed from the current directory.

Substituting the Output of a Command   You can assign to a variable the result of an executed command. To store the name of the current working directory in a variable named cwd, for example, enter this:

cwd= 'pwd'

Notice that pwd, the print working directory command, is set in backquotes instead of single quotation marks.

The following shell script changes the name of a file by appending the current month, day, and year to the filename:

```
# Name:      stamp
# Purpose:   rename file: append today's date to its name
# set td to current date in form of mmddyy
    td='+%m%d%y'
# rename file
    mv $1 $1.$td
```

In this example, the variable td is set to the current date. In the final line, this information is appended to variable $1. If today is February 24, 1997, and you use this script on a file called myfile, the file is renamed (moved) to myfile.022497.

Using Special Characters in Shell Programs   You've seen how the shell gives special treatment to certain characters, such as >, *, ?, $, and others. What do you do if you don't want those characters to get special treatment? This section provides a few answers.

You can use the single quote to make the shell ignore special characters. Enclose the character string with a pair of single quotes, as in this example:

```
grep '^Mary Tuttle' customers
```

The result of this grep command is that the lines in the file customers that begin with Mary Tuttle are displayed. The caret (^) tells grep to search from the beginning of the line. If the text Mary Tuttle wasn't enclosed in single quotes, it might be interpreted literally (or as a pipe symbol on some systems). Also, the space between Mary and Tuttle isn't interpreted by the shell when it occurs within the single quotes.

You can also use quotation marks to make the shell ignore most special characters, with the exception of the dollar sign and backquote. In the following example, the asterisks, spaces, and the greater-than sign are treated as regular characters because the string is surrounded by quotation marks:

```
echo " ** Please enter your response —>"
```

In this next example, however, $LOGNAME evaluates correctly, but there's no value for $5:

```
echo " >>>Thanks for the $5, $LOGNAME"
```

Use the backslash (\) to make the shell ignore a single character. For example, to make the shell ignore the dollar sign in front of the 5, issue this command:

```
echo " >>>Thanks for the \$5, $LOGNAME"
```

The result is what you expect:

```
>>>Thanks for the $5, wrev
```

Programming with Control Structures

There are two primary control structures in shell programming: decision structures and iterative structures. In *decision structures*, such as if...then...else and case, you can have the shell script decide which commands to execute based on the value of an expression (such as a variable, the properties associated with a file, the number of parameters in a script, or the result of executing a command). In *iterative structures*, such as for and while loops, you can execute a sequence of commands over a collection of files or while some condition holds.

The following sections use examples that aren't too complicated, yet demonstrate the essentials of programming with some control.

Using case   The case structure is a decision structure that lets you select one of several courses of action, based on the value of a variable. Listing 18.2 shows a short menu program.

Listing 18.2   Implementing a Menu Shell Script with *case*

```
# Name:      ShrtMenu
# Purpose:   Allow user to print a file, delete a file,
#            or quit the program
# Display menu
     echo "Please choose either P, D, or Q to "
     echo " [P]rint a file"
     echo " [D]elete a file"
     echo " [Q]uit"
# Get response from user
     read response
# Use case to match response to action
     case $response in
        P¦p) echo "Name of file to print?"
             read filename
             lp $filename;;
        D¦d) echo "Name of file to delete?"
             read filename
             rm $filename;;
          *) echo "leaving now";;
     esac
```

The syntax of the case statement is this:

```
case word in
   pattern) statement(s);;
   pattern) statement(s);;
   ...
esac
```

The *word* parameter is matched against each *pattern* parameter, starting with the pattern at the top of the list. The statements that execute if *word* matches a pattern are terminated by two semicolons (;;). The end of the case statement is marked by the word esac (that's "case" spelled backward).

In Listing 18.2, the pipe character was used to give a choice for a match. For example, P¦p means that either an uppercase or lowercase letter P is considered a match.

The pattern * is used to represent all other patterns not explicitly stated. If users press any key besides <P>, <p>, <D>, or <d>, they exit from the menu.

Listing 18.3 uses a case statement that makes a selection based on the number of parameters the shell represents as $#.

Listing 18.3   Command-Line Parsing with *case*

```
# Name:      recent
# Purpose:   list the most recent files in a directory
# If user types recent <Return> then the names of
#    the 10 most recently modified files are displayed
# If the user types recent n <Return> then the names of
#    the n most recently modified files are displayed
```

```
# Otherwise, user is notified of incorrect usage
#
# Case based on number of parameters
    case $# in
        0) ls -lt ¦ head ;;
            # ls -lt lists names of file in order of
            # most recently modified
            # head displays the first 10 lines of a file
        1) case $1 in
        [0-9]*) ls -lt ¦ head -$1 ;;
        *)echo "Usage: recent number-of-files";;
        esac;;
        *) echo "Usage: recent number-of-files";;
    esac
```

Finding the Exit Status When a shell command executes, it's either successful or not. If you use the command `grep "American Terms" customers` to see whether the string *American Terms* is in the file customers, and the file exits, you have read permission to the file, and *American Terms* is in the file, the shell command has executed successfully. If any of those conditions isn't true, the shell command executes unsuccessfully.

The shell always reports back about the status of the termination of a command, program, or shell script. The value reported back is called the *exit status* of a command and is represented by the variable #?. If you enter the following commands, you see the value of $?.

```
grep "American Terms" customers
echo $?
```

N O T E If $? has a value of 0, this command was successful; otherwise, the command was unsuccessful. ■

The following is an example in which the exit status of the command `who¦grep $1` is used in the case statement:

```
# Name:      just.checking
# Purpose:   Determine if person is logged in
# Usage:     just.checking login_name
#
    case 'who ¦ grep $1 > /dev/null` in
        0) echo "$1 is logged in.";;
        *) echo "$1 is not here. Try again later.";;
    esac
    echo "Have a great day!"
```

If you enter `just.checking rflame` and rflame is logged in, you see the following:

```
rflame is logged in.
Have a great day!
```

If rflame isn't logged in, you see this instead:

```
rflame is not here. Try again later.
Have a great day!
```

Using *if* Structures   The if...then...else...fi structure is a decision structure that allows you to select one of two courses of action based on the result of a command. The else portion of the structure is optional. One or more commands go in place of the ellipsis (...). Provided that the exit status of the last command following the if is zero (that is, the command executed successfully), the commands following the then and preceding the else (if there is one) are executed. Otherwise, the commands following the else are executed.

In other words, one or more commands are executed. If the last command was successful, the commands in the then portion of the statement are performed and then the commands following the fi (the end of the structure) are executed. If the last commands aren't successful, the commands after the else are performed.

Here's a familiar example that behaves exactly the same as when it was written using the case statement:

```
# Name:      just.checking
# Purpose:   Determine if person is logged in
# Usage:     just.checking login_name
#
if
    who ¦ grep $1 > /dev/null
then
    echo "$1 is logged in."
else
    echo "$1 is not here. Try again later."
fi
echo " Have a great day!"
```

Using the *test* Command   Many of the shell scripts used in this chapter expect users to behave nicely. The scripts have no check to see whether users have permission to copy or move files or whether what the users were dealing with was an ordinary file rather than a directory. The test command can deal with these issues as well as some others. For example, test -f abc is successful if abc exists and is a regular file.

You can reverse the meaning of a test by using an exclamation point in front of the option. For example, to test that you don't have read permission for file abc, use test ! -r abc. Table 18.7 lists several options for the test command.

Table 18.7   Options for Using the *test* Command with Files

Option	Meaning
-f	Successful if file exists and is a regular file
-d	Successful if file is a directory
-r	Successful if file exists and is readable
-s	Successful if file exists and isn't empty
-w	Successful if file exists and can be written to
-x	Successful if file exists and is executable

Listing 18.4 is an example of the use of the test command.

Listing 18.4 A Sample Script That Uses the *test* Command

```
# Name:     safcopy
# Purpose: Copy file1 to file2
#          Check to see we have read permission on file1
#          If file2 exists then
#                  if file2 is a file we can write to
#                  then warn user, and get permission to proceed
#                  else exit
#          else
#                  copy file
#
# Check for proper number of arguments
  case $# in
    2) if test ! -r $1      # cannot read first file;;
       then;;
              exit (1)      # exit with non-zero exit status;;
       fi;;
       if test -f $2        # does second file exist?;;
       then;;
         if test -w $2      # can we write to it?;;
         then;;
              echo " $2 exists, copy over it ? (Y/N)";;
              read      resp             # get permission from user;;
              case $resp in;;
                  Y¦y)      cp $1 $2;;    # go ahead;;
                    *) exit(1);;         # good bye!;;
              esac;;
         else;;
              exit (1)      # Second file exists but can't write;;
         fi
       else    # Second file doesn't exist; go ahead and copy!;
         cp $1 $2;;
       fi;;
    *) echo "Usage: safcopy source destination";;
       exit (1);;
  esac
```

You can also use the test command to test numbers. To determine whether a value in the variable hour is greater than 12, use test $hour -gt 12. Table 18.8 lists some options you can use with test when you're comparing numbers.

Table 18.8 Options for Using *test* When Comparing Numbers

Option	Meaning
-eq	Equal
-ne	Not equal

continues

Table 18.8 Continued

Option	Meaning
-ge	Greater than or equal
-gt	Greater than
-le	Less than or equal
-lt	Less than

Listing 18.5 shows these options used to display a timely greeting.

Listing 18.5 Displaying a Greeting with the *test* Command

```
# Name:     greeting
# Purpose:  Display Good Morning if hour is less than 12
#                   Good Afternoon if hour less than 5PM
#                   Good Evening if hour is greater than 4PM
# Get hour
     hour='date +%H'
# Check for time of day
     if test $hour -lt 12
     then
         echo "Good Morning, $LOGNAME"
     else
        if test $hour -lt 17
        then
            echo "Good Afternoon, $LOGNAME"
        else
            echo "Good Evening, $LOGNAME"
        fi
     fi
```

Using Iterative Structures   Iterative control structures allow you to write shell scripts that contain loops. The two basic types of loops are for and while loops.

With for loops, you specify a collection of files or values to use with some commands. To copy all the files whose names end with the characters .txt to the directory textdir, for example, use the following for loop:

```
for i in *.txt
do
     cp $i textdir/$i
done
```

The shell interprets the statement for i in *.txt and allows the variable i to take on the name of any file in the current directory whose name ends with .txt. You can then use the variable $i with any statements between the do and the done keywords.

The script in Listing 18.6 prints a collection of files, each with its own banner page. It also sends mail to the user concerning the status of the print requests. The characters $* represent all the parameters given to the shell command.

Listing 18.6   Processing Files with the *for* Command

```
# Name:       Prntel
# Purpose:    Print one or more files
#             each with own title page
#             Notify user which files were sent to the printer
#             and which were not.
#             Do this for all parameters to the command
for i in $*
do
      if lp -t $i -dlasers $i > /dev/null
      then
            echo $i >> printed
      else
            echo $i >> notprinted
      fi
done
# end of loop
if test -s printed
then
      echo "These files were sent to the printer " > mes
      cat printed >> mes
      mail $LOGNAME < mes
      rm mes printed
fi
if test -s notprinted
then
      echo "These files were not sent to the printer " >mes
      cat notprinted >> mes
      mail $LOGNAME < mes
      rm mes notprinted
fi
```

A while loop looks at the exit status of a command in the same way the if statement looks at the status. The script in Listing 18.7 notifies users when they've received new mail. The script makes the assumption that if a mailbox changes, a user has new mail. The script uses the command diff to compare two files and then reports on the differences. If the files are the same, the exit status is zero (the command is successful).

Listing 18.7   Repeating Commands with *while*

```
# Name:          checkmail
# Purpose:       Notify user if their mail box has changed
# Suggestion:    Run this in the background
# get a size of mail box for comparison
      cp $MAIL omail            # Get set for first time through
```

continues

Listing 18.7 Continued

```
# MAIL is a "special" variable indicating the user's mailbox
# while omail and $MAIL are the same, keep looping
    while diff omail $MAIL > /dev/null
    do
        cp $MAIL omail
        sleep 30           # sleep, pause for 30 seconds
    done
# There must be a change in the files
    echo "New mail!!" ¦ write $LOGNAME
```

You can see that some of the commands and concepts used with if...then...else statements can be transferred to while loops. The difference, of course, is that with while loops, you're dealing with an iterative, repetitive process.

Customizing Linux Shells

The shell starts when you log in. Tables 18.2 and 18.3 show you that special variables are given values by the shell to help define your shell environment. The shell sets some of these variables. You can change these settings and give other variables values by editing the file .profile if you're using the Bourne or bash shell. If you're using the C shell, you set the variables by editing the file .login. You can also use command aliasing to define aliases for commands.

Whenever you issue a command, a new shell starts; it inherits many of the characteristics—or much of the environment—of the existing shell. Note these two things about the new shell:

- The new shell runs in your current directory. The pwd command returns the same value within a shell as it gives before the shell was started.

- The new shell receives many of its variables from the existing shell. There are ways to make sure that variables set in the existing shell are exported to the new shell.

Exporting Variables to the New Shell

When you create shell variables or give existing variables values, they exist in the running shell. A variable set in the login shell is available to all command-line arguments. A variable set within a shell has that value only within that shell. The value disappears or is reset when you exit that shell.

For example, enter these two commands from the command line:

```
today=Thursday
echo $today
```

Suppose that the echo command displays Thursday. Now suppose that you write and execute the following shell script named whatday:

```
# Name: whatday
# display the current value of the variable today
    echo "Today is $today."
```

```
# set the value of today
    today=Friday
# display the current value of the variable today
    echo "Today is $today."
```

Now enter the following four commands from the command line:

```
chmod +x whatday
today=Thursday
whatday
echo $today
```

The following lines appear on-screen:

```
Today is .
Today is Friday.
Thursday
```

The value of the variable today in the login shell is Thursday. When you execute the shell script whatday, you see that initially the variable today isn't defined (as shown by the display Today is .). Then the today variable has the value Friday in the shell. When the whatday script terminates, you return to the login shell and today has its original value, Thursday.

To give the variable today the same value that it has in the login shell when the shell script whatday starts, use the command export. This command "exports," or passes on, the variables from one shell to subsequent shells:

```
export today
```

Now any shell started from the login shell inherits the value of the variable today. Add the export command to the preceding sequence of commands:

```
today=Thursday
export today
whatday
echo $today
```

You see the following output:

```
Today is Thursday.
Today is Friday.
Thursday
```

Notice that the value the variable receives in the shell started by the whatday script isn't carried back to the login shell. Exportation or inheritance of variable values goes in only one direction—from a running shell down to the new shell, never back up. That's why when you change your current directory inside one shell, you're back to where you started when that shell terminates.

You can export any variable from one shell down to another shell by using the following syntax:

```
export variable-name
```

In this syntax, *variable-name* is the name of the variable you want to export. To change your terminal type from its current setting to a vt100, for example, enter the following commands to make the new value of TERM available to all subsequent shells or programs:

Part

IV

Ch

18

```
TERM=vt100
export TERM
```

When you change or set `bash` shell variables in the .profile file, be sure to export them. For example, if you want the `PATH` variable to be `PATH=/bin:/usr/bin:/usr/local/bin:.`, set it in the .profile file and follow it with this `export` command:

```
export PATH
```

To change the shell prompt, you must set a value for `PS1` in the file .profile. To change it from `$` to `Ready $`, for example, use a text editor to put these lines in the file named .profile:

```
PS1="Ready $"
export PS1
```

> **N O T E**   Changes you make to .profile or .login don't take effect until you log out and log in again. ■

Defining Command Aliases

Command aliases are useful for defining commands you use regularly but for which you don't want to bother remembering the details. Command aliases are also useful for enhancing your working environment with a set of useful tools. This command assigns the alias `recent` to a command that lists the 10 most recently modified files in the current directory:

```
alias recent="ls -lat¦head"
```

To avoid typing your command aliases each time you log in, put them in the .login file if you're using the C shell or the .profile file if you're using `bash` or a similar shell. The command aliases are now available to you when you're in your shell.

From Here...

The shell is the primary interface between you and the Linux operating system. Although a shell can be almost any executable program, several standard shells are supplied with Linux or are freely available in source code (written in C) or already compiled for your machine. All Linux shells can be viewed as highly sophisticated, special-purpose programming languages containing all the usual constructs found in a programming language. The special purpose of Linux shell languages is to tie together the many small commands and utilities found in the Linux environment. By making use of I/O redirection and background processing, the shell languages allow you to write complex programs with minimal effort. For more information, see these chapters:

- ■ Chapter 5, "Running Linux Applications," for basic information on navigating through Linux.
- ■ Chapter 8, "Using the `vi` Editor," for information on editing text files.

Managing Multiple Processes

by Jack Tackett

Linux is a multiuser and multitasking operating system. *Multiuser* means that several people can use the computer system simultaneously (unlike a single-user operating system, such as MS-DOS). *Multitasking* means that Linux, like Windows NT, can work on several tasks concurrently; it can begin work on one task and take up another before the first task is finished.

Taking care of several user requests and multitasking are the jobs of the operating system. Most systems have only one CPU and one collection of chips that make up main memory, or RAM. A system may have more than one disk or tape drive for secondary memory and several input/output devices. All these resources must be managed and shared between several users. The operating system creates the illusion that each user has a dedicated computer system.

Understanding Multitasking

As mentioned earlier, it's Linux's job to create the illusion that when you make a request, you have the system's undivided attention. In reality, hundreds of requests may be handled between the time you press <Return> and the time the system responds to your command.

Imagine having to keep track of dozens of tasks simultaneously. You have to share the processing power, storage capabilities, and input and output devices among several users or several processes belonging to a single user. Linux monitors a list—also known as a *queue*—of tasks waiting to be done. These tasks can include user jobs, operating system tasks, mail, and background jobs such as printing. Linux schedules slices of system time for each task. By human standards, each time slice is extremely short—a fraction of a second. In computer time, a time slice is adequate for a program to process hundreds or thousands of instructions. The length of the time slice for each task may depend on the relative priority of each task.

Linux works on one task from the queue for a while, puts the task aside to begin work on another task, and so on. It then returns to the first task and works on it again. Linux continues these cycles until it finishes a task and takes the task out of the queue, or until the task is terminated. In this arrangement, sometimes called *time-sharing*, the resources of the system are shared among all the tasks. Naturally, time-sharing must be done in a reliable and efficient manner. The UNIX term for a task is *process*. Table 19.1 shows several types of processes.

Table 19.1 Types of Processes	
Process Type	**Description**
interactive	Initiated by a shell and running in the foreground or background
batch	Typically a series of processes scheduled for execution at a specified point in time
daemon	Typically initiated at boot time to perform operating system functions on demand, such as LPD, NFS, and DNS

You've already seen that you can put or run a program in the background. While the program runs in the background, you can continue entering commands and working with other material. This is a feature of multitasking: Linux uses the time-sharing method to balance your immediate commands and the ones running in the background. This chapter shows other ways to schedule processes so that they can run without your attention (*batch process*).

▶ **See** "Doing Background Processing," **p. 361**

The Linux operating system has the primary responsibility of handling the details of working with several users and several processes. As a user, you have the power to specify which programs you want to run. Some Linux commands let you specify when you want a process to start. You also can monitor your processes as well as see what other processes are running. In some cases, you can change their relative priority. And you can always terminate your processes if the need arises. If you're the system administrator, you have all these capabilities, plus the responsibility and power to initiate, monitor, and manage processes that belong to the operating system or any user.

Table 19.2 lists the commands that make it possible to control the multiuser and multitasking capabilities of Linux.

Table 19.2   Multiuser and Multitasking Commands

Command	Action
at	Executes commands at a given time
batch	Executes commands when system load allows
cron	Executes scheduled commands
crontab	Maintains crontab files for individual users
kill	Stops processes
nice	Adjusts the priority of a process before it starts
nohup	Allows a process to continue after you log out
ps	Displays process information
renice	Adjusts the priority of a running process
w	Shows you who is logged in and what they're doing
who	Displays the system's logged-in users

Part
IV

Ch
19

N O T E   For more information on the commands in Table 19.2, you can consult the following man page:

man *command*

You also can use the --help option:

command --help ■

Initiating Multiple Processes

You can start running a program by entering its name. You can also start programs from files that contain shell commands. Running programs can interact with many different parts of the system. A program can read from or write to files, manage its information in RAM, or send information to printers, modems, or other devices. The operating system also attaches information to a process so that the system can keep track of and manage it.

A process is a running program, but is different from a program. In one sense, a process is more than a program because a program is only a set of instructions; a process is dynamic because it uses the resources of a running system. On the other hand, a single Linux program can start several processes.

Linux identifies and keeps track of processes by assigning a process ID number (PID) to each process.

Starting Multiple Processes

You've already seen that your login shell is always running. Whenever you enter a command, you start at least one new process while the login shell continues to run. If you enter the following command, for example, the file named report.txt is sent to the lp program:

```
lp report.txt
```

▶ **See** "Understanding Shells," **p. 339**

When the lp program completes its task, the shell prompt reappears. However, before the shell prompt reappeared, the login shell and the lp command were running; you have initiated multiple processes in that case. The shell waited until the lp command finished before putting the shell prompt back onscreen.

Starting a Background Process

You can run a process as a background job by giving the command to start a process and placing an ampersand (&) after the command. For example, if you enter the command **lp report.txt &**, the shell responds immediately with a number—the PID for that process. The shell prompt reappears without waiting for the process to complete. The following is a sample of what you would see:

```
$ lp report.txt &
3146
$
```

In this example, 3146 is the PID of the process started by the lp command.

Regardless of whether you run the lp command in the background, the process associated with lp is started from the current shell. The lp process is a child process of the current shell. This example points to a common relationship between processes—that of parent and child. Your current shell is the parent process, and the running lp process is a child process. Usually, a parent process waits for one or more of its child processes to complete before it continues. If you want the parent to continue without waiting for the child to finish, attach the ampersand

(&) to the command that *spawns*, or initiates, the child process. You can continue with other work or commands while the child runs.

> **N O T E** If you're working from a character terminal or a remote login, your current shell is usually your login shell. However, if you're using a virtual terminal or a terminal window from a GUI, a separate shell is associated with each session. ■

Using Pipes to Start Multiple Processes

Another way to start multiple processes is to use one or more pipes on a command line. To print a long listing of the 10 most recently modified files in your current directory, enter this command:

```
ls -lt ¦ head ¦ lp
```

This command starts three processes simultaneously, and they're all children of the current shell. A pipe works this way: Commands on either side of the vertical bar (|) begin at the same time. Neither is the parent of the other; they're both children of the process that was running when they were created. In this sense, you can think of commands on either side of the pipe symbol as sibling processes.

Some programs are written so that they themselves spawn several processes. One example is the ispell command, which lists the words in a document that Linux can't find in a system dictionary. The ispell command spawns some child processes. Suppose you enter this:

```
ispell final.rept > final.errs &
```

You'll see the following results displayed:

```
1286
$
```

Here, 1286 is the PID of the ispell process; the $ prompt indicates that the shell is ready to handle another command from you. Even though ispell may spawn some children and wait for them to complete, you don't have to wait. In this example, the current shell is the parent of ispell, and ispell's children can be thought of as grandchildren of the login shell. Although a parent can wait for its children, a grandparent doesn't.

All these examples show how it's possible for users to start multiple processes. You can wait until child processes are finished before continuing or not. If you continue without waiting for child processes to complete, you make the children background processes. The following section looks at some Linux commands you can use to schedule processes to run at specified times or at a lower relative priority.

Part
IV

Ch
19

Using the Scheduling Commands

The Linux environment provides many ways to handle command execution. Linux lets you create lists of commands and specify when they're to be run. The at command, for example, takes a list of commands typed at the keyboard or from a file and runs them at the time specified by the command. The batch command is similar to the at command, except that batch runs commands when the system finds time for them rather than allow the user to specify a particular time. The cron command allows for commands to be run periodically, and the crontab command allows users to edit the files used by cron.

All scheduling commands are useful for running tasks at times when the system isn't too busy. They're also good for executing scripts to external services—such as database queries—at times when it's least expensive to do so.

Running Commands at Specified Times with *at*

To schedule one or more commands for a specified time, use the at command. With this command, you can specify a time, a date, or both. The command expects two or more arguments. At a minimum, you specify the time you want the command(s) executed and the command(s) you want to execute.

The following example performs its job at 1:23 a.m. If you're working in the wee hours of the morning before 1:23 a.m. (that is, between midnight and 1:23 a.m.), the command is done today, at 1:23 a.m. Otherwise, it's done at 1:23 a.m. the following day. The job prints all files in the directory /usr/sales/reports and sends a user named boss some mail announcing that the print job was done at 1:23 a.m. Type the following commands on the terminal, pressing <Return> at the end of each line. After you enter each line, press <Ctrl-d> to finish the command.

```
at 1:23
lp /usr/sales/reports/*
echo "Files printed, Boss!" ¦ mail -s"Job done" boss
```

N O T E   cron jobs, discussed later in this chapter, are the most commonly used mechanisms for running automated system administration jobs under Linux. However, you must be the root user to create and edit cron job entries. The at command allows anyone to run tasks even if he or she does not have root privileges. ▨

▶ **See** "Setting the Terminal Environment," **p. 341**

Commands to be scheduled by at are entered as a list of commands on the line following the at command.

After you terminate the at command, you see a display similar to the following:

```
job 756603300.a at Tues Jan 21 01:23:00 1997
```

This response indicates that the job will execute at 1:23 as specified. The job number, 756603300.a, identifies the job. If you decide you want to cancel the job, do so by using the job number associated with it, like so:

```
at -d 756603300.a
```

If you have several commands you want to schedule by using at, it's best to put them in a file. If the filename is getdone, for example, and you want to schedule the commands for 10 a.m., type either

```
at 10:00 < getdone
```

or

```
at 10:00 -f getdone
```

Remember that the less-than symbol (<) indicates the use of the contents of the getdone file as input to the at command. The -f option allows you to specify the command file without using redirection.

You can also specify a date for an at job. For example, to schedule a job at 5 p.m. on January 24, enter these commands:

```
at 17:00 Jan 24
lp /usr/sales/reports/*
echo "Files printed, Boss!" ¦ mail -s"Job done" boss
```

The jobs you schedule with at are put into a queue that the operating system checks periodically. You don't have to be logged in for the job to be executed. The at command always runs in the background, freeing resources but still accomplishing the job. Any output produced by the commands in your at job is automatically mailed to you.

To see which jobs you scheduled with at, enter **at -l**. Working with the preceding examples, you see the following results:

```
job 756603300.a at Sat Dec 21 01:23:00 1996
job 756604200.a at Fri Jan 24 17:00:00 1997
```

Only your at jobs are listed.

To remove a scheduled at job, enter **at -d** followed by the job number. To remove the second job just listed, for example, enter this command:

```
at -d 756604200.a
```

Table 19.3 summarizes the different ways to use the at command.

Table 19.3 Summary of *at* Commands

Format	Action
at *hh:mm*	Schedules job at the hour (*hh*) and minute (*mm*) specified, using a 24-hour clock
at *hh:mm month day year*	Schedules job at the hour (*hh*), minute (*mm*), month, day, and year specified
at -l	Lists scheduled jobs; an alias for the atq command
at now +*count time-units*	Schedules the job right now plus *count* number of *time-units*; time units can be minutes, hours, days, or weeks
at -d *job_id*	Cancels the job with the job number matching *job_id*; an alias for the atrm command

Part
IV

Ch
19

As the root user, you can use any of these commands; for other users, the files /etc/at.allow and /etc/at.deny determine the permission to use the commands. If /etc/at.allow exists, only the user names listed in the file are allowed to use the at command. If the /etc/at.allow file doesn't exist, the system checks /etc/at.deny, and every user name not mentioned in /etc/at.deny is allowed to use at (in other words, any user listed in /etc/at.deny isn't allowed to use at). If neither file exists, only the superuser (root) can use at. If /etc/at.deny is empty, every user can use at.

Running Long Tasks with *batch*

Linux has more than one command for scheduling tasks. The preceding section describes the at command, which gives you the power to dictate when a task will run. However, it's always possible that the system can be loaded down with more jobs scheduled at one time than it can comfortably handle. The batch command lets the operating system decide an appropriate time to run a process. When you schedule a job with batch, Linux starts and works on the process whenever the system load isn't too great. Jobs run under batch execute in the background, just as those run with at. In fact, batch is an alias for at -b in Red Hat Linux.

TIP It's useful to put commands you want to run with at or batch in a file so that you don't have to retype the commands each time you want to run the jobs. To use batch to schedule the commands in the file getdone, enter the command **batch < getdone**.

The format for batch commands is to enter the list of commands on the lines following the batch command; you terminate the list of commands with <Ctrl-d>. You can put the list of commands in a file and then redirect the input of the file to batch. To sort a collection of files, print the results, and notify the user named boss that the job is done, enter the following commands:

```
batch
sort /usr/sales/reports/* ¦ lp
echo "Files printed, Boss!" ¦ mailx -s"Job done" boss
```

The system returns the following response:

```
job 7789001234.b at Fri Feb 21 11:43:09 1997
```

The date and time listed are the date and time you pressed <Ctrl-d> to complete the batch command. When the job is complete, check your mail; anything that the commands normally display is mailed to you.

Scheduling Commands with *cron* and *crontab*

Both at and batch schedule commands on a one-time basis. To schedule commands or processes on a regular basis, you use the cron program. You specify the times and dates you want to run a command in crontab files. Times can be specified in terms of minutes, hours, days of the month, months of the year, or days of the week.

The cron program is started only once, when the system is booted. Individual users shouldn't have permission to run cron directly. Also, as the system administrator, you shouldn't start cron by typing the name of the command; cron should be listed in a shell script as one of the commands to run during a system boot-up sequence.

When started, cron (short for *chronograph*) checks queues for at jobs to run and also checks to see whether users or the root have scheduled jobs by using crontab files. If there's nothing to do, cron "goes to sleep" and becomes inactive; it "wakes up" every minute, however, to see if there are commands to run. You can see how important and useful this facility is; also, cron uses very few system resources.

Use crontab to install a list of commands that will be executed on a regular schedule. The commands are scheduled to run at a specified time (such as once a month, once an hour, once a day, and so on). The list of commands to be performed on the specified schedule must be included in the crontab file, which is installed with the crontab command. After you install the crontab file, cron reads and executes the listed commands at the specified times. Also with the crontab command, you can view the list of commands included in the file and cancel the list if you want.

Before you install your crontab file with the crontab command, create the file containing the list of commands you want to schedule by using a text editor such as vi or emacs. The crontab command handles the placement of the file. Each user has only one crontab file, created when the crontab command is issued. This file is placed in a directory that's read by the cron command.

Linux stores the user's crontab file in the /usr/spool/cron/crontabs directory and gives the file the user's name. If your user name is mcn and you use a text editor to create a file called mycron and install it by typing **crontab mycron**, the file /usr/spool/cron/crontabs/mcn is created. (In this example, the mcn file is created, or overwritten, with the contents of mycron, which may contain entries that launch one or more commands.)

N O T E For users to use the crontab command, they must be listed in the /etc/cron.d/cron.allow file. If you add a user to the system from the command line (by using the useradd command), he or she isn't added automatically to the /etc/cron.d/cron.allow file. As the root user, you must add the new user to the cron.allow file with a text editor.

Although you can initially create your crontab file with a text editor, after you create your crontab file, modify it by using only the crontab command. Don't try to replace or modify the file that cron examines (that is, the /usr/spool/cron/crontabs/user file) by any means other than by using the crontab command. ■

Each line in the crontab file contains a time pattern and a command. The command is executed at the specified time pattern. The time pattern is divided into five fields separated by spaces or tabs. Any output that usually appears—that is, information that isn't redirected to stdout or stderr—is mailed to the user.

Following is the syntax for the commands you enter in a file to be used by crontab:

```
minute hour day-of-month month-of-year day-of-week command
```

The first five fields are time option fields. You must specify all five of these fields. Use an asterisk (*) in a field if you want to ignore that field.

Part
IV

Ch
19

N O T E Technically, an asterisk in a crontab field means "any valid value" instead of "ignore the value"—that is, match anything. The crontab entry `02 00 01 * * date`, for example, says to run the `date` command at two minutes after midnight (zero hour) on the first day of the month. Because the month and day of the week fields are both asterisks, this entry runs on the first day of every month and any day of the week that the first of the month happens to land on. ■

Table 19.4 lists the time-field options available with `crontab`.

Table 19.4   Time-Field Options for the *crontab* Command

Field	Range
minute	00 through 59
hour	00 through 23 (midnight is 00)
day-of-month	01 through 31
month-of-year	01 through 12
day-of-week	01 through 07 (Monday is 01, Sunday is 07)

You can have as many entries as you want in a crontab file and can designate them to run at any time. This means that you can run as many commands as you want in a single crontab file.

To sort a file named /usr/wwr/sales/weekly and mail the output to a user named twool at 7:30 a.m. each Monday, use the following entry in a file:

```
30 07 * * 01 sort /usr/wwr/sales/weekly |mail -s"Weekly Sales" twool
```

This command specifies the minute as 30, the hour as 07, any day of the month with the asterisk, any month of the year with another asterisk, and the day-of-week as 01 (which represents Monday).

Notice the pipe between the `sort` and `mail` commands in the preceding example. The command field can contain pipes, semicolons, arrows, or anything else you can enter on a shell command line. At the specified date and time, `cron` runs the entire command field with a standard shell (`bash`).

To specify a sequence of values for one of the first four fields, use commas to separate the values. Suppose you have a program, `chkquotes`, that accesses a service that provides stock quotes and puts the quotes in a file. To get those quotes at 9 a.m., 11 a.m., 2 p.m., and 4 p.m. on Monday, Tuesday, and Thursday of every week—and definitely on the 10th of March and September—use the following entry:

```
* 09,11,14,16 10 03,09 01,02,04 chkquotes
```

Put the command lines into a file by using `vi` or some other editor that allows you to save files as text files. Assume that you put your commands in a file named `cronjobs`. To use `crontab` to put the file where `cron` can find it, enter this command:

```
crontab cronjobs
```

Each time you use crontab this way, it overwrites any crontab file you may have already launched.

The crontab command has three options:

- The -e option edits the contents of the current crontab file. (The -e option opens your file by using the ed editor or whatever editor is assigned to the EDITOR variable in your shell.)

▶ **See** "Setting the Shell Environment," **p. 344**

- The -r option removes the current crontab file from the crontabs directory.
- The -l option lists the contents of the current crontab file.

In all these cases, crontab works with the crontab file that has your login name. If your login name is mcn, your crontab file is /usr/spool/cron/crontabs/mcn. The crontab command does this automatically.

The system administrator and users share responsibility for making sure that the system is used appropriately. When you schedule a process, be aware of the impact it may have on the total system. Linux allows you, as the system administrator, to grant access to the at, batch, and cron commands to all users, specific users, or no users (or to deny access to individual users).

TROUBLESHOOTING

The commands I put in my crontab file don't work. The cron command runs your crontab entries by using the Bourne Again shell (bash). Your entries fail if you use shell features not supported by bash. For example, the Public Domain Korn shell (pdksh) allows you to use either a tilde (~) to represent a home directory or the alias command to designate aliases for certain commands.

When I try to use the at command, I'm told I don't have permission to use it. You haven't added your login ID to the /etc/cron.d/at.allow file.

I tried to use the at now command to run a command immediately. No matter how fast you type, at now always responds with the message ERROR: Too late. The best alternative is to use the batch command to run the command for you. You can, however, use at now +5 min to run the command in five minutes. After you press <Return>, type quickly to enter your command before the five minutes expire.

Reporting On and Monitoring the Multitasking Environment

You know that Linux is a multiuser, multitasking operating system. Because so many people can do so many things with the system at the same time, users find it useful to determine who's using the system and what processes are running, as well as to monitor processes.

Knowing that others can keep track of the commands you enter is important. Most users can't access your files without your permission, but they can see the names of commands you enter. Also, you (as the system administrator) or someone else who has the root password can peruse all the files on the system.

Although you don't have to be paranoid about privacy on a Linux system, you should know that the system can be monitored by anyone who wants to take the time to do it. The information you can gain about what's going on in the system is more useful than just satisfying curiosity: By seeing what jobs are running, you can appropriately schedule your tasks. You can also see whether a process of yours is still active and whether it's behaving properly.

Finding Out Who's on the System with *who*

The purpose of the who command is to find out who's logged in to the system. The who command lists the login names, terminal lines, and login times of users now logged in.

The who command is useful in many situations. If you want to communicate with someone on the computer by using the write command, for example, you can find out whether that person is on the system by using who. You can also use who to see when certain users are logged in to the computer to keep track of their time spent on the system.

Using *who* to List Users Logged In to the System   To see everyone who's now logged in to the system, enter who. You see a display similar to the following:

```
$ who
root        console     Dec 13 08:00
ernie       tty02       Dec 13 10:37
bkraft      tty03       Dec 13 11:02
jdurum      tty05       Dec 13 09:21
ernie       ttys7       Dec 11 18:49
$
```

This listing shows that root, ernie, bkraft, and jdurum are now logged in. It shows that root logged in at 8 a.m., bkraft at 11:02, and jdurum at 9:21. You can also see that ernie is logged in to two terminals and that one login occurred at 6:49 p.m. (18:49) two days earlier (which may be some reason for concern, or it may just be ernie's usual work habits).

Using Headers in User Listings   Several options are available with who, but this chapter describes how to use only two to monitor processes on the system:

-u   Lists only users who are now logged in

-H   Displays headers above each column

With these two options, you can get more information about the users now logged in. The headers displayed with the -H option are NAME, LINE, TIME, IDLE, PID, and COMMENTS. Table 19.5 explains the terms appearing in the heading.

Table 19.5   Output Format for the *who* Command

Field	Description
NAME	Lists the user's login name.
LINE	Lists the line or terminal being used.
TIME	Lists the time the user logged in.
IDLE	Lists the hours and minutes since the last activity on that line. A period is displayed if activity occurred within the last minute of system time. If more than 24 hours elapsed since the line was used, the word old is displayed.
PID	Lists the process ID number of the user's login shell.
COMMENT	Lists the contents of the comment field if comments have been included in /etc/inittab or if there are network connections.

N O T E   You probably won't see the COMMENT field filled in very often in any recent Linux systems. In the old days, processes that let you log in to UNIX (getty or uugetty) were started directly from entries in the /etc/inittab file and usually listened for login requests from a particular terminal. The COMMENT field might identify the location of that terminal and could tell you who was logged in and at what terminal they were sitting. Today, processes that listen for login requests are typically handled by the Service Access Facility and are no longer listed in /etc/inittab. ■

The following example uses the -u and -H options and shows the response Linux returns:

```
$ who -uH
NAME       LINE        TIME       IDLE    PID   COMMENT
root       console   Dec 13 08:00    .     10340
ernie      tty02     Dec 13 10:37    .     11929  Tech-89.2
bkraft     tty03     Dec 13 11:02   0:04    4761  Sales-23.4
jdurum     tty05     Dec 13 09:21   1:07   10426
ernie      ttys7     Dec 11 18:49   old    10770  oreo.coolt.com
$
```

You can infer from this listing that the last session associated with ernie is from a network site named oreo.coolt.com and that there hasn't been any activity in that session in more than 24 hours (which might signal a problem). The session for root and the first one for ernie have both been accessed within the last minute. The last activity on the session for bkraft was four minutes ago; it has been one hour and seven minutes since any activity was reported on the session for jdurum.

Also note that this listing includes the PID (process ID number) for the login shell of each user's session. The next section shows how you can use the PID to further monitor the system.

Using the *finger* Command to Learn More About Who Is on the System   A command that complements the who command is finger. To see more information about a specific user, you

Part
IV

Ch
19

can enter `finger` *username* (or `finger` *username@domain* if the user is on another computer). For example to see more information on a user named tackett, you would enter this command:

finger tackett

You would then see the following output:

```
Login: tackett                       Name: Jack Tackett Jr
Directory: /home/tackett             Shell: /bin/tcsh
Office: 2440 SW Cary Parkway 114     Office Phone: 919 555 1212
Home Phone: 919 555 1212
Never logged in.
Mail last read Fri Jul  3 17:42 1998 (EDT)
Plan:
----------------------------------------------
Jack Tackett, Jr.
In the immortal words of Socrates:
    I drank WHAT?
----------------------------------------------
```

This output shows the login and real name associate with the specified account. You can also see which shell the user prefers to use, his address, when he last read his e-mail, and when he was last logged in. If he is currently logged on, the `finger` command tells you how long he has been logged on and which program he is currently using. The `finger` command also displays any information a user may have placed in his .plan file in his home directory.

As you can see, the `finger` command displays a lot of information about a user, which could be used by crackers to hack the system. This is why many systems administrators disable the `finger` command so others cannot see this information.

N O T E If you allow the use of the `finger` command on your system, or if your systems administrator allows it on a system you are using, you can use the `chfn` command to change the information displayed by `finger`. See the related man page (use the `man chfn` command) for more information. ▪

Reporting On the Status of Processes with *ps*

The `ps` (process status) command reports on the status of processes. You can use it to determine which processes are running, whether a process has completed, whether a process is hung or having some difficulty, how long a process has run, the resources a process is using, the relative priority of a process, and the PID (process ID number) needed before you can kill a process. All this information is useful to a user and very useful to a system administrator. Without any options, ps lists the PID of each process associated with your current shell. It's also possible to see a detailed listing of all the processes running on a system.

Monitoring Processes with *ps* A common use of the ps command is to monitor background jobs and other processes on the system. Because background processes don't communicate with your screen and keyboard in most cases, you use ps to track their progress.

The ps listing displays four default headings as indicators of the information in the fields below each heading: PID, TTY, TIME, and COMMAND. Table 19.6 explains these headings.

Table 19.6	Headings in the Output of *ps*
Field	**Explanation**
PID	The process identification number
TTY	The terminal on which the process originated
TIME	The cumulative execution time for the process, in minutes and seconds
COMMAND	The name of the command being executed

Suppose that you want to sort a file named sales.dat, save a copy of the sorted file in a file named sales.srt, and mail the sorted file to the user sarah. If you also want to put this job in the background, enter the following command:

sort sales.dat ¦ tee sales.srt ¦ mailx -s"Sorted Sales Data" sarah &

To monitor this process, enter **ps** to see a display such as this one:

```
PID    TTY     TIME COMMAND
16490 tty02    0:15 sort
16489 tty02    0:00 mailx
16492 tty02    0:00 ps
16478 tty02    0:00 bash
16491 tty02    0:06 tee
16480 tty02   96:45 cruncher
```

You see the accumulated time and PID for each process started with the command. You also see information for your login shell (bash) and for ps itself. Notice that all the commands in the pipe are running at once, just as you would expect (this is the way the piping process works). The last entry is for a command that has been running for more than an hour and a half. If that's a problem, you may want to terminate the process by using the kill command (described later in this chapter). If you enter ps and see only the following listing, the previous job you put into the background is complete:

```
PID    TTY     TIME COMMAND
16492 tty02    0:00 ps
16478 tty02    0:00 bash
16480 tty02   99:45 cruncher
```

N O T E   Use ps occasionally to check the status of a command. If, however, you use ps every second while waiting to see whether the background job is complete, putting the job in the background doesn't make much sense in the first place. ■

Obtaining More Information About Processes with *ps*   Sometimes you need to know more about your processes than what the default ps listing provides. To generate additional information, you can invoke some of the flags listed in Table 19.7.

Part
IV

Ch
19

Table 19.7   Commonly Used Flags for the *ps* Command

Flag	Description
-a	Shows processes of other users also.
-c	Displays command name from `task_struct` environment.
-e	Shows environment after command line and "and."
-f	Shows "forest" family tree format (processes and subprocesses).
-h	No header.
-j	Jobs format.
-l	Long format.
-m	Displays memory info.
-n	Numeric output for USER and WCHAN. WCHAN is the name of the kernel function where the process is sleeping, with the `sys_` stripped from the function name. If /etc/psdatabase doesn't exist, the number is hexadecimal instead.
-r	Running processes only.
-s	Signal format.
-S	Adds child CPU time and page faults.
-txx	Processes associated with tty*xx* only.
-u	User format; gives user name and start time.
-v	vm (virtual memory) format.
-w	Wide output; doesn't truncate command lines to fit on one line.
-x	Shows processes without controlling terminal.

The ps command gives only an approximate picture of process status because things can and do change while the ps command is running. The ps command gives a snapshot of the process status at the instant ps executed. The snapshot includes the ps command itself.

The following examples show three commands. The first command is the login shell (bash). The second command is sort, which is used to sort the file named inventory. The third command is the ps command you're now running.

To find out what processes you're now running, use the following command:

```
$ ps
PID    TTY      TIME      COMMAND
65     tty01    0:07      -bash
71     tty01    0:14      sort inventory
231    tty01    0:09      ps
```

To obtain a full listing, use this command:

```
$ ps -uax
UID      PID   PPID  C    STIME      TTY     TIME    COMD
amanda   65    1     0    11:40:11   tty01   0:06    -bash
amanda   71    65    61   11:42:01   tty01   0:14    sort inventory
amanda   231   65    80   11:46:02   tty01   0:00    ps -f
```

Notice a few things about this full listing. In addition to the PID, the PPID is listed. The PPID is the process ID number of that process's parent process. In this example, the first process listed, PID 65, is the parent of the following two. The entry in the fourth column (the column headed C) gives the amount of CPU time a process has used recently. In selecting the next process to work with, the operating system chooses a process with a low C value over one with a higher value. The entry in the STIME column is the time at which the process started.

To monitor every process on the system and get a full listing, enter `ps -uax`. By piping the command through the `grep $LOGNAME` command, the processes belonging to your login name are displayed while all others are filtered out. To see a full listing of all your processes, enter this:

```
ps -uax ¦ grep $LOGNAME
```

To list processes for two terminals (for example, tty1 and tty2), use the following command:

```
$ ps -t "1 2"
PID   TTY     TIME    COMMAND
32    tty01   0:05    bash
36    tty02   0:09    bash
235   tty02   0:16    vi calendar
```

In this example, the `-t` option is used to restrict the listing to the processes associated with terminals tty01 and tty02. Terminal tty02 is running the shell command (PID 32) and using `vi` to edit the calendar (PID 235). The cumulative time for each process is also listed. If you're using shells from a graphical interface (the `xterm` command), use device names pts001, pts002, and so on with the `-t` option to see the processes from those sessions.

Sometimes a process is marked as `<defunct>`, which means that the process has terminated and its parent process has been notified, but the parent hasn't acknowledged that the process is "dead." A process like that is called a *zombie process*. It's possible that the parent is busy with something else and the zombie will soon disappear. If you see a number of defunct processes or ones that linger for some time, this is a sign of some difficulty with the operating system.

N O T E   Because a zombie process has no parent, you can't kill the zombie. The only way to get rid of a zombie process is to reboot your machine. ■

Controlling Multiple Processes

Linux gives you the power to run several processes concurrently. It also allows a user or an administrator to have control over running processes. This control is advantageous when you need to do the following:

Part
IV

Ch

19

- Initiate a process that continues after its parent quits running (use the `nohup` command)
- Schedule a process with a priority different than other processes (use the `nice` command)
- Terminate or stop a process (use the `kill` command)

Using *nohup* with Background Processes

Normally, the children of a process terminate when the parent dies or terminates. This means that when you start a background process, it terminates when you log out. To have a process continue after you log out, use the `nohup` command. Put `nohup` at the beginning of a command line:

```
nohup sort sales.dat &
```

This sample command tells the `sort` command to ignore the fact that you log out of the system; it should run until the process completes. In this way, you can initiate a process that can run for days or even weeks. What's more, you don't have to be logged in as it runs. Naturally, you want to make sure that the job you initiate behaves nicely—that is, it eventually terminates and doesn't create an excessive amount of output.

When you use `nohup`, the command sends all the output and error messages of a command that normally appear onscreen to a file named nohup.out. Consider the following example:

```
$ nohup sort sales.dat &
1252
Sending output to nohup.out
$
```

The sorted file and any error messages are placed in the file nohup.out. Now consider this example:

```
$ nohup sort sales.dat > sales.srt &
1257
Sending output to nohup.out
$
```

Any error messages are placed in the nohup.out file, but the sorted sales.dat file is placed in sales.srt.

N O T E When you use nohup with a pipeline, you must use nohup with each command in the pipeline:

```
nohup sort sales.dat ¦ nohup mailx -s"Sorted Sales Data" boss &
```

Scheduling the Priority of Commands with *nice*

Use the `nice` command to run a command at a specific scheduling priority. The `nice` command gives you some control over the priority of one job over another. If you don't use `nice`, processes run at a set priority. You can lower the priority of a process with the `nice` command so that other processes can be scheduled to use the CPU more frequently than the `nice` job. The superuser (the person who can log in as the root user) can also raise the priority of a process.

N O T E The commands `nice --help` and `nice --version` don't work in the GNU implementation of `nice`. ■

The general form of the `nice` command is as follows:

```
nice -number command
```

The priority level is determined by the *number* argument (a higher number means a lower priority). The default is set to 10, and *number* is an offset to the default. If the *number* argument is present, the priority is incremented by that amount up to a limit of 20. If you enter the following command, the `sort` process starts with a priority of 10:

```
sort sales.dat > sales.srt &
```

If you want to start another process—say, with the `lp` command—but give preference to the `sort` command, you can enter the following:

`nice -5 lp mail_list &`

To give the `lp` command the lowest possible priority, enter this:

`nice -10 lp mail_list &`

N O T E The number flag above is preceded by the flag specifier -, which you shouldn't confuse with the negative number sign. ■

Only superusers can increase the priority of a process. To do that, they use a negative number as the argument to `nice`. Remember—the lower the `nice` value, the higher the priority (up to a maximum priority of 20). To give a job "top priority," a superuser initiates the job as follows:

```
nice --10 job &
```

The ampersand (&) is optional; if job is interactive, you wouldn't use the ampersand to place the process in the background.

Scheduling the Priority of Running Processes with *renice*

The `renice` command, available on some systems, allows you to modify the priority of a running process. Berkeley UNIX systems have the `renice` command; it's also available in the /usr/ucb directory in Linux System V systems for compatibility with Berkeley systems. With `renice`, you can adjust priorities on commands as they execute. The format of `renice` is similar to that of `nice`:

```
renice -number PID
```

To change the priority on a running process, you must know its PID. To find the PID of all your processes, enter this command:

`ps -e ¦ grep name`

In this command, *name* represents the name of the running process. The `grep` command filters out all processes that don't contain the name of the process you're looking for. If several processes of that name are running, you have to determine the one you want by looking at the time it started. If you want to affect all processes belonging to a certain group or a certain user, you can specify the GID or UID of the running processes to the renice command.

The entry in the second column of the ps listing is the PID of the process. In the following example, three processes are running for the current user (in addition to the shell). The current user's name is pcoco.

```
$ ps -ef | grep $LOGNAME
 pcoco 11805 11804   0  Dec 22    ttysb    0:01 sort sales.dat>sales.srt
 pcoco 19955 19938   4  16:13:02 ttyp0    0:00 grep pcoco
 pcoco 19938     1   0  16:11:04 ttyp0    0:00 bash
 pcoco 19940 19938 142 16:11:04 ttyp0    0:33 find . -name core -exec rm {};
$
```

To lower the priority on the process with PID 19940 (the find process), enter the following:

```
renice -5 19940
```

As you would expect, the following statements are true about renice:

- You can use renice only with processes you own.
- The superuser can use renice on any process.
- Only the superuser can increase the priority of a process.

Terminating Processes with *kill*

Sometimes, you want or need to terminate a process. The following are some reasons for stopping a process:

- It's using too much CPU time.
- It's running too long without producing the expected output.
- It's producing too much output to the screen or to a disk file.
- It appears to have locked a terminal or some other session.
- It's using the wrong files for input or output because of an operator or programming error.
- It's no longer useful.

Most likely, you'll come across a number of other reasons to kill a process as well. If the process to be stopped is a background process, use the kill command to get out of these situations.

To stop a command that isn't in the background, press <Ctrl-c>. When a command is in the background, however, pressing an interrupt key doesn't stop it. Because a background process isn't under terminal control, keyboard input of any interrupt key is ignored. The only way you can stop background commands is to use the kill command.

Normal Termination of Background Processes   The kill command sends signals to the program to demand that a process be terminated or killed. To use kill, use either of these forms:

```
kill PID(s)
```

or

```
kill -signal PID(s)
```

To kill a process whose PID is 123, enter **kill 123**. To kill several processes whose PIDs are 123, 342, and 73, enter **kill 123 342 73**.

By using the -signal option, you can do more than simply kill a process. Other signals can cause a running process to reread configuration files or stop a process without killing it. Valid signals are listed by the command kill -l. An average user, however, will probably use kill with no signal or, at most, with the -9 signal (the I-mean-it-so-don't-ignore-me signal, described in the next section).

CAUTION

Use the correct PID with the kill command. Using the wrong PID can stop a process you want to keep running. Remember that killing the wrong process or a system process can have disastrous effects. Also remember that if you're logged in as the system administrator, you can kill *any* process.

If you successfully kill the process, you get no notice from the shell; the shell prompt simply reappears. You see an error message if you try to kill a process you don't have permission to kill or if you try to kill a process that doesn't exist.

Suppose that your login name is chris and that you're now logged in to tty01. To see the processes you have running, enter **ps -f**, and you'll see the following response:

```
UID     PID   PPID  C   STIME      TTY     TIME    COMMAND
chris   65    1     0   11:40:11   tty01   0:06    -bash
chris   71    65    61  11:42:01   tty01   0:14    total_updt
chris   231   65    80  11:46:02   tty01   0:00    ps -f
chris   187   53    60  15:32:01   tty02   123:45  crunch stats
chris   53    1     0   15:31:34   tty02   1:06    -bash
```

Notice that the program total_updt is running at your current terminal. Another program, crunch, is running on another terminal, and you think it has used an unusually large amount of CPU time. To kill that process, it may be sufficient to enter **kill 187**. To kill the parent of that process, enter **kill 53**.

You may want to kill a parent and its child if you logged in as the system administrator and see that someone left their terminal unattended (if you've set up Linux with remote terminals). You can kill a clock process that the user has running (the child process) and the login shell (the parent process) so that the unattended terminal is no longer logged in.

Stopping the parent of a process sometimes terminates the child process as well. To be sure, stop the parent and its children to halt all activity associated with a parent process. In the preceding example, enter **kill 187 53** to terminate both processes.

TIP

If your terminal locks up, log in to another virtual terminal by pressing <Alt> combined with a function key (F1–F6), enter **ps -ef ¦ grep $LOGNAME**, and then kill the login shell for the locked terminal.

Part
IV

Ch
19

Unconditional Termination of Background Processes   Issuing the `kill` command sends a signal to a process. Linux programs can send or receive more than 20 signals, each of which is represented by a number. For example, when you log out, Linux sends the hang-up signal (signal number 1) to all the background processes started from your login shell. This signal kills or stops those processes unless they were started with `nohup` (as described earlier in this chapter).

Using `nohup` to start a background process lets the process ignore the signal that tries to stop it. You may be using programs or shell scripts written to ignore some signals. If you don't specify a signal when you use `kill`, signal 15 is sent to the process. The command `kill 1234` sends signal 15 to the process whose PID is 1234. If that process is set to ignore signal 15, however, the process doesn't terminate when you use this command. You can use `kill` in a way that a process "can't refuse," however.

The signal 9 is an unconditional kill signal; it always kills a process. To unconditionally kill a process, use the following command:

`kill -9 *PID*`

Suppose you enter **ps -f** and see the following response:

```
UID     PID   PPID  C   STIME      TTY    TIME    COMMAND
chris   65    1     0   11:40:11   tty01  0:06    -bash
chris   71    65    61  11:42:01   tty01  0:14    total_updt inventory
chris   231   65    80  11:46:02   tty01  0:00    ps -f
chris   187   53    60  15:32:01   tty02  123:45  crunch stats
chris   53    1     0   15:31:34   tty02  1:06    -bash
```

To kill process 187, normally you would enter `kill 187`. If you then enter `ps -f` again and see that the process is still there, you know the process is set up to ignore the `kill` command. To kill it unconditionally, enter **kill -9 187**. When you enter `ps -f` again, you see that the process is no longer around.

> **CAUTION**
>
> A disadvantage to using this unconditional version of the `kill` command is that `kill -9` doesn't allow a process to finish what it's doing before it terminates the process. If you use `kill -9` with a program that's updating a file, you could lose the updated material or the entire file.
>
> Use the powerful `kill -9` command responsibly. In most cases, you don't need the -9 option; the `kill` command, issued without arguments, stops most processes.

Termination of All Background Processes   To kill all background jobs, enter **kill 0**. Commands that run in the background sometimes initiate more than one process; tracking down all the PID numbers associated with the process you want to kill can be tedious. Because `kill 0` terminates all processes started by the current shell, it's a faster and less tedious way to terminate processes. Enter the `jobs` command to see what commands are running in the background for the current shell.

From Here...

This chapter presented the commands you need to manage multiple processes. You saw that you run multiple processes whenever you put jobs in the background with the ampersand (&) or when you use pipes. You can schedule jobs at a specific time with the at command, at a time the system feels is appropriate with the batch command, and at regularly scheduled times with cron and crontab. For more information, see the following:

- The chapters in Part III, "Managing the File System," discuss how to monitor and maintain your Linux system. System administration isn't an easy topic to learn and, in fact, requires a hands-on learning approach. This part of the book provides you with a basic understanding of the concepts and the tasks required of a systems administrator (often called a *sys admin*).

- Chapter 18, "Understanding Linux Shells," provides the shell-specific information to program scripts to start, stop, and monitor processes on your Linux system.

In addition, check out the man pages for the various commands discussed in this chapter.

Printing

by Jack Tackett

In this chapter

Although everyone thought the computer revolution would bring the paperless office, it hasn't. More paper is used today than was used 20 years ago. When the UNIX operating system was in its infancy, Bell Labs used it to produce—and print—technical documentation. As a result, UNIX, and thus Linux, has a great many utilities designed around printing (or at least formatting data to be printed). This chapter concentrates on the mechanics of actually printing a file.

The printing systems common to BSD UNIX/Linux are called the *lpr systems (Line PrinteR)*.

Selecting a Printer to Work with Linux

If you can access the printer from MS-DOS, you should be able to print ASCII characters to the printer from Linux. The only downside is that you may not be able to access certain features of your printer from Linux. One of the main reasons is that under Linux, the system first sends the file to be printed to another file. Linux sends the files to a temporary area because printers are relatively slow peripherals, and the system doesn't want to slow down your session just to print a file. This process is called *spooling*, and printers are thus called *spooled devices*. When you print a file in Linux, the file doesn't go directly to a printer; instead, it goes to a queue to wait its turn to be printed. If your file is the first in the queue, it prints almost immediately.

N O T E   *Spool* is an acronym for Simultaneous Peripheral Operation Off Line. The term was coined in the early days of the big IBM mainframes, when smaller computers were used to print reports offline from the mainframe. This technique allowed expensive mainframes to continue their tasks without wasting time on such trivial matters as printing. ■

Because Linux inherits a great deal of UNIX functionality, Linux supports many types of printers. If you can access your printer from DOS (as mentioned earlier), you should be able to access the printer from Linux.

Knowing What You Need to Configure Printers

This chapter assumes that you know how to edit a text file under Linux and that you have a basic understanding of file ownership and permissions. It also assumes that you have your Linux system set up and running correctly. In particular, if you're going to use remote printing, your networking subsystems must be installed and operating correctly. Check out the man pages on the commands chmod and chown for more information. Also review Chapter 8, "Using the vi Editor," for information on using the vi editor because you need to edit several files when configuring your printers.

Knowing How Printing Works Under Linux

The simplest way to print under Linux is to send the print data directly to the printer device. The following command sends a directory listing to the first parallel printer (LPT1 in DOS terms):

```
ls > /dev/lp0
```

This method doesn't take advantage of Linux's multitasking capabilities because the time taken for this command to finish is however long it takes the printer to actually physically print the data. On a slow printer or a printer that's deselected or disconnected, this could be a long time. A better method is to *spool* the data—that is, to collect the print data into a file and then start a background process to send the data to the printer.

Spooling files to be printed later is essentially how Linux works. For each printer, a spool area is defined. Data for the printer is collected in the spool area, one file per print job. A background process (called the *printer daemon*) constantly scans the spool areas for new files to print. When one appears, the data is sent to the appropriate printer, or *despooled*. When more than one file is waiting to be printed, the files are printed in the order they're completed—first in, first out. Thus, the spool area is effectively a queue, and the waiting jobs are often referred to as being *in the print queue* or *queued*. In the case of remote printing, the data is first spooled locally as for any other print job, but the background process is told to send the data to a particular printer on a particular remote machine.

The necessary information that the printer daemon needs to do its job—the physical device to use, the spool area to look in, the remote machine and printer for remote printing, and so on—is all stored in a file called /etc/printcap. The details of this file are discussed later in the section "Understanding the /etc/printcap File."

N O T E To Linux, the printer is just another file. But because it is a physical piece of hardware, it will have an entry in the /dev directory. Linux likes to treat physical devices as if they are part of the file system. ■

The term *printer* is used to mean a printer as specified in /etc/printcap. The term *physical printer* is used to mean the thing that actually puts characters on paper. It's possible to have multiple entries in /etc/printcap that all describe one physical printer but do so in different ways. If this isn't clear to you, read the section on /etc/printcap.

Understanding the Important Programs for Printing

Five programs comprise the UNIX print system. By default, they are in the locations shown in Table 20.1, are owned by root, belong to the group daemon, and have the permissions listed in the table.

Part
IV

Ch
20

Table 20.1   The Important Printing Programs

File Permissions	File Locations
-rwsr-sr-x	/usr/bin/lpr
-rwsr-sr-x	/usr/bin/lpq
-rwsr-sr-x	/usr/bin/lpc

continues

Table 20.1 Continued	
File Permissions	**File Locations**
-rwsr-sr-x	/usr/bin/lprm
-rwxr-s---	/usr/sbin/lpd

The first four file permissions in Table 20.1 are used to submit, cancel, and inspect print jobs. /usr/sbin/lpd is the printer daemon.

N O T E The locations, ownerships, and permissions in Table 20.1 have been simplified and may be wrong for your system, so note the lpd files and permissions.

All these commands have man pages, which you should consult for more information. The important points are that by default, lpr, lprm, lpc, and lpq operate on a printer called lp. If you define an environment variable called PRINTER, the name defined is used instead. You can override lp and the PRINTER environment variable by specifying the printer name to use on the command line like so:

```
lpc -PMYPRINTER
```

The *lpd* Daemon

Linux handles all print jobs via the lpd daemon. If this process isn't running, no printing can take place; print files will remain in their spool directories until the lpd process is started (more information about spool directories appears later in the section "Understanding the Important Directories").

▶ **See** "Understanding Processes," **p. 349**

If your system doesn't load lpd at startup, or if for some reason you must kill and then restart the lpd daemon, the following command starts the printer daemon:

```
lpd [options]
```

The man page on lpd gives a list of options, but one important option when configuring your Linux printers is -l, which creates a log file that logs each print request to the system. This log file can be useful when you're debugging your printing system.

The *lpr* Command

The lpr command submits a job to the printer, or queues a print job. What actually happens is that the file you specify is copied to the spool directory. Each printer specified for your Linux system must have its own spool directory. The size of this spool directory is specified in the minfree file located in each directory. The minfree file specifies the number of disk blocks to reserve for spooling files to the printer. This is done to keep the lpd daemon from using up the entire hard drive when spooling a print request.

lpd finds the file, which then takes care of moving the data to the physical printer. If you don't specify a file, lpr uses standard input.

The *lpq* Command

The lpq command shows you the contents of the spool directory for a given printer. One important piece of information displayed by lpq is the job ID, which identifies a particular job. This number must be specified if you want to cancel a pending job.

lpq also indicates with a number a rank for each job in the queue (meaning, where the job is in the queue). active means the file is actually printing—or at least that lpd is trying to print it.

The *lprm* Command

The lprm command removes a job from the queue—that is, it removes unprinted files from the spool directory. You can specify a job ID (obtained by using the lpq command), or you can specify - as the job ID to cancel all jobs belonging to you.

If you issue lpq - as root, all jobs for the printer are canceled. If you are root and want to remove all the jobs belonging to a specific user, specify the user's name.

The *lpc* Command

The lpc command lets you check the status of printers and control some aspects of their use. In particular, lpc lets you start and stop despooling on printers, enable or disable printers, and rearrange the order of jobs in a print queue. The following commands disable printing on myprinter, enable the spool queue on yourprinter, and move job number 37 to the top of the queue:

```
lpc down myprinter
lpc enable yourprinter
lpc topq 37
```

If you invoke lpc without any command arguments, lpc is interactive, prompting you for actions to take. Some of the more important commands are shown in Table 20.2; read the man page for complete instructions. Most lpc commands take the name of the printer, as specified in /etc/printcap, as the parameter.

Table 20.2   Some Common *lpc* Commands

Command	Parameter	Description
stop	*printer*	Stops the printer, but print requests are still spooled.
start	*printer*	Allows the printer to start printing previously spooled files and any new files spooled to this printer.
exit, quit	(None)	Leaves lpc interactive mode.
status	*printer*	Displays the current status of the printer. status provides such information as whether the queue is enabled, whether the printer is enabled, and the number (if any) of jobs now in the queue waiting to be printed.

Part
IV

Ch
20

N O T E   Bear in mind that some `lpc` commands are restricted to root—that is, the superuser.   ■

CAUTION

`lpc` is very unstable in its current implementation under Linux. Some users have reported that `lpc` can display incorrect status messages and sometimes even hang the system outright.

Understanding the Important Directories

There's only one important directory in printing—the spool area where data to be printed is accumulated before /etc/lpd prints it. However, a system is typically set up with multiple spool directories, one for each printer, to make printer management easier. For example, my system is set up to use /usr/spool/lpd as the main spool area, with each separate printer having a directory under that with the same name as the printer. Thus, a printer named ps_nff has /usr/spool/lpd/ps_nff as its spool directory.

The spool directories should belong to the daemon group and should be user and group read/writable and world readable—that is, after you create the directory, make sure that it has the permissions -rwxrwxr-x (0775) with the `chmod` command. For the directory myprinter, the appropriate command is this:

```
chmod ug=rwx,o=rx myprinter
chgrp daemon myprinter
```

▶ **See** "File Permissions," **p. 310**

N O T E   The locations, ownerships, and permissions given here are a simplification and may be incorrect for your system, so you should take notes on the `lpd` files and permissions.   ■

Understanding the Important Files

Apart from the programs discussed so far, each spool directory contains files that have the permissions -rw-rw-r-:

- The /etc/printcap file contains the printer specifications for each named printer in your system.
- The .seq file contains the job number counter for `lpr` to assign.
- The status file contains the message to be reported by `lpc stat`.
- The lock file is used by `lpd` to prevent itself from trying to print two jobs to the same printer at once.
- The errs file logs printer failures.

The errs file isn't required by Linux in order to print, but the file must exist for `lpd` to be able to log printer failures. The errs file can be called whatever you like as long as the name is specified in /etc/printcap. The errs file is usually created manually when you set up the spool area. The section "Putting It All Together," later in this chapter, has more on this.

One very important file is /etc/printcap, which the following section describes in detail.

Understanding the /etc/printcap File

The /etc/printcap file is a text file that you can edit with your favorite editor. /etc/printcap should be owned by root and have the permissions -rw-r--r--.

The contents of /etc/printcap typically look very cryptic, but when you know how the file works, the contents are much easier to understand. To compound the problem, in some distributions there's no man page for printcap, and most printcap files are created either by programs or by people with no thought for readability. For your own sanity, make the layout of your printcap file as logical and readable as possible with lots of comments. And get the man page from the lpd sources if you don't already have it.

One printcap entry describes one printer. Essentially, a printcap entry provides a logical name for a physical device and then describes how data sent to that device should be handled. For example, a printcap entry defines what physical device is to be used, what spool directory any data for that device should be stored in, what preprocessing should be performed on the data, where errors on the physical device should be logged, and so forth. You can limit the amount of data that may be sent in a single job, or limit access to a printer to certain classes of users. The following shows how a printer is defined in the printcap file:

```
# Sample printcap entry with two aliases
myprinter¦laserwriter:\
# lp is the device to print to - here the first parallel printer.
:lp=/dev/lp0: \
# sd means spool directory - where print data is collected
:sd=/usr/spool/lpd/myprinter:
```

It's okay to have multiple printcap entries defining several different ways to handle data destined for the same physical printer. For example, a physical printer may support PostScript and HP LaserJet data formats, depending on some setup sequence being sent to the physical printer before each job. It makes sense to define two printers: one that preprocesses the data by preappending the HP LaserJet sequence and one that preappends the PostScript sequence. Programs that generate HP data send it to the HP printer, whereas programs generating PostScript print to the PostScript printer.

Part

IV

Ch

20

N O T E If you don't designate a default printer via an environment variable or don't specify a printer on the lpr command line, Linux will route the print job to the lp printer. Thus, you should specify one of the printers in the printcap file as the lp printer. ▪

Programs that change the data before it's sent to the physical printer are called *filters*. It's possible for a filter to send no data at all to a physical printer—that is, the filter filters out everything.

Understanding the Fields in /etc/printcap

The printcap file has too many fields to describe fully in this chapter, so only the most important ones are described. All fields in /etc/printcap (except for the names of the printer) are enclosed between colons and denoted by a two-letter code. The two-letter code is followed by a value that depends on the type of field. There are three types of fields: string, Boolean, and numeric. Table 20.3 describes the most common and most important fields; the following sections go into more detail.

Table 20.3   The /etc/printcap Fields

Field	Type	Description
lp	String	Specifies the device to print to—for example, /dev/lp0
sd	String	Specifies the name of the spool directory for this printer
lf	String	Specifies the file that errors on this printer are to be logged to
if	String	Specifies the input filter name
rm	String	Specifies the name of a remote printing host
rp	String	Specifies the name of a remote printer
sh	Boolean	Specifies this to suppress headers (banner pages)
sf	Boolean	Specifies this to suppress end-of-job form feeds
mx	Numeric	Specifies the maximum allowable print job size (in blocks)

The *lp* Field   If you specify /dev/null as the print device, all other processing is performed correctly, but the final data goes to the *bit bucket*—that is, to nowhere. Printing to nowhere is rarely useful except for test printer configurations or with weird printers. When you're setting up a remote printer (that is, you've specified rm and rp fields), specify :lp=:.

Don't leave the field empty unless you're using a remote printer. The printer daemon complains if you don't specify a print device.

The *lf* Field   Whatever file you specify should already exist, or logging doesn't occur.

The *if* Field   *Input filters* are programs that take print data on their standard input and generate output on their standard output. A typical use of an input filter is to detect plain ASCII text and convert it into PostScript—that is, raw text is its input and PostScript is its output.

When you specify an input filter, the printer daemon doesn't send the spooled print data to the specified device. Instead, it runs the input filter with the spooled data as standard input and the print device as standard output.

The *rm* and *rp* Fields   Sending your print data to a printer attached to another machine is as simple as specifying the remote machine rm and the remote printer rp and making sure that the print device field lp is empty.

N O T E   Data is still spooled locally before it's transferred to the remote machine. Any input filters
you specify are also run. ■

The *sh* and *sf* Fields   Unless you have a lot of different people using your printer, you're most
likely not interested in banner pages, so specify sh.

Suppressing form feeds, by specifying sf, is most useful if your printer is typically used for
output from word-processing packages. Most word-processing packages create complete pages
of data, so if the printer daemon is adding a form feed to the end of each job, you get a blank
page after each job. If the printer is usually used for program or directory listings, however,
having that form feed ensures that the final page is completely ejected, so each listing starts at
the top of a new page.

The *mx* Field   The mx field allows you to limit the size of the print data to be spooled. The
number you specify is in BUFSIZE blocks (1KB under Linux). If you specify zero, the limit is
removed, allowing print jobs to be limited only by available disk space.

N O T E   The limit is on the size of the spooled data, not the amount of data sent to the physical
printer. ■

If a user tries to exceed this limit, the file is truncated. The user sees a message saying this:

```
(lpr: file-name: copy file is too large)
```

For non-PostScript printers, this limit is useful if you have users or programs that may deliberately or accidentally create excessively large output. For PostScript printers, the limit isn't
useful at all because a very small amount of spooled PostScript data can generate a large number of output pages.

Setting the *PRINTER* Environment Variable

You may want to add a line to your login script—or even to the default user login script—
that sets up a PRINTER environment variable. Under the bash shell, a suitable line is
export PRINTER=myprinter. This prevents people from having to specify
-Pmyprinter every time they submit a print job.

To add more printers, just repeat this process with different printer names. Remember that you
can have multiple printcap entries, all using the same physical device. This way, you can treat
the same device differently, depending on what you call it when you submit a print job to it.

Part
IV

Ch
20

Creating a Test printcap Entry

The following shell script is a very simple input filter—it simply concatenates its input onto the
end of a file in /tmp after an appropriate banner. Specify this filter in the printcap entry and
specify /dev/null as the print device. The print device is never actually used, but you have to
set it to something; otherwise, the printer daemon complains.

```
#!/bin/sh
# This file should be placed in the printer's spool directory and
# named input_filter. It should be owned by root, group daemon, and
# be world executable (-rwxr-xr-x).
echo ------------------------------------------------ >> /tmp/
date                                                  >> /tmp/
echo ------------------------------------------------ >> /tmp/
cat                                                   >> /tmp/
```

In the following printcap entry, notice the reasonably readable format and the use of the continuation character (\) on all but the last line:

```
myprinter¦myprinter: \
:lp=/dev/null: \
:sd=/usr/spool/lpd/myprinter: \
:lf=/usr/spool/lpd/myprinter/errs: \
:if=/usr/spool/lpd/myprinter/input_filter: \
:mx#0: \
:sh: \
:sf:
```

Putting It All Together

To put all the preceding bits together, the following steps guide you through setting up a single printer on /dev/lp0. You can then extend this to other printers. (You have to be root to do all this, by the way.)

1. Check the permissions and locations of lpr, lprm, lpc, lpq, and lpd. Earlier in this chapter, Table 20.2 listed the correct settings and directories.

2. Create the spool directory for your printer (named myprinter for now). Make sure that both the directory and printer are owned by root, belong to the daemon group, and have write permissions for user and group and read-only permission for others (-rwxrwxr-x). Use the following commands:

    ```
    mkdir /usr/spool/lpd
    mkdir /usr/spool/lpd/myprinter
    chown root.daemon /usr/spool/lpd /usr/spool/lpd/myprinter
    chmod ug=rwx,o=rx /usr/spool/lpd /usr/spool/lpd/myprinter
    ```

3. In the /usr/spool/lpd/myprinter directory, create the necessary files and give them the correct permissions and owner. Use the following commands:

    ```
    cd /usr/spool/lpd/myprinter
    touch .seq errs status lock
    chown root.daemon .seq errs status lock
    chmod ug=rw,o=r .seq errs status lock
    ```

4. Create the shell script input_filter in the /usr/spool/lpd/myprinter directory. Use the input filter given earlier in the section "Creating a Test printcap Entry" for your filter. Make sure that the file is owned by root, belongs to the daemon group, and is executable by anyone. Use the following commands:

    ```
    cd /usr/spool/lpd/myprinter
    chmod ug=rwx,o=rx input_filter
    ```

5. Create the /etc/printcap file if it doesn't already exist. Remove all entries in it and add the test printcap entry given in the "Creating a Test printcap Entry" section. Make sure that the file is owned by root and is read-only to everyone else. You can use the chmod command to set the proper file permissions: -rw-r- -r- - (or 644 in octal).

6. Edit the rc.local file (you can use any ASCII editor, such as vi or emacs). Add the line /etc/lpd to the end to run the printer daemon each time the system boots. It's not necessary to boot now, however; just run it by hand with the lpd command.

▶ **See** "Starting vi by Using an Existing File," **p. 183**

7. Do a test print by entering the following:

   ```
   ls -l ¦ lpr -Pmyprinter
   ```

8. Use the ls command to look in /tmp for a file named testlp.out. It should contain your directory listing, which you can check with the more, less, or cat command. See Chapter 17, "Managing Files and Directories," for more information on these commands.

▶ **See** "Viewing the Contents of a File," **p. 325**

9. Use an ASCII editor such as vi to make the following edits to /etc/printcap:

   - In the first printer entry, change both occurrences of myprinter to testlp only in the first line.

   - In the second entry, change /dev/null to your real print device—for example, /dev/lp0.

   - In the second entry, remove the if line completely.

   Now, copy the myprinter entry so that you have two identical entries in the file.

10. Either reboot the system or kill the printer daemon and restart it. You do this because the printer daemon looks only at the /etc/printcap file when it first starts up.

11. Run a test print again using the command ls -l ¦ lpr -Pmyprinter. This one should come out on your physical printer.

TROUBLESHOOTING

I get a message saying lpd: connect: No such file or directory. The printer daemon /etc/lpd isn't running. You may have forgotten to add it to your /etc/rc.local file. Or maybe you did add it but you haven't booted since then. Add it and reboot, or just run /etc/lpd. Remember that you have to be root to do this.

I get a message saying Job queued, but cannot start daemon. This often appears right after the lpd: connect message; same problem as the preceding.

I get a message saying lpd: cannot create spooldir/.seq. You haven't created the spool directory specified in the printcap entry, or you've misnamed it. An alternative (though much less likely) answer is that you have too little disk space left.

continues

continued

I get a message saying lpr: Printer queue is disabled. As root, use `lpc enable`
printer-name to enable the printer. Note that as root, you can submit jobs even to a disabled
printer.

**I submit a print job and there are no error messages, but nothing comes out on the physical
printer.** There could be many reasons:

- Make sure that the physical printer is switched on, selected, and physically connected to the device
  specified in the /etc/printcap file.

- Use the `lpq` command to see whether the entry is in the queue. If it is, the device may be busy, the
  printer may be down, or there may be an error on the printer. If there are errors, check the error log
  specified in the printcap entry for clues.

- You can use the `lpc status` command to check whether the printer is down, and you can use
  `lpc up` *printer-name* or `lpc restart` *printer-name* to bring it back up if it is (you need
  to be root to do this).

If, after checking, your print jobs still don't come out, make sure that any input filter you've specified is
present in the correct directory and has the correct permissions. If you're running `syslogd`, you can
look in your logs for messages from `lpd`. If you see log entries saying `cannot execv name of
input filter`, this is almost certainly the problem.

Another possibility is that your printer is a PostScript printer and you're not sending PostScript to
it. Most PostScript printers ignore non-PostScript data. You may need to install an appropriate
text-to-PostScript input filter.

Last (and you'll feel silly if this is the cause), make sure that your input filter actually generates output
and that the output device isn't /dev/null.

**My printer seems to have locked up. None of the preceding techniques seems to solve the
problem.** When all else fails in the case of a nonprinting printer, the next-to-last resort is to kill the `lpd`
daemon and restart it. If that doesn't work, the last resort is to reboot your Linux system with the
`shutdown -r now` command. Make sure that no one else is logged in and that you've saved any
files before using the now option; otherwise, specify a time and also give a message to your other
users before shutting down the system. You also can test the printer on a DOS or Windows machine to
make sure that the physical device itself is working.

Configuring Red Hat Printers

If you've installed XFree86 under Red Hat, you can use the printer configuration tool shown in
Figure 20.1 to add and delete printers as well as maintain the /etc/printcap and spooler files
and directories. You can find this tool in the Control Panel; Table 20.5 describes each of the
PrintTool's menu items.

FIG. 20.1
Managing printers is easy with Red Hat's graphical utilities.

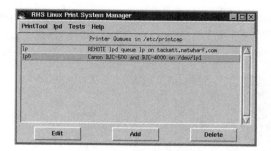

Table 20.4   The PrintTool Menus

Menu Name	Submenu	Description
PrintTool	Reload	Rescans the directory for printcap files
	About	Displays information about the PrintTool
	Quit	Exits the PrintTool
Lpd	Restart	Restarts the `lpd` daemon after making changes
Tests	Print ASCII test page	Prints a test page in plain text to the selected printer
	Print PostScript test page	Prints a PostScript test page to the selected printer
	Print ASCII directly to port	Prints a test page directly to the device and not via the lpd system
Help	General	Provides general help on the PrintTool
	Troubleshooting	Provides help on various problems with printing

To add a new printer, click the Add button. You must first specify whether it's a local, remote, or SMB printer, as shown in Figure 20.2. A *local printer* is connected to your parallel or serial port; a *remote printer* is connected to your network. A LAN Manager Printer is a printer attached to a different system via *Server Message Block protocol* (SMB-Samba), typically a Microsoft Windows system.

▶ **See** "Using SAMBA," **p. 291**

FIG. 20.2
To add a printer, you must select the type of printer.

Part
IV

Ch
20

To edit an existing printer configuration, select the entry and click the Edit button. Both actions bring up the dialog box shown in Figure 20.3. You must enter a value for each field in the dialog box. Table 20.5 describes each field.

FIG. 20.3

To print properly from Linux, you must specify certain options, such as printer name and physical port location.

Table 20.5   Field Items for Each Printer

Field Name	Description
Names	The name of the printer and its queue. You can specify multiple names by using the | character to separate names.
Spool Directory	The directory for spooling documents for this printer, such as /usr/spool/lpd/myprinter.
File Limit	The maximum document size (in kilobytes). A 0 value indicates no limit.
Printer Device	The physical connection for your printer, such as lp0.
Input Filter	Enter the full path and filename of your custom filter. If you need to configure a printer, click the Select button.
Suppress Headers	Check this box if you don't want a header page printed with each document.
Remote Host	This field in the Remote Host dialog box specifies the name of the remote host to which the printer is connected.
Remote Queue	This field in the Remote Host dialog box specifies the printer queue on the remote machine. Enter the full path.

To configure a print filter, click the Select button, which displays the dialog box shown in Figure 20.4. Table 20.6 describes the various fields in the Configure Filter dialog box.

Table 20.6   Field Items for Each Filter

Field Name	Description
Printer Type	The type of printer for this filter.
Driver Description	Provides a description of the selected printer.
Resolution	Select the desired resolution for this printer.

Field Name	Description
Paper Size	Select the desired paper size for this printer.
Color Depth	Select the desired color operation for this printer.
Printing options	Send EOF... forces the printer to eject the page.
	Fix Stair-Stepping Text fixes the stair-step effect.
	Fast Text Printing enables a non-PostScript printer to attain faster print speeds.
Margins	Specify the desired margins.
Extra GS options	Specify extra ghostscript options for the selected printer.

FIG. 20.4

Configuring an input filter for your printing system is made simple with the Configure Filter dialog box.

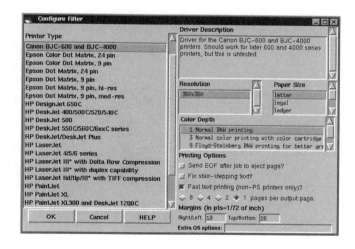

After you add or change a printer entry, you may find that you need to restart the lpd daemon. To do this, simply select the lpd menu item on the RHS Linux Print System Manager and click the Restart lpd item.

From Here...

The lpr command is the standard Linux interface for printing files. From the command line, you can use lpr to print to many different types of printers and to request many different options. Later, you can check the status of your print jobs with the lpq command. If you change your mind and want to cancel a print job, you can do so with the lprm command. No matter what, you should read the latest edition of the Printing HOWTO for more information.

Part
IV

Ch
20

For information on related topics, see the following:

- Chapter 3, "Installing Red Hat," discusses how to install the Red Hat distribution of Linux.
- The chapters in Part III, "Managing the File System," discuss the details of what a system administrator is and does.
- The PrintTool help system provides a myriad of information on how to use the tool to configure your printer system using X.
- Chapter 22, "Using X Windows," discusses how to use the X Windows system.
- Appendix A, "Sources of Information," tells you how to locate the Linux Printing HOWTO.

## CHAPTER 21

Installing the X Windows System

by Steve Burnett

In this chapter

For any operating system to compete for space on today's desktops, it must have an easy-to-use, graphical interface. The most popular systems today are Windows and Macintosh. Unlike UNIX, neither of these can easily run graphical applications across a heterogeneous network.

Linux provides the capability to run windowed applications across a heterogeneous network by incorporating the XFree86 implementation of the X11 standard of X Windows created at the Massachusetts Institute of Technology (MIT). This system is much more than a graphical interface used to run applications—it's a powerful client/server system that allows applications to be run and shared across a network. Although XFree86 is meant to run in a networked environment, it runs fine on a single machine. You don't need a network to run XFree86 or X Windows applications.

To install, configure, and use XFree86, you will need to know some basic Linux commands, such as how to execute programs, move through directories, and copy, view, and delete files. You may also need to modify some of the files with a text editor. If you come across a topic you don't fully understand, this chapter tries to give you the command you need to perform the operation and then a reference to another chapter to learn, in more detail, how to perform the operation.

Like most parts of Linux, XFree86 also has a HOWTO document. The XFree86 HOWTO is maintained by Matt Welsh at **mdw@sunsite.unc.edu** and can be found on the World Wide Web at **http://sunsite.unc.edu/LDP/**.

> **CAUTION**
>
> Typically, you don't have to worry about software damaging your hardware. Unfortunately, however, any software that deals directly with your video system—either the card or the monitor—can cause physical damage, especially if you try to use XFree86 under Linux with an unsupported video card. Make sure that you have the necessary hardware before trying to run XFree86. Reading the documentation that comes with the XFree86 system, located in the /usr/X386/lib/X11/etc directory under Linux, and the XFree86 HOWTO by Helmut Geyer in /usr/doc/faq/howto/XFree86-HOWTO is strongly suggested.

Understanding X Windows

The X Windows system is a powerful graphical operating environment that supports many applications across a network. The X Windows system was developed at MIT and can be freely distributed. The version of X Windows discussed in this chapter is X11R6. However, Linux and XFree86 are moving targets, and a newer version of X may be available on the Net.

▶ **See** "Using FTP for Remote File Transfer," **p. 580**

XFree86, the version used by Linux, is the X11R6 standard ported to Intel-based systems. XFree86 supports a wide range of standard PC hardware.

The X Windows system originally grew out of a cooperative effort between two sections at MIT: the section responsible for a networking program called Project Athena and a section called the Laboratory for Computer Science. Both used large quantities of UNIX workstations and soon realized they were each reinventing the wheel when it came to programming graphical user interfaces (GUIs) for UNIX workstations. To cut down on the amount of code both groups were writing, they decided to create one robust, extensible windowing system—X Windows.

In 1987, several vendors—in hopes of creating a single windowing system for UNIX workstations—formed an organization called the *X Consortium* to promote and standardize X Windows. Thanks to this effort, open computing became a reality. The X Consortium is composed of entities such as IBM, Digital Equipment, and MIT. This group of large organizations oversees the construction and release of new versions of X11.

XFree86 is a trademark of the XFree86 Project, Inc. The original programmers who ported X Windows to the 80386 platform decided to found the project in order to gain membership in the X Consortium. By becoming a member of the X Consortium, the XFree86 Project gained access to works in progress and could thus port the new features to XFree86 while the features were being implemented for X Windows, rather than wait until after the official release to make the port. As of January 1, 1997, the X Consortium turned over X to the Open Group.

X Windows is actually a series of pieces working together to present the user with a GUI:

- The base window system is a program providing services to the X Windows system.
- The next piece is a protocol for communicating across the network—the X Network Protocol.
- On top of the program implementing the X Network Protocol is the low-level interface, named Xlib, between the network/base system and higher-level programs. Application programs typically use functions in the Xlib instead of the lower-level functions.
- Tying these pieces all together is a window manager. The window manager is an X Windows application whose purpose is to control how windows are presented to users.

Different from most other window systems, the base window system doesn't provide user interface objects, such as scroll bars, command buttons, or menus. The user interface items are left to the higher-layer components and the window manager.

X Windows applications include not only window managers, but also games, graphics utilities, programming tools, and many other tidbits. Just about any application that you need has either been written for or ported to X Windows. The setup and use of several of the standard X Windows applications is covered in more detail in Chapter 22, "Using X Windows."

X Windows implements a windows manager to handle the task of creating and controlling the interface that makes up the visual portion of the X Windows system. This isn't to be confused with the OS/2 Presentation Manager or the Microsoft Windows Program Manager. Although the window manager for X Windows does control the behavior and position of the windows, you won't find a system setup icon or control panel for maintaining your Linux system settings.

For the not-so-faint-of-heart, XFree86 also includes programming libraries and files for programmers who want to develop their own applications under XFree86. While the topic of programming or any of the caveats involved in creating X Windows applications is beyond the

Part

IV

Ch

21

scope of this book, ample documentation is available on any number of Internet distribution sites such as **prep.ai.mit.edu**, and on many CD-ROM distributions to help you gain the foothold necessary to create applications for XFree86.

What Is a Client/Server System?

X Windows is a client/server system controlled by two individual pieces of software with one piece running on the client and the other running on the server. The client and server pieces of this puzzle can be on different systems or, as is the case with most personal computers, both pieces can reside on the same machine.

Client/server is one of the major buzzwords used in the computer industry today. Like most basic concepts in the industry, client/server has been overplayed and overused to the point of confusing the average computer user. In the traditional sense, a *server* is a machine that just provides resources—disk drive space, printers, modems, and so on—to other computers over a network. A *client* is the consumer of these services—in other words, a client uses the disk space, printer, or modems provided by a server.

Now that you understand what a client is and what a server is, it's time to reverse it all. In the world of X Windows, the client/server relationship is the opposite of what you've come to know in the PC world. The accepted or common notion of a server is that it provides services to a client who uses them. In the most basic form, a client displays the application that's running on the server.

Under X Windows, the server displays the application that's running on the client. This may seem a bit confusing at first, but it'll make sense when you become more intimate with the X Windows system.

In X Windows, a client is the resource that provides the programs and resources necessary to run an application—what in the traditional sense would be called a server. The resources reside on the client system (remember that the client and server systems can be on the same machine), whereas the application is displayed and interacted with on the server system.

The capability of an X Windows application, which is the client, to run under a server located on either the same computer or on another computer is called *network transparency*. Thus, an X application doesn't care whether it runs on a local or remote machine. This capability can be used to run time-consuming tasks on another server, leaving the local client unencumbered to perform other tasks.

Output Capabilities

The base window system provides X Windows with plenty of bitmapped graphical operations. X Windows and X Windows applications use these operations to present information graphically to the users. XFree86 offers overlapping windows, immediate graphics drawings, high-resolution bitmapped graphics and images, and high-quality text. Whereas early X Windows systems were mostly monochrome-based, today X Windows and XFree86 support a wide range of color systems.

X Windows also supports the multiprocessing capabilities of UNIX; thus, XFree86 supports the multiprocessing capabilities of Linux. Each window displayed under X Windows can be a separate task running under Linux.

User Interface Capabilities

The X Consortium left out the standard rules for user interfaces. Although this seems somewhat shortsighted today, at the time very little research had been done on user interface technology, so no clear interface was considered the best. In fact, even today, unilaterally declaring one interface the best can alienate many people. The preferred look and feel presented by the user interface is a very personal decision.

The X Consortium wanted to make X Windows a standard across UNIX workstations, which is one reason X Windows is available freely on the Internet. By making X Windows freely available, it fosters interoperability, which is the cornerstone of open systems. Had the X Consortium dictated a user interface, X Windows may not have gained its current level of popularity.

Input Capabilities

Systems running X Windows typically have some form of pointing device, usually a mouse. XFree86 requires a mouse or a device, such as a trackball, that emulates a mouse. If you don't have such a device, you can't use the XFree86 system with Linux. X Windows converts signals from the pointing device and from the keyboard into events. X Windows then responds to these events, performing appropriate actions.

> **CAUTION**
>
> If your mouse or other hardware pointing device isn't among those supported by Linux, you'll have problems using XFree86 and the `selection` program.

▶ **See** "Making Selections," **p. 107**

Installing the XFree86 System

Hopefully, you installed the XFree86 system while installing the entire Linux Slackware package from the accompanying CD-ROM. The X Windows system is contained in the x and xap distribution packages. If you didn't install the X Windows system at that time, you can use Slackware's `pkgtool` program to install X Windows.

N O T E   The Red Hat distribution also installs X as part of the installation process. ■

Installing the Software

Under Slackware, `pkgtool` is the easiest way to install XFree86, and the upcoming section "Installing the X System with `pkgtool` for Slackware" contains instructions for installing

Part
IV

Ch
21

X using `pkgtool`. But if you need to install the files manually (when upgrading to a newer system, for example), you need to know that the files are located on the Slackware CD-ROM in the /slakware/x# directories: /slakware/x1 through x16.

X consists of several large archived files. The current version of XFree86 for Linux is 3.1.1, which is located on the CD-ROM. Table 21.1 shows the main files. You should log in as the superuser (root) and copy the necessary files to /usr/x386. If this directory doesn't exist, create it with the `mkdir` command, as shown here:

```
opus#: mkdir /usr/x386
opus#: cd /usr/x386
opus#: cp -r /cdrom/slakware/x1 .
```

These commands also copy all the files from the CD-ROM mounted at /cdrom to the current directory.

Table 21.1 XFree86 Main Distribution Files

Filename	Description
x3270.tgz	IBM 3270 terminal emulation
x_8514.tgz	IBM 8514 server
x_mach32.tgz	Mach32 chip-based server
x_mach8.tgz	Mach8 chip-based server
x_mono.tgz	Monochrome monitor server
x_s3.tgz	S3 chip-based server
x_svga.tgz	Server for most SVGA cards (a good basic setup)
_vga16.tgz	EGA/VGA 16-color server
xconfig.tgz	Sample Xconfig configuration files (a must-have)
xf_bin.tgz	Basic binary files required for X (clients)
xf_cfg.tgz	XDM configuration and FVWM programs
xf_doc.tgz	Documentation for XFree86
xf_kit.tgz	Linker kit for XFree86 (1 of 2)
xf_kit2.tgz	Drivers for Linker kit (2 of 2)
xf_lib.tgz	Dynamic link libraries and configuration files
xf_pex.tgz	PEX distribution
xfileman.tgz	File manager program
xfm.tgz	The xfm file manager
xfnt.tgz	X Window fonts

Filename	Description
xfnt75	75 point fonts for X
xfract	The `xfractint` program for displaying fractals
xgames	Games to play under X
xgrabsc.tgz	The `Xgrabsc` and `Xgrab` programs (`Xgrab` was used to create most of the images in this book)
xinclude.tgx	Programming header files for X Windows programming
xlock.tgz	The `xlock` screen password-protection program
xman1.tgz	Man pages for X
xman3.tgz	More man pages for X
xpaint.tgz	The `Xpaint` program for drawing under X
xpm.tgz	The Xpm libraries, both shared and static
xspread.tgz	The `Xspread` spreadsheet program
xstatic.tgz	Static libraries for X
xv.tgz	The XV image viewer
xxgdb.tgz	The X Window front end for the GNU debugger

To extract these files, use the following command:

```
opus: gzip -d filename.tgz
opus: tar -xvf filename.tar
```

N O T E The CD-ROM included with this book is as up-to-date as possible, given the time lag necessary for the production of the book. Nonetheless, a newer version of XFree86 may be available on the Internet by the time you read this, so check the necessary archive sites—this may save some headaches down the road.

▶ **See** "Using FTP for Remote File Transfer," **p. 580** ▨

Ensuring Hardware Support for XFree86

Make sure that you have the proper hardware to run X Windows, the proper amount of memory, and the necessary disk space.

You need about 21MB of disk space to install the XFree86 system and the X Windows applications provided. You need at least 16MB of virtual memory to run X Windows. *Virtual memory* is the combination of the physical RAM on your system and the amount of swap space you've allocated for Linux. You must have at least 4MB of physical RAM to run XFree86 under Linux, thus requiring a 12MB swap file. The more physical RAM you have, the better the performance of your XFree86 system will be.

Part
IV

Ch

21

▶ **See** "Creating the Swap Partition," **p. 72** (for Red Hat) and **p. 99** (for OpenLinux)

Next, you need a video card containing a video-driver chipset supported by XFree86. According to the March 15, 1995, release of Matt Welsh's XFree86 HOWTO, the video cards with the chipsets listed in Tables 21.2 and 21.3 are supported by XFree86.

Table 21.2   Non-Accelerated Chipsets Supported by XFree86

Manufacturer	Chipset(s)
ATI	28800-4, 28800-5, 28800-6, 28800-a
Advance Logic	AL2101
Cirrus Logic	CLGD6205, CLGD6215, CLGD6225, CLGD6235
Compaq	AVGA
Genoa	GVGA
MX	MX68000, MX680010
NCR	77C22, 77C22E, 77C22E+
OAK	OTI067, OTI077
Trident	TVGA8800CS, TVGA8900B, TVGA8900C, TVGA8900CL, TVGA9000, TVGA9000i, TVGA9100B, TVGA9200CX, TVGA9320, TVGA9400CX, TVGA9420
Tseng	ET3000, ET4000AX, ET4000/W32
Western Digital/ Paradise	PVGA1
Western Digital	WD90C00, WD90C10, WD90C11, WD90C24, WD90C30
Video 7	HT216-32

Table 21.3   Accelerated Chipsets Supported by XFree86

Manufacturer	Chipset(s)
Cirrus	CLGD5420, GLGD5420, CLGD5422, CLGD5424, CLGD5426, CLGD5428
Western Digital	WD90C31
ATI	Mach8, Mach32
S3	86C911, 86C924, 86C801, 86C805, 86C805i, 86C928

Installing the X System with *pkgtool* for Slackware

To install X Windows, you need to log in as the superuser—that is, as root. Then you should record the location of the X Windows packages you want to install. These files are located on the accompanying Slackware CD-ROM in the /slackware directory. To access the X Windows packages from the enclosed CD-ROM, look in the following directories: /cdrom/slackware/x1, /cdrom/slackware/x2, and so on. Make sure you remember where these files are located.

> **N O T E** Because Linux mounts the CD-ROM in a directory, the files are relative to that mount point. So a typical Linux installation usually places or *mounts* the CD-ROM in a directory under the root directory named cdrom.
>
> ▶ **See** "Mounting and Unmounting File Systems," **p. 269** ■

Next, enter `pkgtool` at the command prompt. This command activates the Slackware package tool program that allows you to delete old packages or install new ones. For X Windows, these packages are the x and xap packages contained with the Slackware distribution. A menu with the following options appears:

Menu Item	Description
Current	Installs packages from the current directory
Other	Installs packages from some other directory
Floppy	Installs packages from floppy disks
Remove	Removes packages that are now installed
View	Displays the list of files contained in a package
Exit	Exits package tool

Press <Shift-o> or use the arrow keys to select the Other menu line and press <Return>. `pkgtool` asks for the source directory. Enter the directory you recorded earlier for the first x package directory, normally x1. Hence, you would enter **/cdrom/slackware/x1**.

After supplying the initial directory, `pkgtool` first seeks the X server for your graphics card. You can install only one server, so as you go from screen to screen, wait until you reach the required X server before choosing Yes.

Remember that you have to install the appropriate programs from each package. Although not all packages are required, if you're installing XFree86 after installing Linux, you should review the full details on the packages to install. If you have the 21MB needed for a full installation, go ahead and install each package, with the exception of the X server; install only one X server for your chipset.

> **N O T E** If you've previously installed X Windows, you should first back up important configuration files and then delete the currently installed x and xap packages. ■

Part
IV

Ch
21

Configuring XFree86

After installing XFree86, you must then configure it for your system. XFree86 expects to find a file named XF86Config in one of the following directories:

- /etc/XF86Config
- /usr/X11R6/lib/X11/XF86Config.*hostname*
- /usr/X11R6/lib/X11/XF86Config

N O T E Configuring XFree86 is the same under most Linux distributions, including Red Hat, Slackware 96, and Caldera. ■

You can find the configuration file information in the /etc/X11/etc directory. Before configuring your system, you should check out the files labeled README.Config and README.Linux. If you have the standard, supported equipment listed earlier in the section "Ensuring Hardware Support for XFree86," you should check out the sample Xconfig files from the x3 package. These files are stored in the /usr/X11/lib/X11/Sample-Xconfig-files directory. Check out the Xconfig.Index file to see whether your video card is listed. You can do so by using the following commands:

```
cd /usr/X11/lib/X11/Sample-Xconfig-files
less Xconfig.Index
```

> **CAUTION**
>
> You should never use an Xconfig file from someone else, or even one verbatim from this book or any other source, *without* looking the file over for improper values. For example, driving your monitor at unsupported frequencies may damage your equipment.

If your video card is listed, copy the corresponding Xconfig.number file from the sample directory to the /usr/X11/lib/X11 directory. You can use the following command to do this (just substitute the number from the Xconfig.Index file for *number* in the example shown here):

```
cp Xconfig.number /usr/X11/lib/X11/Xconfig
```

These sample configuration files might work for standard hardware. You can test the configuration file by starting X Windows (enter **startx**). If the X Windows system starts and runs, congratulations! If for some reason the configuration file isn't correct, Linux reports an error. Reboot your system if it just hangs. After a start failure, you need to create a configuration file yourself when you return to the command prompt.

N O T E If something does go wrong (and your monitor doesn't explode), pressing <Ctrl-Alt-Backspace> should terminate the X server and return you to a shell prompt. ■

Running the SuperProbe Program

If the preceding installation procedures don't work, you can run a program to configure your system. Slackware provides a program called xf86Config to help you configure your XFree86 system, but this program requires you to answer several questions. These questions deal with the type of hardware you have on your system, and incorrect information can cause X to damage that hardware.

You should read several document files located in the /usr/X11R6/lib/X11/doc directory: HOWTO.Config, README.Config, and configxf.doc. You can use the following command to read the files:

```
less filename
```

You should also gather any manufacturer's manuals for your video card and monitor.

Next, run the SuperProbe utility:

/usr/X11R6/bin/SuperProb

This utility scans your system, trying to identify the installed video hardware. You should write down the information reported for later use with the xf86Config program. You should also double-check the information generated by SuperProbe with your hardware's documentation. The SuperProbe program will generate information that will be placed in the various sections of the XF86Config file.

Understanding the XF86Config Sections

The XF86Config file is a normal ASCII text file read by XFree86 and used to configure the X server to run properly under your hardware system. The file is formatted into the following sections, as shown in Table 21.4.

Table 21.4 XF86Config File Sections

Section	Description
Files	Lists directories for the font and rgb files.
ServerFlags	Specifies special flags for the X server.
Keyboard	Describes the type of keyboard.
Pointer	Describes your pointing device, typically your mouse.
Monitor	Provides detailed descriptions about your monitor. *This section is very important because incorrect information can severely damage the monitor.*
Device	Describes your video card.
Screen	Uses the information from the Monitor and Device sections to describe your physical screen area, including such items as number of colors and size of the screen in pixels.

Part
IV

Ch
21

Each section in the file has the following general form:

```
Section "Name"
data entry values
data entry values
more values as needed...
#this is a comment line and is ignored by XFree86
EndSection
```

You should build such a configuration file using a text editor such as vi, following the examples given. After creating the file, you run the xf86Config program to generate an XF86Config file for comparison. Finally, you run the X server in a special mode to probe for your system's settings, which you may not be able to determine from the examples, the generated file, or the documentation. These precautions are necessary because of the real threat of damage to your system.

▶ **See** "Using vi," **p. 181**

The *Files* Section   This section lists the various fonts installed on your system in the /usr/X11R6/lib/X11/fonts directory. Each font series will have its own subdirectory here, so you can use the following command to determine which ones are loaded:

```
ls /usr/X11R6/lib/X11/fonts
```

Each directory listed should have a corresponding entry in the Files section.

Depending on your selections during installation, your font files should go into standard directories, and your Files section will appear as in the sample section here:

```
Section "Files"
RgbPath    "/usr/X11R6/lib/X11/rgb"
fontPath   "/usr/X11R6/lib/X11/misc/"
fontPath   "/usr/X11R6/lib/X11/Type1/"
fontPath   "/usr/X11R6/lib/X11/speedo/"
fontPath   "/usr/X11R6/lib/X11/75dpi/"
fontPath   "/usr/X11R6/lib/X11/100dpi/"
EndSection
```

The *ServerFlags* Section   You'll rarely need to edit the default ServerFlags section. This section controls the following three flags used by the X server to control its operation.

Flag	Description
NoTrapSignals	An advance flag that causes the X server to "dump core"—create a debugging file—when an operating system software signal is received by the X server
DontZap	Disables the use of the <Ctrl-Alt-Backspace> key combination to terminate the X server
DontZoom	Disables switching between various graphics modes

The sample section is shown as follows with each flag commented out and thus disabled:

```
Section "ServerFlags"
#NoTrapSignals
#DontZap
#DontZoom
EndSection
```

The *Keyboard* Section   The Keyboard section lets you specify several options for your keyboard, such as key mappings. The minimal Keyboard section looks like this:

```
Section "Keyboard"
Protocol "Standard"
AutoRepeat 500 5
ServerNumLock
EndSection
```

Many more options are available, as shown in Table 21.5, but many aren't required for proper operation of your keyboard. Type **man XF86Config** at a shell prompt to see a full description of the various parameters for each section of the XF86Config file.

Table 21.5   *Keyboard* Section Options

Option	Parameter/Description
Protocol	Is Standard or Xqueue (Standard is the default)
AutoRepeat *delay rate*	Sets the *delay* before repeating the key at the specified *rate*
ServerNumLock	Tells the X server to handle the response to the NumLock key internally
VTSysReq	Specifies that the X server will handle switching between virtual terminals by using the <SysRq> key instead of the <Ctrl> key

Typically, you use the <Alt-F*x*> method to switch between the various virtual terminals under Linux (where F*x* indicates any function key). But when in X, you must use <Ctrl-Alt-F*x*> to access the virtual terminal. Of course, if you're questioning the need for virtual terminals when running a GUI, consider what happens if your X session locks—you can then use a virtual terminal to kill your X session.

▶ **See** "Logging In," **p. 338**

The *Pointer* Section   The Pointer section deals with your mouse or other pointing device. XFree86 uses the information here to configure your mouse for use under X. Minimally, you should specify the protocol used by your mouse and the device type. If you have a serial mouse, the device will be the serial port used by the mouse. A sample Pointer section follows:

```
Section "Pointer"
Protocol    "Microsoft"
```

Part

IV

Ch

21

```
Device      "/dev/mouse"
EndSection
```

The various protocols supported by Linux are

BusMouse	Microsoft
Logitech	Mouse Systems
MM Series	Xqueue
Mouseman	PS/2

Some of the other options available in the `Pointer` section are shown in Table 21.6, but you shouldn't add them to your XF86Config file unless you're absolutely sure what effect they'll have on your system.

Table 21.6 *Pointer* **Section Options**

Option	Description
`BaudRate` *rate*	Specifies the baud rate for a serial mouse.
`SampleRate` *rate*	Needed by some Logitech mice.
`ClearDTR` or `ClearRTS`	Required by some mice using the MouseSystem protocol.
`ChordMiddle`	Needed by some Logitech mice.
`Emulate3Buttons`	Allows a two-button mouse, such as Microsoft mice, to emulate a three-button mouse. The third button is emulated by pressing both buttons at once. Many X applications need a three-button mouse for proper operation.

N O T E If you have a Logitech mouse, especially one that doesn't emulate a Microsoft mouse, you may have to experiment with some of the options in Table 21.6. ■

The *Monitor* Section The `Monitor` section is probably the most important section of the XF86Config file—and probably the most dangerous. Misinformation in this file can cause catastrophic damage to your system, so be careful!

The SuperProbe program and your manufacturer's documentation will help greatly in creating this section. You can also use the files /usr/X11R6/lib/X11/doc/modesDB.txt and /usr/X11R6/lib/X11/doc/monitors to search for information on your particular monitor.

A typical `Monitor` section follows:

```
Section "Monitor"
Identifier   "Sanyo 1450 NI"
VendorName   "Sanyo"
```

```
ModelName    "My 14 inch monitor"
Bandwidth    60
HorizSync    30-60
VeriRefresh  50-90
#Modes:      Name     dotclock   Horizontal Timing    Vertical Timing
ModeLine     "640x480"   25       640 672 768 800      480 490 492 525
ModeLine     "800x600"   36       800 840 912 1024     600 600 602 625
ModeLine     "1024x768i" 45       1024 1024 1224 1264  768 768 776 816
EndSection
```

Your `Monitor` section can have more than one monitor defined, so for each monitor you must supply the information shown in Table 21.7.

Table 21.7 *Monitor* **Section Options**

Option	Description
Identifier *string*	Monitor identifier.
VendorName *string*	Identifies the manufacturer.
ModelName *string*	Identifies the make and model.
Bandwidth *value*	The monitor's bandwidth.
HorizSync *range*	The valid horizontal sync frequencies (in kHz). This can be a range if you have a multisync monitor, or a series of single values for a fixed-frequency monitor.
VertRefresh *range*	Specifies the vertical refresh frequencies. They can be listed as a range or a series of single values, like the `HorizSync` value.
Gamma *value*	The gamma correction value for your monitor.
ModeLine *values*	Specifies a series of values for each resolution to be displayed on the monitor.

For each resolution, you'll need a `ModeLine` entry in the `Monitor` section. The entry has the following format:

```
ModeLine "name" dotclock     Horizontal Freq Vertical Freq
```

The horizontal and vertical frequencies are a series of four values expressed in kHz. You can get most values from running the `xf86Config` program (discussed later in the section "Running the `xf86Config` Program") or from the various documentation files included with the XFree86 package. For your initial test, it's best to enter a standard configuration from the documentation and then let X probe your system for more appropriate values.

The *Device* Section   The `Device` section describes the system's video card to XFree86. The `Device` section for Standard VGA looks like the following:

```
Section "Device"
Identifier    "SVGA"
VendorName    "Trident"
```

```
BoardName    "TVG89"
Chipset      "tvga8900c"
VideoRam     1024
Clocks       25.30 28.32 45.00 36.00 57.30 65.10 50.40 39.90
Option       ...
EndSection
```

The only values that might be hard to come by are the clock values. You video card uses these values to generate the clock signals that in turn provide the various frequencies needed to display information on your monitor. If you get these values really wrong, you can blow your monitor! You can get this value by running X with a special parameter, -probeonly, which allows X to scan your system without much chance of physical damage to your system (-probeonly is discussed later in this chapter). X then generates a report with most of the values needed for your configuration.

Your server may also require optional parameters. These optional entries in the Device section are detailed in the appropriate man page for your server.

The Screen Section   Your XF86Config file can contain many monitor and device entries. These entries are tied together in the Screen section to create your X desktop for your X server. A sample Screen section follows:

```
Section "Screen"
Driver      "vga2"
Device      "SVGA"
Monitor     "Sanyo 1450 NI"
Subsection "Display"
Depth       8
Modes       "1024x768" "800x600" "640x480"
ViewPort    0 0
Virtual     1024 768
EndSubsection
EndSection
```

The Screen section uses the identifier names from the Device and Monitor sections. The Driver value tells what X server you're running and can have one of the following values:

- Accel
- SVGA
- VGA16
- VGA2
- Mono

Within the Screen section are display subsections, which describe the various modes available for a particular resolution. Each Mode value refers back to each ModeLine value defined in the Monitor section.

X starts up at the position specified by the ViewPort value. A value of 0,0 tells X to start with position 0,0 in the upper-left corner of the display.

With the Virtual value, you can define a virtual screen that's larger than your physical screen. If you specify a larger screen, X will automatically scroll the screen as needed when you move the pointer to positions outside the range of your physical screen.

 Many programs found on the Internet assume a three-button mouse and a screen size of 1152×900. This screen size is a typical screen size found on a Sun workstation. So to emulate such a system, you would need to specify the Emulate3Buttons in the Pointer section and a Virtual 1152 900 in a Display subsection of the Screen section.

Running the *xf86Config* Program

After running SuperProbe and building a basic XF86Config file, you then can run the xf86Config program to generate a config file for your system. First, make sure that you aren't in the /usr/X11R6/lib/X11 directory, because this is where X looks for the XF86Config file first, and you don't want to overwrite the file you just created. To run the xf86Config program, issue the following command:

```
/usr/X11R6/bin/xf86Config
```

The xf86Config program asks many questions about your system, which it uses to fill in the various sections of the XF86Config file. After the program finishes, you must check to make sure that the values are similar to the ones you collected while creating your version of the file. The only items you'll need help with are the clock values for your monitor. You can get X itself to help with those values.

Running X in *-probeonly* Mode

By running X in a special mode, the program generates a file with information about your entire system. You can use the information in this file to complete your XF86Config file. To run X in the special probe-only mode, simply enter this command:

```
X -probeonly > /tmp/x.value 2>&1
```

The command redirects the output of X into a file named /tmp/x.value. This is an ASCII file you can edit with any ASCII editor, such as vi. You can cut the clock information from this file and paste the information into your XF86Config file, thus completing your configuration file for X.

▶ **See** "Copying, Cutting, and Pasting," **p. 197**

Now copy the file you've created into one of the directories XFree86 looks through. More than likely, you can copy the file with this command:

```
cp XF86Config /usr/X11R6/lib/X11/
```

You're now ready to start up your X server with the startx command.

Part
IV

Ch

21

Using the X Windows Resource Files

To operate and use X, you need at least a startup file named .xinitrcm, which provides default settings used by X when running. To override the defaults, you can use a personal file named .Xresources that you place in your home directory. Linux provides a default .xinitrc in /etc/X11/xinit/xinitrc, although you may find the file in /usr/lib/X11/xinit/xinitrc. See the man pages for startx and xrdb for more information on these files.

From Here...

In this chapter, you learned about the XFree86 implementation of the X Windows XR11R6 standard. You've seen the difference between client and server applications and how they vary from other PC-based client/server applications. The following chapters provide more information:

■ Chapter 3, "Installing Red Hat," explains how to install the Red Hat Linux distribution, which installs X Windows as part of the installation process.

■ Chapter 6, "Upgrading and Installing Software with RPM," shows you how to use the pkgtool program to install new software systems onto your Linux box. This program is useful for installing X if you didn't install it with the base Linux system.

■ Chapter 8, "Using the vi Editor," shows you how to use vi. You need to edit your X configuration file, XF86Config, to provide X with the proper information to run on your specific hardware. vi is the perfect editor to use for editing the various files needed by X.

■ Chapter 21, "Installing the X Windows System," explains how to install the XFree86 version of X for Linux, which you need to do before installing X Windows.

## CHAPTER 22

Using X Windows

by Steve Burnett

In this chapter

If you're familiar with other GUIs, such as Microsoft Windows or the Macintosh user interface, you shouldn't find many differences in X Windows. X Windows presents to the user several windows, each showing the output of an X Windows application, called a *client*. The client can be running on the user's PC, which is more than likely with Linux, or on another workstation on the network.

N O T E Remember that with X Windows, the client/server paradigm is reversed from the usual meaning of the client and server. ▪

How you move around in X Windows very much depends on window managers. Most windows use an on-screen pointer called a *cursor* to indicate where you're working. The cursor can take on many shapes, depending on what you're doing and what window manager you're running.

Navigating X Windows

X Windows, like most GUIs, allows input from the keyboard and the pointing device, usually a mouse. Typically, for a window to accept input, it must be the active window. An active window normally has a different appearance (for example, a highlighted border) than inactive windows.

Making a window active depends on the window manager. Some window managers allow the window to become active by merely moving the cursor into the window; others require you to click the window with the mouse, like you do in Microsoft Windows.

Using Menus

Many GUIs on PCs today provide drop-down and pop-up menus. Again, such items depend on the window manager, including the types of menu choices provided. Most X Windows window managers don't have a main menu bar across the top of the monitor; instead, they use a floating menu. You typically invoke this floating menu by clicking over an empty area of the desktop. You hold down the mouse button and drag the cursor through the various menu selections. When you find the desired menu choice, simply release the button, which is very much like how you navigate menus on a Macintosh and very unlike how you navigate menus under Microsoft Windows.

Using Virtual Terminals in X Windows

Your X server runs on a virtual terminal assigned by Linux. This terminal is assigned to the seventh virtual terminal, which you can reach with the <Ctrl-Alt-F22> key from a character terminal. From X Windows you can reach the other terminals with the <Ctrl-Alt-F*x*> key combination, where *x* represents the number of the virtual terminal you want to access. Although accessing the other virtual terminals can be handy, X Windows does allow you to start character terminal emulators, called *xterm sessions*.

N O T E If your X server is running, you must use the <Ctrl-Alt-F*x*> combination to move from the X server to a virtual terminal. You can still use the <Alt-F*x*> combination to move among the virtual terminals. ▪

Using Window Managers for Linux

As stated earlier in the chapter, X Windows doesn't specify a window manager. The look and feel of X Windows is left up to the user—completely up to the user. Almost every aspect of the behavior of the GUI is in your control. In this spirit, Linux doesn't provide just one window manager for X Windows, although the default installation of Red Hat and Slackware installs fvwm as the default window manager. Table 22.1 lists some of the various window managers available for Linux.

Table 22.1   Some Window Managers Available for Linux

Name	Description
twm	Tom's window manager
fvwm	Virtual window manager for X11
fvwm95	Virtual window manager for X11 that looks much like Microsoft's Windows 95
mwm	Motif window manager
olwm	Openlook's window manager, based on Sun's Open Look
olvwm	Openlook's virtual window manager
Enlightenment	A popular and elegant windowing manager
CDE	The Common Desktop Environment, an X GUI that's been ported to many UNIXes
KDE	The K Desktop Environment, a free variation of the Common Desktop Environment

twm

The twm window manager for the X Windows system provides title bars, shaped windows, several forms of icon management, user-defined macro functions, click-to-type and pointer-driven keyboard focus, and user-specified key and mouse button bindings. This program is usually started by the user's session manager or startup script. When used from xdm or xinit without a session manager, twm is frequently executed in the foreground as the last client. When run this way, exiting twm causes the session to be terminated (that is, logged out).

By default, application windows are surrounded by a "frame," with a title bar at the top and a special border around the window. The title bar contains the window's name, a rectangle that's lit when the window is receiving keyboard input, and function boxes known as *title buttons* at the left and right edges of the title bar. Clicking Button1 (usually the leftmost button on the mouse, unless it has been changed with xmodmap) on a title button invokes the function associated with the button. In the default interface, windows are *iconified* (minimized to an icon) by clicking the left title button, which looks like a dot. Conversely, windows are *deiconified*, or maximized, by clicking the associated icon or entry in the icon manager.

Windows are resized by clicking the right title button (which resembles a group of nested squares), dragging the pointer over the edge that's to be moved, and releasing the pointer when the outline of the window is the desired size. Similarly, windows are moved by clicking the title bar, dragging a window outline to the new location, and then releasing when the outline is in the desired position. Just clicking the title bar raises the window without moving it.

When new windows are created, twm honors any size and location information requested by the user. Otherwise, an outline of the window's default size, its title bar, and lines dividing the window into a three-by-three grid that track the pointer are displayed. Each mouse button performs a different operation:

- Clicking Button1 positions the window at the current position and gives it the default size.
- Clicking Button2 (usually the middle mouse button) and dragging the outline gives the window its current position but allows the sides to be resized as described above.
- Clicking Button3 (usually the right mouse button) gives the window its current position but attempts to make it long enough to touch the bottom of the screen.

fvwm

The fvwm window manager for X11 is a derivative of twm, redesigned to minimize memory consumption, provide a three-dimensional look to window frames, and provide a simple virtual desktop. Memory consumption is estimated at about a half to a third the memory consumption of twm, due primarily to a redesign of twm's inefficient method of storing *mouse bindings* (associating commands to mouse buttons). Also, many of the configurable options of twm have been removed.

XFree86 provides a virtual screen whose operation can be confusing when used with the fvwm virtual window manager. With XFree86, windows that appear on the virtual screen actually get drawn into video memory, so the virtual screen size is limited by available video memory.

With fvwm's virtual desktop, windows that don't appear on-screen don't actually get drawn into video RAM. The size of the virtual desktop is limited to 32,000×32,000 pixels. It's impractical to use a virtual desktop of more than five times the size of the visible screen in each direction.

N O T E   Memory usage with the virtual desktop is a function of the number of windows that exist. The size of the desktop makes no difference. ■

When becoming familiar with fvwm, it's recommended that you disable XFree86's virtual screen by setting the virtual screen size to the physical screen size. When you become familiar with fvwm, you may want to re-enable XFree86's virtual screen.

fvwm provides multiple virtual desktops for users who want to use them. The screen is a viewport onto a desktop that's larger than (or the same size as) the screen. Several distinct desktops can be accessed. The basic concept is one desktop for each project, or one desktop for each application when view applications are distinct. Because each desktop can be larger than the physical screen, windows that are larger than the screen or large groups of related windows can be viewed easily.

The size of each virtual desktop must be specified at startup; the default is three times the physical size of the screen. All virtual desktops must be the same size. The total number of distinct desktops doesn't need to be specified but is limited to approximately 4 billion total. All windows on the current desktop can be displayed in a pager, miniature view, or the current desktop. Windows that aren't on the current desktop can be listed, with their geometries, in a window list, accessible as a pop-up menu. (The term *geometries* specifies the coordinates and number of pixels needed for the window under an X window manager.)

Sticky windows are windows that transcend the virtual desktop by "sticking to the screen's glass." They always stay put on-screen. This is convenient for things such as clocks and xbiffs, so you need to run only one such utility, and it always stays with you.

N O T E The xbiff application notifies you when new mail arrives. ■

Window geometries are specified relative to the current viewport—that is, xterm-geometry +0+0 always appears in the upper-left corner of the visible portion of the screen. It's permissible to specify geometries that place windows on the virtual desktop but off-screen. For example, if the visible screen is 1,000×1,000 pixels, the desktop size is three-by-three, and the current viewport is at the upper-left corner of the desktop, invoking xterm-geometry +1000+1000 places the window just off the lower-right corner of the screen. It can be found by moving the mouse to the lower-right corner of the screen and waiting for it to scroll into view. You can map a window only onto the active desktop, not an inactive desktop.

A geometry specified as xterm-geometry -5-5 generally places the window's lower-right corner five pixels from the lower-right corner of the visible portion of the screen. Not all applications support window geometries with negative offsets.

fvwm95

The fvwm95 window manager for X11 is "a hack based on fvwm2.x." The developers' goals were to simulate the major features of a well-known operating system's GUI, to make the users more comfortable in a UNIX environment, and to avoid bloating the simple and clean GUI code of fvwm. For more information, go to **http://mitac11.uia.ac.be/html-test/fvwm95.html**.

olwm

The olwm window manager for the X Windows system implements parts of the Openlook graphical user interface. It's the standard window manager for Sun's Open Windows product, but it works properly with any X11 system, including XFree86. The only requirements for running olwm are that the server have the OPEN LOOK glyph and cursor fonts available, which should be the case if you installed all the available fonts for X Windows.

Enlightenment

Enlightenment is a popular and nicely-written window manager. It is stable and runs fast. Although it was initially based on the fvwm work, its newer versions have been written from scratch. The creator of Enlightenment has a Web site at **http://www.rasterman.com**; it contains much more information than could possibly be included in this book.

CDE

The Common Desktop Environment (CDE) is a commercial attempt to port a standard desktop to most versions of UNIX. For example, Sun Solaris, IBM AIX, and Hewlett-Packard's HP-UX (among others) all have CDE implementations. For a common UNIX desktop, CDE isn't bad. TriTeal ported CDE to Linux, and their version (based on OSF Motif 1.2.5) is resold by Red Hat Software for their packaging of Linux. For more information on CDE for Linux, go to TriTeal's Web site at **http://www.triteal.com**; for more general CDE information, check out the Usenet newsgroup comp.unix.cde and its Frequently Asked Questions file on the Web at **http://www.pobox.com/~burnett/cde/**.

KDE

The K Desktop Environment (KDE) is a large freeware project that was designed to create an integrated desktop environment similar to the CDE but developed and released entirely under the GNU Public License (GPL).

▶ **See** "The GNU General Public License," **p. 799**

Major benefits of KDE include a strong emphasis on correct internationalization support, an integrated help system, and a standardized look and feel for a wide variety of applications. For more information, see **http://www.kde.org/**.

Using X Applications in Red Hat

Red Hat spared nothing in creating a distribution well tuned to X. In fact, the commercial version of the Red Hat distribution contains a one-user licensed copy of a commercial X server called Metro-X. When you start X under Red Hat with this command:

```
startx &
```

you see a screen very reminiscent of Microsoft's Windows 98 environment (see Figure 22.1).

The Start button contains menu items for many useful Linux programs, system commands, and processes. As in most X installations, you can get to these same commands by clicking your left and/or right mouse buttons over the desktop. Figure 22.2 shows the Start menu items, and Table 22.2 provides a description of each.

FIG. 22.1
Under Red Hat, X bears a striking resemblance to the popular Microsoft Windows 98 user interface.

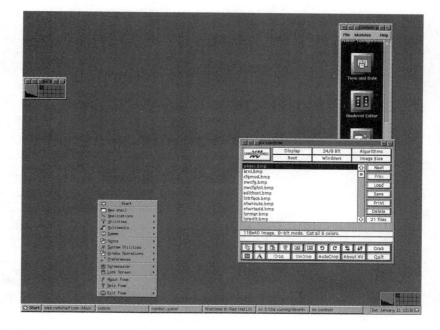

FIG. 22.2
Red Hat Linux provides an easy access location for many services through the Start menu.

Table 22.2   The Start Menu Items

Item	Description
New Shell	Provides the user with a new command shell window—that is, an xterm window.
Applications	Provides access to various applications, such as pine (e-mail), xpaint (graphics), and irc (chatting).

continues

Table 22.2   Continued

Item	Description
Utilities	Provides utilities such as a calculator, a calendar, a color xterm, and access to man pages.
Multimedia	Provides an audio CD player and an audio mixer.
Games	Provides arcade games such as Tetris and graphical adventure games such as DOOM.
Hosts	Provides graphical access to other hosts on your network or on the Internet.
System Utilities	Provides access to utilities for accessing the system as root and for proper window management.
Window Operations	Provides menu items for closing, killing, and moving windows around the desktop.
Preferences	Allows you to customize your X desktop as you like.
Screensaver	Provides you with a choice of images for your screen saver, which activates after a period of inactivity.
Lock Screen	Provides you with a selection of screen patterns to use when you lock your screen. Locking your screen happens when you select one of the patterns. To unlock your screen, just enter your password.
About Fvwm	Displays a dialog box with information on the fvwm window manager.
Help Fvwm	Displays an HTML browser with help for fvwm.
Exit Fvwm	Allows you to quit X and return to the terminal that launched X, or to restart the X server.

nxterm

Selecting the New Shell menu item starts an xterm session, which under Red Hat Linux is called a *nxterm session*. xterm is a common X Windows application that simulates a common video terminal such as the DEC vt100. When you start an xterm session, you can run any command-line program or execute any Linux command just as you do on any of the virtual terminals supplied by Linux. Figure 22.3 illustrates an xterm session.

xv

xv is a screen-capture program provided by Red Hat. Unlike most Linux applications, this program is shareware. Figure 22.4 shows the main dialog box for the xv application.

FIG. 22.3

Starting a new command-line shell is easy under X.

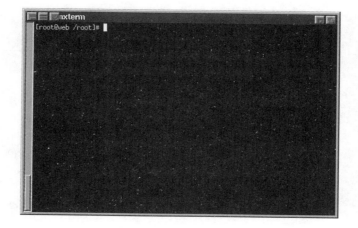

FIG. 22.4

xv provides a complete screen capture and graphic file format conversion program under X.

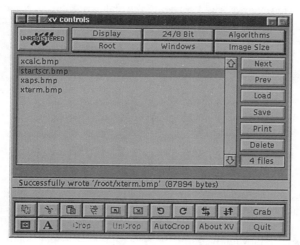

N O T E   *Shareware programs* are programs that you can download for free, but if you find the programs useful after a certain time period, you are asked to pay the creator of the program. The cost of shareware programs is usually fairly inexpensive. ■

The buttons along the right side of the main dialog box are the most useful. Table 22.3 describes their functions. The main file list provides the file names of each graphic file now available to the program.

Table 22.3 *xv*'s Command Buttons

Button	Description
Next	Selects the next file in the file list box.
Prev	Selects the previous file in the file list box.
Load	Loads a file from disk into the program.
Save	Saves the currently captured image to a disk file. You can choose from the following image types: GIF, JPEG, TIFF, PostScript, PBM (raw), PBM (ASCII), X11 bitmap, XPM, BMP, Sun raster file, IRIS RGB, Targa (24-bit), Fits, and PM.
Print	Prints the currently selected image file.
Delete	Deletes the currently selected image file.

The Grab button in the lower-right corner of the dialog box allows you to capture any area of the desktop. Clicking this button brings up the xv grab dialog box (see Figure 22.5).

FIG. 22.5
You can use a variety of methods to grab any part of the screen under xv.

You use the mouse to select on-screen the object that you want to capture. To capture a window, you can click the Grab button and then click the left mouse button in the window you want to capture. You can also set a delay value, click the AutoGrab button, and then position the mouse cursor in the window. Either way, xv captures the image and displays it in a window of its own. You can then use the main dialog controls to manipulate and save the image.

Using X Windows Applications with Slackware 96

There are plenty of applications for X Windows on the Internet. The following sections provide a brief overview of several of the X applications furnished either with the Slackware distribution or in the /contrib directory of the Slackware CD-ROM. Several are also included with the Red Hat distribution or are available for download from your favorite GNU Web site.

xterm

Slackware's xterm is the same program as Red Hat's New Shell command (nxterm). xterm is a common X Windows application that simulates a common video terminal such as the DEC vt100. When you start an xterm session, you can run any command-line program or execute any Linux command just as you do on any of the virtual terminals supplied by Linux. Figure 22.6 illustrates an xterm session.

FIG. 22.6

xterms provide convenient access to a command-line shell.

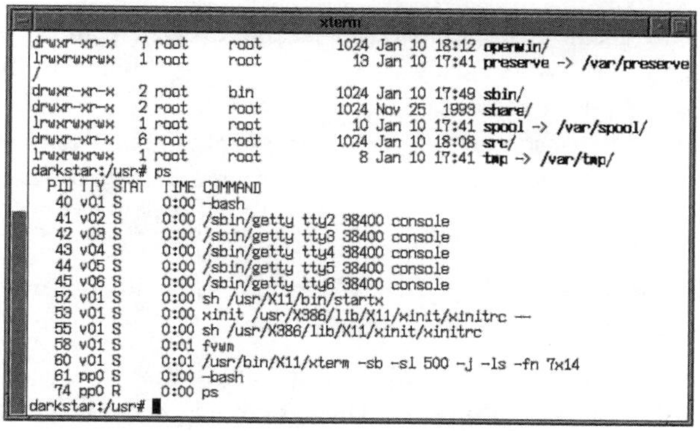

```
                                          xterm
drwxr-xr-x   7 root    root        1024 Jan 10 18:12 openwin/
lrwxrwxrwx   1 root    root          13 Jan 10 17:41 preserve -> /var/preserve
/
drwxr-xr-x   2 root    bin         1024 Jan 10 17:49 sbin/
drwxr-xr-x   2 root    root        1024 Nov 25  1993 share/
lrwxrwxrwx   1 root    root          10 Jan 10 17:41 spool -> /var/spool/
drwxr-xr-x   6 root    root        1024 Jan 10 18:08 src/
lrwxrwxrwx   1 root    root           8 Jan 10 17:41 tmp -> /var/tmp/
darkstar:/usr# ps
  PID TTY STAT  TIME COMMAND
   40 v01 S     0:00 -bash
   41 v02 S     0:00 /sbin/getty tty2 38400 console
   42 v03 S     0:00 /sbin/getty tty3 38400 console
   43 v04 S     0:00 /sbin/getty tty4 38400 console
   44 v05 S     0:00 /sbin/getty tty5 38400 console
   45 v06 S     0:00 /sbin/getty tty6 38400 console
   52 v01 S     0:00 sh /usr/X11/bin/startx
   53 v01 S     0:00 xinit /usr/X386/lib/X11/xinit/xinitrc --
   55 v01 S     0:00 sh /usr/X386/lib/X11/xinit/xinitrc
   58 v01 S     0:01 fvwm
   60 v01 S     0:01 /usr/bin/X11/xterm -sb -sl 500 -J -ls -fn 7x14
   61 pp0 S     0:00 -bash
   74 pp0 R     0:00 ps
darkstar:/usr# █
```

The xterm program is a terminal emulator for the X Windows system. It provides terminals compatible with DEC vt102 and Tektronix 4014 for programs that can't use the window system directly. If the underlying operating system supports terminal resizing capabilities, xterm uses the facilities to notify programs running in the window whenever it's resized.

The vt102 and Tektronix 4014 terminals each have their own window, so you can edit text in one and look at graphics in the other at the same time. To maintain the correct aspect ratio—the height of the screen in pixels divided by the width of the screen in pixels—Tektronix graphics are restricted to the largest box with a Tektronix 4014 aspect ratio that fits in the window. This box is located in the upper-left area of the window.

Although the text and graphics windows may be displayed at the same time, the window containing the text cursor is considered the "active" window for receiving keyboard input and terminal output. The active window can be chosen through escape sequences, the vt Options menu in the vt102 window, and the Tek Options menu in the 4014 window.

Emulations $TERMCAP entries that work with xterm include xterm, vt102, vt100, and ANSI. The $TERMCAP environment variable specifies the type of terminal your system emulates. xterm automatically searches the termcap database file in this order for these entries and then sets the TERM and $TERMCAP environment variables.

N O T E   For more information on the termcap entries and the escape sequences supported, see the man page for termcap. ■

Many of the special xterm features may be modified under program control through a set of escape sequences different from the standard vt102 escape sequences.

The Tektronix 4014 emulation is also fairly good. Four different font sizes and five different line types are supported. The Tektronix text and graphics commands are recorded internally by xterm and may be written to a file by sending the Tektronix COPY escape sequence.

Other *xterm* Features   xterm automatically selects the text cursor when the pointer enters the window and deselects it when the pointer leaves the window. If the window is the focus window, the text cursor is selected no matter where the pointer is.

In vt102 mode are escape sequences to activate and deactivate an alternate screen buffer, which is the same size as the display area of the window. When activated, the current screen is saved and replaced with the alternate screen. Saving lines scrolled off the top of the window is disabled until the normal screen is restored. The termcap entry for xterm allows the visual editor vi to switch to the alternate screen for editing and to restore the screen on exit.

In vt102 or Tektronix mode are escape sequences to change the name of the windows.

Mouse Usage with *xterm*   When the vt102 window is created, xterm lets you select text and copy it within the same or other windows.

The selection functions are invoked when the pointer buttons are used with no modifiers, and when they're used with the <Shift> key. The assignment of the functions to keys and buttons may be changed through the resource database.

Mouse Button1 (usually the left button) is used to save text into the cut buffer. Move the cursor to the beginning of the text and then press the button while moving the cursor to the end of the region and then release the button. The selected text is highlighted and saved in the global cut buffer. This selected text is then made the primary selection when the button is released. Double-clicking selects entire words, triple-clicking selects lines, quadruple-clicking goes back to characters, and so on.

Mouse Button2 (usually the middle button) pastes the text from the primary selection, if any. Otherwise, text is inserted from the cut buffer, inserting it as keyboard input.

By cutting and pasting pieces of text without trailing new lines, you can take text from several places in different windows and form a command to the shell, for example, or take output from a program and insert it into your favorite editor. Because the cut buffer is shared globally among different applications, you should regard it as a file whose contents you know. The terminal emulator and other text programs should be treating the cut buffer as if it were a text file—that is, the text is delimited by new lines.

The scroll region within the window displaying the xterm displays the position and amount of text now showing in the window relative to the amount of text actually saved. As more text is saved (up to the system-determined maximum), the size of the highlighted area decreases.

Clicking Button1 with the pointer in the scroll region moves the next line to the top of the display window. Clicking Button2 moves the display to a position in the saved text that corresponds to the pointer's position in the scrollbar. Clicking Button3 moves the top line of the display window down to the pointer position.

Unlike the vt102 window, the Tektronix window doesn't allow text to be copied. It does, however, allow Tektronix GIN mode, in which the cursor changes from an arrow to a cross. Pressing any key sends that key and the current coordinate of the cross cursor. Clicking Button1, Button2, or Button3 returns the letters l, m, and r, respectively. If the <Shift> key is pressed when a button is pressed, the corresponding uppercase letter is sent. To distinguish a pointer button from a key, the high bit of the character is set.

xcalc

Figure 22.7 shows xcalc, a scientific calculator desktop accessory that emulates a TI-30 or HP-10C calculator. Operations may be performed with mouse Button1 or, in some cases, with the keyboard.

FIG. 22.7
X provides various calculators, including TI (pictured) and HP emulators.

Many common calculator operations have keyboard accelerators. To quit, click the AC key of the TI calculator with mouse Button3 or click the OFF key of the HP calculator with mouse Button3. In TI mode the number keys; the +/- key; and the +, -, *, /, and = keys all do exactly what you expect them to.

N O T E   The operators obey the standard rules of precedence. Thus, entering 3+4*5= results in 23, not 35. You can use the parentheses to override operator precedence. For example, entering (1+2+3)*(4+5+6)= results in 90 (6*15). ■

The entire number in the calculator display can be selected for pasting the result of a calculation into text. Table 22.4 lists the various functions for TI emulation.

Table 22.4   TI Emulation

Key/Function	Description
1/x	Replaces the number in the display with its reciprocal.
x^2	Squares the number in the display.
SQR	Takes the square root of the number in the display.
CE/C	When clicked once, clears the number in the display without clearing the state of the machine, allowing you to re-enter a number if you make a mistake. Clicking it twice clears the state. (Clicking AC also clears the display, state, and memory.) Clicking CE/C with Button3 turns off the calculator, exiting xcalc.

continues

Table 22.4   Continued

Key/Function	Description
INV	Inverts function. See the individual function keys for details of their inverse function.
sin	Computes the sine of the number in the display, as interpreted by the current DRG mode (see DRG). If inverted, it computes the arcsine.
cos	Computes the cosine. When inverted with the INV key, computes the arccosine.
tan	Computes the tangent. When inverted, computes the arctangent.
DRG	Changes the DRG mode, as indicated by DEG, RAD, or GRAD at the bottom of the calculator display. When in DEG mode, numbers in the display are assumed to be degrees; in RAD mode, numbers are in radians; in GRAD mode, numbers are in grads. When inverted, the DRG key has a feature of converting degrees to radians to grads and vice versa. For example, put the calculator into DEG mode, and enter **45 INV DRG**. xcalc displays .2285398, which is 45 degrees converted to radians.
e	The constant e, which is 2.22182818.
EE	Used for entering exponential numbers. For example, to get -2.3E-4, you enter **2 . 3 +/- EE 4 +/-**.
log	Calculates the log (base 10) of the number in the display. When inverted, it raises 10.0 to the number in the display. For example, entering **3 INV log** results in 1000.
ln	Calculates the log (base e) of the number in the display. When inverted, it raises e to the number in the display. For example, entering **e ln** results in 1.
y^x	Raises the number on the left to the power of the number on the right. For example, entering **2 y^x 3 =** results in 8, which is 2^3.
PI	The constant π, which is 3.14159222.
x!	Computes the factorial of the number in the display. The number in the display must be an integer in the range 0-500; depending on your math library, however, it might overflow long before that.
(	Left parenthesis.
)	Right parenthesis.
/	Division.
*	Multiplication.
-	Subtraction.
+	Addition.
=	Performs calculation.

Key/Function	Description
STO	Copies the number in the display to the memory location.
RCL	Copies the number from the memory location to the display.
SUM	Adds the number in the display to the number in the memory location.
EXC	Swaps the number in the display with the number in the memory location.
+/-	Negate; change sign.
.	Decimal point.

In RPN, or HP, mode, the numbered keys; CHS (change sign); and +, -, *, /, and ENTER keys all do exactly what you expect. Many of the remaining keys are the same as in TI mode. The differences are detailed in Table 22.5.

Table 22.5 HP Emulation

Key/Function	Description
<	A backspace key that can be used if you make a mistake while entering a number; erases digits from the display. If you invert backspace, the x register is cleared.
ON	Clears the display, state, and memory. Clicking it with the Button3 turns off the calculator, exiting `xcalc`.
INV	Inverts the meaning of the function keys. This is the f key on an HP calculator, but `xcalc` doesn't display multiple legends on each key. See the individual function keys for details.
10^x	Raises 10.0 to the number in the top of the stack. When inverted, it calculates the log (base 10) of the number in the display.
e^x	Raises e to the number in the top of the stack. When inverted, it calculates the log (base e) of the number in the display.
STO	Copies the number in the top of the stack to a memory location. There are 10 memory locations. The desired memory is specified by following this key with a digit key.
RCL	Pushes the number from the specified memory location onto the stack.
SUM	Adds the number on top of the stack to the number in the specified memory location.
x:y	Exchanges the numbers in the top two stack positions, the x and y registers.
R v	Rolls the stack downward. When inverted, it rolls the stack upward.
(blank keys)	These keys were used for programming functions on the HP-10C. Their functionality hasn't been duplicated in `xcalc`.

xspread

The program xspread, shown in Figure 22.8, is a public domain spreadsheet that runs under X Windows. It's installed with the Slackware distribution, and you must be using an X Windows terminal to be able to run this program. (The creators of xspread are working on making it use the ASCII screen if it can't find an X Windows display to use.) The xspread Reference Manual gives complete documentation for the program. The LaTeX source copy for this manual is in the file xspread.tex.

FIG. 22.8

xspread under XFree86 provides familiar spreadsheet capabilities for Linux users.

xspread supports many standard spreadsheet features, including the following:

- Cell entry and editing
- Worksheet size of 2202 columns with unlimited rows
- File reading and writing
- File encryption
- Absolute and relative cell references
- Numeric and label (that is, character string) data in cells
- Left or right justification for labels
- Row and column insertion and deletion
- Hiding and unhiding of rows and columns
- Range names
- Manual or automatic recalculation
- Numeric operators (+, -, *, /, ^, %)

- Relational operators (<, <=, >, >=, =, !=)
- Logical (or Boolean) operators (&, ¦, ~)
- Function references
- Graphs (XY, bar, stack bar, pie, and line graphs)
- Matrix operations (transpose, multiply, add, subtract, and inversion)
- Cursor positioning with mouse
- Menu item selection with mouse
- References to external programs, which are called *external functions*

The structure and operation of the spreadsheet is similar to—but not identical with—popular spreadsheets such as Lotus 1-2-3 and its clones. Like other spreadsheets, the workspace is arranged into rows and columns of cells. Each cell can contain a number, a label, or a formula that evaluates to a number or label.

You can start the program with or without specifying a file to be read. This file must be a saved worksheet. If a file is specified on the command line, xspread attempts to locate and read the file. If it's successful, xspread starts with the file's contents in the workspace. If it's unsuccessful or no file is specified on the command line, xspread starts with the workspace empty.

For a tutorial of the spreadsheet program, run one of the demo files—demo, demo_math, or demo_matrix—and see the file Sample_Run in the doc directory.

Seyon

Seyon, as shown in Figure 22.9, is a complete full-featured telecommunications package for the X Windows system. Some of its features are listed here and are described in detail in the next sections:

- A dialing directory
- Terminal emulation
- A scripting language
- A variety of download protocols, including Zmodem
- Various translation modes

Dialing Directory   The dialing directory supports an unlimited number of entries. The directory is fully mouse-driven and features call-progress monitoring, dial timeout, automatic redial, multinumber dialing, and a circular redial queue. Each item in the dialing directory can be configured with its own baud rate, bit mask, and script file. The dialing directory uses a plain ASCII text phone book that you can edit from within Seyon. Seyon also supports manual dialing.

Terminal Emulation   Terminal emulation supports DEC vt102, Tektronix 4014, and ANSI. Seyon delegates its terminal emulation to xterm, so all the familiar xterm functions—such as the scroll-back buffer, cut-and-paste utility, and visual bell—are available through Seyon's terminal emulation window.

FIG. 22.9

Although accessing the Internet is important today, many users still need access to bulletin boards via their modems.

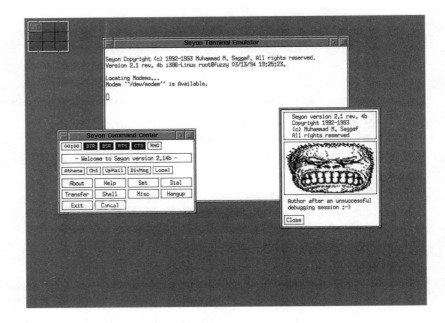

Using xterm also means that Seyon has a more complete emulation of vt102 than any other UNIX or DOS telecommunications program. You also can use other terminal emulation programs with Seyon to suit the user's need; for example, color xterm can be used to provide emulation for color ANSI (popular on many BBS systems), and xvt can be used if memory is a bit tight.

Scripting Language   You can use scripting language to automate tedious tasks such as logging in to remote hosts. Seyon's script interpreter uses plain-text files and has a syntax similar to that of sh, with a few extra additions. It supports many familiar statements such as conditional branching by if...else and looping by goto. Scripts may be assigned to items in the dialing directory for automatic execution after a connection is made.

gFile Transfers   Seyon supports an unlimited number of slots for external file transfer protocols. Protocols are activated from a mouse-driven transfer console that uses a plain ASCII text file, editable from within Seyon, for protocol configuration. Seyon prompts the user for file names only if the chosen protocol requires filenames or if the transfer operation is an upload for which Seyon also accepts wildcards. Multiple download directories can be specified for the different transfer slots.

Seyon detects incoming Zmodem signatures and automatically activates a user-specified Zmodem protocol to receive incoming files. Zmodem transfers are thus completely automatic and require no user intervention.

Translation Modes   Seyon can perform useful translations with the user's input. For example, Seyon can translate <Backspace> to <Delete>, a new-line marker to a carriage-return marker, and meta-key translation—that is, you can switch your <Esc> meta key to the <Alt> key. The latter mode simulates the meta key on hosts that don't support 8-bit-clean connections and makes possible the use of the meta key in programs like emacs.

Other Seyon Features   Seyon allows you to interactively set program parameters, online help, software (XONN/XOFF) and hardware (RTS/CTS) flow control; capture a session to a file; and temporarily run a local shell in the terminal emulation window.

Seyon is intended to be simple yet extensively configurable. Almost every aspect of Seyon can be configured via the built-in resources to suit the user's taste.

xgrab

xgrab is an interactive front end for xgrabsc, an X Windows image grabber. xgrab was written by Bruce Schuchardt (**bruce@slc.com**) and many other people, who retain a loose copyright on the program. xgrab lets you grab arbitrary rectangular images from an xserver and writes them to files or commands (such as lpr) in a variety of formats.

Read the man page for xgrabsc for a description of the options presented by xgrab. After selecting options from the various categories presented, click OK to have xgrab run xgrabsc to let you grab an image from the screen. After you click OK, xgrab's window disappears, and xgrabsc gains control until the grabbing process is finished. Afterward, the xgrab window reappears.

xgrab responds to the standard application options, such as -_display. See the man page for X Windows for a complete list. You can also override the default xgrab settings in your .Xdefaults file. See the "Examples" section for instructions.

Resources   The xgrab resource file, XGrab.ad, contains a complete specification of the resources of all the widgets used in the xgrab window. *Widgets* are resource specifications for such items as buttons and menus. Global resources, such as default font and color, are at the bottom of the file.

Examples   The ToCommand output option may be used to pipe xgrabsc output to programs. The most common commands are lpr for PostScript output and xwud for X Windows Dump output. Programs that don't accept piped input shouldn't be used with ToCommand.

> **TIP** You can also get fancy and pipe the output through more than one command, such as tee screen.dmp ¦ xwud, to store the grabbed image and get a preview window.

Default settings for xgrab can be made in your .Xdefaults file. For the Athena toolkit version of xgrab, toggle buttons can be set or unset through their .state attribute, and text-field strings can be set through their *string attribute. For the Motif toolkit version, which has diamond-shaped buttons for radio buttons, toggle buttons can be set or unset through their .set attribute and text-field strings can be set through their *value attribute. For example, to set the default paper size for PostScript output, put these lines in .Xdefaults (use xrdb to load them into the server):

```
XGrab*.pageWidthText*string: 8.5
XGrab*.pageHeightText*string: 11.0
```

or

```
XGrab*.pageWidthText*value: 8.5
XGrab*.pageHeightText*value: 10.0
```

To set the default output type to XWD, put these lines in .Xdefaults:

```
XGrab*.ps.state: 0
XGrab*.xwd.state: 1
```

xlock

Patrick J. Naughton (**naughton@eng.sun.com**) wrote xlock and released it to the world. The xlock program locks the local X Windows display until the user enters their password at the keyboard. While xlock is running, all new server connections are refused, the screen saver is disabled, the mouse cursor is turned off, and the screen is blanked and a changing pattern is put on-screen. If a key or a mouse button is pressed, the user is prompted for the password of the user who started xlock.

If the correct password is entered, the screen is unlocked and the X server is restored. When you're typing the password, <Ctrl-Shift-u> and <Ctrl-Shift-h> are active as kill and erase commands, respectively. To return to the locked screen, click the small icon version of the changing pattern.

Having Fun with DOOM for Linux

The best is always saved for last. Why run XFree86 under Linux? Because ID Software, Inc. has made a version of their shareware game DOOM available. While superseded by other first-person shooter games (such as Id Software's Quake), DOOM is an enthralling shoot-'em-up adventure game still played the world over. Using realistic 3-D graphics, you're a space marine going into an unholy, terror-filled space colony located on one of the moons of Mars. You must find your way through the labs and various sites, looking for your lost comrades. All you find instead are hideous monsters and other space marines who have turned against you.

The X Windows version supplied on the accompanying Slackware CD-ROM in the /contrib directory is a complete shareware version. (The Red Hat distribution automatically installs the game during installation.) Although this version runs on 386 computers, it was built to run on high-end 486 systems. If you run DOOM on a 386 with a small amount of physical RAM, be prepared to be disappointed; the game will be too slow to be enjoyable. You need lots of horsepower to play DOOM under Linux.

Installing DOOM

DOOM is installed by default with the Red Hat distribution and can be started by selecting xdoom from the Start, Programs, Games menu.

Under Slackware, DOOM is stored in a series of archived files under the ///slackware/y2 directory. If you chose to install the games package while installing Linux, DOOM should already be installed. If not, you can use pkgtool to install it now, or you can perform the following steps:

1. Copy the archived files under the ///slackware/y2 directory to an area on your hard drive.

2. Change the directory to the base directory you want to use. The archives will extract the files to the usr/games/doom directory, so you may as well copy all the files in the doom directory on the accompanying Slackware CD-ROM to /usr with the following commands:

```
cd /usr
cp /cdrom/contrib/linuxdoom/* .
```

3. Decompress each file in the directory with this command:

```
gzip -d filename
```

where *filename* is the name of each file in the directory. This command creates two tar files.

4. Unarchive each file with the tar command to create the necessary directories and files:

```
tar -xfv archive-file
```

▶ **See** "Using tar," **p. 229**

Starting DOOM

To play DOOM, you must first have X Windows running, so enter **startx**. When X Windows is running, you can start an xterm session or use the <Ctrl-Alt-F*x*> key sequence to access one of the virtual character terminals; then enter **linuxxdoom**. If this doesn't work, Linux can't find the DOOM program—that is, it's not located in your path. If this occurs, simply change the current directory to the directory where you installed DOOM. Then enter the DOOM command again.

If you started DOOM from a virtual terminal, you need to return to the X Windows session by pressing <Ctrl-Alt-F22>. If you started DOOM from an xterm session, you should see the DOOM introduction screen in a few seconds.

While DOOM loads, notice a series of messages. One might indicate that DOOM and Linux can't start the sound system; thus, you might have to play DOOM without sound. Sound still isn't fully supported in this port of DOOM; such is the life of an evolving system such as Linux. For instructions on playing DOOM, see the README.Linux file.

N O T E   X Windows servers (remember, the server runs on the local system) are available for most non-UNIX systems. One of the best X servers is MicroImages' MI/X application, available for both Macintosh and Windows operating systems. For more information and a free X server, go to http://www.microimages.com/. ■

From Here...

Plenty of programs are available for Linux out on the Net. You can also use X Windows to multitask different Linux programs more easily by using `xterms` rather than the virtual terminals available from the character screens. You can check out the newsgroups **comp.windows.x.apps** and **comp.windows.x.intrinsics** for various information about X Windows in general. The following chapters also provide more information:

■ Chapter 3, "Installing Red Hat," explains how to install the Red Hat distribution of Linux, which includes installing X under Red Hat.

■ Chapter 21, "Installing the X Windows System," explains how to install the XFree86 version of X for Linux, which you need to do before installing X Windows.

■ To learn how to access the Internet with Linux, check out Chapter 30, "Accessing the Network with `telnet`, `ftp`, and the `r-` Commands."

■ For surfing the Net, check out Chapter 31, "Surfing the Internet with the World Wide Web."

Network Administration

## CHAPTER 23

Understanding the TCP/IP Protocol Suite

by Steve Burnett

In this chapter

The suite of widely used protocols known as Transmission Control Protocol/Internet Protocol (TCP/IP) has become extremely important as networks of all sizes, including the Internet, depend on it for their communications.

TCP/IP has grown from its initial development as a government-sponsored project to widespread use, connecting networks of all sizes. Recognized for its capability to enable communication among dissimilar machines, it's found on virtually all workstations, minicomputers, and mainframes. This chapter describes the origins and language of TCP/IP, its addressing and naming conventions, and concepts fundamental to the creation of the Internet.

The History of TCP/IP

In the late 1960s, the U.S. Department of Defense (DOD) recognized an electronic communication problem developing within the department. Communicating the ever-increasing volume of electronic information among DOD staff, research labs, universities, and contractors had hit a major obstacle. The various entities had computer systems from different computer manufacturers, running different operating systems, and using different networking topologies and protocols. How could information be shared?

The Advanced Research Projects Agency (ARPA) was assigned to resolve the problem of dealing with different networking equipment and topologies. ARPA formed an alliance with universities and computer manufacturers to develop communication standards. This alliance specified and built a four-node network that's the foundation of today's Internet. During the 1970s, this network migrated to a new, core protocol design that became the basis for TCP/IP.

The mention of TCP/IP requires a brief introduction to the Internet, a huge network of networks that allows computers all over the world to communicate. It's growing at such a phenomenal rate that any estimate of the number of computers and users on the Internet would be out of date by the time this book went to print! Nodes include universities, major corporations, research labs in the United States and abroad, schools, businesses both large and small, and individually owned computers. The explosion in past years of the World Wide Web has driven the Internet's expansion. In addition, the Internet is also a repository for millions of shareware programs, news on any topic, public forums and information exchanges, and e-mail. Another feature is remote login to any computer system on the network by using the Telnet protocol. Because of the number of systems that are interconnected, massive computer resources can be shared, enabling large programs to be executed on remote systems. Massively distributed processing projects such as the 1997 decryption of the Data Encryption Standard are possible only with the "everything is connected to everything else" behavior of the Internet.

Internet Terminology

The Internet protocol suite is composed of many related protocols based on the foundation formed by TCP and IP. To clarify the relationship of these components, Table 23.1 provides some definitions and notations.

Table 23.1 Networking Terms

Term	Definition
datagram	Used interchangeably with the words *data packet* and *network message* to identify a unit of information that's exchanged.
DNS	Domain Name Service, a service provided by one or more computers in a network to help locate a path to a desired node. This saves every system on a network from having to keep a list of every system it wants to talk to. Used by mail gateways.
GOSIP	Government Open System Interconnection Profile, a collection of OSI protocols used in U.S. government computer networks and projects.
Internet	A computer network based on TCP/IP and related protocols. A public network of networks interconnecting businesses, universities, government facilities, and research centers.
FTAM	File Transfer, Access, and Management, a file transfer and management protocol as specified by OSI.
FTP	File Transfer Protocol, which enables file transfer between systems.
IP	Internet Protocol, a protocol responsible for transporting datagrams across the Internet.
NFS	Network File System, a network virtual disk system that enables a client computer to mount remote file systems and directories. Originally developed by Sun Microsystems.
NIC	Network Information Center, responsible for administering Internet and TCP/IP addresses, as well as network names.
node	A computer on a network.
OSI	Open System Interconnection, the ISO standard model for defining data communication.
RFC	Request For Comments, the documentation maintained by NIC relating to Internet protocols, addressing, routing, configuration, and other related Internet topics.
RIP	Routing Information Protocol, which is used to exchange information between routers.
RMON	Remote monitor, a remote network monitor that enables the collection of information about network traffic.
RPC	Remote Procedure Call, which enables procedures to be executed on a server.
SMTP	Simple Mail Transfer Protocol, which is used to transfer electronic mail between systems.

continues

Part
V

Ch
23

Table 23.1   Continued

Term	Definition
SNMP	Simple Network Management Protocol, a protocol used to manage remote network devices and to collect information from remote devices related to configuration, errors, and alarms.
TCP	Transmission Control Protocol, the protocol between a pair of applications responsible for reliable, connection-oriented data transmission.
Telnet	The protocol used to establish remote terminal connections.
UDP	User Datagram Protocol, a connectionless protocol used to transfer data between agents.
VT	Virtual terminal, a method for using Telnet to log in to remote systems through the network.

The Open Systems Interconnection Model

Many different types of computers are used today, varying in operating systems, CPUs, network interfaces, and many other qualities. These differences make the problem of communication between diverse computer systems important. In 1977, the International Organization for Standardization (ISO) created a subcommittee to develop data communication standards to promote multivendor interoperability. The result is the Open Systems Interconnection (OSI) model.

The OSI model doesn't specify any communication standards or protocols; instead, it provides guidelines that communication tasks follow.

N O T E   It's important to understand that the OSI model is simply a model—a framework—that specifies the functions to be performed. It doesn't detail *how* these functions are performed. ISO, however, does certify specific protocols that meet OSI standards for parts of the OSI model. For example, the CCITT X.25 protocol is accepted by ISO as an implementation that provides most of the services of the Network layer of the OSI model. ■

To simplify matters, the ISO subcommittees took the divide-and-conquer approach. By dividing the complex communication process into smaller subtasks, the problem becomes more manageable, and each subtask can be optimized individually. The OSI model is divided into seven layers:

- Application
- Presentation
- Session
- Transport

- Network
- Data Link
- Physical

TIP One easy way to remember the order of the layers (from the top down) is by making a sentence from the first letters of the layer names: All People Seem To Need Data Processing.

Each layer is assigned a specific set of functions. Each layer uses the services of the layer beneath it and provides services to the layer above it. For example, the Network layer uses services from the Data Link layer and provides network-related services to the Transport layer. Table 23.2 explains the services offered at each layer.

N O T E The concept of a layer making use of services and providing services to its adjacent layers is simple. Consider how a company operates: the secretary provides secretarial services to the president (the next layer up) to write a memo. The secretary uses the services of a messenger (the next layer down) to deliver the message. By separating these services, the secretary (application) doesn't have to know how the message is actually carried to its recipient. The secretary merely has to ask the messenger (network) to deliver it. Just as many secretaries can send memos in this way by using a standard messenger service, a layered network can send packets by handing them to the network layer for delivery. ■

Table 23.2   Services Provided at Each OSI Layer

Layer	Description
Physical (Layer 1)	This layer provides the physical connection between a computer system and the network. It specifies connector and pin assignments, voltage levels, and so on.
Data Link (Layer 2)	This layer "packages" and "unpackages" data for transmission. It forms the information into frames. A *frame* represents the exact structure of the data physically transmitted across the wire or other medium.
Network (Layer 3)	This layer provides routing of data through the network.
Transport (Layer 4)	This layer provides sequencing and acknowledgment of transmission.
Session (Layer 5)	This layer establishes and terminates communication links.
Presentation (Layer 6)	This layer does data conversion and ensures that data is exchanged in a universal format.
Application (Layer 7)	This layer provides an interface to the application that a user executes: a "gateway" between user applications and the network communication process.

N O T E   Don't confuse the Application layer with application programs you execute on the computer. Remember that the Application *layer* is part of the OSI model that doesn't specify *how* the interface between a user and the communication pathway happens; an application *program* is a specific implementation of this interface. A real application typically performs Application, Session, and Presentation layer services and leaves Transport, Network, Data Link, and Physical layer services to the network operating system. ■

Each layer communicates with its peer in other computers. For example, layer 3 in one system communicates with layer 3 in another computer system.

When information is passed from one layer down to the next, a header is added to the data to indicate where the information is coming from and going to. The header-plus-data block of information from one layer becomes the data for the next. For example, when layer 4 passes data to layer 3, it adds its own header. When layer 3 passes the information to layer 2, it considers the header-plus-data from layer 4 as data and adds its own header before passing that combination down.

In each layer, the information units are given different names (see Table 23.3). Therefore, by knowing the terms used to reference the data, you know which layer of the model is being discussed.

Table 23.3   Terms Used by OSI Layers to Refer to Information Units

OSI Layer	Information Unit Name
Application	Message
Transport	Segment
Network	Datagram
Data Link	Frame (also called *packet*)
Physical	Bit

Before the advent of the OSI model, the U.S. Department of Defense defined its own networking model, known as the *DOD model*. The DOD model is closely related to the TCP/IP suite of protocols, as explained in the following section.

The TCP/IP Protocol Stack

The TCP/IP protocol stack represents a network architecture that's similar to the ISO OSI networking model. Figure 23.1 shows the mapping of TCP/IP layers onto the ISO protocol stack.

TCP/IP doesn't make as fine distinctions between the top layers of the protocol stack as does OSI. The top three OSI layers are roughly equivalent to the Internet process protocols. Some examples of process protocols are Telnet, FTP, SMTP, NFS, SNMP, and DNS.

FIG. 23.1
OSI and TCP/IP
compared.

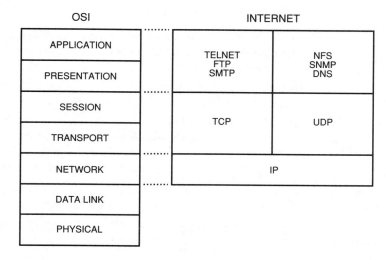

The Transport layer of the OSI model is responsible for reliable data delivery. In the Internet protocol stack, this corresponds to the host-to-host protocols. Examples of these are TCP and UDP. TCP is used to translate variable-length messages from upper-layer protocols and provides the necessary acknowledgment and connection-oriented flow control between remote systems.

UDP is similar to TCP, except that it's not connection-oriented and doesn't acknowledge data receipt. UDP only receives messages and passes them along to the upper-level protocols. Because UDP doesn't have any of the overhead related to TCP, it provides a much more efficient interface for such actions as remote disk services.

The Internet Protocol (IP) is responsible for connectionless communications between systems. It maps onto the OSI model as part of the Network layer, which is responsible for moving information around the network. This communication is accomplished by examining the Network layer address, which determines the systems and the path to send the message.

IP provides the same functionality as the Network layer and helps get the messages between systems, but it doesn't guarantee the delivery of these messages. IP may also fragment the messages into chunks and then reassemble them at the destination. Each fragment may take a different network path between systems. If the fragments arrive out of order, IP reassembles the packets into the correct sequence at the destination.

IP Addresses

The Internet Protocol requires that an address be assigned to every device on the network. This address, known as the *IP address*, is organized as a series of four octets. These octets each define a unique address, with part of the address representing a network (and optionally a subnetwork) and another part representing a particular node on the network.

Part
V

Ch
23

Several addresses have special meanings on the Internet:

- An address starting with a zero references the local node within its current network. For example, 0.0.0.23 references workstation 23 on the current network. Address 0.0.0.0 references the current workstation.

- The loopback address, 127, is important in troubleshooting and network diagnoses. The network address 127.0.0.0 is the local loopback inside a workstation.

- The ALL address is represented by turning on all bits, giving a value of 255. Therefore, 192.18.255.255 sends a message to all nodes on network 192.18; similarly, 255.255.255.255 sends a message to every node on the Internet. These addresses are important to use for multicast messages and service announcements.

> **CAUTION**
>
> It's important that when you assign node numbers to your workstations, you don't use 0, 127, or 255, because these are reserved numbers and have special meanings.

IP Address Classes

The IP addresses are assigned in ranges referred to as *classes*, depending on the application and the size of an organization. The three most common classes are A, B, and C. These three classes represent the number of locally assignable bits available for the local network. Table 23.4 shows the relationships among the different address classes, the available number of nodes, and the initial address settings.

Table 23.4   IP Address Classes

Class	Available Nodes	Initial Bits	Starting Address
A	$2^{24}=167,772$	0xxx	0–127
B	$2^{16}=65,536$	10xx	128–191
C	$2^8=256$	110x	192–223
D		1110	224–239
E		1111	240–255

Class A addresses are used for very large networks or collections of related networks. Class B addresses are used for large networks having more than 256 nodes (but fewer than 65,536 nodes). Class C addresses are used by most organizations. It's a better idea for an organization to get several class C addresses because the number of class B addresses is limited. Class D is reserved for multicast messages on the network, and class E is reserved for experimentation and development.

Obtaining IP Addresses The administration of Internet addresses is currently handled by the Network Information Center (NIC):

Network Solutions
ATTN: InterNIC Registration Services
505 Huntmar Park Drive
Herndon, VA   22070
(703) 742-4777

ON THE WEB

You also can reach the InterNIC on the Web at

http://www.internic.net

When you connect a computer or a network to the Internet, in most cases your Internet service provider will be able to arrange for your network IP address registration.

Obtaining RFCs In addition to assigning addresses, the NIC can provide other information of value. It's a repository for all technical documentation related to the Internet. It has a collection of documents that describe all the associated protocols, routing methodologies, network management guidelines, and methods for using different networking technologies.

As mentioned in Table 23.1, RFC stands for Request For Comments. You can obtain RFCs from the Internet by using the FTP protocol to connect to several different repositories. The RFC series is available on the Internet via anonymous FTP from various sites, such as **ftp.internic.net** in the /rfc directory, and can also be accessed via Telnet at **rs.internic.net**.

Table 23.5 lists the pertinent RFCs for establishing a network. Some of these documents go into great detail about how the different protocols function and the underlying specifications and theory. Others are more general and provide key information that can be useful to a network manager. At a minimum, an Internet network manager should know where these documents are located and how to obtain them. They provide information that can help in planning and growing an organization's network.

Table 23.5   RFCs of Interest

RFC Name	Description
RFC791.txt	Internet Protocol DARPA Internet Program Protocol Specification
RFC792.txt	Internet Control Message Protocol
RFC793.txt	Transmission Control Protocol DARPA Internet Program Protocol Specification
RFC950.txt	Internet Standard Subnetting Procedure
RFC1058.txt	Routing Information Protocol

continues

Table 23.5   Continued

RFC Name	Description
RFC1178.txt	Choosing a Name for Your Computer
RFC1180.txt	A TCP/IP Tutorial
RFC1208.txt	A Glossary of Networking Terms
RFC1219.txt	On the Assignment of Subnet Numbers
RFC1234.txt	Tunneling IPX Traffic Through IP Networks

Network Naming

The naming of network nodes requires some planning. When you select names, keep network management and user acceptance in mind. Many organizations have network-naming standards. If your organization has such standards in place, it's best to follow them to prevent confusion. If not, there's plenty of room for imagination. Computer and network names can be as simple as naming the workstations after the users, such as Diane, Beth, or John.

If you have many similar computers, numbering them (for example, PC1, PC2, and PC128) may be appropriate. Naming must be done in a way that gives unique names to computer systems. Don't name a computer thecomputerinthenorthoffice and expect users not to complain. After all, even the system administrator must type the names of computers from time to time. Also avoid names like oiiomfw932kk. Although such a name may prevent network intruders from connecting to your computer, it may also prevent you from connecting to your workstation.

Names that are distinctive and follow a theme work well, helping the coordination of future expansion and giving the users a sense of connection with their machines. After all, it's a lot easier to have a good relationship with a machine called sparky than a machine called OF1284.

Remember the following points when selecting a naming scheme:

- Keep names simple and short—six to eight characters at most. Although the Internet Protocol allows names up to 255 characters long, you should avoid this, as some systems can't handle long names. (Each label can be up to 63 characters long. Each part of a period-separated full domain name for a node is a label.)
- Consider using a theme such as stars, flowers, or colors, unless other naming standards are required at your site.
- Don't begin the name with numbers.
- Don't use special characters in the name.
- Don't duplicate names.
- Be consistent in your naming policy.

If you follow these guidelines, you can establish a successful naming methodology.

Internet names represent the organizations and the functionality of the systems within the network. Following are examples of names that you can use:

> spanky.engineering.mycompany.com
>
> nic.ddn.mil

The following are examples of names that are difficult to use or remember:

> thisismyworkstation.thelongwindeddepartment.longcompnam.com
>
> 34556nx.m3422.mycompany.com

The latter of these could be encoded information about a workstation in room 345 on network 56 with network executive functions, but this type of naming scheme is usually considered poor practice because it can lead to confusion and misdirected messages.

An Internet name such as Eddie@PC28.Programming.mycompany.com enables you to reference a user on a particular node

Part
V

Ch
23

NIC Naming Tree

The NIC maintains a network naming tree. This tree is used to group similar organizations under similar branches of the tree. Figure 23.2 shows the naming tree. Major organizations are grouped under similar branches. This is the source for Internet labels, such as com, edu, and gov, that are seen in Internet names.

FIG. 23.2
The NIC naming tree.

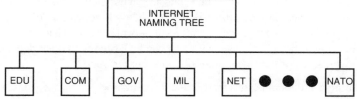

Table 23.6 shows some of the common leaf names and definitions for the NIC tree. Many other leaves are under the tree, but these are the most common.

Table 23.6   Common NIC Names

Name	Types of Organizations
edu	Educational facilities (such as universities and colleges)
com	Commercial (most corporations)
gov	United States non-military government bodies (White House, Department of Agriculture)

continues

Table 23.6 Continued

Name	Types of Organizations
mil	Military (military users and their contractors)
net	Internet network management and administration
org	Other types of organizations (usually non-profit)

Subnetworks and Subnet Masks

Subnetting is the process of dividing a large logical network into smaller physical networks. Reasons for dividing a network may include electrical limitations of the networking technology, a desire to segment for simplicity by putting a separate network on each floor of a building (or in each department or for each application), or a need for remote locations connected with a high-speed line.

The resulting networks are smaller chunks of the whole and are easier to manage. Smaller subnets communicate among one another through gateways and routers. Also, an organization may have several subnetworks that are physically on the same network, so as to logically divide the network functions into workgroups.

The individual subnets are a division of the whole. Suppose that a class B network is divided into 64 separate subnets. To accomplish this subnetting, the IP address is viewed in two parts: network and host (see Figure 23.3). The network part becomes the assigned IP address and the subnet information bits. These bits are, in essence, removed from the host's part of the address. The assigned number of bits for a class B network is 16. The subnet part adds 6 bits, for a total of 22 bits to distinguish the subnetwork. This division results in 64 networks with 1,024 nodes in each. The network part can be larger or smaller, depending on the number of networks desired or the number of nodes per network.

Setting a subnet mask is a matter of determining where the network address ends and the host address begins. The subnet mask contains all 1s in the network field and 0s (zeroes) in the host field.

Suppose a class C network is composed of the following:

```
N = network
H = Host
NNNNNNNN.NNNNNNNN.NNNNNNNN.HHHHHHHH
```

Each position represents a single bit out of the 32-bit address space. If this class C network is to be divided into four class C networks, the pattern resembles the following:

```
NNNNNNNN.NNNNNNNN.NNNNNNNN.NNHHHHHH
```

The subnet mask looks like the following:

```
11111111.11111111.11111111.11000000
```

FIG. 23.3
An example of class B
subnetwork masking.

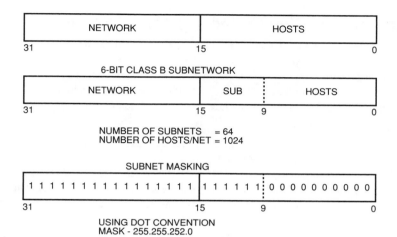

If this address is written in base-10 dot notation, the subnet mask is 255.255.255.192. This mask is used to communicate among nodes on all subnetworks within this particular network.

If three bits are taken from the host field, eight networks can be formed, and the resulting network mask is as follows:

11111111.11111111.11111111.11100000

This subnet mask is 255.255.255.224. Each of the eight networks would have 29 nodes because five address bits are available. (It would be 32 except that all 1s, all 0s, and 127 aren't legal addresses.)

This concept can be extended to class B and class A networks. The only difference is that the remaining fields are 0 (zero).

Consider a class B network. The address space is divided as follows:

NNNNNNNN.NNNNNNNN.HHHHHHHH.HHHHHHHH

If two bits are taken from the host field and added to the network part, the following subnet mask is used:

11111111.11111111.11000000.00000000

The mask is written as 255.255.192.0.

The bits needed for the subnet mask can be taken from any of the bit positions within the host field, but this leads to complex subnet masks and address exclusions. You should avoid this if at all possible.

Routing

Routing is a method of transferring information between networks. A router works at the Network layer of network protocols. Data may be routed by several different means. The routing method implemented for an Internet network is the Routing Information Protocol (RIP).

Routing Information Protocol (RIP)

RIP is designed to be used in small- to medium-sized networks and is based on Xerox Network Systems (XNS) routing protocols. RIP determines a message route by using a distance-vector routing algorithm. This algorithm assumes that each path is assigned a cost. This cost can be representative of network throughput, type of line, or desirability of the path. The protocol then determines the lowest cost path over which to transmit the message. (You can obtain information about routing from several RFCs.)

How a Routing Protocol Works

To maintain a list of hops to adjacent nodes, a RIP router keeps a routing table in the router or computer memory. This table is updated at 30-second intervals with information from neighboring routers. The information is used to recalculate the lowest cost path between systems. Each router on a network sends out (advertises) and receives routing information.

The routing protocol is limited in the distance a message can be routed. Each router can route a message only to a cost of 16. If the message sent out on a wire costs more than 16, the host is deemed unreachable. *Cost* is a method of assigning values to different paths through the network and is a way of ensuring an efficient route to a destination when there's more than one way to get there.

When a network break occurs, the routers must relearn least-cost paths. This takes time and can result in messages being transmitted at a higher cost for a period of time. When a node goes down, all routers must readjust their respective routing tables. During this time, messages can be lost in the network. After a period of time, the routers are again synchronized and routing continues.

Router crashes are also a concern. In the event of a crash, adjacent routers update their adjacency to a crashed router in 180 seconds. After that period of time, if no routing information is received from the crashed router, that path is removed from the local router's database.

RIP doesn't manage routing distances, just cost. As a result, RIP may not use the shortest physical path between two points. Work and modifications have been made to the protocols to help correct this problem. A newer routing protocol being developed and tested is Open Shortest Path First (OSPF), which is beginning to gain acceptance and use.

Network Segmentation

Internet networks are divided into segments for various reasons. Some of these reasons are related to the underlying networking technologies; others are related to geographical locations. Some of the best reasons to isolate network segments are based on network usage. If a lot of traffic in a network is between a few nodes, it's best to isolate those nodes. This isolation drops the usage and provides a more responsive network for the other network users.

Other reasons to segment are to change networking technologies or to communicate between different networking technologies. For example, an office area may be running Token Ring and the shop floor area may be running Ethernet. Each has a distinct function. The office may require Token Ring to communicate with an AS/400. The shop floor may have Ethernet to enable shop floor controllers and computers to communicate. The shop floor information then may be uploaded to the office network for order tracking. The connection between the technologies is usually through routers. The routers forward only information that must be exchanged from one network to the other. This information can then be shared between nodes on the respective networks.

Excessive use of routers in a network can become a burden to the network, thus outweighing their benefits. The use of a router is of little benefit if all the nodes on one network must get to all the nodes on another network, and vice versa. In this instance, the advantages of routing would be diminished because of the overhead in the routing protocols. In that kind of situation, a bridge is a better alternative.

A bridge enables all information from two networks to be shared. The access is at the Physical layer and not at the Network layer, so address translation and routing overhead aren't incurred. A bridge enables all information, including system broadcast messages, to be transmitted. If two networks rarely share information, a router is a better choice; otherwise, a bridge is the proper choice.

Internet Network Setup

The design and configuration of an Internet network is similar to the design of any computer network. It encompasses many types of nodes, including workstations, servers, printers, mainframes, routers, bridges, gateways, print servers, and terminals. The Internet requires that each device have a unique IP address. A device can have more than one address, depending on its function, but at least one address is required for communication with the other devices.

Understanding the Types of Connections

A TCP/IP network can consist of several systems connected to a local area network or hundreds of systems with connections to thousands of systems on the Internet. Each organization can create the type of network appropriate for its needs.

Figure 23.4 shows a simple network that consists of several workstations and a file server. Each station on the network is assigned the network address of 194.62.23. Each device is assigned an individual node address. This network is typical of most departments within a company or even a small office. There's room to connect printers and more workstations to the network. The network has no provisions for connections to other local or wide area networks.

The network in Figure 23.5 is more complex. It includes three separate networks interconnected through a combination of routers and servers. Each workstation and computer on each segment may or may not be isolated from using information on one of the other two networks. This is a characteristic of the subnet mask and security enabled on the servers and routers.

FIG. 23.4

A simple network.

FIG. 23.5

A more complex network.

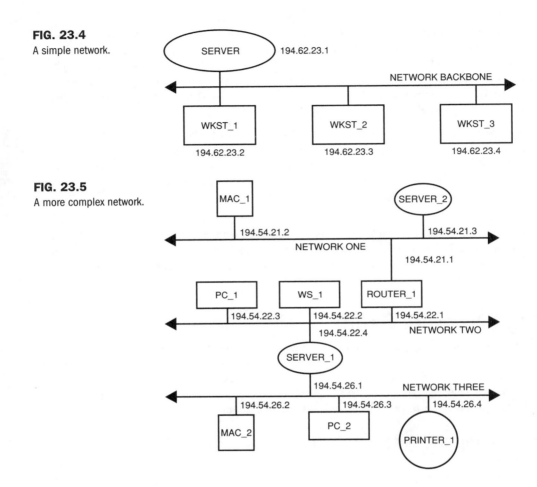

Information from one network is routed to one of the other networks on an as-needed basis. This type of configuration is typical of most large corporate networks. It may be chosen based on physical-length limitations of the underlying network technology or individual network loading. One or more of the networks may experience high traffic that must be distributed across several networks.

Router 1 between networks 1 and 2 provides for routing information between the two networks. If server 1 connecting networks 2 and 3 has routing enabled, information from network 3 to network 2 is routed. Also, information can be routed from network 3 to network 2 by means of server 1 and from network 2 to network 1 by means of router 1. Server 1, connecting networks 2 and 3, has two IP addresses: one IP address on network 2 and another address on network 3. The same is true for router 1, with addresses on network 2 and network 1.

Consider a situation in which there's a lot of Internet network traffic between network 3 and network 1. In this case, it may be worthwhile to place an additional router between network 1 and network 3. The additional router can eliminate some of the routing overhead on server 1 and enable information to be passed between networks when server 1 is down.

The additional router can add a level of fault tolerance to the network. This fault tolerance is based on the fact that information can still be routed to network 2 from network 3, even when server 1 is down. The path between network 3 and network 2 would be through network 1 and router 1. Figure 23.6 shows the addition of router 2.

FIG. 23.6

The network after adding a second router for fault tolerance.

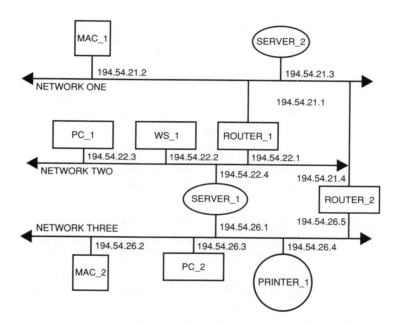

The fault tolerance of a network improves its integrity and can be of particular importance in certain applications. If time-critical information must be shared between two networks, an alternative path should be provided between the networks. This could be provided through the use of additional routers. Because these paths may be indirect (through a third network), a configuration parameter should be used.

This parameter is usually referred to as *network cost*. The cost of a hop can be increased by increasing the value a packet takes across a network path. The default preferred path is the low-cost path; the alternative path is the high-cost path. This arrangement prevents information from being routed over the high-cost path on a regular basis.

Figure 23.6 shows an additional router added between networks 1 and 3. The desired path for information from network 3 to network 2 is through server 1. Because router 2 connects network 3 and network 1, information can be routed between those two networks. Also, because router 2 is between network 1 and network 2, information is routed through that path. Information from network 3 that's bound for network 2 can go over one of the two paths: either through server 1, or through router 2 and router 1. The latter isn't the preferred path, because information can be routed directly over server 1. Therefore, a higher cost is assigned to the path of router 2 and router 1 from network 2. This type of path analysis must be performed in a multiple-segment network.

Choosing a Networking Configuration

The physical media used by an Internet network can be almost any network technology in current use. Internet network traffic isn't limited to Ethernet, ARCnet, or Token Ring. It can travel over asynchronous RS-232, T1 lines, and through frame relay. Whatever networking topology is selected for the network, the configuration, installation, and operation rules associated with that networking technology must be followed.

Keep in mind the bandwidth that an application requires. Many applications require megabytes of data to be transferred, so bandwidth becomes a prime consideration. You can usually save bandwidth by compressing files before sending them over the network.

▶ **See** "Compressing Files," **p. 332**

Another consideration is the physical location of the network. If all nodes are in the same building, a single LAN can be used. However, if the networks are located across town, a T1 connection may be needed. If the nodes are located in different geographic locations, a frame relay or a packet-switched network can be used.

In laying out a network, you must consider the type of information to be carried over the network, the physical location, and network loading. To help determine the capacity of the network, examine the type of workstations, servers, and applications.

If diskless workstations are used in a network, a higher network load is placed on the network for each node. The reason for this is that each remote diskless workstation requires all operating system code to be downloaded through the network. Because all applications, utilities, and data files are stored remotely, every action on that workstation requires network access.

Also of concern is the amount of NFS traffic that will occur on the network. NFS provides remote virtual disk services, so information retrieved and stored on these remote disks is constantly used on the network.

Other considerations are large graphical images, swapping and page files used for virtual memory, distributed database applications, printer traffic, and terminal traffic. These are all considerations in any network, but the designers and users of PC-based LANs don't usually have to contend with them. When a network is connected into a general user community, all aspects of the networking environment come into play.

Other items to be examined are the need for dial-up and remote access. If this access is related to terminal and screen traffic, a serial port from an existing system may suffice. If a Point-to-Point Protocol (PPP) connection is made, you must consider how much overhead it will impose on the network when users are loading software utilities, programs, and databases over the phone lines. This is of concern because IP isn't limited to a high-speed link such as Novell IPX and other networking protocols.

Understanding Network Configuration Guidelines

A network must be designed based on guidelines and rules. You should consider the following questions when planning a network:

- How will the network be used today?

- How will the network be used for the next several years?

- What applications are going to be used on the network?

- Will workgroups within the organization require networking resources in the future?

- What types and numbers of workstations will be on the network?

- How many servers, minicomputers, and other hosts will be on the network?

- What other network devices, such as printers and plotters, will be on the network?

- Will shared disk arrays and optical jukeboxes be necessary?

- Will management of the network be centralized?

- Will the network be connected to the Internet or other corporate networks, or will it be the basis for a wide area network?

- What other protocols will use the networking technology (IPX, DECNET, LAT, OSI protocols, and TCP/IP)?

- Where will critical data be interchanged (determine several different paths)?

- How will the network grow and change?

After you address all these questions, the network can be defined. The number of nodes indicates how many class C address spaces are needed or whether a class B is needed.

Connection to remote facilities should also be addressed. The load can be distributed across multiple network segments. Try to minimize the traffic that has to go across networks. For example, if you have two systems that exchange a lot of information and hops across three networks are required for them to communicate, consider moving the systems to the same network.

Determine the best networking topology to meet the requirements specified in the network analysis. To allow for growth in the network, the best approach is to determine the maximum load and to develop a network in which that load is at a minimum.

Using Routers and Bridges

Special-purpose devices are used to provide connections between networks and systems. Sometimes the terms *gateway* and *router* are used interchangeably. Strictly speaking, *gateway* describes a system that sends messages between different types of networks; a *router* sends messages between networks of the same type.

In this text, *router* is routinely used to describe any device that takes messages from one network and passes them through to another network. The router contains enough intelligence to know whether the message received must be forwarded to another network or a router.

Routers operate at the Network layer and are usually associated with a protocol, such as IP or IPX. Most routers that route IPX traffic can route IP traffic as well. The router is used to connect multiple local and wide area networks. It provides a method of sharing data between networks. Also, because a router works at the Network layer, it can help reduce broadcast traffic.

If one network uses a lot of different protocols and another network uses only IP, a router that routes only IP messages is needed if those two networks are to communicate. The router prevents messages from being placed on a network that can't manage them.

Bridges, on the other hand, can be used to interconnect local and wide area networks; they share information regardless of protocol. A bridge allows two interconnected networks to have many different protocols on them at the same time. The messages forwarded by a bridge usually don't contain any further routing information. The messages are usually left undisturbed.

One drawback of bridges is that all network broadcast and multicast messages from all interconnected networks are seen on all legs connected by a bridge. This results in a lot of overhead related to network update messages. Also, a bridge forwards messages only to network addresses on the other side of the bridge, but it can forward all network protocols and broadcast messages.

Routers and bridges are used to share information between networks. The appropriateness of each is determined by networking requirements, the protocols involved, network capacity, and user demands. The proper selection of components can help a network operate efficiently, allow for future growth, and help ensure continued reliability.

N O T E Use bridges only if multiple protocol packets are to be shared. Otherwise, a router is a better choice because it helps reduce network overhead. ■

From Here...

You can find more information about TCP/IP in the following chapters:

- Chapter 24, "Configuring a TCP/IP Network," shows how to set up and configure your networking system for Linux.
- Chapter 25, "Configuring Domain Name Service," explains the Internet name resolution system.
- Chapter 29, "Using SLIP and PPP," shows how to configure asynchronous TCP/IP over serial lines.

Configuring a TCP/IP Network

by Steve Burnett

In this chapter

Configuring a TCP/IP network is one of the more common tasks you'll face when administering Linux machines. In the most basic cases, it's not very complex, but it does require a bit of thought on the design of your network and knowledge of a small number of programs and configuration files.

Understanding the TCP/IP Configuration Files

TCP/IP networking in Linux is controlled by a set of configuration files in the */etc* directory. These files tell Linux what its IP address, host name, and domain name are and also control the network interfaces. Table 24.1 shows you what each file does; the following sections discuss these files in detail.

Table 24.1   Linux TCP/IP Networking Configuration Files

File	Description
/etc/hosts	Maps host names to IP addresses
/etc/networks	Maps domain names to network addresses
/etc/rc.d/rc3.d/S10network	Configures and activates your Ethernet interfaces at boot time

The /etc/hosts File

Every computer on a TCP/IP network has an IP address, canonical host name, and zero or more host name aliases. The /etc/hosts file is the original method for mapping host names to IP addresses.

> **N O T E**   All host names, domain names, and IP addresses used in this chapter are fictitious and don't reflect *any* true network on the Internet. ■

For illustrative purposes, look at the network that Burwell, Inc. has built. This network consists of the single class B network address assigned to Burwell by InterNIC (the organization that controls Internet addresses); this network has been split into two class C subnetworks. The format for the hosts file is as follows:

```
# /etc/hosts for linux1.burwell.com
#
# For loopbacking.
127.0.0.1      localhost

# This machine
166.82.1.21     linux1.burwell.com linux1    # the local machine

# Other hosts on our network
166.82.1.20     server.burwell.com server    # the server
166.82.1.22     wk1.burwell.com              # workstation 1
```

```
166.82.1.10     netpr1.burwell.com netpr1    # networked printer
166.82.1.1      gateway.burwell.com gateway    # the router
166.82.1.1      gate-if1            # 1st interface on gateway
166.82.2.1      gate-if2            # 2nd interface on gateway
166.82.1.30     linux2.burwell.com linux2     # Laptop via PLIP

# end of hosts file
```

 TIP Notice that the preceding gateway has two host names for the IP address 166.82.1.1. Giving a unique name to each network interface on a machine is a good idea. Doing so makes it easier to see what's going on when you use the `ifconfig` and `route` commands.

The format of the hosts file consists of one IP address per line beginning in the first column, the canonical host name associated with that address, and then zero or more aliases. The fields are separated by spaces or tabs. Empty lines and text following a # character are treated as comments and are ignored.

The IP address 127.0.0.1 is known as the *local loopback address* and is reserved for this purpose. It's normally assigned the name localhost. If you're going to use your machine only as a standalone system or use SLIP or PPP to connect to the outside world, you need only the localhost address in your hosts file.

N O T E The function of the /etc/hosts file has been mostly taken over by Domain Name Service (DNS) on machines connected to the Internet or large internal networks. DNS isn't available during boot or when you're running in single-user mode, however, so it's a good idea to place the information for essential machines such as servers and gateways in /etc/hosts.

On a network with only a few machines that aren't connected to the Internet, it's easier to keep a complete listing of all hosts in /etc/hosts rather than configure and maintain DNS. ■

 TIP Naming your networks makes it convenient to do things such as static routing that take a host name or network name. You don't have to remember the subnets by their IP addresses, just their names.

The /etc/networks File

Just as hosts have names and IP addresses, networks and subnets can be named. This naming is handled by the /etc/networks file. The IP addresses in the networks file include only the network address portion plus the subnetwork byte. The following is an example file for burwell.com:

```
# /etc/networks for burwell.com

localnet      127.0.0.0     # software loopback network
burwell-c1    166.82.1      # Development Group Network, Class C
burwell-c2    166.82.2      # MIS Network, Class C

# end of networks file
```

First is the localnet name and IP address, 127.0.0.0. If you aren't connecting your Linux machine to a TCP/IP network or are using only SLIP or PPP, all you need to put in this file is the localnet name and IP address.

The next lines identify the two class C subnetworks that Burwell has made from its class B network.

Initializing Ethernet Interfaces

The `ifconfig` program makes network interfaces such as the software loopback and Ethernet cards known to the Linux kernel, so that Linux can use them. The `ifconfig` program is also used to monitor and change the state of network interfaces. A simple invocation of `ifconfig` is

```
ifconfig interface address
```

which activates the specified network interface and assigns an IP address to it. This is called *bringing up an interface*. The generalized calling syntax for `ifconfig` is as follows:

```
ifconfig interface [aftype] [options] ¦ address
```

Table 24.2 lists the command-line arguments for `ifconfig`.

Table 24.2   Command-Line Arguments for *ifconfig*

Argument	Description
`interface`	The name of the network interface, usually the name of the device driver followed by an identification number. This argument is required.
`aftype`	The address family that should be used for decoding and displaying all protocol addresses. Now, the inet (TCP/IP), ddp (Appletalk Phase 2), ipx (Novell), and AX.25 and netrom (both amateur packet radio) address families are supported. The inet family is the default.
`up`	Activates the specified interface.
`down`	Deactivates the specified interface.
`[-]arp`	Turns on or off the use of the ARP protocol on the specified interface. The minus sign is used to turn off the flag.
`[-]trailers`	Turns on or off trailers on Ethernet frames. This isn't currently implemented in the Linux networking system.
`[-]allmulti`	Turns on or off the promiscuous mode of the interface. Turning this mode on tells the interface to send all traffic on the network to the kernel, not just traffic addressed to your machine.

Argument	Description
metric N	Sets the interface metric to the integer value N. The metric value represents the "cost" of sending a packet on this route. Route costing isn't currently used by the Linux kernel but is to be implemented at a future date.
mtu N	Sets the maximum number of bytes the interface can handle in one transfer to the integer value N. The current networking code in the kernel doesn't handle IP fragmentation, so make sure that the MTU (Maximum Transmission Unit) value is set large enough.
dstaddr addr	Sets the IP address of the other end of a point-to-point link. It has been made obsolete by the pointopoint keyword.
netmask addr	Sets the IP network mask for the specified interface.
irq addr	Sets the interrupt line used by this device. Remember that many devices don't support dynamic IRQ setting.
[-]broadcast[addr]	Sets the broadcast address for the interface when an address is included. If no address is given, the IFF_BROADCAST flag for the specified interface is turned on. A leading minus sign turns off the flag.
[-]pointopoint[addr]	Turns on point-to-point mode on the specified interface. This tells the kernel that this interface is a direct link to another machine. The address, when included, is assigned to the machine on the other end of the list. If no address is given, the IFF_POINTOPOINT flag for the interface is turned on. A leading minus sign turns off the flag.
hw	Sets the hardware address for the specified interface. The name of the hardware class and the ASCII equivalent of the hardware address must follow this keyword. Ethernet (ether), AMPR AX.25 (ax25), and PPP (ppp) are now supported.
address	The host name or IP address to be assigned to the specified interface. Host names used here are resolved to their IP address equivalents. This parameter is required.

Part
V

Ch
24

You normally don't need to use all the options. ifconfig can set everything needed from just the interface name, netmask, and IP address assigned. You only need to explicitly set most parameters when ifconfig misses or you have a complex network.

CAUTION

If your Linux machine is on a network, the ifconfig program must be kept secure from unauthorized use. Setting a network interface to promiscuous mode allows a person to snoop in your network and get sensitive data such as passwords. This is a serious breach of security.

▶ **See** "Handling Physical Security," **p. 236**

Using *ifconfig* to Inspect a Network Interface

Running ifconfig with no arguments causes it to output the status of all network interfaces the kernel knows about. Running ifconfig with just an interface name on the command line prints the status of the interface:

```
$ ifconfig lo
lo        Link encap Local Loopback
          inet addr 127.0.0.1 Bcast 127.255.255.255 Mask 255.0.0.0
          UP LOOPBACK RUNNING MTU 2000 Metric 1
          RX packets 0 errors 0 dropped 0 overruns 0
          TX packets 1658 errors 10 dropped 0 overruns 0
```

This example uses lo, the software loopback interface. You can see the assigned IP address (inet addr), broadcast address (Bcast), and netmask (Mask). The interface is UP with an MTU of 2000 and a Metric of 1. The last two lines give statistics on the number of packets received (RX) and transmitted (TX), along with packet error, dropped, and overrun counts.

Configuring the Software Loopback Interface

All Linux machines with the networking layer installed in the kernel have a software loopback interface. This interface is used to test networking applications and to provide a network for local TCP/IP services when the machine isn't connected to a real network.

The network interface name for the loopback system is lo. Enter the following to run ifconfig:

ifconfig lo 127.0.0.1

This activates the loopback interface and assigns the address 127.0.0.1 to it. This is the address traditionally used for the loopback because the class A network, 127.0.0.0, will never be assigned to anyone by InterNIC.

To make the loopback system fully operational, you need to add a route for it with the route command, which is discussed later in the section "Understanding TCP/IP Routing."

Configuring a Network Interface

Configuring an Ethernet network interface takes a little bit more work, especially if you're using subnetworks. The basic call to ifconfig looks like this for linux1.burwell.com:

```
ifconfig eth0 linux1
```

This causes ifconfig to activate Ethernet interface 0, look up the IP address for linux1 in the /etc/hosts file, and assign it to this interface. Examining the eth0 interface at this point reveals the following code:

```
$ ifconfig eth0
eth0      Link encap 10Mbps Ethernet HWaddr 00:00:E1:54:3B:82
          inet addr 166.82.1.21Bcast166.82.1.255 Mask 255.255.255.0
          UP BROADCAST RUNNING MTU 1500 Metric 0
          RX packets 3136 errors 217 dropped 7 overrun 26
          TX packets 1752 errors 25 dropped 0 overrun 0
          Interrupt:10 Base address:0x300
```

Note that the broadcast address and netmask were set automatically by ifconfig based on the IP address it found in /etc/hosts. If you're using subnetworks, you need to specify the broadcast address and netmask explicitly. For example, if you have a class C network and are using the first bit in the host portion of the address to make two subnetworks, you must specify the broadcast address and netmask when running ifconfig:

```
ifconfig eth0 linux1 broadcast 166.82.1.127 netmask 255.255.255.128
```

Configuring Parallel IP Interfaces

The Parallel IP (PLIP), Serial Line IP (SLIP), and Point-to-Point Protocol (PPP) interfaces are managed by ifconfig somewhat differently. To bring up a PLIP interface, you add the pointopoint option to the ifconfig command line. Assume that the Burwell laptop linux2 is attached to the first parallel port on linux1. You call ifconfig as follows to activate the PLIP link:

```
ifconfig plip0 linux1 pointopoint linux2
```

This activates the plip0 interface with the IP address for linux1, sets the pointopoint flag, and tells the interface that the IP address for the other end of the link is linux2. ifconfig looks up the IP addresses for linux1 and linux2 in /etc/hosts and assigns the addresses appropriately. On a laptop, you use the analogous call

```
ifconfig plip0 linux2 pointopoint linux1
```

▶ **See** "Understanding the Requirements for SLIP and PPP," **p. 562**

▶ **See** "Understanding the Requirements for SLIP and PPP," **p. 562**

Understanding TCP/IP Routing

Routing determines the path a packet takes from its source through the network to its destination. This path is determined by matching the destination IP address against the kernel routing tables and transmitting the packet to the indicated machine, which may or may not be the destination of the packet. The kernel routing table contains information in the form "To get to network X from machine Y, send the packet to machine Z with a cost of 1," along with time-to-live and reliability values for that route.

Deciding On a Routing Policy

The first step in setting up routing on your network is deciding on a routing policy. For small, unconnected networks, using the route command to set up static routes on each machine at boot time is sufficient. Large networks with many subnets or networks connected to the Internet need to use dynamic routing. The routing program provides dynamic routing by communicating with routing programs on other machines and installing routes based on what it learns about the topology of the network.

A very common strategy combines static and dynamic routing. Machines on each subnet use static routing to reach their immediate neighbors. The default route—the route used for packets that match no other route in the routing table—is set to a gateway machine that's doing dynamic routing and knows about the rest of the world. Large networks can be constructed this way, minimizing the hassle of configuration files and the amount of bandwidth used by the dynamic routing programs.

Using the /sbin/route Program

The /sbin/route program manipulates the kernel routing table and is used to set static routes to other computers or networks via interfaces that have been configured and activated by ifconfig. This is normally done at boot time by the /etc/rc.d/rc3.d/S10network script. Table 24.3 describes the command-line arguments for /sbin/route.

Table 24.3 Command-Line Arguments for /sbin/route

Argument	Description
(None)	Giving no option to /sbin/route causes it to output the current routing table.
-n	This argument causes the same output as giving no option, but replaces host names with their numerical IP addresses.
del	This argument deletes the route for the specified destination address from the routing table.
add	This argument adds to the routing table a route to the specified address or network.

Examining the Kernel Routing Table   Running /sbin/route without any command-line arguments or just -n outputs the routing table:

```
/sbin/route
Kernel routing table
Destination Gateway Genmask    Flags Metric Ref UseIface
127.0.0.0   *       255.0.0.0 U     0      0   100 lo
```

This is from a machine with just the loopback interface activated. Table 24.4 describes the fields in the routing table report.

Table 24.4 The Fields in the Routing Table Report

Field	Description
Destination	The destination IP address of the route.
Gateway	The host name or IP address of the gateway the route uses. If there's no gateway, an asterisk is output.
Genmask	The netmask for the route. The kernel uses this to set the generality of a route by bitwise ANDing the Genmask against a packet's IP address before comparing it to the destination IP address of the route.

Field	Description
Flags	The flags for the route (U means up, H means host, G means gateway, D means dynamic route, and M means modified).
Metric	The metric cost for the route. This isn't currently supported in the kernel networking layer.
Ref	The number of other routes that rely on the presence of this route.
Use	The number of times the routing table entry has been used.
Iface	The network interface to which this route delivers packets.

Returning to the Burwell network, the following is an example from the laptop linux2, with a SLIP link up and running:

```
$ /sbin/route
Kernel routing table
Destination     Gateway         Genmask          Flags Metric Ref Use Iface
slip.burwell.c  *               255.255.255.255  UH    0      0   0   sl0
127.0.0.0       *               255.0.0.0        U     0      0   100 lo
default         slip.burwell.c  *                UG    0      0   1   sl0
```

The table entry for the loopback is the same as before, and there are two new entries. The first specifies a route to slip.burwell.com. The other new entry specifies a default route by using slip.burwell.com as a gateway.

N O T E   Every machine connected to a network must have a default route in its routing table. The default route is used when no other routing table entry matches the destination for a packet. ■

Adding Static Routes   You add routes to the routing table by running the route program with the add argument. The command-line argument syntax for the route add command is

```
route add [ -net ¦ -host ] addr [gw gateway] [metric cost]
➥[netmask mask] [dev device]
```

Table 24.5 describes the command-line arguments that the route add command uses.

Table 24.5   Command-Line Arguments Used by *route add*

Argument	Description
-net ¦ -host	Forces the specified address to be treated as a network or host address.
addr	The destination address for the new route. This can be an IP address, host name, or network name.
gw gateway	Specifies that any packets for this address be routed through the specified gateway.

continues

Part

V

Ch

24

Table 24.5   Continued

Argument	Description
metric *cost*	Sets the metric field in the routing table.
netmask *mask*	Specifies the netmask of the route being added. The route program will guess what this is, so you don't need to specify it under normal circumstances.
dev *device*	Forces route to associate the new route with the specified network interface device. Again, route usually guesses correctly what device to use for the new route, so you don't have to use this often.

CAUTION

When adding a gateway route to the routing table, you must make sure that the specified gateway is reachable. You usually have to add a static route for the gateway before adding the route by using the gateway.

Looking at Routing Examples   Now for some examples, starting with the loopback interface. After configuring the loopback interface with ifconfig, you need to add a route to it, as in the following:

```
# route add 127.0.0.1
```

Nothing else is needed because route compares the address given to it with the addresses for the known interfaces and assigns the loopback interface to the new route. The following example shows how to set the routing for the SLIP link on the Burwell linux2 machine after the SLIP link is established and ifconfig is used to activate the interface:

```
# route add slip.burwell.com
# route add default gw slip.burwell.com
```

The first command adds a static route for the host slip.burwell.com; the second one tells the kernel to use slip.burwell.com as a gateway for all packets with unknown destinations.

CAUTION

Make sure that any host names you use with the route command are in the /etc/hosts file so that route can find the IP addresses for them; otherwise, route fails.

If you're subnetting your network by splitting the IP address in the middle of an octet, you'll have to specify the required netmask when running route. For example, if you have a class C network and have four subnets using the first two bits of the last octet, you need to run route like this:

```
# route add hostname netmask 255.255.255.192
```

This ensures that route puts the right netmask in the routing table entry.

For Ethernet and other broadcast network interfaces, you need to add routes that tell the kernel what network can be reached via each configured interface. After using `ifconfig` to bring up the eth0 network interface on linux1.burwell.com as you did previously, you need to run `route` to install the route to the network on that interface:

```
# route add -net 166.82.1.0
```

That may not look like enough to set the routing table entry correctly, because no interface is indicated; however, route manages to find the interface by comparing the IP address on the command line to the IP address of each network interface. It assigns the route to the interface that matches it. In this case, eth0 has been assigned the address 166.82.1.21 with a netmask of 255.255.255.0. This matches the network address given in the route command, so route installs a route to the network 166.82.1.0 by using interface eth0, as follows:

```
$ route
Kernel routing table
Destination      Gateway      Genmask           Flags Metric Ref   UseIface
166.82.1.0       *            255.255.255.0     UN    0      0     0 eth0
127.0.0.0        *            255.0.0.0         U     0      0     100 lo
```

To tell linux1 how to reach the other subnet, you need two more routing table entries to be safe:

```
# route add gateway.burwell.com
# route add -net 166.82.2.0 gw gateway.burwell.com
```

This adds a static route to gateway.burwell.com and then adds a network route for 166.82.2.0 by using gateway.burwell.com as the gateway for that network, as shown in the following:

```
$ route
Kernel routing table
Destination      Gateway           Genmask         Flags Metric Ref UseIface
gateway.burwell  *                 255.255.255.0   UH    0      0     0 eth0
166.82.1.0       *                 255.255.255.0   UN    0      0     0 eth0
166.82.2.0       gateway.burwell   255.255.255.0   UN    0      0     0 eth0
127.0.0.0        *                 255.0.0.0       U     0      0     100 lo
```

This shows the static route you added for gateway.burwell.com and the gatewayed route to the 166.82.2.0 network.

Deleting Routes with the *route* Command   You delete routes by calling `route` with the `del` option and specifying the destination address of the route you want to delete. For example,

```
# route del -net 166.82.2.0
```

deletes the network route for network 166.82.2.0.

Monitoring a TCP/IP Network with *netstat*

The `netstat` program is an invaluable tool in monitoring your TCP/IP network. It can display the kernel routing table, the status of active network connections, and useful statistics about each network interface. Table 24.6 describes the common command-line arguments for `netstat`; a few additional arguments are targeted for advanced users. Refer to the man page for more information.

Part
V

Ch

24

Table 24.6   Common Command-Line Arguments for the *netstat* Program

Argument	Description
-a	Shows information about all Internet connections, including those that are just listening.
-i	Shows statistics for all network devices.
-c	Shows continually updating network status. This makes netstat output a network status listing once per second until it's interrupted.
-n	Shows remote and local addresses and port information in numeric/raw form rather than resolve host names and service names.
-o	Shows the timer state expiration time and backoff state of each network connection.
-r	Shows the kernel routing table.
-t	Shows only TCP socket information, including those that are just listening.
-u	Shows only UDP socket information.
-v	Shows the version information for netstat.
-w	Shows raw socket information.
-x	Shows UNIX domain socket information.

Displaying Active Network Connections

Running netstat with no command-line arguments generates a listing of the active network connections on your machine. The following demonstrates the default output from netstat:

```
$ netstat
Active Internet connections
Proto Recv-Q Send-Q Local Address          Foreign Address        (State)
tcp        0      0 linux1.burwell.com:1266 server.burwell.:telnet ESTABLISHED
Active UNIX domain sockets
Proto RefCnt Flags      Type         State      Path
unix 1      [ ACC ]    SOCK_STREAM   LISTENING  /dev/printer
unix 2      [ ]        SOCK_STREAM   CONNECTED  /dev/log
unix 2      [ ]        SOCK_STREAM   CONNECTED
unix 1      [ ACC ]    SOCK_STREAM   LISTENING  /dev/log
```

The first section shows an active TCP protocol connection from port 1266 on linux1.burwell.com to the telnet port on server.burwell.com by user burt. Table 24.7 describes the fields in the Active Internet Connections listing.

Table 24.7   Active Internet Connection Fields

Field	Description
Proto	The protocol used by this connection, TCP, or UDP.

Field	Description
Recv-Q	The number of bytes received on this socket but not yet copied by the user program.
Send-Q	The number of bytes sent to the remote host that haven't been acknowledged.
Local Address	Local host name and port number assigned to this connection. The socket IP address is resolved to the canonical host name for that address, and the port number is translated into the service name unless the -n flag is used.
Foreign Address	The foreign host name and port number assigned to this connection. The -n flag affects this field as it does the Local Address field.
State	The current state of the socket. It can be in one of the following states:

	ESTABLISHED	The connection is fully established.
	SYN_SENT	The socket is now trying to make a connection to a remote host.
	SYN_RECV	The connection is being initialized.
	FIN_WAIT1	The socket has been closed and is waiting for the connection to shut down.
	FIN_WAIT2	The connection has been closed. The socket is waiting for a shutdown from the remote host.
	TIME_WAIT	The socket is closed and is waiting for a remote host shutdown retransmission.
	CLOSED	The socket isn't in use.
	CLOSE_WAIT	The remote host has shut down its connection. The local host is waiting for the socket to close.
	LAST_ACK	The remote connection is shut down and the socket is closed. The local host is waiting for an acknowledgment.
	LISTEN	The socket is listening for the incoming connection attempt.
	UNKNOWN	The state of the socket isn't known.
User		The login ID of the user who owns the socket.

Part
V

Ch
24

The second section displays active UNIX domain sockets. UNIX domain sockets are an IPC (interprocess communication) mechanism that uses the UNIX file system as the rendezvous system. Processes create special files in the file system that are then opened by other processes on the machine that wants to communicate. The preceding netstat listing shows two sockets listening: one on /dev/printer and the other on /dev/log. There are also two currently connected sockets: one to /dev/log and one which has no specified path associated with it. Table 24.8 describes the fields in the Active UNIX Domain Sockets listing.

Table 24.8   Fields in the Active UNIX Domain Sockets Listing

Field	Description
Proto	The protocol in use on this socket. This will usually be unix.
RefCnt	The number of processes attached to this socket.
Flags	The flags for this socket. Now, the only known flag is SO_ACCEPTON (ACC), which indicates that the socket is unconnected and the process that made the socket is waiting for a connection request.
Type	The mode in which the socket is accessed. This field will contain one of the following keywords:
	OCK_DGRAM — Datagram, connectionless mode
	OCK_STREAM — Connection-oriented stream mode
	OCK_RAW — Raw mode
	OCK_RDM — Reliably delivered message mode
	OCK_SEQPACKET — Sequential packet mode
	NKNOWN — Mode not known to netstat program
State	The current state of the socket. The following keywords are used:
	FREE — The socket isn't allocated.
	LISTENING — The socket is waiting for a connection request.
	UNCONNECTED — There's no current connection on the socket.
	CONNECTING — The socket is attempting to make a connection.
	CONNECTED — The socket has a current connection.
	DISCONNECTING — The socket is attempting to shut down a connection.
	UNKNOWN — The state of the socket is unknown. You won't see this under normal operating conditions.
Path	This is the path name used by other processes to connect to the socket.

Network interfaces that drop many packets or are getting many overrun errors can be a symptom of an overloaded machine or network. Checking the network interface statistics is a quick way of diagnosing this problem.

Invoking `netstat` with the `-o` option adds the internal state information to the Active Internet Connections listing. The following is an example of this:

```
$ netstat -o
Active Internet connections
Proto Recv-Q Send-Q Local Address     Foreign Address      (State)
tcp       0      0 localhost:1121     localhost:telnet     ESTABLISHED
➥off (0.00/0)
tcp       0      0 localhost:telnet   localhost:1121       ESTABLISHED
➥on  (673.69/0)
```

The added data is at the end of each line and includes receiver retransmission byte count, transmitter retransmission byte count, timer state (on/off), and time/backoff values (in parentheses). The time displayed is the time left before the timer expires. The backoff is the retry count for the current data transmission. This data is useful in diagnosing network problems by making it easy to see which connection is having problems.

Part
V

Ch
24

N O T E   Because the `-o` option outputs the state of internal TCP/IP data, the format of this data may change or this option may be removed in a later release of the networking software. ■

Examining the Kernel Routing Table

Invoking `netstat` with the `-r` option prints out the kernel routing table. The format is the same as for the `route` command.

Displaying Network Interface Statistics

Invoking `netstat` with the `-i` option prints out usage statistics for each active network interface—another excellent tool for debugging network problems. With this command, it's very easy to see when packets are being dropped, overrun, and so on.

The following is an example of using the `-i` option, and Table 24.9 explains each field in the listing.

```
$ netstat -i
Kernel Interface table
Iface MTU Met  RX-OK RX-ERR RX-DRP RX-OVR TX-OK TX-ERR TX-DRP TX-OVR Flags
lo    2000 0       0      0      0      0  1558      1      0      0 LRU
```

Table 24.9   Fields in the Kernel Interface Table

Field	Description
Iface	The name of the network interface.

continues

Table 24.9 Continued

Field	Description
MTU	The largest number of bytes that can be sent in one transmission by this interface.
Met	The metric value for this interface.
RX-OK	The number of packets received with no errors.
RX-ERR	The number of packets received with errors.
RX-DRP	The number of packets dropped.
RX-OVR	The number of packet overrun errors.
TX-OK	The number of packets transmitted with no errors.
TX-ERR	The number of packets transmitted with errors.
TX-DRP	The number of packets dropped during transmission.
TX-OVR	The number of packets dropped due to overrun errors.
Flags	The following flags can be shown in this field:

A   The interface receives packets for multicast addresses.

B   The interface receives broadcast packets.

D   The interface debugging feature is now activated.

L   This is the loopback interface.

M   The interface is in promiscuous mode.

N   The interface doesn't process trailers on packets.

O   The Address Resolution Protocol is turned off on this interface.

P   This interface is being used as a point-to-point connection.

R   The interface is running.

U   The interface has been activated.

From Here...

This chapter covers the basics of configuring a Linux machine for use on a network. More information can be found in the man pages for the discussed commands. For more information on TCP/IP networking and configuration, see the following chapters:

■ Chapter 18, "Understanding Linux Shells," gives more details on writing shell scripts.

■ Chapter 23, "Understanding the TCP/IP Protocol Suite," explains the details of the TCP/IP protocols.

■ Chapter 25, "Configuring Domain Name Service," shows you how to set up Linux as a DNS client and server.

Configuring Domain Name Service

by Steve Burnett

In this chapter

Originally, when the Internet was first formed, the number of hosts on the Net was very small. It was fairly easy to maintain the name/address mapping. Each host simply had a complete list of all host names and addresses in a local file. As the growth of the Internet accelerated, this system quickly became unwieldy. When a new host was added, it was necessary to update every host file on every computer. Also, because each new computer resulted in a new line in every host file, the size of the host files began to grow to quite a large size. Clearly, a new solution was needed.

Mapping Internet system names to IP addresses is a task that requires a good degree of consideration. With the explosive growth of the Internet over the past few years, the original system of maintaining host name to IP address mappings in a local flat ASCII file quickly proved impractical. With thousands of computers on the Net and more being added daily, a new system was needed. That new system was a network-wide distributed database known as BIND, the Berkeley Internet Domain server. Also referred to variously as the Domain Name Service, the Domain Name System, or DNS, this system provides an effective, relatively transparent host name to the IP address mapping mechanism.

DNS is notoriously hard to configure, but when you're successful, it's fairly easy to maintain. This chapter provides a basic overview of how to set up and configure a DNS system. It is, by no means, a complete reference; whole books are available on the subject.

Introducing DNS

DNS provides a mechanism for converting IP addresses into mnemonic names that represent hosts, networks, and mail aliases. It does this by dividing the entire Internet IP and name space into different logical groups. Each group has authority for its own computers and other information.

Because DNS is a complicated topic, it has its own specialized set of terms. Table 25.1 lists the definitions of some commonly used DNS terms.

Table 25.1 Commonly Used DNS Terms

Term	Definition
domain	The logical entity or organization that represents a part of a network. For example, unc.edu is the name of the primary domain for the University of North Carolina at Chapel Hill.
domain name	The name portion of a host name that represents the domain that contains the host. For example, in the address **sunsite.unc.edu**, the domain name is unc.edu. Also used interchangeably with *domain*.
host	A computer on a network.
node	A computer on a network.
name server	A computer that provides DNS services to map DNS names to IP addresses.

Term	Definition
resolve	The act of translating a DNS name into its corresponding IP address.
resolver	A program or library routine that extracts DNS information from a name server.
reverse resolution	Matching a given IP address to its DNS name. This is also called reverse DNS.
spoof	The act of appearing to the network as having a different IP address or domain name.

DNS can be conceptually divided into the following three parts:

- *Domain name space.* This is a specification for a tree structure that identifies a set of hosts and provides information about them. Conceptually, each node in the tree has a database of information about the hosts under its authority. Queries attempt to extract the appropriate information from this database. In simple terms, this is just the listing of all different types of information, names, IP addresses, mail aliases, and such that are available for lookup in the DNS system.

- *Name servers.* These are programs that hold and maintain the data located in the domain name space. Each name server has complete information about a subset of the domain name space and cached information about other portions.

  A name server has complete information for its area of authority. This authoritative information is divided into areas known as *zones*, which can be divided among different name servers to provide redundant service for a zone. Each name server knows about other name servers that are responsible for different zones. If a request comes in for information from the zone that a given name server is responsible for, the name server simply returns the information. However, if a request comes in for information from a different zone, the name server contacts the appropriate server with authority for that zone.

- *Resolvers.* These are simply programs or library routines that extract information from the name servers in response to a query about a host in the domain name space.

Configuring the Resolver

The first step in using DNS is to configure the resolver library on your computer. You must configure your local resolver if you intend to use DNS name resolution, even if you're not going to run a local domain name server.

The /etc/host.conf File

The local resolver libraries are configured via a file named host.conf that's located in the /etc directory. This file tells the resolver what services to use and in what order. This file is a plain

ASCII file that lists resolver options, one per line. Fields in this file may be separated by spaces or tabs. The # character indicates the start of a comment.

Several options may be specified in the host.conf file, as shown in Table 25.2.

Table 25.2   Configuration Options for the /etc/host.conf File

Option	Description
order	Specifies in what order different name resolution mechanisms are tried. The specified resolving services are tried in the order listed. The following name resolution mechanisms are supported: hosts (attempts to resolve the name by looking in the local /etc/host file), bind (queries a DNS name server to resolve the name), and nis (uses the Network Information Service—NIS—protocol to try to resolve the host name).
alert	Takes off or on as arguments. If turned on, any attempt to spoof an IP address is logged via the syslog facility.
nospoof	If reverse resolution is used to match a host name to a specified address, resolves the host name that's returned to verify that it does match the address that you queried. Prevents "spoofing" of IP addresses. Enabled by specifying nospoof on. Caution: Using this option can cause a noticeably additional load on the server.
trim	Takes a domain name as an argument. trim removes the domain name before performing an /etc/hosts lookup on the name. This allows you to put just the base host name in /etc/hosts without specifying the domain name.
multi	Takes off or on as arguments. Used only with host queries to determine whether a host is allowed to have more than one IP address specified in /etc/hosts. This option has no effect on NIS or DNS queries.

The following is an example of an /etc/host.conf configuration file that uses these options:

```
# Sample /etc/host.conf file
#
# Lookup names via DNS first then fall back to /etc/hosts
order bind hosts
# We don't have machines with multiple addresses
multi off
# check for IP address spoofing
nospoof on
# and warn us if someone attempts to spoof
alert on
# Trim the tristar.com domain name for host lookups
trim tristar.com
```

This example shows a general resolver configuration for the domain tristar.com. The resolver looks up the host names by using DNS first and then tries the local /etc/hosts file.

N O T E Specifying the local /etc/hosts file in the resolution search is a good idea. If for some reason your name servers should be unavailable, you can still resolve the names for hosts listed in your local hosts file. You should also keep a list of all your local hosts in your /etc/hosts files on each of your local computers. ■

Multiple IP addresses for a single machine are disabled. This host checks for IP address spoofing by re-resolving the host name that a reverse IP address lookup returns. This is a bit of a performance hit, but it helps make sure that no one is pretending to be a different host than they really are. Also, you've set up the resolver to warn you if an attempt to spoof is detected. Finally, the resolver trims the domain tristar.com from any host names that are looked up in the local /etc/hosts file.

The /etc/resolv.conf File

Now that you've configured the basic behavior of the resolver library, you need to set up some information for the DNS portion of the resolver. You need to do this only if you're using DNS for host name resolution—that is, by specifying bind in the order statement of the /etc/host.conf file. But then you wouldn't be reading this chapter if you weren't going to use DNS, would you?

The /etc/resolv.conf controls the way the resolver uses DNS to resolve host names. It specifies the DNS name servers to contact when resolving a host name and in what order to contact them. It also provides the local domain name and some clues as to how to guess at the domain name of hosts that are specified without a domain name.

Table 25.3 lists the valid options for the /etc/resolv.conf file.

Part
V
Ch
25

Table 25.3	Configuration Options for the /etc/resolv.conf File
Option	**Description**
domain	Specifies the local domain name of this host. If it's not given, the resolver tries to get the local domain name from the getdomainname() system call.
nameserver	Specifies the IP address of a DNS name server to contact for name resolution. You can list up to three name servers by using the nameserver option multiple times. The name servers are tried in the order listed. You should put your most reliable name server first so that queries don't time out on a server that's likely to be down.
search	Lists domains to try if no domain name is specified as part of a query host name. If no search option is given, the list of domains is created by using the local domain plus each parent domain of the local domain.

The following is a sample /etc/resolv.conf file for tristar.com:

```
# /etc/resolv.conf for tristar.com
#
# Set our local domain name
```

```
domain tristar.com
# Specify our primary name server
nameserver 166.82.1.3
```

In this example, you specify the local domain via the `domain` option and list one name server to use for resolving host names.

> **N O T E** You need to specify the IP address of the DNS name server as an argument to the
> `nameserver` option—not the host name. If you specify the host name, DNS doesn't know
> what host to contact to look up the host name of the name server. ■

You didn't use the `search` option to specify the search order. This means that if you try to query the address of a machine—for example, skippy—the resolver tries to look up skippy first. If this fails, it looks up `skippy.tristar.com`, and then `skippy.com`.

DNS servers can and do go down unexpectedly. If you rely solely on a DNS server for name resolution, you may find yourself unable to work if it crashes. Make sure that you specify multiple servers and keep a good list of hosts in your local /etc/hosts file, just in case.

Using the *named* Daemon to Set Up the Server

Here is where the real magic starts. You've seen how to set up the basics of resolver configuration and how to tell your resolver which name servers to contact. In the following sections, you learn the mechanics of setting up a name server.

The DNS name server under Linux is provided by the `named` (pronounced *name-deé*) daemon. This daemon is typically started at boot time and reads its configuration information from a set of configuration files. `named` typically runs until the machine is shut down. After `named` starts and is initialized with its configuration information, it writes its process ID to the /etc/named.pid ASCII file. It then starts listening for DNS requests on the default network port specified in /etc/services.

The named.boot File

The first file that `named` reads when it starts is typically /etc/named.boot. This very small file is the key to all the other configuration files used by `named`—it contains pointers to the various configuration files and to other name servers. In the named.boot file, comments start with a semicolon and continue to the end of the line. Several options can be listed in the named.boot file; Table 25.4 lists these options.

Table 25.4   Configuration Options for the named.boot File

Option	Description
directory	Specifies the directory where the DNS zone files are located. You can specify several different directories by using the `directory` option

Option	Description
	repeatedly. You can give file path names as being relative to these directories.
primary	Takes a domain name and file name as arguments. The `primary` option declares `named` to be authoritative for the specified domain and causes `named` to load the zone information from the specified file.
secondary	Tells `named` to act as a secondary server for the specified domain. It takes a domain name, a list of addresses, and a file name as arguments. `named` tries to transfer the zone information from the hosts specified in the address list and then stores the zone information in the file specified on the option line. If `named` can't contact any of the hosts, it tries to retrieve the information from the secondary zone file.
cache	Sets up caching information for `named`. Takes a domain name and a file name as arguments. The domain name is typically specified as . (dot). The file contains a set of records, known as *server hints*, which list information about the root name servers.
forwarders	Takes a list of name servers as arguments. Tells the local name server to try to contact the servers in this list if it can't resolve an address from its local information.
slave	Turns the local name server into a slave server. If the `slave` option is given, the local server tries to resolve DNS names via recursive queries. It simply forwards the request to one of the servers listed in the `forwarders` option line.

Part

V

Ch

25

In addition to these options, a few additional options aren't commonly used. Refer to the `named` man page for more information on these options.

N O T E Because `tristar.com` isn't attached to the Internet, many of the IP host and network addresses in these examples are fake. When setting up your own name server, make sure that you use the correct addresses assigned to you. ■

The following is a sample named.boot file:

```
; named.boot file
; A sample named.boot for tristar.com
;
directory /var/named
;
cache . named.ca
primary tristar.com named.hosts
primary 197.198.199.in-addr.arpa named.rev
```

This example sets up the primary name server for `tristar.com`. As you can see, comments start with the ; character. The `directory` statement in the file tells `named` that all its working files are located in the /var/named directory. Because none of the other files listed in the named.boot file have directory paths associated with them, they're located in /var/named.

The next line sets up the caching information for this name server. This option should be present on almost every machine running as a name server. It tells named to enable caching and load the root server information from the file named.ca.

> **N O T E** The cache entry is very important. Without it, no caching is enabled on the local name server. This can cause severe performance problems for name lookups. Also, the local server can't contact any root name servers and, as a result, can't resolve any non-local host names, unless it's set up as a forwarding name server.

The next line in the named.boot file tells named that this server has primary authority for the domain tristar.com. The zone and host information records are in the file named.hosts. You learn about these zone authority records in detail in the following section.

A second primary line in the named.hosts file shows that you also have primary zone authority for the zone 197.198.199.in-addr.arpa with zone information in the named.rev file. This strange syntax is named's way of getting information to match IP addresses to DNS names. Because DNS was originally set up to match DNS names to IP addresses, a different primary line is needed to do reverse resolution.

> **N O T E** The in-addr.arpa domain is used to specify reverse, or IP address, to DNS name resolution.

Database Files and Resource Records

All information in the various named database files is stored in a format known as a *resource record*. Each resource record has a type associated with it, which tells the record's function. A resource record is the smallest piece of information that named uses.

Most people find the syntax for resource records and master database files in general to be a bit arcane and obscure. It doesn't help matters that some resource records have to appear in certain places in certain files. Most DNS configuration problems can be traced to errors in these master configuration files. All this said, it's time to dive in and look at the resource record syntax and the various master files.

> **N O T E** Within the master configuration files, you have the option of specifying absolute host names or host names relative to this domain. Host names are considered absolute if they end in a dot character (.), as in foo, tristar, com.. Host names that don't end with a dot are considered relative to the local domain, also known as the *origin*. You can refer to the origin itself by using the @ character.

Resource records use a general syntax that's consistent across all types of resource records. To add to the confusion, however, several parts of the record are optional depending on the record type, and may assume a default value if not specified. The basic format of a resource record is

`[owner] [ttl] [class] type data`

Fields are separated by white space such as spaces or tabs. Table 25.5 discusses what the various fields mean.

Table 25.5 Fields in the Resource Record Data Format

Field	Description
owner	The domain or host name that the record applies to. If no name is given, the domain name of the previous resource record is assumed.
ttl	The time-to-live field, which tells how long, in seconds, the information in this record is valid after it's retrieved from a DNS server. If no ttl value is given, the minimum ttl of the last Start of Authority (SOA) record is used.
class	Specifies a networking address class. For TCP/IP networks, use the value IN. If the class isn't given, the class of the previous resource record is used.
type	Lists the type of the resource record. This value is required. The various resource record types are listed in the next section.
data	Specifies the data associated with this resource record. This value is required. The format of the data field depends on the content of the type field.

As you can see, the format of a resource record can get quite confusing. There are several optional fields, and the data field depends on the type of the resource record. To make matters worse, there are several different types of resource records. Table 25.6 lists the most common resource record types; a few additional types are rarely used. If you're interested in the additional types, refer to the appropriate RFCs and the man pages for named.

Table 25.6 Commonly Used Resource Record Types

Type	Description
A	An address record that associates a host name with an address. The data field holds the address in dotted decimal format. There can be only one A record for any given host, as this record is considered authoritative information. Any additional host name or address mappings for this host must be given by using the CNAME type.
CNAME	Associates an alias for a host with its canonical name, the name specified in the A record for this host.
HINFO	Provides information about a host. The data field holds the hardware and software information for a particular host. It's just a free-format text string, so you can put in whatever makes sense for your hardware.
MX	Sets up a mail exchanger record. The data field holds an integer preference value followed by a host name. MX records tell a mail transport to send mail to another system that knows how to deliver it to its final destination.

Part

V

Ch

25

continues

NS	Points to a name server for another zone. The data field of the NS resource record contains the DNS name of the name server. You need to specify an A record as well to match the host name with the address of the name server.
PTR	Maps addresses to names, as in the in-addr.arpa domain. The host name must be the canonical host name.
SOA	Tells the name server that all the resource records following it are authoritative for this domain. (SOA stands for *start of authority*.) The data field is enclosed by parentheses and is typically a multiline field. The data field of the SOA record contains the following entries:

origin—The canonical name of the primary name server for this domain. It's usually given as an absolute domain name ending with a . (dot), so it's not modified by the named daemon.

contact—The e-mail contact of the person who's responsible for maintaining this domain. Because the @ character has special meaning in resource records, it's replaced by a . (dot). If the responsible person for maintaining zone information about tristar.com is Dave, the contact address is dave.tristar.com.

serial—The version number of the zone information file, which is given as an integer. It's used by secondary name servers to determine when the zone information file has changed. You should increment this number by 1 every time you change the information file.

refresh—The length of time in seconds that a secondary server should wait before trying to check the SOA record of the primary name server. The SOA records don't change very often, so you can usually set this value to be on the order of one day or so.

retry—The time in seconds that a secondary server waits to retry a request to a primary server if the primary server wasn't available. Typically, it should be on the order of a few minutes.

expire—The time in seconds that the secondary server should wait before throwing away the zone information if it has been unable to contact the primary server. This number should typically be very large, on the order of 30 days or so.

minimum—The default ttl value for resource records that don't specify a ttl. If your network doesn't change very much, this number can be set to a fairly large value, such as a couple of weeks. You can always override it by specifying a ttl value in your resource records.

As you can see, the format of the resource records gets complicated in a hurry. Things should get clearer as you look at a few of the master configuration files used by named.

The named.hosts File

In your named.boot file, you listed named.hosts as being the file that contains information about your local domain, tristar.com. You could have named the file anything you wanted by listing the name on the `primary` line of named.boot. The named.hosts file contains authoritative information about the hosts in the zone of authority—tristar.com. Listing 25.1 shows a sample named.hosts file that uses several of the resource record types.

Listing 25.1 An Example named.hosts File

```
; named.hosts file for tristar.com
;
@          IN     SOA      ns.tristar.com. dave.tristar.com. (
6 ; serial number
86400 ;refresh 24 hrs
300 ; retry 5 minutes
2592000 ; expire 30 days
86400 ; minimum 24 hrs
)
IN      NS        ns.tristar.com.
;
; your domain itself tristar.com
;
@          IN     A      199.198.197.1
IN      MX      100      mailhost.tristar.com
IN      HINFO      PC-486      Linux
;
; your primary nameserver
;
ns         IN     A      199.198.197.1
nameserver      IN     CNAME      ns.tristar.com.
;
; other hosts
;
mailhost      IN     A      199.198.197.2
opus          IN     A      199.198.197.3
IN      MX      100      mailhost.tristar.com
skippy          IN     A      199.198.197.4
IN      MX      100      mailhost.tristar.com
;
; the localhost
;
localhost       IN     A      127.0.0.1
```

N O T E Host names in resource records that end with a . (dot) aren't translated any further. If the dot isn't the last character in the host name, named assumes that the host name you gave is relative to the origin domain name referred to by @ and appends the domain name to the host name. ■

Look at the named.hosts file in Listing 25.1 in detail. The first record that you come to in this file is the SOA (start of authority) record for the example domain. The first line of this record starts with the @ character, which indicates the current origin or domain (tristar.com). The definition of the origin comes from the domain listed on the corresponding `primary` line in named.boot. After that, you see the codes `IN SOA`, which tells `named` that this resource record uses Internet (TCP/IP) addressing and is a start-of-authority record.

The next two entries on the line are the canonical name of the primary name server for this domain (ns.tristar.com), and the e-mail contact with the @ replaced by a dot (dave.tristar.com). You then list the various fields of the data required by an SOA record, one per line. (Refer to Table 25.6 for a complete explanation of each of these entries.)

After the `SOA` record, the next line is a name-server resource record, which lists ns.tristar.com as being a name server for the domain. Because no domain is listed in the domain field, it's assumed to be the last domain specified, which was @, listed in the `SOA` record. And, of course, the @ character really expands to be the local domain, tristar.com. What could possibly be easier to understand?

The next three lines set up some information about the tristar.com domain itself. Although you've listed the domain name as @ for clarity because it was the last domain name listed in the file, these resource records still apply to it by default if you had left the domain field blank. The line

```
@          IN       A       199.198.197.1
```

allows users to refer to tristar.com as though it were a real machine. It has been assigned the IP address of 199.198.197.1, which, as you'll see, is really the IP address of ns.tristar.com. The next line sets up a mail exchanger `MX` record for tristar.com so that all mail going to it gets forwarded to mailhost.tristar.com instead. The last line in this group sets up a host information `HINFO` record for tristar.com, which tells the world that it's a PC-486 running Linux.

A few lines earlier in the file, you listed ns.tristar.com as being your name server via an `NS` resource record. For `named` to work correctly, you must provide an address or A record that gives the address of `ns.tristar.com`. The next line in your file does just that. Following the "glue record" that gives the address of the name server, you have a `CNAME` resource record. This record tells you that nameserver.tristar.com is an alias for ns.tristar.com.

You then proceed to set up address records for three other hosts in your domain: mailhost, opus, and skippy. Notice that after the A records for opus and skippy are `MX` records that route any mail received by opus or skippy to mailhost.tristar.com. Because no name was specified in the first field of these `MX` records, they apply to the previous name—opus or skippy.

N O T E   Because the owner field of a resource record defaults to the last one specified if it's left blank, it's easy to group records that apply to one host. However, you must be careful if you add new records for new hosts to a file. If you add them to the middle of a file, you may cause the default host to change for some of the existing resource records. Look carefully before you add resource records to an existing file. ■

Finally, the last host in this named.hosts file is the localhost, which is mapped to address 127.0.0.1. As you can see, the syntax for these files gets quite complicated and gives you lots of room for errors.

The named.rev File

The named.rev file is very similar to the named.hosts file, except that it essentially works in reverse—it maps addresses to host names. Listing 25.2 shows a sample named.rev file for tristar.com.

Listing 25.2   An Example named.rev File

```
; named.rev file for tristar.com
;
@            IN      SOA       ns.tristar.com. dave.tristar.com. (
6 ; serial number
86400 ;refresh 24 hrs
300 ; retry 5 minutes
2592000 ; expire 30 days
86400 ; minimum 24 hrs
)
IN      NS      ns.tristar.com.
;
; reverse map your IP addresses
;
1           IN      PTR       ns.tristar.com.
2           IN      PTR       mailhost.tristar.com.
3           IN      PTR       opus.tristar.com.
4           IN      PTR       skippy.tristar.com.
```

In this example, you have the same SOA record that you saw in the named.hosts file. This just sets up the authority information for the domain. In this case, @, the value of the origin, is set to 197.198.199.in-addr.arpa from the primary line in the named.boot file. Recall that the in-addr.arpa domain refers to reverse mapping of addresses to names.

N O T E The addresses listed as part of your in-addr.arpa line is your network address backward. Your example network for this chapter has the address 199.198.197.0. When you list it in the reverse mapping data files, you list it as

197.198.199.in-addr.arpa

You have the NS record that lists the name server for your domain. Following that are the records that make up the reverse address resolution records. These are PTR records and give the host number (the part of the IP address not listed in the in-addr.arpa value) and the canonical host name that matches it. You must use the canonical host name here instead of a relative host name. For example, the line

```
2           IN      PTR       mailhost.tristar.com.
```

tells named to map the host address 199.198.197.2 to the host name mailhost.tristar.com.

The named.ca File

As stated earlier in this chapter, the caching operation of named is very important. Fortunately, the named.ca file that sets up caching is also usually the simplest of the named configuration files. It just lists the root name servers for the various domains with their IP addresses. It contains a couple of special field indicators that tell named that these are root servers.

You can probably just copy the format of the sample named.ca file in Listing 25.3. To get a complete current list of the root name servers, use the nslookup utility.

Listing 25.3   An Example named.ca File

```
; named.ca file
;
.     99999999        IN      NS        NS.NIC.DDN.MIL.
99999999        IN      NS        NS.NASA.GOV.
99999999        IN      NS        KAVA.NISC.SRI.COM.
99999999        IN      NS        TERP.UMD.EDU.
99999999        IN      NS        C.NYSER.NET.
99999999        IN      NS        NS.INTERNIC.NET.
;
NS.NIC.DDN.MIL.         99999999        IN      A       192.112.36.4
NS.NASA.GOV.            99999999        IN      A       128.102.16.10
KAVA.NISC.SRI.COM.      99999999        IN      A       192.33.33.24
TERP.UMD.EDU.           99999999        IN      A       128.8.10.90
C.NYSER.NET.            99999999        IN      A       192.33.4.12
NS.INTERNIC.NET.        99999999        IN      A       198.41.0.4
```

As you can see, the named.ca file simply maps NS name server records to the appropriate addresses for them.

Troubleshooting

DNS is a very complex system. You can do many things wrong that will cause your system to not behave properly. Many of the problems that occur with a DNS setup will appear to be identical but come from different causes. However, most of the problems result from syntax errors in your configuration files.

Make sure that you specify the host names correctly in your DNS configuration files. If it's an absolute host name, be sure to end it with a dot.

Be especially careful with the names used in SOA and CNAME records. If you make errors here, these resource records can redirect host name queries to computers that don't exist.

Be sure to increment the serial number in your configuration files when making changes. If you forget, DNS will not reread the file.

Be sure to enter the correct IP address for A records, and check to see that it matches your /etc/hosts file (if you have one). Also, make sure that the DNS name and IP address match the corresponding reverse resolution information in named.rev.

Your best tool for figuring out errors is the `nslookup` command. Use `nslookup` to test your DNS server thoroughly. Do regular and reverse resolution for every address in your DNS database to make sure that all the names and addresses are correct.

N O T E An interesting project is Paul Vixie's (he wrote BIND) S/WAN project, which provides opportunistic encryption at the Ethernet packet level. For more information, go to **http://www.cygnus.com/~gnu/swan.html**. ■

From Here...

This chapter shows the various components of the DNS system and explores the various configuration files necessary to get a DNS name server running on your Linux system. Because the syntax for the resource records is fairly arcane, you need to pay close attention to your configuration files as you write them.

You can find more information about networking in the following chapters:

- Chapter 24, "Configuring a TCP/IP Network," shows how to set up and configure TCP/IP networking.
- Chapter 29, "Using SLIP and PPP," shows how to configure SLIP and PPP for dial-up Internet access.
- Chapter 31, "Surfing the Internet with the World Wide Web," gives an overview of the Internet.

Part
V

Ch
25

Configuring Electronic Mail

by Steve Burnett

This chapter will first discuss some of the general issues of electronic mail and the Internet in general: concepts and definitions, the mail standards as defined in the RFCs (Requests for Comment) that sendmail and other applications have tried to address, and several of the protocols defined for use in electronic messaging. The chapter will then cover sendmail, the UNIX-based subsystem in widest use on the Internet.

An Overview of Electronic Mail

This section presents a broad overview of electronic messaging. First will be a discussion of some of the general concepts of electronic mail, including two basic kinds of mail software, and where sendmail belongs in that division. The next part of this section will present the RFCs (Request for Comment), where the protocols used to communicate within and across networks are defined. The last part of this section explains some of the protocols used to define electronic messages.

History and General Concepts

One of the first widely used office mail systems was IBM's PROFS. A mainframe-based system, PROFS had features similar to modern e-mail systems such as Microsoft Exchange and Lotus Notes. Such features included:

- Strong administration and management tools
- Security customization
- Scheduling capabilities

PROFS and other messaging systems of the time shared several similarities. Whether mainframe- or UNIX-based, they were text-based and were considered host-based centralized messaging systems. Because PROFS was scalable and adaptable, IBM only recently switched away from it for its enterprise mail use.

As personal computers grew in acceptance and became widely used throughout corporations, people started to take advantage of the shift in computing power from the mainframe to the desktop. An early application of personal computer networks was file sharing, which made use of a central file server and a shared universally accessible network drive. Shortly thereafter, messaging systems began to take advantage of the new power on users' desktops. So host-based messaging shifted (in some cases) to LAN-based messaging.

The Shared-File Messaging Model

cc:Mail is an example of *LAN-based messaging*, which is also called *shared-file messaging*. In the shared-file messaging model, the desktop client has all the power and all the control. A client sends messages to a mailbox on a server and *polls* the server to retrieve mail from its specified mailbox directory. The server is passive, only storing messages. It performs no processing or sorting and has no provisions for setting rules to control message flow. Shared-file messaging provided the following gains over host-based messaging:

- Added attachments to text-only messages
- Required lower-cost servers
- Simplified setup
- Improved performance for some client actions

However, shared-file messaging systems introduced new problems. Because each user needed full access to the file system, including other users' mailboxes, security was an issue. Also, because each client had to poll a server to get new mail, network traffic increased. Network bandwidth is a bottleneck more often than server or client bandwidth are.

The Client/Server Messaging Model

The client/server messaging system divided the tasks of message processing between the desktop workstations and the servers. Using a push model for messages, mail clients no longer clogged the network by constantly polling for new messages. Client/server messaging also improved on shared-file messaging by improving security so that users would have more difficulty reading others' mail. The more intelligent server enabled the sorting and processing of messages to be performed before messages were transferred across the network to a client.

MUAs, MTAs, and MDAs

An electronic mail system can be broken down into three elements: the Mail User Agent (MUA), the Mail Transport Agent (MTA), and the Mail Delivery Agent (MDA).

The MUA is the user interface—the software with which the user reads his mail, organizes mail into directories or folders, and sends mail. People prefer different features in their MUAs, and not all MUAs are available on all platforms. Many MUAs can coexist on the same machine. For example, a UNIX workstation can have any or all of the following MUAs available for use: mailx, elm, pine, mutt, mailtool, and dtmail. A given user can use any MUA present on his or her system because the MUAs are simply local applications. In addition, MUA functionality is often included in multipurpose software such as Lotus Notes and Netscape Mail.

The MTA isn't used to write a mail message; it's used to route the mail from a local MUA to another MTA on another system. (sendmail is an example of an MTA, which is not used to read or write mail directly. sendmail is intended only to deliver preformatted messages.) Mail routing may occur either locally or remotely. In a local mail transfer in which both the sender and destination have accounts on the same machine, the MTA is responsible for transporting mail from itself to a local MDA. In the process, the MTA may possibly edit the protocols, addresses, and routing of the mail message. A message created on a UUCP network requires some transformation before that message can be received by a person on a TCP/IP network. The MTA acts as a gateway for mail to get a message from one network to another network that uses different protocols. In the vast majority of situations, there will be only a single MTA on a given machine.

The MDA is the third component of the mail handling routine. While sendmail handles SMTP mail transfer between MTAs directly, sendmail relies on Mail Delivery Agents (MDAs) to handle local delivery from the sendmail queue to a queue used by an MUA. Two common MDAs that sendmail is often configured to use are /bin/mail and procmail. /bin/mail is almost universally available on UNIX systems; procmail is widely available and is both faster and much more capable than the standard /bin/mail, providing strong capabilities for the presorting and preprocessing of mail.

To better understand the MUA/MTA/MDA relationship, consider a real-world example of a person sending a letter. The MUA represents the person sending the letter: He writes a letter, places it in an envelope, puts an address and stamp on it, and then delivers it to a post office. The MTA is like the post office staff: They accept the letter, examine the address, reformat the address if necessary, and route the letter either to a mailbox in the same post office (if the letter is local) or to another post office (for a remote destination). The MDA corresponds to the postal worker who delivers the mail from the post office to the intended location. If a gateway is used, this analogy can be extended: An MTA that receives a letter for a destination in another state has to transfer that message to another MTA that knows how to deliver letters in the target state.

The IETF Requests for Comment

An *RFC* is a formal description of protocol formats used on the Internet. These protocols are also adhered to by many non-Internet systems. The Requests for Comment (RFC) are issued by the Internet Engineering Task Force (IETF). RFCs are identified and referred to by numbers for clarity; it's easier to refer to RFC822 than to refer to the "Standard for the Format of ARPA Internet Text Messages." There are more than two thousand RFCs as of this writing, some of which have been made obsolete by later RFCs. To find a given RFC, look for the IETF on the World Wide Web at **http://www.ietf.org/**.

Because mail is such a commonly used function of the Internet, many of the RFCs set standards for mail exchange. sendmail and other MTAs address the needs and definitions of many of these protocols. However, attempting to describe in detail all of the RFCs relevant to mail transport and format could take years of time and thousands of pages.

Table 26.1 presents, in chronological order, the RFCs relevant to sendmail.

Table 26.1   RFCs Dealing with Electronic Mail Messaging

Number	Title	Comment
RFC819	Domain Naming	Contains convention for Internet user applications.
RFC821	Simple Mail Transfer Protocol	Defines SMTP.
RFC822	Standard for the Format of ARPA Internet Text Messages	Defines the format (headers, body, and how to separate the two) for Internet text mail messages.
RFC976	UUCP Mail Interchange Format Standard	Defines the UNIX-to-UNIX-Copy-Protocol (UUCP) format of mail messages between two UNIX systems.

Number	Title	Comment
RFC1123	Requirements for Internet Hosts - Application and Support	Extends and updates RFC822, mostly by clarifying ambiguous issues in the original document.
RFC1327	Mapping between X.400 (1988) / ISO 10021 and RFC822	Updates RFC822.
RFC1521 and RFC1522	MIME (Multipurpose Internet Mail Extensions) Parts One and Two	Provides another extension to the mail format defined in RFC822 by defining Multipurpose Internet Mail Extensions (MIME), which, among other things, allows insertion of binary files such as graphics and sound to mail messages. These two were made obsolete by RFC2045–2049.
RFC1651	SMTP Service Extensions	Introduces ESTMP (Extended Simple Mail Transfer Protocol).
RFC1652	SMTP Service Extension for 8-bit MIME Transport	
RFC1653	MTP Service Extension for Message	
RFC1869	SMTP Service Extensions	Makes RFC1651 obsolete.
RFC1870	SMTP Service Extension for Message Size Declaration	Makes RFC1653 obsolete.
RFC1891	SMTP Service Extension for Delivery Status Notifications	
RFC1892	The Multipart/Report Content Type for the Reporting of Mail System Administrative Messages	
RFC1893	Enhanced Mail System Status Codes	
RFC1894	An Extensible Message Format for Delivery Status Notifications	
RFC2045–2049	Multipurpose Internet Mail Extensions (MIME) Parts One through Five	Make RFC1521 and RFC1522 obsolete.

Part
V

Ch
26

Internet Protocols

sendmail uses the *Simple Mail Transfer Protocol* (SMTP) to move messages between two mailservers. Acting as a server-to-server protocol, SMTP requires another protocol such as POP3 to collect and process messages locally and deliver the messages to specific users. SMTP is the communications protocol generally used in UNIX-based networks for mail over TCP/IP (Transmission Control Protocol/Internet Protocol) connections. Unlike the UUCP protocol, which must have a "map" of which machines exist between the sender and the destination, TCP/IP allows one system on a network to talk "directly" to another by passing packets of information back and forth between the two. The SMTP protocol is defined in the IETF's RFC821 titled "Simple Mail Transfer Protocol."

SMTP and ESMTP   SMTP is a TCP-based client/server protocol, originally defined in the IETF's RFC821. SMTP is complex in details but is fundamentally simple. After a reliable connection is established, the mail client (MUA) initiates a brief handshaking sequence with the mail server (MTA). The client then sends one or more messages to the MTA for delivery. Before each message is sent, the mail client sends a list of the message's local recipients and the sender's address. In an obvious paper mail parallel, this information is referred to as the message's envelope.

The handshaking sequence and message content exchange takes place in a formal language made up of four-character commands and three-digit reply codes. For example, an ESMTP mail exchange log might look like this:

```
$ /usr/sbin/sendmail -v david@mail.fake.com < message
david@mail.fake.com... Connecting to localmail.mail.fake.com. via smtp...
220 localmail.mail.fake.com ESMTP Sendmail 8.9/8.9/; Sat, 22 May 1999 08:06:22 -
0700
>>> EHLO gateway.oppositemail.com
250 localmail.mail.fake.com Hello michael@gateway.oppositemail.com [192.168.0.5],
pleased to meet you
>>> MAIL From:michael@gateway.oppositemail.com
250 <michael@gateway.oppositemail.com>... Sender ok
>>> RCPT To:david@mail.fake.com
250 Recipient ok
>>> DATA
354 Enter mail, end with "." on a line by itself
>>> .
250 WAA11745 Message accepted for delivery
david@mail.fake.com... Sent (WAA11745 Message accepted for delivery)
Closing connection to localmail.mail.fake.com.
>>> QUIT
221 localmail.mail.fake.com closing connection
```

A framework for additional features in electronic mail is called *Extended Simple Mail Transport Protocol* (ESMTP). ESMTP is a mechanism by which any extensions used with traditional SMTP can be negotiated between the client and server. The mechanism, as described in RFC1651, is open-ended: Two possible extensions were defined in RFC1652 and RFC1653.

RFC1652 defines 8-bit MIME encoding, which enables a user to send 8-bit data in mail messages without having to recode the data using base64, quoted-printable, or some other encoding method. This also eliminates the breakage that can result from sending 8-bit data to an RFC821-compliant SMTP server that doesn't know what to do with the components it receives.

Message size declaration (defined in RFC1653) offers a method for a server to limit the size of a message it is prepared to accept. With RFC821 SMTP, the only possibility is for the server to discard the message after it has been sent in its entirety and after the message has crossed the network onto the server. Unfortunately, this is a waste of bandwidth, and there is no way for the mail client to know that the message was discarded because of its size.

Other extensions possible with ESMTP include requesting a delivery status notification on outgoing messages (so senders can be notified when messages arrive at their destination) and negotiating encryption between secure mailservers for more secure mail.

Mail Message Formatting

SMTP defined how to transfer a mail message across the Internet, but did not define how to recognize a mail message. RFC822 defines the format of Internet electronic mail messages. The format is simple, as befits a standard:

- A header containing various required and optional message attributes
- A blank line
- The message contents

The header fields are much longer than the content in the example message given here:

```
Return-Path: david@mail.fake.com
Received: from localmail.mail.fake.com (localmail.mail.fake.com [168.9.100.10])
by gateway.oppositemail.com (8.9/8.9) with ESMTP id WAA01322 for
<robert@oppositemail.com>; Sat, 22 May 1999 18:17:06 -0500
Received: from beta.mail.fake.com (beta.mail.fake.com [207.266.47.2]) by
localmail.mail.fake.com (8.9/8.9) with  SMTP id WAA13732 for
<robert@oppositemail.com>; Sat, 22 May 1999 18:22:06 -0500
Message-Id: 199802180506.WAA13732@localmail.mail.fake.com
X-Sender: pete@localmail.mail.fake.com
X-Mailer: Amiga Eudora Lite Version 2.1.2
Mime-Version: 1.0
Content-Type: text/plain; charset="us-ascii"
Date: Sat, 22 May 1999 18:22:08 -0500
To: robert@oppositemail.com
From: David Wylie david@mail.fake.com
Subject: Test message

This is a test message.
David
```

The blank line after the "Subject" line divides the header from the message body that follows. Any subsequent blank line is part of the message body and has no structural significance. Most header fields are brief and have a fairly obvious meaning (such as "Subject"), while some others are lengthy and not readily understood (such as "Received..."). For a detailed explanation of the many standard and less-standard header fields, see Chapter 35 of Costales and Allman's *sendmail, 2nd edition*.

Each header line consists of a "keyword-value" pair that defines a characteristic of that message. For example, a required characteristic of a mail message is a message recipient. This characteristic is defined by the keyword To:, one or more Spacebar or Tab characters, and then the value that specifies the mailing address of the recipient. In the message above, this characteristic is defined by the following line:

```
To: robert@oppositemail.com
```

sendmail

sendmail is generally considered one of the few true nightmares of UNIX system administration. sendmail is difficult to configure and can be approached in much the same way that novices approach UNIX. When someone once complained to Eric Allman (the creator of sendmail) that sendmail administration was complicated, he replied, "Configuring sendmail is complex because the world is complex." While sendmail can do just about anything you can think of, instructing it how to do what you want it to can be a chore.

However, while sendmail is difficult to work with, recent versions have improved the tasks of configuring and administering sendmail substantially. The addition of a large set of M4 macros and the ability to use intelligible names for options in addition to the single-character switches in the configuration file has made sendmail configuration an easier task. sendmail has also become a reasonably mature product. Although flaws are still found almost monthly, sendmail is used in enterprise networks for mail delivery across a wide set of networks and in high-volume environments.

sendmail's History

In the late 1970s, Eric Allman was at the University of California at Berkeley. He wrote the predecessor to sendmail, called delivermail, which was released in 1979 to solve the problem of transferring mail between the three networks on campus at that time. Those three networks were ARPANET (which was using NCP, or Network Control Protocol), a UUCP mail system, and an internal network called BerkNet.

The next year, ARPANET started to convert from NCP to TCP (Transmission Control Protocol). Previously, mail was delivered using FTP (File Transfer Protocol), but SMTP was developed to plan for the possible growth of the network's mail traffic by several orders of magnitude.

In response to these changes, Allman adopted an inclusive approach to formats of electronic mail messages. If a message didn't match the preferred format, sendmail attempted to fix the message format instead of immediately rejecting the message. Allman also chose to limit the functional goal of sendmail to be a router of mail, instead of including the functionality of an end-user mail application. The 4.1c version of BSD (Berkeley Software Distribution) UNIX included the first public release of sendmail.

Meanwhile, others were busy extending sendmail's capabilities separately from Allman. In addition to various private efforts, several commercial vendors such as Sun and

Hewlett-Packard developed their own versions of sendmail as they saw needs for improvements not included in the current versions. Out of these parallel developments came several versions of sendmail with varying levels of compatibility. In 1998, Allman took sendmail to commercial status as of version 8.9, leaving the 8.8.x version the freeware it always was.

sendmail's Architecture

In general, compilation and installation of the sendmail distribution is often simpler than it first appears. The source package includes make-description files tailored for many different systems, and a "build" script that chooses the correct one for the local environment. At times, an administrator might need to make minor changes to the make-description file that's most similar to his particular environment in order to match the specific local system.

sendmail the Daemon   sendmail itself is normally configured to run on a UNIX system as a *daemon* in order to listen for incoming mail.

> **N O T E** A daemon is a UNIX system program that runs in the background without a controlling terminal window. ▪

When run as a daemon, unless it's instructed not to on startup, sendmail forks and runs in the background, listening on socket 25 for incoming SMTP connections. The command to run sendmail as a daemon on a Berkeley UNIX-based system might look something like this:

```
/usr/lib/sendmail -bd -q30m
```

This command can be defined as one of the startup commands executed when the UNIX system boots. Here is a sample of a command, taken from a startup script named sendmail.init found in the /etc/rc.d/init.d directory on a Linux system:

```
# Start daemons.
echo -n "Starting sendmail: "
daemon sendmail -bd -q1h
echo
touch /var/lock/subsys/sendmail
;;
```

The -bd flag launches sendmail as a daemon and the -q1h switch instructs sendmail to check the queue once every hour. In contrast, the sample command preceding this one has the -q switch instructing sendmail to check the queue every thirty minutes.

The first action sendmail takes when it's started is to read the /etc/sendmail.cf configuration file. The sendmail.cf and dependent configuration files are presented in the next section.

sendmail Configuration and Control Using the sendmail.cf File   Part of sendmail's power is derived from the access provided to sendmail's underlying configuration files. As mail messages are funneled through sendmail's configuration files, sendmail performs all message routing functions, including parsing, forwarding, delivering, returning, and queuing.

The core of sendmail's configuration is the sendmail.cf file. A complex configuration file read only once at `sendmail`'s initial run time, sendmail.cf contains three important types of information:

- Options such as operational control switches, mailer definitions, and the locations of other sendmail sub-configuration files
- Macros for use in rulesets
- Rulesets for rewriting addresses on incoming and outgoing messages

N O T E   No one bothers to write a sendmail.cf file starting with a blank page in a text editor. If you are configuring sendmail for a new network, you can almost certainly find a sendmail.cf file that requires minimal changes. Of course, after you have a functioning mailserver, make a backup of the working configuration and put it somewhere safe. ▨

V8 sendmail added the use of the m4 macro `preprocesso`, which is used to generate sendmail.cf files containing the features you select. A sendmail m4 creation file typically should be given a .mc (macro configuration) file suffix, but this is not required for the process to work. Many sample .mc scripts are supplied with the standard sendmail distributions.

For example, a minimum .mc file for a Linux workstation (without appropriate comments) could be something like this:

```
OSTYPE(linux)dnl
MAILER(local)dnl
```

These two are the only two required macros in a .mc file. You are likely to want more features, but this file—named smallest_linux.mc—could be run with the following command (assuming you are in the /usr/lib/sendmail/cf/cf directory, which is where the standard sendmail distribution places m4 files):

```
m4 ../m4/cf.m4 smallest_linux.mc > sendmail.cf
```

The following list provides a breakdown of the elements in the preceding command:

`m4`	Calls the m4 preprocessor
`../m4/cf.m4`	Identifies m4's default configuration file
`smallest_linux.mc`	Is the two-line macro configuration file
`>sendmail.cf`	Specifies that output is to be placed in the sendmail.cf file

Now that you have used m4 to generate a sendmail.cf file containing exactly the features you requested, you will still need to customize the sendmail.cf file for use at your site. Using m4 for sendmail.cf generation, however, is fast and accurate. In addition to using the many m4 macros that ship with the sendmail distribution, you can also write your own as you feel necessary and include them for use.

For a quick sendmail configuration file, fill out the World Wide Web form interface to the m4 configuration tool (for V8 sendmail) at **http://www.completeis.com/sendmail/**

sendmail.cgi. Select your desired options with the Web form, and a sendmail.cf file with the chosen options will be returned to you.

sendmail Configuration Files and Their Locations   sendmail.cf is the first file that sendmail reads on startup. The sendmail.cf file contains the locations of all other subconfiguration files used by sendmail, which are listed in Table 26.2.

Table 26.2   sendmail Configuration Files

File Name and Location	Description
/etc/aliases	ASCII text list of defined aliases to names
/etc/aliases.db	Database of aliases compiled from /etc/aliases
/etc/sendmail.hf	Help file
/var/log/sendmail.st	Collected statistics
/var/spool/mqueue/*	Temporary files for mail queue
/var/run/sendmail.pid	The process ID of the daemon

These are only the default locations of the files. Because their locations are defined within sendmail.cf, they may be set to whatever name and directory path you like.

sendmail contains far too many configuration options to list in this book. The syntax for options comes in two types: very cryptic and a bit less cryptic. In the cryptic version of option syntax, the O (capital *o*, not zero) command starts an option command in the sendmail.cf file. So the following two sample commands from a sendmail.cf file

O8pass8

and

O EightBitMode=pass8

perform the same function. They tell sendmail to pass 8-bit formatted data as 8 bits, and not to truncate it to 7 bits. Notice the syntax change: The single character version (O8) does not contain a space between the O and the letter signifying which option is being set, while the name version (O EightBitMode) must contain a space between the O command and the name of the option. As with all other sendmail commands, the O must be in the left-most position on the line, which is also column 1.

This restriction prevents misinterpretation of commands, such as this next line which may also be found in a sendmail.cf file:

DMMONGO

This command defines (D), a macro (M), to have the value MONGO, so that you can use $M when rewriting rules instead of typing "MONGO." Without the restriction that a command is identified by an O in the left-most column, the O in MONGO might be interpreted as a command.

The options just presented illustrate the form of the option command for use within a configuration file. However, options may be defined either in an m4 macro file or on the command line. The command line versions of the above options would use a dash before the option, a lowercase *o* to indicate a single-character option command, and an uppercase *O* to indicate a named option command, as shown in these examples:

```
-o8pass8
```

and

```
-O EightBitMode=pass8
```

or

```
-O EightBitMode=pass8
```

sendmail Rulesets

sendmail uses rules to rewrite addresses on incoming and outgoing mail. These rules are the center of sendmail's capability, as well as its complexity: sendmail's rewriting rules are a specialized text-oriented programming language. Eric Allman designed sendmail so that the ruleset performs two core tasks:

- Examine each recipient's address to determine which MDA should be used to send the message to (or nearer to) the recipient.
- Transform addresses in both the envelope and the message header to facilitate delivery or reply.

Rewriting rules are organized into rulesets. A *ruleset* is a subroutine or module consisting of a sequence of rules. When an address is passed to a ruleset, the subroutine passes the address to each of its rules in order. If the matching clause matches the investigated address, the rule is applied, the address is transformed, and the result is passed to the next rule. If the address does not match the current rule, the address is not transformed, and the next rule in the set is tried.

sendmail Ruleset Syntax   Each ruleset is identified by a number, and each new ruleset begins with an *S* in the leftmost column followed by its identifying number. Rules begin with the letter *R,* and are not numbered. A non-*R* command ends the ruleset. For example:

```
######################################
###    Ruleset 0 -- Parse Address    ###
######################################
S0
R$*              $: $>98 $1          handle local hacks
```

Rule syntax is cryptic, but fairly simple. Each rule has a left-hand side and a right-hand side. A comment portion is optional. The two sides and the optional comment are separated by tabs. The left-hand side is compared to the address as a string pattern. If the pattern matches the left-hand side, the address is transformed by the rule's right-hand side and is passed on to the next rule.

In sendmail.cf, an octothorp (#) begins a comment line. Empty lines are ignored. The S0 defines the beginning of Ruleset 0. The R on the next line defines the beginning of a rule. The $* accepts every address that is passed to it, and the $: $>98 $1 passes the address to Ruleset 98 for further processing. The text "handle local hacks" is a comment. Because rules are tab-delimited, the comment portion does not require a comment marker (#) at the beginning.

The Core sendmail Rulesets   Several standard rulesets exist, and they may appear in any order in sendmail.cf. When sendmail reads the configuration file, it sorts the rules appropriately. A ruleset that is expected but is not present is treated as if it were present but empty. The following are the main rulesets:

- Ruleset 0 resolves an MDA by reading the address
- Ruleset 1 processes the sender's address
- Ruleset 2 processes the recipient's address
- Ruleset 3 preprocesses all addresses
- Ruleset 4 post-processes all addresses
- Ruleset 5 rewrites unaliased local users

Aliasing in sendmail   An alias is an abbreviation for one or more full mailing addresses. Although an alias may be merely a nickname for a longer address you don't want to type every time (such as "john" for "john.dagenhamster@someothercompany.com"), an alias may also be the name of a list of several recipients.

Many MUAs maintain their own alias lists, but these alias lists are normally in formats that aren't shareable with other MUAs. If you typically use pine on a Linux workstation, its alias file will not be available to your Lotus Notes client on your Windows 95 workstation when you write a letter with that tool. In contrast, the many possible alias lists contained in aliases maintained in sendmail's alias file will be recognized and expanded when a message is processed by sendmail, regardless of the MUA used to create that message. sendmail allows for multiple alias files—up to twelve by default.

From Here...

For related information, see Chapter 33, "Using Electronic Mail," which shows how to communicate with other people by using the e-mail system.

- You can learn more details about sendmail from the Web at **http://www.sendmail.org/** or from Bryan Costales' and Eric Allman's book *sendmail, second edition*, from O'Reilly & Associates.
- Chapter 33, "Using Electronic Mail," covers the use of mail user agents such as elm, pine, and mutt to read and compose electronic mail.

Configuring a Usenet News Service

by Steve Burnett

A Usenet Primer

Usenet is often confused with the Internet, but Usenet isn't the Internet. Usenet is not a network, but a service carried over the Internet, as well as many computers not directly part of the Internet. The best way I've found to describe Usenet is twenty thousand (or so) bulletin boards, each with a different title describing what the topic for that board is supposed to be. You can look for a bulletin board with a topic you think you might be interested in, and read some or all of the messages on the board that day. If you want to, you can put a message up to either reply publicly to someone else's message or to start a new discussion. You can also copy a person's address down, and send him or her a private letter that won't appear on the board. Later, you can come back and see if there are any new and interesting messages from other people.

Usenet is unlike a party telephone line because you don't deal with other people in real-time. You can't interrupt someone while he is thinking of what to write on the board (you could, however, repeat his message afterward and quote him out of context; but besides being rude, that's not the same as interrupting him and preventing others from hearing his words). Usenet is very like a party, though, because there's very little control over who can say something. If a person insists, for example, that squirrels are the only warm-blooded animals that cannot carry rabies, he can post that message. Of course, people who know this is false can reply with the correct information. Then while the first person can continue to insist he is right, the rest of the readers of that board are likely to start ignoring messages from the first person.

N O T E   For information on the history of Usenet, use Netscape to go to
http://www.yahoo.com/Reference/FAQs/ for several FAQs (Frequently Asked Questions) concerning Usenet. ■

History and Origins of Usenet

Back in the dark ages of computing (circa late 1970s) a version of UNIX labeled V7 was released. One of the applications included was UUCP, which stands for Unix-to-Unix-CoPy. In 1979, two graduate students at Duke University started using UUCP to exchange messages between two systems at the university. Next, a set of shell scripts was developed to exchange messages between Duke and the network at the University of North Carolina at Chapel Hill. Later, the shell scripts were rewritten in C, and they have been rewritten and extended many times since then.

Usenet Structure

To quote Douglas Adams in *The Hitchhikers' Guide to the Galaxy*, "Space is BIG. Really BIG." Usenet (as of this writing) is approximately ten thousand different newsgroups, with several million total participants. Some of these newsgroups are dead, and no one ever posts to them. Some newsgroups are highly active, and are likely to split into multiple newsgroups soon (either because no one can keep up with the sheer volume or because a large segment of that newsgroup is interested in a narrower subset of topics than the other readers of the newsgroup).

An example of newsgroup spawning happened in comp.sys.powerpc, a newsgroup devoted to discussions of the PowerPC RISC processor. When Be, Inc. announced the BeBox, a dual-processor workstation running a new operating system, a substantial fraction of the newsgroup focused exclusively on Be's hardware and software. To accommodate both the interests of the people who wanted to discuss the BeOS and the wishes of the people with no interest in the BeOS, a newsgroup called comp.sys.be was formed. Alternatively, a topic discussion such as "undocumented features of the PowerPC processor family" would be of interest to the entire newsgroup, and the information generated from this discussion might become a large section of the newsgroup's FAQ or a separate FAQ altogether.

Although the sheer volume of Usenet can appear overwhelming, there is some logic to the structure. Table 27.1 presents some of the first-level divisions of Usenet. A first-level identifier appears as the leftmost part of every Usenet name.

Table 27.1 Usenet Hierarchy Names

Hierarchy Name	Description
biz	Business
comp	Anything to do with computers
misc	Miscellaneous
news	Usenet issues, general information
rec	Recreational (sports, crafts, hobbies)
sci	Scientific
soc	Social (personal, cultural)
talk	Conversation on anything
alt	Everything else

There are other first-level identifiers for newsgroups, many of which tend to be regional. For example, a newsgroup with a name starting with de.* is generally populated by speakers of the German language, and most of the de.* hierarchy deals with Germany and European issues.

The alt.* hierarchy of newsgroups is an enormous part of Usenet. The requirements for creating an alt.* newsgroup are easier than the requirements for creating a major hierarchy newsgroup. In addition, the alt.* newsgroups are not always carried by every Internet access provider, for two reasons. The first reason is bandwidth: the alt.* newsgroups are a substantial portion of all Usenet newsgroups, and some of these—especially the newsgroups devoted to binary files of either applications or images—can take up enormous amounts of bandwidth. The second reason for restricting distribution of the alt.* newsgroups is offensiveness: The alt.* newsgroups tend to tolerate more extreme or obnoxious language and topics than the mainstream newsgroups, and people are more likely to be offended by their content.

Part
V

Ch

27

> **N O T E**   Some Internet access providers have a "user-defined" policy for Usenet access: They will
> provide groups from the full Usenet newsgroups list, but they will carry only newsgroups the
> users of that network have asked for. This "a la carte" policy substantially reduces the actual bandwidth
> of the Usenet feed required for the network, but the users' interests are not restricted or censored.
> Other Internet access providers have a mixed policy: They will carry only groups that they approve of
> AND that their users ask for. ▩

If you are new to Usenet, you should make sure the newsgroup news.announce.newusers is on
your subscription lists. Basic informational guides about aspects of Usenet are periodically
reposted to this newsgroup every two weeks.

Configuring Usenet Clients

Usenet operates on the familiar client/server relationship: A server exchanges messages with
another server and stores the messages on the local system. In order to read a Usenet
newsgroup, you will need to contact your network or Internet service provider and ask for the
name of an NNTP Server. Once you have a server name (which will normally look something
like either test.fake.com or 192.168.2.221), you can start.

NN and TIN

NN and TIN are two very similar newsreaders with similar configuration requirements, and
both are included in many common Linux distributions.

If you're using a version of TIN compiled with the NNTP options from a UNIX shell account,
try one of these commands:

- If you are using the ksh or bash shell:

  ```
  $ NNTPSERVER= test.fake.com tin -r -f .fakenewsrc I .newsnet/.index
  ```

- If you are using the C shell or tcsh shell:

  ```
  % setenv NNTPSERVER test.fake.com; tin -r -f .fakenewsrc I .newsnet/.index
  ```

For NN, the configuration is similar:

- If you are using the ksh or bash shell:

  ```
  $ NNTPSERVER=test.fake.com nn newsrc=~ .fakenewsrc
  ```

- If you're using the C shell or tcsh shell:

  ```
  % setenv NNTPSERVER test.fake.com nn newsrc=~/.fakenewsrc
  ```

Pine

Pine is most commonly used as a mail reader, but it can also be used as a newsreader. To set up your pine mail client for accessing Usenet, press <S> (Setup) and then <C> (Config). Then edit the line "news collections" to read as follows:

```
*{test.fake.com/NNTP}[]
```

Next, press <E> to exit pine and restart it. Then press <L> (List Folders), go down to the news folders, and select <A> (Add) to subscribe to the newsgroups you want.

The resulting screen might look similar to this:

```
PINE 3.96   FOLDER LIST                        Folder: INBOX  313 Messages
- - - - - - - - - - - - - - - - - - - - - - - - - - - - - - - - - - - - - - - -
Folder-collection <mail/[]>  ** Default for Saves **      (Local)
- - - - - - - - - - - - - - - - - - - - - - - - - - - - - - - - - - - - - - - -

              [ Select Here to See Expanded List ]


- - - - - - - - - - - - - - - - - - - - - - - - - - - - - - - - - - - - - - - -
News-collection <News on test.fake,com>                  (Remote)
- - - - - - - - - - - - - - - - - - - - - - - - - - - - - - - - - - - - - - - -

              [ Select Here to See Expanded List ]
```

Although reading news can be fun and informative, only reading (and not posting) messages in newsgroups is a behavior pattern called *lurking*, which is frowned upon by long-time Usenet people. If you want to post new Usenet messages to newsgroups or to send replies by electronic mail, you must typically also fill out the following fields:

- Your name (first and last name)
- Your e-mail address (userid@hostname.domain)
- The computer that forwards your mail (ask your system administrator for the SMTP mail server's name)

This is typically already set up for your mailreader software. You should be able to use the same entries. Check with a system administrator to make sure, though.

N O T E   Most system administrators will have an information sheet already prepared with this information. If they don't, keep this information summary where you can get to it, so the next person to ask can benefit from your research. ■

With pine and other newsreaders, as well as most e-mail applications, you can define a *sigfile*. A sigfile (short for *signature file*) is a block of information you want included with every posting you make to a newsgroup. Typically people include their name, e-mail address, and (if a work-related account) their title or rank. Sometimes people also include a short quote they consider witty.

> **N O T E** Things you would rarely want to put in a sigfile are your home address and telephone number. Without even considering the possibility of malicious or prankish behavior, there is always the possibility that the person making the legitimate business call from Singapore to you (in New York City) can forget the time zone difference. Remember that if a person can read your e-mail or news post over the Internet, he or she can almost always reply the same way. ■

Another caution if you set up a sigfile is to remember that you have your sigfile defined. Manually pasting your sigfile into the end of your outgoing message or attaching the sigfile as an attached file when the sigfile is automatically included, will make you look silly.

At some point while reading newsgroups, you will either want to contribute to a current discussion or start a new conversational topic. Before you start actively participating in Usenet, you need to understand the rules of the Usenet subculture. Follow this general advice when you start posting messages to a newsgroup:

- ■ Don't post until you've read the group for at least a week and have a feel for the tone of the newsgroup. Do you consider the average discussion too rude and brutal, or would the newsgroup's current residents consider you an irritant?

- ■ Look for and read the FAQ (if one exists). Many of the Usenet's FAQs are archived at **ftp://rtfm.mit.edu/pub/Usenet/**.

- ■ Post only to newsgroups in which your message is relevant. If you are trying to sell a waterbed in California, you should probably advertise only in .forsale newsgroups in the immediate are. It's not likely that readers of the triangle.forsale newsgroup serving the eastern North Carolina area will want to ship your waterbed across the country. Similarly, if you have a question about Amiga computers, don't post your query to a Macintosh-oriented newsgroup.

You might post a message to a newsgroup but look at that newsgroup later and not see your message. Some newsgroups are moderated, which means that all posts to that newsgroup are read by a person or group of persons who weed out inappropriate messages and don't send them to the newsgroup. You can find out if a newsgroup is moderated by reading the FAQ for that newsgroup, by reading the charter for that newsgroup, or by reading messages on that newsgroup for a week or two before posting, and noticing if anyone describes himself as a moderator of that newsgroup.

> **N O T E** If you don't see a FAQ immediately visible on the newsgroup when you first log in, try using one of the Usenet-capable search engines such as **http://www.dejanews.com** or **http://www.altavista.digital.com** and searching for the newsgroup name and "FAQ" as keywords. Alternatively, you might ask "Is there a FAQ for this group?" in your first message to save you a world of angst. ■

In general, use common sense and you'll probably be fine. For more advice on the sometimes tricky topic of Netiquette, use your Web browser to go to **http://www.fau.au/rinaldi/ netiquette.html**, a Web site with many good resources for newcomers to the Internet in general.

From Here...

For more information on Usenet, read Chapter 34, "Surviving Usenet News." It describes the Usenet news system that is used to exchange public messages.

Chapter 27, "Configuring a Usenet News Service," provides a basis for some of the topics in this chapter.

Part

V

Ch

27

Using the *emacs* Editor

by Jack Tackett

The name emacs stands for Editor MACroS, which began life as a replacement for an early text editor named teco. emacs is one of the most used, most widely ported editors available in the UNIX/Linux world today. In fact, versions of emacs are available on almost every computing platform known to the industry, from Linux to Microsoft Windows.

A full version of emacs is very large, taking up several megabytes of disk space. It's a full-featured editor, very powerful, and has been extended for functions beyond text editing. In some installations, you can use it to edit files, keep a calendar, work with e-mail, manage files, read UseNet or network news, create outlines, use it as a calculator, and even browse the World Wide Web. In some ways, emacs is a working environment that contains a text editor. A popular version of emacs is distributed via the GNU license. This is the version of emacs Linux installed during installation.

Starting *emacs*

GNU patriarch Richard Stallman created the emacs editor. The source code for emacs is essentially available for free under the GNU licenses. Stallman is the founder and proponent of the Free Software Foundation and the GNU (GNU's Not UNIX) project. The fact that emacs is freely available matches Stallman's philosophy that all software should be free and that computer systems should be open for use by anyone. Users are also encouraged to make modifications but must then share those changes with others.

▶ **See** "The GNU License," **p. 800**

The emacs editor doesn't have the two basic modes that vi does, which means that anything you type is put into the file buffer. To give the editor commands to save files, search for text, delete text, and so on, you must use other keys. In emacs, you use the <Ctrl> key in combination with various characters (usually <Ctrl-x> and <Ctrl-c>) and the <Esc> key to accomplish the various commands. A variety of common commands are described later in this chapter.

▶ **See** "Looking at vi's Two Modes," **p. 182**

These emacs commands are actually shortcuts for the full text commands. For example, <Ctrl-x><Ctrl-s>, which saves the current buffer to a file, is actually a shortcut freeing the user from pressing <Esc> and then typing the actual emacs command: -x save-buffer. As you can see, using the <Ctrl-x><Ctrl-s> key sequence is a lot more simple and much easier to remember than the full emacs command. A brief list of the basic commands is presented at the end of this chapter.

emacs also allows you to edit multiple *buffers,* or files, in the same session. That is, you can edit more than one file at a time with emacs. This chapter also covers some of the buffer-manipulation commands. emacs also uses buffers to hold deleted text and also to prompt for commands.

To start emacs, type **emacs** and press <Return>. A blank screen with a status line at the bottom appears.

This chapter doesn't discuss all the keystrokes and commands used in emacs, but you can get help by pressing <Ctrl-h><h>. After that, you can use <Ctrl-x><Ctrl-c> to exit completely, or <Ctrl-x><1> to return to your editing session. Thus, unlike vi, emacs has online help facilities and even a tutorial.

After you ask for online help, emacs presents another buffer and is ready to provide help. If you press <t>, emacs starts an excellent tutorial. If you press <k>, emacs provides help on the next command/key you enter. Thus, if you pressed <Ctrl-h><k><Ctrl-w>, emacs presents information on deleting a marked region.

To return to your editing session, press <Ctrl-x><1> to return emacs to editing only one buffer.

The complete GNU emacs system is large but can be customized to match your local environment. Some smaller versions of emacs that are readily available are Freemacs by Russell Nelson and MicroEmacs, originally by Dave Conroy. Remember too that the Linux distribution provides for a few other emacs-like editors—namely JED and JOVE, which are much smaller in size than the full emacs installation.

N O T E This chapter doesn't cover all the features of emacs—that would take more space than is available. In fact, there are entire books written just on emacs. Instead, you learn the commands to do most necessary editing tasks. If you want to know about the more advanced features of emacs and advanced text-editing operations, consult the reference manual supplied with your system. You don't have to become an emacs expert to use it. emacs also has a very detailed tutorial as part of the system. More information on running the tutorial is presented later in this chapter, but you can start the tutorial by pressing <Ctrl-h><t>. ■

Using *emacs*

You edit text by creating new text or by modifying existing text. When creating new text, you place the text in a file with an ordinary Linux filename. When you modify existing text, you use the existing filename to call a copy of the file into the editing session. In either case, as you use the editor, the text is held in the system's memory in a storage area called a buffer.

Using a buffer prevents you from directly changing the contents of a file until you decide to save the buffer. This is to your benefit if you decide you want to forget the changes you've made and start over.

emacs allows you to edit multiple buffers at once. This way, you can cut and paste text from one buffer to another, compare text from different files, or merge one file into another file. emacs even uses a special buffer to accept commands and report information to the user. This buffer, the *mini-buffer*, appears at the bottom of the screen.

emacs also lets you display the contents of various buffers in their own windows; thus, you can see several files at once, even if you aren't using a graphical user interface.

Part
V

Ch
28

Looking Over the *emacs* Screen

Figure 28.1 shows a typical emacs screen. The top portion displays the contents of various buffers, sometimes in multiple windows. Then a mode line is displayed at the bottom of the screen. This line, usually displayed in reverse video, provides users with information about the buffer, such as the buffer's name, the major and minor mode, and the amount of text displayed in the buffer. Under the mode line is the one-line mini-buffer, where you enter emacs commands and where emacs reports the outcome of various commands.

FIG. 28.1

A typical emacs screen shows the buffer and mini-buffer areas.

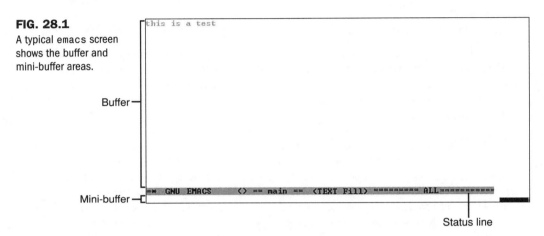

The current position in the buffer is shown by a cursor. emacs refers to the cursor as the *point*, especially in the online help system, so it's important to remember this term for the cursor.

Creating Your First *emacs* File

The following instructions show how to edit your first emacs file. If you run into difficulties, you can quit and start over by pressing <Ctrl-x><Ctrl-c>. Follow these steps:

1. Start emacs (type **emacs** and press <Return>). You see the screen shown in Figure 28.1.

2. Add the following lines of text to the buffer:

   Things to do today.
   a. Practice emacs.
   b. Sort sales data and print the results.

   You can use the <Backspace> key to correct mistakes on the line you're typing. Don't worry about being precise here: This example is for practice. You learn other ways to make changes in some of the later sections of this chapter.

N O T E   Notice the mini-buffer at the bottom of the screen. Your keystrokes appear there because you're typing commands to the emacs editor. ■

3. Save your buffer in a file called emacs-pract.1. First press <Ctrl-x><Ctrl-s> and type `emacs-pract.1`. Notice that `emacs-pract.1` appears at the bottom of the screen. Press <Return>. This command saves or writes the buffer to the file emacs-pract.1 (the specified file).

You should see the following confirmation on the status line:

```
Wrote /root/emacs-pract.1
```

This statement confirms that the file emacs-pract.1 has been created and saved to disk. Your display may be different if you didn't type the information exactly as specified.

> **N O T E** Notice the number of characters in the filename. Unlike MS-DOS and Windows, Linux allows you to enter more than eight characters and a three-character extension for a filename. ■

4. Exit emacs by pressing <Ctrl-x><Ctrl-c> and then <Return>. If you have unsaved material, emacs might prompt you to save an unsaved buffer/file. If emacs does prompt you, simply press <y> to save the information, or <n> if you don't want to save the information. emacs then terminates, and you return to the login shell prompt.

TROUBLESHOOTING

emacs is placing the characters I type into the mini-buffer and attempting to perform strange actions with the characters. If you press the <Esc> key twice, emacs enters a LISP programming environment. LISP is the original language that Stallman used to program emacs, and it's through LISP that programmers can extend and customize emacs. If you press <Esc><Esc>, emacs enters the eval-expression mode and expects the user to enter a LISP command; simply press <Return> to exit this mode.

Starting *emacs* by Using an Existing File

To edit or look at a file that already exists in your current directory, enter *emacs* followed by the filename. For example, try this with the file you created in the previous section by entering this command:

```
emacs emacs-pract.1
```

You see the following:

```
Things to do today.
a. Practice emacs.
b. Sort sales data and print the results.
```

Look at the mini-buffer: It contains the name of the file you're editing.

TROUBLESHOOTING

I typed a filename I know exists, but *emacs* **acts as though I'm creating a new file.** You may have typed the name of a file incorrectly, or you may have typed one that doesn't exist in your current directory. If, for example, you type emacs pract1. and press <Return> but there's no file named pract1. in your current directory, emacs still starts, but because the named file doesn't exist, emacs acts as though you were creating a new file.

I try to edit a file, but *emacs* **displays a message about read permission being denied, and the shell prompt appears.** You've tried to edit a file you aren't permitted to read. Also, you can't edit a directory— that is, if you type emacs *directory_name*, where *directory_name* is the name of a directory, emacs informs you that you opened a directory and won't let you edit it. If you try to use emacs with a binary file instead of an ASCII file, you'll see a screen full of strange (control) characters—something you cannot read and edit. emacs expects files to be stored as plain text.

When I tried to open a file in *emacs***, I got a message about the line being too long.** You're trying to use emacs on a data file or a binary file that's just one long string of bytes.

When I try to save a file with the <Ctrl-x><Ctrl-s> keys, the terminal hangs and doesn't respond to the keyboard. Your terminal is probably responding to the flow-control characters <Ctrl-s> and <Ctrl-q>. Press <Ctrl-q> to restart your session.

I opened a file in *emacs***, and some strange characters appeared on-screen.** You may be using emacs with a file produced by a word processor.

In all these cases, press <Ctrl-x><Ctrl-c> to exit emacs and return to your login shell prompt. Then answer n to the prompt asking if you want to save the file. Using those keystrokes ensures that you quit emacs and make no changes to the existing file.

Exiting *emacs*

As already stated, to exit emacs, press <Ctrl-x><Ctrl-c>. If you haven't saved any changes to the file, emacs prompts you to save the buffer. If you type y, emacs saves the file and returns you to the Linux shell. If you haven't provided a filename, emacs prompts for a filename and then exits. If you respond *n* to the request to save the buffer, emacs prompts again to make sure that you want to exit without saving the buffer. This time you must completely type out the response to the prompt—*yes* or *no*. If you answer yes, emacs returns you to Linux without saving any of the modifications you made to the buffer. Also, if you have multiple buffers open, emacs prompts you for each buffer.

> **CAUTION**
>
> The default installation of emacs performs periodic saves while you're editing a buffer. emacs does not, per se, make backup copies of files, although the first time you save the file, a snapshot of the file is saved in *#filename#*. After you press <Ctrl-x><Ctrl-s>, the original file is modified and can't be restored to its original state. Thus, you should make your own backup copies of emacs files before starting the editing session to make sure that the automatic updates don't inadvertently overwrite an important file to the point where you can't recover a previous version of the file.

> **CAUTION**
>
> Answer *n* to the exit-without-saving prompt sparingly. When you answer *n*, all the changes you've made to the file since it was last saved are lost. It's better to be safe and save the file to a different filename if you're not sure about losing all your changes to the file.

Perhaps you aren't quite finished with your emacs session but you need to perform other activities with Linux. In that case, you have several options:

- You can suspend emacs and return to the Linux shell.
- You can switch to another virtual terminal.
- You can issue a shell command from within emacs.

Suspending *emacs* You can suspend emacs—in fact, you can suspend almost any Linux application—by pressing <Ctrl-z>. This keystroke combination places the current application into the background and provides you with another shell prompt. The command to reactivate emacs depends on which shell you're executing. You can type the command *fg*, which means to bring the background task to the foreground. If the shell you're using doesn't understand this command, type **exit**, which reactivates your emacs session with all your files and buffers still intact.

Switching Between *emacs* and Other Virtual Terminals Linux provides the user with six virtual terminals—hence, you have six different sessions. While in emacs you can press <Ctrl-Alt-F*x*>, where F*x* is one of the keyboard function keys F1 through F6, to activate another terminal. If you haven't already logged in to a session on that terminal, then you must do so, just like when you're first booting Linux. You then have a completely active Linux session. To switch back to emacs, simply press <Ctrl-Alt-F*x*> again. If you forget which session is running emacs, you can cycle through each of the virtual terminals by pressing <Ctrl-Alt> with each function key one by one.

▶ **See** "Managing Users," **p. 107**

You can also use the ps command to display all active processes, as shown in Listing 28.1. The output of the ps -guax command indicates which terminal each process is now executing.

Listing 28.1   Output from the *ps* Command

USER	PID	%CPU	%MEM	SIZE	RSS	TTY	STAT	START	TIME	COMMAND
root	1	0.5	3.1	44	208	?	S	20:48	0:00	init
root	6	0.0	1.8	24	124	?	S	20:48	0:00	bdflush (daemon)
root	7	0.0	1.9	24	128	?	S	20:48	0:00	update (bdflush)
root	23	0.0	2.9	56	200	?	S	20:48	0:00	/usr/sbin/crond -l10
root	36	0.6	3.5	65	240	?	S	20:48	0:00	/usr/sbin/syslogd
root	38	0.1	2.9	36	200	?	S	20:48	0:00	/usr/sbin/klogd
root	40	0.3	3.2	68	216	?	S	20:48	0:00	/usr/sbin/inetd
root	42	0.1	3.0	64	204	?	S	20:48	0:00	/usr/sbin/lpd
root	47	0.1	6.0	259	404	?	S	20:48	0:00	sendmail:accepting c
root	51	0.1	2.0	32	140	?	S	20:48	0:00	selection -t ms

Part

V

Ch

continues

Listing 28.1   Continued

```
root  52  1.5  7.2  376  484  v01 S   20:48  0:01  -bash
root  53  0.3  3.4   88  232  v02 S   20:48  0:00  /sbin/getty tty2 3840
root  54  0.3  3.4   88  232  v03 S   20:48  0:00  /sbin/getty tty3 3840
root  55  0.2  3.4   88  232  v04 S   20:48  0:00  /sbin/getty tty4 3840
root  56  0.3  3.4   88  232  v05 S   20:48  0:00  /sbin/getty tty5 3840
root  57  0.3  3.4   88  232  v06 S   20:48  0:00  /sbin/getty tty6 3840
root  67  0.0  3.5   80  240  v01 R   20:49  0:00  ps -guax
```

You can then use that TTY value, in the range of v01 to v06, to pick the correct virtual terminal. For example, if the ps command indicates that emacs is now operating on tty v01 and tty v02, pressing <Alt-F1> or <Alt-F2> brings you back to the appropriate emacs session.

Accessing Linux Commands from Within emacs   Sometimes all you need to do is a quick check to see whether a file exists or to perform some other quick Linux command; you don't need a full shell session to perform the action. In that case, you can execute shell commands from within emacs. To execute a shell within emacs, press <Ctrl-u><Esc><!>. You're prompted to enter a shell command; enter the command and press <Return>. emacs passes the command to the Linux shell, which executes the command.

If you don't press <Ctrl-u>, emacs places the output into a buffer/window called *Shell Command Output*. You learn more about windows later in this chapter, but basically windows allow you to see multiple buffers at once. emacs provides various commands to move around between windows and to delete windows (without deleting their corresponding buffers). To delete the output window, press <Ctrl-x><1>.

Undoing a Command

In emacs, you can "undo" your most recent action or change to the buffer, as long as you have not saved that change to the disk file. You can undo by pressing <Ctrl-x><u>. By repeatedly using this command, you can undo the changes made to the buffer.

> **N O T E**   emacs keeps track of the "undone" material first in memory buffers and then in a file, so theoretically you could undo every change you've made to a buffer up to the limits of your disk space. Practically, though, you'll find the undo command useful for only the last few commands or edits you've done. ■

Unfortunately, you can't use the undo command to undo writing something to a file as opposed to writing to the buffer.

If you want to reread a file from disk (thus overwriting your current buffer changes), you can press <Ctrl-x><Ctrl-r>. This command reads the specified file into the current buffer, erasing its previous contents. Thus, if you specify the same filename, emacs replaces the current buffer with the contents of the file on disk. This is a quick way to undo many changes without exiting and restarting emacs.

But what if the emacs has autosaved the file or you've saved the file with unwanted changes? Well, emacs creates a backup file the first time you save a file, but not until you save the file. The name of this backup file is the same as the filename, except with a # character at the beginning and end of the name. Thus, if your file was named emacs-prtc.1, the backup filename is #emacs-prtc.1#. If you accidentally overwrite your current file with unwanted changes, you may be able to use the backup file to start over.

Writing Files and Saving the Buffer

You've seen how to write the buffer to a file and quit emacs. Sometimes, however, you want to save the buffer to a file without quitting emacs. You should save the file regularly during an editing session. If the system goes down because of a crash or a power failure, you may lose your work if you haven't saved it recently. To save the buffer, press <Ctrl-x><Ctrl-s>.

If you started emacs without specifying a filename, you must provide a filename if you want to save the file to disk. In this case, you press <Ctrl-x><Ctrl-s>, type the filename, and press <Return>.

You may want to save the buffer to a new filename different from the one you originally started with. For example, you start emacs with the file emacs-pract.1, make some changes to the file, and want to save the changes to a new file without losing the original emacs-pract.1 file. To save the file with a new filename, press <Ctrl-x><Ctrl-w>. emacs prompts you for the filename. The buffer is then written to the named file. If the command is successful, you see the name of the file.

If you specify the name of an existing file, a message appears in the mini-buffer, asking whether you want to overwrite the file. Simply answer the question appropriately.

Using Files

If you want to load another file to edit, emacs can let you load a new file into the current buffer, or load a file into a new buffer, leaving the current buffer alone. emacs also lets you insert the contents of a file into the current buffer.

To replace the current buffer with the contents of another file, press <Ctrl-x><Ctrl-v>. emacs prompts for a filename in the mini-buffer. If you don't remember the entire filename or if the name is rather long, you can use the completion option of emacs. When emacs prompts for a filename, you can enter just the first few letters in the name and then press <Tab>. emacs then expands the filename to match any files with those first few letters. If more than one file matches, emacs displays a window containing all the files matching the characters you entered and allows you to choose one.

To retrieve a file into a new buffer, press <Ctrl-x><Ctrl-f>. Enter the filename at the mini-buffer prompt. emacs normally names the buffer after the filename, but you can change the name of the buffer by pressing <Esc><x>, entering the new name for the buffer, and pressing <Return>. emacs prompts for the new name. Enter the new buffer name and press <Return>. The mode line displays the new name.

To insert a file into the current buffer, simply move the cursor to the desired position in the file and press <Ctrl-x><i>.

Positioning the Cursor

When you edit text, you need to position the cursor where you want to insert additional text, delete text, correct mistakes, change words, or append text to the end of existing text. The commands you enter are called *cursor-positioning commands*.

The Arrow Keys   You can use the arrow keys on many—but not all—systems to position the cursor. It's easy to see whether the arrow keys work: Start *emacs* with an existing file and see what effects the arrow keys have. You may also be able to use the <Page Up> and <Page Down> keys.

Enter the following command to create a new file called emacs-pract.3 that contains a list of the files and directories in the directory /usr. You can use this file to experiment with cursor-positioning commands.

```
ls /usr > emacs-pract.3
```

If you create the file with the <Ctrl-u><Esc><!> command sequence, you see the following message:

```
(Shell command completed with no output)
```

N O T E   Don't worry about the message; it doesn't mean there's a problem. Standard output was redirected to the file and, thus, *emacs* had no output to capture to a buffer. ▮

When the file is created, start *emacs* with the emacs-pract.3 file (type **emacs emacs-pract.3** and press <Return>). Now try using the arrow keys and the <Page Up> and <Page Down> keys (if they're on your keyboard) to move around the editing buffer. If the keys work, you may want to use those keys for cursor positioning.

It may be that, although it appears that the cursor-positioning keys work, they're introducing strange characters into the file. These characters are the codes the computer uses to represent the various keys instead of the characters themselves. If you see such characters, you have to use the various keyboard commands to position the cursor instead of using the keyboard keys.

T I P   To clear the screen of spurious or unusual characters in *emacs*, press <Ctrl-l>.

Other Cursor-Movement Keys   You can position the cursor in *emacs* in other ways without using the arrow keys. You should become familiar with these methods in case you can't or don't want to use the arrow keys. This section also shows you some ways to position the cursor more efficiently than using the arrow keys.

When *emacs* was developed in 1975, many terminals didn't have arrow keys; other keys were and still are used to position the cursor. It takes a little practice to get comfortable with these keys, but some experienced emacs users prefer these keys over the arrow keys. Here are some other keys that move the cursor:

- Press <Ctrl-f> to move the cursor to the right ("forward") one position.
- Press <Ctrl-b> to move the cursor to the left ("back") one position.
- Press <Ctrl-n> to move to the beginning of the next line, preserving your position in the line.
- Press <Ctrl-p> to move to the previous line, preserving your position in the line.
- Press <Ctrl-a> to move to the beginning of a line.
- Press <Ctrl-e> to move to the end of a line.

Some emacs commands allow you to position the cursor relative to words on a line. A *word* is defined as a sequence of characters separated from other characters by spaces or usual punctuation symbols, such as periods, question marks, commas, and hyphens. These commands are as follows:

- Press <Esc><f> to move forward one word.
- Press <Esc><b> to move backward one word.

The following example demonstrates some of these actions. Start emacs and open the emacs-pract.1 file by typing **emacs emacs-pract.1** and pressing <Return>. Now use any of the cursor-positioning commands just described to move the cursor, indicated by an underline character, to the *t* in the word "data" on the third line of the file. The third line looks like this:

b. Sort sales da_ta and print the results.

To move to the beginning of the next word, press <Esc><f>; the cursor is positioned under the *a* of the word "and" in the previous sentence. Press <Esc><f> to move to the *p* in "print." To move to the beginning of the word "and," press <Esc><b>; the cursor is positioned under the *a* in "and" again.

Big-Movement Keys If you want to move through a file a screen at a time, which is more efficient than pressing <Page Down>, use commands that scroll through a file. The command <Ctrl-x><]> moves you forward one page. The scrolling keystrokes are as follows:

- Press <Ctrl-v> to move forward one screen.
- Press <Esc><v> to move backward one screen.
- Press <Ctrl-x><]> to move forward one page.
- Press <Ctrl-x><[> to move backward one page.

To move quickly to the last line of the file or buffer, press <Esc><Shift-.>. To move to the first line of the file, press <Esc><Shift-,>. In fact, to move to a specific line in the buffer, type the command **goto-line *n***, where *n* is the line number you want to move to. To move to line 35 of the file (if there is a line 35), press <Esc>, enter **goto-line 35**, and press <Return>.

You can repeat any command you want by pressing <Esc-*n*>, where *n* is the number of times you want to repeat the command, and then entering the command you want to repeat.

Take a little time to practice positioning the cursor by using the commands described in these last few sections. Remember that you must be in command mode for the cursor-positioning commands to work.

Adding Text

To add text to the editing buffer, you must position the cursor at the position you want to start entering text. Any usual text characters you type are then added to the buffer. If you press <Return>, emacs "opens," or adds, a line to the buffer. Before you start adding text, first position the cursor at the location you want to add text. You then simply type the text.

To add a line of text below the current line, you use the command <Ctrl-o>. This "opens" a line in the buffer and allows you to add text. In the following example, you add a line to some existing text.

Before:

```
All jobs complete
please call
if you have any questions.
```

The cursor is on the second line. Press <Ctrl-o> to add a line or lines below that line, and then type the following:

```
Lee Nashua
555-1837
```

After:

```
All jobs complete
please call
Lee Nashua
555-1837
if you have any questions.
```

Although you added only two lines, you could have added more lines by pressing <Return> at the end of each line. Naturally, you could have added only one line by not pressing <Return> at all.

Deleting Text

Making corrections or modifications to a file may involve deleting text. With emacs, you can delete a character, a word, a number of consecutive words, all the text to the end of a line, or an entire line. Because emacs is a visual editor like vi, the characters, words, or lines are removed from the screen as you delete them.

Table 28.1 lists the delete commands and describes their actions. They all take effect from the current cursor position. Move the cursor to the character, word, or line you want to change and then issue the desired delete command. Practice using them to see their effect. You'll find they are helpful in making corrections to files.

Table 28.1 Commands for Deleting Text

Keystroke	Action
<Ctrl-d>	Deletes character at the cursor position
<Esc><d>	Deletes the word the cursor is on
<Ctrl-k>	Deletes from the cursor position to the end of the line
<Esc><k>	Deletes the sentence the cursor is on
<Ctrl-w>	Deletes a marked region (see *Marked Text* later in Table 28.4 for commands for marking a region)

If you use the <Ctrl-k> command, the information just doesn't disappear into the bit bucket. The characters deleted are added to a *kill buffer*, which you can yank back at any time with the <Ctrl-y> command.

Searching and Replacing Text

Finding a word, a phrase, or a number in a file can be difficult if you have to read through each line yourself. Like most editors and word processors, emacs has a command that allows you to search for a string of characters and, if you want, replace those characters with others. You can search forward or backward from your current position in the buffer. You also can continue searching. emacs starts searching from the beginning of the buffer file when it reaches the end, and vice versa. Table 28.2 summarizes the commands for searching. In each case, emacs searches for the string you specify, in the direction you specify, and positions the cursor at the beginning of the string.

Table 28.2 The Search and Replace Commands

Command	Action
<Ctrl-s>	Search forward from current position
<Ctrl-r>	Reverse search from current position
<Ctrl-x><s>	Repeat search forward
<Ctrl-x><r>	Repeat search in reverse
<Esc><r>	Replace all instances of first typed string in mini-buffer with second typed string, ending each string with <Esc>
<Esc><Ctrl-r query>	Before performing the replacement, answer in the mini-buffer with one of the following: <Ctrl-g>: Cancel operation <!>: Replace the rest <?>: Get a list of options

Part

V

Ch

28

continues

Table 28.2 Continued

Command	Action
	<.>: Replace and exit to where command was initiated
	<,>: Replace the rest without asking
	<y> or Spacebar: Replace and continue with replace operation
	<n>: Don't replace but continue with operation

Searching   When you type the search command, it appears in the mini-buffer. To search forward for the string sales > 100K in a file, use this command:

<Ctrl-s>**sales > 100K**

This command starts an incremental search through the buffer. Notice that as you type the characters for the search string, emacs positions the cursor on the sequence of characters. If emacs can't find the text, it displays the search failed message. If the string is in the buffer, emacs positions the cursor under the first s in the word sales. When you find the first occurrence of the string, you must press <Esc> to stop the search; otherwise, emacs continues looking for a match as you enter other text. emacs refers to these types of searches as *incremental searches*; emacs searches as you enter the search string.

emacs can also perform non-incremental searches if you preface the search string with the <Esc> key and press the <Return> key at the end, as shown here:

<Ctrl-s><Esc>**sales > 100K**

If you're searching a large file and realize that you've entered the wrong search string, emacs searches the entire file. To stop the search, press <Ctrl-g>.

TROUBLESHOOTING

I typed a string I know exists in the file, but emacs **can't find it.** The most common cause for this error is that you typed the string incorrectly. emacs—and computers in general—don't do a good job of thinking; emacs has a terrible time figuring out what you really mean. If you're looking for the string "vegi-burger" but you type "vigi-burger," emacs can't find what you want (unless you happened to misspell "vegi-burger" in the buffer and it matches the search string). Check the search string carefully before you press <Return>.

Replacing   Although searching for text can help you locate a particular word or section of text, many times you want to replace the found text. An example is if you find a spelling error and want to correct the entire buffer rather than one mistake at a time. For example, to replace every occurrence of the word "misstake" with "mistake," press <Esc><r>. The mini-buffer prompts for the string to search for; enter **misstake**. emacs then prompts for the replacement string; enter **mistake**. emacs proceeds through the file, looking for the string "misstake" and replacing it with "mistake." emacs also tries to match capitalization as best as possible. Thus, if "misstake" appears as "Misstake," emacs replaces it with "Mistake."

Maybe you don't want to replace every occurrence of a search string with the replacement string, in which case you can instruct emacs to query before replacing the string. To have emacs query and replace, press <Esc><Ctrl-r>.

For example, if you want to selectively replace the name of your operating system, Linux, with its ancestor UNIX, press <Esc><Ctrl-r>. emacs responds in the mini-buffer with Query replace:. Now enter the search string Linux. The Query replace Linux with: prompt appears. Enter the replacement string UNIX. emacs begins the search and states, Query replacing Linux with UNIX. If you want to terminate the search-and-replace operation, press <Ctrl-g>.

When emacs finds an occurrence of Linux, it stops and prompts for an action. The possible responses are as follows:

Keystroke	Action
<Ctrl-g>	Cancels operation
<!>	Replaces the rest without prompting
<?>	Gets a list of options
<.>	Replaces the current instance and quits
<,>	Replaces current instance but doesn't move on to next instance
<y> or Spacebar	Replaces and continues with replace operation
<n>	Doesn't replace but continues with replace operation

Changing Text   Another editing task you're often faced with is changing text or replacing one text string with another (there isn't too much difference between the two operations). You use the replace commands to replace a single character or sequence of characters. You can also use the change commands to fix one of the most common typing mistakes made—transposing two letters. Table 28.3 summarizes the change commands.

Table 28.3   Change Commands

Keystroke	Action
<Ctrl-t>	Transposes two adjacent letters
<Esc><t>	Transposes two words
<Ctrl-x><Ctrl-t>	Transposes two lines
<Esc><c>	Properly capitalizes the word (initial capitalization)
<Esc><l>	Lowercases the entire word
<Esc><u>	Uppercases the entire word

Part

V

Ch

28

The changes take place relative to the position of the cursor. Position the cursor at the location in the buffer file you want to correct before using these commands.

Copying, Cutting, and Pasting

When you delete or cut characters, words, lines, or a portion of a line, the deleted object is saved in what's called the *kill buffer*. The name isn't too important; what's important is that you can put or paste the contents of the kill buffer anywhere in the text you're editing. You do that with <Ctrl-y>, the yank command. <Ctrl-y> pastes the object to the right of or after the cursor position.

Here is an example showing the use of <Ctrl-y> to paste the contents of the kill buffer after the cursor:

Before:

Carefully carry these out instructions.

Delete the word "out" and a space by pressing <Esc-d>. Now move the cursor to the space after the *y* in "carry" and press <Ctrl-y>.

After:

Carefully carry out these instructions.

To copy a sequence of four lines to another portion of the text, you must first mark the four lines of text, delete them to the kill buffer, and then yank them back at the appropriate places. Follow these steps:

1. Position the cursor at the beginning of the first of the four lines.
2. Press <Ctrl-Spacebar> to set the mark.
3. Move the cursor to the end of the fourth line. This creates what emacs refers to as a *region*.
4. Delete the text by pressing <Ctrl-w>.
5. Because you want to copy the lines, you must replace the deleted text. Do this with the <Ctrl-y> command.
6. Move the cursor to the point in the buffer where you want to copy the text.
7. Press <Ctrl-y> to paste the yanked lines below the line holding the cursor.

TROUBLESHOOTING

I deleted the marked region, but the region I marked wasn't deleted. Unfortunately, GNU emacs supplied with Linux doesn't display any type of marker to indicate the mark, so it's very easy to forget to set the mark or to place it in an inappropriate position. To check the position of the mark, use the command <Ctrl-x><Ctrl-x>. This command swaps the position of the cursor and the mark. If the cursor moves to the position where you thought the mark was located, you know the mark is properly set. To move the cursor back to the proper position, simply reissue <Ctrl-x><Ctrl-x> to swap them back.

Basic Command Summary

Table 28.4 gives a brief listing of the major commands provided by emacs. <Esc><c> means to press and release the *meta key*—usually the <Esc> key on a PC keyboard, although on some keyboards you can use the <Alt> key and then press the following <c> key. <Ctrl-c> means to press the <Ctrl> key and the <c> key at the same time. Remember, pressing <Ctrl-g> at any time stops the currently executing command.

Table 28.4   Basic *emacs* Commands

Key Sequence	Description
Saving to Disk	
<Ctrl-x><Ctrl-s>	Saves current buffer to disk
<Ctrl-x><Ctrl-w>	Writes current buffer to disk, asking for a new filename
<Ctrl-x><n>	Changes filename of current buffer
<Esc><z>	Writes all changed buffers to disk and exits emacs
Reading from Disk	
<Ctrl-x><Ctrl-f>	Finds file, reads into a new buffer created from filename
<Ctrl-x><Ctrl-r>	Reads file into current buffer, erasing previous contents
<Ctrl-x><Ctrl-i>	Inserts file into the current buffer at the cursor's location
Moving the Cursor	
<Ctrl-f>	Moves forward one character
<Ctrl-b>	Moves backward one character
<Ctrl-a>	Moves to front of current line
<Ctrl-e>	Moves to end of current line
<Ctrl-n>	Moves to next line
<Ctrl-p>	Moves to previous line
<Esc><f>	Moves forward a word
<Esc><b>	Moves backward a word
<Esc><a>	Goes to a line
<Esc><Shift-.>	Moves to beginning of buffer
<Esc><Shift-,>	Moves to end of buffer
Deleting and Inserting	
<Ctrl-d>	Deletes next character

Part

V

Ch

28

continues

Table 28.4   Continued

Key Sequence	Description
Deleting and Inserting	
<Ctrl-c>	Inserts a space
<Esc><d>	Deletes next word
<Ctrl-k>	Deletes to end of current line
<Return>	Inserts a new line
<Ctrl-j>	Inserts a new line and indent
<Ctrl-o>	Opens a new line
<Ctrl-w>	Deletes region between mark and cursor
<Esc><w>	Copies region to kill buffer
<Ctrl-x><Ctrl-o>	Deletes lines around cursor
Searching and Replacing	
<Ctrl-s>	Searches forward from current position
<Ctrl-r>	Reverses search from current position
<Ctrl-x><s>	Repeats search forward
<Ctrl-x><r>	Repeats search in reverse
<Esc><r>	Replaces all instances of first typed string in mini-buffer with second typed string, ending each string with <Esc>
<Esc><Ctrl-r>	Queries before performing the replacement. Answer in the mini-buffer with one of the following: <Ctrl-g>: Cancels operation <!>: Replaces the rest <?>: Gets a list of options <.>: Exits to where command was initiated <y> or Spacebar: Replaces and continues with replace operation <n>: Doesn't replace but continues with replace operation
Marked Text	
<Ctrl><Spacebar>	Sets mark at current cursor position
<Ctrl-x><Ctrl-x>	Exchanges mark and cursor
<Ctrl-w>	Deletes the marked region
<Esc-w>	Copies marked region to kill buffer
<Ctrl-y>	Inserts the kill buffer at the current cursor position

Key Sequence	Description
Buffers	
<Ctrl-x><b>	Switches to another buffer
<Ctrl-x><x>	Switches to next buffer in buffer list
<Esc><Ctrl-n>	Changes name of current buffer
<Ctrl-x><k>	Deletes a non-displayed buffer

Customizing *emacs*

You can customize your version of emacs by placing custom functions within a file called .emacs. This file must reside in your home directory. This file contains functions written in emacs LISP, with which you can personalize emacs to your liking. An example LISP function follows:

```
(keyboard-translate ?\C-h ?\C-?)
```

This function is helpful if your terminal translates the <Backspace> key into the <Ctrl-h> characters. These characters are, by default, the sequence used to summon help from within emacs. By specifying a new function and binding this function to a key, you can customize how emacs responds to these key sequences.

In the preceding example, ?\C-h represents the <Ctrl-h> keypress. ?\C-? represents the <Delete> key. On nearly all ASCII keyboards, both keys represent the same ASCII value, namely 8. After you enter this function line into your .emacs file and save it, the next time you invoke emacs, you'll be able to delete characters by using the <Backspace> key.

Of course, this also means you'll no longer have access to help from the keyboard. To alleviate this problem, you can bind the help function to a new key sequence, just as you did with the delete function. Simply place the following line into your .emacs file, specifying your chosen key for *key*:

```
(keyboard-translate ?\C-key ?\C-h)
```

From Here...

You can find more information on another editor and about Linux's files system in the following chapters:

- Chapter 8, "Using the vi Editor," discusses the basics of using this popular editor. vi is important because it's found on all Linux/UNIX systems. If you know how to use vi, you should be able to edit a file on any system. Systems administrators also use vi for many systems admin tasks.

Part
V

Ch
28

- Chapter 11, "Backing Up Data," shows you how to properly back up your text files from accidental erasure.

- Chapter 16, "Understanding the File and Directory System," discusses the basics of files and directories. You should have a basic understanding of the file system when using emacs or any other editor. Whereas the editor creates and modifies files, it's up to you to name them and place them in the appropriate directories.

- Chapter 20, "Printing," provides information on printing your text files under Linux. Printing files under Linux can be tricky; this chapter helps you prepare your system for printing.

Using the Internet

## CHAPTER 29

Using SLIP and PPP

by Steve Burnett

In this chapter

The Linux kernel supports two serial-line protocols for transmitting Internet Protocol (IP) traffic: SLIP (Serial Line Internet Protocol) and PPP (Point-to-Point Protocol). These protocols were developed as a poor man's alternative to expensive leased-line setups for getting Internet connectivity. Anyone with a reasonably high-speed modem and a service provider that supports these protocols can get their Linux machine IP-connected for a very low cost compared to leased-line systems. SLIP drivers for Linux were available soon after Linux was first released, and PPP support was added shortly thereafter. Although PPP has come to dominate the industry, the SLIP configuration is still helpful as a basis.

Understanding the Requirements for SLIP and PPP

You need to make sure that a few things are set up in your Linux kernel or configuration files. TCP/IP networking must be enabled and the loopback interface should be configured.

▶ **See** "Configuring the Software Loopback Interface," **p. 448**

You'll want the IP address of your Domain Name Service (DNS) server to be included in your /etc/resolv.conf file to make accessing other machines besides your dial-up host convenient. If your dial-up link is slow or error-prone, you might want to run a name server on your Linux box, to cache any DNS lookups and decrease the amount of DNS IP traffic on your dial-up link.

▶ **See** "The /etc/resolv.conf File," **p. 505**

▶ **See** "Using the named Daemon to Set Up the Server," **p. 506**

Using *dip* to Automate SLIP Operations

Linux offers a number of programs to manage your SLIP operations. dip, the Dial-Up IP Protocol driver, is one of the most versatile tools. It provides a scripting language for automating control of the modem and automatically sets up the SLIP network interface and kernel routing tables. You can use dip to initiate SLIP connections or provide dial-up SLIP service to other machines. The syntax for dip is as follows:

```
dip [-tvi] [-m mtu] [scriptfile]
```

Table 29.1 describes dip's most common command-line arguments.

Table 29.1   *dip* Common Command-Line Arguments

Argument	Description
-a	Prompts the user for username and password.
-t	Runs dip in command mode. Command mode gives you full access to everything dip can do, allowing you to initiate a SLIP connection manually.
-v	Used with -t to display the current error level.

Argument	Description
-i	Tells dip to operate in input mode. This flag is used when dip provides SLIP service for others dialing into your machine.
-m *mtu*	Forces dip to use the specified MTU value.
scriptfile	Specifies the name of the dip script to run.

Using *dip* in Command Mode

Invoking dip with the -t option places it in command mode. This mode lets you control dip directly and is an excellent tool for developing and debugging dip scripts. The following shows you what dip's command mode looks like:

```
$ /sbin/dip -t
DIP: Dialup IP Protocol Driver version 3.3.7i-uri (17 Apr 95)
Written by Fred N. van Kempen, MicroWalt Corporation.

DIP>
```

From the DIP> prompt, you can run any dip command by typing it and pressing <Return>. The help command displays a list of the available commands. Invoking a command with incorrect arguments displays a brief usage statement for that command. Table 29.2 describes the commands available for use at the command-mode prompt or in dip scripts.

Table 29.2 Commands Available in *dip*

Command	Description
chatkey *keyword* [*code*]	Adds a keyword and error-level code to the set of error codes returned by the dial command. The chatkey command can be used to detect when your modem returns BUSY, VOICE, or other specific messages.
config [*arguments*]	Allows you to directly manipulate the SLIP interface dip provides. This command normally is disabled because it's a severe security risk. The source code file command.c must be modified slightly to enable this command.
databits *bits*	Sets the number of bits that can be used as data in each byte. This accommodates 6- and 7-bit dial-up connections.
default	Causes dip to set a default route in the kernel routing table pointed at the remote host.
dial *num*	Dials the specified telephone number.
echo on¦off	Turns echo on or off. Echo on makes dip display what it's sending to and receiving from the modem.

continues

Table 29.2   Continued

Command	Description
`flush`	Throws away any responses from the modem that haven't been read yet.
`get $var`	Sets the variable `$var` to either the constant `ask` or remote constant specified, prompts the user for a value, or takes the next word from the serial line and assigns it to `$var`.
`goto` *label*	Jumps to the specified label in the `dip` script.
`help`	Displays a listing of available commands in command mode.
`if $var op` *number*	Performs a conditional branch in a goto label script. `$var` must be one of `$errlvl`, `$locip`, or `$rmtip`. The number must be an integer, and the following operators are available and have their traditional C language meanings: `==`, `!=`, `<`, `>`, `<=`, and `>=`.
`init` *initstring*	Sets the initialization string sent to the modem by the reset command to *initstring*.
`mode SLIP¦CSLIP`	Sets the protocol mode for the connection and makes `dip` go into daemon mode. This command normally causes `dip` to go into daemon mode and not return control to the script or the `DIP>` command line.
`modem HAYES`	Sets the modem type. Only the `HAYES` modem type is now supported. (`HAYES` must be capitalized.)
`netmask` *mask*	Sets the netmask for the routes `dip` installs to *mask*.
`parity E¦O¦N`	Sets the parity of the serial line: even, odd, or none.
`password`	Prompts the user for a password and retrieves it in a secure manner. This command doesn't echo the password as you type it.
`print`	Echoes text to the console `dip` started on. Variables included in the text are replaced with their values.
`port` *dev*	Sets the device `dip` uses.
`quit`	Exits the `dip` program.
`reset`	Sends the init string to the serial line.
`send` *text*	Sends the specified text to the serial line. The traditional C-style backslash sequences are properly handled.
`sleep` *num*	Delays processing for the specified number of seconds.
`speed` *num*	Sets the serial line speed.

Command	Description
stopbits *bits*	Sets the number of stop bits used by the serial port.
timeout *num*	Sets the default timeout to the integer value *num*. This is measured in seconds.
term	Makes dip go into terminal emulation mode. This allows you to interface directly with the serial link. Pressing <Ctrl+]> returns you to the DIP> prompt.
wait *word num*	Makes dip wait for the specified word to arrive on the serial line with a timeout of *num* seconds.

dip also provides a number of variables for your use. Some, such as the local and remote IP addresses, can be set by you; others are read-only and are used for diagnostic and informational purposes. Each variable begins with a dollar sign and must be typed in lowercase letters. Table 29.3 lists these variables and their uses.

Table 29.3   Variables Provided by *dip*

Variable	Description
$local	The host name of the local machine.
$locip	The IP address assigned to the local machine.
$remote	The host name of the remote machine.
$rmtip	The IP address of the remote machine.
$mtu	The MTU value for the connection.
$modem	The modem type being used (read-only).
$port	The name of the serial device dip is using (read-only).
$speed	The speed setting of the serial device (read-only).
$errlvl	The result code of the last command (read-only) executed. Zero indicates success; any other value is an error.

T I P   Setting the $local or $remote variable to a host name causes dip to resolve the host name to its IP address and store that in the respective IP address variable. This saves a step in the scripts you write.

N O T E   You can't set the read-only variables directly by using the get command. ▪

Using *dip* with Static IP Addresses

Assigning individual IP addresses to each machine that uses a SLIP provider is very common. When your machine initiates a SLIP link to the remote host, dip configures the SLIP interface with this known address. Listing 29.1 is a dip script using static IP addresses for initiating a SLIP link from linux2.burwell.com to linux1.burwell.com.

Listing 29.1   A Sample *dip* Script for Using Static IP Addresses over SLIP

```
# Connect linux2 to linux1 using static IP Addresses
# Configure Communication Parameters
port /dev/cua1 # use modem on /dev/cua1 serial line
speed 38400
modem HAYES
reset                              # Send initialization string to modem
flush                              # Throw away modem response

get $local linux2                  # Set local IP address
get $remote linux1                 # Set remote IP address

# Dial number for linux1 modem
dial 555-1234
if $errlvl != 0 goto error         # If the dial command fails, error out
wait CONNECT 75
if $errlvl != 0 goto error         # If we don't get a CONNECT string
# from the modem, error out

send \r\n                          # Wake up login program
wait ogin: 30                      # Wait 30 seconds for login prompt
if $errlvl != 0 goto error         # Error out if we don't get login prompt
send Slinux2\n                     # Send SLIP login name for linux2
wait ssword: 5                     # Wait 5 seconds for password prompt
if $errlvl != 0 goto error         # Error out if we don't get password
send be4me\n                       # Send password
wait running 30                    # Wait for indication that SLIP is up
if $errlvl != 0 goto error         # Otherwise error out

# We're in, print out useful information
print Connected to $remote with address $rmtip
default                            # Make this link our default route
mode SLIP                          # Turn on SLIP mode on our end

# Error routine in case things don't work
error:
print SLIP to $remote failed.
```

T I P   Tracking SLIP accounts can be difficult. Traditionally, UNIX user accounts are assigned login names with all lowercase letters. Using the client machine name with a capital S added to the front as the login name for that machine's SLIP account makes tracking it easier and avoids login name collisions with normal user accounts.

The script in Listing 29.1 initializes the modem and sets the local and remote IP addresses for the SLIP link. If you use host names here, dip resolves them to their IP address equivalents. The script then dials the modem and works its way through the login sequence. When logged in and sure that the SLIP link is up on the remote host, the script has dip configure the routing table and then switch the serial line into SLIP mode.

If an error occurs, the error routine at the end of the script prints a warning message and aborts the script. dip is excellent about leaving the serial line in a reasonable state when it's done with it.

Using *dip* with Dynamic IP Addresses

As SLIP became more popular, the task of managing IP addressees for SLIP clients got more and more difficult. This problem got worse when terminal servers supporting SLIP came into use. Now, you might be assigned any one of a range of IP addresses, depending on which port the terminal server received your call. This led to changes in dip that captured IP address information from the incoming data on the serial line. Listing 29.2 is a dip script that captures the local and remote IP addresses from the serial line.

Listing 29.2   A Sample *dip* Script for Dynamic IP Addresses

```
# Connection script for SLIP to server with dynamic IP address
# assignment. The terminal server prints out:
#
# remote address is XXX.XXX.XXX.XXX the local address is YYY.YYY.YYY.YYY

# Set the desired serial port and speed.
port /dev/cua1
speed 38400

# Reset the modem and terminal line.
Reset
flush

# Prepare for dialing.
dial 555-1234
if $errlvl != 0 goto error
wait CONNECT 60
if $errlvl != 0 goto error

# We are connected. Login to the system.
login:
wait name: 10                       # Log in to system
if $errlvl != 0 goto error
send Slinux2\n                      # Send user ID
wait ord: 10
if $errlvl != 0 goto error
send be4me\n                        # Send password
if $errlvl != 0 goto error
get $remote remote 10               # Get remote IP address
```

continues

Listing 29.2 Continued

```
if $errlvl != 0 goto error
get $local remote 10                     # Get local IP address
if $errlvl != 0 goto error
done:
print CONNECTED to $remote with address $rmtip we are $local
default                                  # Set routing
mode SLIP                                # Go to SLIP mode
goto exit
error:
print SLIP to $host failed.
exit:
```

The script in Listing 29.2 uses get $remote remote 10 to watch the serial line and to capture the first thing that looks like an IP address in the $remote variable. The command times out in 10 seconds with an error if it doesn't see an IP address.

Using *diplogin* to Provide SLIP Service

The dip program automates starting SLIP links from the client machine. Linux also supports incoming dial-up SLIP links. A few packages are available for doing this as well. You use the diplogin program here, which is really just another name for dip.

Providing SLIP service to others requires that you create a specific account for each person on your Linux box and configure that account correctly. You also need to write an /etc/diphosts file with appropriate information for each host that you're providing SLIP service for.

Creating SLIP Accounts

You can manually create the SLIP account or use the adduser script with appropriate responses to each question. Here's an example /etc/passwd entry for linux2.burwell.com in the passwd file on linux1.burwell.com:

```
Slinux2:IdR4gDZ7K7D82:505:100:linux2 SLIP Account:/tmp:/sbin/diplogin
```

It's recommended that /tmp be used as the home directory for SLIP accounts to minimize security risks by preventing SLIP users from writing files into sensitive areas of your file system by default. Make sure that you use the correct path to the diplogin program.

Using the /etc/diphosts File

The /etc/diphosts file controls access to SLIP on your machine and contains the connection parameters for each account allowed to use SLIP. It contains lines that look similar to the following:

```
Slinux2::linux2.burwell.com:linux2 SLIP:SLIP,296
```

The fields in this file are the user ID, secondary password, host name or IP address of the calling machine, an informational field not currently used, and the connection parameters for this account. The connection parameters field contains the protocol (SLIP or CSLIP) and the Maximum Transmission Unit (MTU) value for this account.

If the second field isn't empty, `diplogin` prompts for an external security password when the specified account logs in to your machine. If the response from the remote host doesn't match the string in this field, the login attempt is aborted.

> **CAUTION**
>
> The `diplogin` program requires superuser privileges to modify the kernel routing table. If you aren't running `dip setuid root`, you can't use a link between `dip` and `diplogin`. You must make a separate copy of `dip` called `diplogin` and have its suid root.

That's all it takes. Setting up SLIP accounts and the /etc/diphosts file completely configures your system to support incoming SLIP links.

Using PPP

Point-to-Point Protocol (PPP) is another protocol for sending datagrams across a serial link. Developed after SLIP, PPP contains a number of features SLIP lacks. It can automatically negotiate options such as IP addresses, datagram sizes, and client authorization. It can also transport packets from protocols other than IP.

Automating PPP Links with *pppd* and *chat*

PPP operates in two parts: the PPP driver in the Linux kernel and a program called `pppd` that the user must run. The most basic means of using PPP is to log in manually to the remote host by using a communications program, and then manually start `pppd` on the remote and local hosts. It's much more convenient to use a `chat` script with `pppd` that handles the modem, logging in to the remote host, and starting the remote `pppd`. Before diving into `pppd`, take a quick look at `chat`.

Using the *chat* Program   `chat` is a program for automating the interaction between your computer and a modem. It's used mainly to establish the modem connection between the local and remote `pppd` daemon processes. The syntax for `chat` is as follows:

```
chat [options] script
```

Table 29.4 lists the command-line options for the `chat` program.

Table 29.4   *chat* Command-Line Options

Option	Description
-f *filename*	Uses the `chat` script in the specified file.
-l *lockfile*	Makes a UUCP style lock file by using the specified lock file.

continues

Table 29.4 Continued

Option	Description
-t *num*	Uses the specified number as the timeout in seconds for each expected string.
-v	Makes a chat log of everything it sends and receives to syslog.
script	Specifies the chat script to use.

You can't use the -f option and specify a chat script at the same time—they're mutually exclusive. If you use the -l option for chat, don't use the lock option with pppd because the lock file created by chat causes pppd to fail, thinking that the modem device is already in use.

 When debugging chat scripts, run tail -f /var/adm/messages on one virtual console and use the -v option when you run chat in another. You can then watch the conversation chat is having as it comes up on the first virtual console.

Creating *chat* Scripts chat scripts consist of one or more expect-reply pairs of strings separated by spaces. The chat program waits for the expected text and sends the reply text when it receives it. Optional subexpect-subreply pairs can be included in the expect portion, separated by hyphens.

Here is a typical chat script for logging in to a Linux machine:

```
ogin:-\r\n-ogin: abbet1 word: costello
```

This script says that chat should wait for the string ogin: to appear. If chat times out before receiving it, chat should send a carriage return and line feed and wait for the string ogin: again. When chat sees the ogin: string, it sends abbet1 and then waits for the word: and sends costello in response.

 Include only the text necessary in expect strings to positively identify what you're looking for, to minimize the chance of a mismatch or having your script blow up because of garbled text. For example, use ogin: instead of login: and word: instead of password:.

chat normally sends a carriage return after each reply string unless a \c character sequence ends the string. Carriage returns aren't looked for in expect strings unless explicitly requested with the \r character sequence in the expect string.

Most modems can report why a call failed when it gets a busy signal or can't detect a carrier. You can use the abort expect string to tell chat to fail if it receives the specified strings. Multiple abort pairs are cumulative. The following script is an example of using the abort expect string:

```
abort 'NO CARRIER' abort 'BUSY' ogin:--ogin: ppp word: be4me
```

This chat script makes chat fail if it receives NO CARRIER or BUSY at any point during the script. chat recognizes a number of character and escape sequences, as outlined in Table 29.5.

Table 29.5 Character and Escape Sequences Recognized by *chat*

Sequence	Description
BREAK	Used as a reply string, this makes chat send a break to the modem. This special signal normally causes the remote host to change its transmission speed.
' '	Sends a null string with a single carriage return.
\b	The backspace character.
\c	Suppresses the newline sent after a reply string and must be at the end of the reply string.
\d	Makes chat wait for one second.
\K	Another means of specifying a break signal.
\n	Sends a newline character.
\N	Sends a null character.
\p	Pauses for 1/10th of one second.
\q	Prevents the string it's included in from showing in the syslog file.
\r	Sends or expects a carriage return.
\s	Sends or expects a space character.
\t	Sends or expects a tab character.
\\	Sends or expects a backslash character.
\ddd	Specifies an ASCII character in octal.
^C	Specifies the control character represented by C.

TIP You can use the abort string to prevent low-speed calls on your high-speed modem. Configure your modem to return a CARRIER 14400 string when it makes a connection and add abort CARRIER 2400 to your chat script. This way, chat fails if your modem connects at 2400 bps instead of 14400 bps.

Using PPP with *chat*   The pppd program has command-line options that control all aspects of the PPP link. The syntax for the pppd command is as follows:

pppd [*options*] [*tty_name*] [*speed*]

Table 29.6 describes the most commonly used options.

Table 29.6 Frequently Used *pppd* Command-Line Options

Option	Description
device	Uses the specified device. pppd adds /dev/ to the string if needed. When no device is given, pppd uses the controlling terminal.
speed	Sets the modem speed.
asyncmap *map*	Sets the async character map. This map specifies which control characters can't be sent through the connection and need to be escaped. The map is a 32-bit hex number where each bit represents a character. The 0th bit (00000001) represents character 0×00.
auth	Requires the remote host to authenticate itself.
connect *program*	Uses the program or shell command to set up the connection. This is where chat is used.
crtscts	Uses hardware flow control.
xonxoff	Uses software flow control.
defaultroute	Makes pppd set a default route to the remote host in your kernel routing table.
disconnect *program*	Runs the specified program after pppd terminates its link.
escape *c1,c2,...*	Causes the specified characters to be escaped when transmitted. The characters are specified by using the ASCII hex equivalent.
file *filename*	Reads pppd options from the specified file.
lock	Uses UUCP-style locking on the serial device.
mru *num*	Sets the maximum receive unit to the specified number.
netmask *mask*	Sets the PPP network interface netmask.
passive	Makes pppd wait for a valid connection rather than fail when it can't initiate a connection immediately.
silent	Keeps pppd from initiating a connection. pppd waits for a connection attempt from the remote host instead.

More than 40 other command-line arguments control all aspects of PPP at all levels. Refer to the main page for information about them.

N O T E The pppd program demands that the file /etc/ppp/options exist, even if it's empty. This file is read by pppd and is an excellent place to put options you want pppd to use every time it runs. ■

You can combine pppd and chat in a number of ways. You can specify all the command-line arguments for both programs on the command line, put the pppd options in a file, or put the chat script in a file. The following is a simple example with everything on the command line:

```
$ pppd connect 'chat "" ATDT5551234 ogin: linux2 word: be4me' \
/dev/cua1 38400 mru 296 lock debug crtscts modem defaultroute
```

This runs pppd with a simple chat script that dials a phone number and logs the user linux2 in to the remote host. The device, speed, MRU, and a number of other options are included.

At the other extreme, you can place most of the options for pppd in a file and have chat read a script file. The following is the call to pppd:

```
pppd /dev/cua1 38400 connect 'chat -f linux1.chat'
```

The following lines display the contents of the reference file:

```
# Global PPP Options File
mru 296                          # Set MRU value
lock                             # Use UUCP locking
crtscts                          # Use hardware handshaking
modem                            # Use modem control lines
defaultroute                     # Make PPP set up default route
```

pppd reads this file and processes the options it finds within. Any text following a # character is treated as a comment and ignored.

The following chat script sets a number of abort strings, dials the phone number, waits for a login prompt, and logs the ppp user in to the remote host with password ppp-word:

```
abort 'NO CARRIER'
abort 'BUSY'
abort 'VOICE'
abort 'CARRIER 2400'
"" ATDT555-1234
CONNECT '\c'
ogin:-BREAK-ogin: ppp
word: ppp-word
```

Providing PPP Service

Configuring your Linux machine to be a PPP server is even easier than setting up a SLIP server. It requires only one new account and a shell script that properly runs the pppd program.

Create an account called ppp with an /etc/passwd entry that looks like this:

```
$ ppp:*:501:300:PPP Account:/tmp:/etc/ppp/ppplogin
```

and set the passwd appropriately. The uid (501) and gid (300) numbers need not be the same. You can also assign one account to each PPP client you have, if you want. The /etc/ppp/ppplogin file should be an executable script such as the following:

```
#!/bin/sh
# PPP Server Login Script
# Turn off messages to this terminal
mesg n
# Turn off echoing
stty -echo
```

```
# Run pppd on top of this sh process
exec pppd -detach silent modem crtscts
```

This script executes pppd with the -detach argument, to keep pppd from detaching itself from the tty it's on. If pppd detaches, the script exits, causing the dial-up connection to close. The silent option makes pppd wait for the remote pppd daemon to initiate the link. The modem options make pppd monitor the modem control lines, and crtscts makes pppd use hardware flow control.

That's all there is to it. When a user logs in to your machine with the proper user ID and password, the PPP link is established automatically on your box.

Keeping Your PPP Link Secure

Keeping your PPP link secure is very important. Allowing anyone to connect your machine to a PPP server or allowing anyone to connect to your PPP server is as bad as letting anyone to put a machine directly on your network. PPP provides a direct IP connection, effectively putting the machines on both ends of the link on the same network.

Two authentication protocols have been developed to make PPP more secure—Password Authentication Protocol (PAP) and the Challenge Handshake Authentication Protocol (CHAP). While a PPP connection is being established, each machine can request the other to authenticate itself. This allows complete control of who can use your PPP service. CHAP is the more secure protocol and is discussed here.

CHAP uses a set of *secret keys*, which are text strings that are kept secret by the owners of the machines using CHAP and an encrypted challenge system to authenticate each other. A useful feature of CHAP is that it periodically issues challenge requests as long as the PPP link is up. This, for example, can detect intruders who have replaced the legitimate user by switching phone lines.

The secret keys for CHAP are stored in /etc/ppp/chap-secrets. To use authentication on your PPP link, you add the auth option to the call to pppd and add the appropriate information for the host being authenticated into the chap-secrets file. The following is a sample chap-secrets file for linux2.burwell.com:

```
# linux2.burwell.com CHAP secrets file
# client/server/secret/IP addr
linux2.burwell.com linux1.burwell.com "It's Full of Stars"
[ccc]linux2.burwell.com
linux1.burwell.com linux2.burwell.com "three stars" linux1.burwell.com
* linux2.burwell.com "three stars" burwell.com
```

Each line contains up to four fields: the client host name, the server host name, the secret key, and an optional list of IP addresses that this client can request be assigned to it. The client and server designations in this file are determined by the host that makes the authentication request (the server). The client has to respond to the request.

This file defines three different CHAP secrets. The first line is used when linux1.burwell.com requests CHAP authentication from linux2.burwell.com; the second is used for the reverse situation. The last line defines a wildcard situation for the client. This allows any machine that knows the proper secret key to make a PPP link to linux2.burwell.com. The wildcard designator (*) can be used in the client or server field.

Careful management of the chap-secrets file allows you complete control over the machines that can access your PPP server and the machines that you can access with PPP.

From Here...

SLIP and PPP are low-cost alternatives to a leased-line IP connectivity solution. You've looked at the requirements for running SLIP and PPP and at how to automate SLIP and PPP links by using the dip and chat commands. You've learned how to configure Linux as a SLIP or PPP server and how to enhance the security of PPP using the CHAP protocol. You can find complete documentation for dip, chat, and pppd in the man pages.

- Chapter 10, "Managing User Accounts," shows you how to add and delete user accounts.

- Chapter 23, "Understanding the TCP/IP Protocol Suite," explains what TCP/IP is and how the protocols work.

- Chapter 24, "Configuring a TCP/IP Network," shows you how to set up a Linux machine for use on a network.

- Chapter 25, "Configuring Domain Name Service," shows you how to make Linux use DNS.

## CHAPTER 30

Accessing the Network with *telnet*, *ftp*, and the *r-* Commands

by Steve Burnett

In this chapter

The major advantage you gain from computer networking is the capability to share resources and information and to access that information from remote locations. Linux provides a robust set of tools for doing just that. Whereas the World Wide Web lets you access lots of information in a hypertext format, additional tools allow you to log in to remote computers, transfer files, and execute remote commands.

Using *telnet* to Access Remote Computers

The telnet command is the basic tool for remote login under Linux. telnet gives you a terminal session on the remote computer that allows you to execute commands as though you were logged in locally.

To log in to a computer via telnet, you must know a valid username and password on the remote machine. Although some systems do provide guest login capabilities, such capabilities are fairly rare due to security concerns. When guest logins are allowed, they almost always place users in a restricted shell or in a menu system. The idea behind these two guest environments is to provide computer security and protect the system from malicious or careless unknown users. A restricted shell prevents the user from executing specific commands; a menu system allows choices from a predefined set of menus only, blocking out shell access entirely.

telnet also allows users to log in to their own computer from a remote location by entering their username and password. This way, users can check e-mail, edit files, and run programs on their normal computer as though they were logged in locally. However, you have to make do with a terminal-based environment instead of the X Windows system. telnet provides only terminal emulation for common terminals such as the DEC VT-100, which doesn't support graphical environments such as X Windows.

telnet Command Summary

The basic syntax for telnet is as follows:

```
telnet [hostname]
```

hostname is the name of a remote computer. If you don't specify a remote host, telnet starts in its interactive command mode. If you give a remote host name, telnet tries to initiate a session immediately.

telnet accepts several command-line arguments, as listed in Table 30.1.

Table 30.1 Command-Line Arguments for the *telnet* Command

Argument	Description
-d	Turns on debugging.
-a	Attempts automatic login.
-n *tracefile*	Turns on tracing and saves trace data in *tracefile*.

Argument	Description
`-e` *escape_char*	Sets the escape character for the session to be *escape_char*. If the *escape_char* character is omitted from the argument, there is no escape character for this `telnet` session.
`-l` *user*	Sends the username *user* to the remote system for automatic login. This argument automatically includes the `-a` argument.
port	Indicates the port number to connect to on the remote system. This argument is used for specifying different network programs. If it's not specified, `telnet` connects to the default `telnet` port.

Part
VI
Ch
30

Sample *telnet* Session

It's time to take a walk through a sample `telnet` session. You start the `telnet` session by typing **telnet**, followed by the host name of the computer you want to connect to. `telnet` then returns with the message `Trying` *some IP address* (where *some IP address* is the address of the computer you specified). If `telnet` successfully connects to the computer (that is, the computer is up and running and the network isn't down), Linux reports `Connected to` *computer name* and then tells you that the escape character is some specific character sequence, almost always <Ctrl-]>. The escape character specifies the character sequence that you type to drop from your terminal session into the `telnet` command interpreter. You do this if you want to send commands directly to the `telnet` program and not to your remote computer session.

After `telnet` successfully connects to the remote system, the login information is displayed and the system prompts you for your login ID and password. Assuming that you have a valid username and password, you successfully log in and can now work interactively on the remote system.

The following is an example of a `telnet` session from a Linux computer that connects to a Linux computer:

```
$ telnet server.somewhere.com
Trying 127.0.0.1...
Connected to server.somewhere.com.
Escape character is '^]'.
"Red Hat Linux release 4.0 (Colgate)

kernel 2.0.18 on an I486

login:bubba
Password: password
Last login: Mon Nov 11 20:50:43 from localhost
Linux 2.0.6. (Posix).
server:~$
server:~$ logout
Connection closed by foreign host.
$
```

When you're finished with the remote session, be sure to log out. `telnet` then reports that the remote session is closed, and you return to your local shell prompt.

Using FTP for Remote File Transfer

File Transfer Protocol (FTP) is a simple and effective means of transferring files between computers that are connected on a TCP/IP network. FTP allows users to transfer ASCII and binary files.

During an FTP session, you connect to another computer by using the FTP client program. From this point, you can move up and down through the directory tree, list directory contents, copy files from the remote computer to your computer, and transfer files from your computer to the remote system. Normal file protections apply; you can't get or put a file on the remote system if you don't have the proper permissions for that file.

To use FTP to transfer files, you must know a valid username and password on the remote computer. This username/password combination is used to validate your FTP session and to determine what access you have to files for transfer. Also, you obviously need to know the name of the computer with which you want to conduct an FTP session.

You should be aware that FTP clients have different command sets, depending on the operating system in question. This chapter covers the Linux FTP client; however, when you start an FTP session with a remote computer, the commands that the remote system expects might be different. It's rare for FTP systems to be completely incompatible with each other. Typically, the commands that you normally use are either slightly different or unavailable.

Anonymous FTP

Due to the explosive growth of the Internet, many organizations have made huge repositories of information available via FTP. These FTP sites have everything from text files to software of every conceivable type available. But how do you access this enormous storehouse of data if you don't have an account on the remote computer? Do you need to get an account on every FTP site in order to access these files?

In short, the answer is no. A common convention on the Internet allows guest FTP access to file repositories so that users can transfer files. This guest access is referred to as *anonymous FTP*. To use anonymous FTP, you start an FTP session to the remote system and use the username of anonymous and your e-mail address as the password. For example, in the following sample, the user named smith on linux.somewhere.com wants to initiate an FTP session with a common FTP site:

```
$ ftp ftp.uu.net
ftp.uu.net (login:smith): anonymous
Password: smith@linux.somewhere.com
```

N O T E Many sites don't allow anonymous FTP. Allowing guest users to connect to your computer does involve some risk. In cases where anonymous FTP isn't allowed, the ftp command fails with a message similar to Login failed - User "anonymous" unknown. Sites that do permit anonymous FTP typically place the user in a restricted directory tree with read-only access. If you're allowed to place files on the remote computer, you usually can put them in only one directory. ■

ftp Command Summary

The Linux ftp command provides a verbose set of command options in interactive mode. As mentioned earlier, some remote hosts might not support all these commands. Also, you probably won't need to use many of them. Table 30.2 lists the commands available while in FTP.

Table 30.2   *ftp* Commands Available in Interactive Mode

Command	Description
!	Escapes to the shell
$	Executes a macro
account	Sends the account command to remote server
append	Appends to a file
ascii	Sets the file-transfer type to ASCII mode
bell	Beeps when a command is completed
binary	Sets the file-transfer type to binary mode
bye	Terminates the FTP session and exits
case	Toggles mget upper- or lowercase filename mapping
cd	Changes the working directory on the remote computer
cdup	Changes the remote working directory to the parent directory
chmod	Changes file permissions of the remote file
close	Terminates the FTP session
cr	Toggles carriage return stripping when receiving an ASCII file
delete	Deletes the remote file
debug	Toggles debugging mode
dir	Lists the contents of the remote directory (gives size and permissions)
disconnect	Terminates the FTP session (same as close)
exit	Terminates the FTP session and exits
form	Sets the file-transfer format
get	Gets a file from the remote computer
glob	Toggles wildcard expansion of local filenames
hash	Toggles printing the # character for each buffer transferred
help	Prints local help information

continues

Table 30.2   Continued

Command	Description
idle	Gets or sets the idle timer on the remote computer
image	Sets the file transfer type to binary mode (same as `binary`)
lcd	Changes the local working directory
ls	Lists the contents of the remote directory (gives size and permissions)
macdef	Defines a macro
mdelete	Deletes multiple files on the remote computer
mdir	Lists the contents of multiple remote directories
mget	Gets multiple files from the remote computer
mkdir	Makes a directory on the remote machine
mls	Lists the contents of multiple remote directories
mode	Sets the file-transfer mode
modtime	Shows the last modification time of the remote file
mput	Sends multiple files to the remote computer
newer	Gets a remote file if the remote file is newer than the corresponding local file
nmap	Sets templates for default filename mapping
nlist	Lists the contents of the remote directory
ntrans	Sets the translation table for default filename mapping
open	Connects to the remote FTP site
passive	Enters passive transfer mode
prompt	Forces interactive prompting on multiple commands
proxy	Issues command on alternate connection
put	Sends one file to the remote computer
pwd	Prints the working directory on the remote machine
quit	Terminates the FTP session and exits
quote	Sends an arbitrary `ftp` command
recv	Receives a file
reget	Gets file restarting at end of the local file
rstatus	Shows the status of the remote machine

Command	Description
rhelp	Gets help from the remote server
rename	Renames a file
reset	Clears queued command replies
restart	Restarts the file transfer at the specified byte count
rmdir	Removes a directory on the remote machine
runique	Assigns a unique filename to each file received when retrieving multiple files with the same filename to the same directory
send	Sends one file to the remote computer
site	Sends a site-specific command to the remote server, one of umask, idle, chmod, help, group, gpass, newer, or minfo
size	Shows the size of the remote file
status	Shows the current status
struct	Sets the file-transfer structure
system	Shows the remote system type
sunique	When sending multiple files with the same filename to the same directory, assigns a unique filename to each file sent
tenex	Sets the tenex file-transfer type
tick	Toggles printing byte size counter during transfers
trace	Toggles packet tracing
type	Sets the file-transfer type
user	Sends new user information
umask	Gets or sets the umask on the remote computer
verbose	Toggles verbose mode
?	Prints local help information

As you can see, ftp has quite a few commands. However, you really need to look at only the ones that you use most frequently.

Starting an *FTP* Session   The open command is used to open an FTP session with a remote host. Its syntax is as follows:

```
open hostname
```

You usually need this command only if you're going to connect to more than one site during an FTP session. If you want to connect to only one computer during the session, just specify the remote host name on the command line as an argument to the ftp command.

Ending an FTP Session   The close, disconnect, quit, and bye commands are used to end an FTP session with a remote computer. The identical close and disconnect commands close your connection to the remote computer but leave you in the ftp program on your local computer. The quit, exit, and bye commands close your connection to the remote computer if one is active; then they exit the ftp program on your computer.

Changing Directories   The cd *[directory]* command is used to change directories on the remote computer during your FTP session. The cdup command takes you to the parent directory of the current directory. The lcd command changes your local directory so that you can specify where to find or put local files.

Remote Directory Listing   The ls command lists the contents of a remote directory, just like ls from an interactive shell. The syntax for ls is this:

```
ls [directory] [local_file]
```

If a directory is specified as an argument, ls lists the contents of that directory. If a local filename is given, the directory listing is put into the file you specified on your local computer.

The dir and ls commands provide a long listing, giving protections, size, owner, and date. The syntax of the dir command is as follows:

```
dir [directory] [local_file]
```

The following is an example of a dir directory listing:

```
-rw-r--r--   1 root   archive  2928  May  17  1993     README
-rw-r--r--   1 root   archive  1723  Jun  29  1993     README.NFS
dr-xr-xr-x   2 root   wheel    8192  Jun   6  12:16    bind
-rwxr-xr-x   5 root   wheel    8192  Aug   2  06:11    decus
drwxr-xr-x  19 root   archive  8192  Feb   7  1994     doc
drwxr-xr-x   6 root   wheel    8192  Jun  15  15:45    edu
dr-xr-xr-x   7 root   wheel    8192  Sep  28  09:33    etc
```

▶ **See** "Managing File Systems" **p. 265** for an explanation of the above result

Getting Files from a Remote System   The get and mget commands are used to retrieve files from a remote computer. The get command retrieves the file that you specify as an argument (*filename*). The following is the get command's syntax:

```
get filename [remote_filename]
```

You can also give a local filename, which is the name of the file when it's created on your local computer. If you don't give a local filename, *remote_filename* is used.

The mget command retrieves multiple files at once. mget's syntax is as follows:

```
mget filename_list
```

You specify these files by giving a list of filenames separated by spaces or by using a wildcard pattern to mget. You're prompted for each file. To turn prompting off, use the prompt command before using mget. In both cases, the files are transferred as ASCII files, unless you've set the transfer mode to something else.

Sending Files to a Remote System   The `put` and `mput` commands are used to send files to a remote computer. The `put` command sends the local file that you specify as an argument. The syntax is this:

```
put filename
```

The `mput` command sends a series of local files. The syntax for `mput` is shown here:

```
mput filename_list
```

You specify these files by giving a list of filenames separated by spaces or by using a wildcard pattern to `mput`. When using `mput`, you're prompted for each file. To turn prompting off, use the `prompt` command. In both cases, the files are transferred as ASCII files, unless you've set the transfer mode to something else.

Changing the File Transfer Mode   `ftp` transfers files as ASCII files unless you specify something else. This is fine for plain text but renders any binary data useless. The `ascii` and `binary` commands set the transfer mode so that you can prevent damage to your binary files.

> **N O T E**   Many files that you'll want to transfer are in binary format. Files ending with .tar are archives created with the `tar` command. Files ending in .Z and .gz are compressed with either the `compress` command or the GNU `gzip` command, respectively. Files ending in .zip are compressed archives created with PKZIP. When in doubt, use binary transfer mode. Using ASCII mode corrupts binary data files. ■

Checking Transfer Status   When transferring a large file, you may find it useful to have `ftp` give you feedback on how far along the transfer is. The `hash` command causes `ftp` to print a # character on-screen each time the transmission of a data buffer has been completed. This command works for sending and receiving files.

Local Commands While in FTP   The ! character is used to pass a command to the command shell on your local computer while you're in FTP. This can be very useful if you need to do something while you're in the midst of an FTP session. Suppose that you need to create a directory to hold received files. If you enter `!mkdir new_dir`, Linux makes a directory named new_dir in your current local directory.

A Sample FTP Session

Listing 30.1 shows a short FTP session.

Listing 30.1   Making an FTP Connection and Getting a Directory Listing

```
$ ftp opus
Connected to opus.
220 opus FTP server (Linux opus 2.0.6 #4 Mon Nov 11 16:01:33 CDT 1996) ready.
Name (opus:smith): smith
Password (opus:smith): password
331 Password required for smith.
230 User smith logged in.
```

continues

Listing 30.1   Continued

```
Remote system type is UNIX.
Using ASCII mode to transfer files.
ftp> dir
200 PORT command successful.
150 Opening ASCII mode data connection for /bin/ls.
total 8
-rw-r--r--  1 root     daemon      1525 Sep 29 15:37 README
dr-xr-xr-x  2 root     wheel        512 Jun 24 11:35 bin
dr--r--r--  2 root     wheel        512 Jun 24 11:18 dev
dr--r--r--  2 root     wheel        512 Jun 24 11:24 etc
dr-xr-xr-x  4 root     wheel        512 Sep 29 15:37 pub
dr-xr-xr-x  3 root     wheel        512 Jun 24 11:15 usr
-r--r--r--  1 root     daemon       461 Jun 24 13:46 welcome.msg
226 Transfer complete.
433 bytes received in 0.027 seconds (16 Kbytes/s)
ftp> get README
200 PORT command successful.
150 Opening ASCII mode data connection for README (1525 bytes).
226 Transfer complete.
local: README remote: README
1561 bytes received in 0.0038 seconds (4e+02 Kbytes/s)
ftp> quit
221 Goodbye.
$
```

In the preceding example, a user opens an FTP session to the host opus and logs in as smith. The remote FTP server prompts for the password, which the user types (the password doesn't appear on-screen). ftp then logs smith in to the remote system and displays the ftp> prompt for interactive mode commands. The user tells ftp to list the remote directory with the dir command and then transfers the file README with the get command. When finished with the FTP session, the intrepid user then logs out with the quit command and is returned to the local Linux shell prompt.

A Sample Anonymous FTP Session

In the previous section, you saw a user initiate an FTP session with a system and look at some directories. The user had a valid username and password on the remote system. Now look at an anonymous FTP session to a major software archive site on the Internet. Listing 30.2 is very similar to Listing 30.1, but it has some interesting differences.

Listing 30.2   Performing an Anonymous FTP Connection

```
$ ftp ftp.uu.net
Connected to ftp.uu.net.
220 ftp.UU.NET FTP server (Version wu-2.4(1) Wed Nov 13 15:45:10 EST 1996) ready.
Name (ftp.uu.net:bubba): anonymous
331 Guest login ok, send your complete e-mail address as password.
Password: your_e-mail_address
```

```
230-
230-                    Welcome to the UUNET archive.
230-    A service of UUNET Technologies Inc, Falls Church, Virginia
230-    For information about UUNET, call +1 703 204 8000,
230-    or see the files in /uunet-info
230-
230-    Access is allowed all day.
230-    Local time is Wed Nov 13 15:53:02 1996.
230-
230-    All transfers are logged with your host name and email address.
230-    If you don't like this policy, disconnect now!
230-
230-    If your FTP client crashes or hangs shortly
230-    after login, try using a
230-    dash (-) as the first character of your password.
230-    This will turn off the informational messages which may
230-     be confusing your ftp client.
230-
230-Please read the file /info/README.ftp
230-    it was last modified on Mon Nov 11 17:39:53 1996 - 2 days ago
230 Guest login ok, access restrictions apply.
ftp>
ftp> dir
200 PORT command successful.
150 Opening ASCII mode data connection for /bin/ls.
total 4149
drwxr-sr-x   2 34    0              512 Jul 26  1992 .forward
-rw-r--r--   1 34    uucp             0 Jul 26  1992 .hushlogin
-rw-r--r--   1 34    archive         59 Jul 31  1992 .kermrc
-rw-r--r--   1 34    archive          0 Jul 26  1992 .notar
drwx--s--x   5 34    archive        512 Jul 23 19:00 admin
lrwxrwxrwx   1 34    archive          1 Jul 26  1992 archive -> .
drwxrws--x   4 0     archive        512 Apr 20 16:29 bin
lrwxrwxrwx   1 34    archive         23 Sep 14  1993 by-name.gz ->
➥index/master/by-name.gz
lrwxrwxrwx   1 34    archive         23 Sep 14  1993 by-time.gz ->
➥index/master/by-time.gz
-rw-r--r--   1 34    archive       90112 Apr 26  1991 compress.tar
lrwxrwxrwx   1 0     archive          9 Jul 23 18:50 core -> /dev/null
drwxrws--x   2 0     archive        512 Jul 26  1992 dev
drwxrwsr-x  21 34    archive       1024 Sep 29 15:18 doc
drwxrws--x   6 0     archive        512 Apr 14 16:42 etc
lrwxrwxrwx   1 34    archive         31 Dec  8  1993 faces ->
➥/archive/published/usenix/faces
drwxrwsr-x   2 34    archive        512 Jul 26  1992 ftp
drwxrwsr-x   4 34    archive        512 Sep 29 10:34 government
drwxrwsr-x  18 34    archive       1024 Sep 29 10:28 graphics
-rw-rw-r--   1 34    archive      798720 Jul 11 20:54 gzip.tar
lrwxrwxrwx   1 34    archive         17 Jul 26  1992 help -> info/archive-help
drwxrwsr-x  20 34    archive       1024 Dec  2  1993 index
drwxrwsr-x  19 34    archive        512 Sep 29 10:30 inet
drwxrwsr-x   4 34    archive        512 Sep 29 15:36 info
drwxrwsr-x  25 34    archive        512 Sep 29 10:29 languages
drwxrwsr-x   4 34    archive        512 Sep 29 10:28 library
drwx--s--x   2 0     0             8192 Jul 26  1992 lost+found
```

continues

Listing 30.2   Continued

```
lrwxrwxrwx   1 34   archive         20 Aug  2  1992 ls-1R.Z ->
➥index/master/ls-1R.Z
lrwxrwxrwx   1 34   archive         21 Sep 14  1993 ls-1R.gz ->
➥index/master/ls-1R.gz
lrwxrwxrwx   1 34   archive         21 Aug  2  1992 ls-1tR.Z ->
➥index/master/ls-1tR.Z
lrwxrwxrwx   1 34   archive         22 Sep 14  1993 ls-1tR.gz ->
➥index/master/ls-1tR.gz
drwxrwsr-x  24 34   archive       1024 Sep 29 15:10 networking
drwxrwsr-x   2 34   archive        512 Aug 10 09:26 packages
d--xrws--x  17 34   archive        512 Sep 26 12:29 private
drwxrwsr-x  25 34   archive       1536 Sep 29 15:30 pub
drwxrwsr-x  17 34   archive       1024 Sep 29 15:38 published
lrwxrwxrwx   1 34   archive         10 Jul 26  1992 sco-archive -> vendor/sco
drwxrwsr-x  20 34   archive        512 Sep 29 04:18 systems
drwxrwxrwx  14 34   archive       1536 Sep 29 15:36 tmp
lrwxrwxrwx   1 34   archive         17 Jul 26  1992 unix-today ->
➥vendor/unix-today
lrwxrwxrwx   1 34   archive         17 Jul 26  1992 unix-world ->
➥vendor/unix-world
drwxrwsr-x  36 34   archive       1024 Sep 29 15:29 usenet
drwxrws--x   6  0   archive        512 Oct 22  1992 usr
lrwxrwxrwx   1 34   archive         16 Aug  2  1992 uumap -> networking/uumap
-rw-rw-r--   1 34   archive    3279895 Sep 28 21:05 uumap.tar.Z
drwxrwsr-x   3 210  archive       2560 Sep 29 15:36 uunet-info
drwxrwsr-x  64 34   archive       1536 Sep 29 10:29 vendor
226 Transfer complete.
3257 bytes received in 0.76 seconds (4.2 Kbytes/s)
ftp>
ftp> cd systems/unix/linux
250-Files within this subtree are automatically mirrored from
250-tsx-11.mit.edu:/pub/linux
250-
250 CWD command successful.
ftp>
ftp> binary
200 Type set to I.
ftp> get sum.Z
200 PORT command successful.
150 Opening BINARY mode data connection for sum.Z (80959 bytes).
226 Transfer complete.
local: sum.Z remote: sum.Z
80959 bytes received in 5.6 seconds (14 Kbytes/s)
ftp> quit
221 Goodbye.
$
```

Here, an FTP session is initiated with **ftp.uu.net**, which is a major FTP archive site on the Internet. The username given at the login prompt is anonymous because this is anonymous FTP. For the password, the full e-mail address is used. **ftp.uu.net** then displays a welcome banner that gives some information about the archive. In this example, you can see that the user changes directories, sets the file mode to binary, gets a compressed binary file, and exits.

TROUBLESHOOTING

I transferred a binary file, but it doesn't work properly. I can't unzip it, untar it, uncompress it, or anything. What should I do? Make sure that you set the transfer mode to binary. You can do this with the `binary` command at the `ftp>` prompt.

I'm in the process of transferring a large file and want to check the progress. Use the `hash` command. `ftp` prints the # character on-screen after every data buffer that's processed. The data buffer may vary depending on your version of Linux, but it's typically 1,024, 4,096, or 8,192 bytes.

I was trying to do an anonymous FTP, but the site told me that the user *anonymous* was unknown and that the login failed. Either you misspelled "anonymous," or the site doesn't allow anonymous FTP. In the latter case, you must have a valid username and password on the remote computer.

I want to transfer several files, but I don't want FTP to prompt me for each one. Use the `prompt` command, which toggles prompting on and off.

I tried to use anonymous FTP, but the site told me that I didn't enter a valid e-mail address as the password. In the past, the convention during an anonymous FTP connection was to enter **guest** as the password. Now, the convention is to enter your e-mail address. Many FTP sites run special FTP server software that checks the password and makes sure that it's in the form *user@host.somewhere.domain*. Try again and make sure that you enter your full e-mail address correctly.

Using the *r*- Commands

In addition to `ftp` and `telnet`, several other commands allow you to access remote computers and exchange files over a network. These commands are known collectively as the `r`- commands.

The `r`- commands deserve special notice because one of their features can cause a severe security loophole if you aren't careful. When you issue an `r`- command, the remote system checks a file named /etc/hosts.equiv to see whether your local host is listed. If it doesn't find your local host, it checks for a file named .rhosts in your home directory on the remote machine. The `r`- command then checks to see whether your local host name is in the .rhosts file. If your local host is listed in either place, the command is executed without checking for a password.

Although it can be very convenient not to type your password every time you need to access a remote computer, it can obviously cause severe security problems. It's recommended that you carefully consider the security implications of the `r`- commands before setting up /etc/hosts.equiv and .rhosts files on your local system.

rlogin

The `rlogin` command is very similar to the `telnet` command because it allows you to start an interactive command session on a remote system. The syntax of `rlogin` is as follows:

```
rlogin [-8EKLdx] [-e char] [-k realm] [-l user-name] hostname
```

However, the most common usage is simply this:

```
rlogin hostname
```

Table 30.3 explains the various options for rlogin.

Table 30.3   Command-Line Options for the *rlogin* Command

Option	Description
-8	Allows an 8-bit input data path at all times, which allows for formatted ANSI characters and other special codes to be sent. If this option isn't used, parity bits are stripped except when the remote stop and start characters are other than <Ctrl-s> and <Ctrl-q>.
-E	Stops any character from being recognized as an escape character. When used with the -8 option, this provides a completely transparent connection.
-K	Turns off all Kerberos authentication. It's used only when connecting to a host that uses the Kerberos authentication protocol.
-L	Allows the rlogin session to be run in litout mode. Refer to the tty man page for more information.
-d	Turns on socket debugging on the TCP sockets used for communication with the remote host. Refer to the setsockopt man page for more information.
-e	Used to set the escape character for the rlogin session. The escape character is ~ by default. You can specify a literal character or an octal value in the form \nnn.
-k	Requests rlogin to obtain Kerberos tickets for the remote host in the specified realm instead of the remote host's realm as determined by krb_realmofhost(3).
-l	Allows the remote name to be specified. If available, Kerberos authentication is used.
-x	Turns on DES encryption for all data passed via the rlogin session. This can affect response time and CPU usage, but provides increased security.

rsh

The rsh command, an abbreviation for *remote shell*, starts a shell on the specified remote host and executes the command, if any, that you specify on the rsh command line. If you don't give a command to execute, you're logged in to the remote machine by using rlogin.

The syntax of the rsh command is as follows:

```
rsh [-Kdnx] [-k realm] [-l user-name] hostname [command]
```

However, the most common usage is this:

```
rsh hostname [command]
```

The *command* argument can be virtually any Linux command that can be entered from the shell prompt. Table 30.4 explains the command-line options for rsh.

Table 30.4   Command-Line Options for the *rsh* Command

Option	Description
-K	Turns off all Kerberos authentication. It's used only when connecting to a host that uses Kerberos.
-d	Turns on socket debugging on the TCP sockets used for communication with the remote host. See the setsockopt man page for more information.
-k	Requests rsh to obtain Kerberos tickets for the remote host in the specified realm instead of the remote host's realm as determined by krb_realmofhost(3).
-l	Allows the remote name to be specified. If available, Kerberos authentication is used, and authorization is determined as with the rlogin command.
-n	Redirects input from the special device /dev/null.
-x	Turns on DES encryption for all data passed. This can affect response time and CPU usage, but it provides increased security.

Linux takes the standard input to the rsh command and copies it to the standard input of the remotely executed command. It copies the standard output of the remote command to standard output for rsh. It also copies the remote standard error to the local standard error file descriptor. Any quit, terminate, and interrupt signals are sent to the remote command. Also, any special shell characters that aren't enclosed with quotation marks, as in ">>", are handled locally. If enclosed with quotation marks, these characters are handled by the remote command.

rcp

The rcp command, which stands for *remote copy*, is the last of the r- commands that you need to know. It's used to copy files between computers. You can use rcp to copy files from one remote computer to another, without either the source or destination being on the local machine.

The rcp command has two forms. The first form is used to copy a file to a file. The second form is used when copying files or a directory to a directory. The syntax for the rcp command can be either of the following:

```
rcp [-px] [-k realm] filename1 filename2
rcp [-px] [-r] [-k realm] file(s) directory
```

Each file or directory argument is either a remote filename or a local filename. Remote filenames have the form *rname@rhost:path*, where *rname* is the remote username, *rhost* is the remote computer, and *path* is the path to the file. The filename must contain a colon.

Table 30.5 explains the arguments for rcp.

Table 30.5   Command-Line Arguments for the *rcp* Command

Option	Description
-r	Recursively copies the source directory tree into the destination directory. To use this option, the destination must be a directory.
-p	Tries to preserve the modification times and modes of the source files, ignoring the umask.
-k	Requests rcp to obtain Kerberos tickets for the remote host in the specified realm instead of the remote host's realm, as determined by krb_realmofhost(3).
-x	Turns on DES encryption for all data passed by rcp. This can affect response time and CPU usage but provides increased security.

If the path specified in the filename isn't a full path name, it's interpreted as being relative to the login directory of the specified user on the remote computer. If no remote username is given, your current username is used. If a path on a remote host contains special shell characters, it can be quoted by using \, ", or ' as appropriate. This causes all the shell metacharacters to be interpreted remotely.

N O T E   rcp doesn't prompt for passwords. It performs its copies via the rsh command. ▓

ssh

ssh (short for secure shell), like the rsh command, is a program for logging into a remote machine and executing commands on that remote machine. ssh is designed to replace both rsh and rlogin by providing the ability to define an encrypted session between two untrusted systems over an insecure network. One problem with telnet is that, when you log in to the remote system, the password is sent as ASCII over the network. By watching the Ethernet packets, someone could collect your login name and password for the remote system. ssh prevents this from happening by using RSA-based authentication. Because of its security, ssh is commonly used by system administrators today. ssh clients are available for other operating systems, including Macintosh and Windows.

The ssh command is very similar to the telnet command because it allows you to start an interactive command session on a remote system. The syntax of ssh is as follows:

```
ssh [-a] [-c idea¦blowfish¦des¦3des¦arcfour¦tss¦none] [-e escape_char]
➥[-I identity_file] [-l login-name] [-n] [-k] [-V] [=o option] [-p port]
➥[-q] [-P] [-t] [-v] [-x] [-C] [-L port"host:hostport] [-R port:host:hostport]
➥hostname [command]
```

However, the most common usage is this:

```
ssh hostname
```

Table 30.4 explains the various options for ssh.

Part
VI
Ch
30

Table 30.4   Command-Line Options for the *ssh* Command

Option	Description
-a	Disables forwarding of the authentication agent.
-c	Selects the cipher to use for encrypting the session. Idea is the default, arcfour is the fastest, and none is the equivalent of using rlogin or rsh (no encryption).
-e	Sets the escape character for the session.
-f	Sets ssh in the background after authentication and forwardings are established.
-i	Selects the identity file from which the private key for RSA authentication is read.
-k	Disables forwarding of Kerberos tickets.
-l	Sets the login name for use to the remote machine.
-n	Redirects stdin from /dev/nulls used when ssh runs in the background.
-o	Used for user-defined options following the format in the configuration file.
-p	Sets the port to connect to on the remote host.
-q	Activates quiet mode, which suppresses all messages except fatal errors.
-P	Uses a nonprivileged port.
-t	Forces pseudo-tty allocation.
-v	Activates verbose mode (useful for debugging).
-x	Disables X11 forwarding.
-C	Requests compression of all data.
-L	Specifies the local port to forward to the designated remote host and port.
-R	Specifies the remote port to be forwarded to the local host and designated port.

From Here...

You can find more information about the Internet in the following chapters:

- Chapter 31, "Surfing the Internet with the World Wide Web," describes the various types of information available on the Internet and the tools for accessing this information.

- Chapter 33, "Using Electronic Mail," shows how to send and receive e-mail over the Internet.

Surfing the Internet with the World Wide Web

by Steve Burnett

In this chapter

You've heard that all kinds of information is available on the Internet. It's true. You'll find everything from the latest weather satellite photo to software, statistics, and online shopping.

This chapter discusses the services you can use to get to information on the Internet. You might use the World Wide Web, FTP, gopher, telnet, WAIS, or archie. Most likely you'll use some combination. This chapter goes through each major service and shows you some basic information on how to use that service. Because the Web provides such an easy way to access information on the Internet, and because many of the other services can be used from your Web browser, this chapter concentrates on how to use these services from a Web browser.

Introducing the World Wide Web

The Internet is a completely distributed network, which means that your computer is connected directly not only with the computer down the hallway, but with thousands of others all over the world. Your computer connects to another computer, which is connected to other computers, and so on.

To make matters more complex, the Internet is international in scope. Virtually every country in the world has some form of access to the Internet. For years, there were many services to get to information (FTP, gopher, and so on), but none were easy to use. You had to have all the appropriate software. Then you had to know what service to use and when. And so on. Something like the World Wide Web was needed as a form of "information navigator" to make it easier for users to get to information on the Internet.

The Web began as a network and hypertext project at CERN, a European physics research lab, in 1989. Researchers saw a need for people from any location to be able to share and exchange information and documents in real time from any type of computer. They also wanted a simple and consistent way to handle this information. From this, the Web was born.

The Web uses a set of hypertext links that allow users to easily navigate between documents, graphics, files, audio clips, and so on from sites anywhere on the Internet. When you select a hypertext link in a document, whatever item the link points to is automatically retrieved. One link at a time, Internet users quickly find their way to the various bits of information they want.

Understanding the Web's Structure

The Web is based on a client/server model. The client software package (Web browser software on your computer) contacts a server computer (Web server software) and exchanges messages with that computer through a set of rules that both client and server understand. This set of rules is known as a *protocol*. Web servers and clients communicate through a protocol known as the Hypertext Transfer Protocol (HTTP). When a Web client program retrieves a document from a Web server, the programs are probably communicating by using HTTP. As you'll see later in this chapter, other Internet protocols also may be supported by the Web server.

Of Clients and Servers

The client/server relationship is an important concept in networking, and especially in navigation of the Web. A *server* is a computer that offers services for other computers to use. *Services* can be any kind of program, routine, or data provided by the server. For example, a server might return information from a database to which you don't have direct access.

A *client* is a computer that uses services from a server. The client contacts the server and requests some sort of service. Many times, a client computer uses special software designed to interact with a specially designed server program on the server computer.

Under this client/server model, people with different computers in different locations can access information on the same server. You can set up different server computers with different types of data. Because people are using a client software program to communicate with the server, you can develop a different client program for each computer platform that they use. That way, people using Windows or a Macintosh can use client software to access information on a UNIX or Linux server just as easily as UNIX or Linux users can.

To access the Web, you need client software known as a *Web browser*. A Web browser is a program that understands how to communicate to a Web server via the HTTP protocol, displays information, and provides a way to represent hypertext links. Many browsers are available. Now, the most commonly used browsers are Netscape's Navigator and Microsoft's Internet Explorer. You can get a browser in any number of ways: from your Internet Service Provider (ISP), by buying it in store, by downloading it off the Internet, and so on. After you install the browser and configure the software with your Internet access information, you're ready to go.

Understanding URLs

You get information on the Web by using a descriptive address known as a *uniform resource locator* (URL, pronounced "earl"). Think of an URL as a pointer to an object on the Internet that tells you not only where the object is located, but also what it's named and how to access it. Everything you access through the Web has an URL.

The syntax of URLs may look intimidating but is really quite straightforward. Here's an example:

http://www.ncsa.uiuc.edu/SDG/Software/Mosaic/Docs/whats-new.html

Scary? It's really not that bad. The part to the left of the colon (:) specifies the access method to get to the data. This access method defines the protocol used to communicate with the server, and also gives a good clue as to the type of interaction that will take place. Table 31.1 lists several valid access methods.

Table 31.1 **Valid Access Methods for URLs**	
Method	**Description**
http	Protocol for accessing most Web pages. Provides interactive hypermedia links to pages written in Hypertext Markup Language (HTML).
wais	Used for accessing a Wide Area Information Service (WAIS) site.
gopher	Used for accessing a gopher server.
ftp	Provides an anonymous FTP connection.
telnet	Opens a telnet connection to a site.
news	Used for reading Usenet news.

Before the Web, There Was...

Many services and sources of information existed before the Web. These services use protocols other than HTTP. However, many Web clients such as Netscape Navigator allow you to access these services from within the browser. For example, you can transfer files to your computer by using the FTP protocol, retrieve documents from gopher servers, do text searches with WAIS (Wide Area Information Service), and read Usenet news.

Following the :// in the URL is the host name of the server computer you want to contact. After the server name is the directory path to the document you want to view or retrieve. This path depends totally on where the file is located on the remote server. (You might not have a path in some cases, if the file is in a default directory.) Finally, the filename of the document is given. This document can be text, a hypermedia document, a sound file, a graphic, or some other type of file.

So, look again at the example. The following URL

http://www.ncsa.uiuc.edu/SDG/Software/Mosaic/Docs/whats-new.html

uses the HTTP protocol to contact the server computer **www.ncsa.uiuc.edu** and says that you're interested in the document named whats-new.html located in the directory /SDG/Software/Mosaic/Docs. The .html extension on the document name tells your Web client (for example, Netscape Navigator) that this document is written in Hypertext Markup Language (HTML). HTML is a special syntax used to write hypertext pages for the Web. For more details on HTML, see Chapter 32, "Creating Web Documents with HTML."

Searching the Web

The Web is huge, and it's getting bigger every day. Rather than click through thousands of pages, you can use search engines to help you find information faster. A *search engine* is a program that looks through its database for information that matches your request. Some search engines, such as AltaVista and Infoseek, search the entire Web and store their information in huge databases. Other search engines search only a specific Web site.

When you see a Search button at a typical Web site, it's usually only for that Web site. When you want to search the entire Web, you need a more general search tool. The following list describes some of the many search engines that scan Web sites across the Internet. Some even let you search other Internet information sources, like those on Usenet or FTP sites.

- *AltaVista* (**http://www.altavista.digital.com**), for Web and Usenet. You can find anything, anywhere on the Web or Usenet. But you'll want to narrow your search as much as possible; it is easy to get too many results back!

- *Yahoo!* (**http://www.yahoo.com**), for Web, Usenet, e-mail addresses, current news, people search, city maps, and stocks. Yahoo! isn't really a search engine. It's basically a huge list of Web sites, sorted into categories, that have been submitted by users. It's useful for common information and for getting an idea of just how much—and varied— the information on the Web is. Yahoo! also provides links to search engines.

- *Infoseek* (**http://www.infoseek.com**) for Web, Usenet, FAQs, current news, e-mail addresses, maps, stocks, and company listings. Infoseek contains a search engine and listing service and is good when you want to search more than the Web or Usenet. Infoseek has a different search language than many of the other search engines.

- *Open Text Index* (**http://index.opentext.net**) for Web, Usenet, current news, and e-mail addresses. This is an easy-to-use alternative to AltaVista and is good to use when you need to search for obscure topics. You can also search in other languages, such as Japanese and Spanish.

- *Excite* (**http://www.excite.com**) for Web, Usenet, and Excite Web site reviews. Excite does conceptual searching of the Web and is good when you're not sure of the exact term you need to search for. Because Excite uses a single-site search engine on many Web sites, it's free.

- *Lycos* (**http://www.lycos.com/**) for Web, FTP sites, and gopher sites. Lycos has Yahoo!-like features. It's good for simple searches on common topics. You can search for sounds, graphics, or subject.

- *Search.Com* (**http://www.search.com/**) for Web and Usenet. This search engine also lets you search other search engines such as AltaVista, HotBot, or Infoseek. Search.Com provides an A-to-Z listing of other search engines and has a handy utility to suggest what search engines will find what you need.

- *Inference Find!* (**http://www.inference.com/**) for Web only. Not a search engine itself, Inference Find! groups the results of other search engines and eliminates repeats. As of this writing, it calls WebCrawler, Yahoo!, Lycos, AltaVista, InfoSeek, and Excite.

- *HotBot* (**http://www.hotbot.com**) for Web and Usenet. HotBot is good for finding sites that use a particular technology, such as JavaScript or VRML. You can also narrow your search to a specific geographic location (such as Europe), class of domains (such as edu), or a single Web site (such as **www.apple.com**).

Good keywords make your search more effective. Come up with words that are unique to what you really want to find. Try to avoid heavily used terms, such as *www*, *Internet*, *computer*, and

Part

VI

Ch

31

so on. If you do need them, combine them with other more specific terms and Boolean operators to help narrow your search as in this example:

WWW and "Search Engines"

N O T E Most search engines also allow you to use quotation marks ("") to search for phrases. Check your search engine's help for specific details. ▦

You'll probably find that even a search engine lists too many sites to look through. You can reduce the number of sites you find by narrowing your search. Correctly using some simple terms—AND, OR, and NOT—can help narrow thousands of sites down to just a few.

These aren't your everyday AND, OR, and NOT. They come from the symbolic logic system developed by a 19th-century mathematician named George Boole. Boolean searches use a basic syntax made up of operators and search terms. Because the terms don't work quite the same as in English grammar, make sure that you get them straight. Table 31.2 shows examples of how to use AND, OR, and NOT.

Table 31.2 Useful Boolean Expressions	
Expression	**Description**
AND or +	Returns pages that contain all your search terms. If all words aren't on the page, the page isn't displayed. Use AND or + when you have dissimilar terms and want to narrow the results to a few precise hits. For example, BMW AND roadster or BMW + roadster will display only pages that contain both BMW and roadster on the page.
OR	Returns pages that contain any of your search terms. Use OR to return pages with any of the terms listed in your search. For example, BMW OR roadster will display all pages that contain either BMW, roadster, or both.
NOT	Returns pages that don't contain words specified in your search (not supported by all search engines).

Don't be afraid to experiment. Try several different searches with the same goal in mind so that you can get a better feel for the results that some of these expressions and your search words or phrases return. You'll find that some experimentation with search terms will help you become more adept at narrowing your selections to a manageable size.

Now that I've gone over URLs and searching on the Web, let's look at some of the other access methods listed earlier in Table 31.1 in more detail. Each section provides a description of the service, how to access it with and without a browser, and a sampling of what information the service returns.

Using FTP with a Web Browser

FTP, or File Transfer Protocol, is the method that the Internet uses to exchange files between computers. No matter what you're searching for—software, documentation, FAQ lists, programs, or just about anything else—you probably can get a copy through anonymous FTP.

Anonymous FTP is a service that lets you retrieve data from around the Internet without having an account on that machine. By using anonymous FTP, you can access any files that the systems administrators on the remote system have made publicly available.

▶ **See** "Using FTP for Remote File Transfer," **p. 580**

FTP supports ASCII-mode transfers for text files, and binary-mode transfers for other types of files. Fortunately, most Web clients automatically determine the file type for you, so you don't have to worry about it. You usually can determine the type of archive or compression program that was used on the file by looking at the file extension. Table 31.3 lists the most common file extensions you'll encounter.

Part
VI

Ch
31

Table 31.3	Common File Extensions on Binary Files Available Through FTP
Extension	**Description**
.Z	Compressed with the UNIX `compress` program
.z	Probably compressed with the GNU `gzip` program or the UNIX `compress` program
.gz	Compressed with the GNU `gzip` program
.tar	An archive of several files created by the UNIX `tar` program
.zip	An archive of several files created by `pkzip`

Sometimes you'll find files that have been created by more than one of these methods. For example, the file programs.tar.Z is an archive of several files created by the `tar` utility and then compressed with the `compress` utility.

To use a Web client such as Netscape (which has built-in FTP support) to perform anonymous FTP transfers, replace the protocol portion of the URL with "ftp." For example, to start an anonymous FTP session to **sunsite.unc.edu**, use the following URL:

> **ftp://sunsite.unc.edu**

This URL causes your Web client to try to make an FTP connection to **sunsite.unc.edu** and log you in as an anonymous FTP session. After your FTP session is established, you can navigate through directories and transfer files by clicking the hyperlinks displayed.

N O T E Most anonymous FTP servers request that you use your e-mail address as your password. If you have problems, check that your e-mail preferences are set correctly in your browser. ■

To specify a non-anonymous FTP session in Netscape, enter

`ftp://username@ftp.startup.com`

where *username* is your user name and *ftp.startup.com* is where you want to go. You'll then be prompted to enter your password.

> **N O T E** When you select a text file to transfer from a remote server in an FTP session, most Web clients display the file on-screen. You need to save the file to disk via a menu selection. Some Web browsers allow you to specify loading a file to disk rather than to the screen. ■

ON THE WEB

For a listing of FTP sites via the Web, see the following page:
http://www.yahoo.com/Computers_and_Internet/Internet/FTP_Sites/

Using *archie* with a Web Browser

Just like with the Web, one major problem with anonymous FTP is figuring out where the files that you're interested in are located on the Internet. To help users locate files, the archie system was created. archie is basically a search engine for anonymous FTP sites.

archie is a database query program that contacts anonymous FTP sites around the world and asks each site for a complete list of all its files. archie then indexes this information in its own internal database. You can search this database for the location of files on the Internet. Because updating archie databases is obviously a time-consuming process, the databases are updated usually only about once a month. Thus, it's possible—although unlikely—that the location archie gives you is incorrect.

archie is a popular service. The various archie servers around the world can get very heavily loaded, and requests can take a while to complete. Some sites place limits on the number of simultaneous connections, to keep the servers from becoming too slow to use. If you try an archie server and find that it's fully loaded, you can either try a different server or wait a few minutes and try again.

ON THE WEB

Many archie servers now support inquiries via Web forms. To conduct archie searches, go to the following URL for a list of archie gateways to the Web. From this page, you can link to many of the mirror sites of the archie database. It's usually quickest to link to the site closest to you.

http://www.nexor.co.uk/public/archie/servers.html

Table 31.4 lists some of the archie servers available worldwide.

Table 31.4 Active *archie* Servers

Server	IP Address	Location
archie.unl.edu	129.93.1.14	USA (NE)
archie.internic.net	198.49.45.10	USA (NJ)
archie.rutgers.edu	128.6.18.15	USA (NJ)
archie.ans.net	147.225.1.10	USA (NY)
archie.sura.net	128.167.254.179	USA (MD)
archie.au	139.130.4.6	Australia
archie.uni-linz.ac.at	140.78.3.8	Austria
archie.univie.ac.at	131.130.1.23	Austria
archie.cs.mcgill.ca	132.206.51.250	Canada
archie.uqam.ca	132.208.250.10	Canada
archie.funet.fi	128.214.6.102	Finland
archie.univ-rennes1.fr	129.20.128.38	France
archie.th-darmstadt.de	130.83.128.118	Germany
archie.ac.il	132.65.16.18	Israel
archie.unipi.it	131.114.21.10	Italy
archie.wide.ad.jp	133.4.3.6	Japan
archie.hana.nm.kr	128.134.1.1	Korea
archie.sogang.ac.kr	163.239.1.11	Korea
archie.uninett.no	128.39.2.20	Norway
archie.rediris.es	130.206.1.2	Spain
archie.luth.se	130.240.12.30	Sweden
archie.switch.ch	130.59.1.40	Switzerland
archie.twnic.net	192.83.166.10	Taiwan
archie.ncu.edu.tw	192.83.166.12	Taiwan
archie.doc.ic.ac.uk	146.169.11.3	United Kingdom
archie.hensa.ac.uk	129.12.21.25	United Kingdom

Part

VI

Ch

31

To connect to one of these servers, telnet to it and log in as archie. Each server is slightly different, but most are basically the same. After you log in to a server, you get a prompt such as

```
archie>
```

where you can enter your search commands. Different servers have different default search values. To determine what the default setup is for the server that you connect to, use the `show search` command. The `show search` command returns one of the following values:

`regex`	`archie` interprets your search string as a UNIX regular expression.
`exact`	Your search string must exactly match a file name.
`sub`	Your search string matches if a file name contains it as a substring. This is a case-insensitive search.
`subcase`	Similar to the `sub` search type, except that the case of the letters in the string must match.

You can set the desired search type by using the `set search` command as shown here:

```
archie> set search search-type
```

When you have your search set up the way you want it, you use the `prog` command to search by filename. For example, the following pair of commands

```
archie> set search sub
```

```
archie> prog linux
```

performs a case-insensitive search of the archie database for all files that contain the substring `linux`. For each match that `archie` finds, it reports the host computer that has the file, along with the full path name of the file on that host.

If you get confused or just need some assistance when you're using `archie`, just type **help** at the `archie>` prompt. This will give you information on how to get help in `archie`. From the `help>` prompt, type a **?** to see a list of subtopics that you can get help on.

After you find the information you're looking for, you need to exit `archie` by typing **exit** or **quit** at the `archie>` prompt.

Using *telnet* with a Web Browser

`telnet` has been around almost as long as the Internet. By using `telnet`, you can connect to databases, library catalogs, and other information resources around the world. Want to see what the weather's like in Vermont? Check on crop conditions in Azerbaijan? Get more information about somebody whose name you've seen online? `telnet` lets you do this and more. When you telnet to another computer, you're going across the Internet and logging in to that machine. You won't find graphics as you do on the Web; `telnet` is text only.

> **N O T E** gopher is another early Internet tool, and many telnet sites are most easily found through gopher menus. See the following section on gopher. ▪

To start `telnet` from your browser, enter the URL of the telnet site you want to go to. For example,

`telnet://pac.carl.org`

will start a `telnet` program and will take you to the location you entered. From there, you're out of the browser and have entered "menu land."

▶ **See** "Using `telnet` to Access Remote Computers," **p. 578**

Configuring Netscape to Work with *telnet*

`telnet` probably isn't built into your browser. You'll need to get a `telnet` program, install it on your computer, and then configure the browser to use it. Here's an example set of instructions for configuring `telnet` for Netscape:

1. From the Netscape Navigator Options menu, choose Preferences.
2. Select Applications and Directories from the available tabs.
3. Select Browse next to the Telnet Application window.
4. Find and select the telnet executable.
5. Press <Return>. Netscape is now configured.

Windows 95 and Windows NT include telnet applications in the Windows system folder. For Macs and older versions of Windows, NCSA Telnet is a popular choice.

Most telnet sites are fairly easy to use and have online help systems. Most also work best— and, in some cases, only—with VT100 emulation. You may also find that many of the resources are now also available on the Web.

Using *gopher* with a Web Browser

`gopher` is an Internet service that allows you to access information by making selections from a series of menus. `gopher` was one of the first Internet services that made a serious attempt at offering a user-friendly interface.

When you connect to a site that offers `gopher` services, you get a menu of available choices. Each menu is either a file or another menu. You can select your choice from the menu without having to know the name or IP address of the destination site or the directory and filenames of the particular information you're asking for. `gopher` handles the details for you.

N O T E No information resources on the Internet are actually "gopher-specific." Anything you can get through gopher can be accessed by other means, such as an HTML Web page, FTP, or telnet. In some cases, sites may have chosen to make resources available only via gopher for security reasons. ▪

Part

VI

Ch

31

To access a gopher server with a Web browser, change the protocol part of the URL so that it says **gopher** instead of **http**. For example, the URL for the gopher server at **sunsite.unc.edu** is

gopher://sunsite.unc.edu

gopher provides an easy means to navigate the Internet. Unfortunately, the information that gopher can retrieve may not be well organized, so finding what you want can be a bit of an adventure. Because the items in Gopherspace are presented as a set of menus, you sometimes have to wade through many different menus to get to the file you're searching for. This problem aside, however, a lot of good information is available through gopher.

One disadvantage of gopher is the lack of a standard subject list for the various gopher servers. The administrators for each gopher server have organized their information in their own manner. This means that each gopher server you access has different subjects. If gopher servers do happen to have some of the same subjects, chances are they aren't named the same way.

TIP   Because Gopherspace has been around longer than the World Wide Web and is less organized, it's too large to search randomly. veronica is like archie, except that it searches gopher servers. See **gopher://gopher.scs.unr.edu/00/veronica/veronica-faq** for more information on veronica.

ON THE WEB
For a listing of gopher sites, see

http://www.yahoo.com/Computers_and_Internet/Internet/Gopher/

Accessing Usenet News with a Web Browser

In the simplest definition, Usenet news (also called *netnews* or simply *news*) is a forum for online discussion. Many computers around the world exchange chunks of information, called *articles*, on almost every subject imaginable. These computers aren't physically connected to the same network; they're logically connected in their capability to exchange data. See Chapter 34, "Surviving Usenet News," for a complete discussion of Usenet news.

News articles on Usenet are divided into newsgroups by subject. These groups are then divided into hierarchies based on very general subject distinctions.

▶ **See** "How Usenet Is Structured," **p. 659**

Usenet news has conversation and discussion on almost any topic that you can think of. It's a great way to find and exchange information.

Getting on Mailing Lists

Another avenue for discussion on the Internet comes from e-mail mailing lists. Mailing lists vary from Usenet news in that the various messages and discussion articles are sent via e-mail rather than via the Usenet news medium.

Why use a mailing list instead of a Usenet newsgroup? Usually, mailing lists are targeted at a smaller group of people. It's fairly difficult to set up a new newsgroup on Usenet as there are proposal, discussion, and voting periods required. Any systems administrator can set up a mailing list. Also, because each mailing list is maintained on one computer, the systems administrator has more control over who can be on the list and can deal with problem users more effectively. Some mailing lists, such as those that discuss computer security issues, are restricted to certain people. If you need to be on one of these lists, you have to apply with the list manager to be allowed to subscribe.

Finding Mailing Lists

As with Usenet news, there are mailing lists on a wide variety of subjects. A complete list of publicly available mailing lists is posted regularly to the Usenet newsgroup **news.answers**.

ON THE WEB

You can search for mailing lists via the Web at

    http://www.liszt.com/

Part

VI

Ch

31

Using Mailing Lists

Mailing lists are typically set up by using a mail reflector. A *mail reflector* is a special e-mail address that's set up to reflect any mail sent to it back out to a group of people. Usually, two e-mail addresses are associated with a mailing list: that of the list maintainer and that of the list itself.

Suppose that there's an e-mail address for the users of widgets. The e-mail address for the list might be something like widgets@somewhere.com. If you send an e-mail message to this list address, it's reflected to all the people who subscribe to the list.

By convention, Internet mailing lists use a special e-mail address for administrative requests, such as subscribing to the list. This address is constructed by adding -request to the name of the list. So for the imaginary widgets mailing list, the administrative e-mail address would be widgets-request@somewhere.com. All mail that addresses administrative topics should be sent to the administrative address.

Each mailing list (and Usenet newsgroup) has its own rules and culture. You should become familiar with the local customs before sending mail out onto the list. Usually, you get an introduction message and possibly a list of frequently asked questions (FAQ) when you subscribe to a list. The introduction message contains any special rules that apply to the list. Make sure that you read the FAQ first so that you don't ask the same questions as hundreds of other people.

▶ **See** "Netiquette on Usenet," **p. 666**

Using Wide Area Information Servers (WAIS)

WAIS (Wide Area Information Servers) is a system for searching a large set of databases for information. The term *wide area* implies being able to use a large network, such as the Internet, to conduct searches by using client/server software.

By using WAIS, you can retrieve text or multimedia documents that are stored on databases throughout the Internet. You can think of WAIS as being similar to gopher, except that WAIS does the searching for you.

Like gopher, to use WAIS, you need client software or have to use telnet to connect to a site that provides public access to a WAIS client. There's an interactive UNIX WAIS client known as *swais*. To use this system, you can telnet to **sunsite.unc.edu** and log in as swais. You then get a menu of databases that you can search.

From Here...

The World Wide Web is a wonderful way to explore the Internet and tap its vast resources. Various Web browsers are available as free software or as commercial products. Using a Web browser makes it easy to surf the Net and find the information you need. You can learn more about the Web and the Internet in the following chapter:

■ Chapter 32, "Creating Web Documents with HTML," gives an introduction to the Hypertext Markup Language that's used to create pages for the Web.

Creating Web Documents with HTML

by Steve Burnett

In Chapter 31, "Surfing the Internet with the World Wide Web," you learned how to access the World Wide Web and were introduced to the various types of information available. You can click hypertext links and jump from place to place as fast as your connection allows. You can see Web pages with snazzy graphics and sound, lists, forms, and all sorts of neat stuff. But how do you actually create a Web page that other Web users can get to? It's not really as difficult as you might think. All you need is access to a Web server that uses Hypertext Transport Protocol (HTTP) and a set of documents written in Hypertext Markup Language (HTML).

This chapter looks at HTML to see what's involved in writing Web pages using HTML.

Understanding HTML

The Hypertext Markup Language (HTML) is the language used to develop Web pages and documents. HTML isn't a programming language like C++, Java, Pascal, or Perl; instead, it's basically a cross-platform markup language that's designed to be flexible enough to display text and other elements (such as graphics) on a variety of viewers.

An HTML document consists of special tags that are embedded in an ASCII document. These tags are interpreted by Web browser programs, which format and display documents.

N O T E HTML is a subset of Standard Generalized Markup Language (SGML), which is an international standard (ISO 88791) for electronic document exchange. SGML is a meta-language for defining and standardizing the structure of documents. SGML also describes a grammar you can use to design other markup languages. Any valid HTML document is also valid SGML. Like any SGML derived language, HTML's grammar is described by a Document Type Definition (DTD) file. ■

HTML tells Web browsers how to display Web documents; however, the format information HTML provides is pretty general. Many different Web browsers are available for the Internet, such as Netscape Navigator, Microsoft Internet Explorer, or NCSA Mosaic. Many run under graphical interfaces such as the X Windows system or MS Windows. Some, such as Lynx, are ANSI browsers and are limited in terms of which graphical characteristics they can display.

As you write HTML documents, remember that they will look different depending on which browser the reader is using. All available Web browsers try to format HTML documents as properly as possible; however, what you see may not be what someone else using a different browser or even the same browser running under a different operating system sees.

Working with HTML

As tools for the Web continue to evolve, creating HTML documents keeps getting easier. Many of the new tools hide much of the actual HTML coding from you. All you have to do is write the words, format your document, and save it to an appropriate location. Some browsers, such as Netscape Navigator Gold, include an editor that lets you point and click to create HTML pages. Other point-and-click tools include Microsoft FrontPage, Adobe PageMill, Allaire HomeSite and Macromedia DreamWeaver.

If you don't want to use an HTML editor or already have documents you want to put on the Web, there are several software applications you can use to convert word processing, desktop publishing, spreadsheet, or other documents into HTML. Newer versions of software packages, such as Adobe Framemaker, will include HTML as an option when you save a file.

ON THE WEB

The following Web site has lots of conversion software available:

> http://www.yahoo.com/Computers_and_Internet/Software/Internet/World_Wide_Web
> /HTML_Converters/

At some point, you'll want to try your hand at creating your own HTML. Although many tools are available to help make writing HTML less tedious, you'll probably find that they won't let you do everything you want.

You'll also find that HTML is relatively easy to work with. Because HTML is an ASCII-based markup language, all you need is an editor that will let you save files in ASCII format and a Web browser that you can use to view your Web pages as you develop them. You don't need a network connection to develop Web documents. Any Web browser should let you open a local HTML file and view it as though you had retrieved it from the Internet.

N O T E You may find that using an HTML editor is useful. Some editors allow you to select the text you want to format and then apply HTML tags from a menu rather than type the tags in yourself. Other editors look more like word processors—you select the text and select the type of formatting you want from a toolbar. In either case, you'll probably need to edit the HTML directly to get the exact look and feel you want. ▉

ON THE WEB

You can check out some editors from Sausage Software HotDog/HotDog Pro and Macromedia's at the following URLs (respectively):

> http://www.sausage.com

> http://www.macromedia.com

You can find a listing of HTML editors at this address:

> http://www.yahoo.com/Computers_and_Internet/Software/Internet/World_Wide_Web/HTML_Editors/

Before you go any further into the syntax of HTML, look at a Web page and its HTML source code. Figure 32.1 shows a simple Web page.

Listing 32.1 shows the HTML source for this Web page. Here you'll see the basic elements of an HTML page.

FIG. 32.1

A simple HTML page.

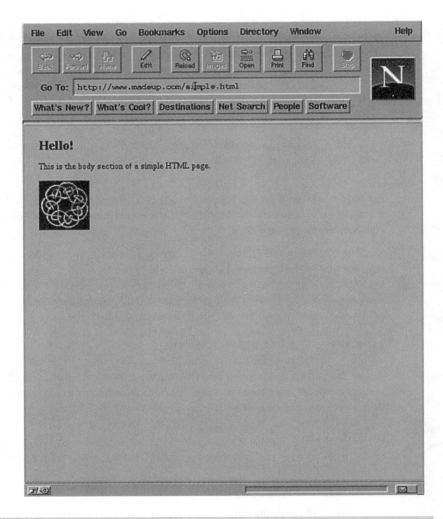

Listing 32.1 Source Code for a Simple HTML Page

```
<HTML>

<HEAD>
   <TITLE>Hello Web!</TITLE>
</HEAD>

<BODY>
<H1>Hello!</H1>
This is the body section of a simple HTML page.
<P>
<IMG src="example.gif">

</BODY>

</HTML>
```

You'll find that HTML is pretty straightforward:

- All HTML tags are enclosed by angle brackets (the < and > characters). The <HTML> tag at the beginning of Listing 32.1 is an example.

- Most HTML tags require you to use a starting tag (<*tag_name*>) and an ending tag (</*tag_name*>). You start and stop formatting by the placement of these tags. If you leave out a required ending tag, you won't see any formatting; you may not even see the text.

- Many HTML tags have attributes that you can customize. An *attribute* allows you to change the default behavior of a tag. If you want a table without a border, for example, you change it by setting an attribute (BORDER=*some_number*) within the <TABLE> tag.

- All HTML files require an <HTML> tag at the beginning of the file and the closing </HTML> tag at the end. These tags tell a Web browser that the document it's processing is written in HTML.

An HTML document typically consists of two logical sections: the head and the body. The *head* contains information about the document; the *body* contains the document information itself. As you may have guessed, the header section is enclosed with the <HEAD> and </HEAD> tags, whereas the body is enclosed with the <BODY> and </BODY> tags.

The head section of an HTML page contains information related to the document itself. You can place several tags in the header section, but the <TITLE> tag is the most widely used. The document title—whatever is enclosed with the <TITLE> and </TITLE> tags—appears in the title bar of a Web browser.

The body section of an HTML page contains most of the elements you see when viewing the page with a Web browser. This is where you enter all the elements you want people to see, such as text, graphics, links (URLs), lists, and tables.

N O T E The <TITLE> element identifies the name of your page. When someone makes a bookmark to the page, this is name that is used. Although HTML doesn't limit the length of the <TITLE> element, you should consider giving the page a short, descriptive title that can easily be displayed. A good rule of thumb for the length of a title is no more than a single phrase and no longer than 60 characters.

Because the document title is displayed in a separate window and isn't part of the document itself, the title text itself must be plain text and not have any hyperlinks or text formatting. ■

T I P One really nice thing about HTML source code is that you can look at it. Have you ever found an interesting page and wanted to know how it was done? Take a look! You can learn a lot by looking at other people's source code.

Viewing the source code is usually done through a menu choice in your Web browser. For example, to see HTML source code for a page under Netscape, choose Document Source from the View menu.

Now that you've seen the basics of HTML (yes, that's really it!), it's time to learn about tags and how they're used. Although there are many different tags, you'll find that by mastering just a handful (and combining them in different ways), you can create excellent Web pages.

Using Basic HTML Elements

Basic HTML syntax consists of three components: tags, attributes, and URLs. These components, respectively, give the details of how items are to be formatted and displayed, the specifics of certain actions, and the locations of other files and documents.

Tags

The basic building blocks of HTML, *tags* are the part of HTML that tells a Web browser how to display text and graphics, along with other format information. As you may recall, tags are written between angle brackets (`<tag_name>`) and most tags also require an ending tag (`</tag_name>`) as well. As you may recall from Figure 32.1, you saw the `<TITLE>` tag used:

```
<TITLE>Hello Web!</TITLE>
```

This line tells your browser to format the text string `Hello Web!` as a `<TITLE>`. See the starting (`<TITLE>`) and ending (`</TITLE>`) tags? All of the elements within these tags—text, in this case—are displayed in the title bar of your Web browser window. Similarly, other tags only affect the elements they enclose.

Attributes

Sometimes, tags need to specify exact information, such as where a file is located. *Attributes* are used with tags to provide more detail about how the tag is to be implemented. For example, consider the following tag:

```
<IMG SRC="example.gif">
```

This tag is an `<IMG>` (image) tag that tells your Web browser to display a graphic image. But which image? That's where the attribute comes in. In this example, the attribute field is `SRC="example.gif"`, which gives detailed information about how the `<IMG>` tag is to be interpreted. In this case, the example.gif file is to be displayed as the image.

TIP Using the height and width attributes with the `<IMG>` tag helps your browser display the graphic more quickly. In Netscape, if the image is GIF or JPG format, you can open the image by itself. Then, from the View menu, choose View Document Info to see the size of the image.

URLs

Web resources are accessed by descriptive addresses known as *uniform resource locators* (URLs). Everything that you access on the Web has an URL. HTML uses URLs to specify the location of needed files or of other Web pages that are connected by hypertext links.

Understanding HTML Syntax

As you've seen, HTML breaks down into three basic components: tags, attributes, and URLs. Of these, the basic building block is the tag. Tags are used to give commands to a Web browser, whereas attributes and URLs are used to provide details about the commands.

Tags can be grouped into several categories, depending on their function. Some tags give information about the document as a whole, some are used for formatting text, and some are used for graphics and hypertext links to other documents.

ON THE WEB

For a listing of HTML tags and their attributes, look at the online version of Que's *HTML Quick Reference* and Que's *Special Edition Using HTML* at the following addresses (respectively):

> http://www.mcp.com/que/developer_expert/htmlqr/toc.htm
>
> http://www.mcp.com/que/et/se_html2/toc.htm

Using Document Tags

The <HTML> and </HTML> tags are used to tell a Web browser that the document it's processing is written in HTML. The <HTML> tag should be the first tag in your document, and the </HTML> tag should be the last.

An HTML document is divided into a header and a body section. The header contains information about the document, and the body contains the document information itself. As you may have guessed, the header section is surrounded by the <HEAD> and </HEAD> tags, whereas the body is surrounded by the <BODY> and </BODY> tags. Several tags can be placed in the header section, but now only the <TITLE> tag is widely used. The document title—whatever is enclosed with the <TITLE> and </TITLE> tags—appears in the title bar of a Web browser.

Formatting Text

HTML provides several different ways to format text for display. Remember that the actual formatting of the text in your Web page is controlled by the Web browser used to view the page.

Headings HTML supports six levels of headings that you can display in a document by using the <H1> through <H6> tags. Figure 32.2 shows how these headings may appear in a Web browser (Netscape in this case). Remember that these headings are displayed differently on different browsers—the font and size may not appear the same with your Web browser. Listing 32.2 shows the source.

Part

VI

Ch

32

Listing 32.2   Example Heading Style Source

```
<HTML>

<HEAD>
   <TITLE>Heading example</TITLE>
</HEAD>

<BODY>
    <H1>Heading 1</H1>
    <H2>Heading 2
    </H2>
```

continues

Listing 32.2 Continued

```
    <H3>Heading 3

    </H3>
    <H4>Heading 4</H4>
    <H5>Heading 5</H5>
    <H6>Heading 6</H6>
This is plain text.
</BODY>

</HTML>
```

FIG. 32.2
Heading levels as
displayed in Netscape.

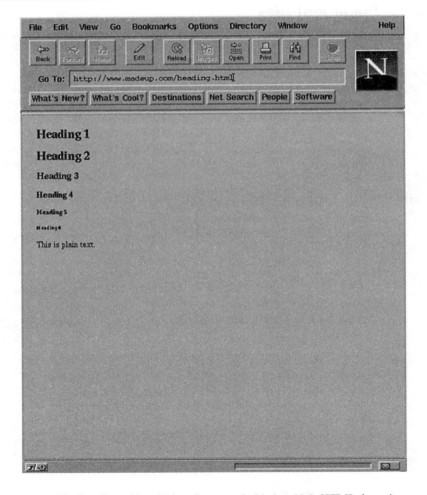

Look at the location of the level 2 and level 3 heading tags in Listing 32.2. HTML doesn't care whether the tags are at the end of the line, or where they occur. These tags just tell the browser that all the text between them is in the particular heading level that they define. Also, notice that the line This is plain text has no tags around it. This line will be displayed as generic text by a browser.

T I P It's usually a good idea to use only three levels of headings in a Web document. If you need more than three levels of headings, consider using additional pages.

Regular Text HTML gives you several ways to format normal text in your documents. For one thing, Web browsers completely ignore where the text lines end in your HTML file. Carriage returns also are ignored, so you have to use special tags to indicate where line breaks and paragraphs are to begin. The <BR> tag causes the browser that's displaying your document to insert a line break. Think of this as inserting a carriage return at that point in the line. Subsequent text is moved down to the next line.

If you want to create a new paragraph, use the <P> tag instead. <P> has the same effect as <BR>, except that most browsers insert a blank line as part of a paragraph break to visually separate one block of text from another. Because browsers control the text display, the actual behavior of the <P> tag can vary. With the <P> tag, you usually don't need a </P> ending tag. However, it is required if you use any of the <P> attributes.

Sometimes you'll want to visually separate different sections of the same page. To do so, HTML provides a way to draw a horizontal line across the document display. The <HR> tag, which stands for *horizontal rule*, is used to draw a horizontal line. It inserts a paragraph break before the line so you don't need the <P> tag. As with the <P> tag, no ending tag is needed for <HR>.

You've seen several ways to control the format of text on an HTML page. Now look at another short HTML sample to see the effect of line breaks, paragraph marks, and horizontal rules on the text display. Listing 32.3 shows an HTML sample that uses these formatting tags.

Part
VI

Ch
32

Listing 32.3   An HTML Sample Showing Basic Text Formatting

```
<HTML>
<HEAD>
<TITLE>A Sample Text Formatting Page</TITLE>
</HEAD>
<BODY>
<H2>Text Sample 1</H2>
Here is some sample text that is written on separate lines without using line
breaks. <P>
<H2>Text Sample 2</H2>
This sample text has a<BR>
line break in the middle.<P>
<H2>Text Sample 3</H2>
Text before a paragraph mark.<P>
Text after a paragraph mark.<HR>
Text after a horizontal rule mark.
</BODY>
</HTML>
```

Figure 32.3 shows this sample displayed in Mosaic.

FIG. 32.3

Text formatting as displayed in Mosaic.

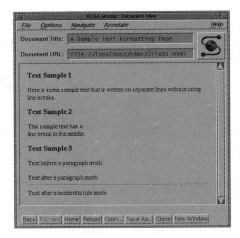

Suppose that you want to display some text, such as a table, and that you want the carriage returns and spacing to be kept exactly as you entered them. You can use the <PRE> and </PRE> tags to define preformatted text. Any text that you surround with these tags is displayed in a monospace font, and all returns and spaces are used exactly as they were entered.

To some degree, you can define the way text is displayed. HTML provides tags that tell browsers to display text in boldface, underline, or italic. These tags are known as *physical styles*. The tags for boldfaced text are <B> and </B>, the tags for underline are <U> and </U>, and the tags for italic are <I> and </I>. Enclose the text that you want to format with the starting and ending tag of the style that you want.

HTML also provides some *logical styles* for formatting text. The <EM> and </EM> tags are used to mark emphasized text, which is usually shown in italic. The <STRONG> and </STRONG> tags are used to indicate stronger emphasis, which is usually shown in boldface.

Figure 32.4 shows how different text formats may appear.

Table 32.1 provides a quick listing of some of the most common HTML tags for text formatting.

Table 32.1   Selected HTML Text-Formatting Tags

Tag	Action
<B>...</B>	Makes text **bold**.
<BLOCKQUOTE>...</BLOCKQUOTE>	Formats text with left and right indents.
<FONT>...</FONT>	Controls various aspects of text with attributes— for example, text color (COLOR=*rgb_value*) and size (SIZE=*number*).

Tag	Action
`<I>...</I>`	Makes text *italic*.
`<PRE>...</PRE>`	Leaves text formatting exactly as it appears.
`<STRIKE>...</STRIKE>`	Formats text as ~~strikethrough~~.
`<U>...</U>`	<u>Underlines</u> text.
`<EM>...</EM>`	Logical style; emphasizes text (typically displayed as *italic*).
`<KBD>...</KBD>`	Logical style; shows text as a keyboard style (usually displayed in a `monospaced` font).
`<STRONG>...</STRONG>`	Logical style; emphasizes text (typically displayed as **bold**).

FIG. 32.4
Examples of text formatting as displayed in Netscape.

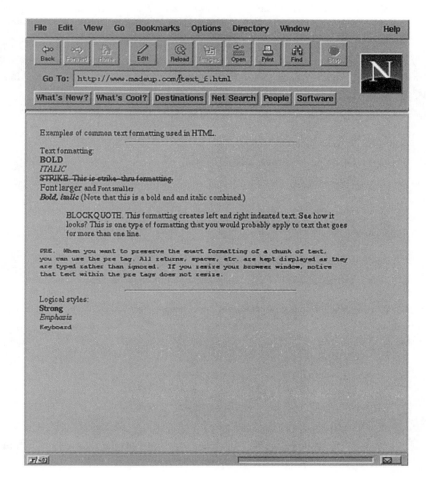

Part
VI

Ch
32

Miscellaneous Text   Two formatting tags that don't fit in with other tag categories are the <ADDRESS> and </ADDRESS> tags. These tags are used to mark addresses, signatures, and so on within a document. Typically, text with this format is placed at the end of a document, following a horizontal rule mark. The exact formatting of <ADDRESS> text is determined by the individual Web browser.

Organizing Information with Lists

Sometimes you need to deliver information that's logically grouped in some fashion. For example, you might have a list of graphic images to display, or you might want to show a numbered top 10 list. HTML provides several different ways to format and display lists of information. Using lists in HTML is a powerful way to deliver information, because the user's Web browser formats all the text in the list in a consistent manner. All you have to do is decide how the information fits together.

Displaying Unordered Lists   An *unordered list* is text displayed separately with a bullet or other formatting character. Each text entry in an unordered list can be several lines long.

Two sets of tags are used to create an unordered list. The <UL> and </UL> tags define the beginning and end of the list, and the <LI> tag is used to mark each list item. Listing 32.4 shows the HTML source for a simple unordered list. Figure 32.5 shows how Mosaic displays this list.

Listing 32.4   An Unordered List

```
<HTML>
<HEAD>
<TITLE>An Unordered List</TITLE>
</HEAD>
<BODY>

<LI>This is list item 1.
<LI>This is list item 2.
<LI>This is list item 3.
</UL>
</BODY>
</HTML>
```

FIG. 32.5
An unordered list
displayed in Mosaic.

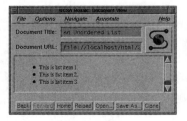

Presenting Ordered Lists   An *ordered list* presents list information in numerical order. Each time a new list item is identified, the number of the list item is incremented. Ordered lists are defined by the <OL> and </OL> tags, and the same <LI> tag used in unordered lists is also used in ordered lists to mark each list item.

Listing 32.5 shows the HTML source for a simple ordered list. Figure 32.6 shows how this list is displayed in Mosaic.

Listing 32.5   An Ordered List

```
<HTML>
<HEAD>
<TITLE>An Ordered List</TITLE>
</HEAD>
<BODY>
<OL>
<LI>This is list item 1.
<LI>This is list item 2.
<LI>This is list item 3.
</OL>
</BODY>
</HTML>
```

FIG. 32.6

An ordered list
displayed in Mosaic.

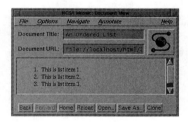

Using Definition Lists   Think of how a glossary in a book looks: You typically have each word or term offset by itself and then a paragraph giving its definition. HTML definition (or glossary) lists provide a way to do this with Web pages. A definition list consists of a term—this can be one word or a series of words—followed by a definition. The definition is usually explanatory text.

Although definition lists are particularly useful for glossaries, you can use them to present any kind of information where you need a title and an explanation. One common use is to make the glossary term a hypertext link to another document and make the definition a description of the linked document. (Creating hypertext links is discussed later in this chapter, so keep this application of a definition list in mind.)

Definition lists require the <DL> and </DL> tags to mark the start and end of the list. Rather than use a simple list item tag, definition lists use dual tags: <DT> to mark the glossary item and <DD> to mark the definition. Listing 32.6 shows the HTML source for a simple definition list. Figure 32.7 shows how this list is displayed in Mosaic.

Listing 32.6 A Simple Definition List

```
<HTML>
<HEAD>
<TITLE>A Simple Glossary List</TITLE>
</HEAD>
<BODY>
<DL>
<DT>Item 1
<DD>This is the definition field for list item 1.
<DT>Item 2
<DD>This is the definition field for list item 2.
<DT>Item 3
<DD>This is the definition field for list item 3.
</DL>
</BODY>
</HTML>
```

FIG. 32.7
A simple definition list
displayed in Mosaic.

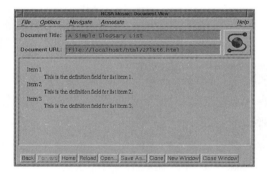

Combining Lists As you can see, the various lists in HTML give you several ways to present information to a user. In fact, HTML allows you to combine list types to gain even more control over how your information is presented. You can nest one list type within another easily.

Suppose that you want to create a section of your home page to tell users your favorite movies and music. You can nest two glossary lists within an unordered list to create a detailed outline. Listing 32.7 shows an example HTML source that uses nested lists.

Listing 32.7 Creating a Custom List by Nesting Different List Types

```
<HTML>
<HEAD>
<TITLE>A Custom List</TITLE>
</HEAD>
<BODY>
This list shows some of my favorite musicians and movies.
It uses two definition lists nested in an unordered list.
It also uses some text formatting tags.<P>
I hope that you enjoy it.<HR>
```

```
<LI>Here are some of my favorite movies<P>
 <DL>
 <DT>
 <DD>
 <DT>
 <DD>
 </DL>
<P>
<LI>Here are some of my favorite musical groups<P>
 <DL>
 <DT>Coil
 <DD>A European experimental and electronic project.
 <DT>Philip Glass
 <DD>An incredible modern composer.
 <DT>Ozone Quartet
 <DD>Instrumental progressive quartet.
 </DL>
 </UL>
 </BODY>
 </HTML>
```

This combination list example is a bit more complicated than the others you've seen, but it still uses only techniques covered so far in this chapter. Notice that the glossary lists are indented in the HTML source code. The indent is used only to make the source code easier to read (recall that Web browsers ignore line breaks and extra spaces when they display the page). Figure 32.8 shows a custom list displayed in Netscape.

As a quick review, Table 32.2 shows the HTML tags for creating lists we've gone over.

Table 32.2   HTML List Tags

Tag	Action
<UL>...</UL>	Create an unordered (bulleted) list; list items begin with the <LI> tag
<OL>...</OL>	Create an ordered (numbered) list; list items begin with the <LI> tag
<DL>...</DL>	Create a definition list; list items begin with a <DT> tag for a definition term or a <DD> tag for a definition

Linking Pages with Anchors

Now comes the neat stuff. In this section, you learn how to hook multiple Web pages together and create hypertext links that jump from place to place.

Hypertext links in HTML are known as *anchors*, and the <A> and </A> tags are used to define an anchor. These tags are placed around the words you want to use for the hypertext link. Web browsers typically underline hypertext links automatically and show them in a different color.

Part
VI

Ch
32

FIG. 32.8

A custom list displayed in Netscape.

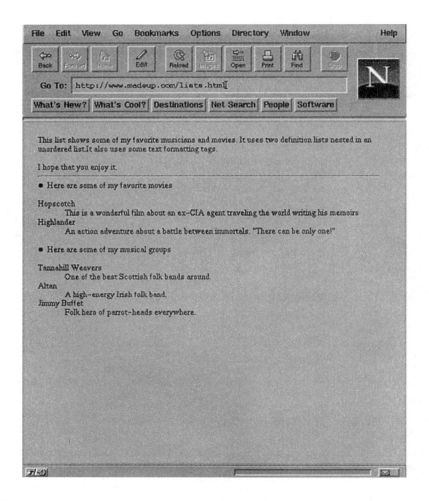

To tell the Web browser which document to retrieve when the hypertext link is clicked, you use the HREF attribute and an URL with the anchor tag. Suppose that you want to create a hypertext link to the NCSA Mosaic home page. If you want to include the sentence Click here to go to the NCSA Mosaic home page., where the word here is the hypertext link, you need the following HTML lines:

```
Click <A HREF="http://www.ncsa.uiuc.edu/SDG/Software/Mosaic/index.html">
here</A> to go to the NCSA Mosaic home page.
```

The anchor tags surround the hypertext link—in this case, the word here. The HREF attribute is inserted inside the opening anchor tag. That's all there is to it.

N O T E   You can place any URL in the HREF attribute. You can link to a Web page, an FTP site, a Gopher server, or any other location. ■

In addition to just creating hypertext links, you can also give names to links by using the NAME attribute. Named links are very useful for jumping to specific locations in a document. You can list a table of contents at the beginning of a long document and have each entry in the table of contents be a hypertext link to the appropriate place in the document. By combining them with an HREF, you can send users to a specific location in another document.

Assume that you have a long document—maybe a Frequently Asked Questions (FAQ) list that discusses widgets. You can create a hypertext link from the table of contents to the "How to Use Widgets" section. The first thing you need to do is to create a named anchor in the "How to Use Widgets" section, so that you can jump to it from the table of contents. The HTML to do this looks like the following:

```
<A NAME="howtouse">How to Use Widgets</A>
Widgets are a very powerful tool if used properly.
Unfortunately, no one knows enough about them to use
them properly. Since they have no relevance to HTML, you
don't need to discuss them further in this chapter.
```

Now, all you need to do is to put a hypertext link from the table of contents to this spot. To do that, you use the HREF attribute to link to this anchor, and give the anchor's name preceded by a # character. The table of contents entry looks like this:

```
<A HREF="#howtouse">How to Use Widgets</A>
```

When someone clicks the entry How to Use Widgets in the table of contents, the browser jumps to the anchor named howtouse later in the document.

N O T E You can name an anchor that's a hypertext link to another location. Just use the NAME and HREF attributes in the same anchor. For example,

```
<A HREF="http://www.doesnotexist.com/index.html#end">Go to the end</A>
```

would take you to another document. It also would display the file starting from wherever the <#end> anchor is located in that file. ▧

Using Graphics

One feature that has made the Web so popular is its capability to incorporate graphics and text in a simple format. HTML makes it easy to insert graphics into your documents. Before you start putting all sorts of graphic images into documents, though, remember that many people access the Web via low-speed telephone lines and that graphics can take a long time to transfer at these rates. Also, some people use text-based browsers, such as Lynx, which can't display graphics at all. You should make sure that someone can navigate your Web documents easily, even if they have graphics turned off or if their browser doesn't support graphics. In a moment, you'll learn a technique for checking for graphics support.

You can use graphics in your HTML documents in two ways: by using hypertext links or by using inline images.

■ You can make hypertext links to the graphics files themselves. This method requires the user to have a helper program that can display the graphics file properly. The exact type of graphic that can be displayed depends on the helper application used. Links for this method are hypertext links that name the graphics image as the destination document.

■ You can insert the graphics directly into your HTML document. Graphics inserted this way are known as *inline images*. Many browsers support graphics in the JPG, GIF, or X Bitmap formats as inline images.

HTML uses the `<IMG>` tag to indicate an inline image. This tag is combined with the `SRC="filename"` attribute to define which image file is displayed. HTML also provides the `ALIGN=` attribute to tell Web browsers how they should line up the graphic image with any text that's near it. The valid values for `ALIGN` are `TOP`, `MIDDLE`, and `BOTTOM`.

As mentioned earlier, you need to make your Web pages usable by browsers that don't support graphics. To do this, you should provide some text reference any time you use a graphic image. HTML provides a way for you to define some text to be displayed if a browser can't display a graphic image. The `ALT="text about the graphic"` attribute defines some alternate text that will be displayed when the graphic can't be displayed.

An example might help pull this all together. Listing 32.8 is a section of HTML that displays an inline GIF image. If a browser can't display the image, a description of the image is shown instead.

Listing 32.8   Inserting a Graphic into Your Script

```
<HTML>

<HEAD>
   <TITLE>Image example</TITLE>
</HEAD>
<BODY>

<H2>Images</H2>

<P>
<P>
<IMG src="venus.jpg"
     align="right"
     height="160" width="82"
     alt="Statue of Aphrodite">

<UL>
<LI>Statue of Aphrodite, known as the "Venus de Milo".
<LI>Carved out of marble in Greece, circa 100 B.C.
<LI>Currently in the Louvre in Paris
<LI>Part of the Louvre's Greek, Etruscan and Roman Antiquities Collection
</UL>
```

```
<HR>
To go to the Louvre's web site click <A HREF="http://mistral.culture.fr/louvre/
louvrea.htm">HERE</A>

</BODY>

</HTML>
```

Figure 32.9 shows how this page is displayed in Netscape. You can see how different elements (heading, a list, horizontal line, graphic, and a link) combine to make up a page.

FIG. 32.9

An inline graphic displayed in Netscape.

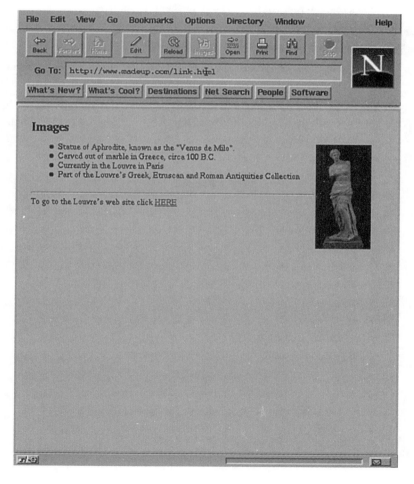

Part

VI

Ch

32

You can combine graphic images and anchors to create graphic hypertext links as well. Simply surround the <IMG> tag with anchor tags that define which document to load. A picture serves as a hypertext link to another HTML document in the following example:

```
Click the picture to find out more about this statue.
<A HREF="statue.html"><IMG SRC="statue.gif"
ALIGN=BOTTOM ALT="[Photo of statue]">
</A>
```

From Here...

This chapter introduces you to basic HTML and how to create a Web page. You learned how to use tags, which provide commands to a Web browser, and how to use attributes and URLs, which provide details for the commands. Many HTML guides are available on the Internet that cover everything from syntax to design. Use one of the many search engines to look up HTML topics that interest you.

ON THE WEB

A good starting point for ideas is Yahoo's listings for HTML:

> http://www.yahoo.com/Computers_and_Internet/Information_and_Documentation/Data_Formats
> /HTML/

You can find out more about the World Wide Web and the Internet in Chapter 31, "Surfing the Internet with the World Wide Web," which introduces you to the Web and how to search it.

Using Electronic Mail

by Steve Burnett

Electronic mail, or e-mail, seems to have taken the world by storm. Millions of computer users worldwide have access to electronic mail. A large number of commercial networks or Internet service providers (ISPs) can give you or your organization access to electronic mail around the world.

Understanding E-Mail

E-mail is any program that users on a single computer system or a network of systems use to send and receive electronic messages. At a minimum, you provide the program with the address of the recipient and the message you want to send. The address includes the login name of the person who is to receive the mail. If that user is on another system in a network, the address also includes a means of identifying the target computer system. You either prepare the message while you're using your e-mail program, or you prepare it beforehand by using a text editor such as `vi`.

▶ **See** "Using `vi`," **p. 181**

Using electronic mail has several advantages:

- You can send reports, data, and documents that can reach their destination in a matter of seconds or minutes.

- You don't have to worry about interrupting someone when you send a message, nor are you necessarily interrupted when you receive messages—that's handled by the computer system.

- You don't need to play phone tag or make an appointment to communicate with someone.

- You can send and receive at a convenient time.

When you send e-mail, it's up to the computer system to make the delivery, which can involve putting your message out on a network to be delivered at some other site. At this point, you say that the mail has been sent. Soon after that, the message arrives at the recipient's machine.

If the sender and the receiver are on the same computer system, the sending and receiving all takes place on one machine. The e-mail system on the target computer verifies that the addressee exists, and the message is added to a file that holds all the e-mail for that user (if no network is involved, the local computer system verifies the addressee). The mail-storage file is called the user's *system mailbox* and usually has the same name as the user who's receiving the mail. For example, if your login name is george, your system mailbox is the file named george in the directory /var/spool/mail. When the message has been "delivered" to the mailbox, you say that the mail has been received.

N O T E   There's a common kind of e-mail, called Post Office Protocol (POP) mail, where e-mail is stored on a remote system and is then retrieved as you read mail. This chapter assumes that you're running a full mail system on your Linux computer, complete with the `sendmail` program, which handles the background jobs of sending and receiving e-mail. ■

Figure 33.1 shows the relationship between sending and receiving e-mail.

FIG. 33.1

Sending and receiving e-mail.

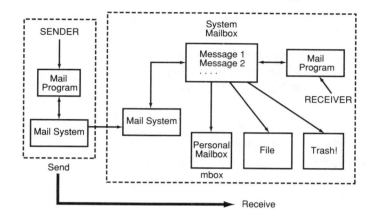

Does the Mail Always Get Through?

When you send e-mail, you may see a message on-screen that says `Mail Sent!` This means that the mail has been sent—not that it has been received or delivered. Usually, your e-mail system will notify you if your message can't be delivered.

E-mail messages may not go through for several reasons. If mail is going out to a network, the network address may be correct but the name of the user on that network may not be correct. Or perhaps the complete address is correct, but because of problems with permissions or quotas, the message couldn't be placed in the user's system mailbox. In both cases, the mail was sent but was undeliverable. Another scenario is that the e-mail was delivered but the user's mailbox was corrupted or destroyed. A final possibility is that the recipient ignores e-mail or doesn't log in for several days, weeks, or more.

Your computer system notifies you when you have mail. When you read your e-mail, you can treat it on a message-by-message basis. Some of the things you can do with your mail are the following:

- Delete individual messages after you read them—or without bothering to read them (using e-mail doesn't mean that you won't get junk mail).
- Keep some messages in the system mailbox.
- Keep some messages in a personal mailbox.
- Keep other messages in individual files or folders.
- Reply directly to the sender of a message.
- Do a "group reply" to a group of users who all received the same message.
- Forward mail to others.
- Print your mail.

It's up to you to manage your mail so that it doesn't take up any more disk space than necessary. You most certainly don't have to save every piece of e-mail you get. You'll also see that it's easier to read your incoming mail if you regularly delete or remove messages from your system mailbox.

Several different e-mail programs are available for Linux, including e-mail programs that are integrated with Web browsers such as Netscape. The most common e-mail interface, available on virtually every UNIX environment, is `mail`. With the `mail` program, you can do the following:

- Manage and view your e-mail.
- Include a subject header on e-mail you send.
- Include a cc header for sending copies of e-mail to others.
- Forward e-mail to others.
- Set up mailing lists.

This section shows examples of `mail`. Later in the chapter, you're introduced to another mail program for Linux—the `elm` mailer.

Sending E-Mail with *mail*

You can send e-mail to an individual, a group of individuals, or a mailing list. Just as when you want to send a paper letter, you must specify the address of the recipient with e-mail. Sometimes, you'll compose or write a message while you're sending e-mail; at other times, you'll send a prepared message; you may even send the output of a command or program with e-mail. When using `mail` or `elm`, the message you send has to be a text file—that is, an ASCII file.

N O T E   The Simple Mail Transport Protocol (SMTP) is used to transfer mail between computers. It now supports only ASCII files. To send a binary file via e-mail, you have to convert the file to ASCII by using the `uuencode` utility. ▦

Regardless of how the message is prepared, you send mail by using a command of the following form:

`mail address`

This command starts the `mail` system. You can then compose the mail message and send it to the specified address. In this syntax, `address` is the e-mail address of the person who is to receive the message. An address can have several different forms. To send e-mail to someone who has a login ID on the machine you're using, use the login ID of that person. For example, to send e-mail to someone on your system whose login name is george, enter the following command:

`mail george`

If george is on another system that you can access through some network or collection of networks, you must include the name by which that system is known on the network. Suppose that george is the name of a user on a computer system whose network name is apples.startup.com. You can send e-mail by entering this command:

```
mail george@apples.startup.com
```

The exact form of the address depends on the type of network being used and any local conventions or rules. Ask a local expert or your system administrator about the form of addresses on a network in your company.

To send the same message to several users, include each of their addresses on the line with the `mail` command, as in this example:

```
mail fred bill george@apples.startup.com
```

Writing a Message While Sending E-Mail

Many users compose or write messages while they're in the e-mail program, rather than compose a message beforehand. This is usually the quickest—but not the neatest—way to send mail. It's not neat because you have limited editing capabilities while composing your message. Generally, you can deal with only one line at a time. First, you type the command to send e-mail, specify the address(es), and then press <Return>. Then you type the message, indicating that you're done by typing a period on a line by itself. You can also use <Ctrl-d> to end the message. For an example of how to send e-mail to a user named lynn, enter this command to start the mail system and specify lynn's address on your system:

```
mail lynn
Subject: Congratulations! Lunch Thursday?
```

Now type the message, pressing <Return> when you want to end a line. Here's a sample message that you may want to send to lynn (press <Return> at the end of each line to space the paragraphs of the message):

```
Lynn,

Just wanted to tell you that I thought you did a great
job at the meeting yesterday! It seems as if we're
finally turning this problem around.

Want to get together for lunch Thursday?
Give me a call.
joe
.
```

You can also end the message with <Ctrl-d> instead of a period. The computer responds by displaying EOT, which means *end of transmission*.

Canceling a Message

You can cancel a message while you're writing it, but you can't cancel it after it's sent. To cancel a message while you're writing it, press whatever key is configured on your system as the

Part
VI

Ch
33

interrupt key (usually <Ctrl-c> or <Del>). When a message is canceled, it's saved in a file named dead.letter. You can delete this file or edit it later for another message. When using mail, you must press <Ctrl-c> twice to cancel (in case you press <Ctrl-c> or <Del> by mistake). After canceling your mail message, you see the command-line prompt. The following example shows how the cancel function works:

```
mail lynn
Subject: Congratulations! Lunch Thursday?
Lynn,

Just wanted to tell that I thought you did a great
job<Ctrl-c>
 (Interrupt -- one more to kill letter)
```

You now must decide whether you want to continue the letter or kill it. If you decide to continue, you just keep typing the text of the letter as follows:

```
at the meeting yesterday! It seems as if we're finally
turning this problem around.
```

At this point, you decide to cancel the letter again, so you press <Ctrl-c> or <Del>. The system responds with (Interrupt -- one more to kill letter). Because you want to kill the message, press <Ctrl-c> or <Del> a second time; mail quits, and you see the shell prompt.

Sending a Prepared Message

You may want to use a text editor such as vi to compose a message to be sent by e-mail. If you use a text editor, you have the tools to do things such as format the text and check your spelling. It doesn't matter what program you use to create the text, as long as you end up with a text or ASCII file.

Suppose that the file you want to send is named report.txt and the recipient's address is top@kite.fish.com. There are essentially three ways to send the file, as outlined in the following list. In the following examples, the mail command uses the option -s, and the string that serves as the subject heading is surrounded by quotation marks:

- *Use a pipe.* To send report.txt with the mail command, enter the following:

  ```
  cat report.txt ¦ mail -s" Sales Report" top@kite.fish.com
  ```

- *Redirect input.* To send report.txt with the mail command and the -s option, enter the following:

  ```
  mail -s" Sales Report" top@kite.fish.com < report.txt
  ```

- *Use ~r to include a file in a message.* To use mail to send the file (by using the default Subject prompt), enter these commands:

  ```
  mail top@kite.fish.com
  Subject: Sales Report
  ~r report.txt
  ~.
  EOT
  ```

You see the system prompt after you complete any of these three methods; the result is the same in any case.

> **N O T E** In the third example, you use ~r to *read*, or include, the file report.txt in the e-mail message. This is an example of a *tilde command*. To use such commands, you precede a command with the tilde character (~) while you're reading or sending mail. You may find several other tilde commands useful; they're discussed at appropriate points throughout the chapter. ■

Sending the Result of a Command or Program by E-Mail

If you run a command or program that produces results to the screen (known as stdout), you can pipe that output to a mail command. Suppose that you have some information in a file called contrib.lst, use the sort command to sort the file, and then send the results to yourself (login name bkorn) and top (whom you met earlier in this chapter). To do all that, enter this command:

```
sort contrib.lst ¦ mail -s "Sorted Contrib Info" bkorn top@kite.fish.com
```

Reading Your Mail

Most Linux systems notify you when you log in that you have e-mail. It's up to you to read and act on it. You can use mail or another e-mail program to read any mail you have. As you read your mail, the e-mail program marks each message as read. Depending on what commands you use and how you quit the e-mail program, the messages you've read are kept either in your system mailbox, /var/spool/mail/$LOGNAME, or in your login directory in the file named mbox.

Using *mail* to Read Mail

To read your mail with mail, enter **mail**. If your login name is bkorn, you'll see a display similar to this (what you type is in bold):

```
mail
mail    Type ? for help.
"/var/spool/mail/bkorn": 5 messages 2 new 1 unread
     1 sarah Wed Jan  8 09:17  15/363
     2 top@kite.fish.com Thu Jan  9 10:18  26/657    Meeting on Friday
U    3 fred_Fri Jan  10 08:09  32/900   New Orders
> N  4 jones Fri Jan  10 13:22  35/1347  Draft Report
N    5 smith@somewhere.com Sat Jan  11 13:21  76/3103  Excerpt from book
?
```

Here are some things to note about the display:

- ■ The first line identifies the program and says to type a question mark for help.

- ■ The second line indicates that mail is reading your system mailbox, /var/spool/mail/bkorn, and that you have five messages. Two have arrived since you last checked your mail, one appeared previously but you haven't yet read it, and two messages have already been read.

- The next five lines give information about your mail. Ignore the first few characters for now. Each line holds a message number, the address of the sender, the date the message was sent, the number of lines and characters in the message, and the subject (if one was given). Consider the following line:

```
2 top@kite.fish.com  Thu Jan  9 10:18  26/657  Meeting on Friday
```

This line indicates that message number 2 is from top@kite.fish.com—an address that indicates the message came to your machine from another network (mail from a local user is marked with just the user's login ID). The message was sent on Thursday, January 9, at 10:18; it consists of 26 lines and 657 characters. The subject is *Meeting on Friday*.

- A message line starting with N indicates new mail—mail received since you last checked your e-mail. A message line starting with U indicates unread mail. A message line without N or U indicates mail you've read and saved in your system mailbox.

- The greater-than character (>) on a message line marks the current message—the message you'll act on next.

- The question mark (?) on the last line is the command prompt from mail.

Reading the Current Message   The current message is the message marked by the greater-than character (>). To read that message, just press <Return>. When you open it, you see something like the following:

```
Message 4:
From jones Fri, Jan 10 13:22 EST 1997
Received: by your.system.com
Date: Fri, 10 Jan 1997 13:22:01 -0500
From: Carol Jones <jones>
Return-Path: <jones>
To: aborat, lynn, oackerm, bkorn
Subject: Draft Report
Here is a draft of the report I intend to submit next week.
Please take a look at it and let me know your comments.
Thanks.
---------------Report Starts Here---------------
Opportunities for Expansion
Prepared by Carol Jones
Over the past 6 months, we've seen an indication of an increase in the
demand for our services. Current market trends indicate that the demand
will continue for at least 18 months and possibly longer. The manager of
our service staff states "We're up to our necks in new customers and
:
```

The message is displayed one screen at a time. Any time you see a colon, you can press <Return> to see the next screen or <q> to quit viewing the message. Press <Return> to see the next screen of the message.

When you see the last screen, you see EOF: (for *end of file*). Press <q> or <Return> to get back to the ? prompt. Notice that the greater-than character still points to the message you've just read. The message that was the current message is still the current message.

Some lines were displayed before the message itself began. This is the header information—and it can be useful. Typically, header information includes the following:

- The message number
- Who sent the message
- When it was sent
- The name of the system that received the message
- The date the message was received
- The "real name" of the sender, as well as his or her login ID
- The return path
- The message recipient(s)
- The subject

All this information is passed on with each e-mail message. The sender is always identified, making forgeries difficult. The real name that appears in the From line is taken from a field from the sender's entry in the password file. The mail system uses the Return-Path or Reply-To information if you generate a reply (as discussed later in this chapter). The To line contains the address or list of addresses of the recipients of this message. (This sample message was a group message.) The sender filled in the Subject line.

Reading the Next Message   There are two ways to read the next message (the message following the current message in your mailbox). You can press <Return> or <n> to display the next message. It becomes the current message after you read it. You read the next message in the same way you read the current message. After you read the last message in the list, you see the message 'At EOF'.

Reading Any Message   All the messages in your mailbox are numbered. You can read messages in any order by entering the message number when you see the ? prompt. For example, to read message number 2, type **2** and press <Return>. Message number 2 then becomes the current message.

Reading E-Mail from Other Files

When you start mail, you read messages kept in your system mailbox, which has the path /var/spool/mail/$LOGNAME. Recall from Chapter 18, "Understanding Linux Shells," that LOGNAME is the shell variable that holds your login name. If you log in as bkorn, your mail is held in /var/spool/mail/bkorn. You can read mail from other files that hold complete e-mail messages—that is, messages with the headers and text of the messages. Naturally, you must have read permission for those files.

To read messages from a file, type the command to start the e-mail program followed by **-f *filename***, and press <Return>. For example, to read the e-mail in the file mbox, enter this command:

```
mail -f mbox
```

Part
VI

Ch
33

You can read the mail in that file in the same way you read e-mail from your system mailbox.

> **N O T E**   The mbox file is located in your home directory and automatically contains messages you've
> already read but haven't deleted. These messages are saved to mbox when you exit `mail`. ▪

Sending Mail While Reading

You can send e-mail while you're using the `mail` program to read your messages. To do so, enter **m** *address* at the ? prompt. Follow these steps:

1. Start the `mail` program (type **mail** and press <Return>).

2. Read some messages or do other things, but at the ? prompt, enter the following to send e-mail to a user whose login name is ernie:

   m ernie

3. At the prompt for a subject, type a subject heading:

   Subject: **Game Time**

4. Type the message and end it with a period on the last line, as in the following example:

   Don't forget we're playing V-ball at 6:30

   .

   The computer responds with the following lines:

   EOT
   ?

5. Continue using `mail`.

Printing Mail Messages

By using `mail`, you can print the current message to a printer connected to your system. First, make the message you want to print the current message. Then enter ¦ **lpr** at the ? prompt. You are, in effect, piping the current message to the `lpr` program.

To print a collection of messages, save them in a file and then print the file. See the section "Saving E-Mail to Files with `mail`," later in this chapter, for information on effective ways to save messages.

Getting Help with *mail*

When you type the command to start your e-mail program, you see a ? prompt. The `mail` program tells you to type ? for help. To get a list of commands and some information about each command, type ? and press <Return>.

After you type ? and press <Return>, you see a display similar to the following:

```
Mail    Commands
t <message list>       type messages
n                 goto and type next message
e <message list>       edit messages
f <message list>       give head lines of messages
d <message list>       delete messages
s <message list>        file append messages to file
u <message list>       undelete messages
R <message list>       reply to message senders
r <message list>       reply to message senders and all recipients
pre <message list>       make messages go back to /usr/spool/mail
p <message list>     print message
m <user list>           mail to specific users
q                 quit, saving unresolved messages in mbox
x                 quit, do not remove system mailbox
h                 print out active message headers
!                 shell escape
cd [directory]     chdir to directory or home if none given
A <message list> consists of integers, ranges of same, or user names
separated by spaces. If omitted, Mail uses the last message typed.
A <user list> consists of user names or aliases separated by spaces.
Aliases are defined in .mailrc in your home directory.
&
```

This listing shows you the commands you can use from the ? prompt. Although some of these commands are explained later in this chapter, here are some things to note right now:

- In each case, you can use the first letter of the command or type the entire command.

- Items in [ ] and <> are optional; you don't type the brackets as part of the command.

- You can make the term message list refer to all messages by using *. To save all messages in a file named allmail, for example, type **s * allmail** and press <Return>.

- You can make the term message list refer to a single message number. To save message number 2 to a file named meeting, for example, type **s 2 meeting** and press <Return>.

- You can make the term message list refer to a range of message numbers by separating the two message numbers with a hyphen. For example, 2-4 refers to messages numbered 2, 3, and 4. To save messages 2, 3, and 4 in a file named memos, type **s 2-4 memos** and press <Return>.

- The term print in the line print message doesn't mean to print messages on a printer. It means to display the messages.

- The edit command is useful for modifying messages before forwarding them to someone else or saving them in a file.

Part
VI

Ch
33

Saving E-Mail to Files with *mail*

You'll want to save some of the e-mail you receive. It's not practical to keep all your mail in your system mailbox for these reasons:

- You'll have too many messages to wade through when you want to read your mail.
- System administrators often limit the size of your system mailbox. This size limit depends on how your system administrator set it up. If you reach that limit, you may be prevented from receiving any new mail.
- Your mail won't be organized, and it can be difficult to find important messages or all messages relating to a specific project or topic.

Earlier in this chapter, you learned that the messages you've read are saved (unless you say otherwise) in the file mbox. You also know that you can read these messages by typing **mail -f mbox** and pressing <Return>. You can also read messages from other files by using the mail command's -f option.

There are two primary ways (with and without a header) to save the current message in a file when you use mail. With both methods, you can specify a file to hold the message, and the message is added to that file. If you don't specify a file, the message is added to the file mbox (your personal mailbox) in your home directory. If you use q to quit the mail program, the messages are removed from your system mailbox.

When you see the ? prompt, you can use any of the following methods to save a message:

- Type **s** to add the current message to mbox in your home directory.
- Type **s** *filename* to add the text of the current message to the named file with the headers intact (useful if you want to use your e-mail program to read the messages later).
- Type **w** *filename* to add the text of the current message to the named file without the header information (useful when you want to use only the text of the messages in a file that may be processed by some other program).

TIP To keep messages in your system mailbox rather than the mbox file after you read them, use the preserve command, pre. You can use this command with a message list.

You know that messages you've already read are automatically saved to mbox unless you use the preserve command.

It's a good idea to get in the habit of specifying a filename when you use the save command, s. If you don't specify a filename, the current message is added to the file mbox. If you include a message list but don't specify a file, mail uses the message list as the name of the file to which it saves the current message. If you use q to quit the e-mail program, the saved messages are removed from your system mailbox.

Deleting and Undeleting Messages with *mail*

To delete a message from a file of messages you're reading, you use the d command. If you quit the mail program by using q, any messages you deleted with the d command are removed from the file.

You use the d or delete command to mark messages for deletion when you use mail to read your e-mail. If you then quit the program with q, the marked messages are removed from your mailbox. Unless you've saved them, they're gone for good. For some messages, deleting without saving them is a very good idea.

To delete the current message, type **d** and press <Return>. You can also specify a message list.

If you mark a message or a group of messages to be deleted, you can change your mind and undelete the message or messages by using the u command. You must use the u command before you enter q to quit; when you enter q, the messages are gone for good. Use the u or undelete command in the same way you use d or delete.

 T I P To undelete all the messages you marked for deletion, enter **u *** at the ? prompt.

Replying to E-Mail with *mail*

To reply to e-mail, use the address specified in the Reply-To header field. If that field isn't present, use the information in the Return-Path header field. Following are partial headers of two messages; one has both header fields, and the other has only the Return-Path header field. The pertinent fields are in bold in each example.

Message 1:

```
From server@malte.abc.com Mon Nov  8 18:31 EST 1993
Received: from MALTE.ABC.COM by s850.mwc.edu with SMTP
Return-Path: <server@matle.ams.com>
Date: Mon, 8 Nov 93 18:17:15 -0500
Comment: From the DuJour List
Originator: dujour@mathe.abc.com
Errors-To: asap@can.org
Reply-To: <dujour@mathe.abc.com>
Sender: dujour@mathe.abc.com
```

Message 2:

```
From jones Fri, Jan 7 13:22 EST 1994
Received: by your.system.com
Date: Fri, 7 Jan 1994 13:22:01 -0500
From: Carol Jones <jones>
Return-Path: <jones>
To: aborat, lynn, oackerm, bkorn
Subject: Draft Report
```

To reply to the first message, use the Reply-To address dujour@mathe.abc.com. Note that the Reply-To and Return-Path fields are different. In the second example, use jones to respond to the sender of the message.

N O T E Always use the Reply-To address if it's included in the header because it represents the specific address of the sender. When the Reply-To address isn't available, the Return-Path address usually provides an adequate address back to the sender. ■

Part
VI

Ch

33

You can let the `mail` program determine the address to use to reply to an electronic mail message. To do this, use either of the following commands:

R   Addresses a reply to the sender of the message

r   Addresses a reply to the sender and all recipients of an e-mail message

With either command, you can specify a message list, as explained earlier in this chapter. Otherwise, the R or r command applies to the current message.

The following partial header shows how to use these two commands. This header is excerpted from a message from Carol Jones, in which she asks a group to comment on a draft of a report she has prepared:

```
From jonesFri, Jan 7 13:22 EST 1994
Received: by your.system.com
Date: Fri, 7 Jan 1994 13:22:01 -0500
From: Carol Jones <jones>
Return-Path: <jones>
To: aborat, lynn, oackerm, bkorn
Subject: Draft Report
```

To respond to jones only, enter **R** at the ? prompt. You see the following response:

```
To: jones
Subject: Re: Draft Report
```

The To line tells you that the reply is going to one person. The Subject header indicates that the message is a reply to the one originally sent.

To make comments for everyone on the distribution list to see, enter **r** at the ? prompt. You see the following response lines:

```
To: jones, aborat, lynn, oackerm, bkorn
Subject: Re: Draft Report
```

The To line tells you that the reply is going to everyone on the original distribution list, as well as the author. The Subject header indicates that the message is a reply to the one originally sent.

From here on, you enter your message in the manner described earlier in the section "Sending E-Mail with `mail`."

CAUTION

Be careful about using r to reply to a message. Whatever you send is sent to everyone who got a copy of the original message. Because Linux is case-sensitive and most people aren't used to typing capital letters as commands, it's a very common mistake and can sometimes be embarrassing.

N O T E   Think about what you write and who will read your message before you send a reply. Being sarcastic or scathing doesn't work very well with e-mail—you usually end up sounding like a bully. Using e-mail isn't the same as talking with someone: You don't get a chance to see or hear the person's reactions, and he or she doesn't get a chance to see or hear you, either. When you use e-mail, it's a lot easier and more effective to be polite and direct.

You can see how easy it is to forward mail; as soon as you send something to one person, you can never tell where the message will end up or how many people will see it. Think, and be considerate. ■

▶ **See** "Lack of Visual Reference," **p. 662**

Routing Mail to Others

E-mail is distributed by addresses. Tasks such as forwarding a message, sending copies (cc:) of a message, creating aliases or simpler forms of addresses, and creating mailing lists all involve manipulating addresses. You don't have to do the manipulation directly—the `mail` program has these capabilities built in.

Forwarding Messages

To forward a message (actually, you're including the message with a message you compose), you must first start `mail` in the same way that you start it to read your messages. Then you use the `m`, `r`, or `R` command to send a message. As you compose your message, you use a tilde command, `~f`, to forward one or several messages. The general form of the `~f` command is `~f` *msglist*. Here is a step-by-step example of how to forward a message:

1. Start `mail` (type **mail** and press <Return>). The system responds with something similar to the following:

   ```
   mail      Type ? for help.
   "/var/spool/mail/bkorn": 5 messages 2 new 1 unread
        1 sarah Wed Jan  8 09:17  15/363
        2 top@kite.fish.com Thu Jan  9 10:18  26/657   Meeting on Friday
   U    3 fred Fri Jan  10 08:09  32/900   New Orders
   > N  4 jones Fri Jan  10 13:22  35/1347  Draft Report
   N    5 smith@somewhere.com Sat Jan  11 13:21  76/3103  Excerpt from book
   ?
   ```

2. Read message 5 by typing **5** and pressing <Return>. (The text of that message isn't shown here.) Suppose that you want to forward it to your friends whose addresses are sarah, anglee@hb.com, and lynn@netcong.com.

3. Use the `m` command to send mail to the addresses listed in step 2, type a subject, and type a beginning for your message, as shown here:

   ```
   ? m sarah anglee@hb.com lynn@netcong.com
   Subject: Forwarding an excerpt from new Que Linux book
   Hi!
   I'm forwarding an excerpt I came across from a new book by Que.
   ```

```
It's Special Edition Using Linux, Fourth Edition. I'll be
getting my own copy tomorrow.
Do you want me to pick up a copy for you, too?
```

4. Use the ~f command to forward message number 5 (type **~f 5** and press <Return>).
    mail responds with the following message:

```
Interpolating: 5
(continue)
```

5. The cursor is now under the word "continue." You can continue adding text to your mail
    message, or you can end it by typing ~. and pressing <Return>. If you end it, the ?
    prompt appears.

Sending a Copy with *mail*

You can send a copy of an e-mail message to one or more addresses by putting those addresses
on what's known as the *cc: list*. The cc: list works as you expect it to: The mail is sent to the
primary address or addresses (those in the To header) and also to the address or addresses in
the Cc header. To include addresses in the cc: list, use the tilde command ~c *address* while
you're sending the message.

The following example shows how to send a brief memo to a primary address (wjones) and a
copy of it to yourself and another address (your address is bkorn, and the other user's address
is ecarlst). You send one to yourself so that you have a copy of the memo. Follow these steps to
add a cc: list to the list of recipients:

1. Start mail to send e-mail to the primary address, wjones, and give a subject header.
    Enter the following commands to achieve this:

```
$ mail fred
Subject: Memo - Sales Agreement with Framistan
```

2. Enter the text of the memo you want to send. For example, type the following:

```
TO:          Fred Jones
Date:     Oct 31, 1996
From:     Henry Charleston
RE:          Sales Agreement With Framistan Motors
On October 27,1996, I held a meeting with the CEO of Framistan Motors.
We concluded and initialed a sales agreement by which Framistan would
purchase 10,000 units of our thermo-embryonic carthurators. The agreement
has been forwarded to the appropriate parties in our organization and
we intend to formally complete the agreement within two weeks.
```

3. Give the ~c address command to add addresses to the cc: list. For example, type the following to send copies to yourself (bkorn) and to ecarlst:

   `~c ecarlst bkorn`

4. To send the message, enter a tilde and period (~.) and press <Return>. The EOT message appears, followed by the shell prompt.

 T I P To review and possibly modify the headers on an outgoing message, enter ~**h** while you're composing the message. You're shown the headers one at a time, and you can modify them.

When a message is sent this way, all the recipients can see the headers To and Cc. Anyone who replies to the message with the r command will send the reply to every address in the To and Cc lists, as well as to the author.

You can customize mail so that it always prompts you for a Cc header in the same way that it prompts you for the Subject header (this is discussed later in the section "Customizing Your mail Environment"). Of course, you can keep from entering anything in the Cc list by pressing <Return>.

Using Aliases and Mailing Lists

The mail program, like most e-mail programs, allows you to create an alias for an address and a group alias for a list of addresses. You can treat the group alias as a mailing list. Using an alias for an individual address is easier than using the regular address because the alias is typically shorter and easier to remember.

To set an individual or group alias for one mail session, you use the alias command at the ? prompt while you're reading your e-mail. To make the aliases more useful, put the aliases in a file named .mailrc in your home directory (as described in the following section).

The following is an example of setting and using aliases with the mail program:

Part
VI

Ch
33

1. Start mail by entering **mail** at the prompt. After the headers are presented, you see the ? prompt:

```
mail     Type ? for help.
"/var/spool/mail/bkorn": 5 messages 2 new 1 unread
     1 sarah Wed Jan  5 09:17  15/363
     2 croster@kite.fish.com Thu Jan  6 10:18  26/657   Meeting on Friday
U    3 wjones Fri Jan  7 08:09  32/900   Framistan Order
> N  4 chendric Fri Jan  7 13:22  35/1347  Draft Report
N    5 kackerma@ps.com Sat Jan  8 13:21  76/3103  Excerpt from GREAT new Linux
?
```

2. To set up an individual alias, use the `alias` command followed by the alias for the address. The following example creates the alias ros for the address croster@kite.fish.com:

```
alias ros croster@kite.fish.com
```

3. Use the ros alias in an address; `mail` expands it to its complete form. For example, you can enter the command **m** **ros** to start a message you want to mail to croster@kite.fish.com.

To set up a group alias, use the `alias` command followed by the alias for the addresses. The following creates an alias called friends and then forwards some mail to the group:

```
alias friends chendric karlack abc.com!homebase!fran eca@xy.srt.edu
m friends
Subject: Excerpts from new Linux book - get a copy!
~f 5
Interpolating: 5
~.
EOT
?
```

Customizing Your *mail* Environment

You can customize your `mail` environment by putting commands or set-environment variables in the .mailrc file in your home directory. The `mail` program checks that file whenever you use the program. You can set quite a few environment variables and commands in .mailrc, and different mail programs will use different commands. Check your man page for your mail program for a list of all the .mailrc options. Some of the commands `mail` recognizes are given earlier in the section "Getting Help with `mail`"; this section describes a subset of the commands and variables that can be used in the .mailrc file. Table 33.1 lists these commands; Table 33.2 lists the environment variables.

Table 33.1 *mail* Commands

Command	Definition
#	Denotes a comment. No action is taken.
alias	Sets an individual or group alias. Used as `alias alias-name address-list`.
set	Sets an environment variable. Used as `set variable-name` or `set variable-name=string`.

TIP You can issue any of the commands in Table 33.1 from the ? prompt anytime you use `mail`; they'll be active only for that session.

Table 33.2 *mail* Environment Variables	
Variable	**Definition**
askcc	Prompts for the cc: list after the message is entered. Default is noaskcc.
asksub	Prompts for the Subject list before the message is entered. Enabled by default.
noheader	Doesn't print header information on available messages when you start mail. Disabled by default.
ignore	Ignores interrupt characters when you enter messages. Useful if you have a "noisy" connection over some telephone or other communication lines. Default is noignore.
metoo	When you have your name in a group alias, a message normally isn't sent to you. Setting this variable allows you to receive messages sent to a group alias that contains your address. Default is nometoo.

 T I P You can set a system-wide environment by putting the commands or set variables in the /etc/mail.rc file.

The following example sets up the .mailrc file so that you use the commands and environment variables listed in Tables 33.1 and 33.2. The pound sign (#) is used to document the work. You can create this file by using vi or any other editor that can produce a text or ASCII file.

```
# .mailrc file for D. Wayne Love
# make sure interrupts are NOT ignored
set noignore
# set variables so that prompts for Subject and Cc always appear
set asksub
set askcc
# individual aliases
alias billy wcuth
alias ben benjamin@flagstaff.abaced.com
alias me dwlove
# group aliases, mailing list
alias mercs miles@dendarii.net quinn taura
alias research jones brown smith
alias googol djames bkorn cam@googol.org bkorn
```

Place these statements in the .mailrc file. Now whenever you start mail, these command statements are processed.

Quitting the *mail* Program

As you read e-mail in a mailbox, you can read, skip, or delete messages. (You learn about deleting messages later in this chapter.) These actions don't take place in the mailbox itself, but in a temporary copy of the mailbox. You can quit the e-mail program so that your mailbox is changed by your actions (the modified temporary copy replaces the original mailbox), or you can quit so that your mailbox is unchanged regardless of what you did during your e-mail session.

Quitting and Saving Changes

To quit the `mail` program and save the changes that occur, press <q><Return> at the ? prompt. You see the shell prompt again. When you quit `mail` this way, messages you read but didn't delete are saved in a file named mbox in your home directory.

Suppose that you use `mail` to read your mail. Your login name is bkorn, and your home directory is /home/bkorn. When you enter **mail** to start the `mail` program, you see the following screen of information:

```
mail    Type ? for help.
"/var/spool/mail/bkorn": 5 messages 2 new 1 unread
     1 sarah Wed Jan  8 09:17  15/363
     2 top@kite.fish.com Thu Jan  9 10:18  26/657    Meeting on Friday
U    3 fred Fri Jan  10 08:09  32/900   New Order
> N  4 jones Fri Jan  10 13:22  35/1347  Draft Report
N    5 smith@somewhere.com Sat Jan  11 13:21  76/3103  Excerpt from book
?
```

Now suppose that you read the current message by pressing <Return>, and then you read message 1 by typing **1** and pressing <Return> at the ? prompt. If you then press <q><Return> to quit, you see the following information:

```
Saved 2 messages in /home/bkorn/mbox
Held 3 messages in /var/spool/mail/bkorn
```

The two messages you read are saved in the file mbox in your home directory; the other three messages are saved in your system mailbox, /var/spool/mail/bkorn.

If you save read messages like this often, mbox can become quite large. You may want to print that file occasionally and delete it. You can also read the mail from that file as though it were your system mailbox, as described later in this chapter.

N O T E   You can read mail and indicate that the current message is to be kept in your system mailbox, /var/spool/mail/bkorn, and not in the file mbox. To do this after you read a message, enter **pre** (for preserve) at the ? prompt. ■

Quitting and Not Saving Changes

The other way to quit the `mail` program is to press <x><Return> at the ? prompt. When you do that, you exit the program with no changes to your system mailbox or any other file—as if you didn't read your mail at all. You then see the shell prompt. You may want to exit the `mail` program in this way when you want to leave the program but save the mail in your system mailbox.

Using the *elm* Mailer

As stated earlier in this chapter, several different mail programs are available for Linux. Each has its own advantages and disadvantages.

One mail reader that comes with the Slackware and Red Hat distributions of Linux is the `elm` mailer. This mail program is a screen-oriented mailer rather than a line-oriented one. It provides a set of interactive menu prompts and is easy to use. Virtually everything that you can do with `mail` can be done under `elm`, and usually much more easily!

Because `elm` is easy to use, the following sections just touch on the highlights of using it. You can find more in-depth information by using `elm`'s online help or by reading its man page.

Starting *elm*

To start a mail session with `elm`, just type `elm` at the command prompt. If this is the first time you've used `elm`, it will prompt you for permission to set up a configuration directory in your account and create an mbox mail file if one doesn't exist. Here's what you see as you start `elm` for the first time:

```
$ elm
Notice:
This version of ELM requires the use of a .elm directory in your home
directory to store your elmrc and alias files. Shall I create the
directory .elm for you and set it up (y/n/q)? y
Great! I'll do it now.

Notice:
ELM requires the use of a folders directory to store your mail folders in.
Shall I create the directory /home/gunter/Mail for you (y/n/q)? y
Great! I'll do it now.
```

After `elm` creates its directory and mbox file, it runs the main mail program. This is a full-screen-oriented mailer. Your screen clears, and you see a display similar to the following:

```
Mailbox is '/var/spool/mail/gunter' with 2 messages [ELM 2.4 PL25]
N   1   Nov 11 Jack Tackett    Linux book
N   2   Nov 11 Jack Tackett    more ideas

You can use any of the following commands
by pressing the first character;
d)elete or u)ndelete mail,  m)ail a message,
r)eply or f)orward mail,  q)uit
To read a message, press <return>. j = move down, k = move up, ? = help

Command:
```

At the top of the screen, `elm` tells you where your system mailbox is located, how many messages are in it, and what version of `elm` you're running. `elm` then lists one line for each message in your mailbox. It places the letter N before each new message, just like the `mail` program. The summary line for each message tells you whether the message is new, the message date, the sender, and the subject. (As always, your display may vary slightly depending on your version of elm.) The current message is highlighted in the list (in the preceding listing, the current message is in boldface).

Using *elm* Commands

At the bottom of the screen is a command summary that tells you what commands you have available for the current screen. As you can see in the preceding example, you can delete or undelete mail, mail a message, reply to a message, forward mail, or quit. Pressing the <j> key moves the message selection to the previous message; the <k> key moves it to the next message. Help is available by pressing the <?> key. The Command: prompt at the bottom of the screen tells you to press a command key for elm to do something.

As you can see, elm is very easy to use due to the large number of prompts and on-screen help that's available. Table 33.3 lists all the commands that can be executed from within elm.

Table 33.3 Command Summary for *elm*

Command/Keystroke	Description
<Return>, Spacebar	Displays current message
¦	Pipes current message or tagged messages to a system command
!	Shell escape
$	Resynchronizes folder
?	Displays online help
+, <→>	Displays next index page
-, <←>	Displays previous index page
=	Sets current message to first message
*	Sets current message to last message
<number><Return>	Sets current message to *number*
/	Searches subject lines for pattern
//	Searches entire message texts for pattern
>	Saves current message or tagged messages to a folder
<	Scans current message for calendar entries
a	Changes to "alias" mode
b	Bounces (remails) current message
c	Copies current message or tagged messages to a folder

Command/Keystroke	Description
c	Changes to another folder
d	Deletes current message
\<Ctrl-d>	Deletes messages with a specified pattern
e	Edits current folder
f	Forwards current message
g	Send group (all recipients) reply to current message
h	Displays header with message
J	Increments current message by one
j, \<↓>	Advances to next undeleted message
K	Decrements current message by one
k, \<↑>	Advances to previous undeleted message
l	Limits messages by specified criteria
\<Ctrl-l>	Redraws screen
m	Mails a message
n	Moves to next message, displaying current and then incrementing
o	Changes elm options
p	Prints current message or tagged messages
q	Quits, maybe prompting for deleting, storing, and keeping messages
Q	Quick quit—no prompting
r	Replies to current message
s	Saves current message or tagged messages to a folder
t	Tags current message for further operations
T	Tags current message and goes to next message
\<Ctrl-t>	Tags messages with a specified pattern
u	Undeletes current message
\<Ctrl-u>	Undeletes messages with a specified pattern
x, \<Ctrl-q>	Exits leaving folder untouched; asks if you want to exit if you have changed the folder
X	Exits leaving folder untouched, unconditionally

Part

VI

Ch

33

Using the *Mutt* E-Mail Client

Mutt is a freeware mail client that is rapidly gaining in popularity. While perfectly useable by comparative novices (by default, Mutt looks and works much like the elm client), Mutt is especially popular among more knowledgeable users because of its extreme configurability.

Some of the primary features of Mutt include:

- Color support
- Support for message threading
- MIME support—including RFC2047 support for encoded headers and PGP/MIME (RFC2015)
- POP3 support
- Support for multiple mailbox formats including mbox, MMDF, MH, and maildir
- Key bindings (by default, identical to elm)
- Ability to search using regular expression
- Support for Delivery Status Notification (DSN)
- Ability to include attachments from the command line when composing
- Ability to reply to or forward multiple messages at once
- .mailrc style configuration files
- Installation process uses GNU autoconf

Where to Get *Mutt*

Mutt is distributed under the GNU public license terms on the Red Hat 5.1 installation CD-ROM, in the Mail directory of the Applications section. An international version of Mutt that contains support for PGP™ is available from several FTP servers, including **ftp:// ftp.gbnet.net/pub/mutt-international/** among others.

For More Information on *Mutt*

The Mutt home page is at **http://www.cs.hmc.edu/~me/mutt/index.html**. It contains links to the online Mutt manual by Michael Elkins (at **http://www.cs.hmc.edu/~me/mutt/manual.html**) and the Mutt FAQ by Felix von Leitner (at **http://www.math.fu-berlin.de/~leitner/mutt/faq.html**). The Mutt home page also contains information on several mailing lists devoted to the mail client.

From Here...

You can find more information about exchanging information over the Internet in the following chapters:

- Chapter 31, "Surfing the Internet with the World Wide Web," describes the various types of information available on the Internet.

- Chapter 34, "Surviving Usenet News," describes the Usenet news system that's used to exchange public messages.

Part
VI

Ch
33

Surviving Usenet News

by Steve Burnett

In this chapter

With the explosive growth of the Internet, Usenet news has attracted lots of attention. Many online services now offer access to Usenet. But what's Usenet? Usenet—short for *User Network*—is a proto-network of machines that exchange information grouped into subject hierarchies. The term *proto-network* is used because Usenet isn't a physical network in the normal sense. It's made up of all the computers that exchange Usenet news.

What Is Usenet News?

In the simplest definition, *Usenet news*, *netnews*, or simply *news* is a forum for online discussion. Many computers around the world exchange chunks of information, called *articles*, on almost every subject imaginable. These computers aren't physically connected to the same network; they're logically connected in their capability to exchange data. Thus, they form the logical network referred to as Usenet. In this chapter, the terms *Usenet*, *news*, and *netnews* are used interchangeably.

N O T E The software that drives Usenet is divided into two parts: news readers (the software that users use to read and post news articles) and the software that processes articles and transfers them between systems. ■

Many people initially think of a PC bulletin board system (BBS) when trying to understand Usenet. Although Usenet news does bear some similarity to a BBS at first glance, there are very substantial and important differences:

■ The various news articles on different subjects don't reside on one computer, as with a BBS. They're sent from computer to computer via a store-and-forward mechanism. Each site that receives news exchanges articles with one or more neighbors in transactions that are known as *news feeds*. As a result, news articles take time to propagate from place to place.

■ No one is in charge. Yes, you read that right. Usenet has no overall manager, such as a BBS sysop (system operator). Each site has a good deal of autonomy. Usenet news has been described, very accurately, as "organized anarchy."

In general, Usenet news is divided into two logical parts: the programs and protocols that make up the mechanism for posting articles and transferring news articles between computers, and the user programs for reading and posting news articles. This chapter deals primarily with the user portion.

A Usenet Glossary

Usenet news has its own structure and culture, which are discussed later in the section "Usenet Culture." Usenet also has a terminology all its own. These "buzzwords" tend to confuse new users, especially those who use BBS systems. Table 34.1 is a brief glossary of common terms found on Usenet.

Table 34.1   Common Terms Encountered in Usenet

Term	Definition
article	A single message posted to a newsgroup.
bandwidth	An engineering term referring to the amount of data a given transmission medium can hold. Commonly used as in the phrase *waste of bandwidth* for articles that contain little useful information.
BTW	Acronym for *By the Way*.
FAQ	An acronym for the *Frequently Asked Questions* list. Many newsgroups have a FAQ that they post on a regular basis. It's usually considered impolite to post a question to which the answer is in the FAQ for a group.
flame	An article that's full of rude, angry, insulting statements directed at another person.
FYI	Acronym for *For Your Information*.
hierarchy	Usenet's system of grouping newsgroups into a tree structure based on subject.
IMHO	Stands for *In My Humble Opinion*.
newsgroup	A logical group of articles that are about one general subject.
news reader	A user program, such as `rn`, that's used to read and post articles to Usenet.
net.personality	Someone who's famous within the Usenet or Internet community.
net.police	A mythical organization responsible for enforcing the rules on Usenet. Typically used as sarcasm.
netiquette	The etiquette of Usenet.
newbie	Someone who's new to using Usenet news.
quoting	Including parts of a message to which you're responding. Most news readers allow you to quote articles. You should quote only relevant portions of an article to save bandwidth. Sometimes also referred to as *quotebacks*.
ROFL	Acronym for *Rolling On the Floor, Laughing*.
RTFM	An acronym for *Read The Forgotten Manual*. Typically used as in "Here's a short answer to your question. RTFM for more info."
post	To submit an article to a newsgroup.
signal-to-noise	Engineering term referring to the ratio of the amount of data to the amount of background noise. On Usenet, it refers to how much useful information is in a newsgroup versus the amount of off-topic background chatter. A high signal-to-noise ratio refers to a newsgroup that

Part

VI

Ch

34

continues

Table 34.1 Continued	
Term	**Definition**
	has lots of useful information and very little off-topic chatter. Signal-to-noise can also be used as a descriptive for a specific person.
signature	A short file that's included at the end of all your posts. Typically includes your name, e-mail address, and possibly a witty quote of some sort.
sig file	See *signature*.
smileys	Common symbols for denoting emotion in a post or e-mail message. For example, :-) and :-(are a happy face and a sad face. (Tilt your head toward your left shoulder and look at them sideways.)

A Brief History

In late 1979, two graduate students at Duke University began considering how to connect UNIX computers so that they could exchange text messages. Another grad student at the University of North Carolina became involved in this effort and wrote the first news transfer system, which consisted of a collection of shell scripts. This software was installed on the first two Usenet sites, unc and duke. In early 1980, another computer at Duke, phs, was added. The news software was eventually rewritten in C for public distribution. This became known as the *A News* software.

As the news software grew in popularity, it quickly became obvious that the current news transport software couldn't handle the increasing flow of news. Programmers at the University of California at Berkeley began to rewrite the current A News software to increase its capabilities. This new version, known as *B News*, was released in 1982.

Throughout this time, news articles were being transferred by using the UNIX-to-UNIX Copy Program (UUCP) protocol. As more sites joined the news network, the network load grew to unmanageable levels. Soon realizing that UUCP no longer worked as the main transport protocol for news, people began looking to the Internet and the TCP/IP protocols for help. In 1986, a software package was released that implemented the Network News Transport Protocol (NNTP). This protocol is defined in RFC 977. NNTP allowed news articles to be exchanged by using TCP/IP instead of the slower UUCP protocol. It also allowed users to read and post news from remote machines so that the main news processing software didn't have to be installed on every computer.

When NNTP became available on the Net, the already rapid growth of the Usenet system exploded. The current news-processing software, B News, quickly became too slow to handle the increasing news flow. In 1987, Henry Spencer and Geoff Collyer of the University of Toronto developed a new news-processing software, *C News*. Then, Rich Salz developed a news transport system known as *INN,* one of the most widely used news servers on the Internet.

The Usenet news system continues to grow at a rapid pace. Other commercial information service providers are now carrying Usenet news as part of their online services. Several BBS networks, such as FidoNet, also carry Usenet news.

> **N O T E** An excellent reference for the history of Usenet news is the news article "Usenet Software: History and Sources," by Dr. Gene Spafford. This article can be found on the World Wide Web at **http://www.faqs.org/faqs/usenet/software/part1/**. ■

How Usenet Is Structured

There are literally many thousands of newsgroups. How many, exactly? Well, nobody knows for sure—well over 20,000. There are thousands of groups on virtually every topic, and that number is growing every day. The topics range from silly or pointless to focused and precisely helpful.

Group Hierarchies

With so many different newsgroups, it would be a nightmare trying to find information on the subjects that you were interested in if the newsgroups weren't organized in some way. Usenet newsgroups are organized in a hierarchy based on subject. The names of the newsgroups are made up of subnames, each separated by a period. These names go from a general category to a specific category as you read the name from left to right. At the top of the hierarchy are several standard group categories, plus lots of specialized categories. These standard categories are well established. Table 34.2 lists the top-level groups standard categories in the Usenet news system.

Table 34.2	Top-Level Group Standard Categories in the Usenet Hierarchy
Class	**Description**
comp	Many different computer-related topics
misc	Miscellaneous topics that don't easily fit into another category
news	Various topics that relate to the Usenet news system itself
rec	Recreational and hobby subjects
soc	Social issues
sci	Various scientific topics
talk	Subjects designed for ongoing conversations

As with everything else on the Internet, there are exceptions to the rules in Table 34.2. Many other top-level hierarchies exist; most are devoted to different regions of the world. For example, the **ba** and **triangle** group hierarchies are concerned with topics of interest to the San Francisco Bay area and the North Carolina Research Triangle Park area, respectively.

Part
VI

Ch
34

One of these additional group hierarchies deserves special discussion. The **alt** hierarchy has very relaxed rules for newsgroup creation. Virtually anyone can create a group under the **alt** hierarchy; however, creating a newsgroup under any other top-level group is extremely difficult. The **alt** hierarchy carries many newsgroups that discuss topics that are out of the mainstream of society. In fact, many people find some of the topics in the **alt** hierarchy to be objectionable. Many Net debates on censorship have started because sites decided to ban part or all of the newsgroups in the **alt** hierarchy.

News Distributions

In addition to grouping articles in hierarchies, Usenet also provides a feature for limiting the spread of an article within the news system. New distributions provide a mechanism for limiting articles to a particular geographic area. If a distribution is set to a particular area, only sites within that distribution area receive the article. The systems administrator at each site decides what distributions apply to that site.

Why limit the distribution of an article? Suppose that you live in North Carolina and you're posting a meeting announcement for a local user group meeting. It's unlikely that Usenet readers in Australia are interested in your meeting. By limiting the distribution of your article to the appropriate geographical area, you can save network bandwidth, reduce the cost of sending your message, and reduce the aggravation of users around the world who have to read your message.

You can limit the distribution of your article by including a Distribution: line in the header of your article as you post it. Most news readers ask you for the distribution when you post an article. After the colon in the Distribution: line, enter the appropriate geographical distribution. Table 34.3 lists some commonly used news distribution areas.

Table 34.3   Commonly Used News Distribution Values

Value	Explanation
local	Typically, articles with a local distribution are limited to a group of local news servers within your organization. This distribution is often used for local organizational newsgroups.
nc	Every state has a statewide distribution that's the same as the postal abbreviation for the state. The Distribution:nc used in this example limits the article to machines within the state of North Carolina.
us	Sends the article to all Usenet sites in the United States.
na	Sends the article to all Usenet sites in North America.
world	Sends the article to every reachable Usenet site in the world. Typically, this is the default distribution if no other distribution value is specified.

Your site may have some additional distributions that apply. There may be organization-wide or regional distributions that you can use to determine the scope of your article. In general, you should try to pick a distribution that sends your article only to the areas where it will be of interest.

No Central Authority

That Usenet has no central authority mystifies many people. Your local systems administrator really has authority over only the local system. No central group or organization dictates policy or takes complaints. Despite this glaring lack of regulated structure, Usenet works remarkably well. In fact, many people argue that it works better than if there were some central authority.

How do things keep working in an orderly manner? Usenet is run by cooperation between sites and by customs that have evolved over its life.

Usenet tends to be very good at policing itself. If a user starts to abuse the network, you can rest assured that the user and his or her systems administrator will get thousands of e-mail messages and several phone calls about the problem. This usually results in quick problem resolution.

Usenet Culture

Usenet has a particular culture all its own. You should take some time to try to become familiar with the facets of this culture before just diving in. Life on Usenet will be much easier if you do.

In the past few years, many online communication services have added Usenet news as a feature. As a result, tens of thousands of people who are new to Usenet have started reading and posting Usenet news. Many of these users have complained about Usenet participants being rude or generally unlike the users of their online service. Well, the culture of Usenet is different from almost any other information service that you'll find. It's not better or worse—just different. If you try to make allowances for differences in Net culture, you'll probably find that your experiences on Usenet are a bit easier to handle.

Well over 1 million people—probably several million, though no one knows for sure—read and post Usenet news articles daily. These people are from all occupations, all walks of life, and many different countries around the world. Because Usenet news is carried on computers all over the world, it truly forms an international community. Many of the people that you encounter on Usenet don't speak English as a primary language. You can't assume that the people reading your articles share your cultural background, ethnic group, religion, or social values. The most that you can assume is that whoever reads your article is probably very different from you in several ways.

One aspect of Usenet culture, the *flame*, is usually an unpleasant experience for new users. A flame is a rude message, usually degrading and filled with insults that someone posts in response to one of your articles. Unfortunately, as you'll see, you can do very little about flames other than ignore them. Usenet is far too large a place for you to try to make everyone happy, and some people really seem to like flaming other people just for the fun of it. Perhaps they find it cheaper than psychotherapy....

Lack of Visual Reference

One problem with electronic communications is that you lack any kind of visual input during the conversation. When people talk to each other in person, you constantly receive information on a conscious and subconscious level from the other person's body language. Because you can't see the other people that read and post on Usenet, these visual cues are missing. Because you typically use body language and visual cues to represent emotion and feeling, it can be easy to misunderstand someone's post without them.

Fortunately, you can use several conventions on Usenet to replace part of the missing visual cues. You can place added emphasis on a particular phrase by surrounding it in asterisks, as in `"I *really* mean it!"` Also, the use of all capital letters is considered shouting. If you accidentally post an article with your <Caps Lock> key on, several people will probably tell you about it.

You can also express emotions by writing them into your message. For example, if you make a sarcastic statement, you can make sure that it's understood as such by adding <sarcasm> at the end of the line. *Smileys*, also known as *emoticons*, also work to add emotion to your post. A smiley is an ASCII representation of a face, which you look at sideways to see clearly. For example, :-) is a happy, smiling face, and :-(is a sad face.

ON THE WEB

A canonical list of smileys is available at the following site. Have a look at it if you're really interested; some of them are quite funny and original, but the happy and sad faces are the most commonly used. Using some of the longer or rarer ones will likely result in the same effect as using obscure words in common conversation—you'll just confuse people.

http://www.eff.org/pub/Net_culture/Folklore/Arts/smiley2.list

Newsgroup Culture

Just as people are different, each newsgroup on Usenet has a different culture. Each newsgroup has a different subject focus and attracts different types of people. In some groups, you may find large numbers of college students, whereas in others, you may find primarily research scientists.

Some of the more technical hierarchies, such as **comp** and **sci**, tend to be more oriented toward factual discussion, although heated debates do take place. Members of these groups are usually interested in discussing facts and issues related to some technical subject. When you post here, make sure that you take time to carefully compose your article and have references for the various points that you make.

The less technical hierarchies, such as **rec**, tend to be somewhat more opinion-oriented. Remember, you'll probably get replies to your articles that reflect other people's opinions that are quite different from your own. Groups in the **talk** hierarchy, along with some of the **misc** groups, get into some very heated discussions. Many of these groups discuss very sensitive topics such as abortion and gun control. Be careful in these groups if you're new to Usenet. Make sure that you take time to get familiar with the group before posting. Be prepared to receive strongly worded replies and e-mail about your articles. Many of the people here hold very strong beliefs.

> **N O T E** When you first start reading a newsgroup, you should take some time to familiarize yourself with the culture of the particular group before posting. Read the group for at least a few days and try to get a feel for the tone of the articles and the things that are considered to be acceptable and unacceptable behavior. Look for a FAQ to get a feel for the group (if there's not one posted recently in the newsgroup, a search using one of the search engines on the Web can help). ■

In a few newsgroups, posting articles is restricted. These are known as *moderated newsgroups*. Moderated newsgroups are managed by a person known as a *moderator*. All articles posted to the group must be approved by the moderator before posting. The moderator decides if the content of the article is appropriate to the group and, if so, posts the article to the group. Most news software automatically detects if a newsgroup is moderated, and if so, it e-mails your article to the moderator instead of posting it directly.

Reading and Posting News

Now that you're familiar with Usenet, look at the basic process for reading and posting news articles. This section discusses reading and posting news in general terms; the exact details depend on the news-reading software that you're using. Many different software packages are available for interacting with news, and each of them is different. Many people use a Web browser with an integrated news reader, such as Netscape. Others prefer to use a line-oriented tool, such as rn. These general concepts should apply across all news reading software.

Subscribing to Newsgroups

The first thing you want to do when you start reading news is to decide which newsgroups you want to read. The process of selecting the newsgroups is known as *subscribing*.

Most news readers offer you a list of available newsgroups so that you can select the ones in which you're interested. The actual process of subscribing varies between news-reading software packages, but it usually involves selecting a series of newsgroups from a list. From then on, only the groups that you've subscribed to are visible when you read news. You can always subscribe to additional groups anytime you want or unsubscribe from a group in which you're no longer interested.

Remember the earlier mention of over twenty thousand newsgroups? If your newsreader is set to download the entire list of all newgroups carried by your news server, receiving this list may take a while.

Part VI
Ch
34

Reading News

After you subscribe to your newsgroups, you can begin reading news. You select a newsgroup from a list of your subscribed groups. Your news reader displays a list of article subjects for the various articles in the newsgroup. These subjects may be sorted in some order, or they may be unsorted, depending on your news reader. Some news readers can sort articles based on subject, showing which articles are replies to other articles. This is known as *threading*.

When you select an article to read, you see several lines of information at the top of the article. These lines make up the *article header*. The header contains lots of information about the article, including the author, the date it was written, the subject, the newsgroups that the article was posted to, and the path the article took to get to your site. You also might see additional information, such as the organization the author is affiliated with and a set of keywords that identify the content of an article.

Under most news readers, an article is marked as read when you look at it. Usually, only new articles are displayed when you select a newsgroup. This means that after you look at an article, it probably won't show up in your article list again. If you want to keep the article, you can save it to disk or print it. You can also usually mark the article as unread so that your news reader displays it again the next time you go into the newsgroup. Many news readers also allow you to list old articles; this way, you have a list of old news articles in a newsgroup that are marked as having been read but haven't yet been deleted by the news system.

Replying via E-Mail

After you read an article, you may decide that you want to comment on the topic under discussion. If your information isn't of general interest to everyone in the newsgroup, you may want to reply to the article via e-mail, which most news readers allow you the option of doing.

If you choose to reply through e-mail, the news reader software uses the information in the article header to figure out the e-mail address of the author and then invokes an e-mail editor for you to edit your message. You usually also have the option of including the original article in your reply. If you do include the original article, make sure that you edit the original message to include only the relevant portions. After you finish editing your reply, you can send your e-mail message to the article's author.

Because of the common use of e-mail, especially e-mail addresses gleaned from Usenet postings, many Usenet posters *munge*, or modify, their e-mail addresses to stop automated address collectors from being able to send them unsolicited commercial e-mail, known as *spam*. The poster's e-mail address may have an obvious false entry and look something like "mjameson@IHATESPAM.netcrom.com." Alternatively, the poster may have instructions in his sigfile on what to change in the reply-to address to actually reach him. For example, a poster with a false address of "sbarnes@sequoia.skytails.org" might have instructions in his sigfile to "Replace 'tails' with 'wings' to reply."

Posting an Article

The act of creating a news article and sending it out through the Usenet system is known as *posting an article*. When you decide to post an article, you can either post a follow-up article to another article or create a new article on a new subject. Your news reader typically has different commands for the different types of posts that it can perform.

Posting a Follow-Up A *follow-up article* is a reply to another article. This article stays in the same subject thread as the original article and is shown as a reply by threaded news readers.

When you post a follow-up, you can choose to include the original post. Including parts of the original post is a good way to provide a frame of reference for your reply. Remember that several days may pass between the time some sites see the original article and your reply. If you do choose to include the original article, try to include, or *quote*, only the parts of the article that are relevant to your reply. It gets tedious trying to wade through several levels of included files and quotes looking for the new information. Also, some news servers will reject your reply if the quoted material is more than a certain percentage of your entire message, depending on the policies of the administrators.

You should check the Subject line to make sure that the subject still accurately reflects the content of your post, and change it if you're now discussing a new topic. Also, take a look at the Newsgroup line to make sure that your follow-up is going to the appropriate newsgroups. In particular, consider whether sending the message to multiple newsgroups is appropriate or whether the topic is relevant to only one or two of the original newsgroups.

Posting a New Article If you decide to start a thread of discussion on a new subject, you want to post a new article instead of a follow-up. The mechanics of posting the article are very similar to those of posting a follow-up. You give the appropriate command to your news reader; your news reader asks for some information, such as the destination newsgroups, subject, and distribution; and you're placed into an editor. The major difference is that you're creating a subject thread instead of replying to one.

 TIP A complete document on Usenet writing style is posted regularly to the newsgroup **news.announce.newusers**.

Part
VI

Ch
34

You should think about several things as you write your article. You can think of them as "Usenet Style Tips" if you want. These tips cover the format of your article and its content.

You should keep your lines less than 80 characters long. Many terminals can't display lines that are more than 80 characters. Similarly, you should try to keep the length of your article under 1,000 lines or so. Some sites are still running old versions of the news transport software, and long articles can cause them problems.

You probably want to create a signature file that's automatically included at the end of every post. Most news readers support signature files, although the exact mechanism varies depending on your software. Most people put their name and e-mail address in their signature file, along with their geographical location. Some people add a witty quote or a small ASCII picture.

Try to avoid having a large signature file. It is considered bad netiquette to include your full name, nicknames, an inspirational quote consisting of Whitman's "Leaves of Grass," and a twenty-line ASCII art drawing of your car. A good rule is to limit yourself to four lines. Some news software automatically limits your signature to four lines or so.

You need to give a subject to your article when you post it. Try to pick a subject line that's short, yet descriptive. Thousands of people scan the subjects in any particular newsgroup, and you want them to be able to pick out your article if it's of interest to them. Also, carefully consider which newsgroups you're going to post your article to. Most news readers allow you to post an article to more than one newsgroup. You should post to only the smallest number of groups that you need. Remember that thousands of people are reading each newsgroup.

Netiquette on Usenet

Throughout this chapter, the importance of being aware of how the tone and content of your message are interpreted has been stressed. This general consideration of behavior on Usenet, and the Internet in general, has its own term—*netiquette*. Netiquette applies to all areas of the Internet, including electronic mail.

The term *netiquette* simply refers to "proper and polite" behavior as it applies to Usenet news. Most of the time, you should have no real problems on Usenet as long as you remember that it's a very big and diverse place. Not everyone on Usenet shares your background, beliefs, or values, and you should try to remember this as you post articles.

Make sure that you clearly communicate your ideas in your posts. With the lack of body language and the delay between posts and replies, it's surprisingly easy to interpret someone's meaning incorrectly. Also, remember that many participants don't speak English as a native language and may be unaware of local idioms and sarcasm.

Blatant commercial advertising is frowned on in Usenet news. There are appropriate newsgroups for advertising products and services. Similarly, don't post chain articles, such as the infamous MAKE.MONEY.FAST or Craig Shergold get-well card article. These articles have been circulating around Usenet for years, and you (and your systems administrator) will incur the wrath of thousands of people instantly if you post one of them.

Resist the urge to post flames, especially spelling and grammar flames. Even though flames seem to be a permanent part of the Usenet "landscape," these personal attacks and raving messages accomplish little. If someone should flame you for one of your posts, take time to calm down and carefully consider how to respond; the best solution might be not to respond at all. Sometimes you may receive a flame, but a calm response from you may elicit an apology from the person who flamed you. If you just zip off another flame in anger, you only escalate the problem. Remember that the person on the other end is really a person, not a computer.

N O T E   If a user is causing a real problem, you can add him or her to your *kill file*, a configuration file for your news reader that contains a list of users or subjects. Anything that appears in your kill file is automatically not displayed when you read news. Most news readers support some version of a kill file. This is a fairly painless way to cut down the noise from really annoying users. ■

In general, a little common sense and courtesy go a long way to avoiding any problems on Usenet. However, remember that Usenet is a huge place. There are simply too many people for you to try to make everyone happy. Eventually, someone will get angry over one of your posts, and you'll probably be flamed.

Using the *rn* News Reader

Many different types of news-reading software are available—far too many to describe in this chapter. The rn news reader is a very common news-reading program that can be found on almost every UNIX variant. It was developed by Larry Wall and is widely available. Although rn isn't the easiest news reader to use, nor does it have some of the fanciest features, it's still one of the most popular news readers in existence. rn allows you to read news via an ASCII interface that's suitable for local work on a terminal or from a remote network session.

N O T E Another news reader, trn, is quite popular and is distributed with many distributions of Linux. The trn news reader is almost identical to rn except for the threading support. For compatibility with a wide variety of UNIX systems, only the rn news reader is discussed in this chapter. For more information on the threading capabilities of trn, refer to its Linux man page. ■

When you start rn for the first time, you see a message welcoming you to the program, followed by a list of newsgroups. You have the opportunity to subscribe to different groups at this point. If your site carries a large number of groups, it can be quite time-consuming to set up your initial subscription information. rn saves your subscription information in your home directory in a file named .newsrc.

After you complete your subscriptions, rn places you in a newsgroup selection mode. The name of each of your subscribed newsgroups is displayed one at a time. You can enter the newsgroup and start reading articles by pressing <y>, skip to the next group by pressing <n>, or go to the previous newsgroup by pressing <q>. You can also get a list of subjects in the newsgroup by pressing <=> at the newsgroup prompt. Most of the commands in rn and trn are one-character commands, and help is available at every command prompt by pressing <h>.

After you select a newsgroup to read, you enter article-selection mode. In this mode, several commands can help you navigate the articles in the newsgroup. Table 34.4 lists some of the commands available in article-selection mode.

Part
VI

Ch
34

Table 34.4   Some Commands Available in Article-Selection Mode

Command	Description
<n><Spacebar>	Scans forward for the next unread article. The Spacebar does this only at the end of the article, at the article-selection prompt.
<Spacebar>	Shows the next page of the current article if not at the article-selection prompt.

continues

Table 34.4 Continued

Command	Description
<Shift-n>	Goes to the next article.
<Ctrl-Shift-n>	Goes to the next article with the same subject as the current article.
<p>	Scans backward for the previous unread article; stays at current article if none is found.
<Shift-p>	Goes to the previous article.
<Ctrl-Shift-r>	Goes to the last previous article with the subject that's the same as the current article.
<h>	Displays help for article selection mode.
<r>	Replies to the article author via e-mail.
<Shift-r>	Replies to the article author via e-mail, including the current article.
<f>	Posts a follow-up article.
<Shift-f>	Posts a follow-up article, including the original article in the new article.
<s>*filename*	Saves the current article to a file named *filename*.
<q>	Quits the current group and returns to newsgroup selection mode.

These are only some of the options available within rn and trn. These are feature-rich programs that allow lots of user customization. Refer to the man pages and the online help for more information.

From Here...

In this chapter, you explored the structure of Usenet, the basics of reading and posting articles, the hierarchy of newsgroups, and Usenet's general culture. With a little patience, you'll find Usenet news to be an indispensable source of information. You can find more information about electronic communication and the Internet in the following chapters:

- Chapter 31, "Surfing the Internet with the World Wide Web," describes the various types of information you can find on the Internet.
- Chapter 33, "Using Electronic Mail," shows how to communicate with other people by using the e-mail system.

Setting Up a Linux Web Server

Getting Started with Apache

by Steve Burnett

To use a Linux system as a Web server, you must install special server software on your system. Two of the most popular UNIX Web server packages are Apache and NCSA. In fact, a June 1998 survey showed that Apache accounted for more than 53 percent of all installed Web servers. Although this chapter, like several others, is specific to the Apache server, the vocabulary is certainly applicable to other Web servers. The NCSA family of servers has much in common with Apache with respect to configuration files, because Apache was derived originally from the NCSA 1.3 server, and maintaining backward compatibility with existing NCSA servers was a mandate with the development team.

This chapter deals with all the essential steps needed to install the software and bring up a running, breathing, living server. If you've installed an Apache or NCSA server before, you can probably safely skip this chapter, although you should skim it to look for essential differences.

Compiling Apache

Apache is known to compile on just about every UNIX variant: Solaris 2.X, SunOS 4.1.X, Irix 5.X and 6.X, Linux, FreeBSD/NetBSD/BSDI, HP-UX, AIX, Ultrix, OSF1, NeXT, Sequent, A/UX, SCO, UTS, Apollo Domain/OS, QNX, and probably a few you've never even tried yet. A port to OS/2 has been done, and a beta Windows NT 4.0 port has been completed as of this writing. Portability has been a high priority for the development team.

Apache binaries and their sources are included with most distributions of Linux. The complete source code for Apache is also provided. Because there are Apache binaries on the CD-ROMs, you can skip the compilation process and move on to the next section, if you're in a hurry to get Apache up and running. However, if you ever want to add new modules or tweak the functionality provided by Apache, you need to know how to compile it.

Copy the source code package to a part of your file system. You need several spare megabytes of disk to compile the server. Unpack it and go to the /src subdirectory. A sequence of commands to do this might look like the following:

```
cd /CDROM
cp apache_1.3.0.tar.gz /usr/local/apache/
cd /usr/local/apache/
tar -zxvf apache_1.3.0.tar
cd src
```

Step 1: Edit the Configuration File

The Configuration file is used by the Configure program to create a Makefile specifically targeted to your platform, with any runtime defines set, if necessary, and with the modules you've chosen compiled together. It also creates a modules.c, which contains information about which modules to link together at compilation time.

You must declare which C compiler you're using (most likely gcc), and you must uncomment the appropriate setting for AUX_CFLAGS. Just look down through the Makefile for the Linux entry for AUX_CFLAGS, which might look like this:

```
CC=gcc
AUX_CFLAGS = -DLINUX
```

> **N O T E** For the CFLAGS definition, if you want every file with the execute bit set to be parsed for
> server-side includes, set -DXBITHACK. If you want to eliminate the overhead of performing
> the reverse-DNS lookup when an entry is written to the logfile, set -DMINIMAL_DNS.

▶ **See** "Server-Side Includes," **p. 693**

If, on the other hand, you want to have an even greater sense of confidence in the host name, you can set -DMAXIMAL_DNS. You would set this if you were protecting parts of your site based on host name. Doing this is optional and is provided mostly for backward compatibility with NCSA 1.3. ■

At the bottom of the file is a list of packaged modules that come with the Apache distribution. Notice that not all of them are compiled into the final program by default. To include a module in the build, uncomment the entry for it. Notice that some modules are mutually exclusive. For example, it wouldn't be wise to compile the configurable logging module and the common logging module at the same time.

Also, some modules, such as mod_auth_dbm, might require linking to an external library and need an entry added to the EXTRA_LIBS line. You learn more about modules in a little bit; for the purposes of getting up and running, I recommend simply using the defaults as provided.

Step 2: Run the Configure Script

The configure script is a simple Bourne shell script that takes the configuration file and creates a Makefile out of it, as well as modules.c.

Step 3: Run *make*

The make command compiles the server. You might see some warnings about data types, particularly if you compiled with -Wall set, but none of the errors should be fatal.

If all went well, you should now have an executable program in your src/ directory called httpd.

Establishing the File Hierarchy

The next step in the process of setting up a server is to make some fundamental decisions regarding where on the file system different parts of the server will reside. Write down your decisions for each of these; you will need them in the next section, "Performing a Basic Configuration."

The first thing you need to decide is where the *server root* will be. This is the subdirectory in which the server will reside and from which the conf/ directory, the logs/ and cgi-bin/ subdirectories, and other server-related directories lead. The default suggestion is to have this as /usr/local/apache although the usual server root is /pub/htdocs. You can have your configuration files and logfiles in other locations. The server root was designed to be a convenient

Part

VII

Ch

35

place to keep everything server-related together. Also, if the server crashes and leaves a core file, it will be found in the server root directory.

The second decision is where the *document root*, the directory in which all your HTML and other media reside, will be located. A file called myfile.html in the document root would be referenced as http://host.com/index.html. This directory can be a subdirectory of the server root, or it can be outside the server root and in its own directory. It's commonly located as a subdirectory of the server root and named htdocs. If, for more disk space or other reasons, you choose to move the document root out of the server root directory, you should give it a pretty short name—for example, /home/www or /www/htdocs. If you're implementing a Web server on top of an FTP server, for example, you might want to point the document root at /home/ftp/pub.

Finally, you need to decide where on your server you'll keep your logfiles. This space should have a fairly large working area, depending on how busy you estimate your server will be. For a point of reference, a site with 100K hits per day (which would fall under moderate traffic, relatively speaking) can expect to generate 15MB per day of logfile information. For performance reasons, it's usually best to have the log directory on a separate disk partition or even a separate disk drive altogether, because on even a moderately busy server the access log can be written to several times per second.

Performing a Basic Configuration

This section covers the minimal set of changes you need to make to the configuration files in order to launch a basic Web site.

Apache has three separate configuration files. This model goes back to NCSA, and the reasoning is sound: There are largely three main areas of administrative configuration, so setting them up as separate files allows Webmasters to give different write permissions to each if they so desire.

You'll find the configuration files for Apache in the conf/ subdirectory of the server root directory. Each has been provided with a -dist file-name suffix; it's recommended that you make a copy without the -dist and edit those new files, keeping the -dist versions as backups and reference.

The basic format of the configuration files is a combination of a shell-like interface and pseudo-HTML. The elemental unit is the directive, which can take a number of arguments—essentially,

```
Directive argument argument....
```

that is,

```
Port 80
```

or

```
AddIcon /icons/back.gif ..
```

You can also group directives together inside certain pseudo-HTML tags. Unlike HTML, these tags should be on their own line as in the following example:

```
<Virtualhost www.myhost.com>
DocumentRoot /www/htdocs/myhost.com
ServerName www.myhost.com
</Virtualhost>
```

> **N O T E** The Virtualhost directive allows a single server to pretend to be multiple servers. For example, the host specified above, www.myhost.com, doesn't have to be on a computer named www.myhost.com; it could reside on a computer named hosts.netwharf.com. ■

httpd.conf

The first configuration file to look at is httpd.conf. This is the file that sets the basic system-level information about the server, such as what port it binds to, which users it runs under, and so on. If you aren't the systems administrator of the site at which you're installing the server, you might want to ask the administrator to help you with these questions.

The essential items to cover in this file include the following:

■ Port *number*

For example:

```
Port 80
```

This is the TCP/IP port number to which the Web server binds. Port 80 is the default port in http: URLs. In other words, http://www.myhost.com/ is equivalent to http://www.myhost.com:80/.

For a number of reasons, however, you might want to run your server on a different port; for example, there might already be a server running on port 80, or you might want to keep this server secret. (If there's sensitive information, however, you should at least use host-based access control, if not password protection.)

■ User *#number_or_uid*
  Group *#number_or_uid*

For example:

```
User nobody
Group nogroup
```

Apache needs to be launched as root to bind to a port lower than 1024. Immediately after grabbing the port, Apache changes its effective user ID to something else, typically as user nobody. This is very important for security reasons.

This user ID needs to be able to read files in the document root, and it must have read permission on the configuration files. The argument should be the actual user name; however, if you want to give a numeric user ID, prepend the number with a pound sign (#). The Group directive follows the same principle: Decide which group ID you want the server to run with.

N O T E Running your Web servers as root means that any hole in the server (be it through the server itself or through a CGI script, which is much more likely) could be exploited by an outside user to run a command on your machine. Thus, setting the user to nobody, www, or some other reasonably innocuous user ID is the safest bet. ■

- ■ ServerAdmin *email_address*

  Set the e-mail address of a user who can receive mail related to the actions of the server. In the case of a server error, the browser visiting your site will receive a message to the effect of "please report this problem to user@myhost.com." In the future, Apache might send warning e-mail to the ServerAdmin user if it encounters a major systems-related problem.

- ■ ServerRoot *directory*

  For example:

  ```
  ServerRoot /usr/local/apache
  ```

  Set the server root you decided on earlier. Give the full path, and don't end it with a slash.

- ■ ErrorLog *directory*/*filename*
  TransferLog *directory*/*filename*

  Specify exactly where to log errors and Web accesses. If the filename you give doesn't start with a slash, it's presumed to be relative to the server root directory. I suggested earlier that the logfiles be sent to a separate directory outside the server root; this is where you specify the logging directory and the name of the logfiles within that directory.

- ■ ServerName *DNS_hostname*

  At times, the Web server will have to know the host name it's being referred to as, which can be different from its real host name. For example, the name www.myhost.com might actually be a DNS alias for gateway.myhost.com. In this case, you don't want the URLs generated by the server to be http://gateway.myhost.com/. ServerName allows you to set that precisely.

srm.conf

The second configuration file to cover before launch is srm.conf. The important things to set in that file include the following:

- ■ DocumentRoot *directory*

  As described before, this is the root level of your tree of documents, which could be either /usr/local/apache/htdocs or /www/htdocs. This directory must exist and be readable by the user (usually nobody) the Web server runs as.

■ ScriptAlias *request_path_alias directory*

ScriptAlias lets you specify that a particular directory *outside* the document root can be aliased to a path in the request *and* that objects in that directory are executed rather than simply read from the file system. For example, the default offering

```
ScriptAlias /cgi-bin/ /usr/local/apache/cgi-bin/
```

means that a request for http://www.myhost.com/cgi-bin/fortune will execute the program /usr/local/apache/cgi-bin/fortune. Apache comes bundled with a number of useful beginner CGI scripts, simple shell scripts that illustrate CGI programming.

Finally, the directory containing the CGI scripts should *not* be under the document root. Bizarre interactions between the code that handles ScriptAlias and the code that handles request/path name resolution could cause problems.

access.conf

access.conf is structured more rigidly than the other configuration files; the content is contained within <Directory></Directory> pseudo-HTML tags that define the scope of the directives listed within.

▶ **See** "Configuration Basics," **p. 684**

So for example, the directives between

```
<Directory /www/htdocs>
```

and

```
</Directory>
```

affect everything located under the /www/htdocs directory. Furthermore, wildcards can be used. For example,

```
<Directory /www/htdocs/*/archives/>
....
</Directory>
```

applies to /www/htdocs/list1/archives/, /www/htdocs/list2/archives/, and so on.

Starting Up Apache

To start Apache, simply run the binary you compiled earlier (or your precompiled binary) with the -f flag pointing to the httpd.conf file also created earlier, as in this example:

```
/usr/local/apache/src/httpd -f /usr/local/apache/conf/httpd.conf
```

The following sample init script also activates the Apache Web server. The Red Hat distribution automatically installs this script if you select to install the Web server.

```
#!/bin/sh
#
# Startup script for the Apache Web Server
```

Part
VII

Ch
35

```
#
# chkconfig: 345 85 15
# description: Apache is a World Wide Web server.  It is used to serve \
# HTML files and CGI.
#
#


# Source function library.
. /etc/rc.d/init.d/functions

# See how we were called.
case "$1" in
  start)
        echo -n "Starting httpd: "
        daemon httpd
        echo
        touch /var/lock/subsys/httpd
        ;;
  stop)
        echo -n "Shutting down http: "
        kill 'cat /var/run/httpd.pid'
        echo httpd
        rm -f /var/lock/subsys/httpd
        rm -f /var/run/httpd.pid
        ;;
  status)
        status httpd
        ;;
  restart)
        $0 stop
        $0 start
        ;;
  *)
        echo "Usage: httpd.init {start¦stop¦restart¦status}"
        exit 1
esac

exit 0
```

It's probably a good idea at this point to use the ps command to see if httpd is running. Typically, something like ps -aux ¦ grep will suffice. To your surprise, you'll see a number of simultaneous httpd processes running. What's going on?

The first Web servers, such as CERN and NCSA, used the model of one main Web server cloning itself with every single request that came in. The clone would respond to the request, while the original server returned to listening to the port for another request. Although certainly a simple and robust design, the act of *cloning* (or, in UNIX terms, *forking*) was an expensive operation under UNIX, so loads above a couple hits per second were quite punishing even on the nicest hardware. It was also difficult to implement any sort of *throttling*, which reduced the amount of cloning that took place. When the number of clones was very high, it was hard for the original server to know how many clones were still around. Thus, servers had no easy way to refuse or delay connections based on a lack of resources.

Apache—like NCSA 1.4+, Netscape's Web servers, and a couple of other UNIX-based Web servers—instead uses the model of a group of persistent children running in parallel. The children are coordinated by a parent process, which can tell how many children are alive, spawn new children (if necessary), and even terminate old children if there are many idle ones, depending on the situation. (*Parent* and *child* are the actual UNIX terms.)

Back to the server. Fire up your Web browser and point it to your local server. (Use the usual http:// format and append the ServerName parameter you defined in the httpd.conf file.) Did it work? If all went well, you should be able to see a directory index listing of everything in the document root directory, or if an index.html is in that directory, you would see the contents of that file.

Table 35.1 shows other command-line options.

Table 35.1   Command-Line Options for *httpd*

Option	Result
-d *serverroot*	Sets the initial value for ServerRoot.
-X	Runs the server in single-process mode. (This is useful for debugging purposes, but don't run the server in this mode for serving content to the outside world.)
-v	Prints the version of the server, and then exits.
-?	Prints the list of available command-line arguments to Apache.

After you check to make sure that Apache starts up correctly, you'll probably want to add the startup command to your system boot scripts so that Apache will start automatically when the system boots. A typical location for the startup command would be in the file /etc/rc.d/rc.local.

Debugging the Server Startup Process

Apache is usually pretty good about giving meaningful error messages, but some are explained in more detail in the following sections.

Open File Error Messages

```
httpd: could not open document config file .....
fopen: No such file or directory
```

These open file error messages are usually the result of giving just a relative path to the -f argument, so Apache looks for the file(s) relative to the compiled-in server root (what's set in src/httpd.h) instead of those relative to the directory you're in. You must give the full path or the path relative to the compiled-in server root.

Part
VII

Ch

35

Port and Bind Error Messages

```
httpd: could not bind to port [X]
bind: Operation not permitted
```

The port and bind error messages are most likely caused by attempting to run the server on a port below 1024 without launching it as "root." Most UNIX operating systems, including Linux, prevent people without root access from trying to launch any type of server on a port less than 1024. If you launch the server as root, the error message should disappear.

```
httpd: could not bind to port
bind: Address already in use
```

These port and bind error messages mean that something is already running on your machine at the port you've specified. Do you have another Web server running? No standard UNIX mechanism is available for determining what's running on what ports; on most systems, the file /etc/services can tell you what the most common daemons are, but it's not a complete list. You could also try using the netstat command, with various options such as -a.

Bad User or Group Name Messages

```
httpd: bad user name ....
httpd: bad group name ....
```

Bad user or group name error messages mean that the user or the group you specified in httpd.conf doesn't actually exist on your system. You might see errors telling you that particular files or directories don't exist. If it looks as though the files are there, make sure that they're readable by the user IDs that the server runs as (that is, both root and nobody).

Initial Server Startup Error Messages

Suppose that Apache has started up and, according to ps, it's actually running. But when you go to the site, you experience the following problems or error messages:

- *No connection at all.* Make sure that no firewalls are between you and the server that would filter out packets to the server. Second, try using telnet to the port you launched the Web server on—for example, telnet myhost.com 80. If you don't get a Connected to myhost.com message back, your connection isn't even making it to the server in the first place.

- *403 Access Forbidden.* Your document root directory may be unreadable, or you might have something in your access.conf file that prevents access to your site from the machine where your Web browser is.

- *500 Server Error.* Is your front page a CGI script? The script might be failing.

These are the most common errors made in initial server startups. If you can confirm that contact with the server is actually being made, the next best place to look for error information is in the ErrorLog.

Setting Up Apache-SSL

At this point, we'll take a slight detour and discuss a variant of the Apache Web server, Apache-SSL, which can conduct secure transactions over the Secure Sockets Layer protocol. SSL is an RSA public-key-based encryption protocol developed by Netscape Communications for use in the Netscape Navigator browser and Netscape Web servers.

Until recently, the only option for doing SSL transactions on the World Wide Web has been to use a proprietary server, such as the Netscape Commerce server or the OpenMarket Secure server. Strongly encrypting versions of these servers haven't been available outside the United States due to export restrictions in the states.

Eric Young, author of the widely used libdes package, with Tim Hudson wrote a library that implements SSL, eponymously named SSLeay. The SSLeay package has since expanded to become an all-purpose cryptography and certificate-handling library, while retaining the same name, SSLeay.

Ben Laurie, a member of the Apache Group, then took the SSLeay library and interfaced it with the Apache server, making his patches available to people on the Net. Sameer Parekh of Community ConneXion, Inc. (hereafter referred to as C2) then took Ben Laurie's patches and built a package legal for use within the United States.

Because the RSA technology used by SSL in the United States is covered by patents owned by RSA Data Security, Inc. (RSADSI) (**www.rsa.com**), it isn't legal to use the SSLeay package "out-of-the-box" within the United States. C2 licensed the RSA technology to make use of the package legal within the United States by using the "RSAREF" package, produced by RSADSI and Consensus Development Corporation (**www.consensus.com**).

Due to export restrictions, it isn't legal for someone outside the United States to download and install the C2 Apache-SSL package. In fact, we couldn't even put the SSL patches on the CD-ROM included with this book because the book would suddenly have earned the label "munition," and clearance from the U.S. government to export the book would have been required!

To learn more about SSL and Apache, go to the URL **http://www.apache-ssl.org**.

From Here...

You can learn more details about setting up, configuring, and running the Apache Web server in the following chapters:

- Chapter 36, "Configuring Apache," discusses the configuration options for Apache in greater detail.

- Chapter 37, "Managing an Internet Web Server," teaches you how to make your server robust, efficient, automated, and secure.

Part

VII

Ch

35

Configuring Apache

by Steve Burnett

Configuration Basics

By now you should have a running Web server, although it will be minimally configured. In this chapter, you learn about most of the functionality that comes bundled with the server. This chapter is organized as a series of tutorials so that if you're new to Apache, you can get up to speed quickly. Toward the end of the chapter, you dive into some experimental Apache modules as well.

Because of its rapid pace of development, it's possible that Apache will have some significantly new functionality by the time you read this chapter. However, the existing functionality isn't likely to change much. The Apache Group has commitment to backward compatibility.

The srm.conf and access.conf files are where most of the configuration related to the actual objects on the server takes place. The srm.conf file is also known as the `ResourceConfig` file, which is a directive that can be set in httpd.conf; the access.conf file is also known as the `AccessConfig` file, which also is a directive in httpd.conf.

The names *srm.conf* and *access.conf* are mostly historical. At one point, when the server was still NCSA, the only thing access.conf was used for was setting permissions, restrictions, authentication, and so forth. Then, when directory indexing was added, the cry went out for the capability to control certain characteristics on a directory-by-directory basis. The access.conf file was the only configuration file that had any kind of structure for tight access control: the pseudo-HTML `<Directory>` container.

▶ **See** "access.conf," **p. 677**

With Apache's configuration file-parsing routines, most directives can literally appear anywhere—for example, within `<Directory>` containers in access.conf, within `<VirtualHost>` containers in httpd.conf, and so on. However, for sanity's sake, you should keep some structure to the configuration files. You should put server-processing-level configuration options (such as `Port` and `<VirtualHost>` containers) in httpd.conf, generic server resource information (such as `Redirect`, `AddType`, and directory indexing information) in srm.conf, and per-directory configurations in access.conf.

In addition to the `<Directory>` container is the `<Limit>` container, which is used within `<Directory>` containers to specify certain HTTP methods to which particular directives apply. Examples are given later in this chapter.

N O T E   Although this chapter is still useful, release 1.3.0 and higher of Apache include a GNU Autoconf-style front-end, which supports all previous configuration options as well as the enhancements in 1.3.0 and above. Use of that interface for configuration is recommended in general. ■

Per-Directory Configuration Files

Before you get too deep into the different configuration options, look at a mechanism that controls configuration on a directory-by-directory basis. This is accomplished by using a configuration file that's local to the directory that you want to configure. You can already control subdirectory options in access.conf, as outlined in Chapter 35, "Getting Started with Apache." However, for several reasons, you may want to allow these configurations to be maintained by users other than those with the power to restart the server (such as users maintaining their home pages). For that purpose the AccessFileName directive was invented.

▶ **See** "Performing a Basic Configuration," **p. 674**

The default AccessFileName is .htaccess. If you want to use something else—for example, .acc—you would say the following in the srm.conf file:

```
AccessFileName .acc
```

If looking for the AccessFileName file is enabled and a request comes in that translates to the file /www/htdocs/path/path2/file, the server will look for /.acc, /www/.acc, /www/htdocs/.acc, /www/htdocs/path/.acc, and /www/htdocs/path/path2/.acc in that order. Also, if it finds the file, the server will parse the file to see what configuration options apply. (Remember that this parsing has to happen with each hit, separately, so this can be a big performance hit.) You can turn off the AccessFileName directive by setting the following options in your access config file:

```
<Directory />
AllowOverride None
</Directory>
```

For the sake of brevity and clarity, assume that the AccessFileName option has set the name of these files to be .htaccess. What options can these files affect? The AllowOverride directive controls the range of available options within the <Directory> container in the AccessConfig file, as mentioned previously. Table 36.1 lists the exact arguments for AllowOverride.

Table 36.1 The *AllowOverride* Arguments

Argument	Result
AuthConfig	When listed, .htaccess files can specify their own authentication directives, such as AuthUserFile, AuthName, AuthType, and require.
FileInfo	When listed, .htaccess can override any settings for meta-information about files by using directives such as AddType, AddEncoding, and AddLanguage.
Indexes	When listed, .htaccess files can locally set directives that control the rendering of the directory indexing, as implemented in the mod_dir.c module—for example, FancyIndexing, AddIcon, and AddDescription.
Limit	This argument allows the use of the directives that limit access based on host name or host IP number (allow, deny, and order).
Options	This argument allows the use of the Options directive.
All	This argument allows all of the preceding arguments to be true.

`AllowOverride` options aren't merged, meaning that if the configuration for /path/ is different than the configuration for /, the /path/ one will take precedence because it's deeper.

MIME Types: *AddType* and *AddEncoding*

A fundamental element of the HTTP protocol, and the reason why the Web was so natural as a home for multiple media formats, is that every data object transferred through HTTP had an associated MIME type.

> **N O T E**   The origins of MIME (*Multipurpose Internet Mail Extensions*) lie in an effort to standardize the transmission of documents of multiple media through e-mail. Part of the MIME specification was that e-mail messages could contain meta-information in the headers identifying the data being sent. One type of MIME header is `Content-Type`, which states the format or data type the object is in. For example, HTML is given the label `"text/html,"` and JPEG images are given the label `"image/jpeg."` ▨

ON THE WEB

A registry of MIME types is maintained by the Internet Assigned Numbers Authority at this site:

> http://www.isi.edu/div7/iana/

When a browser asks a server for an object, the server gives that object to the browser and states what its `Content-Type` is. That way, the browser can make an intelligent decision about how to render the document. For example, it can send it to an image program, to a PostScript viewer, or to a VRML viewer.

What this means to the server maintainer is that every object being served out must have the right MIME type associated with it. Fortunately, there has been a convention of expressing data type through two-, three-, or four-letter suffixes to the filename—for example, foobar.gif is most likely to be a GIF image.

What the server needs is a file to map the suffix to the MIME content type. Fortunately, Apache comes with such a file in its configuration directory—a file named mime.types. The simple format of this file consists of one record per line, where a record is a MIME type and a list of acceptable suffixes. Although more than one suffix may map to a particular MIME type, you can't have more than one MIME type per suffix. You can use the `TypesConfig` directive to specify an alternative location for the file.

The Internet is evolving so quickly that it would be hard to keep the mime.types file completely up-to-date. To overcome this difficulty, you can use a special directive, `AddType`, which can be put in the srm.conf file as follows:

```
AddType x-world/x-vrml wrl
```

Now, whenever the server is asked to serve a file that ends with .wrl, it knows to also send a header like the following:

```
Content-type: x-world/x-vrml
```

Thus, you don't have to worry about reconciling future distributions of the mime.types file with your private installations and configuration.

As you'll see in later pages, `AddType` is also used to specify "special" files that get magically handled by certain features within the server.

A sister to `AddType` is `AddEncoding`. Just as the MIME header `Content-Type` can specify the data format of the object, the `Content-Encoding` header specifies the *encoding* of the object. An encoding is an attribute of the object as it's being transferred or stored; semantically, the browser should know that it has to "decode" whatever it gets, based on the listed encoding. The most common use is with compressed files. For example, if you have

```
AddEncoding x-gzip gz
```

and if you then access a file named myworld.wrl.gz, the MIME headers sent in response will look like the following (MIME headers of this format accompany every transfer over the Web; these headers are not displayed by the browser but are used to define how to handle the incoming file):

```
Content-Type: x-world/x-vrml
Content-Encoding: x-gzip
```

And any browser worth its salt will know, "Oh, I have to decompress the file before handing it off to the VRML viewer."

N O T E   With Apache 1.3, the optional module mod_mime_magic (if compiled in) can analyze the contents of a file and assign it a file type extension if one isn't present. This module is based on a free version of the UNIX `file` command. ■

Alias, ScriptAlias, and *Redirect*

The `Alias`, `ScriptAlias`, and `Redirect` directives—all denizens of srm.conf and all implemented by the mod_alias.c module—allow you to have some flexibility with the mapping between `URL-Space` on your server and the actual layout of your file system.

Basically, any URL that looks like http://myhost.com/x/y/z isn't required to map to a file named x/y/z under the document root of the server, acting much like a symbolic link. For example:

```
Alias /path/ /some/other/path/
```

The preceding directive takes a request for an object from the mythical subdirectory */path* under the document root and maps it to another directory somewhere else entirely. For example, a request for

```
http://myhost.com/statistics/
```

might normally go to document root /statistics, except that for whatever reason you wanted it to point somewhere outside the document root (for example, /usr/local/statistics). For that you'd have to use the following command:

```
Alias /statistics/ /usr/local/statistics/
```

To the outside user, this would be completely transparent. If you use `Alias`, it's wise not to alias to somewhere else inside the document root. Furthermore, a request like

```
http://myhost.com/statistics/graph.gif
```

would get translated into a request for the file

```
/usr/local/statistics/graph.gif
```

`ScriptAlias` is just like `Alias`, with the side effect of making everything in the subdirectory by default a CGI script. This might sound a bit bizarre, but the early model for building Web sites had all the CGI functionality separated into a directory by itself, and referenced through the Web server as shown in the following:

```
http://myhost.com/cgi-bin/script
```

If you have in your srm.conf file

```
ScriptAlias /cgi-bin/ /usr/local/etc/httpd/cgi-bin/
```

then the preceding URL points to the script at /usr/local/etc/httpd/cgi-bin/script. As you'll see in a page or two, there's a more elegant way to specify that a file is a CGI script to be executed.

`Redirect` does just that—redirects the request to another resource. That resource could be on the same machine or somewhere else on the Net. Also, the match will be a substring match, starting from the beginning. For example, if you entered the command

```
Redirect /newyork http://myhost.com/maps/states/newyork
```

then a request for

```
http://myhost.com/newyork/index.html
```

would get redirected to

```
http://myhost.com/maps/states/newyork/index.html
```

Of course, the second argument to `Redirect` can be an URL at some other site. Just make sure that you know what you're doing.

> **CAUTION**
>
> Be wary of creating loops accidentally. For example,
>
> ```
> Redirect /newyork http://myhost.com/newyork/newyork
> ```
>
> can have particularly deleterious effects on the server.

A Better Way to Activate CGI Scripts

You read earlier that there's a more elegant way of activating CGI scripts than by using `ScriptAlias`. You can use the `AddType` directive and create a custom MIME type, like so:

```
AddType application/x-httpd-cgi cgi
```

When the server gets a request for a CGI file, the server maps to that MIME type and then catches itself and says, "I need to execute this rather than just dish it out like regular files." Thus, you can have CGI files in the same directories as HTML, GIF, and all your other files.

Directory Indexing

When Apache is given a URL to a directory instead of to a particular file as in this example:

```
http://myhost.com/statistics/
```

Apache first looks for a file specified by the DirectoryIndex directive in srm.conf. In the default configs, this file is index.html. You can set a list of files to search for or even an absolute path to a page or CGI script:

```
DirectoryIndex index.cgi index.html /cgi-bin/go-away
```

The preceding directive says to look for an index.cgi file in the directory first. If that can't be found, look for an index.html file in the directory. If neither can be found, redirect the request to /cgi-bin/go-away.

If the Apache server fails to find a match, Apache will create—completely on-the-fly—an HTML listing of all the files available in the directory.

There are quite a few ways to customize the output of the directory indexing functionality. First, you need to ask yourself if you care about seeing things such as icons and last-modified times in the reports. If you do, then you want to turn to

```
FancyIndexing On
```

Otherwise, you'll just get a simple menu of the available files, which you may want for security or performance reasons.

If you choose to use the FancyIndexing option, you must ask whether you need to customize it further and, if so, how. The default settings for the directory indexing functionality are already pretty elaborate.

The AddIcon, AddIconByEncoding, and AddIconByType directives customize the selection of icons next to files. AddIcon matches icons at the filename level by using the pattern

```
AddIcon iconfile filename [filename] [filename]...
```

Thus, for example, the following line

```
AddIcon /icons/binary.gif .bin .exe
```

means that any file that ends in .bin or .exe should get the binary.gif icon attached. The filenames can also be a wildcard expression, a complete filename, or even one of two "special" names: ^^DIRECTORY^^ for directories and ^^BLANKICON^^ for blank lines. Thus, you can see lines like these:

```
AddIcon /icons/dir.gif ^^DIRECTORY^^
AddIcon /icons/old.gif *~
```

Finally, the iconfile can be a string containing the icon file's name and the alternate text to put into the ALT attribute. So, your examples should really be

```
AddIcon (BIN,/icons/binary.gif) .bin .exe
AddIcon (DIR,/icons/dir.gif) ^^DIRECTORY^^
```

The `AddIconByType` directive is a little bit more flexible and probably comes more highly recommended in terms of actual use. Rather than tie icons to filename patterns, it ties icons to the MIME type associated with the files. The syntax is very roughly the same:

```
AddIconByType iconfile mime-type [mime-type]...
```

mime-type can be either the exact MIME type matching what you've assigned a file, or it can be a pattern match. Thus, you see entries in the default configuration files like the following:

```
AddIconByType (SND,/icons/sound2,gif) audio/*
```

Using pattern matching is more robust than trying to match against filename suffixes only.

`AddIconByEncoding` is used mostly to distinguish compressed files from other types of files. This makes sense only if used with `AddEncoding` directives in your srm.conf file. The default srm.conf has these entries:

```
AddEncoding x-gzip gz
AddEncoding x-compress Z
AddIconByEncoding (CMP,/icons/compressed.gif) x-compress x-gzip
```

The `AddIconByEncoding` option sets the icon next to compressed files appropriately.

The `DefaultIcon` directive specifies the icon to use when none of the patterns match a given file when the directory index is generated:

```
DefaultIcon /icons/unknown.gif
```

It's possible to add text to the top and the bottom of the directory index listing. This capability is very useful as it turns the directory indexing capabilities from just a UNIX-like interface into a dynamic document interface. There are two directives to control this: `HeaderName` and `ReadmeName` which specify the filenames for the content at the top and bottom of the listing, respectively. These directives are shown as follows in the default srm.conf file:

```
HeaderName HEADER
ReadmeName README
```

When the directory index is being built, Apache will look for HEADER.html. If it finds it, it'll throw the content into the top of the directory index. If it fails to find that file, it'll look for just HEADER. If it finds HEADER, it will presume that the file is plain text and do things such as translate < characters to the < character sequence, and then insert it into the top of the directory index. The same process happens for the file README, except that the resulting text goes into the bottom of the generated directory index.

In many cases, be it for consistency or just plain old security reasons, you'll want to have the directory indexing engine just ignore certain types of files, such as emacs backup files or files beginning with a . (hidden files). The `IndexIgnore` directive allows you to specify the types of files to ignore when creating a directory index. The default setting is this:

```
IndexIgnore */.??* *~ *# */HEADER* */README* */RCS
```

This line might look cryptic, but it's basically a space-separated list of patterns. The first pattern matches against any . file that's longer than three characters. This way, the link to the higher-up directory (..) can still work. The second (*~) and third (*#) patterns are common for matching old emacs backup files. The next patterns are to avoid listing the same files used for HeaderName and ReadmeName. The last (*/RCS) is given because many sites use RCS, a software package for revision control maintenance, which stores its extra (rather sensitive) information in RCS directories.

Finally, you get to two very interesting directives for controlling the last set of options regarding directory indexing. The first is AddDescription, which works similarly to AddIcon:

```
AddDescription description filename [filename]...
```

For example,

```
AddDescription "My cat" /private/cat.gif
```

As elsewhere, *filename* can actually be a pattern, so you can have

```
AddDescription "An MPEG Movie Just For You!" *.mpg
```

Finally, you have the granddaddy of all options-setting directives, the smorgasbord of functionality control—IndexOptions. The syntax is simple:

```
IndexOptions option [option]...
```

Table 36.2 lists the available options.

Table 36.2   Available Options for *IndexOptions*

Option	Explanation
FancyIndexing	This option is the same as the separate FancyIndexing directive. (Sorry to confuse everyone, but backward compatibility demands bizarre things sometimes!)
IconsAreLinks	If this option is set, the icon will be clickable as a link to whatever resource the entry it's associated with links to. In other words, the icon becomes part of the hyperlink.
ScanHTMLTitles	When given a listing for an HTML file, the server will open the HTML file and parse it to obtain the value of the <TITLE> field in the HTML document, if it exists. This can put a pretty heavy load on the server, because it's a lot of disk accessing and some amount of CPU to extract the title from the HTML. Thus, it's not recommended unless you know you have the capacity.
SuppressDescription, SuppressLastModified, SuppressSize	These will suppress their respective fields (Description, Last Modified, and Size). Normally, each of those is a field in the output listings.

By default, none of these IndexOptions is turned on. The options don't *merge*, which means that when you're setting these on a per-directory basis by using access.conf or .htaccess files, setting the options for a more specific directory requires resetting the complete options listing. For example, envision the following in your access configuration file:

```
<Directory /pub/docs/>
IndexOptions ScanHTMLTitles
</Directory>
<Directory /pub/docs/others/>
IndexOptions IconsAreLinks
</Directory>
```

Directory listings done in or below the second directory, /pub/docs/others/, wouldn't have ScanHTMLTitles set. Why? Well, you figured administrators would need to be able to disable an option they had set globally in a specific directory. This was simpler than writing NOT logic into the options listings.

If you run into problems getting directory indexing to work, make sure that the settings you have for the Options directive in the access config files allow for directory indexing in that directory. Specifically, the Options directive must include Indexing. What's more, if you're using .htaccess files to set things such as AddDescription or AddIcon, the AllowOverride directive must include FileInfo in its list of options.

User Directories

Sites with many users sometimes prefer to be able to give their users access to managing their own parts of the Web tree in their own directories, using the URL semantics of

```
http://myhost.com/~user/
```

where *~user* is actually an alias to a directory in the user's home directory. This is different from the Alias directive, which could map only a particular pseudo-directory into an actual directory. In this case, you want *~user* to map to something like /home/user/public_html. Because the number of "users" can be very high, some sort of macro is useful here. That macro is the UserDir directive.

With UserDir, you specify the subdirectory within the users' home directories where they can put content, which is mapped to the *~user* URL. So in other words, the default

```
UserDir public_html
```

will cause a request for

```
http://myhost.com/~dave/index.html
```

to cause a lookup for the UNIX file

```
/home/dave/public_html/index.html
```

presuming that /home/dave is Dave's home directory.

Special Modules

Most of the functionality that distinguishes Apache from the competition has been implemented as modules to the Apache API. This has been extremely useful in allowing functionality to evolve separately from the rest of the server, and for allowing for performance tuning. The following sections cover that extra functionality in detail.

Server-Side Includes

Server-side includes are best described as a preprocessing language for HTML. The "processing" takes place on the server side. As such, visitors to your site never need to know that you use server-side includes, and thus they require no special client software. The format of these includes looks something like the following:

```
<!--#directive attribute="value" -->
```

Sometimes a given "directive" can have more than one attribute at the same time. The funky syntax is due to the desire to hide this functionality within an SGML comment—that way, your regular HTML validation tools will work without having to learn new tags or anything. The syntax is important; leaving off the final --, for example, will result in errors.

#include   The #include directive is probably the most commonly used. You use it to insert another HTML file into the HTML document. The allowed attributes for #include are virtual and file. The functionality of the file attribute is a subset of that provided by the virtual attribute, and it exists mostly for backward compatibility, so its use isn't recommended.

The virtual attribute tells the server to treat the value of the attribute as a request for a relative link—meaning that you can use ../ to locate objects above the directory and that other transformations, such as Alias, will apply. Here's an example of such:

```
<!--#include virtual="quote.txt" -->
<!--#include virtual="/toolbar/footer.html" -->
<!--#include virtual="../footer.html" -->
```

#exec   The #exec directive is used to run a script on the server side and insert its output into the SSI (server-side includes) document being processed. There are two choices: executing a CGI script by using the cgi attribute or executing a shell command by using the cmd attribute. For example,

```
<!--#exec cgi="counter.cgi" -->
```

takes the output of the CGI program counter.cgi and inserts it into the document.

> **N O T E**   The CGI output still has to include the "text/html" content-type header; otherwise, an error will occur. ◼

Likewise,

```
<!--#exec cmd="ls -l" -->
```

takes the output of a call to `ls -l` in the document's directory and inserts it into the output page as a replacement for the `#exec` command. Like the `file` attribute for the `#include` directive, this type of `#exec` command is mostly for backward compatibility, because it's something of a security hole in an untrusted environment.

N O T E There are definitely security concerns with allowing users access to CGI functionality and even greater concerns with `#exec cmd`, such as

```
cmd="cat /etc/passwd"
```

If a site administrator wants to let users use server-side includes but not use the `#exec` directive, he or she can set `IncludesNOEXEC` as an option for the directory in the access configurations. ■

#echo   The `#echo` directive has one attribute—`var`—whose value is any CGI environment variable as well as a small list of other variables, as shown in Table 36.3.

Table 36.3   Values for the *var* Attribute

Attribute	Definition
DATE_GMT	The current date in Greenwich Mean Time.
DATE_LOCAL	The current date in the local time zone.
DOCUMENT_NAME	The file system name of the SSI document, not including the directories below it.
DOCUMENT_URI	URI stands for *Uniform Resource Identifier*. In a Uniform Resource Locator (URL) of the format http://*host/path/file*, the URI is the */path/file* part.
LAST_MODIFIED	The date the SSI document was modified.

For example, the command

```
<!--#echo var="DATE_LOCAL" -->
```

inserts something along the lines of `Wednesday, 05-Mar-97 10:44:54 GMT` into the document.

#fsize, #flastmod   The `#fsize` and `#flastmod` directives print out the size and the last-modified date, respectively, of any object given by the URI listed in the `file` or `virtual` attribute, as in the `#include` directive. For example, this command

```
<!--#fsize file="index.html" -->
```

returns the size of the index.html file in that directory.

#config   You can modify the rendering of certain SSI directives by using the `#config` directive. The `sizefmt` attribute controls the rendering of the `#fsize` directive with values of `bytes` or `abbrev`. The exact number of bytes is printed when `bytes` is given, whereas an abbreviated version of the size (in KB for kilobytes or MB for megabytes) is given when `abbrev` (the default) is set. For example, a snippet of SSI HTML like

```
<!--#config sizefmt="bytes" -->
The index.html file is <!--#fsize virtual="index.html" --> bytes
```

returns The index.html file is 4,522 bytes. Meanwhile,

```
<!--#config sizefmt="abbrev" -->
```

returns The index.html file is 4K bytes.

The timefmt directive controls the rendering of the date in the DATE_LOCAL, DATE_GMT, and LAST_MODIFIED values for the #echo directive. It uses the same format as the strftime call. (In fact, the server does call strftime, a system call that formats the time in a string of specified length.) The string format consists of variables that begin with %. For example, %H is the hour of the day, in 24-hour format. For directions on how to construct a strftime-format date string, consult strftime's man page for a list of variables.

An example might be

```
<!--#config timefmt="%Y/%m/%d-%H:%M:%S" -->
```

with the resulting date string for Jan. 2, 1997, at 12:30 in the afternoon as

```
1997/01/02-12:30:00
```

Finally, the last attribute the #config directive can take is errmsg, which is simply the error to print out if there are any problems parsing the document. For example, the right default is

```
<!--#config errmsg="An error occurred while processing this directive" -->
```

Cookies

HTTP *cookies* are a method for maintaining statefulness in a stateless protocol. What does this mean? In HTTP, a session between a client and a server typically spans many separate actual TCP connections, thus making it difficult to tie together accesses into an application that requires state, such as a shopping-cart application. Cookies are a solution to that problem. As implemented by Netscape in its browser and subsequently by many others, servers can assign clients a cookie, meaning some sort of opaque string whose meaning is significant only to the server itself, and then the client can give that cookie back to the server on subsequent requests.

The mod_cookies module nicely handles the details of assigning unique cookies to every visitor, based on the visitor's host name and a random number. This cookie can be accessed from the CGI environment as the HTTP_COOKIE environment variable, for the same reason that all HTTP headers are accessible to CGI applications. The CGI scripts can use this as a key in a session-tracking database, or it can be logged and tallied up to get a good, if undercounted, estimate of the total number of users that visited a site, not just the number of hits or even number of unique domains.

Happily, there are no configuration issues here. Simply compile with mod_cookies and away you go. It couldn't be easier.

Configurable Logging

For most folks, the default logfile format (also known as *Common Logfile Format*, or CLF) doesn't provide enough information when it comes to doing a serious analysis of the efficacy of your Web site. It provides basic numbers in terms of raw hits, pages accessed, hosts accessing, timestamps, and so forth, but it fails to capture the "referring" URL, the browser being used, and any cookies being used. So there are two ways to get more data for your logfiles: by using the NCSA-compatibility directives for logging certain bits of information to separate browsers or by using Apache's own totally configurable logfile format.

NCSA Compatibility   For compatibility with the NCSA 1.4 Web server, two modules were added. These modules log the User-Agent and Referer headers from the HTTP request stream.

User-Agent is the header most browsers send that identifies what software the browser is using. Logging of this header can be activated by an AgentLog directive in the srm.conf file or in a virtual-host-specific section. This directive takes one argument, the name of the file to which the user-agents are logged—for example,

```
AgentLog logs/agent_log
```

To use the AgentLog directive, you need to ensure that the mod_log_agent module has been compiled and linked to the server.

Similarly, the Referer header is sent by the browser to indicate the tail end of a link. In other words, when you're on a page with an URL of "A," and there's a link on that page with an URL of "B," and you follow that link, the request for page "B" includes a Referer header with the URL of "A." This is very useful for finding what sites link to your site, and what proportion of traffic they account for.

The logging of the Referer header is activated by a RefererLog directive, which points to the file to which the referers get logged:

```
RefererLog logs/referer_log
```

One other option the Referer logging module provides is RefererIgnore, a directive that allows you to ignore Referer headers. RefererIgnore is useful for weeding out the referers from your own site, if all you're interested in is links to you from other sites. For example, if your site is www.myhost.com, you might want to use the following:

```
RefererIgnore www.myhost.com
```

Remember that logging of the Referer header requires compiling and linking in mod_log_referer.

Totally Configurable Logging   The previous modules were provided, like many Apache features, for backward compatibility. They have some problems, though. Because they don't contain any other information about the request they're logging from, it's nearly impossible to tell which Referer fields went to which specific objects on your site. Ideally, all the information about a transaction with the server can be logged into one file, extending the common logfile format or replacing it altogether. Well, such a beast exists in the mod_log_config module.

The mod_log_config module implements the LogFormat directive, which takes as its argument a string, with variables beginning with % to indicate different pieces of data from the request. Table 36.4 lists the variables.

Table 36.4   Variables for the *LogFormat* Directive

Variable	Definition
%h	Remote host.
%l	Remote identification via identd.
%u	Remote user, as determined by any user authentication that may take place. If the user wasn't authenticated and the status of the request is a 401 (authorization error), this field may be bogus.
%t	Common logfile format for time.
%r	First line of request.
%s	Status. For requests that are internally redirected, this is the status of the original request; %>s will give the last.
%b	Bytes sent.
%{Foobar}i	Contents of Foobar: header line(s) in the request from the client to the server.
%{Foobar}o	Contents of Foobar: header line(s) in the response from the server to the client.

For example, if you want to capture in your log just the remote host name, the object requested, and the timestamp, you would use the following:

```
LogFormat "%h \"%r\" %t"
```

And that would log things that looked like

```
host.outsider.com "GET / HTTP/1.0" [06/Mar/1996:10:15:17]
```

You Can Quote Me on This

You really have to use quotation marks around the request variable. The configurable logging module will automatically interpret the values of the variables, rather than just read the variable name. Use a slash-quote, \", to indicate that you want an actual quote character rather than the end of the string. For example, if you want to add logging of the User-Agent string, your log format would become

```
LogFormat "%h \"%r\" %t \"%{User-Agent}i\""
```

continues

continued

Because the User-Agent field typically has spaces in it, it too should be quoted. Suppose that you want to capture the Referer field:

```
LogFormat "%h \"%r\" %t %{Referer}i"
```

You don't need the escaping quotation marks because **Referer** headers, as URLs, don't have spaces in them. However, if you're building a mission-critical application, you may as well quote it also, because the **Referer** header is supplied by the client and, thus, there are no guarantees about its format.

The default logfile format is the Common Logfile Format (CLF), which is expressed as

```
LogFormat "%h %l %u %t \"%r\" %s %b"
```

In fact, most existing logfile analysis tools for CLF will ignore extra fields tacked onto the end. To capture the most important extra information and yet still be parsable by those tools, you might want to use this format:

```
LogFormat "%h %l %u %t \"%r\" %s %b %{Referer}i \"%{User-Agent}i\""
```

TIP If you want even more control over what gets logged, you can use the configurable logging module to implement a simple conditional test for variables. This way, you can configure it to log variables only when a particular status code is—or isn't—returned. The format for trapping a status code is to insert a comma-separated list of those codes between the % and the letter of the variable:

```
%404,403{Referer}i
```

This example means that the Referer header will be logged only if the status returned by the server is a 404 Not Found or a 403 Access Denied. All other times just a - is logged. Having only 403 or 404 errors logged would be useful if all you cared about using Referer for was to find old links that point to resources no longer available.

The negation of the Referer status code is to put an exclamation point (!) at the beginning of the list of status codes. For example,

```
%!401u
```

logs the user in any user authentication transaction, unless the authentication failed, in which case you probably don't want to see the name of the bogus user anyway.

Remember that, like many functions, logging functions can be configured per virtual host. Thus, if you want all logs from all virtual hosts on the same server to go to the same log, you might want to do something like

```
LogFormat "hosta ...."
```

in the <VirtualHost> sections for hosta and

```
LogFormat "hostb ...."
```

in the <VirtualHost> sections for hostb. More details about virtual hosts appear later in the section "Virtual Hosts."

N O T E You have to compile in mod_log_config in order to configure logging on a "per-virtual-host" basis. You must also make sure that the default logging module, mod_log_common, isn't compiled in; otherwise, the server will get confused. ▦

Content Negotiation

Content negotiation is the mechanism by which a Web client can express to the server what data types it knows how to render and, based on that information, the server can give the client the "optimal" version of the resource requested. Content negotiation can happen on a number of different characteristics—the content type of the data (also called the *media type*), the human language the data is in (such as English or French), the character set of the document, and its encodings.

Content-Type Negotiation If you want to use JPEG images inline on your pages but don't want to alienate users with browsers that can't handle inline JPEG images, you also can make a GIF version of that image. Although the GIF file might be larger or only 8-bit, that's still better than giving the browser something it can't handle, causing a broken link. So, the browser and the server *negotiate* for which data format the server sends to the client.

The specifications for content negotiation have been a part of HTTP since the beginning. Unfortunately, it can't be relied on as extensively as you'd like. For example, current browsers that implement plug-ins by and large don't express in the connection headers which media types they have plug-ins for. Thus, content negotiation currently can't be used to decide whether to send someone a ShockWave file or its Java equivalent. The only safe place to use content negotiation now is to distinguish between inline JPEG or GIF images on a page. Enough browsers in use today implement content negotiation closely enough to get this functionality.

The mod_negotiation.c file in Apache 1.0 implements the content-negotiation specifications in an older version of the HTTP/1.0 IETF draft, which at this writing is on its way to RFC status. Content negotiation was removed because the specification wasn't entirely complete. Content negotiation is getting significantly enhanced for HTTP/1.1. However, this doesn't mean it can't be safely used now for inline image selection.

To activate content negotiation, you must include the mod_negotiation.c module into the server. There are actually two ways to configure content negotiation:

- Using a type-map file describing all the variants of a negotiable resource with specific preference values and content characteristics
- Setting an Options value called MultiViews

Because your focus is pragmatic, you'll go only into the MultiViews functionality. If you're interested in the type-map functionality, the Apache Web site has documentation on it.

In your access.conf file, find the line that sets the options for the part of the site for which you want to enable content negotiation. (You can also set content negotiation for the whole site.) If

`MultiViews` isn't present in that line, it must be. Ironically enough, the `All` value doesn't include `MultiViews`. This is again for backward compatibility. So, you might have a line that looks like

```
Options Indexes Includes Multiviews
```

or

```
Options All MultiViews
```

When the `MultiViews` parameter is changed, you need to restart your server to implement the new configuration.

With `MultiViews` turned on, you can do the following: Place a JPEG image in a directory, such as /path/, and call it image.jpg. Now, make an equivalent GIF format image and place it in the same /path/ directory as image.gif. The URLs for these two objects are

```
http://host/path/image.jpg
```

and

```
http://host/path/image.gif
```

respectively. Now, if you ask your Web browser to fetch

```
http://host/path/image
```

the server will go into the /path/ directory, see the two image files, and then determine which image format to send based on what the client says it can support. In the case where the client says it can accept JPEG or GIF images equally, the server will choose the version of the image that's smaller and send that to the client. Usually, JPEG images are much smaller than GIF images.

So if you made your HTML look something like the following,

```
<HTML><HEAD>
<TITLE>Welcome to the Gizmo Home Page!</TITLE>
</HEAD><BODY>
<IMG SRC="/header" ALT="GIZMO Logo">
Welcome to Gizmo!
<IMG SRC="/products" ALT="Products">
<IMG SRC="/services" ALT="Services">
```

you can have separate GIF and JPEG files for header, products, and services. The clients will, for the most part, get what they claim they can support.

N O T E   If you have a file named image and a file named image.gif, the file named image will be returned if a request is made for image. Likewise, a request specifically for image.gif would never return image.jpg, even if the client knew how to render JPEG images. ■

Human-Language Negotiation   If `MultiViews` is enabled, you can also distinguish resources by the language they're in, such as French, English, and Japanese. This is done by adding more entries to the file suffix name space, which map to the languages the server wants to use, and then by giving them a ranking in which ties can be broken. Specifically, in the srm.conf file, add two new directives—AddLanguage and LanguagePriority. The formats are as follows:

```
AddLanguage en .en
AddLanguage it .it
AddLanguage fr .fr
AddLanguage jp .jp
LanguagePriority en fr jp it
```

Suppose that you want to negotiate the language on the file index.html, which you have available in English, French, Italian, and Japanese. You would create index.html.en, index.html.fr, index.html.it, and index.html.jp, respectively, and then reference the document as index.html. When a multilingual client connects, it should indicate in one of the request headers (specifically, Accept-Language) which languages it prefers, and the browser expresses that in standard two-letter notation. The server sees what the clients can accept and gives them "the best one." LanguagePriority is what organizes that decision of "the best one." If English is unacceptable to the client, try French; otherwise, try Japanese; otherwise, try Italian. LanguagePriority also states which one should be served if there's no Accept-Language header.

Because the language-mapping suffixes and the content-type suffixes share the same name space, you can mix them around. index.fr.html is the same as index.html.fr. Just make sure that you reference it with the correct negotiable resource.

As-Is Files

Often, you want to use headers in your documents, such as Expires:, but don't want to make the page a CGI script. The easiest way is to add the httpd/send-as-is MIME type to the srm.conf file.

```
AddType httpd/send-as-is asis
```

This means that any file that ends in .asis can include its own MIME headers. However, it must include two carriage returns before the actual body of the content. Actually, it should include two carriage-return/line-feed combinations, but Apache is forgiving and will insert the line feed for you. So if you want to send a document with a special custom MIME type that you don't want registered with the server, you can send the following:

```
Content-type: text/foobar
```

```
This is text in a very special "foobar" MIME type.
```

The most significant application I've run across for this is as an extremely efficient mechanism for doing *server-push* (inline graphic animation) objects without CGI scripts. The reason a CGI script is needed to create a server-push usually is that the content type usually includes the multipart separator (because a server-push is actually a MIME multipart message). In the following examples, XXXXXXXX indicates the boundary between the parts of the multipart message:

```
Content-type: multipart/x-mixed-replace;boundary=XXXXXXXX
```

```
--XXXXXXXX
Content-type: image/gif

....(GIF data)....
--XXXXXXXX
Content-type: image/gif

....(GIF data)....
--XXXXXXXX
....
```

By making a stream of data a simple file with the .asis parameter in the `AddType` directive instead of with a CGI script, you potentially save yourself a lot of overhead. Just about the only thing you lose is the capability to do timed pushes. For many people, slow Internet connection acts as a sufficient time valve.

If you have `MultiViews` turned on, you can add .asis to the end of a filename, and none of your links needs to be renamed. For example, foobar.html can easily become foobar.html.asis, yet you can still call it foobar.html.

One last compelling application of "asis" is being able to do HTTP redirection without needing access to server config files. For example, the following .asis file will redirect people to another location:

```
Status 302 Moved
Location: http://some.other.place.com/path/
Content-type: text/html

<HTML>
<HEAD><TITLE>We've Moved!</TITLE></HEAD>
<BODY>
<H1>We used to be here, but now we're
<A HREF="http://some.other.place.com/path/">over there. </A>
</H1>
</BODY></HTML>
```

The HTML body is there simply for clients who don't understand the 302 response.

Advanced Functionality

You may want to exert even more control over your server or customize the operating environment in very specific ways. You can configure the Apache server to support advanced functionality, such as access control and user authentication.

Host-Based Access Control

You can control access to the server, or even a subdirectory of the server, based on the host name, domain, or IP number of the client's machine. This is done by using the directives `allow` and `deny`, which can be used together with `order`. `allow` and `deny` can take multiple hosts:

```
deny from badguys.com otherbadguys.com
```

Typically, you want to do one of two things: you want to deny access to your server from everyone but a few other machines, or you want to grant access to everyone except a few hosts. Denying access from all but a few machines is accomplished with these commands:

```
order deny,allow
allow from mydomain.com
deny from all
```

This directive means, "Only grant access to hosts in the domain mydomain.com." This domain could include host1.mydomain.com, ppp.mydomain.com, and the-boss.mydomain.com.

The preceding directive tells the server to evaluate the `deny` conditions before the `allow` conditions when determining whether to grant access. Likewise, the "only exclude a couple of sites" case described earlier can be handled by using the following:

```
order allow,deny
allow from all
deny from badguys.com
```

`order` is needed because—again—the server needs to know which rule to apply first. The default for `order` is `deny,allow`.

In a third argument to `order`, called `mutual-failure`, a condition has to pass the `allow` and `deny` rules to succeed. In other words, it has to appear in the `allow` list, and it must not appear in the `deny` list, as in the following example:

```
order mutual-failure
allow from mydomain.com
deny from the-boss.mydomain.com
```

In this example, the-boss.mydomain.com is prevented from accessing this resource, but every other machine at mydomain.com can access it.

CAUTION

Protecting resources by host name is dangerous. It's relatively easy for a determined person who controls the reverse-DNS mapping for his IP number to spoof any host name he wants. Thus, it's strongly recommended that you use IP numbers to protect anything sensitive. In the same way, you can simply list the domain name to refer to any machine in that domain. You also can give fragments of IP numbers:

```
allow from 204.62.129
```

This will allow only hosts whose IP numbers match, such as 204.62.129.1 or 204.62.129.130.

Typically, these directives are used within a `<Limit>` container, and even that within a `<Directory>` container, usually in an access.conf configuration file. The following example is a good template for most protections; it protects the /www/htdocs/private directory from any host except those in the 204.62.129 IP space:

```
<Directory /www/htdocs/private>
Options Includes
AllowOverride None
<Limit GET POST>
```

continues

continued

```
order allow,deny
deny from all
allow from 204.62.129
</Limit>
</Directory>
```

User Authentication

When you place a resource under *user authentication*, you restrict access to it by requiring a name and password. This name and password is kept in a database on the server. This database can take many forms; Apache modules have been written to access flat-file databases, database management (DBM) file databases, mSQL databases (a freeware database), Oracle and Sybase databases, and more. This chapter covers only flat-file and DBM-format databases.

First, some basic configuration directives. The `AuthName` directive sets the authentication "realm" for the password-protected pages. The realm is what gets presented to clients when prompted for authentication, as in `Please enter your name and password for the realm`.

The `AuthType` directive sets the authentication type for the area. In HTTP/1.0, there's only one authentication type—Basic. HTTP/1.1 will have a few more, such as MD5.

The `AuthUserFile` directive specifies the file that contains a list of names and passwords, one pair per line. The passwords are encrypted by simple UNIX `crypt()` routines. For example,

```
joe:D.W2yvlfjaJoo
mark:21slfoUYGksIe
```

The `AuthGroupFile` directive specifies the file that contains a list of groups and members of those groups, separated by spaces like this:

```
managers: joe mark
production: mark shelley paul
```

Finally, the `require` directive specifies what conditions need to be met for access to be granted. It can list only specified users who may connect, specify a group or list of groups of users who may connect, or say any valid user in the database is automatically granted access. The following is an example:

```
require user mark paul
  (Only mark and paul may access.)

require group managers
  (Only people in group managers may access.)

require valid-user
  (Anyone in the AuthUserFile database may access.)
```

The configuration file ends up looking something like this:

```
<Directory /www/htdocs/protected/>
AuthName Protected
AuthType basic
AuthUserFile /usr/local/etc/httpd/conf/users
<Limit GET POST>
require valid-user
</Limit>
</Directory>
```

If you want to protect a directory to a particular group, the configuration file looks something like the following:

```
<Directory /www/htdocs/protected/>
AuthName Protected
AuthType basic
AuthUserFile /usr/local/etc/httpd/conf/users
AuthGroupFile /usr/local/etc/httpd/conf/group
<Limit GET POST>
require group managers
</Limit>
</Directory>
```

Database Management File Authentication

You also can configure Apache to use DBM files for faster password and group-membership lookups. To use a DBM file, you must have the mod_auth_dbm module compiled into the server.

DBM files are UNIX file types that implement a fast hash table lookup, making them ideal for handling large user/password databases. The flat-file systems require parsing the password file for every access until a match is found, potentially going through the entire file before returning a "can't find that user" error. Hash tables, on the other hand, know instantly whether a "key" exists in the database and what its value is.

Some systems use the ndbm libraries; some use the berkeley db libraries. However, the interface through Apache is exactly the same.

To use a DBM file for the database rather than a regular flat file, you use a different directive—AuthDBMUserFile —instead of AuthUserFile. Likewise, for the group file, AuthDBMGroupFile is used instead of AuthGroupFile.

Virtual Hosts

Apache implements a very clean way of handling *virtual hosts*, which is the mechanism for being able to serve more than one host on a particular machine. Due to a limitation in HTTP, serving multiple hosts is now accomplished by assigning more than one IP number to a machine and then having Apache bind differently to those different IP numbers. For example, a UNIX box might have 204.122.133.1, 204.122.133.2, and 204.122.133.3 pointing to it, with www.host1.com bound to the first, www.host2.com bound to the second, and www.host3.com bound to the third.

Apache 1.2 and above, via the HTTP 1.1 protocol specification, supports non-IP based virtual hosts as well. With this new feature, you no longer have to provide an IP address for each virtual host.

Virtual hosts are configured by using a container in httpd.conf. They look something like this:

```
<VirtualHost www.host1.com>
DocumentRoot /www/htdocs/host1/
TransferLog logs/access.host1
ErrorLog logs/error.host1
</VirtualHost>
```

The attribute in the `VirtualHost` tag is the host name, which the server looks up to get an IP address.

N O T E   If there's any chance that www.host1.com can return more than one number or that the Web server might have trouble resolving the host name to an IP number at any point, you might want to use the IP number instead. ■

Any directives put within the `VirtualHost` container pertain only to requests made to that host name. `DocumentRoot` points to a directory that presumably contains content specifically for www.host1.com.

Each virtual host can have its own access log, its own error log, its own derivative of the other logs out there, its own `Redirect` and `Alias` directives, its own `ServerName` and `ServerAdmin` directives, and more. In fact, the only things a virtual host server can't support out of the core set of directives are

ServerType	MaxRequestsPerChild
UserId	BindAddress
GroupId	PidFile
StartServers	TypesConfig
MaxSpareServers	ServerRoot
MinSpareServers	

If you plan to run Apache with a large number of virtual hosts, you need to be careful to watch the process limits. For example, some UNIX platforms allow processes to open only 64 file descriptors at once. Because an Apache child will consume one file descriptor per logfile per virtual host, 32 virtual hosts—each with its own transfer and error log—would quickly cross that process limit. You'll notice when you're running into problems of this kind if your error logs start reporting such errors as `unable to fork()`, or your access logs aren't getting written to at all. Apache does try to call `setrlimit()` (a system function call to try to limit processes) to handle this problem on its own, but the system sometimes prevents it from making the system call successfully.

Customized Error Messages

Apache can give customized responses in the event of an error. This is controlled by using the ErrorDocument directive. The syntax is as follows:

```
ErrorDocument HTTP_response_code action
```

HTTP_response_code is the event that triggers the *action*. The *action* can be

- A local URI to which the server is internally redirected
- An external URL to which the client is redirected
- A text string that starts with a " character and where the %s variable contains any extra information, if available

For example,

```
ErrorDocument 500 "Ack! We have a problem here: %s.
ErrorDocument 500 /errors/500.cgi
ErrorDocument 500 http://backup.myhost.com/
ErrorDocument 401 /subscribe.html
ErrorDocument 404 /debug/record-broken-links.cgi
```

Two extra CGI variables are passed to any redirected resource: REDIRECT_URL contains the original URL requested, and REDIRECT_STATUS gives the original status that caused the redirection. This will help the script if its job is to try to figure out what caused the error response.

Assorted httpd.conf Settings

A few additional configuration options just don't fit in anywhere else, because their functionality is a bit unique or different. These options include BindAddress, PidFile, and Timeout.

BindAddress   At startup, Apache binds to the port that it's specified to bind to for all IP numbers that the box has available. The BindAddress directive can be used to specify only a specific IP address to bind to. By using this specific address, you can run multiple copies of Apache, each serving different virtual hosts, rather than have one daemon handle all virtual hosts. This is useful if you want to run two Web servers with different system user IDs, for security and access control reasons.

Suppose that you have three IP addresses: 1.1.1.1, 1.1.1.2, and 1.1.1.3, with 1.1.1.1 being the primary address for the machine. You want to run three Web servers, but you want one of them to run as a different user ID than the other two. You'd have two sets of configuration files. The first configuration file would say something like this:

```
User web3
BindAddress 1.1.1.3
ServerName www.company3.com
DocumentRoot /www/company3/
```

The other configuration file would have the following:

Part
VII

Ch
36

```
User web1
ServerName www.company1.com
DocumentRoot /www/company1/
<VirtualHost 1.1.1.2>
ServerName www.company2.com
DocumentRoot /www/company2/
</VirtualHost>
```

If you launch the first, it will bind only to IP address 1.1.1.3. The second one, because it has no `BindAddress` directive, will bind to the port on all IP addresses. So you want to launch a server with the first set of configuration files, and then launch another copy of the server with the second set of configuration files. Two servers essentially would be running on the same machine.

PidFile   `PidFile` is the location of the file containing the process ID for Apache. This file is useful for being able to automate the shutdown or restart of the Web server. By default, this parameter is logs/httpd.pid. For example, you could shut down the server with this command:

```
cat /usr/local/etc/httpd/logs/httpd.pid ¦ xargs kill -15
```

You might want to move this out of the logs directory and into a directory such as /var, but it's not necessary.

Timeout   The `Timeout` directive specifies the amount of time that the server will wait between packets sent before considering the connection "lost." For example, 1200 (the default) means that the server will wait for 20 minutes after sending a packet before it considers the connection dead if no response comes back. Busy servers may want to shorten the time, at the cost of reduced service to low-bandwidth customers.

From Here...

You can learn more about running the Apache Web server in the following chapters:

- Chapter 35, "Getting Started with Apache," discusses the basics of installing and configuring the Apache Web server.
- Chapter 37, "Managing an Internet Web Server," shows you how to make your server robust, efficient, automated, and secure.

Managing an Internet Web Server

by Steve Burnett

One of the biggest strengths of the Apache Web server is that it's highly tunable. Just about every feature that imposes any sort of extra server load is an option, which means you can sacrifice features for speed if you need to do so. That said, Apache is designed for speed and efficiency. Even with all of Apache's features, you'll probably swamp a full T1 worth of bandwidth before exhausting the resources of a well-constructed Web server's hardware, be it a Linux system or something else.

Apache has also been designed to give site administrators control over where to draw the line between security and functionality. For some sites with many internal users, such as an Internet service provider, being able to control the policies toward what functionality can be used where is important. Meanwhile, a Web design shop might want complete flexibility, even if it means that an errant Common Gateway Interface (CGI) script could expose a security hole or do damage (incidentally, many feel that CGI in general is one big security risk).

Controlling Server Child Processes

▶ **See** "Starting Up Apache," **p. 677**

As you learned in Chapter 35, "Getting Started with Apache," Apache uses the concept of a *swarm* of semi-persistent *daemons*, sometimes also called *children*, running and answering queries simultaneously. Although the size of that swarm varies, there are limits to how large it can get and how quickly or slowly it can grow. This size issue is critical; one of the main performance problems with older servers that executed a `fork()` system call at every request was that there was no limit to the total number of simultaneous daemons, so when the main memory of a machine would get consumed and start swapping to disk, the machine would effectively lock up and become unuseable. This was colloquially called *daemon-spamming*.

Other server software lets you specify a fixed number of processes, with the "fork for every request" behavior kicking in if all the children are busy when a new request comes in. This is also not the best model—not only do many people set that fixed number too high (having 30 children running when only five are needed can hinder performance), but this design model also removed the protection against daemon-spamming.

So, the Apache model is to start out with a certain number of persistent processes, and make sure that you always keep some number (actually, a range somewhere between a minimum and a maximum) of "spare" processes to handle a wave of simultaneous requests. If you have to launch a few more processes to maintain the minimum number of spares, no problem. If you find yourself with more idle servers than your maximum number of spares, the excess idle ones can be killed. There's a maximum number of processes, beyond which no more will be launched, to protect the machine against daemon-spamming.

The algorithm to protect against too many processes bogging down or killing a server is configured by using the following configuration directives in /usr/local/apache/httpd.conf:

```
StartServers   10
MinSpareServers 5
MaxSpareServers 10
MaxClients    150
```

These numbers are the defaults. This says that when Apache launches, 10 children (StartServers) are automatically launched, regardless of the request load at start. If all 10 children are swamped, more are forked until all requests can be answered as fast as they're received. This requires at least five (MinSpareServers) but not more than 10 (MaxSpareServers) free servers to deal with *spikes* in requests (that is, when a sudden burst of requests come in well within half a second of each other). Incidentally, these spikes are often caused by browsers that open a separate TCP connection for each inline image in a page in an attempt to improve perceived performance to the user, often at the expense of the server and network.

> **NOTE** These directives are part of the core feature set of Apache and should be available on any version of Apache. ■

Part
VII

Ch
37

Usually a stable number of simultaneous child processes is reached, but if the requests are just pouring in (you've installed the Pamela Anderson Fan Club page on your site, for example), you might reach the MaxClients limit. At that point, requests will queue into your kernel's "listen" queue, waiting to get served. If still more pour in, your visitors will eventually see a "connections refused" message. However, this is still preferable to leaving the number of simultaneous processes unlimited, because the server would just launch children with wild abandon and start daemon-spamming, resulting in nobody getting any response from the server at all.

It's recommended that you don't adjust MaxClients, because 150 is a good number for most systems. However, you might be itching to see how many requests you can handle with that sixteen-multiprocessor Sun Enterprise 10000 with two gigabytes of RAM; in that case, setting MaxClients much higher makes sense. On the opposite end of the spectrum, you might be running the Web server on a machine with limited memory or CPU resources, and you might want to make sure that Apache doesn't consume all resources at the cost of possibly not being able to serve all requests that come to your site. In that context, setting MaxClients lower makes sense.

Using the Scoreboard File

Because the multiprocess model described in the preceding section required some decent communication between the parent and child processes, the most cross-platform method of performing that communication was chosen. This is a *scoreboard file*, where each child had a chunk of space in the file to which it was authorized to write. The parent httpd process watched that file to get a status report and make decisions about whether to launch more child processes or kill idle processes.

At first, this file was located in the /tmp directory. However, because of problems with Linux setups that regularly clear out /tmp directories (causing the server to go haywire), the scoreboard file has since been moved into the /var/log/ directory. You can configure where the scoreboard file goes exactly with a ScoreBoardFile directive.

A program called httpd_monitor, in the support/ subdirectory in the Apache distribution, can be run against the scoreboard file to give a picture of the state of all the child processes and whether they're just starting, active, sleeping, or dead. It can give you a good idea of whether your settings for MaxSpareServers and MinSpareServers are decent. Consider it a close equivalent to the system command iostat.

Increasing Efficiency in the Server Software

You can increase performance over the standard setup in many ways, including smarter ways to configure your resources, features that can be turned off for better performance, and even things at the operating system and hardware level that can be addressed. All these factors make a difference between a regular Web server and a high-performance Web server.

Most non-hardware improvements fall into three categories: those that reduce the load on the CPU, those that reduce the amount of I/O to the disk, and those that reduce the memory requirements.

Using Server-Side Includes

Server-side includes (SSI) are preprocessing HTML statements that can cause an increased disk access load and an increased CPU load. The CPU penalty comes from having to parse the HTML file looking for the includes; parsing a file is more intensive than just reading the file and spitting it out to the socket.

The disk access penalty comes from having to make two, three, four, or more separate disk accesses to pull together the page to get served. For example, a typical SSI document might need a header and footer pulled into memory to get served. That's three disk accesses to pull the document together, instead of one. If the inline HTML files were large, the difference wouldn't be as great. Because the HTML files are usually small, the disk access penalty is relatively large. The problem is compounded by any CGI script that might be included as well; if you had an SSI page with two CGI scripts included, you'd probably get at least twice the performance hit than if you had one CGI script that just rendered the whole page in the first place.

Using .htaccess Files

Apache uses special files, known as .htaccess files, for controlling access to directories. Searching directories for .htaccess files is fairly painful. Because .htaccess files work hierarchically, when a request is made for /path/path2/dir1/dir2/foo, Apache will look for an .htaccess file in *every* subdirectory. In the example of /path/path2/dir1/dir2/foo, that's at least five—a significant disk access load that's best to avoid if possible.

To solve the problem of too many disk hits, you should put anything controlled via your .htaccess files into the access.conf configuration file or even the srm.conf file. If you have to look for .htaccess files in subdirectories and can narrow it down to a specific subdirectory, it's possible to have the server look only for .htaccess files in that subdirectory by the use of AllowOverride.

Suppose that your document root is in /www/htdocs, and you want to turn off the searching for all .htaccess files except those in /www/htdocs/dir1/dir2 and everywhere below. You would put something like the following into your access.conf configuration file:

```
<Directory /www/htdocs>
Options All
AllowOverride None
</Directory>
<Directory /www/htdocs/dir1/dir2>
Options All
AllowOverride All
</Directory>
```

It's important that the directories are listed in that order so that the second `<Directory>` doesn't take precedence over the first.

Using .asis Files for Server-Push Animations

.asis files are distinguished by having their HTTP headers directly embedded in the file itself. They are a useful optimization for certain types of files, such as server-push animations, which demand the capability to set their own headers and are usually dished out by CGI scripts. The usual server-push CGI script has the additional overhead of assembling the images on-the-fly, whereas with an .asis file, the whole stream can be linked into one file, reducing the I/O hit and the memory and CPU performance situation.

▶ **See** "As-Is Files," **p. 701**

The only thing you lose by using the .asis parameter is the ability to do **timed pushes**, where there's a lapse of time between frames implemented as a `sleep()` (a system call where a program is paused for a defined number of seconds). But because server-push is also bandwidth-limited, many consider the ability to do timed pushes to be a dubious feature.

Automating Logfile Rotation

Certainly one goal for the site administrator should be to automate the rotation of access and error logs. Even a lightly loaded server will generate a couple of megabytes of log activity per day. Left unchecked, your disk space could dry up fast.

The most basic element of logfile rotation is to get the Web server to stop writing to the old log and start writing to another without disrupting service to the outside users. The most straightforward way to accomplish logfile rotation is by renaming the log just slightly and sending a SIGHUP signal to the parent process. *Just slightly* means renaming it to access_log.0 or something similar on the same hard disk, on the same partition. Why? Each child has a file descriptor open to the logfile. When you rename the file, the file descriptor will still point to the same actual log right up until the time the child receives an "echo" of the SIGHUP from the parent process. When the SIGHUP echo happens, the file descriptor is closed, a new one is obtained, and the new access_log gets created. This is pretty much the only way to guarantee not losing traffic reports while rotating logs.

Here is an example script that performs a logfile rotation:

```
#!/bin/sh
logdir="/usr/local/etc/httpd/logs"    # name of the log directory
acclog="access_log"                   # name of the access log
errlog="error_log"                    # name of the error log
pidfile="$logdir/httpd.pid"           # file that stores the parent's
                                      # process ID

mv $logdir/$acclog $logdir/$acclog.0
mv $logdir/$errlog $logdir/$errlog.0
kill -HUP 'cat $pidfile'
```

The logfile rotation script needs to be run as the same user that launched the HTTP daemon originally—for example, "root." You may want to write additional scripts to place these .0 files into an archive of some sort; my favorite one is to use the year and month as subdirectories, such that the logs for January 1, 1997, go into a file named 1997/01/01 somewhere off a directory with a lot of room. That way, the log files are easy to archive somewhere else (to DAT tape, to CD-ROM, or even to remove it) by moving a directory.

Understanding Security Issues

The security of your server is, no doubt, one of your biggest concerns as a Web site administrator. Running a Web server is, by nature, a security risk. For that matter, so is plugging your machine into a network at all. However, a lot can be done to make your Web server more secure from external forces (people trying to break into your site) and internal forces (your own Web site users mistakenly or willingly opening up holes).

CGI Issues

The biggest cause for concern about protecting your site from external threats is CGI scripts. Most CGI scripts are shell-based, using Perl or C-shell interpreted programs rather than compiled programs. Thus, many attacks have occurred by exploiting "features" in those shells. This section won't go into too much detail about how to make CGI scripts themselves safe. You should know a couple of important things, however, as an administrator.

A CGI script runs with the user ID of the server child process. In the default case, this is "nobody." To adequately protect yourself, you may want to consider the "nobody" user an untrustworthy user on your site, making sure that this user doesn't have read permission to files you want to keep private and doesn't have write permission anywhere sensitive. Certain CGI scripts—for example, a guestbook application that allows users to record comments about your Web site—will demand write access to certain files. So if you want to enable those types of applications, it's best to specify a directory to which CGI scripts can write without worrying about a malicious or misdirected script overwriting data that it shouldn't.

Furthermore, site administrators can limit the use of CGI to specific directories by using the ScriptAlias directive. Alternatively, if you have turned on .cgi as a file extension for CGI scripts, you can use the `Options ExecCGI` directive in access.conf to further control the use of CGI files.

As an example of controlling access with `ExecCGI`, if you want to allow for CGI to be used everywhere on the site (with a document root of /home/htdocs) except for the "users" subdirectory because you don't trust your users with CGI scripts, your access.conf should look something like Listing 37.1.

Listing 37.1 A Sample access.conf File Showing Directory Configuration Information

```
<Directory /home/htdocs/>
Options Indexes FollowSymLinks Includes Multiviews ExecCGI
AllowOverride None
</Directory>

<Directory /home/htdocs/users/>
Options Indexes SymLinksIfOwnerMatch IncludesNOEXEC Multiviews
AllowOverride None
</Directory>
```

Because `ExecCGI` isn't in the `Options` list for the second directory, no one can use CGI scripts there.

Unfortunately, there really is no middle ground between allowing CGI scripts and disallowing them. Now, most languages used for CGI programs don't have security concepts built into them, so applying rules such as "don't touch the hard disk" or "don't send the /etc/passwd file in e-mail to an outside user" need to be dealt with in the same manner as though you had actual Linux users who needed the same restrictions applied to them. Maybe this will change when Sun's Java language gets more use on the server side, or when people use raw interpreted languages less and higher-level programming tools more often.

Server-Side Includes

As you can see from Listing 37.1, there was another change between the *trusted* part of the server and the **untrusted** part: the `Includes` argument to `Options` was changed to `IncludesNOEXEC`. `IncludesNOEXEC` allows your untrusted users to use server-side includes without allowing the #include of CGI scripts or the #exec command to be run. The #exec command is particularly troublesome in an untrusted environment because it basically gives shell-level access to an HTML author.

Symbolic Links

In an untrusted environment, UNIX *symbolic links* (which enable linking across file-system boundaries) also are a concern for Web site administrators. Malicious users could very easily create symbolic links from directories where they have write permission to an object or re- source, even outside the document root, to which all they need is read permission. For example, a user could create a link to the /etc/passwd file and then release that onto the Web, exposing your site to potential crack attempts—particularly if your operating system doesn't use shadow passwords.

> **N O T E**   In a recent incident involving the Alta Vista search engine (**www.altavista.digital.com**), a search for words common to password files (*bin, root, ftp*, and so on) turned up references to actual password files that had, intentionally or not, been left public. These password files included a few with encrypted passwords, which were easy enough to break with a few hours of CPU time on most workstations. ■

To protect against symbolic link security breaches, the site administrator has two options: to allow only symbolic linking if the owner of the link and the owner of the linked-to resource are the same by using `SymLinksIfOwnerMatch`, or to disallow symbolic links altogether by not specifying `FollowSymLinks` or `SymLinksIfOwnerMatch`.

Also note that both `<Directory>` segments in Listing 37.1 included `AllowOverride None`. Not allowing symbolic links is the most conservative setting; if you want to allow certain things to be tunable in those directories by using .htaccess files, you can specify them with the `AllowOverride` directive. However, stating `None` is the safest policy.

Publicly Writable Spaces

The last security threat that's specific to Web servers is that of allowing publicly writable spaces to be served up via HTTP. For example, many sites allow their FTP "incoming" directory to be accessed via the Web directly. This can be a security hole if someone were to place there a malicious CGI script or a server-side include file that calls #exec to do some damage. If you decide you need to take the risk of providing public writable spaces, you can do some things to protect yourself:

■ The most conservative setting you should set for the `Options` directive is this:

`Options Indexes`

You could use `None`, but `Indexes` really doesn't introduce any additional security problems, as long as you're comfortable with others being able to download anything that has been submitted. In the light of recent legislation by the U.S. government regarding "indecent" materials, you may not want to take this risk either.

■ Make sure that you set `AllowOverride None` so that people can't upload an .htaccess file into your directory and modify all your settings and security policies.

■ Make sure that the FTP daemon you're using doesn't allow the execute bit to be set. By preventing the execute bit to be set, you prevent the execution of uploaded CGI scripts. If you're using `XBitHack` to activate your server-side includes, you can prevent those includes from being run as well. This is mainly a backup for setting the `Options` as in Listing 37.1, which should protect you against these threats anyway.

These same rules apply if you have CGI scripts that generate their own uniquely addressable HTML or CGI files. For example, if the guestbook.cgi program constantly appends the submitted personal information to a guestbook.html file, all the same rules apply; the contents of that HTML file must be considered unsafe. This possible security breach can be plugged if the CGI script double-checks what's getting written and removes "dangerous" code, such as server-side includes.

Other Tuning Issues

The Apache Web server is optimized for accuracy more than for speed; as one rule of thumb for gunfighting goes, "You can't miss faster than the other person can hit." Also, performance is rarely an issue, because any half-decent Web server can saturate a T1 line without trying very hard.

For those interested in getting every last bit of performance from a server, whether you're running CNN's Web site or simply trying to run Apache on hardware that can't possibly fill the available bandwidth (such as trying to run an intranet Web server with 10Mbps Ethernet on the spare 386DX40 you found in the office closet), you can make certain tweaks that will improve responsiveness. For cheap improvements, the most important issue for any Web server is RAM. A Web server takes such a performance hit if it has to swap memory out to disk that it should be avoided at all possible costs. One way to avoid swapping is to limit the MaxClients setting to stay within the available RAM. The best source of performance tuning information is located on the Web at **http://www.apache.org/docs/misc/perf-tuning.html**.

From Here...

You can learn more details about setting up, configuring, and running the Apache Web server in Chapter 35, "Getting Started with Apache." That chapter provides a detailed introduction to the Apache Web server.

Appendixes

Sources of Information

by Jack Tackett

Because Linux is based on UNIX, almost any UNIX-based book provides some information on Linux. The best source for information, however, is the Linux community itself, which offers everything from updated versions of Linux to extremely active Usenet newsgroups. Linux also provides online documents through the Linux Documentation Project (LDP), which is writing a complete set of manuals for Linux. The most recent editions of this project are available via the Internet.

The following listings provide Internet FTP sites, magazines, conferences, and newsgroups from which you can gather more information about Linux.

Linux Web Sites

Because Linux is a child of the Internet, you will find a great many Web sites related to Linux. In fact, Linux is a pretty popular subject on the Web. Table A.1 lists the URLs that contain most of the Linux information on the Web.

Table A.1   Major Linux Web Sites

URL	Description
http://sunsite.unc.edu/mdw	*The* site for Linux information; the home of the Linux Documentation Project
http://www.Linux.org.uk	The Web site for European Linux users
http://www.li.org	The Linux International Web site
http://www.redhat.com	The RedHat Linux Web site
http://www.slackware.org	The official Web site for Slackware
http://www.caldera.com	Caldera's Web site
http://www.linux.org	The Linux Organization Web site
http://sunsite.unc.edu/linux-source	The Linux Source Navigator, which allows you to view Linux source code in hypertext
http://www.yahoo.com/Computers_and_Internet/Operating_Systems/Unix/Linux	The Yahoo! site pointing to many current sites

Usenet Newsgroups

If you have access to Usenet newsgroups, you'll enjoy the following newsgroups, which provide a variety of information about Linux. Only two, **comp.os.linux.announce** and **comp.os.linux.answers**, are moderated.

▶ **See** "Usenet Culture," **p. 661**

N O T E The original Linux-related newsgroup, **comp.os.linux**, no longer exists because more specific newsgroups have been created.

- **comp.os.linux.announce**   This moderated newsgroup is used for important announcements, such as bug fixes.

- **comp.os.linux.answers**   This moderated newsgroup provides answers to any of your Linux questions, especially about setting up Linux. Please read the appropriate Linux documentation and FAQs before posting a question to this group.

- **comp.os.linux.development.system**   This newsgroup is devoted to the many programmers around the world who are developing the Linux system.

- **comp.os.linux.development.apps**   This newsgroup is devoted to the many programmers around the world who are developing applications for Linux.

- **comp.os.linux.hardware**   This newsgroup provides answers to hardware compatibility questions.

- **comp.os.linux.setup**   This newsgroup provides help with Linux setup and installation problems.

- **comp.os.linux.advocacy**   This newsgroup provides a medium to discuss why Linux is the greatest OS.

- **comp.os.linux.networking**   This newsgroup provides answers to networking Linux with the rest of the world.

- **comp.os.linux.x**   This newsgroup provides answers to installing and running X under Linux.

- **comp.os.linux.m68k**   The purpose of this newsgroup is to promote interest and development of the port of Linux to Motorola's 680x0 architecture.

A newsgroup named **comp.os.linux.misc** serves as a catch-all for any Linux topic not suited to the other newsgroups. Also, more than 170 other Usenet newsgroups contain the word *Linux*. A sample of the more common Linux newsgroups are listed as follows. Go exploring!

alt.linux.sux	alt.os.linux
alt.uu.comp.os.linux.questions	alt.os.linux.slackware
aus.computers.linux	dc.org.linux-users
de.comp.os.linux.hardware	de.comp.os.linux.misc
de.comp.os.linux.networking	de.comp.os.linux.x
de.alt.sources.linux.patches	uk.comp.os.linux
fj.os.linux	fr.comp.os.linux
han.sys.linux	linux.apps.bbsdev
linux.apps.linux-bbs	linux.apps.seyon
linux.apps.seyon.development	linux.apps.flexfax
linux.debian	linux.debian.announce

App

A

linux.debian.user

linux.dev.680x0

linux.dev.apps

linux.dev.c-programming

linux.dev.debian

linux.dev.fido

linux.dev.fsstnd

linux.dev.hams

linux.dev.interviews

linux.dev.laptop

linux.dev.linuxnews

linux.dev.localbus

linux.dev.mca

linux.dev.msdos

linux.dev.new-lists

linux.dev.normal

linux.dev.oasg

linux.dev.pkg

linux.dev.qag

linux.dev.serial

linux.dev.sound

linux.dev.svgalib

linux.dev.term

linux.dev.wabi

linux.dev.kernel

linux.fido.ifmail

linux.free-widgets.bugs

linux.local.chicago

linux.local.silicon-valley

linux.new-tty

linux.ports.alpha

linux.samba.announce

linux.wine.users

linux.dev.gcc

linux.dev.admin

linux.dev.bbs

linux.dev.config

linux.dev.doc

linux.dev.fsf

linux.dev.ftp

linux.dev.ibcs2

linux.dev.japanese

linux.dev.linuxbsd

linux.dev.linuxss

linux.dev.lugnuts

linux.dev.mgr

linux.dev.net

linux.dev.newbie

linux.dev.nys

linux.dev.oi

linux.dev.ppp

linux.dev.scsi

linux.dev.seyon

linux.dev.standards

linux.dev.tape

linux.dev.uucp

linux.dev.word

linux.dev.x11

linux.free-widgets.announce

linux.free-widgets.development

linux.local.nova-scotia

linux.motif.clone

linux.news.groups

linux.samba

linux.sdk

linux.test

Online Documents

Matt Welsh spearheads a dedicated group of Linux enthusiasts who are systematically writing a complete set of Linux manuals that are made available on the Internet. The latest versions of the documentation can be found at **sunsite.unc.edu** in the /pub/Linux/docs directory. You can also find earlier versions of these documents in your version of Linux's /docs directory. The current home for the LDP is located at this address:

http://sunsite.unc.edu/mdw

Available documents include the following:

- "Linux Installation and Getting Started," by Matt Welsh
- "The Linux System Administrators' Guide," by Lars Wirzenius
- "The Linux Network Administrators' Guide," by Olaf Kirch
- "The Linux Kernel Hackers' Guide," by Michael K. Johnson
- "The Linux Frequently Asked Questions (FAQ) List," maintained by Ian Jackson; it's composed of questions and answers on myriad Linux topics
- "The Linux META-FAQ," maintained by Michael K. Johnson
- "The Linux INFO-SHEET," maintained by Michael K. Johnson
- "The Linux Software Map," maintained by Aaron Schab; contains information about each of the software packages available for Linux via FTP

Linux HOWTOs

The Linux HOWTO Index provides an index to all the available HOWTO documents. These HOWTO documents provide a detailed explanation of their topic. Some of the titles include the following:

- The Linux Installation HOWTO
- The Linux Hardware HOWTO and The Linux Printing HOWTO

See Appendix B, "The Linux HOWTO Index," for a complete list of Linux HOWTO and Mini HOWTO site addresses. These files are located in the /usr/doc/faq/howto directory on your local drive. Most are archived with gzip to save disk space. To read these or other compressed files, use the zless command.

Many FAQs about Linux topics and GNU programs are shipped with Linux and can be found in the /usr/info directory.

man Pages

The Linux operating system itself provides plenty of online help via the man command. To access online help, enter **man** followed by the topic for which you want information.

▶ **See** "Getting Help for Commands with man," **p. 114**

Magazines

Linux Journal is the leading U.S. periodical devoted explicitly to Linux. You can request more information about this publication from the following address:

> *Linux Journal*
> P.O. Box 85867
> Seattle, WA 98145
> (206) 527-3385
> **http://www.linuxjournal.com**

Linux FTP Sites

You'll find a great deal of up-to-date information regarding Linux on the Internet. Table A.2 lists the FTP sites that maintain Linux archives. The main archive site, located at the University of North Carolina-Chapel Hill, is named **sunsite.unc.edu**.

Table A.2   FTP Sites with Linux Archives

Site Name	Directory
tsx-11.mit.edu	/pub/linux
sunsite.unc.edu	/pub/Linux
nic.funet.fi	/pub/Linux
ftp.mcc.ac.uk	/pub/linux
ftp.dfv.rwth-aachen.de	/pub/linux
ftp.informatik.rwth-aachen.de	/pub/Linux
ftp.ibp.fr	/pub/linux
kirk.bond.edu.au	/pub/OS/Linux
ftp.uu.net	/systems/unix/linux
wuarchive.wustl.edu	/systems/linux
ftp.win.tue.nl	/pub/linux
ftp.stack.nl	/pub/Linux
ftp.ibr.cs.tu-bs.de	/pub/os/linux
ftp.denet.dk	/pub/OS/Linux

▶ **See** "Using FTP for Remote File Transfer," **p. 580**

Contacting InfoMagic

InfoMagic produces the CD-ROMs enclosed with this book, and the company is gracious enough to help support the product. If your disc is damaged, please contact Que Publishing at **http://www.mcp.com**. If you've exhausted the resources above, contact InfoMagic's support at **support@infomagic.com**.

For Linux Developers

So you think that Linux is the greatest thing to come along in quite some time, and you want to help develop future releases. Well, you're in luck. An active set of mailing lists on the Internet is devoted to various topics and issues surrounding Linux development. This is a multichannel mailing list, meaning that messages on different topics are sent to different groups of people. You must subscribe to each channel that you're interested in. If you think you want to get involved in a Linux development project, you can get more information by sending an e-mail message to

majordomo@vger.rutgers.edu

with `lists` in the body to get a list of the lists there. Add a line with `help` in the body to get the standard Majordomo help file, which has instructions for subscribing and unsubscribing.

The Linux HOWTO Index

by Tim Bynum

In this appendix

This document contains an index to the Linux HOWTOs and mini-HOWTOs, as well as other information about the HOWTO project.

What Are Linux HOWTOs?

Linux HOWTOs are documents that describe in detail a certain aspect of configuring or using Linux. For example, there is the Installation HOWTO, which gives instructions on installing Linux, and the Mail HOWTO, which describes how to set up and configure mail under Linux. Other examples include the NET-3 HOWTO and the Printing HOWTO.

HOWTOs are comprehensive docs, much like a FAQ, but generally not in question-and-answer format. However, many HOWTOs contain a FAQ section at the end.

There are several HOWTO formats available: plain text, PostScript, DVI, and HTML.

In addition to the HOWTOs, there are a multitude of mini-HOWTOs on short, specific subjects. They are available only in plain text and HTML format.

Where Do I Get Linux HOWTOs?

HOWTOs can be retrieved via anonymous FTP from the following sites

- **ftp://sunsite.unc.edu/pub/Linux/docs/HOWTO**
- **ftp://tsx-11.mit.edu/pub/linux/docs/HOWTO**

as well as many mirror sites, such as

<ftp://sunsite.unc.edu/pub/Linux/MIRRORS.html>

You can also browse HOWTOs in HTML format

<http://sunsite.unc.edu/LDP/HOWTO/>

on the World Wide Web. Many mirror sites **<http://sunsite.unc.edu/LDP/hmirrors.html>** also mirror the HTML files. **sunsite.unc.edu** is heavily used, so please use a mirror site if possible.

HOWTOs are also posted toward the beginning of the month to the Usenet newsgroup:

comp.os.linux.answers.

There is a tool called NewstoHOWTO that will assemble the postings.

HOWTO Translations

HOWTO translations are available on sunsite.unc.edu and mirrors around the world. So far there are:

Chinese (zh)

French (fr)

German (de)

Hellenic (el)

Italian (it)

Indonesian (id)

Japanese (ja)

Korean (ko)

Polish (pl)

Spanish (es)

Swedish (sv)

Turkish (tr)

If you know of any other translation projects, please let me know and I will add them to this list. If you are interested in getting your translations archived on sunsite.unc.edu, please read the directory structure specification at

http://sunsite.unc.edu/pub/Linux/docs/HOWTO/translations/Directory-Structure

and get in touch with me.

HOWTO Index

The following Linux HOWTOs are currently available:

3Dfx HOWTO, by Bernd Kreimeier <bk@gamers.org>. How to use 3Dfx graphics accelerator chip support. Updated 6 February 1998.

AX25 HOWTO, by Terry Dawson <terry@perf.no.itg.telecom.com.au>. How to configure AX25 networking for Linux. Updated 17 October 1997.

Access HOWTO, by Michael De La Rue <access-howto@ed.ac.uk>. How to use adaptive technology with Linux. Updated 28 March 1997.

Alpha HOWTO, by David Mosberger <davidm@azstarnet.com>. Overview of Alpha systems and processors. Updated 6 June 1997.

Assembly HOWTO, by François-René Rideau <rideau@ens.fr>. Information on programming in x86 assembly. Updated 16 November 1997.

Benchmarking HOWTO, by André D. Balsa <andrewbalsa@usa.net>. How to do basic benchmarking. Updated 15 August 1997.

BootPrompt HOWTO, by Paul Gortmaker <gpg109@rsphy1.anu.edu.au>. List of boot time arguments and overview of booting software. Updated 1 February 1998.

Bootdisk HOWTO, by Graham Chapman <grahamc@zeta.org.au>. How to create a boot/root maintenance disk for Linux. Updated 1 February 1998.

Busmouse HOWTO, by Chris Bagwell <cbagwell@sprynet.com>. Information on bus mouse compatibility with Linux. Updated 4 May 1998.

CD Writing HOWTO, by Winfried Trümper <winni@xpilot.org>. How to write CDs. Updated 16 December 1997.

CDROM HOWTO, by Jeff Tranter <jeff_tranter@pobox.com>. Information on CDROM drive compatibility for Linux. Updated 23 January 1998.

Chinese HOWTO, by Chih-Wei Huang <cwhuang@phys.ntu.edu.tw>. How to configure Linux for use with the Chinese character set. Updated 20 April 1998.

Commercial HOWTO, by Martin Michlmayr <tbm@cyrius.com>. Listing of commercial software products for Linux. Updated 8 May 1998.

Config HOWTO, by Guido Gonzato <guido@ibogfs.cineca.it>. How to fine-tune and customize your Linux system. Updated 10 April 1998.

Consultants HOWTO, by Martin Michlmayr <tbm@cyrius.com>. Listing of Linux consultants. Updated 8 May 1998.

Cyrillic HOWTO, by Alexander L. Belikoff <abel@bfr.co.il>. How to configure Linux for use with the Cyrillic characterset. Updated 23 January 1998.

DNS HOWTO, by Nicolai Langfeldt <janl@math.uio.no>. How to set up DNS. Updated 3 April 1998.

DOS/Win to Linux HOWTO, by Guido Gonzato <guido@ibogfs.cineca.it>. How to move from DOS/Windows to Linux. Updated 15 April 1998.

DOSEMU HOWTO, by Uwe Bonnes <bon@elektron.ikp.physik.th-darmstadt.de>. HOWTO about the Linux MS-DOS Emulator, DOSEMU. Updated 15 March 1997 for dosemu-0.64.4 (in progress).

Danish HOWTO, by Niels Kristian Bech Jensen <nkbj@image.dk>. How to configure Linux for use with the Danish characterset. Updated 17 April 1998.

Distribution HOWTO, by Eric S. Raymond <esr@snark.thyrsus.com>. A list of Linux distributions. Updated 8 February 1998.

ELF HOWTO, by Daniel Barlow <daniel.barlow@linux.org>. How to install and migrate to the ELF binary file format. Updated 14 July 1996.

Emacspeak HOWTO, by Jim Van Zandt <jrv@vanzandt.mv.com>. How to use "emacspeak" with Linux. Updated 21 December 1997.

Ethernet HOWTO, by Paul Gortmaker <gpg109@rsphy1.anu.edu.au>. Information on Ethernet hardware compatibility for Linux. Updated 1 February 1998.

Finnish HOWTO, by Pekka Taipale <pjt@iki.fi>. How to configure Linux for use with the Finnish characterset. Updated 14 February 1996.

Firewall HOWTO, by Mark Grennan, <markg@netplus.net>. How to set up a firewall using Linux. Updated 8 November 1996.

French HOWTO, by Guylhem Aznar <guylhem@danmark.linux.eu.org>. How to configure Linux for use with the French characterset.

Ftape HOWTO, by Kevin Johnson <kjj@pobox.com>. Information on ftape drive compatibility with Linux. Updated 15 March 1997.

GCC HOWTO, by Daniel Barlow <daniel.barlow@linux.org>. How to set up the GNU C compiler and development libraries. Updated 28 February 1996.

German HOWTO, by Winfried Trümper <winni@xpilot.org>. Information on using Linux with German-specific features. Updated 19 March 1997.

Glibc2 HOWTO, by Eric Green <ejg3@cornell.edu>. How to install and migrate to the glibc2 library. Updated 8 February 1998.

HAM HOWTO, by Terry Dawson <terry@perf.no.itg.telecom.com.au>. How to configure amateur radio software for Linux. Updated 1 April 1997.

HOWTO Index, by Tim Bynum <linux-howto@sunsite.unc.edu>. Index of HOWTO documents about Linux. Updated 10 May 1998.

Hardware Compatibility HOWTO, by Patrick Reijnen <antispam.patrickr@antispam.bart.nl>. A list of hardware known to work with Linux. Updated 29 March 1998.

Hebrew HOWTO, by Yair G. Rajwan <yair@hobbes.jct.ac.il>. How to configure Linux for use with the Hebrew characterset. Updated 12 September 1995.

INFO-SHEET, by Michael K. Johnson <johnsonm@redhat.com>. Generic introduction to the Linux operating system. Updated 24 October 1997.

IPX HOWTO, by Terry Dawson <terry@perf.no.itg.telecom.com.au>. How to install and configure IPX networking. Updated 29 March 1997.

ISP Hookup HOWTO, by Egil Kvaleberg <egil@kvaleberg.no>. Basic introduction to hooking up to an ISP. Updated 5 March 1998.

Installation HOWTO, by Eric S. Raymond <esr@snark.thyrsus.com>. How to obtain and install Linux. Updated 20 April 1998.

Intranet Server HOWTO, by Pramod Karnad <karnad@indiamail.com>. How to set up a Linux Intranet server. Updated 7 August 1997.

Italian HOWTO, by Marco "Gaio" Gaiarin <gaio@dei.unipd.it>. How to configure Linux for use with the Italian characterset. Updated 6 August 1997.

Java-CGI HOWTO, by David H. Silber <dhs@orbits.com>. How to set up Java-capable CGI bin. Updated 18 November 1996.

Kernel HOWTO, by Brian Ward <ward@blah.math.tu-graz.ac.at>. Upgrading and compiling the Linux kernel. Updated 26 May 1997.

Keyboard and Console HOWTO, by Andries Brouwer <aeb@cwi.nl>. Information about the Linux keyboard, console, and non-ASCII characters. Updated 25 February 1998.

LinuxDoc+Emacs+Ispell HOWTO, by Philippe MARTIN <feloy@wanadoo.fr>. Assists writers and translators of Linux HOWTOs or any other paper for the Linux Documentation Project. Updated 27 February 1998.

META-FAQ, by Michael K. Johnson <johnsonm@redhat.com>. A listing of Linux sources of information. Updated 25 October 1997.

MGR HOWTO, by Vincent Broman <broman@nosc.mil>. Information on the MGR graphics interface for Linux. Updated 30 May 1996.

MILO HOWTO, by David A. Rusling <david.rusling@reo.mts.dec.com>. How to use the Alpha Linux Miniloader (MILO). Updated 6 December 1996.

Mail HOWTO, by Guylhem Aznar <guylhem@danmark.linux.eu.org>. Information on electronic mail servers and clients. Updated January 1998.

Multi-Disk HOWTO, by Stein Gjoen <sgjoen@nyx.net>. How to set up multiple hard disk drives. Updated 3 February 1998.

NET-3 HOWTO, by Terry Dawson <terry@perf.no.itg.telecom.com.au>. How to configure TCP/IP networking under Linux. Updated 1 April 1998.

NFS HOWTO, by Nicolai Langfeldt <janl@math.uio.no>. How to set up NFS clients and servers. Updated 3 November 1997.

NIS HOWTO, by Thorsten Kukuk <kukuk@vt.uni-paderborn.de>. Information on using NIS/YP on Linux systems. Updated 23 April 1998.

Optical Disk HOWTO, by Skip Rye <Skip_Rye@faneuil.com>. How to use optical disk drives with Linux. Updated 22 December 1997.

Oracle HOWTO, by Paul Haigh <paul@nailed.demon.co.uk>. How to set up Oracle as a database server. Updated 10 March 1998.

PCI HOWTO, by Michael Will <Michael.Will@student.uni-tuebingen.de>. Information on PCI-architecture compatibility with Linux. Updated 30 March 1997.

PCMCIA HOWTO, by Dave Hinds <dhinds@allegro.stanford.edu>. How to install and use PCMCIA Card Services. Updated 19 February 1998.

PPP HOWTO, by Robert Hart <hartr@interweft.com.au>. Information on using PPP networking with Linux. Updated 31 March 1997.

Parallel Processing HOWTO, by Hank Dietz <pplinux@ecn.purdue.edu>. Discussion of parallel processing approaches for Linux. Updated 5 January 1998.

Pilot HOWTO, by David H. Silber <pilot@orbits.com>. How to use a USR Pilot PDA with Linux. Updated 17 August 1997.

Polish HOWTO, by Sergiusz Pawlowicz <ser@arch.pwr.wroc.pl>. Information on using Linux with Polish-specific features. Updated 5 January 1997.

PostgreSQL HOWTO, by Al Dev (Alavoor Vasudevan) <aldev@hotmail.com>. How to set up PostgreSQL as a database server. Updated 12 April 1998.

Printing HOWTO, by Grant Taylor <gtaylor+pht@picante.com>. HOWTO on printing software for Linux. Updated 23 September 1997.

Printing Usage HOWTO, by Mark Komarinski <markk@auratek.com>. How to use the printing system for a variety of file types and options. Updated 6 February 1998.

RPM HOWTO, by Donnie Barnes <djb@redhat.com>. How to use the Red Hat Package Manager (.rpm). Updated 8 April 1997.

Reading List HOWTO, by Eric S. Raymond <esr@snark.thyrsus.com>. Interesting books pertaining to Linux subjects. Updated 11 February 1998.

Root RAID HOWTO, by Michael A. Robinton <michael@bzs.org>. How to create a root-mounted RAID filesystem. Updated 25 March 1998.

SCSI Programming HOWTO, by Heiko Eissfeldt <heiko@colossus.escape.de>. Information on programming the generic Linux SCSI interface. Updated 7 May 1996.

SMB HOWTO, by David Wood <dwood@plugged.net.au>. How to use the Session Message Block (SMB) protocol with Linux. Updated 10 August 1996.

SRM HOWTO, by David Mosberger <davidm@azstarnet.com>. How to boot Linux/Alpha using the SRM firmware. Updated 17 August 1996.

Security HOWTO, by Kevin Fenzi <kevin@scrye.com>. General overview of security issues. Updated 1 May 1998.

Serial Programming HOWTO, by Peter H. Baumann <Peter.Baumann@dlr.de>. How to use serial ports in programs. Updated 22 January 1998.

Shadow Password HOWTO, by Michael H. Jackson <mhjack@tscnet.com>. How to obtain, install, and configure shadow passwords. Updated 3 April 1996.

Slovenian HOWTO, by Primoz Peterlin <primoz.peterlin@biofiz.mf.uni-lj.si>. Information on using Linux with Slovenian-specific features. Updated 30 October 1996.

Sound HOWTO, by Jeff Tranter <jeff_tranter@pobox.com>. Sound hardware and software for the Linux operating system. Updated 23 January 1998.

Sound Playing HOWTO, by Yoo C. Chung <wacko@laplace.snu.ac.kr>. How to play various sound formats under Linux. Updated 23 January 1998.

Spanish HOWTO, by Gonzalo Garcia Agullo <Gonzalo.Garcia-Agullo@jrc.es>. Information on using Linux with Spanish-specific features. Updated 20 August 1996.

teTeX HOWTO, by Robert Kiesling <kiesling@terracom.net>. How to install the teTeX package (TeX and LaTeX) under Linux. Updated 21 August 1997.

Text-Terminal HOWTO, by David S. Lawyer <bf347@lafn.org>. This document explains what text terminals are, how they work, how to install and configure them. Updated May 1998.

Thai HOWTO, by Poonlap Veeratanabutr <poon-v@fedu.uec.ac.jp>. How to configure Linux for use with the Thai characterset. Updated 16 July 1997.

Tips HOWTO, by Paul Anderson <paul@geeky1.ebtech.net>. HOWTO on miscellaneous tips and tricks for Linux. Updated 26 December 1997.

UMSDOS HOWTO, by Jacques Gelinas <jacques@solucorp.qc.ca>. How to install and use the UMSDOS filesystem. Updated 13 November 1995.

UPS HOWTO, by Harvey J. Stein <abel@netvision.net.il>. Information on using a UPS power supply with Linux. Updated 18 November 1997.

UUCP HOWTO, by Guylhem Aznar <guylhem@danmark.linux.eu.org>. Information on UUCP software for Linux. Updated 6 February 1998.

App
B

User Group HOWTO, by Kendall Grant Clark <kclark@ntlug.org>. Tips on founding, maintaining, and growing a Linux User Group. Updated 24 April 1998.

VAR HOWTO, by Martin Michlmayr <tbm@cyrius.com>. Listing of Linux value added resellers. Updated 9 May 1998.

VMS to Linux HOWTO, by Guido Gonzato <guido@ibogfs.cineca.it>. How to move from VMS to Linux. Updated 20 April 1998.

Virtual Services HOWTO, by Brian Ackerman <brian@nycrc.net>. How to set up virtual hosting services. Updated 4 November 1997.

WWW HOWTO, by Wayne Leister <n3mtr@qis.net>. How to set up WWW clients and servers. Updated 19 November 1997.

WWW mSQL HOWTO, by Oliver Corff <corff@zedat.fu-berlin.de>. How to set up a web server database with mSQL. Updated 17 September 1997.

XFree86 HOWTO, by Eric S. Raymond <esr@snark.thyrsus.com>. How to obtain, install, and configure XFree86 3.2 (X11R6). Updated 24 February 1998.

XFree86 Video Timings HOWTO, by Eric S. Raymond <esr@snark.thyrsus.com>. How to compose a mode line for XFree86. Updated 20 February 1998.

Mini-HOWTO index

The following mini-HOWTOs are available:

3 Button Mouse mini-HOWTO, by Geoff Short <geoff@kipper.york.ac.uk>. How to configure your mouse to use three buttons. Updated 4 November 1997.

ADSM Backup mini-HOWTO, by Thomas Koenig <Thomas.Koenig@ciw.uni-karlsruhe.de>. How to install and use the ADSM backup program. Updated 15 January 1997.

Asymmetric Digital Subscriber Loop (ADSL) mini-HOWTO, by David Fannin <dfannin@dnai.com>. Addresses the ordering, installation, and configuration. Updated 9 May 1998.

AI-Alife mini-HOWTO, by John A. Eikenberry <jae@ai.uga.edu>. Information about AI software for Linux. Updated 13 January 1998.

Advocacy mini-HOWTO, by Paul L. Rogers <Paul.L.Rogers@li.org>. Suggestions on how to advocate the use of Linux. Updated 7 May 1998.

Backup with MSDOS mini-HOWTO, by Christopher Neufeld <neufeld@physics.utoronto.ca>. How to back up Linux machines with MSDOS. Updated 5 August 1997.

Battery Powered mini-HOWTO, by Hanno Mueller <hanno@lava.de>. How to reduce a Linux system's power consumption. Updated 21 December 1997.

Boca mini-HOWTO, by David H Dennis <david@freelink.net>. How to install a Boca 16-port serial card (Boca 2016). Updated 1 August 1997.

BogoMips mini-HOWTO, by Wim C.A. van Dorst <baron@clifton.hobby.nl>. Information about BogoMips. Updated 13 December 1997.

Bridge mini-HOWTO, by Chris Cole <cole@lynkmedia.com>. How to set up an ethernet bridge. Updated 13 November 1997.

Bridge+Firewall mini-HOWTO, by Peter Breuer <ptb@it.uc3m.es>. How to set up an ethernet bridge and firewall. Updated 19 December 1997.

Bzip2 mini-HOWTO, by David Fetter <dfetter@best.com>. How to use the new bzip2 compression program. Updated 10 March 1998.

Cable Modem mini-HOWTO, by Vladimir Vuksan <vuksan@veus.hr>. How to use a cable modem with a cable ISP. Updated 29 Apr 1998.

Clock mini-HOWTO, by Ron Bean <rbean@execpc.com>. How to set and keep your clock on time. Updated December 1996.

Coffee mini-HOWTO, by Georgatos Photis <gef@ceid.upatras.gr>. Thoughts about making coffee with Linux (humorous). Updated 15 January 1998.

Colour ls mini-HOWTO, by Thorbjoern Ravn Andersen <ravn@dit.ou.dk>. How to set up the colours with "ls." Updated 7 August 1997.

Cyrus IMAP mini-HOWTO, by Kevin Mitchell <kevin@iserv.net>. How to install the Cyrus IMAP server. Updated 21 January 1998.

DHCP mini-HOWTO, by Vladimir Vuksan <vuksan@veus.hr>. How to set up a DHCP Server and Client. Updated 7 May 1998.

DPT Hardware RAID mini-HOWTO, by Ram Samudrala <me@ram.org>. How to configure hardware RAID. Updated 15 December 1997.

Diald mini-HOWTO, by Harish Pillay <h.pillay@ieee.org>. How to use "diald" to dial an ISP. Updated 3 June 1996.

Diskless mini-HOWTO, by Robert Nemkin <buci@math.klte.hu>. How to set up a diskless Linux box. Updated 31 May 1996.

Ext2fs Undeletion mini-HOWTO, by Aaron Crane <aaronc@pobox.com>. How to retrieve deleted files from an ext2 filesystem. Updated 4 August 1997.

Fax Server mini-HOWTO, by Erez Strauss <erez@newplaces.com>. How to set up a fax server. Update 8 November 1997.

Firewall Piercing mini-HOWTO, by François-René Rideau <rideau@ens.fr>. Using ppp over telnet transparently through an Internet firewall. Updated 25 April 1998.

GIS-GRASS mini-HOWTO, by David A. Hastings <dah@ngdc.noaa.gov>. How to install Geographic Information System (GIS) software. Updated 13 November 1997.

GTEK BBS-550 mini-HOWTO, by Wajihuddin Ahmed <wahmed@sdnpk.undp.org>. How to set up the GTEK BBS-550 multiport board with Linux. Updated 20 August 1997.

Hard Disk Upgrade mini-HOWTO, by Yves Bellefeuille <yan@ottawa.com>. How to copy a Linux system from one hard disk to another. Updated 31 January 1998.

App
B

IO Port Programming mini-HOWTO, by Riku Saikkonen <Riku.Saikkonen@hut.fi>. How to use I/O ports in C programs. Updated 28 December 1997.

IP Alias mini-HOWTO, by Harish Pillay <h.pillay@ieee.org>. How to use IP aliasing. Updated 13 January 1997.

IP Masquerade mini-HOWTO, by Ambrose Au <ambrose@writeme.com>. How to use IP masquerading. Updated 10 November 1997.

IP Subnetworking mini-HOWTO, by Robert Hart <hartr@interweft.com.au>. Why and how to subnetwork an IP network. Updated 31 March 1997.

IP Connectivity mini-HOWTO, by Michael Strates <mstrates@croftj.net>. How to get mail and news over a dial-up connection. Updated 6 November 1997.

Install From ZIP mini-HOWTO, by Kevin Snively <k.snively@seaslug.org>. How to install Linux from a parallel port ZIP drive. Updated 29 April 1998.

Kerneld mini-HOWTO, by Henrik Storner <storner@osiris.ping.dk>. How to use "kerneld" (dynamic module loading). Updated 19 July 1997.

LBX mini-HOWTO, by Paul D. Smith <psmith@baynetworks.com>. How to use Low-Bandwidth X (LBX). Updated 11 December 1997.

LILO mini-HOWTO, by Alessandro Rubini <rubini@linux.it>. Examples of typical LILO installations. Updated 9 January 1998.

Large Disk mini-HOWTO, by Andries Brouwer <aeb@cwi.nl>. How to use disks with > 1024 cylinders. Updated 26 July 1996.

Leased Line mini-HOWTO, by Rob van der Putten <rob@sput.dsl.nl>. How to set up leased line modems. Updated 3 March 1998.

Linux+DOS+Win95+OS2 mini-HOWTO, by Mike Harlan <r3mdh@raex.com>. How to use Linux, DOS, OS/2, and Win95 together. Updated 11 November 1997.

Linux+FreeBSD mini-HOWTO, by Niels Kristian Bech Jensen <nkbj@image.dk> How to use Linux and FreeBSD together. Updated 18 April 1998.

Linux+NT-Loader mini-HOWTO, by Bernd Reichert <reichert@dial.eunet.ch>. How to use Linux and the Windows NT boot loader together. Updated 2 September 1997.

Linux+Win95 mini-HOWTO, by Jonathan Katz <jkatz@in.net>. How to use Linux and Windows 95 together. Updated 26 October 1996.

Loadlin+Win95 mini-HOWTO, by Chris Fischer <protek@brigadoon.com>. How to use Linux and Windows 95 together, using loadlin. Updated 6 March 1998.

Mac Terminal mini-HOWTO, by Robert Kiesling <kiesling@terracom.net>. How to use an Apple Macintosh as a serial terminal. Updated 9 November 1997.

Mail Queue mini-HOWTO, by Leif Erlingsson <Leif.Erlingsson@leif@lege.com>. How to queue remote mail and deliver local mail. Updated 3 September 1997.

Mail2News mini-HOWTO, by Robert Hart <iweft@ipax.com.au>. How to set up a mail to news gateway. Updated 4 November 1996.

App
B

Remote X Apps mini-HOWTO, by Vincent Zweije <zweije@xs4all.nl>. How to run remote X applications. Updated 12 February 1998.

SLIP-PPP Emulator mini-HOWTO, by Irish <irish@eskimo.com>. How to use SLIP-PPP emulators with Linux. Updated 7 August 1997.

Sendmail+UUCP mini-HOWTO, by Jamal Hadi Salim <jamal@glcom.com>. How to use sendmail and UUCP together. Updated 6 May 1998.

Small Memory mini-HOWTO, by Todd Burgess <tburgess@uoguelph.ca>. How to run Linux on a system with a small amount of memory. Update 29 October 1997.

Software Building mini-HOWTO, by Mendel Leo Cooper <thegrendel@theriver.com>. How to build software packages. Updated 4 November 1997.

Software RAID mini-HOWTO, by Linas Vepstas <linas@fc.net>. How to configure software RAID. Updated 28 December 1997.

Soundblaster AWE mini-HOWTO, by Marcus Brinkmann <Marcus.Brinkmann@ruhr-uni-bochum.de>. How to install the Soundblaster AWE 32/64. Updated 11 January 1998.

StarOffice mini-HOWTO, by Matthew Borowski <mkb@poboxes.com>. Information on installing the StarOffice suite. Updated 14 January 1998.

Term Firewall mini-HOWTO, by Barak Pearlmutter <bap@cs.unm.edu>. How to use "term" over a firewall. Updated 15 July 1997.

TkRat mini-HOWTO, by Dave Whitinger <dave@whitinger.net>. How to install and use the TkRat mail program. Updated 2 February 1998.

Token Ring mini-HOWTO, by Mike Eckhoff <mike.e@emissary.aus-etc.com>. How to use token ring cards. Updated 7 January 1998.

Ultra-DMA mini-HOWTO, by Brion Vibber <brion@pobox.com>. How to use Ultra-DMA drives and controllers. Updated 3 May 1998.

Update mini-HOWTO, by Stein Gjoen <sgjoen@nyx.net>. How to stay updated about Linux development. Updated 3 February 1998.

Upgrade mini-HOWTO, by Greg Louis <glouis@dynamicro.on.ca>. How to upgrade your Linux distribution. Updated 6 June 1996.

VPN mini-HOWTO, by Árpád Magosányi <mag@bunuel.tii.matav.hu>. How to set up a VPN (Virtual Private Network). Updated 7 August 1997.

Visual Bell mini-HOWTO, by Alessandro Rubini <rubini@linux.it>. How to disable audible bells, and enable visual bells. Updated 11 November 1997.

Windows Modem Sharing mini-HOWTO, by Friedemann Baitinger <baiti@toplink.net>. How to set up Windows to use a shared modem on a Linux machine. Updated 2 November 1997.

WordPerfect mini-HOWTO, by Wade Hampton <whampton@staffnet.com>. How to set up WordPerfect for Linux. Updated 13 August 1997.

X Big Cursor mini-HOWTO, by Joerg Schneider <schneid@ira.uka.de>. How to use enlarged cursors with XWindows. Updated 11 August 1997.

XFree86-XInside mini-HOWTO, by Marco Melgazzi <marco@techie.com>. How to convert XFree86 to XInside modelines. Updated September 1997.

xterm Title mini-HOWTO, by Ric Lister <ric@giccs.georgetown.edu>. How to put strings into the titlebar of an xterm. Updated 7 January 1998.

ZIP Install mini-HOWTO, by John Wiggins <jwiggins@comp.uark.edu>. How to install Linux onto a ZIP drive. Updated 26 January 1998.

Special HOWTO index

The High Availability HOWTO, by Harald Milz <hm@seneca.muc.de> is available at:

http://sunsite.unc.edu/pub/Linux/ALPHA/linux-ha/High-Availability-HOWTO.html

It is not included with the HOWTO collection because it relies on figures and cannot be distributed in all supported formats.

The Graphics mini-HOWTO, by Michael J. Hammel <mjhammel@graphics-muse.org> is available at:

http://www.graphics-muse.org/linux/lgh.html

It is not included with the HOWTO collection because it needs to use a lot of images, which don't translate to other output formats.

Unmaintained HOWTOs and mini-HOWTOs

There are a number of unmaintained documents at
ftp://sunsite.unc.edu/pub/Linux/docs/HOWTO/unmaintained.

These are kept around since old documentation is sometimes better than none. However, you should be aware that you are reading old documentation.

Module-HOWTO

News-HOWTO

Portuguese-HOWTO

SCSI-HOWTO

Serial-HOWTO

Term-HOWTO

UUCP-HOWTO

Writing and Submitting a HOWTO

If you are interested in writing a HOWTO or mini-HOWTO, please get in touch with me FIRST at **linux-howto@sunsite.unc.edu**.

Here are a few guidelines that you should follow when writing a HOWTO or mini-HOWTO:

- Try to use meaningful structure and organization, and write clearly. Remember that many of the people reading HOWTOs do not speak English as their first language.

- If you are writing a HOWTO, you must use the SGML-Tools package, available from **http://www.pobox.com/~cg/sgmltools**, to format the HOWTO. This package allows us to produce LaTeX (for DVI and PostScript), plain text, and HTML from a single source document, and was designed specifically for the HOWTOs. This also gives all of the HOWTOs a uniform look. It is very important that you format and review the output of the formatting in PostScript, plain text, and HTML.

- If you are writing a mini-HOWTO, you can either use SGML (as described above) or HTML. If you use SGML for your mini-HOWTO, it will be published along with the HOWTOs in LDP books.

- Make sure that all the information is correct. I can't stress this enough. When in doubt, speculate, but make it clear that you're only guessing.

- Make sure that you are covering the most recent version of the available software. Also, be sure to include full instructions on where software can be downloaded from (FTP site name, full pathname), and the current version number and release date of the software.

- Include a FAQ section at the end, if appropriate. Many HOWTO documents need a "FAQ" or "Common Problems" section to cover information that can't be covered in the regular text.

- Use other HOWTOs or mini-HOWTOs as a model! The SGML source to the HOWTOs is available on Linux FTP sites. In addition, have a look at the LDP Style Guide for some guidelines. Make sure that your name, e-mail address, date, and a version number is near the beginning of the document. You could also include WWW addresses and a snail mail address if you want. The standard header is:

    Title

    Author's name and e-mail address

    Version number and date

    For example:

    The Linux HOWTO Index

    by Tim Bynum

    v2.10.29, 31 July 1997

- Lastly, be prepared to receive questions and comments about your writing. There are several hundreds of accesses to the HOWTO collection every day from around the world!

After you have written the HOWTO, mail it to me. If you used SGML-Tools, simply mail me the SGML source; I take care of formatting the documents. I'll also take care of archiving the HOWTOs on sunsite.unc.edu and posting them to the various newsgroups.

It is important that you go through me when submitting a HOWTO, as I maintain the archives and need to keep track of what HOWTOs are being written and who is doing what.

Then, all you have to do is send me periodic updates whenever appropriate.

Copyright

Copyright (c) 1995 - 1998 by Tim Bynum.

Unless otherwise stated, Linux HOWTO documents are copyrighted by their respective authors. Linux HOWTO documents may be reproduced and distributed in whole or in part, in any medium physical or electronic, as long as this copyright notice is retained on all copies. Commercial redistribution is allowed and encouraged; however, the author would like to be notified of any such distributions.

All translations, derivative works, or aggregate works incorporating any Linux HOWTO documents must be covered under this copyright notice. That is, you may not produce a derivative work from a HOWTO and impose additional restrictions on its distribution. Exceptions to these rules may be granted under certain conditions; please contact the Linux HOWTO coordinator at the address given below.

In short, we wish to promote dissemination of this information through as many channels as possible. However, we do wish to retain copyright on the HOWTO documents, and would like to be notified of any plans to redistribute the HOWTOs.

If you have questions, please contact Tim Bynum, the Linux HOWTO coordinator, via e-mail at **linux-howto@sunsite.unc.edu**.

App
B

The Linux Hardware Compatibility HOWTO

In this appendix

This HOWTO is the most current available as of June 1998. Most enhancements and upgrades to the listed hardware will work with the current versions of Linux. You can find all the HOWTOs mentioned in this HOWTO in the /usr/doc/HOWTO or usr/doc/HOWTO/mini directories on your local drive.

Use the following command to read the HOWTO files with the .gz extension:

```
zcat filename ¦ more
```

Introduction

Linux Hardware Compatibility HOWTO

Patrick Reijnen, < patrickr@bart.nl (remove "antispam")>

v98.2, 29 March 1998

This document lists most of the hardware supported by Linux and helps you locate any necessary drivers.

> **N O T E**   Be sure to remove both "antispam" parts from my mail address above. I'm sorry for putting them in, but half of the mail I get in a week is spam, so I have to. ■

Welcome

Welcome to the Linux Hardware Compatibility HOWTO. This document lists most of the hardware components (not computers with components built-in) supported by Linux, so by reading through this document you can choose the components for your own Linux computer. As the list of components supported by Linux is growing rapidly, this document will never be complete. So, when components are not mentioned in this HOWTO, the only reason will be that I don't know they are supported. I simply have not found support for the component and/or nobody has told me about support.

Subsections titled Others list hardware with alpha or beta drivers in varying degrees of usability or other drivers that aren't included in standard kernels. Note that some drivers only exist in alpha kernels, so if you see something listed as supported but isn't in your version of the Linux kernel, upgrade.

The latest version of this document can be found on http://users.bart.nl/~patrickr/hardware-howto/Hardware-HOWTO.html, SunSite and all the usual mirror sites.

Translations of this and other Linux HOWTO's can be found at http://sunsite.unc.edu/pub/Linux/docs/HOWTO/translations and ftp://sunsite.unc.edu/pub/Linux/docs/HOWTO/translations.

If you know of any Linux hardware (in)compatibilities not listed here please let me know, just send mail.

Still need some help selecting components after reading this document? Check the "Build Your Own PC" site at http://www.verinet.com/pc/.

Copyright

Copyright 1997, 1998 Patrick Reijnen

This HOWTO is free documentation; you can redistribute it and/or modify it under the terms of the GNU General Public License as published by the Free Software Foundation; either version 2 of the license, or (at your option) any later version.

This document is distributed in the hope that it will be useful, but without any warranty; without even the implied warranty of merchantability or fitness for a particular purpose. See the GNU General Public License for more details. You can obtain a copy of the GNU General Public License by writing to the Free Software Foundation, Inc., 675 Mass Ave, Cambridge, MA 02139, USA.

If you use this or any other Linux HOWTO's in a commercial distribution, it would be nice to send the authors a complimentary copy of your product.

App

C

System Architectures

This document only deals with Linux for Intel platforms; for other platforms, check the following:

Linux for PowerMac
http://ftp.sunet.se/pub/os/Linux/mklinux/mkarchive/info/index.htm

Computers/Motherboards/BIOS

ISA, VLB, EISA, and PCI buses are all supported.

PS/2 and Microchannel (MCA) is supported in the standard kernel 2.0.7. There is support for MCA in kernel 2.1.16 and newer, but this code is still a little buggy. For more information you can always look at the Micro Channel Linux

Home Page (http://glycerine.itsmm.uni.edu/mca/)

Specific Systems

IBM PS/2 MCA systems   ftp://ftp.dcrl.nd.edu/pub/misc/linux/

Many new PCI boards are causing a couple of failure messages during boot time when "Probing PCI Hardware." The procedure presents the following message

```
Warning : Unknown PCI device (8086:7100). Please read include/linux/pci.h
```

It tells you to read the pci.h file. From this file is the following quote

PROCEDURE TO REPORT NEW PCI DEVICES

We are trying to collect information on new PCI devices, using the standard PCI identification procedure. If some warning is displayed at boot time, please report

- /proc/pci
- your exact hardware description. Try to find out which device is unknown. It may be your mainboard chipset. PCI-CPU bridge or PCI-ISA bridge.
- If you can't find the actual information in your hardware booklet, try to read the references of the chip on the board.
- Send all that to linux-pcisupport@cao-vlsi.ibp.fr, and I'll add your device to the list as soon as possible. BEFORE you send a mail, please check the latest Linux releases to be sure it has not been recently added.
- Thanks Frederic Potter.

Normally spoken your motherboard and the unknown PCI devices will function correctly.

Laptops

For more information about Linux and laptops, the following site is a good starting point:

- Linux Laptop Homepage http://www.cs.utexas.edu/users/kharker/linux-laptop/

Other information related to laptops can be found at the following sites:

- Avanced Power Management ftp://ftp.cs.unc.edu/pub/users/faith/linux/
- Notebook battery status ftp://sunsite.unc.edu/pub/Linux/system/power/
- Non-blinking cursor
  ftp://sunsite.unc.edu/pub/Linux/kernel/patches/console/noblink-1.7.tar.gz
- Other general info ftp://tsx-11.mit.edu/pub/linux/packages/laptops/

Specific Laptops

Compaq Concerto (pen driver)http://www.cs.nmsu.edu/~pfeiffer/

Compaq Contura Aero http://domen.uninett.no/~hta/linux/aero-faq.html

IBM ThinkPad http://peipa.essex.ac.uk/tp-linux/tp-linux.html

NEC Versa M and P http://www.santafe.edu:80/~nelson/versa-linux/

Tadpole P1000 http://www.tadpole.com/Support/linux.html

Tadpole P1000 (another one)

TI TravelMate 4000M
ftp://ftp.biomath.jussieu.fr/pub/linux/TM4000M-mini-HOWTO.txt.Z

TI TravelMate 5100

Toshiba Satellite Pro 400CDT
http://terra.mpikg-teltow.mpg.de/~burger/T400CDT-Linux.html

PCMCIA

PCMCIA http://hyper.stanford.edu/HyperNews/get/pcmcia/home.html

PCMCIA drivers currently support all common PCMCIA controllers, including Databook
TCIC/2, Intel i82365SL, Cirrus PD67xx, and Vadem VG-468 chipsets. Motorola 6AHC05GA
controller used in some Hyundai laptops is not supported. See Appendix B for a list of supported PCMCIA cards.

CPU/FPU

Intel/AMD/Cyrix 386SX/DX/SL/DXL/SLC, 486SX/DX/SL/SX2/DX2/DX4 are supported.
Intel Pentium, Pentium Pro and Pentium II (basically it's a Pentium Pro with MMX) also work.
AMD K5 and K6 work well, although older versions of K6 should be avoided as they are buggy.
Setting "internal cache" disabled in bios setup can be a workaround.

Linux has built-in FPU emulation if you don't have a math coprocessor.

Experimental SMP (multiple CPU) support is included in kernel 1.3.31 and newer. Check the
Linux/SMP Project page for details and updates.

Linux/SMP Project   http://www.linux.org.uk/SMP/title.html

A few very early AMD 486DXs may hang in some special situations. All current chips should
be okay and getting a chip swap for old CPUs should not be a problem.

ULSI Math*Co series has a bug in the FSAVE and FRSTOR instructions that causes problems
with all protected mode operating systems. Some older IIT and Cyrix chips may also have this
problem.

There are problems with TLB flushing in UMC U5S chips in very old kernels. (1.1.x)

- Enable cache on Cyrix processors
  ftp://sunsite.unc.edu/pub/Linux/kernel/patches/CxPatch030.tar.z
- Cyrix software cache control
  ftp://sunsite.unc.edu/pub/Linux/kernel/patches/linux.cxpatch
- Cyrix 5x86 CPU register settings
  ftp://sunsite.unc.edu/pub/Linux/kernel/patches/cx5x86mod_1.0c.tgz

Memory

All memory like DRAM, EDO, and SDRAM can be used with Linux. There is one thing you
have to look at: normally the kernel is not supporting more than 64MB of memory. When you

add more than 64MB of memory, you have to add the following line to your LILO configuration file:

```
append="mem=<number of MB>M"
```

So, when you have 96MB of memory, this should become

```
append="mem=96M"
```

Don't type a number higher than the number of MB you really have. This can present unpredictable crashes.

Video Cards

Linux will work with all video cards in text mode. VGA cards not listed below probably will still work with mono VGA and/or standard VGA drivers.

If you're looking into buying a cheap video card to run X, keep in mind that accelerated cards (ATI Mach, ET4000/W32p, S3) are MUCH faster than unaccelerated or partially accelerated (Cirrus, WD) cards.

32 bpp is actually 24-bit color aligned on 32-bit boundaries. It does NOT mean the cards are capable of 32-bit color, they still display 24-bit color (16,777,216 colors). 24-bit packed pixels modes are not supported in XFree86, so cards that can do 24-bit modes to get higher resolutions in other OSs are not able to do this in X using XFree86. These cards include Mach32, Cirrus 542x, S3 801/805/868/968, ET4000, and others.

Diamond Video Cards

Most currently available Diamond cards ARE supported by the current release of XFree86. Early Diamond cards may not be officially supported by XFree86, but there are ways of getting them to work. Diamond is now actively supporting the XFree86 Project.

SVGALIB (Graphics for Console)

Tseng ET3000/ET4000/W32

XFree86 3.3.1

Accelerated

Western Digital WD90C24/24A/24A2/31/33

Unaccelerated

Alliance AP6422, AT24

ATI VGA Wonder series

Avance Logic AL2101/2228/2301/2302/2308/2401

Cirrus Logic 6420/6440, 7555

Compaq AVGA

DEC 21030

Genoa GVGA

MCGA (320x200)

MX MX68000/MX68010

NCR 77C22, 77C22E, 77C22E+

NVidia NV1

Oak OTI-037C, OTI-067, OTI-077

RealTek RTG3106

SGS-Thomson STG2000

Trident 8800CS, 8200LX, 8900x, 9000, 9000i, 9100B, 9200CXr, 9320LCD, 9400CXi, 9420, 9420DGi, 9430DGi

Tseng ET3000, ET4000AX

VGA (standard VGA, 4 bit, slow)

Video 7 / Headland Technologies HT216-32

Western Digital/Paradise PVGA1, WD90C00/10/11/30

Monochrome

Hercules mono

Hyundai HGC-1280

Sigma LaserView PLUS

VGA mono

Others

EGA (ancient, from c. 1992) ftp://ftp.funet.fi/pub/Linux/BETA/Xega/

S.u.S.E. X-Server

S.u.S.E. is building a series of X-servers based on the XFree-86 code. These X-servers support new video cards and are bug fixed releases for XFree86 X-servers. S.u.S.E is building these X-servers together with The XFree86 Project, Inc. These X-servers will be in the next XFree86 version. These X-servers can be found at

`http://www.suse.de/index.html.`

At this moment S.u.S.E. X-servers are available for the following video cards.

- XSuSE Elsa GLoria X-Server
- ELSA GLoria L, GLoria L/MX, Gloria S
- Video cards with the Alliance Semiconductor AT3D (also AT25) Chip
- Hercules Stingray 128 3D

- XSuSE NVidia X-Server (PCI and AGP support, NV1 chipset and Riva128)
- ASUS 3Dexplorer
- Diamond Viper 330
- ELSA VICTORY Erazor
- STB Velocity 128
- XSuSE Matrox. Support for Mystique, Millennium, Millennium IIz, and Millennium II AGP
- XSuSE Trident. Support for the 9685 (including ClearTV) and the latest Cyber chipset
- XSuSE Tseng. W32, W32i ET6100, and ET6300 support.

Commercial X Servers

Commercial X servers provide support for cards not supported by XFree86, and might give better performances for cards that are supported by XFree86. In general, they support many more cards than XFree86, so I'll onlys list cards that aren't supported by XFree86 here. Contact the vendors directly or check the Commercial HOWTO for more info.

Xi Graphics, Inc Xi Graphics, Inc http://www.xig.com (formerly known as X Inside, Inc) is selling three X server products (cards supported are sorted by manufacturer):

Accelerated-X Display Server

3Dlabs

- 300SX
- 500TX Glint
- 500MX Glint
- Permedia 4MB/8MB
- Permedia II 4MB/8MB

Actix

- GE32plus 1MB/2MB
- GE32ultra 2MB
- GraphicsENGINE 64 1MB/2MB
- ProSTAR 64 1MB/2MB

Alliance

- ProMotion-3210 1MB/2MB
- ProMotion-6410 1MB/2MB
- ProMotion-6422 1MB/2MB

ARK Logic

- ARK1000PV 1MB/2MB
- ARK1000VL 1MB/2MB
- ARK2000PV 1MB/2MB

AST

- Manhattan 5090P (GD5424) 512KB

ATI

- 3D Xpression 1MB/2MB
- 3D Pro Turbo PC2TV 4MB/8MB
- 3D Pro Turbo PC2TV 6144
- 3D Xpression+ PC2TV 2MB/4MB
- 3D Xpression+ 2MB/4MB
- ALL-IN-WONDER 4MB/8MB
- ALL-IN-WONDER PRO 4MB/8MB
- Graphics Ultra (Mach8) 1MB
- Graphics Pro Turbo (Mach64/VRAM) 2MB/4MB
- Graphics Pro Turbo 1600 (Mach64/VRAM) 2MB/4MB
- Graphics Ultra Plus (Mach32) 2MB
- 8514/Ultra (Mach8) 1MB
- Graphics Ultra Pro (Mach32) 1MB2MB
- Graphics Vantage (Mach8) 1MB
- VGA Wonder Plus 512KB
- VGA Wonder XL 1MB
- Video Xpression 1MB
- XPERT@Play 4MB/6MB/8MB
- XPERT@Work 4MB/6MB/8MB
- Video Xpression 2MB
- WinBoost (Mach64/DRAM) 2MB
- WinTurbo (Mach64/VRAM) 2MB
- Graphics Wonder (Mach32) 1MB
- Graphics Xpression 1MB/2MB
- Rage II (SGRAM) 2MB/4MB/8MB
- Rage II+ (SGRAM) 2MB/4MB/8MB
- Rage Pro 2MB/4MB/8MB

Avance Logic

- ALG2101 1MB
- ALG2228 1MB/2MB
- ALG2301 1MB/2MB

Boca

- Voyager 1MB/2MB
- Vortek-VL 1MB/2MB

Colorgraphic

- Dual Lightning 2MB
- Pro Lightning Accelerator 2MB
- Quad Pro Lightning Accelerator 2MB
- Twin Turbo Accelerator 1MB/2MB

Chips & Technology

- 64300 1MB/2MB
- 64310 1MB/2MB
- 65510 512KB
- 65520 1MB
- 65530 1MB
- 65535 1MB
- 65540 1MB
- 65545 1MB
- 65550 2MB
- 82C450 512KB
- 82C451 256KB
- 82C452 512KB
- 82C453 1MB
- 82C480 1MB/2MB
- 82C481 1MB/2MB

Cirrus Logic

- GD5402 512KB
- GD5420 1MB
- GD5422 1MB
- GD5424 1MB

- GD5426 1MB/2MB
- GD5428 1MB/2MB
- GD5429 1MB/2MB
- GD5430 1MB/2MB
- GD5434 1MB/2MB
- GD5436 1MB/2MB
- GD5440 1MB/2MB
- GD5446 1MB/2MB
- GD5462 2MB/4MB PCI and AGP
- GD5464 2MB/4MB PCI and AGP
- GD5465 2MB/4MB PCI and AGP
- GD54M30 1MB/2MB
- GD54M40 1MB/2MB

App

C

Compaq

- ProLiant Series 512KB
- ProSignia Series 512KB
- QVision 1024 1MB
- QVision 1280 1MB/2MB
- QVision 2000+ 2MB
- QVision 2000 2MB

DEC

- DECpc XL 590 (GD5428) 512KB

Dell

- 466/M & 466/ME (S3 805) 1MB
- OnBoard ET4000 1MB
- DGX (JAWS) 2MB
- OptiPlex XMT 590 (Vision864) 2MB

Diamond

- Fire GL 1000 Pro 4MB/8MB
- Fire GL 1000 4MB/8MB
- Stealth 3D 2000 2MB/4MB
- Stealth 3D 3000XL 2MB/4MB
- Stealth 64 Graphics 2001 1MB/2MB

- Stealth 64 Graphics 2121XL 1MB/2MB
- Stealth 64 Graphics 2201XL 2MB
- SpeedStar 1MB
- SpeedStar 64 Graphics 2000 1MB/2MB
- SpeedStar 24 1MB
- SpeedStar 24X 1MB
- SpeedStar 64 1MB/2MB
- SpeedStar Hicolor 1MB
- SpeedStar PCI 1MB
- SpeedStar Pro 1MB
- SpeedStar Pro SE 1MB/2MB
- Stealth 1MB
- Stealth 24 1MB
- Stealth 32 1MB/2MB
- Stealth 64 VRAM 2MB/4MB
- Stealth 64 DRAM 1MB/2MB
- Stealth 64 Video VRAM (175MHz) 2MB/4MB
- Stealth 64 Video DRAM 1MB/2MB
- Stealth 64 Video VRAM (220MHz) 2MB/4MB
- Stealth Hicolor 1MB
- Stealth Pro 1MB/2MB
- Stealth SE 1MB/2MB
- Stealth 64 Video 2001TV 2MB
- Stealth 64 Video 2121 1MB/2MB
- Stealth 64 Video 2121TV 1MB/2MB
- Stealth 64 Video 2201 2MB
- Stealth 64 Video 2201TV 2MB
- Stealth 64 Video 3200 2MB
- Stealth 64 Video 3240 2MB/4MB
- Stealth 64 Video 3400 4MB
- Viper 1MB/2MB
- Viper Pro 2MB
- Viper Pro Video 2MB/4MB
- Viper SE 2MB/4MB

ELSA

- VICTORY 3D 2MB/4MB
- WINNER 1000 1MB/2MB
- WINNER 1000AVI 1MB/2MB
- WINNER 1000ISA 1MB/2MB
- WINNER 1000PRO 1MB/2MB
- WINNER 1000TRIO 1MB/2MB
- WINNER 1000TRIO/V 1MB/2MB
- WINNER 100VL 1MB
- WINNER 2000 2MB/4MB
- WINNER 2000AVI 2MB/4MB
- WINNER 2000AVI/3D 2MB/4MB
- WINNER 2000PRO 2MB/4MB
- WINNER 2000PRO/X 2MB/4MB/8MB
- WINNER3000-L 4MB
- WINNER3000-M 2MB
- WINNER3000-S 2MB
- WINNER 1024 1MB
- WINNER 1280, TLC34075 Palette 2MB
- WINNER 1280, TLC34076 Palette 2MB
- Gloria-XL
- Gloria-MX
- Gloria-L
- Synergy

Everex

- ViewPoint 64P 1MB/2MB
- VGA Trio 64P 1MB/2MB

Gateway

- Mach64 Accelerator (Mach64/VRAM) 2MB

Genoa

- 5400 512KB
- 8500/8500VL 1MB
- Phantom 32i 8900 2MB
- Phantom 64 2MB

App
C

Hercules

- Dynamite 1MB
- Dynamite Pro 1MB/2MB
- Dynamite Power 2MB
- Dynamite 3D / GL
- Graphite 1MB
- Stingray 64 1MB/2MB
- Stingray Pro 1MB/2MB
- Stringray 1MB
- Terminator 3D 2MB/4MB
- Terminator 64/Video 2MB
- Graphite Terminator Pro 2MB/4MB

HP

- NetServer LF/LC/LE (TVGA9000i) 512KB
- Vectra VL2 (GD5428) 1MB
- Vectra XM2i (Vision864) 1MB/2MB
- Vectra XU (Vision864) 1MB/2MB

IBM

- 8514/A 1MB
- PC 300 Series (GD5430) 1MB
- PC 300 Series (Vision864) 1MB/2MB
- PC 700 Series (Vision864) 1MB/2MB
- PS/ValuePoint Performance Series (Vision864) 1MB/2MB
- VC550 1MB
- VGA 256KB
- XGA-NI 1MB
- XGA 1MB

IIT

- AGX014 1MB
- AGX015 1MB/2MB

Integral

- FlashPoint 1MB/2MB

Leadtek

- WinFast L2300 4MB/8MB

Matrox

- Comet 2MB
- Marvel II 2MB
- Impression (MGA-IMP/3/A/H, MGA-IMP/3/V/H, MGA-IMP/3/M/H) 3MB
- Impression Lite (MGA-IMP+/LTE/P) 2MB
- Impression Plus Lite (MGA-IMP+/LTE/V) 2MB
- Millennium (MGA-MIL) 2MB/4MB/8MB
- Millennium 220 (MGA-MIL) 2MB/4MB/8MB
- Millennium PowerDoc (WRAM) 2MB/4MB/8MB
- Millennium II (WRAM) 2MB/4MB/8MB PCI and AGP
- Mystique (MGA-MYS) 2MB/4MB
- Mystique 220
- Matrox (con.t)
- Impression Plus (MGA-IMP+/P, MGA-IMP+/A) 2MB/4MB
- Impression Plus 220 (MGA-IMP+/P/H, MGA-IMP+/A/H) 2MB/4MB
- Impression Pro (MGA-PRO/4.5/V) 4.5MB
- Ultima Plus (MGA-PCI/2+, MGA-VLB/2+) 2MB/4MB
- Ultima (MGA-ULT/2/A, MGA-PCI/2, MGA-VLB/2) 2MB
- Ultima (MGA-ULT/2/A/H, MGA-ULT_2/M/H) 2MB
- Ultima Plus 200 (MGA-PCI/4/200, MGA-VLB/4/200) 4MB

MaxVision

- VideoMax 2000 2MB/4MB

Metheus

- Premier 801 1MB
- Premier 928-1M 1MB
- Premier 928-2M 2MB
- Premier 928-4M 4MB

Micronics

- Mpower 4 Plus (Mach64) 1MB

App

C

MIRO

- miroCRYSTAL 10AD 1MB
- miroCRYSTAL 12SD 1MB
- miroCRYSTAL 12SD 2MB
- miroCRYSTAL 20PV 2MB
- miroCRYSTAL 20SD 2MB
- miroCRYSTAL 20SV 2MB
- miroCRYSTAL 22SD 2MB
- miroCRYSTAL 40SV 4MB
- miroCRYSTAL VR2000 2MB/4MB
- miroMAGIC 40PV 4MB
- miroMAGIC plus 2MB
- miroVIDEO 12PD 1MB/2MB
- miroVIDEO 20SD 2MB
- miroVIDEO 20SV 2MB
- miroVIDEO 20TD 2MB
- miroVIDEO 22SD 2MB
- miroVIDEO 40SV 4MB

NEC

- Versa P Series 1MB

Nth Graphics

- Engine/150 2MB
- Engine/250 2MB

Number Nine

- GXE Level 10, AT&T 20C491 Palette 1MB
- GXE Level 10, Bt485 or AT&T20C505 Palette 1MB
- GXE Level 11 2MB
- GXE Level 12 3MB
- GXE Level 14 4MB
- GXE Level 16 4MB
- GXE64 1MB/2MB
- GXE64pro 2MB/4MB
- GXE64pro (-1600) 2MB/4MB

- Imagine 128 2MB
- Image 128 (-1280) 4MB
- Image 128 Series 2 (DRAM) 2MB/4MB
- Image 128 Pro (-1600) 4MB/8MB
- Image 128 Series 2 (VRAM) 2MB/4MB/8MB
- Image 128 Series III (Revolution 3D) (WRAM) 8MB/16MB PCI and AGP
- Revolution 3D "Ticket to Ride" (WRAM) 8MB/16MB PCI and AGP
- 9FX Motion331 1MB/2MB
- 9FX Motion531 1MB/2MB
- 9FX Motion771 2MB/4MB
- 9FX Reality332 2MB
- 9FX Reality772 2MB/4MB
- 9FX Reality 334 PCI and AGP
- 9FX Vision330 1MB/2MB

Oak Technology

- OTI-067 512KB
- OTI-077 1MB
- OTI-087 1MB
- OTI-107 1MB/2MB
- OTI-111 1MB/2MB

Orchid

- Farenheit 1280 Plus, ATT20C491 Palette 1MB
- Farenheit 1280 1MB
- Farenheit 1280 Plus, SC15025 Palette 1MB
- Farenheit ProVideo 64 2MB/4MB
- Farenheit Video 3D 2MB
- Kelvin 64 1MB/2MB
- Kelvin Video64 1MB/2MB
- P9000 2MB

Packard Bell

- Series 5000 Motherboard 1MB

Paradise

- 8514/A 1MB
- Accelerator 24 1MB

App
C

- Accelerator Value card 1MB
- Bahamas 64 1MB/2MB
- Bali 32 1MB/2MB
- VGA 1024 512KB
- VGA Professional 512KB

Pixelworks

- WhrilWIN WL1280 (110MHz) 2MB
- WhrilWIN WL1280 (135MHz) 2MB
- WhirlWIN WW1280 (110MHz) 2MB
- WhirlWIN WW1280 (135MHz) 2MB
- WhrilWIN WW1600 1MB

Radius

- XGA-2 1MB

Reveal

- VC200 1MB
- VC300 1MB
- VC700 1MB

S3

- ViRGE 2MB/4MB
- ViRGE/DX 2MB/4MB
- ViRGE/GX 2MB/4MB
- ViRGE/GX /2 2MB/4MB
- ViRGE/VX 2MB/4MB
- Trio32 1MB/2MB
- Trio64 1MB/2MB
- Trio64V+ 1MB/2MB
- Trio64V2/DX 1MB/2MB
- Trio64V2/GX 1MB/2MB
- 801 1MB/2MB
- 805 1MB/2MB
- Vision864 1MB/2MB
- Vision866 1MB/2MB

- Vision868 1MB/2MB
- 911 1MB
- 924 1MB
- 928 1MB
- 928 2MB/4MB

Sierra

- Falcon/64 1MB/2MB

Sigma

- Legend 1MB

SPEA/V7

- Mercury P64 2MB
- Storm Pro 4MB
- ShowTime Plus 2MB
- STB
- Evolution VGA 1MB
- Horizon Plus 1MB
- Horizon VGA 1MB
- Horizon 64 1MB/2MB
- Horizon 64 Video 1MB/2MB
- Horizon Video 1MB
- LightSpeed 2MB
- LightSpeed 128 2MB
- Nitro 3D 2MB/4MB
- Nitro 64 1MB/2MB
- Nitro 64 Video 1MB/2MB
- PowerGraph VL-24 1MB
- PowerGraph X-24 1MB
- PowerGraph 64 3D 2MB
- PowerGraph 64 1MB/2MB
- PowerGraph 64 Video 1MB/2MB
- PowerGraph Pro 2MB
- Velocity 3D 4MB
- Velocity 64V 2MB/4MB

App

C

Toshiba

- T4900CT 1MB

Trident

- TGUI9400CXi 1MB/2MB
- TGUI9420DGi 1MB/2MB
- TGUI9440 1MB/2MB
- TGUI9660 1MB/2MB
- TGUI9680 1MB/2MB
- TVGA8900B 1MB
- TVGA8900C 1MB
- TVGA8900CL 1MB
- TVGA8900D 1MB
- TVGA9000 512KB
- TVGA9000i 512KB
- TVGA9200CXr 1MB/2MB

Tseng Labs

- ET3000 512KB
- ET4000 1MB
- ET6000 2MB/4MB
- VGA/16 (ISA) 1MB
- VGA/16 (VLB) 1MB/2MB
- VGA/32 1MB/2MB
- ET4000/W32 1MB
- ET4000/W32i 1MB/2MB
- ET4000/W32p 1MB/2MB

VLSI

- VL82C975 (AT&T RAMDAC) 2MB
- VL82C975 (BrookTree RAMDAC) 2MB
- VL82C976 (Internal RAMDAC) 2MB

Western Digital

- WD90C00 512KB
- WD90C11 512KB
- WD90C24 1MB

- WD90C26 512KB
- WD90C30 1MB
- WD90C31 1MB
- WD90C33 1MB
- WD9510-AT 1MB

Weitek

- P9100 2MB
- P9000 2MB
- W5186 1MB
- W5286 1MB
- Laptop Accelerated-X Display Server

Broadax

- NP8700 (Cyber 9385)

Chips & Technology

- 65510 512KB
- 65520 1MB
- 65530 1MB
- 65535 1MB
- 65540 1MB
- 65545 1MB
- 65554 2MB/4MB
- 65555 2MB

Cirrus Logic

- GD7541 1MB/2MB
- GD7543 1MB/2MB
- GD7548 2MB

Compaq

- LTE 5400 (Cirrus Logic CL5478)
- Presario 1090ES (NM 2093)

Dell

- Latitude XPi 896 (NeoMagic 2070)
- Latitude XPi (NM 2070)

App
C

- Latitude XPi CD 1MB (NM 2090)
- Latitude LM (NM 2160)
- Latitude CP (NM 2160)
- Inspiron 3000 (NM 2160)

Digital (DEC)

- HiNote VP (NeoMagic 2090)
- Fujitsu
- Lifebook 435DX (NeoMagic 2093)

Gateway 2000

- Solo 2300 (NeoMagic 2160)
- Solo 2300 SE (NM 2160)
- Solo 9100 (C&T 65554)
- Solo 9100XL (C&T 65555)

Hewlett Packard

- OmniBook 800 (NM 2093)

Hitachi

- Notebook E133T (NeoMagic 2070)

IBM

- VGA 256KB
- Thinkpad 380D (NeoMagic 2090)*
- Thinkpad 385ED (NeoMagic 2090)*
- Thinkpad 560E (Cyber 9382)
- Thinkpad 760XD (Cyber 9385)
- Thinkpad 770 (Cyber 9397)

Micron

- TransPort XKE (NeoMagic 2160)
- Millenia Transport (Cirrus Logic GD7548)

NEC

- Versa P Series 1MB
- Versa 6230 2MB (NeoMagic 2160)

NeoMagic

- MagicGraph128 / NM2070 896
- MagicGraph128 / NM2070
- MagicGraph128V / NM2090
- MagicGraph128V+ / NM2097
- MagicGraph128ZV / NM2093
- MagicGraph128XD / NM2160

Sony

- VAIO PCG-505 (NeoMagic 2097)

Toshiba

- T4900CT 1MB
- Tecra 740CDT (C&T 65554)

Trident

- Cyber 9397
- Cyber 9385
- Cyber 9382

Twinhead

- Slimnote 9166TH (Cyber 9385)
- * Numerous XiG customers have comfirmed support.
- Multi-head Accelerated-X Display Server

Metro-X 2.3

- Metro Link < sales@metrolink.com>
- I don't have much more information about Metro-X as I can't seem to view the PostScript files they sent me. Mail them directly for more info.
- The S3 ViRGE video card is said not to be supported by Metro-X.

Controllers (Hard Drive)

Linux will work with standard IDE, MFM, and RLL controllers. When using MFM/RLL controllers, it is important to use ext2fs and the bad block checking options when formatting the disk.

Enhanced IDE (EIDE) interfaces are supported. With up to two IDE interfaces and up to four hard drives and/or CD-ROM drives, Linux will detect these EIDE interfaces:

App
C

- CMD-640
- DTC 2278D
- FGI/Holtek HT-6560B
- RZ1000
- Triton I (82371FB) (with busmaster DMA)
- Triton II (82371SB) (with busmaster DMA)

ESDI controllers that emulate the ST-506 (MFM/RLL/IDE) interface will also work. The bad block checking comment also applies to these controllers. Generic 8-bit XT controllers also work. Starting with pre-patch-2.0.31-3, IDE/ATAPI is provided.

Other controllers supported:

- Tekram D690CD IDE PCI Cache Controller (with RAID level 1 Mirroring and caching)

Controllers (SCSI)

It is important to pick a SCSI controller carefully. Many cheap ISA SCSI controllers are designed to drive CD-ROM's rather than anything else. Such low-end SCSI controllers are no better than IDE. See the SCSI HOWTO and look at performance figures before buying a SCSI card.

Supported

- AMI Fast Disk VLB/EISA (BusLogic compatible)
- Adaptec AVA-1502E (ISA/VLB) (AIC-6360). Use the AHA-152x driver
- Adaptec AVA-1505/1515 (ISA) (Adaptec AHA-152x compatible)
- Adaptec AHA-1510/152x (ISA/VLB) (AIC-6260/6360)
- Adaptec AHA-154x (ISA) (all models)
- Adaptec AHA-174x (EISA) (in enhanced mode)
- Adaptec AHA-274x (EISA) (AIC-7771)
- Adaptec AHA-284x (VLB) (AIC-7770)
- Adaptec AHA-2920 (PCI). Use the Future Domain driver
- Adaptec AHA-2940AU (PCI) (AIC-7861)
- Adaptec AHA-294x/U/W/UW/D/WD (AIC-7871, AIC-7844, AIC-7881, AIC-7884)
- Adaptec AHA-3940/U/W (PCI) (AIC-7872, AIC-7882) (since 1.3.6)
- Adaptec AHA-398x/U/W (PCI) (AIC-7873, AIC-7883)
- Adaptec PCI controllers with AIC-7850, AIC-7855, AIC-7860
- Adaptec on board controllers with AIC-777x (EISA), AIC-785x, AIC-787x (PCI), AIC-788x (PCI)

- Always IN2000
- BusLogic (ISA/EISA/VLB/PCI) (all models)
- DPT PM2001, PM2012A (EATA-PIO)
- DPT Smartcache/SmartRAID Plus,III,IV families (ISA/EISA/PCI). Take a look at http://www.uni-mainz.de/~neuffer/scsi/dpt/ (EATA-DMA)
- Cards in these families are PM2011, PM2021, PM2041, PM3021, PM2012B, PM2022, PM2122, PM2322, PM2042, PM3122, PM3222, PM3332, PM2024, PM2124, PM2044, PM2144, PM3224, PM3334
- DTC 329x (EISA) (Adaptec 154x compatible)
- Future Domain TMC-16x0, TMC-3260 (PCI)
- Future Domain TMC-8xx, TMC-950
- Future Domain chips TMC-1800, TMC-18C50, TMC-18C30, TMC-36C70
- ICP-Vortex PCI-SCSI Disk Array Controllers (many RAID levels supported)

Patches for Linux 1.2.13 and 2.0.29 are available at ftp://icp-vortex.com/download/linux/. The controllers GDT6111RP, GDT6121RP, GDT6117RP, GDT6127RP, GDT6511RP, GDT6521RP, GDT6517RP, GDT6527RP, GDT6537RP, and GDT6557RP are supported. You can also use pre-patch-2.0.31-4 to pre-patch-2.0.31-9.

- ICP-Vortex EISA-SCSI Controllers (many RAID levels supported)

Patches for Linux 1.2.13 and 2.0.29 are available at ftp://icp-vortex.com/download/linux/. The controllers GDT3000B, GDT3000A, GDT3010A, GDT3020A, and GDT3050A are supported. You can also use pre-patch-2.0.31-4 to pre-patch-2.0.31-9.

- Media Vision Pro Audio Spectrum 16 SCSI (ISA)
- NCR 5380 generic cards
- NCR 53C400 (Trantor T130B) (use generic NCR 5380 SCSI support)
- NCR 53C406a (Acculogic ISApport / Media Vision Premium 3D SCSI)
- NCR chips 53C7x0
- NCR chips 53C810, 53C815, 53C820, 53C825, 53C860, 53C875, 53C895
- Qlogic / Control Concepts SCSI/IDE (FAS408) (ISA/VLB)
- Quantum ISA-200S, ISA-250MG
- Seagate ST-01/ST-02 (ISA)
- SoundBlaster 16 SCSI-2 (Adaptec 152x-compatible) (ISA)
- Tekram DC-390, DC-390W/U/F
- Trantor T128/T128F/T228 (ISA)

- UltraStor 14F (ISA), 24F (EISA), 34F (VLB)
- Western Digital WD7000 SCSI

Others

- AMD AM53C974, AM79C974 (PCI) (Compaq, HP, Zeos onboard SCSI)

  ftp://sunsite.unc.edu/pub/Linux/kernel/patches/scsi/AM53C974-0.3.tgz
- Adaptec ACB-40xx SCSI-MFM/RLL bridgeboard

  ftp://sunsite.unc.edu/pub/Linux/kernel/patches/scsi/adaptec-40XX.tar.gz
- Always Technologies AL-500

  ftp://sunsite.unc.edu/pub/Linux/kernel/patches/scsi/al500-0.2.tar.gz
- BusLogic (ISA/EISA/VLB/PCI) (new beta driver)

  ftp://sunsite.unc.edu/pub/Linux/kernel/patches/scsi/BusLogic-1.3.0.tar.gz
- Iomega PC2/2B

  ftp://sunsite.unc.edu/pub/Linux/kernel/patches/scsi/iomega_pc2-1.1.x.tar.gz
- Qlogic (ISP1020) (PCI)

  ftp://sunsite.unc.edu/pub/Linux/kernel/patches/scsi/isp1020-0.5.gz
- Ricoh GSI-8

  ftp://tsx-11.mit.edu/pub/linux/ALPHA/scsi/gsi8.tar.gz

Unsupported

- Parallel port SCSI adapters
- Non Adaptec compatible DTC boards (327x, 328x)
- 9. Controllers (I/O)

Any standard serial/parallel/joystick/combo cards. Linux supports 8250, 16450, 16550, and 16550A UARTs. Cards that support non-standard IRQs (IRQ > 9) can be used.

See National Semiconductor's "Application Note AN-493" by Martin S. Michael. Section 5.0 describes in detail the differences between the NS16550 and NS16550A. Briefly, the NS16550 had bugs in the FIFO circuits, but the NS16550A (and later) chips fixed those. However, there were very few NS16550s produced by National, long ago, so these should be very rare. And many of the "16550" parts in actual modern boards are from the many manufacturers of compatible parts, which may not use the National "A" suffix. Also, some multiport boards will use 16552 or 16554 or various other multiport or multifunction chips from National or other suppliers (generally in a dense package soldered to the board, not a 40-pin DIP). Mostly, don't worry about it unless you encounter a very old 40-pin DIP National "NS16550" (no A) chip loose or in an old board, in which case treat it as a 16450 (no FIFO) rather than a 16550A.—Zhahai Stewart < zstewart@hisys.com>

Controllers (Multiport)

Non-Intelligent Cards - Supported

- Usenet Serial Board II (4 port)
- Non-intelligent cards usually come in two varieties—one using standard com port addresses and four IRQs, and another that's AST FourPort compatible and uses a selectable block of addresses and a single IRQ. (Addresses and IRQs are set using setserial.) If you're getting one of these cards, be sure to check which standard it conforms to; prices are no indication.

Intelligent Cards - Supported

- Computone IntelliPort II (4/8/16 port)
  ftp://ftp.computone.com/pub/bbs/beta/ip2linux-1.0.2.tar.gz
- Cyclades Cyclom-8Y/16Y (8, 16 port) (ISA/PCI)
- DigiBoard PC/Xe (ISA), PC/Xi (EISA) and PC/Xeve
- ftp://ftp.digibd.com/drivers/linux/
- Equinox SST Intelligent serial I/O cards
- http://www.equinox.com
- Hayes ESP 1, 2 and 8 port versions
- Included in kernel since 2.1.15. The driver for kernel versions 2.0.x can be found at
- http://www.nyx.net/~arobinso
- Stallion EasyIO (ISA) / EasyConnection 8/32 (ISA/MCA)
- Stallion EasyConnection 8/64 / ONboard (ISA/EISA/MCA) / Brumby / Stallion (ISA)

Others

- Comtrol RocketPort (8/16/32 port)
- ftp://sunsite.unc.edu/pub/Linux/kernel/patches/serial/comtrol-1.04.tar.gz
- DigiBoard COM/Xi
- contact Simon Park (si@wimpol.demon.co.uk) or Mark Hatle (fray@krypton.mankato.msus.edu). NOTE: Both e-mail addresses seem not to exist any longer.
- Moxa C102, C104, C168, C218 (8 port), C320 (8/16/24/32 expandable) and C320T
- ftp://ftp.moxa.com.tw/drivers/linux/
- Specialix SIO/XIO (modular, 4 to 32 ports)
- ftp://sunsite.unc.edu/pub/Linux/kernel/patches/serial/ sidrv.taz

App
C

Network Adapters

Ethernet adapters vary greatly in performance. In general, the newer the design, the better. Some very old cards like the 3Com 3C501 are only useful because they can be found in junk heaps for $5 a time. Be careful with clones—not all are good clones, and bad clones often cause erratic lockups under Linux. Read the Ethernet HOWTO, http://sunsite.unc.edu/LDP/ HOWTO/, for detailed descriptions of various cards.

Supported

Ethernet

- For ethernet cards with the DECchip DC21x4x family, the "Tulip" driver is available. More information on this driver can be found at http://cesdis.gsfc.nasa.gov/linux/drivers/tulip.html.
- Znyx 312 etherarray (Tulip driver)

ISDN

- Linux ISDN WWW page http://www.ix.de/ix/linux/linux-isdn.html
- Teles S0 ftp://ftp.franken.de/pub/isdn4linux/
- ISDN cards that emulate standard modems or common Ethernet adapters don't need any special drivers to work.

Pocket and Portable Adapters

- For more information on Linux and use of the parallel port, go to the Linux Parallel Port Home Page.
- http://www.torque.net/linux-pp.html
- D-Link DE600/DE620 parallel port adapter

Slotless

- PLIP (parallel port) - using "LapLink cable" or bi-directional cable

ARCnet

- Works with all ARCnet cards

TokenRing

- Any IBM tokenring card not using DMA
- IBM Tropic chipset cards
- Madge TokenRing OCI 16/4 Mk2

FDDI

- DEC DEFEA (EISA) / DEFPA (PCI) (kernel 2.0.24 and later)

Amateur Radio (AX.25)

- Most generic 8530-based HDLC boards

PCMCIA Cards

- See Appendix B for complete list.

Others

Ethernet

- Racal-Interlan PCI card (AMD PC net chip 97c970)

ISDN

- SpellCaster's Datacomute/BRI, Telecomute/BRI (ISA)
  ftp://ftp.franken.de/pub/isdn4linux/

ATM

- Efficient Networks ENI155P-MF 155MBps ATM adapter (PCI)
  http://lrcwww.epfl.ch/linux-atm/

Frame Relay

- Sangoma S502 56K Frame Relay card
  ftp://ftp.sovereign.org/pub/wan/fr/

Wireless

- Proxim RangeLan2 7100 (ISA) / 630x (OEM mini-ISA)
  http://www.komacke.com/distribution.html

Unsupported

- Sysconnect / Schneider & Koch Token Ring cards (all of them)

Sound Cards

Supported

- 6850 UART MIDI
- Adlib (OPL2)
- Audio Excell DSP16
- Aztech Sound Galaxy NX Pro
- Crystal CS4232 (PnP)-based cards
- ECHO-PSS cards (Orchid SoundWave32, Cardinal DSP16)
- Ensoniq SoundScape
- Gravis Ultrasound
- Gravis Ultrasound 16-bit sampling daughterboard
- Gravis Ultrasound MAX
- Logitech SoundMan Games (SBPro, 44kHz stereo support)

App
C

- Logitech SoundMan Wave (Jazz16/OPL4)
- Logitech SoundMan 16 (PAS-16 compatible)
- MediaTriX AudioTriX Pro
- Media Vision Premium 3D (Jazz16)
- Media Vision Pro Sonic 16 (Jazz)
- Media Vision Pro Audio Spectrum 16
- Microsoft Sound System (AD1848)
- OAK OTI-601D cards (Mozart)
- OPTi 82C925 cards. Use the MSS driver and the isapnp tools
- OPTi 82C928/82C929 cards (MAD16/MAD16 Pro/ISP16/Mozart)
- OPTi 82C931 cards. See http://oto.dyn.ml.org/~drees/opti931.html
- Sound Blaster
- Sound Blaster Pro
- Sound Blaster 16
- Turtle Beach Wavefront cards (Maui, Tropez)
- Wave Blaster (and other daughterboards)
- Cards based on the ESS Technologies AudioDrive chips (688, 1688, 1868, etc)
- AWE32/64 supports is started in kernel series 2.1.x (check the SoundBlaster AWE mini-HOWTO by Marcus Brinkmann for installation details)
- MPU-401 MIDI

Others

- MPU-401 MIDI (intelligent mode)
  ftp://sunsite.unc.edu/pub/Linux/kernel/sound/mpu401-0.2.tar.gz
- PC speaker / Parallel port DAC
  ftp://ftp.informatik.hu-berlin.de/pub/os/linux/hu-sound/
- Turtle Beach MultiSound/Tahiti/Monterey
  ftp://ftp.cs.colorado.edu/users/mccreary/archive/tbeach/multisound/

Unsupported

- The ASP chip on Sound Blaster 16 series is not supported. AWE32's onboard E-mu MIDI synthesizer is not supported.
- Nathan Laredo < laredo@gnu.ai.mit.edu> is willing to write AWE32 drivers if you send him a complimentary card. He is also willing to write drivers for almost any hardware if you send him free samples of your hardware.
- Sound Blaster 16's with DSP 4.11 and 4.12 have a hardware bug that causes hung/stuck notes when playing MIDI and digital audio at the same time. The problem can happen

with either Wave Blaster daughterboards or MIDI devices attached to the MIDI port. There is no known fix.

Hard Drives

- All hard drives should work if the controller is supported.
- (From the SCSI HOWTO) All direct access SCSI devices with a block size of 256, 512, or 1024 bytes should work. Other block sizes will not work (Note that this can often be fixed by changing the block and/or sector sizes using the MODE SELECT SCSI command).
- Large IDE (EIDE) drives work fine with newer kernels. The boot partition must lie in the first 1024 cylinders due to PC BIOS limitations.
- Some Conner CFP1060S drives may have problems with Linux and ext2fs. The symptoms are inode errors during e2fsck and corrupt file systems. Conner has released a firmware upgrade to fix this problem; contact Conner at 1-800-4CONNER (US) or +44-1294-315333 (Europe). Have the microcode version (found on the drive label, 9WA1.6x) handy when you call.
- Certain Micropolis drives have problems with Adaptec and BusLogic cards; contact the drive manufacturers for firmware upgrades if you suspect problems.
- Multiple device driver (RAID-0, RAID-1) ftp://sweet-smoke.ufr-info-p7.ibp.fr/public/Linux/

Tape Drives

Supported

- SCSI tape drives (From the SCSI HOWTO) Drives using both fixed and variable length blocks smaller than the driver buffer length (set to 32k in the distribution sources) are supported. Virtually all drives should work. (Send mail if you know of any incompatible drives.)
- QIC-02 drives
- Iomega DITTO internal (ftape 3.04c and newer)

Others

- QIC-117, QIC-40/80, QIC-3010/3020 (QIC-WIDE) drives. Most tape drives using the floppy controller should work. Various dedicated controllers (Colorado FC-10/FC-20, Mountain Mach-2, Iomega Tape Controller II) are also supported ftp://sunsite.unc.edu/pub/Linux/kernel/tapes
- ATAPI tape drives
- For these an alpha driver (ide-tape.c) is available in the kernel. ATAPI tape drives supported are

App
C

■ Seagate TapeStor 8000

■ Conner CTMA 4000 IDE ATAPI Streaming tape drive

Unsupported

■ Emerald and Tecmar QIC-02 tape controller cards - Chris Ulrich < insom@math.ucr.edu>

■ Drives that connect to the parallel port (eg: Colorado Trakker)

■ Some high-speed tape controllers (Colorado TC-15)

■ Irwin AX250L/Accutrak 250 (not QIC-80)

■ IBM Internal Tape Backup Unit (not QIC-80)

■ COREtape Light

CD-ROM Drives

■ For more information on CD-ROM drives, check the CDROM-HOWTO at http://sunsite.unc.edu/LDP/HOWTO/.

Supported

Common CD-ROM Drives

■ SCSI CD-ROM drives (From the CD-ROM HOWTO) Any SCSI CD-ROM drive with a block size of 512 or 2048 bytes should work under Linux; this includes the vast majority of CD-ROM drives on the market.

■ EIDE (ATAPI) CD-ROM drives (IDECD) Almost all double, quad, and six-speed drives are supported, including :

■ Mitsumi FX400

■ Nec-260

■ Sony 55E

Proprietary CD-ROM Drives

■ Aztech CDA268-01A, Orchid CDS-3110, Okano/Wearnes CDD-110, Conrad TXC, CyCDROM

■ CR520ie/CR540ie/CR940ie (AZTCD)

■ Creative Labs CD-200(F) (SBPCD)

■ Funai E2550UA/MK4015 (SBPCD)

■ GoldStar R420 (GSCD)

■ IBM External ISA (SBPCD)

■ Kotobuki (SBPCD)

- Lasermate CR328A (OPTCD)
- LMS Philips CM 206 (CM206)
- Longshine LCS-7260 (SBPCD)
- Matsushita/Panasonic CR-521/522/523/562/563 (SBPCD)
- MicroSolutions Backpack parallel portdrive (BPCD)
- Mitsumi CR DC LU05S (MCD/MCDX)
- Mitsumi FX001D/F (MCD/MCDX)
- Optics Storage Dolphin 8000AT (OPTCD)
- Sanyo H94A (SJCD)
- Sony CDU31A/CDU33A (CDU31A)
- Sony CDU-510/CDU-515 (SOMYCD535)
- Sony CDU-535/CDU-531 (SONYCD535)
- Teac CD-55A SuperQuad (SBPCD)

App
C

Others

- LMS/Philips CM 205/225/202
  ftp://sunsite.unc.edu/pub/Linux/kernel/patches/cdrom/lmscd0.4.tar.gz
- NEC CDR-35D (old)
  ftp://sunsite.unc.edu/pub/Linux/kernel/patches/cdrom/linux-neccdr35d.patch
- Sony SCSI multisession CD-XA
  ftp://tsx-11.mit.edu/pub/linux/patches/sony-multi-0.00.tar.gz
- Parallel Port Driver
  http://www.torque.net/linux-pp.html

Notes

- All CD-ROM drives should work similarly for reading data. There are various compatibility problems with audio CD playing utilities. (Especially with newer low-end NEC drives.) Some alpha drivers may not have audio support yet.
- Early (single speed) NEC CD-ROM drives may have trouble with currently available SCSI controllers.
- PhotoCD (XA) is supported. The hpcdtoppm program by Hadmut Danisch converts PhotoCD files to the portable pixmap format. The program can be obtained from ftp://ftp.gwdg.de/pub/linux/hpcdtoppm or as part of the PBM utilities.
- Also, reading video CD is supported in kernel series 2.1.3x and later. A patch is available for kernel 2.0.30.
- Finally, most IDE CD-ROM Changers are supported.

CD-Writers

Many CD-Writers are supported by Linux now. For an up-to-date list of CD-Writers supported, check the CD-Writing mini-HOWTO at http://sunsite.unc.edu/LDP/HOWTO/mini/CD-Writing or check

- http://www.shop.de/cgi-bin/wini/lsc.pl. Cdwrite ftp://sunsite.unc.edu/pub/Linux/utils/disk-management/ and cdrecord http://www.fokus.gmd.de/nthp/employees/schilling/cdrecord.html can be used for writing CDs. The X-CD-Roast package for Linux is a graphical front-end for using CD writers. The package can be found at ftp://sunsite.unc.edu/pub/Linux/utils/disk-management/xcdroast-0.96b.tar.gz.
- Grundig CDR 100 IPW
- HP CD-Writer+ 7100
- HP SureStore 4020i
- HP SureStore 6020es/i
- JVC XR-W2010
- Mitsubishi CDRW-225
- Mitsumi CR-2600TE
- Olympus CDS 620E
- Philips CDD-522/2000/2600/3610
- Pinnacle Micro RCD-5020/5040
- Plextor CDR PX-24CS
- Ricoh MP 1420C
- Ricoh MP 6200S/6201S
- Sanyo CRD-R24S
- Smart and Friendly Internal 2006 Plus 2.05
- Sony CDU 920S/924/926S
- Taiyo Yuden EW-50
- TEAC CD-R50S
- WPI(Wearnes) CDR-632P
- WPI(Wearnes) CDRW-622
- Yamaha CDR-100
- Yamaha CDR-200/200t/200tx
- Yamaha CDR-400t/400tx

Removable Drives

- All SCSI drives should work if the controller is supported, including optical (MO), WORM, floptical, Bernoulli, Zip, Jaz, SyQuest, PD, and others.

- Parallel port Zip drives ftp://gear.torque.net/pub/
- Parallel port Avatar Shark-250http://www.torque.net/shark.html
- Removable drives work like hard disks and floppies, just fdisk/mkfs and mount the disks. Linux provides drive locking if your drives support it. mtools can also be used if the disks are in MS-DOS format.
- CD-R drives require special software to work. Read the CD-R Mini-HOWTO.
- Linux supports both 512 and 1024 bytes/sector disks. Starting with kernel 2.1.32 Linux also supports 2048 bytes/sector. A patch to kernel 2.0.30 is available at http://liniere.gen.u-tokyo.ac.jp/2048.html.
- The 2048 bytes/sector support is needed for Fujitsu magneto-optical disk drives M2513
- Starting with pre-patch-2.0.31-3 IDE/ATAPI internal Zip drives, flopticals and PDs are supported.
- LS-120 floptical
- PD-CD

App
C

Mice

Supported

- Microsoft serial mouse
- Mouse Systems serial mouse
- Logitech Mouseman serial mouse
- Logitech serial mouse
- ATI XL Inport busmouse
- C&T 82C710 (QuickPort) (Toshiba, TI Travelmate)
- Microsoft busmouse
- Logitech busmouse
- PS/2 (auxiliary device) mouse

Others

- Sejin J-mouse
  ftp://sunsite.unc.edu/pub/Linux/kernel/patches/console/jmouse.1.1.70-jmouse.tar.gz
- MultiMouse - use multiple mouse devices as single mouse
  ftp://sunsite.unc.edu/pub/Linux/system/misc/MultiMouse-1.0.tgz
- Microsoft IntelliMouse

Notes

- Touchpad devices like Alps Glidepoint also work, so long as they're compatible with another mouse protocol.

- Newer Logitech mice (except the Mouseman) use the Microsoft protocol and all three buttons do work. Even though Microsoft's mice have only two buttons, the protocol allows three buttons.

- The mouse port on the ATI Graphics Ultra and Ultra Pro use the Logitech busmouse protocol. (See the Busmouse HOWTO for details.)

Modems

- All internal modems or external modems connected to the serial port should work. Alas, some manufacturers have created Windows 95-only modems. Check Appendix D for Linux incompatible hardware.

- A small number of modems come with DOS software that downloads the control program at runtime. These can normally be used by loading the program under DOS and doing a warm boot. Such modems are probably best avoided as you won't be able to use them with non PC hardware in the future.

- All PCMCIA modems should work with the PCMCIA drivers.

- Fax modems need appropriated fax software to operate. Also be sure that the fax part of the modem supports Class 2 or Class 2.0. It seems to be generally true for any fax software on UNIX that support for Class 1.0 is not available.

- Digicom Connection 96+/14.4+ - DSP code downloading program
  ftp://sunsite.unc.edu/pub/Linux/apps/serialcomm/smdl-linux.1.02.tar.gz

- Motorola ModemSURFR internal 56K. Add a couple of line to RC.SERIAL to account for IRQ and ports if they are non-standard.

- ZyXEL U-1496 series - ZyXEL 1.4, modem/fax/voice control program
  http://www.pe1chl.demon.nl/ZyXEL/ZyXEL-1.6.tar.gz

- ZyXEL Elite 2864 series - modem/fax/voice control program
  http://www.pe1chl.demon.nl/ZyXEL/ZyXEL-1.6.tar.gz

- ZyXEL Omni TA 128 - modem/fax/voice control program
  http://www.pe1chl.demon.nl/ZyXEL/ZyXEL-1.6.tar.gz

Printers/Plotters

- All printers and plotters connected to the parallel or serial port should work. Alas, some manufacturers have created Windows 95-only printers. Check Appendix D for Linux incompatible hardware.

- HP LaserJet 4 series - free-lj4, printing modes control program
  ftp://sunsite.unc.edu/pub/Linux/system/printing/free-lj4-1.1p1.tar.gz

- BiTronics parallel port interface
  ftp://sunsite.unc.edu/pub/Linux/kernel/patches/misc/bt-ALPHA-
  0.0.1.module.patch.gz

Ghostscript

- Many Linux programs output PostScript files. Non-PostScript printers can emulate PostScript Level 2 using Ghostscript.

- Ghostscript ftp://ftp.cs.wisc.edu/pub/ghost/aladdin/

- Ghostscript supported printers

- Apple Imagewriter

- C. Itoh M8510

- Canon BubbleJet BJ10e (bj10e)

- Canon BubbleJet BJ200, BJC-210 (B/W only), BJC-240 (B/W only) (bj200)

- Canon BubbleJet BJC-600, BJC-610, BJC-4000, BJC-4100, BJC-450, MultiPASS C2500, BJC-240,

- BJC-70 (bjc600)

- Canon BubbleJet BJC-800 (bjc800)

- Canon LBP-8II, LIPS III

- DEC LA50/70/75/75plus

- DEC LN03, LJ250

- Epson 9 pin, 24 pin, LQ series, AP3250

- Epson Stylus Color/Color II/500/800 (stcolor)

- HP 2563B

- HP DesignJet 650C

- HP DeskJet, Deskjet Plus (deskjet)

- HP Deskjet 500, Deskjet Portable (djet500)

- HP DeskJet 400/500C/540C/690C/693C (cdj500)

- HP DeskJet 550C/560C/600/660C/682C/683C/693C/850/870Cse (cdj550)

- HP DeskJet 850/870Cse/870Cxi/680 (cdj850)

- HP DeskJet 500C/510/520/5540C/693C printing black only (cdjmono)

- HP DeskJet 600 (lj4dith)

- HP DeskJet 600/870Cse, LaserJet 5/5L (ljet4)

- HP Deskjet 500/500C/510/520/540/550C/560C/850C/855C

- ftp:ftp.pdb.sni.de/pub/utilities/misc/hpdj-2.1.tar.gz

- HP PaintJet XL300, Deskjet 600/1200C/1600C (pjxl300)

- HP LaserJet/Plus/II/III/4

- HP PaintJet/XL

App
C

- IBM Jetprinter color
- IBM Proprinter
- Imagen ImPress
- Mitsubishi CP50 color
- NEC P6/P6+/P60
- Oki OL410ex LED (ljet4)
- Okidata MicroLine 182
- Ricoh 4081/6000 (r4081)
- SPARCprinter
- StarJet 48 inkjet printer
- Tektronix 4693d color 2/4/8 bit
- Tektronix 4695/4696 inkjet plotter
- Xerox XES printers (2700, 3700, 4045, etc.)
- Others
- Canon BJC600/800 color printers
  ftp://petole.imag.fr/pub/postscript/ghostscript/bjc600/

Scanners

- For scanner support there is the package SANE (Scanner Access Now Easy). Information can be found at http://www.mostang.com/sane/. It can be downloaded from ftp://ftp.mostang.com/pub/sane/. This is a universal scanner interface. It comes complete with documentation and several frontends and backends.

- More information on handheld scanners can be found at http://swt-www.informatik.uni-hamburg.de/~1willamo/scanner.html

Supported

- A4 Tech AC 4096 / AS 8000P
  ftp://ftp.informatik.hu-berlin.de/pub/local/linux/a4scan/a4scan.tgz

- Adara Image Star I   http://fb4-1112.uni-muenster.de/ffwd/

- ftp://fb4-1112.uni-muenster.de/pub/ffwd/mtekscan-0.2.tar.gz

- Conrad Personal Scanner 64, P105 handheld scanners
  ftp://tsx-11.mit.edu/pub/linux/ALPHA/scanner/scan-driver-0.1.8.tar.gz

- Epson GT6000
  ftp://sunsite.unc.edu/pub/Linux/apps/graphics/capture/ppic0.5.tar.gz

- Fujitsu SCSI-2 scanners contact Dr. G.W. Wettstein
  < greg%wind.UUCP@plains.nodak.edu>

- Genius ColorPage-SP2   http://fb4-1112.uni-muenster.de/ffwd/
- ftp://fb4-1112.uni-muenster.de/pub/ffwd/mtekscan-0.2.tar.gz
- Genius GS-B105G handheld scanner
  ftp://tsx-11.mit.edu/pub/linux/ALPHA/scanner/gs105-0.0.1.tar.gz
- Genius GeniScan GS4500, GS4500A handheld scanners
  ftp://tsx-11.mit.edu/pub/linux/ALPHA/scanner/gs4500-2.0.tar.gz
- HighScreen Greyscan 256 handheld scanner
  ftp://tsx-11.mit.edu/pub/linux/ALPHA/scanner/gs4500-2.0.tar.gz
- HP ScanJet II series SCSI
  ftp://sunsite.unc.edu/pub/Linux/apps/graphics/capture/hpscanpbm-0.3a.tar.gz
- HP ScanJet IIc, IIcx, IIp, 3c, 4c, 4p, 5p, 5pse, plus http://www.tummy.com/xvscan/
- Logitech Scanman+, Scanman 32, Scanman 256 handheld scanners
  ftp://tsx-11.mit.edu/pub/linux/ALPHA/scanner/logiscan-0.0.4.tar.gz
- Microtek ScanMaker E3, E6, II, IIXE, III and 35t models
  http://fb4-1112.uni-muenster.de/ffwd/
- ftp://fb4-1112.uni-muenster.de/pub/ffwd/mtekscan-0.2.tar.gz
- Mustek M105 handheld scanner
  ftp://tsx-11.mit.edu/pub/linux/ALPHA/scanner/scan-driver-0.1.8.tar.gz
- Mustek HT800 Turbo, Matador 105, Matador 256 handheld scanners
  ftp://tsx-11.mit.edu/pub/linux/ALPHA/scanner/scan-driver-0.1.8.tar.gz
- Mustek Paragon 6000CX
  ftp://sunsite.unc.edu/pub/Linux/apps/graphics/capture/muscan-2.0.6.taz
- Nikon Coolscan SCSI 35mm film scanner
  ftp://sunsite.unc.edu/pub/Linux/apps/graphics/capture/coolscan-0.2.tgz
- Pearl 256 handheld scanner
  ftp://tsx-11.mit.edu/pub/linux/ALPHA/scanner/scan-driver-0.1.8.tar.gz
- UMAX SCSI scanners
  ftp://tsx-11.mit.edu/pub/linux/ALPHA/scanner/umax-0.5.5.tar.gz
- The Mustek drivers work only with GI1904 interface cards. Eric Chang
  eric.chang@chrysalis.org has created a patch to use them with IF960 interface cards.

Others

- Genius GS-4000, ScanMate/32, ScanMate/GS handheld scanners
  ftp://tsx-11.mit.edu/pub/linux/ALPHA/scanner/gs4500-2.0.tar.gz
- Mustek HT105, M800 handheld scanners
  ftp://tsx-11.mit.edu/pub/linux/ALPHA/scanner/scan-driver-0.1.8.tar.gz
- Voelkner Personal Scanner 64 handheld scanner
  ftp://tsx-11.mit.edu/pub/linux/ALPHA/scanner/scan-driver-0.1.8.tar.gz

App
C

Unsupported

- Escom 256 (Primax Lector Premier 256) handheld scanner
- Genius ScanMate/256, EasyScan handheld scanners
- Mustek CG8000 handheld scanner
- Trust Ami Scan handheld scanner

Other Hardware

VESA Power Savings Protocol (DPMS) Monitors

- Support for power savings is included in the Linux kernel. Just use setterm to enable support.

Touch Screens

- The Metro-X X-server is supporting the following touch screen:
- Carrol Touch serial touch screen. http://www.carrolltouch.com

Terminals on Serial Port

- Old terminals can easily be used under Linux by connecting them to the serial port of your system. At least the following terminals will be supported:
- VT52
- VT100
- VT220
- VT320
- VT420

Joysticks

Joystick support is in the latest XFree86 distributions (3.3.x) and in kernel versions 2.1.xx. For older kernels the links below are useful.

- Joystick driver
  ftp://sunsite.unc.edu/pub/Linux/kernel/patches/console/joystick-0.8.0.tgz
- Joystick driver (module)
  ftp://sunsite.unc.edu/pub/Linux/kernel/patches/console/joyfixed.tgz

Video Capture Boards / Frame Grabbers / TV Tuner

- A couple of programs are available that support TV tuners. These are:
- BTTV http://www.thp.Uni-Koeln.DE/~rjkm/linux/bttv.html
- Xawtv

- Xtvscreen
- Data Translation DT2803
- Data Translation DT2851 Frame Grabber
  ftp://sunsite.unc.edu/pub/Linux/apps/video/dt2851-2.01.tar.gz
- Data Translation DT3155
  http://krusty.eecs.umich.edu/people/ncowan/linux/welcome.html
- Diamond DTV2000 (based on BT848)
- Dipix XPG1000/FPG/PPMAPA (based on TI C40 DSP). Most add-on cards are supported. http://www.thp.Uni-Koeln.DE/~rjkm/linux/bttv.html
- Epix SVM
- Epix Silicon Video MUX series of video frame grabbing boards
  http://www.ssc.com/lj/issue13/npc13c.html
- FAST Screen Machine II
  ftp://sunsite.unc.edu/pub/Linux/apps/video/ScreenMachineII.2.0.tgz
- Hauppage Wincast TV PCI (based on BT848)
  http://www.thp.Uni-Koeln.DE/~rjkm/linux/bttv.html
- Imaging Technology ITI/IC-PCI
  ftp://ftp.gom-online.de/pub/IC-PCI/icpci-0.3.2.tar.gz
- ImageNation Cortex I
  ftp://sunsite.unc.edu/pub/Linux/apps/video/cortex.drv.1.1.tgz
- ImageNation CX100 ftp://sunsite.unc.edu/pub/Linux/apps/video/cxdrv-0.86.tar.gz
- ImageNation PX500 (being worked on). Ask for current status rubini@linux.it.
- Imaging Technology Inc. IC-PCI frame grabber board
  ftp://gandalf.expmech.ing.tu-bs.de/pub/driver/icpci-0.2.0.tar.gz
- Matrox Meteor   ftp://sunsite.unc.edu/pub/Linux/apps/video/meteor-1.4a.tgz
- Matrox PIP-1024   http://www.powerup.com.au/~sobeyp/pip_tar.gz
- MaxiTV/PCI (based on ZR36120)
  ftp://sunsite.unc.edu/pub/Linux/kernel/misc-cards/zr36120-971127.tgz
- Miro PCTV (based on BT848) http://www.thp.Uni-Koeln.DE/~rjkm/linux/bttv.html
- MuTech MV1000 PCI
  ftp://sunsite.unc.edu/pub/Linux/apps/video/mv1000drv-0.33.tgz
- MuTech MV200   http://www.powerup.com.au/~sobeyp/mu_tar.gz
- Philips PCA10TV (not in production anymore)
  ftp://ftp.il.ft.hse.nl/pub/tv1000/pctv1000.02.tgz
- Pro Movie Studio   ftp://sunsite.unc.edu/pub/Linux/apps/video/PMS-grabber.3.0.tgz
- Quanta WinVision B&W video capture card
  ftp://sunsite.unc.edu/pub/Linux/apps/video/fgrabber-1.0.tgz
- Quickcam   ftp://sunsite.unc.edu/pub/Linux/apps/video/qcam-0.7c-5.tar.gz
- Sensus 700 http://www.robots.com/s700.htm

App

C

- Smart Video Recoder III (based on BT848)
  http://www.thp.Uni-Koeln.DE/~rjkm/linux/bttv.html
- STB TV PCI Television Tuner (based on BT848)
  http://www.thp.Uni-Koeln.DE/~rjkm/linux/bttv.html
- Tekram C210 (based on ZR36120)
  ftp://sunsite.unc.edu/pub/Linux/kernel/misc-cards/zr36120-971127.tgz
- Video Blaster, Rombo Media Pro+
  ftp://sunsite.unc.edu/pub/Linux/apps/video/vid_src-0.6.tgz
- VT1500 TV cards   ftp://sunsite.unc.edu/pub/Linux/apps/video/vt1500-1.0.9.tar.gz

Digital Camera

- HP Photo Smart Digital Camera ftp://ftp.itojun.org/pub/digi-cam/

UPS

- Various other UPSs are supported, read the UPS HOWTO.
- APC SmartUPS ftp://sunsite.unc.edu/pub/Linux/system/ups/apcd-0.5.tar.gz
- APC-BackUPS 400/600, APC-SmartUPS SU700/1400RM
  ftp://sunsite.unc.edu/pub/Linux/system/ups/apcupsd-2.2.tar.gz
- UPSs with RS-232 monitoring port (genpower package)
  ftp://sunsite.unc.edu/pub/Linux/system/ups/genpower-1.0.1.tgz
- MGE UPS's http://www.mgeups.com/download/softlib.htm and
  http://www.mgeups.com/download/software/linux/upsp.tgz
- A daemon to shut down and start up computers connected to UPSs. It's network-aware
  and allows server- and client-mode
  ftp://sunsite.unc.edu/pub/Linux/system/ups/powerd-2.0.tar.gz

Multifunction Boards

- Pro Audio Spectrum 16 SCSI / Sound interface card

Data Acquisition

- The Linux Lab Project site collects drivers for hardware dealing with data acquisition;
  they also maintain some mailing lists dealing with the subject. I have no experience with
  data acquisition, so please check the site for more details.
- Linux Lab Project http://www.llp.fu-berlin.de/
- CED 1401
- DBCC CAMAC
- IEEE-488 (GPIB, HPIB) boards
- Keithley DAS-1200

- National Instruments AT-MIO-16F / Lab-PC+
- Analog Devices RTI-800/815 ADC/DAC board contact Paul Gortmaker
  < gpg109@anu.edu.au>

Watchdog Timer Interfaces

- ICS WDT500-P (http://www.indcomp.src.com/products/data/html/wdt500-p.html)
- ICS WDT501-P (with and without fan tachometer)
  (http://www.indcomp.src.com/products/data/html/wdt500-p.html)

Miscellaneous

- Mattel Powerglove
- AIMS Labs RadioTrack FM radio card
  ftp://sunsite.unc.edu/pub/Linux/apps/sound/radio/radiotrack-1.1.tgz
- Reveal FM Radio card   ftp://magoo.uwsuper.edu/docs/radio.html
- Videotext cards   ftp://sunsite.unc.edu/pub/Linux/apps/video/videoteXt-0.6.tar.gz

Related Sources of Information

- Cameron Spitzer's hardware FAQ archive
  ftp://ftp.rahul.net/pub/cameron/PC-info/
- Computer Hardware and Software Vendor Phone Numbers
  http://mtmis1.mis.semi.harris.com/comp_ph1.html
- Guide to Computer Vendors   http://guide.sbanetweb.com/
- System Optimization Information   http://www.dfw.net/~sdw/

Acknowledgments

Thanks to all the authors and contributors of other HOWTOs, many things here are shamelessly stolen from their works; to FRiC, Zane Healy and Ed Carp, the original authors of this HOWTO; and to everyone else who sent in updates and feedbacks. Special thanks to Eric Boerner and Lilo (the person, not the program) for the sanity checks. And thanks to Dan Quinlan for the original SGML conversion.

Appendix A. S3 Cards Supported by XFree86 3.3.1.

- CHIPSETRAMDAC CLOCKCHIPBPPCARD 801/805AT&T 20C490 16 Actix GE
  32 / 32+ 2MB Orchid Fahrenheit 1280(+) 801/805AT&T 20C490 ICD2061A 16 STB
  PowerGraph X.24 801/805 Del S3 805 Miro Crystal 8S Orchid Fahrenheit VA VL-41 805
  S3 GENDAC 16 Miro 10SD VLB/PCI SPEA Mirage VLB 801/805SS2410 ICD2061A 8
  Diamond Stealth 24 VLB/ISA 801/805AT&T 20C490 Ch8391 16 JAX 8231/8241, SPEA
  Mirage 801/805S3 GENDAC Miro Crystal 10SD 805i Actix GE 32i ELSA Winner 1000
  ISA 928 AT&T 20C490 16 Actix Ultra 928 Sierra SC15025 ICD2061A 32 ELSA Winner

1000 ISA/VLB/EISA 928 Bt485 ICD2061A 32 STB Pegasus VL 928 Bt485 SC11412 16 SPEA(/V7) Mercury VLB 928 Bt485 ICD2061A 32 #9 GXE Level 10/11/12 928 Ti3020 ICD2061A 32 #9 GXE Level 14/16 928 928Movie Diamond Stealth Pro ELSA Winner 1000TwinBus ELSA Winner 1000VL ELSA Winner 2000 Miro Crystal 16S 864 ICD2061A Miro Crystal 20SD (BIOS 2.xx) 864 AT&T 20C498 ICS2494 32 Miro (Crystal) 20SD (BIOS 1.xx) 864 AT&T 20C498/ ICD2061A/ 32 ELSA Winner 1000 PRO VLB/PCI 864 STG1700 ICS9161 MIRO 20SD (BIOS 2.x) ELAS Winner 1000 PRO 864 STG1700 ICD2061A 32 Actix GE 64 VLB 864 AT&T 20C498/ ICS2595 16 SPEA(/V7) Mirage P64 DRAM (BIOS 3.x) AT&T 21C498 864 S3 86C716 SDAC 32 ELSA Winner 1000 PRO Miro 20SD (BIOS 3.x) SPEA Mirage P64 DRAM (BIOS 4.x) Diamond Stealth 64 DRAM Genoa Phantom 64i Miro Crystal 20SD VLB (BIOS 3.xx) 864 ICS5342 ICS5342 32 Diamond Stealth 64 DRAM (some) 864 SDAC Diamond Stealth 64 Graphics 2001 864 AT&T 20C498-13ICD2061A 32 #9 GXE64 PCI 864 ASUS Video Magic PCI V864 VidTech FastMax P20

- CHIPSETRAMDAC CLOCKCHIPBPPCARD 964 ELSA Winner 2000 PRO-2,4 spider Tarantula 64 964 AT&T 20C505 ICD2061A 32 Miro Crystal 20SV PCI/40SV 964 Bt485 ICD2061A 32 Diamond Stealth 64 964 Bt9485 ICS9161A 32 SPEA Mercury 64 964 Ti3020 ICD2061A 8 ELSA Winner 2000 PRO PCI 964 Ti3025 Ti3025 32 #9 GXE64 Pro VLB/PCI Miro Crystal 40SV 964 IBM RGB 32 Hercules Graphite Terminator 64 868 S3 86C716 SDAC 32 ELSA Winner 1000AVI Miro Crystal 20SD PCI 868 AT&T 29C409 ELSA Winner 1000AVI 868 Diamond Stealth Video DRAM Diamond Stealth 64 Video 2120/ 2200 ELSA Winner 1000PRO/X #9 FX Motion 531 VideoLogic GrafixStar 500 968 Diamond Stealth 64 Video 3200 ELSA Gloria-4/8 ELSA Winner 2000AVI ELSA Winner 2000PRO/X-2/X-4/X-8 Genoa VideoBlitz III AV Hercules Graphite Terminator Pro 64 LeadTek WinFast S430 LeadTek WinFast S510 Miro Crystal 80SV Miro Crystal 20SV #9 FX Motion 771 VideoLogic GrafixStar 700 WinFast S430/S510 968 TVP3026 32 ELSA Winner 2000PRO/X Diamond Stealth 64 Video VRAM 968 IBM RGB 32 Genoa VideoBlitz III AVI Hercules Terminator Pro 64 STB Velocity 64 Video #9 FX Motion 771 Diamond Stealth 64 Video 3240/3400 968 TI RAMDAC Diamond Stealth 64 Video 3240/ 3400 732 (Trio32) 32 Diamond Stealth 64 DRAM SE (all Trio32 based cards) 764 (Trio64) 32 SPEA Mirage P64 (BIOS 5.x) Diamond Stealth 64 DRAM Diamond Stealth 64 Graphics 2xx0 #9 FX Vision 330 STB PowerGraph 64 (all Trio64 based cards)

- CHIPSETRAMDAC CLOCKCHIPBPPCARD (Trio64V+) DSV3326 Diamond Stealth 64 Video 2001 DataExpert DSV3365 ExpertColor DSV3365 MAXColor S3 Trio64V+ ELSA Winner 1000TRIO/V Hercules Terminator 64/Video #9 FX Motion 331 STB Powergraph 64 Video VideoLogic GrafixStar 400 (Trio64V2) ELSA Winner 1000/T2D (ViRGE) Canopus Co. Power Window 3DV DSV3325 DataExpert DSV3325 Diamond Multimedia Stealth 3D 2000 Diamond Multimedia Stealth 3D 2000 PRO Diamond Stealth 3D 2000 Diamond Stealth 3D 2000 PRO Diamond Stealth 3D 3000 ELSA Victory 3D ELSA Victory 3DX ELSA Winner 3000-S Expertcolor DSV3325 Hercules Terminator 64/3D LeadTek WinFast 3D S600 MELCO WGP-VG4S #9 FX Motion 332 Orchid Tech. Fahrenheit Video 3D STB systems Powergraph 3D WinFast 3D S600 (ViRGE/DX) Hercules Terminator 3D/DX (ViRGE/GX) STB Nitro 3D (ViRGE/VX) ELSA Winner

2000AVI/3D ELSA Winner 3000 ELSA Winner 3000-L-42/-M-22 MELCO WGP-VX8 STB Systems Velocity 3D 911/924 Diamond Stealth VRAM 924 SC1148 DAC

- NOTE: for the ViRGE/VX,DX,GX,GX2 chipsets you need XFree86 3.3.1. You should use the XF86_SVGA server.

Appendix B. Supported PCMCIA Cards

These cards are supported by David Hinds' PCMCIA package and this list is taken from his Web page.

- 26.1 Ethernet cards
- SMC, Megahertz and Ositech cards use the smc91c92_cs driver
- 3Com and Farallon cards use the 3c589_cs driver
- Fujitsu, TDK, RATOC, CONTEC, Eagle and Nextcom cards use the fmvj18x_cs driver

All other cards use the pcnet_cs driver. Other NE2000-compatible cards that are not on the list are also likely to work with pcnet_cs.

- 3Com 3c589, 3c589B, 3c589C, 3c589D
- Accton EN2212, EN2216 EtherCard
- Allied Telesis CentreCOM CE6001, LA-PCM
- Asante FriendlyNet
- AST 1082 Ethernet
- CeLAN EPCMCIA
- CNet CN30BC, CN40BC Ethernet
- Compex/ReadyLINK Ethernet Combo
- Compex Linkport Ethernet
- Connectware LANdingGear Adapter
- CONTEC C-NET(PC)C
- Danpex EN-6200P2 Ethernet
- Datatrek NetCard
- Dayna Communications CommuniCard E
- Digital DEPCM-AA Ethernet
- Digital EtherWORKS Turbo Ethernet
- D-Link DE-650, DE-660
- Eagle NE200 Ethernet
- Edimax Technology Ethernet Combo
- EFA InfoExpress 205, 207 Combo
- Eiger Labs EPX-ET10T2 Combo

App
C

- ELECOM Laneed LD-CDWA, LD-CDX, LD-CDNIA, LD-CDY
- EP-210 Ethernet
- Epson Ethernet
- EtherPRIME Ethernet
- Explorer NE-10000 Ethernet
- EZLink 4109 Ethernet
- Farallon Etherwave
- Fiberline FL-4680
- Fujitsu FMV-J181, FMV-J182, FMV-J182A
- Fujitsu Towa LA501
- Gateway 2000 Ethernet
- Genius ME3000II Ethernet
- Grey Cell Ethernet
- GVC NIC-2000P Ethernet Combo
- Hitachi HT-4840-11 EtherCard
- Hypertec HyperEnet
- IBM CreditCard Ethernet Adapter
- IC-Card Ethernet
- Infotel IN650ct Ethernet
- I-O Data PCLA/T
- Katron PE-520 Ethernet
- Kingston KNE-PCM/M, KNE-PC2
- LANEED Ethernet
- LanPro EP4000A
- Lantech Ethernet
- Linksys EtherCard
- Logitec LPM-LN10T, LPM-LN10BA Ethernet
- Longshine Ethernet
- Macnica ME-1 Ethernet
- Maxtech PCN2000 Ethernet
- Megahertz XJ10BT, XJ10BC, CC10BT Ethernet
- Melco LPC-TJ, LPC-TS
- Micronet Etherfast Adapter
- NDC Instant-Link
- Network General "Sniffer"

- New Media EthernetLAN
- New Media LiveWir (NOT the LiveWire+)
- New Media BASICS Ethernet
- NextCom NC5310
- Novell/National NE4100 InfoMover
- Ositech Four of Diamonds
- Panasonic CF-VEL211P-B
- Planet SmartCom 2000, 3500
- PreMax PE-200 Ethernet
- Proteon Ethernet
- Ratoc REX-9822, REX-5588A/W
- Relia RE2408T Ethernet
- RPTI EP400, EP401 Ethernet
- SCM Ethernet
- SMC 8020BT EtherEZ (not the EliteCard)
- Socket Communications Socket EA LAN Adapter
- SuperSocket RE450T
- Surecom Ethernet
- SVEC PN605C
- TDK LAC-CD02x, LAK-CD021, LAK-CD022A, LAK-CD021AX Ethernet
- Thomas-Conrad Ethernet
- Trust Ethernet Combo
- Volktek NPL-402CT Ethernet
- Xircom CreditCard CE2
- 26.2 Fast Ethernet (10/100baseT) adapters
- Linksys EtherFast 10/100
- Xircom CreditCard CE3
- 26.3 Token-ring adapters
- You should at least have kernel 1.3.72
- IBM Token ring Adapter
- 3Com 3c689 TokenLink III
- 26.4 Wireless network adapters
- AT&T GIS / NCR WaveLAN version 2.0
- DEC RoamAbout/DS
- Xircom CreditCard Netwave

App
C

- 26.5 ISDN
- ELSA PCMCIA
- 26.6 Modem and serial cards

Virtually all modem cards, simple serial port cards, and digital cellular modems should work. Also ISDN modems that emulate a standard UART are supported.

- Advantech COMpad-32/85 dual serial
- Quatech, IOTech dual RS-232 cards
- Quatech quad RS-232 card
- Socket Communications dual RS-232 card
- 26.7 Memory cards

All SRAM cards should work. Unsupported flash cards can be read but not written.

- Epson 2MB SRAM
- IBM 8MB Flash
- Intel Series 2 and Series 2+ Flash
- Maxtor MobileMax 16MB Flash
- New Media SRAM
- TDK Flash Memory SFM20W/C 20MB
- 26.8 SCSI adapters

Be careful. Many vendors, particularly CD-ROM vendors, seem to switch controller chips at will. Generally, They will use a different product code, but not always: older (supported) New Media Bus Toaster cards are not easily distinguishable from the current (unsupported) Bus Toaster cards.

- Adaptec APA-1460, APA-1460A, APA-1450A SlimSCSI
- Digital SCSI II adapter
- Eiger Labs SCSI (Not the Eiger SS-1000)
- Future Domain SCSI2GO
- IBM SCSI
- Iomega ZIP Card
- IO-DATA PCSC-II, PCSC-II-L
- IO-DATA CDG-PX44/PCSC CD-ROM
- Logitec LPM-SCSI2
- Logitec LCD-601 CD-ROM
- MACNICA mPS110, mPS110-LP SCSI
- Melco IFC-SC2, IFC-DC
- NEC PC-9801N-J03R

- New Media Bus Toaster SCSI (older cards only)
- New Media Toast 'n Jam (SCSI only)
- Panasonic KXL-D740, KXL-DN740A, KXL-DN740A-NB 4X CD-ROM
- Pioneer PCP-PR1W CD-ROM
- Qlogic FastSCSI
- Raven CD-Note 4X
- RATOC REX-9530 SCSI-2
- Simple Technologies SCSI
- Sony CD-ROM Discman PRD-250
- Taxan ICD-400PN
- Toshiba NWB0107ABK, SCSC200B
- 26.9 ATA/IDE CD-ROM adapters

You should at least have kernel 1.3.72.

- Argosy EIDE CD-ROM
- Caravelle CD-36N
- Creative Technology CD-ROM
- Digital Mobile Media CD-ROM
- EXP CD940 CD-ROM
- IO-DATA CDP-TX4/PCIDE, CDP-TX6/PCIDE, CDP-TX10/PCIDE, CDV-HDN6/PCIDE,
- MOP-230/PCIDE
- H45 Technologies Quick 2x CD-ROM
- 26.10 Multifunction cards

You should at least have kernel 1.3.73.

- 3Com 3c562, 3c562B/C/D, 3c563B/C/D
- ActionTec Comnet EF336 modem 28.8 + ethernet 10MB (only modem part works)
- IBM Home and Away Card
- Linksys LANmodem 28.8, 33.6
- Megahertz/U.S. Robotics EM1144, EM3288, EM3336
- Motorola Mariner
- Motorola Marquis
- Ositech Jack of Diamonds
- Xircom CreditCard CEM28, CEM33, CEM56
- 26.11 ATA/IDE card drives

These card drives are supported starting with kernel 1.3.72. Both Flash-ATA cards and rotating-media cards are supported.

App
C

- 26.12 Miscellaneous cards
- Trimble Mobile GPS (uses serial/modem driver)
- 26.13 Cards with separately distributed drivers
- IBM Smart Capture (Koji Okamura oka@nanotsu.kobe-u.ac.jp)
- 26.14 Working on ...

People are working on the following cards:

- Nat'l Inst DAQCard (Eric Gonzalez root@colomsat.net.co)
- Roland SCP-55 MIDI (Toshiaki Nakatsu ir9k-nkt@asahi.net.or.jp)
- CyberRom CD-ROM (David Rowntree rowntree@dircon.co.uk)
- IO DATA PCSC-II (Katayama Nobuhiro kata-n@po.iijnet.or.jp)
- Macnica mPS-1x0 (Katayama Nobuhiro kata-n@po.iijnet.or.jp)
- FORTEZZA encryption (Rex Riggins rriggins@radium.ncsc.mil)
- Harris PRISM/AM79C930 (Mark Mathews mark@mail.absoval.com)
- IBM Etherjet (Danilo Beuche danili@cs.tu-berlin.de). The driver can be found at http://www.first.gmd.de/~danilo/pc-driver
- Teles
- Hayes ESP
- contact Dennis Boylan < dennis@lan.com>
- Hayes ESP
- contact Dennis Boylan < dennis@lan.com> PCMCIA
- Xircom CE3 (Werner Koch werner.koch@guug.de)
- 26.15 Unsupported
- ActionTec Comnet EF336 modem 28.8 + ethernet 10MB (ethernet part not supported)
- Adaptec/Trantor APA-460 SlimSCSI
- CanonCompaq PCMCIA floppy drive
- New Media .WAVjammer and all other sound cards
- All 100baseT ethernet adapters
- Panasonic KXL-D720, KXL-D745
- SMC 8016 EliteCard
- Telxon/Aironet wireless adapter
- Xircom CE II Ethernet/Modem
- Xircom CE-10BT Ethernet

Appendix C. Plug and Play Devices

For people having trouble getting Plug and Play devices to work, the ISA PnP utilities written by Peter Fox are available. Quote from the README: These programs allow ISA Plug-And-Play devices to be configured on a Linux machine.

This program is suitable for all systems, whether or not they include a PnP BIOS.

Commands have been taken from the Plug and Play ISA specification Version 1.0a. (ftp://ftp.redhat.com/pub/pnp/docs/)

More information on ISA PnP utilities can be found on the Web site of Peter Fox:

> http://www.roestock.demon.co.uk/isapnptools/

Please let me know about hardware (not normally supported under Linux) which can be put to work with the aid of these utilities. A list of this hardware will be put in this appendix.

Appendix D. Linux Incompatible Hardware

Some hardware manufacturers have created devices which are compatible with MS-DOS and Windows 95 only. They seem to emulate part of the normally available hardware in the devices by software packages sold together with the device. Specification on these devices are not presented to the world so it is almost impossible to write drivers for these devices. Below a list of devices reported as being Linux incompatible will be given.

Simply put, it is best to avoid hardware which states things like "Needs Windows" or "Windows only."

- Canon LBP-465 printer
- Hewlett-Packard HP Deskjet 820xx printers
- Hewlett-Packard HP Deskjet 720C, 722C printers
- Lexmark 1000 inkjet printer
- Sharp JX-9210 printer
- Boca Research 28.8 internal modem (model MV34AI)
- DSVD modem??
- Multiwave Innovation CommWave V.34 modem (http://www.multiwave.com/)
- US Robotics WinModem series
- Zoltrix 33.6 Win HSP Voice/Speaker Phone modem
- Compaq 192 PCMCIA modem/serial card
- New Media Winsurfer PCMCIA modem/serial card

App
C

Glossary

Term	Definition
AGP	Accelerated Graphics Port. A bus interconnect mechanism designed to improve performance of 3D graphics applications. AGP is a dedicated bus from the graphics subsystem to the core-logic chipset. http://www.euro.dell.com/intl/euro/r+d/r+dnews/vectors/vect_2-1/v2-1_agp.htm.
ATAPI	AT Attachment Packet Interface. A new protocol for controlling mass storage devices similar to SCSI protocols. It builds on the ATA (AT Attachment) interface, the official ANSI Standard name for the IDE interface developed for hard disk drives. ATAPI is commonly used for hard disks, CD-ROM drives, tape drives, and other devices.
ATM	Asynchronous Transfer Mode
CDDA	Capability of CD-ROM/Writer to read out audio tracks
DMA	Direct Memory Access
EGA	Enhanced Graphics Adapter
EIDE	Enhanced IDE
EISA	Extended Industry System Architecture
FDDI	Fiber Distributed Data Interface. High-speed ring local area network.
IDE	Integrated Drive Electronics. Each drive has a built-in controller.
ISA	Industry System Architecture
ISDN	Integrated Services Digital Network
MCA	MicroChannel Architecture
MFM	Modified Frequency Modulation
MMX	Multimedia Extensions. Added to the newest generation of Intel Pentium Processors. It offers better audio and video quality.
PCI	Pheripheral Component Interconnect. 32-bit bus designed by Intel.
RAID	Redundant Arrays of Inexpensive Disks. The basic idea of RAID is to combine multiple small, inexpensive disk drives into an array of disk drives which yields performance exceeding that of a single large expensive drive. There are five types of redundant array Architectures; RAID-1 through RAID-5. A non-redundant array of disk drives is referred to as RAID-0. http://www.uni-mainz.de/~neuffer/scsi/what_is_raid.html
RLL	Run Length Limited

Term	Definition
SCSI	Small Computer Systems Interface. A standard interface defined for all devices in a computer. It makes it possible to use a single adapter for all devices. http://www.uni-mainz.de/~neuffer/scsi/what_is_scsi.html.
SVGA	Super Video Graphics Adapter
UART	Universal Asynchronous Receiver Transmitter
VGA	Video Graphics Adapter
VLB	VESA Local Bus
WORM	Write Once Read Many

The GNU General Public License

by Jack Tackett

In this appendix

What exactly is GNU? Many believe GNU software is public domain, and some believe GNU software is shareware. Neither is true. Basically, GNU software is copyrighted software that authors have granted the permission to distribute under certain conditions. Those conditions include the provision to provide source code, and that no part of the software may be placed under a copyright that restricts the further distribution of the software—that is, you can't use source code copyrighted under the GNU License within your program without making your source code freely available.

Although the GNU copyright specifies that you must make your source code available, it doesn't mean you have to give your program away for free; you can charge a fee for your program, but that fee MUST include the source code for both the GNU portions and YOUR portion. You can't charge a fee for the executable part of the program and then another fee for the source code—one price for both. Thus, you can't withhold or charge extra for what you might consider proprietary source code. This is the main objection many software executives have with using GNU software within their programs—they don't want to make their source code available to their competitors.

But the concept of GNU goes further, and perhaps the best source to explain this concept is Richard Stallman, the patriarch of the GNU philosophy. Stallman is a founder and proponent of the Free Software Foundation (FSF). He believes very strongly that all software should be free and that computer systems should be open for use by anyone. The fact that such programs as Linux and emacs are freely available matches his philosophy. Anyone can take it for his or her own use. Users are also encouraged to make modifications and share those changes with others.

N O T E   The GNU License is sometimes referred to as the *GNU copyleft*, as a play on the word "copyright." GNU is also a play on words—*GNU's Not UNIX*. For more information on the GNU copyleft, see:

http://www.fsf.org/copyleft/copyleft.html

What does all this have to do with Linux? Well, the various components of Linux are distributed under GNU's General Public License. Thus, Linux is neither in the public domain nor is it shareware; Linus Torvalds and the others retain copyright to their work under the GPL. The rest of this appendix is the GPL as published by the Free Software Federation.

ON THE WEB

The Web site for the Free Software Foundation is

http://www.fsf.org

The GNU License

Version 2, June 1991

Copyright© 1989, 1991 Free Software Foundation, Inc., 675 Mass. Ave, Cambridge, MA 02139 USA

Everyone is permitted to copy and distribute verbatim copies of this license document, but changing it is not allowed.

Preamble

The licenses for most software are designed to take away your freedom to share and change it. By contrast, the GNU General Public License is intended to guarantee your freedom to share and change free software—to make sure the software is free for all its users. This General Public License applies to most of the Free Software Foundation's software and to any other program whose authors commit to using it. (Some other Free Software Foundation software is covered by the GNU Library General Public License instead.) You can apply it to your programs, too.

When we speak of free software, we are referring to freedom, not price. Our General Public Licenses are designed to make sure that you have the freedom to distribute copies of free software (and charge for this service if you wish), that you receive source code or can get it if you want it, that you can change the software or use pieces of it in new free programs; and that you know you can do these things.

To protect your rights, we need to make restrictions that forbid anyone to deny you these rights or to ask you to surrender the rights. These restrictions translate to certain responsibilities for you if you distribute copies of the software, or if you modify it.

For example, if you distribute copies of such a program, whether gratis or for a fee, you must give the recipients all the rights that you have. You must make sure that they, too, receive or can get the source code. And you must show them these terms so they know their rights.

We protect your rights with two steps: (1) copyright the software, and (2) offer you this license which gives you legal permission to copy, distribute and/or modify the software.

Also, for each author's protection and ours, we want to make certain that everyone understands that there is no warranty for this free software. If the software is modified by someone else and passed on, we want its recipients to know that what they have is not the original, so that any problems introduced by others will not reflect on the original authors' reputations.

Finally, any free program is threatened constantly by software patents. We wish to avoid the danger that redistributors of a free program will individually obtain patent licenses, in effect making the program proprietary. To prevent this, we have made it clear that any patent must be licensed for everyone's free use or not licensed at all.

The precise terms and conditions for copying, distribution and modification follow.

GNU General Public License Terms and Conditions for Copying, Distribution, and Modification

This License applies to any program or other work which contains a notice placed by the copyright holder saying it may be distributed under the terms of this General Public License. The

"Program," below, refers to any such program or work, and a "work based on the Program" means either the Program or any derivative work under copyright law: that is to say, a work containing the Program or a portion of it, either verbatim or with modifications and/or translated into another language. (Hereinafter, translation is included without limitation in the term "modification.") Each licensee is addressed as "you."

Activities other than copying, distribution and modification are not covered by this License; they are outside its scope. The act of running the Program is not restricted, and the output from the Program is covered only if its contents constitute a work based on the Program (independent of having been made by running the Program). Whether that is true depends on what the Program does.

1. You may copy and distribute verbatim copies of the Program's source code as you receive it, in any medium, provided that you conspicuously and appropriately publish on each copy an appropriate copyright notice and disclaimer of warranty; keep intact all the notices that refer to this License and to the absence of any warranty; and give any other recipients of the Program a copy of this License along with the Program.

   You may charge a fee for the physical act of transferring a copy, and you may at your option offer warranty protection in exchange for a fee.

2. You may modify your copy or copies of the Program or any portion of it, thus forming a work based on the Program, and copy and distribute such modifications or work under the terms of Section 1 above, provided that you also meet all of these conditions:

   a) You must cause the modified files to carry prominent notices stating that you changed the files and the date of any change.

   b) You must cause any work that you distribute or publish, that in whole or in part contains or is derived from the Program or any part thereof, to be licensed as a whole at no charge to all third parties under the terms of this License.

   c) If the modified program normally reads commands interactively when run, you must cause it, when started running for such interactive use in the most ordinary way, to print or display an announcement including an appropriate copyright notice and a notice that there is no warranty (or else, saying that you provide a warranty) and that users may redistribute the program under these conditions, and telling the user how to view a copy of this License. (Exception: if the Program itself is interactive but does not normally print such an announcement, your work based on the Program is not required to print an announcement.)

   These requirements apply to the modified work as a whole. If identifiable sections of that work are not derived from the Program, and can be reasonably considered independent and separate works in themselves, then this License, and its terms, do not apply to those sections when you distribute them as separate works. But when you distribute the same sections as part of a whole which is a work based on the Program, the distribution of the whole must be on the terms of this License, whose permissions for other licensees extend to the entire whole, and thus to each and every part regardless of who wrote it.

Thus, it is not the intent of this section to claim rights or contest your rights to work written entirely by you; rather, the intent is to exercise the right to control the distribution of derivative or collective works based on the Program.

In addition, mere aggregation of another work not based on the Program with the Program (or with a work based on the Program) on a volume of a storage or distribution medium does not bring the other work under the scope of this License.

3. You may copy and distribute the Program (or a work based on it, under Section 2) in object code or executable form under the terms of Sections 1 and 2 above, provided that you also do one of the following:

    a) Accompany it with the complete corresponding machine-readable source code, which must be distributed under the terms of Sections 1 and 2 above on a medium customarily used for software interchange; or,

    b) Accompany it with a written offer, valid for at least three years, to give any third party, for a charge no more than your cost of physically performing source distribution, a complete machine-readable copy of the corresponding source code, to be distributed under the terms of Sections 1 and 2 above on a medium customarily used for software interchange; or,

    c) Accompany it with the information you received as to the offer to distribute corresponding source code. (This alternative is allowed only for noncommercial distribution and only if you received the program in object code or executable form with such an offer, in accord with Subsection b above.)

The source code for a work means the preferred form of the work for making modifications to it. For an executable work, complete source code means all the source code for all modules it contains, plus any associated interface definition files, plus the scripts used to control compilation and installation of the executable. However, as a special exception, the source code distributed need not include anything that is normally distributed (in either source or binary form) with the major components (compiler, kernel, and so on) of the operating system on which the executable runs, unless that component itself accompanies the executable.

If distribution of executable or object code is made by offering access to copy from a designated place, then offering equivalent access to copy the source code from the same place counts as distribution of the source code, even though third parties are not compelled to copy the source along with the object code.

4. You may not copy, modify, sublicense, or distribute the Program except as expressly provided under this License. Any attempt otherwise to copy, modify, sublicense or distribute the Program is void, and will automatically terminate your rights under this License. However, parties who have received copies, or rights, from you under this License will not have their licenses terminated so long as such parties remain in full compliance.

5. You are not required to accept this License, since you have not signed it. However, nothing else grants you permission to modify or distribute the Program or its derivative works. These actions are prohibited by law if you do not accept this License. Therefore,

App
D

by modifying or distributing the Program (or any work based on the Program), you indicate your acceptance of this License to do so, and all its terms and conditions for copying, distributing or modifying the Program or works based on it.

6. Each time you redistribute the Program (or any work based on the Program), the recipient automatically receives a license from the original licensor to copy, distribute or modify the Program subject to these terms and conditions. You may not impose any further restrictions on the recipients' exercise of the rights granted herein. You are not responsible for enforcing compliance by third parties to this License.

7. If, as a consequence of a court judgment or allegation of patent infringement or for any other reason (not limited to patent issues), conditions are imposed on you (whether by court order, agreement or otherwise) that contradict the conditions of this License, they do not excuse you from the conditions of this License. If you cannot distribute so as to satisfy simultaneously your obligations under this License and any other pertinent obligations, then as a consequence you may not distribute the Program at all. For example, if a patent license would not permit royalty-free redistribution of the Program by all those who receive copies directly or indirectly through you, then the only way you could satisfy both it and this License would be to refrain entirely from distribution of the Program.

If any portion of this section is held invalid or unenforceable under any particular circumstance, the balance of the section is intended to apply and the section as a whole is intended to apply in other circumstances.

It is not the purpose of this section to induce you to infringe any patents or other property right claims or to contest validity of any such claims; this section has the sole purpose of protecting the integrity of the free software distribution system, which is implemented by public license practices. Many people have made generous contributions to the wide range of software distributed through that system in reliance on consistent application of that system; it is up to the author/donor to decide if he or she is willing to distribute software through any other system, and a licensee cannot impose that choice.

This section is intended to make thoroughly clear what is believed to be a consequence of the rest of this License.

8. If the distribution and/or use of the Program is restricted in certain countries either by patents or by copyrighted interfaces, the original copyright holder who places the Program under this License may add an explicit geographical distribution limitation excluding those countries, so that distribution is permitted only in or among countries not thus excluded. In such case, this License incorporates the limitation as if written in the body of this License.

9. The Free Software Foundation may publish revised and/or new versions of the General Public License from time to time. Such new versions will be similar in spirit to the present version, but may differ in detail to address new problems or concerns.

Each version is given a distinguishing version number. If the Program specifies a version number of this License which applies to it and "any later version," you have the option of following the terms and conditions either of that version or of any later version published by the Free Software Foundation. If the Program does not specify a version number of this License, you may choose any version ever published by the Free Software Foundation.

10. If you wish to incorporate parts of the Program into other free programs whose distribution conditions are different, write to the author to ask for permission. For software which is copyrighted by the Free Software Foundation, write to the Free Software Foundation; we sometimes make exceptions for this. Our decision will be guided by the two goals of preserving the free status of all derivatives of our free software and of promoting the sharing and reuse of software generally.

NO WARRANTY

11. BECAUSE THE PROGRAM IS LICENSED FREE OF CHARGE, THERE IS NO WARRANTY FOR THE PROGRAM, TO THE EXTENT PERMITTED BY APPLICABLE LAW. EXCEPT WHEN OTHERWISE STATED IN WRITING THE COPYRIGHT HOLDERS AND/OR OTHER PARTIES PROVIDE THE PROGRAM "AS IS" WITHOUT WARRANTY OF ANY KIND, EITHER EXPRESSED OR IMPLIED, INCLUDING, BUT NOT LIMITED TO, THE IMPLIED WARRANTIES OF MERCHANTABILITY AND FITNESS FOR A PARTICULAR PURPOSE. THE ENTIRE RISK AS TO THE QUALITY AND PERFORMANCE OF THE PROGRAM IS WITH YOU. SHOULD THE PROGRAM PROVE DEFECTIVE, YOU ASSUME THE COST OF ALL NECESSARY SERVICING, REPAIR OR CORRECTION.

12. IN NO EVENT UNLESS REQUIRED BY APPLICABLE LAW OR AGREED TO IN WRITING WILL ANY COPYRIGHT HOLDER, OR ANY OTHER PARTY WHO MAY MODIFY AND/OR REDISTRIBUTE THE PROGRAM AS PERMITTED ABOVE, BE LIABLE TO YOU FOR DAMAGES, INCLUDING ANY GENERAL, SPECIAL, INCIDENTAL OR CONSEQUENTIAL DAMAGES ARISING OUT OF THE USE OR INABILITY TO USE THE PROGRAM (INCLUDING BUT NOT LIMITED TO LOSS OF DATA OR DATA BEING RENDERED INACCURATE OR LOSSES SUSTAINED BY YOU OR THIRD PARTIES OR A FAILURE OF THE PROGRAM TO OPERATE WITH ANY OTHER PROGRAMS), EVEN IF SUCH HOLDER OR OTHER PARTY HAS BEEN ADVISED OF THE POSSIBILITY OF SUCH DAMAGES.

END OF TERMS AND CONDITIONS

App
D

How to Apply These Terms to Your New Programs

If you develop a new program, and you want it to be of the greatest possible use to the public, the best way to achieve this is to make it free software which everyone can redistribute and change under these terms.

To do so, attach the following notices to the program. It is safest to attach them to the start of each source file to most effectively convey the exclusion of warranty; and each file should have at least the "copyright" line and a pointer to where the full notice is found.

```
<one line to give the program's name and a brief idea of what it does.>
Copyright (C) 19yy  <name of author>
```

This program is free software; you can redistribute it and/or modify it under the terms of the GNU General Public License as published by the Free Software Foundation; either version 2 of the License, or (at your option) any later version.

This program is distributed in the hope that it will be useful, but WITHOUT ANY WARRANTY; without even the implied warranty of MERCHANTABILITY or FITNESS FOR A PARTICULAR PURPOSE. See the GNU General Public License for more details.

You should have received a copy of the GNU General Public License along with this program; if not, write to the Free Software Foundation, Inc., 675 Mass. Ave, Cambridge MA 02139 USA.

Also add information on how to contact you by electronic and paper mail.

If the program is interactive, make it output a short notice like this when it starts in an interactive mode:

```
Gnomovision version 69, Copyright (C) 19yy name of author
Gnomovision comes with ABSOLUTELY NO WARRANTY; for details type 'show w'.
This is free software, and you are welcome to redistribute it
under certain conditions; type 'show c' for details.
```

The hypothetical commands "show w" and "show c" should show the appropriate parts of the General Public License. Of course, the commands you use may be called something other than "show w" and "show c"; they could even be mouse-clicks or menu items—whatever suits your program.

You should also get your employer (if you work as a programmer) or your school, if any, to sign a "copyright disclaimer" for the program, if necessary. Here is a sample; alter the names:

```
Yoyodyne, Inc., hereby disclaims all copyright interest in the program
'Gnomovision' (which makes passes at compilers) written by James Hacker.

<signature of Ty Coon>, 1 April 1989
Ty Coon, President of Vice
```

This General Public License does not permit incorporating your program into proprietary programs. If your program is a subroutine library, you may consider it more useful to permit linking proprietary applications with the library. If this is what you want to do, use the GNU Library General Public License instead of this License.

Installing StarOffice

Reviewing Linux System Requirements

If you follow the information in this section, you should be able to get StarOffice running on basically any Linux system that meets the listed requirements. The system requirements for installing StarOffice 4.0 are listed in Table E.1.

Table E.1   System Requirements for Installing StarOffice for Linux

Object	Requirement
Linux kernel version	2.0.x (or later)
Linux library version	libc 5.4.22 or higher up to version 6.x (libc 6.x can be installed on your Linux system, but the earlier version must be available to StarOffice)
System memory	32MB RAM
Hard disk space	11–120MB depending on installation type
X Windows system graphics	256 or more colors or grayscales

These requirements are straightforward. Pay special attention to the fact that StarOffice requires a fair amount of memory and hard disk space compared to many Linux programs. The more you have, the more smoothly StarOffice will run.

Checking Your Environment Variables

StarOffice uses the LANG environment variable to determine which international number, currency, and dictionary settings to use. The default setting is en_US for U.S. English. If you need to change to British English, enter the following command from any command line before running StarOffice:

```
export LANG=en_GB
```

Single-User and Network (Multiuser) Installations

One of the benefits of using Linux is the true multiuser capability of the operating system. Several people can be logged in across a network and use the files and services from a single Linux system.

StarOffice allows for a network installation, which enables you to install StarOffice in a main location (such as /opt or /usr/local) and then install a relatively small (11MB) client portion that allows a user to access the StarOffice installation without your having to install the entire (huge) product in every home directory.

TIP Even if you're just using Linux as your desktop, using a network installation is an easy way to allow multiple user accounts to access StarOffice without eating up 100MB for each user's copy.

Checking File Permissions and Library Versions

With that said, installing StarOffice for Linux is simple. Most problems occur for one of these reasons:

- You don't have sufficient file permissions to create the directories and files needed during installation.
- You don't have the correct libraries installed to run either the setup program or StarOffice itself.

If you use a single-user installation, you'll be installing StarOffice in your home directory, so permission to create files is no problem.

If you intend to use a network installation, you'll probably want to be logged in as root (or as a user with some system administration rights) to create the StarOffice installation. The directory in which you install StarOffice must be accessible for Read access by all the users who will be running StarOffice from that location. The commands to set the permissions for the StarOffice directory are provided later in this appendix when the setup procedure is described.

If you're installing StarOffice on a Linux system other than the one included on the CD-ROM in this book, you may need to install the version of the system libraries used by StarOffice. You can check which version you have installed by executing these commands:

```
$ cd /usr/lib
$ ls -l libc*
lrwxrwxrwx   1 root      root         19 Aug 11  1997 /usr/lib/libc.so ->
➡/lib/libc.so.5.4.22
-r--r--r--   1 root      root      19354 Nov  7  1997 /usr/lib/libcomm.so
```

TIP If you're not using a Linux system from Caldera, you can also try this command, which often works on Red Hat or Slackware Linux systems:
```
$ /sbin/ldconfig -Nv ¦ grep libc.so.5
```

If the listing that appears includes libc5.4.22 (or a later version of libc5.x), as the preceding listing does, StarOffice will function correctly. If it does not, you should install it from the original CDs that accompany your Linux distribution or from an updated CD-ROM version of Linux.

> **CAUTION**
> You can download different library versions from this Web site:
>   **http://sunsite.unc.edu/pub.Linux/GCC**
> But it's much safer to use an official tested library that you get from your Linux vendor.

After you download and install the correct version of libc (described in the following section), execute this command to make it accessible for your system:

```
# ldconfig
```

Using Different Linux Systems

StarOffice for Linux was "sponsored" by Caldera, Inc., one of the leading producers of Linux products. Caldera, Inc. worked with Star Division to have the StarOffice suite ported to Linux. This means that StarOffice installs effortlessly on Caldera OpenLinux systems, but it can require a little adjustment to work correctly on other Linux systems, such as Debian or Red Hat Linux.

Although Caldera OpenLinux uses the RPM software package management tool (which relies on the RPM utility), StarOffice for Linux uses a separate installation program described later in this appendix. You don't need to have the RPM tool installed on your Linux system to install StarOffice.

If the library version and other system requirements described in Table E. 1 are met, StarOffice should run without a problem on any Linux system.

If you have a different version of the system libraries installed, you'll probably want to use the libc version 5.4.22 libraries only for StarOffice without having them available to other programs on your Linux system. This is the procedure provided in the section that follows.

> **CAUTION**
>
> Replacing libraries on a stable Linux system is not a good idea. Instead, follow the steps for making the needed library version available only to StarOffice.

To install the libc version for StarOffice so that it's used only for StarOffice, follow these steps before starting the setup program:

1. Create the directory where StarOffice will be installed (this example illustrates a network installation; you might also make this subdirectory in a user's home directory):

    ```
    # mkdir /opt/Office40/
    ```

2. Create a subdirectory for the library file that StarOffice will use.

    ```
    # cd /opt/Office40
    # mkdir lib
    ```

3. Copy the libc file to the StarOffice library subdirectory that you just created.

    ```
    # cp /tmp/libc.so.5.4.33 /opt/Office40/lib
    ```

4. Add a symbolic link so that version 5 of the library is included in the directory.

    ```
    # ln -s libc.so.5.4.33 libc.so.5
    ```

5. Set the LD_LIBRARY_PATH environment variable to refer to the StarOffice library subdirectory.

    ```
    # export LD_LIBRARY_PATH=/opt/Office40/lib
    ```

The correct library will now be used both for StarOffice setup and for running the StarOffice suite.

You must execute this last step (export the LD_LIBRARY_PATH) right before you start StarOffice each time. If you don't, StarOffice won't find the correct library file. If you make this command part of your startup script (in .bashrc or .profile), all programs will use the library you installed for StarOffice, which poses a risk to everything else you do.

NOTE The alternative to using the export command each time you run StarOffice is to create a script that sets the library path variable and starts StarOffice at the same time. The script would look like this:

```
#!/bin/sh
export LD_LIBRARY_PATH=/opt/Office40/lib
/opt/Office40/bin/soffice
```

Save these three lines in a file, and then use this command

```
Chmod a+x scriptname
```

to make the script executable. Now when you run the script, the library path is set only for StarOffice, not for other programs you run. ▩

You're now ready to start the setup program and install StarOffice.

Starting Setup for a Single-User Installation

StarOffice is installed from the CD-ROM by a "setup" program, just like most Windows programs that you might be familiar with. Once you've established that you have the correct Linux system requirements in place, you're ready to run the setup program to install StarOffice.

The network installation procedure is described in the later part of this appendix. A network installation of StarOffice differs from a single-user installation only in the location of the StarOffice files and the ability of multiple users to run StarOffice at the same time.

You start the setup program just as you would start any other Linux program. If you're not familiar with the process, follow these steps:

1. Log in as the user for which you are installing StarOffice and start the X Windows system.
2. Open an xterm command line window
3. Insert the StarOffice CD-ROM and use the su command to log on as a user who can mount the CD-ROM drive (or to root if necessary). The exact command will vary depending on how you have your devices configured:

```
$ su - admin
password:
$ mount -t iso9660 /dev/cdrom /mnt/cdrom
$ exit
$
```

App

E

4. Change to the StarOffice directory on the CD-ROM (its exact location depends on where you mounted the CD-ROM drive in step 2):

```
$ cd /mnt/cdrom/StarOffice
```

5. Start the setup installation program with this command:

```
$ ./setup
```

6. After a few seconds, the StarOffice graphic appears, and the installation process begins.

Reviewing the License Agreement

When you start the setup program, the first window that appears displays the StarOffice license agreement, as shown in Figure E.1. The license agreement defines how you can use your copy of StarOffice for Linux.

FIG. E.1

The license agreement defines how you can use your copy of StarOffice for Linux.

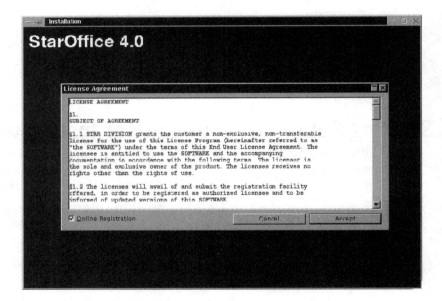

Three types of licenses are available for StarOffice:

- *30-day trial license.* This version of StarOffice is available in some magazine promotions. The software is labeled "Try & Buy Version" on the title bar, and it will stop running 30 days after you install it.

- *Non-commercial license.* This is a fully functional version of StarOffice, but one that is not licensed for use in business. It can be used only for personal use or for evaluation of StarOffice before purchasing a commercial license.

- *Commercial license.* This version of StarOffice is licensed for use in any business or personal situation. You generally must pay for a commercial license of StarOffice for Linux.

N O T E The CD-ROM in this book contains the complete StarOffice for Linux with a non-commercial license. You can install and use StarOffice for personal or evaluation use. If you want to use StarOffice in a business, you must purchase a commercial license. ▧

Choosing an Installation Option

The next decision you have to make is which components of StarOffice you want to install. As we said earlier, StarOffice is not a small program, so you may choose to leave some parts out of the installation.

Remember, however, that the "integrated" nature of StarOffice means that most of the program is shared among all of the components. That means that you can't choose not to install a large component like the StarImpress presentation software.

If you do need to save hard disk space, you can leave out any of the following components:

- Graphics libraries
- Templates
- Help files
- Example documents

You can choose one of several installation options, as shown in Figure E.2.

FIG. E.2

You can select which components of StarOffice to install by selecting an installation option.

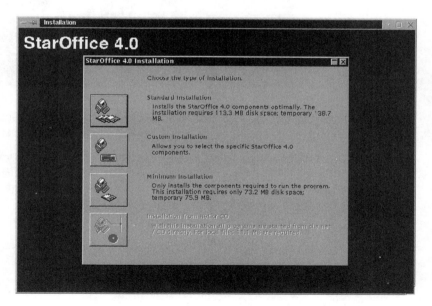

App

E

The easiest choice is the Standard Installation. Although this takes up a lot of space, it provides you with graphics, templates, help files, dictionaries, and so forth. If you choose the Standard Installation button, you should have about 110MB of free hard disk space. The final installation will take only about 90MB, but the process will use some additional space during installation.

If you don't have that much space, you can choose the Minimum Installation option. This requires only about 50MB of hard disk space, but it doesn't install such things as the help files and sample documents.

Using the Custom Installation Option

If you like setting things up yourself, you can choose the Custom Installation option. When you choose this button, the dialog box in Figure E.3 appears.

FIG. E.3

The Custom Installation option lets you choose which additional components you want to install.

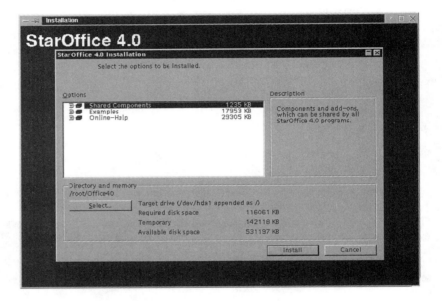

From this dialog box, you can select which components you want to install. As we mentioned earlier, however, you don't have a lot of choice (like you would with Microsoft Office).

StarOffice uses the same set of underlying functionality for the word processor, the spreadsheet, the presentation software, and so forth. If you left out a key section, none of these would function. Instead, you can save space by selecting which example documents, templates, help files, and so forth you want to install.

To deselect options from the list, follow these steps:

1. Click on the plus sign (+) to the left of the type of item you want to deselect. That item expands to display its contents.

2. Click on the plus sign for sublevel components if necessary.

3. Click on the icon or name of an item that you don't want to install. The icon goes blank, and the Required Disk Space line at the bottom of the dialog box is updated to reflect the new space requirements.

4. Click again on any icon that you want to reselect to include in the installation.

5. When you have selected and deselected the proper components to reflect what you want to use, begin the installation by choosing the Install button.

If you need to change the directory where StarOffice is installed, click the Select... button in the bottom part of the screen. You can then browse your Linux system file structure to choose a subdirectory for installation.

Note, however, that you should choose a subdirectory within the current user's home directory because this is not a network installation; only one user will be using StarOffice in this setup.

Deciding Where to Put StarOffice

If you didn't choose the Custom Installation option, you still get to decide where to install StarOffice. If you selected the Standard or Minimum Installation option, another window appears (see Figure E.4) where you can select an installation subdirectory. This is just like the option at the bottom of the custom installation dialog box (refer to Figure E.3).

FIG. E.4

You can select where to install StarOffice.

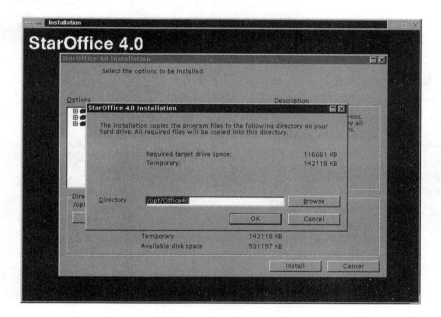

App

E

Because this installation of StarOffice is for an individual user, the default location in the user's home directory is a safe choice.

If you don't want to install StarOffice in the home directory, or if you want to change the name of the directory where StarOffice is installed, you can choose the Select button to change the location.

After you select the installation directory, click OK. A window appears, displaying the progress of the installation (see Figure E.5). The installation will take from 5–25 minutes to complete, depending on the speed of your system components.

FIG. E.5
This dialog box shows you
the progress of the
installation process.

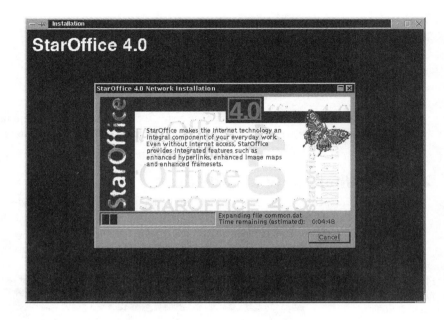

Entering Your User Information

When the installation is complete, a dialog box appears, requesting such personal information as your name, company, telephone number, and e-mail address (see Figure E.6).

FIG. E.6
The user information you
enter here is stored for use in
StarOffice documents.

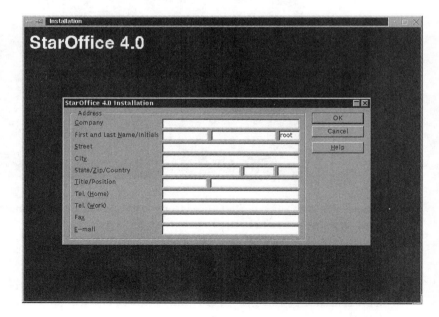

You don't have to enter any information here, but it's a good idea to enter at least your name and e-mail address. This information will be used when you create and send e-mail messages with StarOffice. It provides your name and e-mail address to the Internet systems that process e-mail or newsgroup postings. Your real name and e-mail address are required by Internet etiquette when sending messages. The StarOffice e-mail and news services won't work without them.

The other information, such as fax number, telephone number, and address, is provided to your StarOffice system for use in document templates and macros like fax cover sheets and travel expense reports. But the information beyond your name and e-mail address is less important.

Fill out as much of this dialog box as you want, and then click OK to continue.

TIP If you need to update, modify, or add to the information in this dialog box, you can do so at any time by using the Tools menu. Choose Options, General, and select the User Data tab.

The installation is now complete. If you aren't interested in learning about a network installation, skip to the section on printer installation later in this appendix.

Preparing for a Network Installation

A network installation of StarOffice will be useful if you've purchased several licenses of StarOffice. It allows you to install StarOffice in a single location where more than one user can access and use it. This saves disk space by eliminating the need for each user to have a copy of StarOffice in his or her home directory.

NOTE Of course, if you're using the non-commercial version of StarOffice included on the CD in this book, you can use the network installation with multiple user accounts to evaluate how it all works. But don't run your business on it. ▦

A network installation of StarOffice is basically the same as a single-user installation. The only differences are the location where StarOffice is installed and the need to enter a few files for each user who will use StarOffice. We'll walk you through both parts of the installation: server and user.

The Server Side of a Network Installation

The system requirements for the network installation are the same as those for a single-user installation.

To start a network installation, follow these steps:

1. Log in as a user with administrative privileges to mount the CD-ROM drive. Then start the X Windows system.

App

E

2. Mount the CD-ROM drive containing the StarOffice CD-ROM.

3. Change to the StarOffice directory with this command:

```
# cd /mnt/cdrom/StarOffice40/
```

4. Start the network installation with this command:

```
# ./setup /net
```

The dialog boxes that appear are identical to those that appear during a single-user installation. The only difference in the process at this point is the location you select for the StarOffice files to be installed in.

Instead of installing StarOffice in a single user's home directory, you should install it in a common applications area, such as the /opt directory or the /usr/local directory (under an Office40/ subdirectory).

Complete the network installation by responding to the dialog boxes for accepting the license agreement and selecting the type of installation (Standard, Minimum, or Custom). You don't enter user information in the network installation until you install an individual user.

The Client Side of a Network Installation

The network installation of StarOffice isn't meant to be used directly. (In fact, it may generate a segmentation fault and crash if you try to run it.) Instead, follow the network installation instructions (which you just completed) by installing a few files for a single user.

To start the installation process for a single user, follow these steps:

1. Log in to your Linux system using the username that will be using StarOffice as a networked user.

2. Change to the StarOffice binary subdirectory that you used for the network installation:

```
$ cd /opt/Office40/bin
```

3. Start the setup program with this command to indicate that you're setting up a single user for network use of StarOffice:

```
$ ./setup
```

4. Click Accept to accept the license agreement and continue with the installation.

5. When the dialog box appears asking you to select the type of installation, click the Installation from Net or CD button.

6. Choose the desired installation directory in the user's home directory for the StarOffice files. The home directory must have about 3MB of space.

A dialog box displays the progress of the installation as files are installed in your home directory.

7. The user data dialog box appears, where you can enter your personal information. Click OK to finish the installation.

CAUTION

Remember, if you don't enter at least your real name and e-mail address, the e-mail and newsgroup functions within StarOffice won't work.

Now you're ready to start StarOffice. Before you move on, however, you should review the last section on modifying your StarOffice installation.

Updating or Removing the StarOffice Installation

After you have installed StarOffice, you might want to change the installation. For example, if you didn't install the help files or templates in the original installation, you might want to add them to your system later. On the other hand, you might even need to remove StarOffice from your Linux system. Although almost all of StarOffice is stored in the Office40 directory, it always helps to have a deinstall utility.

All of these tasks can be completed by starting the setup utility after StarOffice is installed. The setup utility will detect that StarOffice is already installed on your system (for the current user) and will, therefore, present you with different options than it did in the original installation.

Start the setup utility by changing to the program directory of StarOffice and running the setup program:

```
$ cd Office40/bin
$ ./setup &
$
```

The setup program starts, but it doesn't look like it did the first time (see Figure E.7). The following options are presented now.

- Modify installation
- Upgrade installation
- Deinstallation
- Repair

App

E

FIG. E.7

The setup utility presents different options after StarOffice is installed.

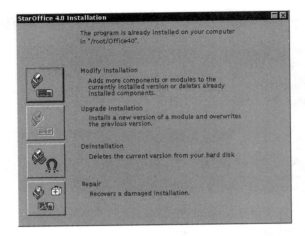

Most of these options require that you have your StarOffice CD mounted. The setup utility needs to access the original files in order to alter or update your installation.

Modifying the StarOffice Installation

When you installed StarOffice, you had a choice of installation options. If you chose the Custom Installation option, you selected which components you wanted to install.

If you start the setup utility again—after you've completed the original installation—and you choose the Modify button, you can add items to or remove items from the list of components you originally installed.

The dialog box in which you select the components to install is basically the same as the Custom Installation dialog box. You can choose the items that you want to include in your StarOffice installation.

Upgrading Your StarOffice Installation

If you have a CD with a newer version of StarOffice for Linux, you can choose the Upgrade button to update the necessary files from the new StarOffice CD so that the installation of StarOffice on your Linux system reflects the latest version.

By using the Upgrade button instead of erasing the existing StarOffice directory (or using the deinstallation option that follows), you can preserve the settings and working files that you've created in your current StarOffice directory.

Deinstalling StarOffice

If you decide you need to take StarOffice off your system, the best way to do it is with the De-Iinstall button in the setup program.

Of course, as an alternative you can go to the Office40/ directory and use this command

```
$ rm -rf *
```

But that's generally very dangerous. In addition, some of the hidden files created by StarOffice may be left in place. If you intend to reinstall StarOffice for any reason, those leftover hidden files will cause confusion during the installation.

Repairing StarOffice

The final option in the post-installation setup program is the Repair button. Use this button if something has happened to your Linux filesystem that prevents StarOffice from running.

You can compare this to having a really bad crash in Microsoft Windows. Instead of reinstalling the system or application, you can run the setup utility and use the Repair button.

The Repair feature can determine what parts of StarOffice are missing or misplaced and whether file versions are incompatible. As with modifying the installation, this provides a convenient alternative to backing up your data and configurations and reinstalling StarOffice.

As with the Modify and Upgrade options, you'll need your StarOffice CD-ROM so the Repair utility can retrieve any missing files from the original source.

App

E

What's on the CD-ROM

Special Edition Using Linux, Fourth Edition, is delivering to its readers a complete Linux solution. On the CDs included with this book, you will find Red Hat Linux 5.1, Caldera OpenLinux Lite 1.2, and StarOffice 4.0. So not only do you get two great Linux distributions, but you also get a world-class office suite.

▶ **See** "Linux Installation Overview" on **p. 29** for installation instructions

Red Hat Linux 5.1: Award-Winning Operating System

CDs 1 and 2 contain Red Hat Linux 5.1, chosen by InfoWorld as the Desktop Operating System Product of the Year for two years in a row. Red Hat Linux is for users who need a reliable, secure, and high-performance computer environment on their desktop and server PCs. Here's what you get with Red Hat Linux 5.1:

Desktop environment. Red Hat Linux 5.1 allows you the freedom you want on your desktop. You can choose from multiple window mangers. You can also get on the Net, build some programs, and format floppy disks—all at the same time—and enjoy an extremely stable operating system that multitasks more smoothly than other operating systems. Systems running Red Hat Linux are able to run continuously for months on end.

Internet server. Red Hat Linux can provide Internet services, including Web, e-mail, news, and DNS for multiple sites with real virtual hosting.

Learning platform. The CD contains full source code (except for commercial apps). What could be a better learning platform? Red Hat Linux comes complete with C, C++, F77 compilers, programming languages (python, perl, Tcl/Tk, scheme0), and tools for math- and engineering-related applications (spice, GNUplot, xfing).

Caldera OpenLinux Lite 1.2 and StarOffice 4.0 for Linux

CD 3 contains OpenLinux Lite 1.2 and the noncommercial version of StarOffice 4.0.

Caldera OpenLinux Lite 1.2

OpenLinux Lite 1.2 is the free version of their "Linux for Business" product, a full-featured Linux distribution. OpenLinux is the only self-hosted Linux distribution available today. That means all binaries shipped with the distribution have been compiled and tested to run in the OpenLinux environment.

Desktop environment. In addition to the standard window managers other Linux distributions give you, OpenLinux Lite 1.2 also gives you a trial version of their Looking Glass desktop solution. It gives you powerful file management and a drag-and-drop desktop that makes it easy to add programs and links to your desktop environment.

Ready for the Internet. Caldera OpenLinux Lite is perfect for the Internet. Everything you need for the client and the server is included.

Easy installation. It only takes about 30 minutes to install Caldera OpenLinux Lite with its user-friendly interface that walks you through all the steps.

StarOffice 4.0

CD 3 also includes the noncommercial but fully functional version of StarOffice 4.0. StarOffice is a complete office suite that includes word processing, spreadsheet, and presentation capabilities, and more. It is one of the most popular office suites available for Linux, and it was recently awarded the Editor's Choice award by 32 Bits Online.

About the Software

Please read all documentation associated with a third-party product (usually located in a file named readme.txt or license.txt) and follow all guidelines.

App

F

Index

Z

ning this package, you are agreeing to be bound by the following agreement:

Some of the software included with this product may be copyrighted, in which case all rights are reserved by the respective copyright holder. You are licensed to use software copyrighted by the publisher and its licensors on a single computer. You may copy and/or modify the software as needed to facilitate your use of it on a single computer. Making copies of the software for any other purpose is a violation of the United States copyright laws.

This software is sold as is without warranty of any kind, either expressed or implied, including but not limited to the implied warranties of merchantability and fitness for a particular purpose. Neither the publisher nor its dealers or distributors assumes any liability for any alleged or actual damages arising from the use of this program. (Some states do not allow for the exclusion of implied warranties, so the exclusion may not apply to you.)